The Psychology of Learning

The Psychology
of Learning

B. R. BUGELSKI

University of Buffalo

HENRY HOLT AND COMPANY
New York

For my daughters

Vicky and Cathy

Preface

This book is an attempt to clarify the major issues in the controversial fields of learning and motivation. It would be presumptuous to pretend that the numerous areas of conflict in the theoretical developments of the last decades have all been resolved or that any of the questions which divide theoretical camps has been answered to everyone's satisfaction. It is of advantage, however, in a developing science occasionally to step aside and look over the area of study, to appraise progress, note changes, and examine the questions that persist and those new questions that inevitably arise when old ones are answered.

The present text in part stems from the writer's observations that on the one hand learning theory is being attacked as impractical and inapplicable while on the other hand ambitious attempts are being made in the name of learning theory to make applications that may not be justified. Before learning psychologists go too far in the areas of education, personality analysis, and clinical practice, a severe appraisal of the current status of learning theory is in order. At the same time, the genuinely useful findings from learning studies must not be allowed to fall into obscurity because some practitioners fail in ill-advised and too hasty applications.

Discussions in the area of learning have frequently been reported on such a high plane that the unsophisticated student has difficulty in appreciating the meaning, to say nothing of the contribution, of a given theorist. The present text is designed to provide a reasonably comprehensible introduction to the problems over which learning psychologists worry. The theories themselves are not described in any formal style, although major premises are considered as they pertain to various questions.

In the present text no attempt is made to offer a new theory to replace the many now competing for attention and support. The writer admits to a bias in favor of the views of Hull and the more recently developed proposals of Hebb. To some extent the text is an attempt to integrate the views of these students to the extent that integration appears possible.

The writer has made no attempt to include reference to some schools of thought, notably that of Lewin. This omission is deliberate and is based on the opinion that Lewin's views do not represent a learning theory. The conclusion of the Dartmouth group in *Modern Learning Theory* reflects the same opinion and the writer takes courage from this report.

The text does not pretend to cover the entire area of behavior. It is believed that behavior is a function of at least some other variables besides learning and that there is room for a book dealing with learning alone.

Because so many problems interlock or overlap with each other, the writer has felt constrained to make extensive use of cross references. It appears quite impossible to stick to a given question without getting involved in numerous side issues, some of which are of great importance. It seemed to be more efficient, even at the risk of almost constant irritation of the reader, to postpone discussions of questions that crop up in connection with the issue at hand. The subject of extinction, for example, is discussed late in the text even though a knowledge of extinction would help in understanding questions discussed earlier.

Every book is the result of the cumulative influence of many individuals. This one is no exception. The writer is greatly in debt to many patient students who, over the years, listened to a constantly revised and changing story with various degrees of doubt. The colleagues who patiently argued against the writer's varying views are particularly appreciated. Among these Dr. Walter Cohen, Dr. Herbert Lansdell, and Dr. Donald Bullock helped develop whatever breadth the reader may find in the text. The encouragement and material support of Dr. Olive P. Lester and Dr. Carleton F. Scofield are gratefully acknowledged. The writer's graduate students, some of whose work is reported here, are chiefly responsible for the writing of the text. Their encouragement and willingness to investigate questions which appeared to be closed issues were the strongest motivational influences. In this connection the writer is indebted to Dr. Robert A. Coyer, Dr. Robert T. White, Dr. Donald Scharlock, Dr. Donald Woodward, William A. Rogers, Thomas Cadwallader, Walter Flakus, and Yasuko Matsuoka. Miss Matsuoka, besides being the writer's experimental assistant, typed the entire manuscript and deserves special mention for eliminating a great deal of obscurity. Miss Ruth Duncan was extremely helpful and patient with numerous revisions. Robert Riddle prepared the bibliography, all the line drawings, and did much of the indexing.

The greatest debt of all is owed to my wife, who urged me to try to make some sense out of the psychology of learning and to indicate the limitations as well as the virtues of learning theory. Her sympathy for students is the basic inspiration of this volume.

B. R. B.

The University of Buffalo
April, 1956

Contents

Chapter

1

The Central Status of Learning in Psychology

There are many branches and divisions of psychology and, while psychologists are engaged in many kinds of functions, there appears to be a basic agreement among them that the principles of learning are the fundamental theoretical tools of modern psychology.

The science of psychology has developed around the S→R formula in one modification or another. Organisms are presumed to react in certain ways because they are stimulated into doing so. The reaction is either native or learned. If learned, it is because some stimulus which did not originally bring out a certain response now has come to do so because of "past experience" or "learning."

In civilized societies many natural reactions are found undesirable. We frown on people who spit in the street or cough in our faces. The organism must not react "naturally" but in some other way, a way dictated by society. Attaching a different response to a stimulus is again "learning." From infancy on, the to-be-civilized human being is subjected to a training process calculated to make him an acceptable member of society. He is taught where and when to sleep, eat, wash behind the ears, read, write, and calculate, to earn his living, and even to grow old gracefully or die nobly, depending upon how the great divisions of society are getting along with each other at the time.

If the subject of all this training turns out delinquent, stupid, maladjusted, or otherwise a nuisance, it is usually assumed that the training process went wrong somewhere, and retraining is usually recommended by the more enlightened segments of society.

Psychologists, in general, have adopted as their sphere of interest this process of training and retraining. Putting this interest in other terms, we can think of psychologists as basically concerned with the role of the environment in determining behavior. While there are exceptions, and many of them, most psychologists operate with the open avowal or tacit assumption that behavior can be predicted, controlled, or altered by manipulating the environment. This assumption, of course, is basic to many educational and child-rearing practices.

The environmentalist bias was first put in its boldest form by John Locke (1690), the English philosopher, when he described the human mind as a blank tablet on which experience would write the biography of the subject. Locke can be described as an "empiricist" as opposed to a "nativist." The nativists since Plato have held to the belief that humans, at least, come equipped by nature with some basic ideas, emotions, and reactions which are used on suitable occasions. The more extreme among them would endorse the common man's assertion, "You can't change human nature."

The history of psychology, to some extent, can be described in terms of a controversy between supporters of "nature" as against "nurture." As with most black-white controversies, the searchers for truth have found themselves forced to compromise from time to time with occasional swings of the pendulum from one extreme to the other.

The nature-nurture controversy still persists. In an interesting and disturbing article, Verplanck (1955) asked, "Since learned behavior is innate, and vice versa, what now?" This quotation, which is the title of his paper, expresses a question that is intriguing more and more psychologists since the publication of Hebb's (1949) monograph, the *Organization of Behavior*.

Learning psychologists are beginning more and more to recognize the role of the organism in behavior. Because of the nature of their tools and techniques they are pretty much limited to the manipulation of stimuli. The preoccupation with stimuli sometimes leads learning psychologists to forget about "nature" and act as if learning is all that matters.

It is basic to our needs to attempt an outcome which will place learning in its proper role in the total behavior pattern. Propaganda about how important learning is does not actually make it so, however much it pleases the psychologist. In his presidential address to the American Psychological Association, Guthrie (1946a) states: "In the two fields of learning and of motivation will be worked out the basic theory that will eventually make the science of psychology a much more powerful instrument than it now is. When we are able to state the general principles which govern human learning we shall have the most important tool needed for the prediction and control of human behavior." Guthrie may be right. On the other hand, it may turn out that when we do understand the general principles of learning, we will be in no position to predict and control behavior or anything else, in any matters of significance. In the same address, Guthrie also points out: "But a scientific theory of learning has yet to be agreed upon by psychologists." The statement, made in 1945, is perhaps even a bit truer today.

If a scientific theory of learning is not yet agreed upon (although agreement is no necessary criterion of truth or correctness) it is somehow disconcerting to the modest learning psychologists to find how readily various types of behavior from the cradle to the grave are attributed to learning. The plasticity of man is taken for granted. The environmental forces are assumed to mold the many-faceted personalities among us. Brains are washed; generations are brought up to fit desires of various types of czars; emotions are conditioned into or out of humanity; slaves or liberators, poets and peasants all fall prey to environmental influence.

In spite of their allegiance to environmentalism there are probably no psychologists today who are willing to act on Watson's (1930, p. 104) dramatic proposal: "Give me a dozen healthy infants, well-formed, and my own specified world to bring them up in and I'll guarantee to take any one at random and train him to become any type of specialist I might select—doctor, lawyer, artist, merchant-chief and, yes, even beggarman and thief, regardless of his talents, penchants, tendencies, abilities, vocations, and race of his ancestors." The proposal is usually dismissed as "extreme." To fail to take up the challenge, however, while retaining the postulates of environmentalism suggests a weakness or lack of faith which is hardly in keeping with the tough-mindedness that is so frequently espoused.

It may be that some of our difficulty is due to a short-term view of life and of history. We want to get things done, institute changes, make a better life, certainly for ourselves, and often enough, for others. Unless we can believe in the efficacy of our actions we may find it difficult to act. Once we raise the question of "to spank or not to spank" our aim and efficiency become poorer. If the psychologist loses confidence in the effectiveness of the possible changes he can institute in the environment he can no longer operate.

The historian and the evolutionary biologist also have to deal with the role of the environment. But they take the long view and recognize, sometimes better than the psychologist, how not only does the environment change man but also how man changes his environment and ways of life. They note also how attempts at control over a population may succeed for a time, perhaps for centuries, but they note also the frequent failures of control. The rise and growth leads to the decline and fall, the new replaces the old. The concept of change is as ancient as philosophy. The causes of change, however, remain an unchanging problem.

To summarize, then, we note that the environment is there, and we recognize that it acts on the organism from before birth till after death; the only difficulty is that the organism also acts on the environment which also changes, and the interaction makes a problem of such complexity that it is difficult to isolate and ferret out the relative roles and principles involved. The chemistry of man and his physics (especially in terms of an active brain) cannot be ignored. We can approach the problem, then, by setting up situations where chemistry and physics are controlled and observe the process of learning in relative purity, or we can hope to take account of the chemistry and physics as we go along. In either case, the difficulties are tremendous and apt to lead us into error. Our problem is to render unto Caesar without knowing what is owed to Caesar. The analysis that we are about to begin will be the analysis of learning. We cannot hope to account for the behavior of organisms or the principles of behavior. Those more comprehensive ambitions would take us too far afield. We must, for the present, be content with trying to determine what changes can be brought about in behavior through the learning process alone. Sometimes this will prove difficult, because the learning psychologist does not stick to purely "educational" processes in his experiments. He resorts, when it is permissible, to punishment by shocks, immersion in cold water, drugs, starvation, loud noises, dehydration, solitary confinement, and other forms of interference with

natural proclivities or activities. The effects of such more or less physical or physiological manipulations might produce changes in the
physiological mechanism of the subject which are then reflected as
alterations in behavior and are attributed to learning. Whether learning is responsible for all the changes is, of course, debatable. Or, we
might ask, does the punished organism, the fearful, the starved organism learn in the same way as one not subjected to those forms of
psychological attention? Does the well-fed and intellectually curious
college student learn like the enraged and fearful rat? Since almost
nothing is known of the nature of the effects of the stimulation
process or the preparation for learning on the kinds of subjects normally used, it behooves us to go carefully.

Obviously, as a first step, we should define our field. We should
set the limits of our subject, we should define learning. In spite of
the tremendous literature in the field, there are precious few attempts
at defining learning which are taken seriously or offered by the leading students of the subjects. Textbook writers are, of course, duty
bound to supply a definition, but we cannot regard their definitions as
binding on the leading workers in the field. If we turn to these we find
a curious reluctance to offer a definition of learning. Where definitions are offered, they are presented as tentative and in general terms,
they tell us something about what learning is not, but frequently include undefined terms which leave us with a feeling that a good deal
more should be specified. An examination of some of these definitions
is in order with the hope of, perhaps, finding some common denom-
inators.

SOME DEFINITIONS OF LEARNING

Guthrie, in his *Psychology of Learning* (1935), offers a series of
definitions: "We shall call these changes in behavior which follow
behavior learning." He proceeds: "The ability to learn, that is, to
respond differently to a situation because of past response to the
situation . . ." and, further, "I prefer to reserve the word 'learning'
for the more lasting effects of practice." And, "behavior which
changes with use or practice." Since in the rest of the book Guthrie
takes a dim view of "practice" and emphasizes "one-trial learning,"
the remarks just quoted might leave one with a few questions. But
before we ask these questions other offerings might better be presented.

In his *Principles of Behavior,* Hull (1943) gives his definition thus: "The essential nature of the learning process may, however, be stated quite simply. Just as the inherited equipment of reaction tendencies consists of receptor-effector connections, so the process of learning consists in the strengthening of certain of these connections as contrasted with others, or in the setting up of quite new connections." Although Hull does go on to talk about the meaning of strengthening and connections, it is obvious that both these terms must be separately defined before we can even have an inkling of his meaning. Unless we are prepared to accept his later definitions we do not have, here, a starting point, but rather a terminus.

The Handbook of Experimental Psychology (Stevens, ed., 1951) contains a number of essays on learning. Hilgard (1951), in his chapter, feels no need to define learning positively. He tells us: "Learning is always an inference, derived from changes in performance, and learning is not the only factor that can cause these changes." (The other factors are listed as age, fatigue, drugs, motivation, state of the organism.) Later he states: "A precise definition of learning is not necessary, so long as we agree that the inference to learning is made from changes in performance that are the result of training or experience, as distinguished from changes such as growth or fatigue and from changes attributable to the temporary state of the learner. The experiments themselves define the field ostensibly."

Here we find definition by exclusion, by pointing, and by introduction of the terms "experience," "training," and "practice," each of which needs definition, and by suggestion that the experiments define the field. The latter point may be of great merit or of great danger; it remains to be seen. Hilgard's point that no definition is needed may have some value. On the other hand, an examination of what learning psychologists have accomplished may make us wish to revise this position.

In a chapter on animal learning, Brogden (1951) presents various misgivings which bear on Hilgard's reliance on experiments as defining the field: "No matter what the efficiency of experimental design, the variation in conditions from one experiment to another is appalling. This is often true of experiments that purport to examine the effect of the same variables on the same phenomenon of learning. Even the same researcher may not maintain standard conditions in a series of experiments on similar problems. Lack of standardization makes most experiments wholly unique." Brogden recognizes the desirability of developing proper definitions for learning phenomena and presents a schema for categorizing the phenomena under the headings of acquisition, transfer, and retention, with acquisition being basic to the other two.

After presenting the characteristics of acquisition, he offers the following definition: "Acquisition is a progressive incremental change in the proficiency of performance by an organism; the direction, rate, and extent of change in the proficiency of performance are functions of the repetitive or continuous presentation of the conditions under which measurement of the change in performance is made." Here we can raise questions about almost every term used, both with regards to definition and to factual support. Whether learning is going to turn out to be progressive, or incremental, or reflect increasing proficiency and whether such proficiency is related to repetitive or continuous presentation of conditions are questions over which there is much disagreement. The definition is an admirable attempt and much can be said for it, but the operations of learning theorists suggest that one will not get far with this definition.

In his chapter, Hovland (1951), after noting that scores of definitions have been proposed and none universally accepted, falls back on a definition supplied by Hunter (1934) as one that best fits the specifications that a definition include reference to a trend of improvement in performance that comes about as a result of practice and to exclude changes due to fatigue, adaptation, drugs, maturation, and artifacts in measurement. Hunter's definition does all this apparently in these terms: "Learning will be defined as the change in performance associated with practice and not explicable on the basis of fatigue, of artifacts of measurement, or of receptor and effector changes."

In a more sophisticated effort, Spence (1951) carries Hilgard's notion of "learning as an inference" several steps beyond any of the definitions so far encountered. He recognizes, as some do not, that learning is in some way different from performance; that performance is observable, empirical, and learning is not, at least at present; that learning must be recognized as a hypothetical construct, that is, the term "learning" must refer to some kind of activity or state of the organism which we infer from behavior. It is assumed to be a state which is dependent upon ". . . past interactions of the individual with his environment . . . and . . . one of the conditions that determines his performance at any moment." To learn something about learning, then, according to Spence, it is necessary: (a) to specify the experimental variables, environmental and organic, that determine the observed behavioral changes that occur with practice, and (b) formulate the laws or functional interrelations that hold between the variables. This program, we can readily appreciate, is a large order, and it remains for us to discover how many variables have been specified, how many laws have been stated, and how many interrelationships have been determined.

Implicit in Spence's definition is the notion that learning, as a state of the organism, has some kind of physiological or neural foundation. Other definitions that have been cited are more or less concerned with behavioral correlations. Some learning psychologists deny interest in neural substrates, others give lip service to the general proposition that something must happen in the nervous system, and some, like Hebb (1949), make serious attempts to inquire into what might possibly be happening. While Hebb does not attempt a behavioral definition of learning because he views the whole question as extremely complicated and involved, he does favor a connectionism of a neural nature as the basic feature of the learning process. We will have many occasions to introduce his views on the great variety of problems that arise as we begin an examination of what learning psychologists do.

It should be quite clear from the definitions presented that there is no clearly operational definition of learning available as a starting point for our study. Some attempts have been made by Hull and Spence to set up such definitions for parts of the problems of behavior that they have studied, but as far as a general and basic definition of learning, comparable to a definition of some basic process in physics, we are still far afield. To pretend otherwise would be nonsensical and dangerous. To speak of past experience is to say nothing operationally. To talk about "practice" without defining it may get us past the introductory section of our story, but it contributes nothing. Consider McGeoch's (1942) definition: "Learning is a change in performance as a result of practice." It is obvious that no statement has been made, but rather several questions asked: What do you mean by change, how much, which direction? What do you mean by performance, and what has that got to do with it? What kind of performance? What is practice? After all, Thorndike has filled many pages of various books pooh-poohing the idea that practice, by itself, has anything to do with learning.

Perhaps the psychologists who make light of the need for a definition of learning have made a real point. It would be better if they carried their lightness a little further and openly refused to try. To pass off the question with a semiserious definition may be more harmful than humorous since it implies that either one does know what learning is or that progress can be made without a definition.[1] There is no question but that experiments can be performed, but whether or not that is progress is a different question. Without a constant watchfulness over the meaning of the experiments we emerge with the present-day results of a wide assortment of unrelated experiments and violently opposed points of view, disagreements about fundamental issues, and very little that can be offered as an example of the scientific work of learning psychologists. We do not even ask the psychologist to train our bird dogs, we go instead to a bird-dog man. How much further are we from telling our kindergarten teachers how to teach our children? Noneducational psychologists generally hold schools of education in some degree of contempt. Can they do better with the problems of the educator?

The question of definition cannot be ignored. But beyond this question there is a greater question. What is it that we are trying to define? If learning proves not to be a process that operates in the same way at all levels of behavior, at all ages, with all species, with all individuals with different backgrounds, then we are chasing a wild goose. It may be that what we have taken as a general process is, in fact, a series of different kinds of processes that require more and more specific definition and differentiation. Brogden may have been on the right track or at least facing in the right direction when he suggested that he thought of learning as consisting of at least three stages of categories of phenomena: acquisition, transfer, and retention. Whether these are too few or too many we can decide after we examine the phenomena. This appears to be the necessary next step.

A definition of learning which reflects the orientation of this text appears on page 120 It is presented after some important preliminary considerations are reviewed.

Chapter
2

The Learning
Psychologist
at Work

For the moment we can leave aside the question of what is learning, if indeed it is something, and, taking Hilgard's advice, look at the experiments that learning psychologists perform, hoping thereby to discover the varieties of phenomena in which Brogden is interested. We must also take account of his warning about the devious ways in which the experimenters tend to treat the variables and their varying interpretations of the same data. We shall, in effect, be searching for the variables that Spence wants to inter-relate as before-and-after factors with the hypothetical learning in between.

To look at everything learning psychologists have done and written about would be impossible. There is simply too voluminous a litera-ture for anyone to know it adequately in detail. We can, at best, select samples and hope to get a rough representation of what has been done. Later we can supplement these samples with more studies bearing on points that turn out to be of interest. Our objective for the present will be a purely practical one. We can take an empirical look at some learning studies, see what is going on, note the generalizations that appear to be pertinent to the data, and leave the theoretical interpretation for later. In our selection of samples we shall pick more or less representative situations and try not to duplicate too exten-sively. Let us begin at the beginning with a dog in Leningrad.[1]

---

[1] A much more extensive selection of illustrations has been presented by Hull (1934a).

AN ASSORTMENT OF LEARNING EXPERIMENTS

The Classical Pavlovian experiment. The general picture of Pavlov's experiments is commonly appreciated today. Virtually every educated person has some familiarity with the dog who salivated when a bell rang. For our purposes we can examine an experiment by one of his students, Frolov (in Pavlov 1927). In the experiment involved, a dog is surgically prepared so that the flow of saliva from the parotic duct is led outside the cheek and through a tube to a recording device. The dog is harnessed into the "Pavlov Frame" to limit its movements. It is stationed in a room that is separated from the experimenter who observes the dog by a periscope arrangement. By suitable means food powder is blown into the dog's mouth at intervals with a resulting discharge of saliva. When the experiment begins formally, a metronome is set beating and after a few seconds food powder is injected into the dog's mouth. The metronome stops and after a rest the procedure is repeated. After several such trials it is observed that the flow of saliva starts before the food is presented. The flow is generally less in quantity than when food is presented, but it does occur and will continue to occur in the absence of food for a number of additional tests trials. (If trials without food are continued, the flow of saliva diminishes and eventually stops altogether. After a longer rest than the usual intertrial interval, the animal may again respond to some degree.) Now, after the "conditioned response" has been established, Frolov occasionally presents food along with the metronome. The response then appears consistently and upon demand. After the conditioned response is considered reasonably securely established, a black card is exposed to the dog's view for 10 seconds and the metronome started at that time for about 15 seconds of ticking. Card and metronome trials are repeated, and metronome-food trials are interspersed. After 10 trials the black card is presented alone and the dog salivates. Pavlov employed the term "higher order" conditioning to describe or label such responding to a stimulus that had *never* been followed or accompanied by food.

Assuming the facts to be as described for this and numerous other experiments of the same type, what generalizations can be drawn? What questions should we and can we raise? Why did the dog salivate to the metronome? Why did the dog stop salivating to the metronome if food was not presented for several trials? Why did not the dog respond as much to the "conditioned stimuli" (card, metronome) as to the "unconditioned" stimulus (food)? Will such "conditioning" occur only to metronomes and cards, or can any stimulus agent be used? Can only salivation be so "conditioned," or only glandular activity? Why did the salivary response occur *before* the food appeared? After the black card became an effective stimulus, what would happen if we presented a grey card or a white one? Or a red flag?

Voluntary control. Roessler and Brogden (1943) [2] performed an experiment that, in its way, is as exciting as that of Frolov. They chose to "condition" the vasoconstrictive reaction (contraction of blood vessels) in human subjects. This reaction is presumably under control of the autonomic nervous system and can be elicited in some subjects by many intense stimuli, presumably as an accompaniment or feature of fear. The experimenters used a high-voltage shock applied to the lower arm. They measured the amount of vasoconstriction in the other arm by recording changes with a plethysmograph. The conditioning stimulus was a buzzer, which sounded for 20 seconds. During the last 5 seconds the shock was applied. As a special feature of the experiment, the subject repeated out loud the nonsense syllable "wek" for the duration of the buzzer. Of 15 subjects originally selected for the experiment, only 4 were found suitable (these gave the response to the shock, and not to the buzzer in preliminary tests). In 15, 20, 20, and 55 trials, respectively, the four subjects gave responses to the buzzer and simultaneous repetition of "wek." The conditioned response was faster but of much lesser magnitude than the response to shock. Two of the subjects were then found to be able to make the response to the repetition of "wek" alone, without the buzzer (this took an additional 5 and 25 trials, respectively; the other two subjects failed in 70 and 110 trials). The two surviving subjects were tested further and required to repeat the syllable "zub" on some trials (not followed by shock) and "wek" still followed by shock. One of the two subjects never responded to "zub" but continued to react to "wek," the other subject required 25 additional trials to make this "conditioned differentiation." As a final step, the subjects were asked to repeat the syllables subvocally when a red light was flashed. Within 5 and 25 trials, respectively, the subjects were reacting with vasoconstriction to subvocal repetitions of the syllables. (Subvocal speech is

---

[2] A condensed version of this report can be found in Crafts *et al* (1950), p. 266.

frequently identified with or related to "thinking" by psychologists.) In a final check experiment the subjects would produce the response when "thinking" "wek" but not "thinking" "zub." This achievement was attained without any additional training.

What questions can we ask about the Roessler-Brogden investigation? What points deserve analysis? Why did only two subjects survive the investigation? Is the vasoconstrictive response in humans similar to salivation in a dog? Both are usually considered "involuntary." What does "involuntary" mean? When the subjects could produce the response by thinking "wek" did the response now become a voluntary one? Why did Roessler and Brogden introduce the negative stimulus "zub"? How did the "conditioned differentiation" come about? What actually happened in the sense of a chain of events in the subjects? Did the shock produce the constriction directly or did the subject first become frightened and did the "fear" then produce the constriction? Why did the experimenters use 20 seconds of buzzer stimulation first? Could they have gone directly to the thinking phase of the experiment without the preliminary training with the buzzer?

Trial and error (?) learning. In *Principles of Behavior*, Hull (1943) describes a pair of experiments he calls *"demonstrations."* In Demonstration A, a rat is placed in a box divided into two compartments by a barrier which the rat can jump or scramble over. The floor of either side can be charged electrically at the whim of the experimenter. If the side on which the rat reposes is charged, the animal begins to hop about, to bite the bars, to stand on its hind feet, and go through a variety of routines. Sooner or later it gets over the barrier and is allowed to rest for a period. After an interval the floor is charged again and once more the rat engages in a variety of reactions which terminates with crossing the barrier. As the trials are repeated, the rat gets over the barrier sooner and sooner. Eventually it gets over the fence almost as soon as the shock is turned on. The first "escape" might have taken minutes, the last in a series of 10 might require only a second or two.

If the time interval is not too long between shocks, and if the procedure is repeated frequently, the rat may develop a pattern of jumping over the barrier at about the time the shock would normally be applied. Bugelski and Coyer (1950) found a 15-second period between shocks most effective and had rats performing almost like clockwork for some time.

In Demonstration B, a buzzer is sounded about 5 seconds before the floor is charged. The rat's behavior is similar to that just described. It again hops about, bites, prances, rears up, and eventually gets over the fence. In about 10 trials, however, the rat begins to scale the wall as soon as the buzzer sounds and gets over into the other compartment before the shock is turned on. The rat may continue to jump when the buzzer sounds for 10 or more trials before it fails to get over before the shock is applied. Again, if the time between trials is regular and brief the rat may start jumping *before* the buzzer sounds. A rat so trained by the writer jumped 95 times without any buzzer stimulus and this after over 100 jumps to a buzzer alone. In other words, for about 200 trials the rat jumped a barrier without any shock. It should be noted that this rat had been carefully prepared by repeated shocks on failure to jump to the buzzer for a two-week period of daily sessions of 24 jumps.

What questions do these demonstrations by Hull suggest? Did the rat learn to jump the fence? Did it already know how? Why did the rat jump to the buzzer? Why did it stop jumping after a number of trials? What stimuli were provoking the rat to jump when neither buzzer nor shock was applied? Was the rat rewarded for learning to cross the barrier? If so, what is the reward? Are there any conditioned stimuli in Demonstration A? In Demonstration B? Is jumping the fence a conditioned response, a learned response, or just the intelligent thing to do?

Acquired drives. Let us now turn to a similar experiment done with animal subjects by Miller (1948). This experiment is famous as a foundation for a theory of *acquired drives*. Miller made use of a two-compartment box with one compartment painted white, the other black. The white compartment had a grid floor through which rats could be shocked. The compartments were separated by a door. In the preliminary phases of the experiment, rats were shocked in the white compartment and allowed to run into the black compartment where they remained for 30 seconds. Ten such trials were given. In these trials the experimenter dropped the door before the animals got to it. In the next stage, the experimenter opened the door for the animals for 5 trials without shock. The animals continued to run. At this time, the door was fastened in such a way that it would open only if a little paddle wheel mounted above it were rotated slightly. Thirteen of the 25 albino rats originally selected learned to turn the wheel, thereby dropping the door and gaining access to the black room. All animals were given 16 trials under this condition.

Their time of turning the wheel decreased progressively. Following the sixteenth trial the door was fastened so that turning the wheel had no effect. A little bar was inserted at the side of the box, pressing of which would open the door. Within 6 trials the median rat failed to turn the wheel even once. The rats in the meantime began to press the bar with progressively shorter intervals and by the tenth trial they had given up turning the wheel and were pressing the bar in about 2 seconds after being dropped into the white compartment. It should be remembered that no shocks were given during any of the wheel turning or bar-pressing trials, and that only during the first 10 trials with the experimenter opening the door was the shock present.

Is this experiment similar to that of Roessler and Brogden? Do we have a "conditioned differentiation" here? Do the rats voluntarily turn the wheel and then press the bar? Why do the rats continue to leave the white compartment when there is no shock? Why did not all of the 25 do so? Why did they give up turning the wheel within 10 trials? (If the door is set to drop when the bar is pressed, Miller reports that animals will continue to press the bar as often as 600 times (see Miller [1951], p. 449). Did the animals fear the white compartment and want to leave it or did they want to get into the black compartment? Why did they learn to press the bar so quickly? Was previous training on the wheel responsible for the rapid bar-pressing learning? Was the white compartment a conditioned stimulus? Was being dropped on the bars the conditioned stimulus? What was the conditioned response here? What was the unconditioned stimulus for turning the wheel? What, for that matter, was the unconditioned response? What did the rats learn? To open doors?

Operant conditioning. Let us turn now to a type of experiment introduced into psychology laboratories by B. F. Skinner (1938) in the early thirties. In this type of experiment, a hungry rat is placed in a simple box with a little lever protruding into the box over a food cup. Pressure on the lever closes a circuit that controls an automatic mechanism which discharges a small pellet of food into the cup. Depending on the size of the box and a number of other factors, the rat can be expected to approach the level and food-cup location fairly soon. If we wait a bit the rat may bump or push the bar with his nose or bite at it or place a paw on it. One of these moves may result in the release of a food pellet. If we wait some more, the lever may again be depressed, then again, and again; the number of presses per minute

FIG. 2.1. Does behavior become stereotyped? The first three pictures will probably be seen as very similar. The fourth, taken minutes later, is quite different. The fifth and sixth again are similar to the others.

keeps increasing until there is barely time to consume the pellet before the lever is pressed again. As the pellets are consumed and the animal's hunger might be assumed to decrease, the lever-pressing slows down and becomes spasmodic.

The experiment could be done using any other animal and arranging for the animal to do something which it does more or less naturally. Skinner (1950) himself has turned to the pigeon as a subject and used the natural pecking behavior of the pigeon. The experimenter waits until a pigeon pecks at a target mounted on a cage wall or at some other place *chosen by the experimenter* and then drops grain to the pigeon. The whole affair can be mechanized and the pigeon put to work at the business of pecking. Pigeons will build up tremendous work totals and anyone who likes data can accumulate as much as he can use with only one active pigeon.

Getting back to our rat, suppose that at some point in the period when the pressing is well established we disconnect the feeding mechanism so that pressing the bar no longer results in the appearance of a pellet. The rat continues to press and pokes its nose into the food cup time after time. But the pressing becomes less and less rapid and finally the rat stops for minutes at a time. It might press several hundred times in an hour after the last pellet was delivered.

It might be mentioned that in connection with a box of this sort, the lever-pressing is recorded automatically and many experimenters pay little attention to the rat after it is placed in the box. The experimenters concern themselves with the record of lever presses. It might be difficult for them to answer many of the questions that this type of experiment might raise. For example, how does the rat press the bar? Is it just an accident? How often does it approach and touch the lever without actually pressing hard enough to operate the mechanism? Does the rat always visit the food cup after each press?

Perhaps more serious questions can be raised about the behavior of the rat in the box which we may have trouble with even if we watch the rat. Does the rat "know" what it is doing? Has the rat learned anything? Has he learned to *press levers in order to get food?* Does the rat press the bar because it wants to, or chooses to, or *must* it press? Why does the rat continue pressing for an hour without a single pellet? Why does it gradually stop pressing instead of all at once? Is this conditioning? Are there any conditioned or unconditioned stimuli? Skinner calls behavior like bar-pressing "operant" conditioning. The term indicates that the organism is *operating* upon its environment. In Skinner's view, the typical Pavlovian procedure is considered as "respondant" conditioning because it appears that in these cases the environment is operating on the organism which merely *responds*. Skinner does not imply that there are no stimuli affecting the organism in his experiment, but rather that the experimenter may not be concerned with the stimuli and is content with recording the responses alone. We will have to consider this distinction carefully later on.

Secondary rewards. In Frolov's experiment we saw how a dog responded to a card which had never accompanied food. We have just noted Skinner's distinction between Pavlovian and operant conditioning. A number of experiments have been performed in which something related to Frolov's finding, if not quite analogous, occurs in the Skinner situation. The writer, for example, noticed that a rat working in one Skinner box might run to the food cup if a rat in another box pressed the lever and activated the somewhat noisy food dispenser. Apparently the sound of the mechanism had some bearing on food-cup behavior.

In an experiment designed to observe the effects of the clicking sound (Bugelski, 1938), some rats were trained to press levers. On the following day half the rats were allowed to work in boxes where the mechanism was disconnected from the lever and produced no noise while the other half worked under the original noisy condition. Neither group obtained any food, however, and the question to be answered was: how long would each group work? The rats that worked with the sound effects produced 30 percent more responses than those in the silent boxes. At the time of the report, the writer suggested that the noise was serving some sort of "subgoal," a part of the total goal situation, and that in some fashion the occurrence of the sound was rewarding or reinforcing to the rat. Since such value, if there was one, had been acquired in the box, the function of such an irrelevant and unconsumable stimulus came to be called a "secondary reinforcer." A great many experiments have been performed in which secondary reinforcers are said to operate. The writer no longer would describe the function of the noise as he did originally and a different explanation will be suggested at a more appropriate time (see p. 91). The experiment does, however, raise its own questions as already implied by the suggestion of a different explanation.

Are there such processes or mechanisms as secondary reinforcers? How do they work? Do they bring pleasure to the organism? Are hundred-dollar bills secondary reinforcers? What about the sound of a dinner gong or the appearance of a waiter in a restaurant? Is praise nothing more than a noise that formerly accompanied a nursing bottle or spoonful of Pablum? How does a secondary reinforcer acquire its powers? Can secondary reinforcers serve as a basis for developing third- or fourth-order reinforcers? Is the noise of the Skinner box like Frolov's black card? Wherein lies the difference?

Punishment. Although psychologists frequently use shock stimuli in learning situations, they have not paid much attention to the effects of punishment in terms of the general public's orientation to the problem. Ordinarily, for example, a child might be punished for doing something someone else regards as bad or undesirable behavior. The parent or teacher might be interested in the effectiveness of punishment in such situations, but psychologists have not quite approximated these situations in the laboratory. Thorndike (1932) reported studies on punishment where a college student would be told that he was "wrong" when he chose one word out of a chance list of five. Thorndike usually found no negative effect of saying "wrong" and concluded that punishment was ineffective. Similarly, Tolman (1930) shocked students when they entered right alleys in stylus-maze experiments. He found improvement in learning. Such studies raise more questions than they answer. Perhaps the outstanding study of punishment effects is that of Estes (1944) who performed a series of experiments with rats in Skinner boxes. After a rat "learned" to press a lever a shock would be given if the lever was touched. Estes found, in general, that a shocked rat would refrain from touching the bar *for a while*, but if Estes allowed the rat to return to the box after a week or two, the bar-pressing would be resumed as if it had never been interrupted. We shall come back to Estes again (see p. 274), but now we can pause for questions.

Does the severity of punishment enter into the situation? Frequency? What does the punished subject learn? Does he learn *not* to do something or does he learn to do something else? Does it remain a matter of choice? Can we "straighten" somebody out by keeping him after school or paddling him? Can we eliminate any kind of behavior by punishment? How could punishment work, if it does? Since there might be a history of reinforcement prior to punishment, how much punishment should be administered? Is the pleasure of three stolen apples counteracted by three spankings or is one stolen apple adequate reinforcement to keep a habit alive through twenty spankings? Can psychologists suggest a formula by which the Mikado could fit the punishment to the crime?

Puzzle-box experiments. Before we leave the subject of animals in boxes, and we have seen a number of types already, we might look at some cats placed in boxes, with food outside. The door of the box can be opened by pulling a string or operating some other device. This is the situation that Thorndike invented back in the early part of the century. It is opposite, in function, to Skinner's box where the food comes to the animal. Skinner has a strong advantage in his box as he does not have to capture his rat after every lever press. Guthrie and Horton's (1946) cat box represents the highest development of this device. In this box, a cat is allowed to enter the main portion of the box from a smaller starting box which is then closed behind it. The main section is built of glass walls with a door at one end. The door opens only if a small pole placed somewhere in the middle of the box is tilted enough to break contact with a switch beneath the pole. The moment contact is broken, the door opens, and at the same time a photograph is taken automatically of the cat at the moment of contact with the pole. Upon leaving the box, the cat may partake of fish or milk placed just beyond the door or, as happens, it may just take off.

At first a cat may wander about the box, moving and scratching. This may take some time, often 20 minutes. Sooner or later it bumps into or nudges the pole. The door opens and the cat may leave immediately. Sometimes the cat may be facing in the wrong direction and its departure is delayed. What do the photographs show? Guthrie examined and compared successive pictures and reports that there was a striking correspondence between pictures in a sequence. If a particular cat happened to bump the pole with its nose on the first occasion, there was a strong probability that it would do so on the next occasion. Another cat might poke the pole with a paw the first time and continue doing so later on. Still another might back up into the pole and adopt that technique. Guthrie bases much of his theorizing on what looks like a strong tendency toward stereotyping of movements. If the pole is moved to a new location, a cat seems not to take this into account and paws or waves away at the place where the pole used to be.

Although the cat must be captured between trials the situation is not unlike that in the Skinner box. The writer has arranged for automatic picture-taking by rats in a Skinner box and has found some remarkably consistent sequences. One rat works left-pawed, another right-pawed. A third uses his teeth, a fourth noses the bar, and so on. But, to return to the cat, does it "know" what it is doing? Has it learned to open doors like Miller's rats? Why does the cat work? Because it is hungry? It frequently ignores the food. Because it does not like boxes? The writer once had a cat that used to hop back into a Thorndike-type box as soon as it had escaped by displacing a latch. Why does the cat scratch away at emptiness when the pole is moved? Why does stereotyping appear to develop?

Cognitive learning. One more type of box and we will have done with them. This time the boxes are small containers which are attached to the ends of a T-maze. A T-maze consists of a narrow runway which connects with a cross-member in the form of a T. At the "choice point," that is, the intersection of the starting runway and the crosspiece, the animal can turn in either direction and arrive at one of the end boxes which may contain food. A T-maze is frequently elevated about 3 feet above the floor.

Using such an elevated T-maze, Tolman and Gleitman (1949) trained 25 rats to run to each of the boxes for food. On half the trials they ate in one box, and in the remaining trials they ate in the other. The two boxes differed in color, illumination, and general construction details, material, and so on. After this preliminary training all the rats were shocked after being placed directly in one of the end boxes. The boxes had been detached from the T. Half the group was shocked in one box and half in the other. Each rat was shocked for two 20-second periods. After a 2-hour wait, the rats were replaced on the starting leg of the T-maze and 23 of the 25 rats "avoided" the pathway that led to the particular box in which they had been shocked, that is, "turned to the side opposite to that which contained the end-box they had been shocked in." We are told no more of what the rats did. Did they actually run down and enter the "safe" boxes? How did they behave in their running? Three rats did make the "wrong" turn. How so?

This is an example of what Tolman calls "place" learning. By this term he suggests that the rat learns the location of various features of his environment; such learning can then be considered to amount to serving as a "cognitive map" of the situation. The rat, according to Tolman, knows "what leads to what." Does he, really? What does the Tolman-Gleitman experiment prove? That the rats knew the location of the particular boxes and that they used this knowledge to deduce the conclusion that the road to one would be dangerous? This conclusion certainly has no logical validity unless we presume that the rats introduced a premise that the same box which is ordinarily supplied with food when found at the end of the maze now contains the fearful shock. Actually a bright rat might well fear a detached box and carry on in the original situation. This might happen with or without a cognitive map. Tolman need not be distressed no matter how the experiment comes out. In a repetition of this experiment, the writer found substantially the same results as did Tolman and Gleitman. The history of many similar experiments, however, leads one to at least wonder about possible unobserved influences that might have been operating on the rats. Many psychologists would like to have a means of manipulating the variables that result in the "cognitive map" rather than to use the concept itself as a variable when it appears to be a possible explanatory device. The original report leaves out much that might be interesting. Was the avoidance apparent at the "choice point" itself? How fast did the rats run on the postshock trials? What would they do on a second run? What factors in the different features of the two end boxes were important? Were these factors related to the external appearance of the boxes? To movements that had to be made to enter, leave, or remain in them? We shall find such details of considerable significance later on.

Human learning.

NONSENSE SYLLABLES. But enough of cats and dogs and rats and boxes. Do psychologists never study human behavior and human learning? We did mention people a while back, the ones studied by Roessler and Brogden. True there were only two of them, and the reaction observed was a change in blood volume which the subjects did not even know was taking place although they could bring it about by saying "wek."

Thousands of other human subjects have been studied as they said "wek," and "kem," "mel," "nuv," "yik," and similar noises. These noises or "nonsense syllables" were introduced into psychological experimentation by Ebbinghaus (1885) many years ago. It is generally recognized that when human subjects are asked to learn verbal material, it is necessary to select materials of equal difficulty in order to compare one condition with another. Furthermore, familiarity with one material, or a sympathy with it, might help its retention over unpopular or strange material. For better or worse, many psychologists have had subjects learn many sets of nonsense syllables in a great variety of circumstances and a great deal of lore has been acquired about the process of learning them. We will look at some of this lore later but right now we can consider a sample experiment of considerable interest. It is an experiment by Lester (1932) and deals with something she called "mental set." The concept of set is so significant for the discussions to follow that we should at least attempt a glimpse at this furtive factor in learning theory.

Lester's experimental arrangements were not complicated. Subjects learned a list of syllables and were told to come back the next day. The next day they were told to learn another list, and then were asked to recall or relearn the original list. The experimental conditions consisted only in different instructions to the subjects about what would take place on the next day. Nothing was done to the subjects other than simply telling them about the next day's work. The subjects were divided into groups according to the instructions as follows:

    I. Told to learn the list and return the next day.
   II. Told that another list would be learned tomorrow and the first relearned.
  III. Told learning a new list the next day might interfere with recall of the list about to be learned.
  IV. Told about possible interference effect and asked to resist it as much as possible.
   V. Told the same as group I but not required to learn another list on the next day.

The results of Lester's experiment lead to a great many questions. In the first place, all but group V lost a great deal of what had been learned on the previous day. The new list of syllables apparently prevented adequate recall or retention of the old. Why? Why should something you learn later affect something you learned before? The somewhat astonishing side of the results is that retention was better and better down the line-up of groups. Group I suffered the most, group IV the least, with the rest in order. We are brought to the conclusion that if one knows he is to learn something later and also knows that this may have a deleterious effect, he can, somehow, avoid this negative effect. By doing what? The subjects could not tell. The data offer no cues. The mere warning of future learning has some virtue. The additional information about its possible "interference" effects helps, and trying to resist something that does not even come into existence until the next day helps even more. How? We can speculate, of course, and we will later, but for the moment we must leave the subject with a bit of verbal magic—"mental set."

Generalization and discrimination. We should not conclude our illustrations without some mention of a commonly accepted principle, that of generalization. We are all familiar with the process, at least on one level. If we are bitten by a kitten, we might avoid all cats, even gentle ones. Folklore expresses it as "once bitten, twice shy." The ever-handy and all-wise folklore also tells us that "one swallow does not make a summer" and thereby we are warned against hasty conclusions. Pavlov's dogs would salivate not only to the original bell that preceded the food but to other bells as well. In a famous experiment Hovland (1937) tried to determine the nature of this *generalization* phenomenon. He shocked human subjects immediately after sounding a pure tone of 1000 cycles per second. The subjects ordinarily are somewhat disturbed by the shock and a measure of this disturbance can be obtained by recording a decrease in the electrical resistance of the skin. This drop in skin resistance is called the "psychogalvanic reflex" or PGR. (It is frequently employed in so-called lie detector studies.) An interesting feature of the PGR is that the subject cannot feel it or know that it is occurring. After a number of trials in which tone and shock are paired, the subjects begin to give the PGR to the tone without shock. Hovland recorded the amount of PGR obtained when tones differing from the original by known steps were used. His results showed that less and less response was made when the tones were more and more distant from the original. Plotting his findings, Hovland discovered a negatively accelerated curve, falling off from the point of origin. We shall have to look more closely at Hovland's experiment later, but for the moment we can ask a few questions.

Is the generalization of the PGR related to such generalizations as fears of cats and dogs? Do we dislike people with mustaches because someone with a mustache hurt us when we were young? Is the child that calls every man "daddy" generalizing? How do we ever come to call only one particular man "daddy"? Is generalization useful or harmful? Why do we not fear lions at the zoo? Is generalization a genuine phenomenon or could it be some sort of artifact of experimental procedures? Could generalization be a real enough and empirically observable affair and yet not necessarily represent the operation of some law or principle? It might be that certain kinds of behavioral events are a function of the number of component stimuli in a situation and that changing the stimuli in the pattern may involve changes in the behavior such that a "generalization" principle might be postulated to account for the event, without actually being warranted. But this problem can wait.

Mediated generalization. We can round out an even dozen illustrations by picking one from an area that has begun to receive increasing attention from psychologists, that of "thinking." Learning psychologists seem to be fascinated by the nature of thinking, reasoning, or problem solving, and sometimes their experiments are more in the nature of observations of puzzle solutions than of "learning." We, too, will look into this engrossing question, but first we want to look at an experiment that might serve as a model or paradigm of a problem solution even though no one involved in the experiment has a problem, unless it be the psychologist.

The original experiment was reported only briefly by Lumsdaine (1939). He arranged to photograph eyelid blinks by attaching a little extension to the eyelids of his subjects. A shadow cast by this extension could be recorded on sensitive paper. Any movement of the eyelid could be timed and measured. To make the subjects blink, a small striker was arranged to hit the cheek just below the eye. A light served as a "conditioned" stimulus and when light and striker were paired a number of times, the onset of the light would be followed by a blink. This was only a routine conditioning setup. Lumsdaine then paired the striker with a shock to the finger and recorded the finger withdrawal. A number of striker-shock combinations resulted in a conditioned withdrawal response. The subject is now equipped with two conditioned responses: (a) light-blink, and (b) striker-finger withdrawal. What will happen to the subject if he now is placed in position for seeing the light and has his finger on the electrode and the light is turned on? Lumsdaine reports that his subjects reacted to the light by withdrawing their fingers even though the light had never accompanied shock.

Is this a case of adding two and two and getting four? Was it the right answer? Is this experiment in any way like a problem? Why would a subject react with his finger to a light? It should be pointed out that the whole affair is over and done with before the subject knows what he is doing. Do we have to know what we are doing to solve problems or give the right answers?

At the beginning of this section we used the label "mediated generalization." What does this expression mean? Where is the generalization? What is mediated? What is the mediator? What has this experiment to do with thinking? Do we have here an illustration of something for nothing? Can we say that the subject learned something without practicing it? What does this experiment suggest about "thinking" or problem solving? How does this experiment differ from those of Thorndike and Guthrie who used "puzzle" boxes? Did the cats have problems, too? Perhaps you have more questions; if you have, save them for later. We had best step back and try to get an over-all view of what these experiments represent.

AN OVERVIEW

We have now seen some learning psychologists at work. What have they been doing, and why? What have they found out, what have they seen, what have they said they have seen? These are the questions that are of the first importance and to these we can now turn.

What have they been doing? We have seen the psychologist handling various types of organisms and subjecting them to various situations. Psychologists have used almost every species commonly available—the rat, the guinea pig, the cockroach, the turtle, the fish, the chicken, the pigeon, the cat and dog, the soldier, and the college sophomore. We have, or could have, seen the psychologist capture these "subjects" and in one way or another place them in a situation. Some have come quietly, others have to be strapped down or penned up in some chamber. Some have been allowed no food or drink for various periods of time, others either come equipped or are provided with other reasons for cooperating with the psychologist.

Once in the situation we have seen the psychologist present various stimuli (lights, buzzers, bells, et cetera) or other more intimate stimuli like food, shock, water. The actual range of stimuli employed has been limited only by the ingenuity of the psychologist. In some situations the psychologist has acted as if the stimuli he presents can be expected to *evoke* some behavior from the animal, more or less directly, as a tap on the knee elicits a knee jerk; in other cases, the psychologist has set the stage and then waited for his actors to *emit* behavior, such as bar-pressing, pecking, running, wheel-turning, and so forth. Whether there is a real difference between *emitting* and being *provoked* into action is a question to which we shall return a little later. In any case, sooner or later, the animal does something, and this "something" is assumed to be related to what the psychologist has done with regard to stimulus, situation, or preparation of the subject. What does the subject actually do? We have seen some subjects salivate, jump over barriers, undergo vasoconstriction, press bars, turn wheels, knock over little poles, mutter nonsense syllables, turn left or right on runways. If we are really strict, we must be a little careful in describing what we have seen. The notorious invalidity of eye-witness testimony is well known. In some of the experiments considered, the psychologist can actually testify that he saw some change in an instrument or that he observed an organism moving. It is doubtful, however, that any psychologist ever saw a subject "turn a wheel." The turning is something that happens to a wheel. The animal places weight against it, perhaps, or extends and flexes his limbs; what happens after that is of the nature and business of wheels. When we get right down to the actual observations, we find psychologists rather indifferent and unnoticing observers of the reactions of their subjects. Frequently they place the animal in a box of one kind or another where the animal can be seen with difficulty, if at all, and the psychologist may never know these things if he observes only the moving paper and its markers. We must, of course, be careful not to endow the animal with "knowledge" of how the gadgets work. The psychologist himself might not know. We may have to distinguish between "acts" and "movements."

In many of the situations we looked at, the subject was first forced to submit to some type of physical insult—a blow to the face or the pride, a puff of air to the eye, starvation or dehydration, electric shock or other nocuous stimulation. Following the insult the psychologist frequently offers apologies in the form of food, drink, rest, or freedom (for a time). The manipulations of these "punishments" and "rewards" will occupy us a great deal, shortly; but for the moment, we merely note that they are used. The use of these "punishments" and "rewards" actually involves a two-pronged problem. The punishment can be provided *before* as well as after the event. In fact, the introduction of some unpleasant state of affairs appears to be almost universal in creating the situation in which the learning is to take place. If we ask the psychologist why he "prepares" his subject in this fashion he can answer by saying that he knows, empirically, that if he does not make things unpleasant for the subjects, they will not learn; the more theoretically inclined will say that some degree of motivation is necessary for learning to take place. Hilgard (1953), in his introductory text, goes so far as to say, "If we could control the variable of motivation, learning would take care of itself." Many psychologists talk about the significance and importance of "drives" in learning. Some feel that no learning can take place without some drive being present, and since the identification of the drive is often difficult with human learning, they suggest that the drive itself might be a learned or "acquired" drive. For other psychologists, not only must there be a drive, native or learned, but such a drive must be satisfied or decreased at least to some degree if learning is to occur. Other students of learning are of different minds on this subject and have varying views In any case, so important has this question become in the learning literature that psychologists are grouped into camps by the position they take on the relation of motivation to learning. This will be a major concern of ours as we develop our appreciation of learning problems and phenomena.

In considering the several experiments that have been reviewed, we might have noticed that a variety of species of subjects has been employed. Most readers of this book will have decided long ago that they have little in common with the rat and tend to resent any suggestion that this might not be the case. What do rats and cats and dogs have to do with the problems of human learning anyhow? Do these "lower" creatures learn in the same way that the human does? Are we men or mice? Why do not the psychologists study human learning? The nonsense syllable experiment? Who learns nonsense syllables outside of laboratories? Would not the psychologist have dogs learn nonsense syllables if he could get the brutes to talk? Why do they avoid people in favor of rats? This question has many aspects and will have to be considered as fully as possible if we are to appreciate the relation of the psychologists' work to human problems. For the moment we leave it as a question.

What other questions have occurred to you? A close look at the experiments reported will reveal two interesting and important phenomena. In every case reported, the subject began to make his responses sooner and sooner as the learning progressed. The rat began to jump the fence before the shock came on. If it did not, we might have felt that it had not learned very much. The students began to recite the nonsense syllables before they appeared in the memory drum. The vasoconstriction occurred before the shock, and so on. The coming-forward-in-time of the response is an outstanding feature of learning. Is it only a sign that learning has occurred or does it have additional importance? Does it mean that a rat "anticipates" a shock and decides to do something about it? Does a blood vessel anticipate a shock and decide to contract also? Or is this a matter not of "anticipation" but of "antedating"? Does it have a significance of its own? Having posed the problem we can leave it for the future and turn to another.

From Hovland's experiment we note that a response can be given by a subject to a variety of stimuli that have some similarity to the original training stimulus. The subject is said to have "generalized," or, more properly, the learning has generalized. What is the significance of such generalization? Does it mean we can know something without learning it? Is this good or bad for us? Can we get into trouble by heading for the dinner table when the fire bell sounds? How does this generalization take place? How do we get rid of undesirable generalized responses? When the child with a bleeding finger says, "Look at the jelly," is it generalizing? How does it learn not to describe blood with the term "jelly"? Or, in more technical language, how does it learn to discriminate? Brogden and Roessler's subjects would constrict to "wek" but not to "zub." Had they learned this discrimination? Did they learn it in the experiment? By what process? Is human learning actually much different from generalization and discrimination? Are we not always learning what not to do as well as what to do?

In thinking about the behavior of the subjects under study in the various experiments, you might have noticed that the experimenters frequently chose responses of a glandular or autonomic nervous control type (salivation, PGR, vasoconstriction) and that some of these, including perhaps the eyelid blink, can happen without our being able to say when or how often or to what degree the response does take place. Other experimenters used responses that appear to be more conscious and voluntary (pressing bars, turning wheels, saying nonsense syllables). Are all these different kinds of behavior learned in the same way, according to the same principles? For some of these we employed the terms "conditioned" and "unconditioned" stimuli. For others such terms did not appear readily appropriate. Is there a difference between conditioning and learning? Are there two, three, or more kinds of learning?

We might have noticed also that the learned behavior on occasion disappears, is lost, forgotten, or interfered with in some fashion. Psychologists frequently use the term "extinction" to refer to the disappearance of a response when its occurrence is not followed by a reward or "unconditioned" stimulus. Is this disappearance related to forgetting? Are they the same?

In one of the experiments (Lumsdaine's) we saw how a response was given to a stimulus although it had never been associated directly with this stimulus. As in the question of generalization we have here an example of "knowing" something without having learned it. Is this a psychological freak event or is it, on the contrary, quite a common feature of human behavior? Do we actually know many things without learning them? Or, putting the question more operationally, are we capable of solving problems or coming up with the right answers without having had the specific behavior patterns or movements learned in the specific situation? If we are, how does this come about? Psychologists talk about this as the problem of "transfer" or "mediated generalization." We shall have a lot to say about it in the future.

Perhaps we have asked enough questions for awhile. Others will come up as we try to answer the ones already raised. We can now restate and rephrase some of the questions in a more systematic fashion. The questions and the answers, if any, will form the substance of the following chapters. The questions that we have considered are arranged in the sequence in which they will be discussed. The sequence is meant to be a logical one, rather than one of relative importance. Whether a question comes early or late has no bearing on its importance. We can probably rest assured that they are all important.

1. What is the relationship of the learner to learning? Does it make any difference whether the learner is a rat, a horse, a human infant, a college student? Do all individuals within a species learn alike?

2. Are there different kinds of learning or only different kinds of learning theories? Are learning and conditioning the same? What is the relation of performance to learning?

3. What is learned? What behavior is unlearned? Does learning have to do with ideas, "acts," or movements? How do individual responses or sensory-motor units become integrated into serial combinations, skills, problem solutions? Can we arrive at a definition of learning?

4. What are the characteristics of learned behavior? This includes the question of generalization, discrimination, anticipation. The relation of learning to perception enters here; so does the relation of learning to external manipulations such as the nature of stimuli, temporal intervals, drugs, fatigue, and so on. The efficiency of learning enters the picture. Does learning take place in one trial? Is it continuous and mechanical or insightful?

5. How do we measure learning? What are the units? How does learning develop? Is there such a thing as a "learning curve"?

6. On what conditions does learning depend? This is the major problem. It includes the question of how motivation is related to learning. What are drives, and how do they fit into the problem? What of acquired drives? What of attention and mental set? Can learning occur without rewards or motivation? Can we entertain the concepts of "latent" learning or "incidental" learning?

7. There is the other side of the problem just considered. What is the effect of reinforcement or reward? What are secondary rewards and how do they work? What is the effect of punishment or negative reinforcement?

8. Are there any other conditions or principles besides motivation and reinforcement that might account for learning? How about recency, frequency, insight?

9. What happens during extinction? Is it the same as forgetting? What factors determine the efficiency of retention? Why do we forget?

10. What is the nature of the influence of past experience on present activity and learning efficiency? Does early training (in infancy) have any effect on adult learning? Does practicing one activity help in acquiring or retaining another? Can there be negative effects of practice? How does learning enter into the matter of thinking and problem solving?

11. How do emotional and temperamental factors relate to learning? Can emotions be conditioned? Are disturbed personalities the victims of faulty training? Are conflicts subject to the same laws as learned behavior? Can maladjusted personalities be retrained or re-educated?

12. What can the learning psychologist offer to the educator? Can we apply the laws of learning to the school, the home, the factory, and the world we live in?

Chapter

3 The Capacity of the Learner

Before we can undertake a consideration of the nature of learning, it is necessary to examine the question of who is going to learn. It is possible that learning is learning, no matter where in the animal kingdom, and no matter what is being learned. If it should turn out, however, that different species or individuals are more or less different in their manner of learning or in what they will learn, we should, indeed, be in difficulty trying to generalize about learning as learning. We would be continually under the obligation to point out the necessary modifications and compromises that might have to be made in our eventual principles.

Sometimes psychology is defined as the science of the white rat and the college sophomore, and it is true that by far the greatest number of studies is devoted to these interesting species. It might even be said that the college sophomore is used, when he is used, because the white rat happens to be unable to do one thing that the college sophomore has been called on to do by the psychologist, and that is, learn nonsense syllables. As was suggested earlier, if the rat could learn nonsense syllables, the psychologist would use it, and then, even the college sophomore would be pretty much out of the picture. Why this tremendous preoccupation with rats? Are they the noblest species of them all, something to admire or emulate? Students frequently object to rat data as irrelevant for human problems. Their reasons are usually superficial and sentimental and are probably based on antipathies developed in childhood. They resent the implication that there is any basis for comparison but seem to be unable to point out the fallacy in a syllogism which roughly appears to them to read: All rats are mammals, man is a mammal; therefore man is a rat. Their objections, however, never seem to carry any weight, even to themselves, because of some uneasy feeling that scientists could not possibly be wasting their time on rats without some proper justification. The justification, however, is seldom spelled out; and so the uneasiness remains, suppressed for the duration of a psychology course, perhaps.

The rat in psychological experiments. Since a great deal of the remainder of this book will be concerned with the twistings and turnings of rats, it behooves us to consider immediately what might be the purpose of using these lowly creatures in the pursuit of learning about learning. The notion that in the rat we have a simple creature in which the principles of learning will appear in some type of magnification for ready scrutiny is, after all, just an old bromide.[1] The principles have not appeared, at least not in any clear-cut form. The existence of numerous antithetical points of view among psychologists should be enough evidence to suggest that the rat is not a simple creature, nor does the rat demonstrate learning in color and in three dimensions. The suggestion that because the rat is a mammal, and a vertebrate, and has a central nervous system with a brain is not quite enough to make an equation with man. Although some psychologists like to imagine the rat's brain as being a miniature human type, any suggestion that there is any exact functional similarity between the rat's brain and that of the human is simply not true (Herrick, 1926). It is true that the rat's brain has the same general component parts as does that of man, but there the similarity ends. The really important question is rather: what does the rat's brain do? And the answer to that question, based on both behavior and anatomical proportions is roughly: sense and "emote." The rat's brain to a considerable degree consists of an extension of his smelling organs, the rhinencephalon,[2] with the remainder of the brain functioning to receive other sensory impulses and to regulate motor activity. The relative proportion of "association" areas in the rat's brain is meager. By contrast, as Hebb (1949) points out, the greater part of man's brain is devoted to cortical areas with no apparent sensory or motor functions of a direct nature, but which, because of their presence, and because we like to

---

[1] The writer has dealt with this problem in greater detail in an earlier text (1951). See especially Chap. 5, The Choice of Subjects for Experimental Work.
[2] The rhinencephalon is now presumed to be functionally involved in emotional behavior (Krieg, 1953).

believe that nature is not too wasteful, must serve a purpose, and that purpose, for Hebb, is to function as *association* areas.

In developing his own argument, Hebb concludes that the brain of the rat might best be described as a sensory type of brain, that of man as an association type. In behavioral terms, we would expect the rat to react more or less directly to any stimulus which impinged upon him in at least threshold strength. The rat would then be extremely sensitive to odors, sounds, lights, cutaneous, and other stimulation and would react quickly to stimuli of these orders. A sound would result in pricking up the ears, an odor in a quivering of the nose, a touch on the vibrissae in a turn of the head, and so on. There would be little hesitation in reaction and little variety in response. We could expect the same thing to happen over and over again, within limits of fatigue, adaptation, frustration, or emotion. Variability would be (although high enough) relatively low compared to that of man or monkey. We would call the rat a relatively "stimulus-bound" organism.

Consider now the behavior of man and his relative independence from direct action. From childhood we are taught to inhibit our actions, motor and verbal. We are cautioned to stop and think, to look before we leap, to examine, to "watch out," to "shut up." The child, to be sure, is "impulsive," that is to say, like the rat to some degree "stimulus-bound," but the entire program of its training is geared to destroy such bonds. We learn gradually to ignore stimuli of many kinds, to suppress, to subjugate impulses, to postpone comforts, to delay reaction, to hesitate. By the time we reach college age we have so learned to be quiet and withhold replies that the reverse process is attempted by college professors who frequently bemoan, "If we could only get them to talk."

What of the variety of possible alternatives that are available in the responses that might be made to any stimulus? Noises are not heard unless our "attention" is called to them. We learn to hold our noses in the air. Odors are ignored deliberately; it is not polite to sniff. The multitude of visual stimuli encountered on a street in the form of buildings, traffic, passersby, the natural environment itself is ignored or responded to *selectively*. We can bump and jostle our way through a crowded department store and scarcely notice the people or the merchandise, the sounds, the pain in our feet, the hunger in our stomachs. We can flip through a book not seeing words until we come to a sentence for which we are searching. What a human being will do when a bell rings depends largely on what kind of bell it is, when it rings, how often, in what musical quality, and on the particular human being. To a degree, of course, this is true of the rat also, but his possible range of responses is extremely limited in comparison. Steam and ice only differ "to a degree." The rat's action can be predicted, within limits, depending upon what some experimenter has done to the rat on previous occasions when that or different bells have been rung. The reaction of the rat will be an either-or kind. Either he will do what the experimenter expects him to do or he will not. The human might also do or not do what some experimenter expects, but that is not all that the human will do. He will also engage in considerable additional behavior either explicitly or implicitly, and depending upon his relative freedom of action, his associations not only with bells but experimenters, with any number of surrounding details, with past events and verbalizations of future possibilities, his behavior may be quite unpredictable and unique, at least as far as the experimenter is concerned. The behavior may be far more predictable in a laboratory because of what the subject himself believes to be proper and depends on his "sets." [3]

To get back to Hebb's analysis for a moment, we can consider behavior to be in some respects dependent upon the relative amounts of sensory and association structures within the nervous system. Hebb expresses this as an A/S ratio and makes it a key principle for evaluation of the kinds of behavior we can expect from different organisms. A large association area will tend to facilitate diversified behavior, delayed activity, multiple possibilities of response. A relatively large sensory area will tend to make the behavior less flexible, more in direct control of the external stimulus world. We will come back to the concept of the A/S ratio later in this chapter, but another problem of more immediate concern now confronts us. We must not limit our interpretation of "association areas" to a function of merely providing additional response outlets for connection with incoming stimulus impulses. Rather, the association areas must be conceived as providing for more and more complex integrations, facilitation, and inhibitions from cortex to thalamus and back again, for proprioceptive and

---

[3] The writer once tried to "frustrate" some 40 freshmen of Yale College. In spite of the most abusive treatment, the freshmen maintained considerable poise, restraint, and gentlemanly dignity. The experimenters were more frustrated than the subjects. See *Frustration and Aggression* by Dollard et al. (1939).

other "feedback," for arousal of a great variety of cortical activity which may include the stimulation of outlets never before "associated" with the incoming impulses.

If it is true that the rat is a stimulus-bound organism and that man is relatively not so, why do psychologists go on using rats in their studies, why do they not turn directly to the subject that probably concerns them all, namely the behavior of man? There are probably many answers to this question, most of them not too satisfying or correct, but a speculation of Hebb's (1951) in a brief paper on personality suggests a possible explanation.

In this paper on the role of neurological ideas in personality theory, Hebb emphasizes that most of the currently prominent theorists of learning are operating either avowedly or implicitly within the framework of their appreciation of how the nervous system works, and that framework, for most theorists of today was constructed when they first studied the nervous system, approximately between 1915 and 1935. During that period which we can identify with the growth and development of behaviorism and neo-behaviorism, the general interpretation of the nervous system was a more or less static one. The nervous system, like a telephone exchange, was assumed to exist to make connections between incoming and outgoing messages. The analogy to afferent and efferent fibers was obvious. The conception of a nervous system in terms of incoming impulses (S) and outgoing impulses (R) was a perfect match for the telephone-exchange metaphor. The exchange itself did nothing, or at least was not supposed to do anything, to hamper the smooth flow of stimuli and responses. The fact that telephone exchanges are not such passive and innocent cooperators, that they frequently get out of order, that operators strike, that wrong wires are connected with the inevitable "wrong numbers," that lines are busy, that "your party does not answer," and even the occasional inability of the caller to get through to the exchange, none of these irritating features of telephone exchanges seemed to impress the students of behavior in the twenties and thirties. They proceeded to consider the nervous system as a connecting system and that only, and built their behavioral theories on that basis. Some even went so far, as does Skinner (1938), as to deny that the exchange was of any importance at all, and that the only thing that mattered was that the caller make his call, that the stimulus occur, and that the response occur. In his actual theoretical speculations, which Skinner even denies are theory (1950), he even ignores the caller or the stimulus to considerable degree and concentrates on the callee, or the response, on the grounds that the response and its features are more readily observable and describable than the stimulus situation. In taking this position Skinner might have erred in the right direction. It may turn out that concentration on a "stimulus" will prove barren. On the other hand, concentration on the "response" may prove equally fruitless if we ignore the central nervous activity which must precede the response. A response with *unknown* antecedents is not likely to facilitate our understanding of the complexities of behavior.

If the nervous system did, in fact, function in the docile and dutiful manner that Skinner apparently assumes it does, he is perfectly justified in ignoring it and proceeding with his investigations of the relationships between stimulus conditions and subsequent response variations. A static nervous system deserves to be ignored. In fact, those who do not ignore the nervous system, so conceived, are wasting considerable time, as Skinner correctly points out, trying to relate their manipulations of stimuli and observations of responses to the nervous system. They have gotten no place and will get no place. We can hardly expect to achieve realistic results with an unrealistic conception of the nervous system. The analogy of the telephone exchange might be a fair approximation, but only that, of the nervous system of the rat. Learning theory based on such a view might prove quite satisfactory for some features of rat learning.

The nervous system of man is not a simple, passive, quiescent affair, existing for the convenience of the orthodox S-R psychologist. Although the conception of the telephone exchange is not completely incorrect, it is like many other partial truths, a dangerous one. The exchange features are there, but so are many others which were not brought to our attention until the late thirties and forties with the development of electrophysiology and the discovery of the various brain rhythms, the discovery of the constant activity of the brain, the discovery of persistent chains of impulses, the observation of apparently spontaneous discharge of neural cells, the recognition that the impulse does not enter a quiet domain and demand a connection with a particular outlet and immediately get it.

Quite the contrary appears to be the case, not only neurologically but also behaviorally. It is not our interest, at the moment, to go into the details of neural function. To be completely frank about it, these are not adequately enough known to permit a significant behavioral correlation, and as Hebb takes pains to point out, we must still, unfortunately, deal with a CNS which is translated as a *conceptual nervous system* rather than as a *central* nervous system. From both sides of the picture, neural and behavioral, however, we have enough observations to recognize that behavior is extremely variable in its details, if not in major aspects, and that the nervous system seems to lead a life of its own in many respects.

If we accept the common working assumption that the behavior of organisms is mediated by the nervous system, we cannot avoid accepting what goes along with the neural activity that occurs in the absence of obvious external stimulation. It is not enough to accept the nervous system as a conduction system or a connector of stimuli with responses. Sometimes connections are not made, or they are made with unexpected outlets; and sometimes responses are made without any external stimulation at all. Penfield & Rasmussen (1950) have reported long chains of thought from conscious subjects undergoing surgery for tumors of the brain when a small area of the cortex is given a weak (1 volt) shock. The shock can hardly be thought of as a "stimulus." In any event a chain of "behavioral" activity is reported by the subject from a single shock. Apparently there is evidence also that neurones will, from time to time, discharge themselves spontaneously if they are not stimulated into firing (Lorente de Nó, 1938). Our conceptual picture of the brain, to follow Hebb, is one of a dynamic, live, complex organ which permits of a wide variety of different connections to be made to *any* stimulus and which permits almost any kind of response to occur with or without stimulation from the outside world. Rather than be astounded by this variability, we should be more astounded at the regularity that apparently prevails in our daily routine existences.

More recently Hebb (1955)[4] has become interested in the functions of the reticular system in the brain stem which appears to function as a diffuse, nonspecific, projection system.[5] According to Hebb, this formation functions as an "arousal system" whose activity "in effect makes organized cortical activity possible." When the "arousal system" is active, sensory impulses can have their proper effect; with-

---

[4] This paper expresses the general orientation of this text so succinctly that it is recommended as a "must" reference.

[5] An excellent description of the reticular formation for students unfamiliar with nervous mechanisms is available in *Fortune Magazine*, January, 1955. (Bello, 1955) For more advanced students several articles in the Laurentian Symposium publication (Delafresnaye [ed.] 1954) will be more appropriate sources.

out this system sensory impulses cannot go beyond the sensory cortex and cannot affect the rest of the cortex so that "learned stimulus—response relations are lost." Hebb considers the "arousal system" to be equated with a general "drive" state which controls the functions of sensory input and efferent output. Sensory impulses will have weak, strong, positive, or negative effects depending upon the operations of the "arousal system." The "arousal system" can be activated by cortical activity itself (this Hebb identifies with *cognitive* processes in psychological terms) and, if this is the case, we have what Hebb calls "the immediate drive value of cognitive processes." Such a picture of an active, live, controlling, nervous system is indeed a far cry from the nervous system of the 1920's and even the 1940's. It calls for a major reorientation of psychological thinking about the determiners of behavior.

Lest the notion develop that the Hebbian picture is one of a capricious brain toying about with neural impulses, now making this or that connection out of petulance or whimsy, we must recognize that the problem is not that of lawlessness or rebellion but rather of complexity. Some "antinervous system" writers like Kantor (1947) have complained of too much attention to the brain and too little to other systems of the body like the endocrine, the circulatory, the digestive, or other systems all of which are significant for behavior. It is exactly this point which must be recognized in connection with neural function. The brain, like the rest of us, depends on oxygen, on a constant supply of nutritive elements, on a proper circulation, on endocrine secretions, on freedom from invasion by infection or foreign growths, and on freedom from concussion, scarring, or other forms of injury. Sexual behavior, for example, is to a considerable degree under the control of variables that have little to do with environment, training, and past experience. Kinsey (1953) has pointed out how little the human female is affected by "psychological" stimulation. Beach (1951) has emphasized, besides environmental factors like illumination, habit, stimulation by a partner, such physiological factors as drugs, diets, and hormonal secretions as significant variables in sexual and parental behavior of many species.

If behavior is to be explained by scientific effort, it is necessary that the problem of behavior be perceived as it is and not as we might like it to be. If a person is experiencing hallucinations because he has pellagra, we must not diagnose him as an alcoholic. If a patient needs vitamins, let us not give him psychotherapy, or at least not psychotherapy alone. As a matter of speculation, he might need psycho-therapy too; there may be behavioral reasons which might account for his vitamin deficiency!

To return to our problem, it is not so much one of understanding how the brain works, although this would presumably solve our dif-ficulty, but rather one of *not misunderstanding* how it works. The proper business of psychologists is usually presumed to be that of behavior, and most psychologists are ill-equipped to study anything else. They should not, however, put on the straightjackets of a 1920 nervous system and consequently see behavior as a matter of simple S-R connections or even uniform R's.

The view of the nervous system presented by Hebb provides the psychologist with a looser fitting garment. There is room to move around in it, to admit that behavior is complicated and depends on many variables including *physiological* ones. It permits of the pos-sibility that someone might do something completely new and dif-ferent at any moment, quite out of keeping with his routine. If some-one jumps off a bridge that he has driven over daily for 20 years, we no longer have a right to say, "It couldn't be." If someone gets a new "idea" and cannot account for it, we can hardly deny that it happened. If he reports that it came "out of the blue" we can prob-ably translate it to mean "out of his brain" and proceed to look for how it happened.

We are now in a better position to answer the question of why psychologists have done so much with rats and so little with other organisms. Beach (1950) complains about the overwhelming atten-tion paid to an organism that represents an almost insignificant pro-portion of life forms. The simple answer to the question is that the rat behaves more or less faithfully to the 1920 conception of a human nervous system. From that point on, we have one rationalization after another which is advanced to defend the use of the rat. The most satisfying of such rationalizations is that the rat studies might provide sources of ideas that might be checked further along in the animal scale. It is unfortunately true, however, that relatively few psychol-ogists run comparative studies, and in their thinking the jump from rat to man is made quite easily and with but few qualms.

What is wrong with rat studies? Nothing at all so long as the be-havior observed is related to the "stimulus-bound" nature of the rat. Applications to man are not out of order if we are trying to account for some kinds of behavior in which man, too, is stimulus bound.

A man in a maze, for example, may *be forced* to operate on a stimulus-bound level. Any "thinking" he does may merely get him into trouble. When no brains are required, it is folly to use them.[6] It is difficult, however, to conjure up situations where the human is truly stimulus-bound. Children sometimes appear to be chained to stimuli and develop various habit patterns about going to bed, bathing, eating, playing, and so on. There may be a considerable range of application of rat studies to children's behavior although it is awkward to check the applications to child learning. For various reasons we do not require children to traverse mazes to a food cup. Some Skinnerian enthusiasts (Fuller, 1949) managed to train a feeble-minded youth, an idiot, to develop an operant (raising his arm) by "reinforcing" the response with a squirt of milk; they took some satisfaction in finding that the subject, for the first time in his life, had learned something. Some studies with normal (Siegel and Foshee 1953) and feeble-minded children (Mitrano 1939) made use of Skinner lever-pressing setups and found behavior patterns similar to those of rats. The scope of these experiments, however, leaves much to be questioned about the kinds of learning in which humans like to take pride.

INDIVIDUAL AND SPECIES DIFFERENCES

It is not our intent in this chapter to deal with the comparative psychology of learning. The topic is too formidable in scope and very adequately handled in the various volumes dealing with comparative findings. It is not our concern to decide whether the octopus can learn better than a mole or a blue jay. The relative intelligence of dogs or horses may be of some concern to dog lovers, betting commissioners, or Saturday matinée movie fans. Students sometimes like to know if a cow is smarter than a pig or if sheep are stupid. If there is an answer to such a question, it is not our problem to supply it. We are concerned, rather, with another form of the problem, namely: what difference does being a cow, or a horse, or a platypus make in learning? As Beach and Jaynes (1954) have pointed out, certain

---

[6] Human subjects (college students) usually do not excel rats in mazes of similar pattern. Rats, in fact, usually have a better error score. Human subjects, perhaps unfortunately, can hardly help "thinking" about their performance and may be introducing obstacles to the mastery of the maze.

kinds of behavior patterns may be part of the basic equipment, that is, be innate, or "instinctive" in one species, and the same *kind* of behavior might have to be learned, if it is at all possible, by another species. Some cats become good mouse-catchers (we can skip the question of whether it is innate [7]), but it is doubtful that a horse could be trained to be even a fair "mouser." A dog (or almost any other mammal) will swim when thrown into the water for the first time; humans have to learn to swim. It is a well-known fact that only certain breeds of dogs serve well as guides for the blind. This, perhaps, might be better stated as meaning that some breeds are more unsuitable. Long and careful breeding of dogs has resulted in dog types so specialized that some make superior guides, shepherds, or guards; others make more suitable companions for children, hunters, or dowagers. Teaching a Boston terrier to "point" might be possible, but his performance in the field is not likely to win any honors. Pavlov (1927) was strongly impressed by differences in susceptibility to conditioning in different breeds. Not only would one breed "condition" more quickly than another, but some breeds would develop certain kinds of conditioned responses more readily than others. We will return to these observations of Pavlov later (see p. 54). To consider any species for use in learning experiments poses a difficult question, or, better, a series of questions: (1) Is the learning situation suited for this organism? Or is it too easy a matter or too difficult? (2) Does this organism have a special advantage over other organisms in this kind of situation? (3) If this organism behaves in a given fashion or displays a certain learning speed in a given situation, is it because it happens to have, for example, pigmented eyes? Certain experimenters favor "hooded" rats with pigmented eyes. Albino rats' eyes are not pigmented. Sometimes experiments done with albino rats cannot reproduce results obtained with hooded rats. Are we studying learning or the effects of visual pigmentation in such cases? The cardinal sin of experimentation is self-deception. Unfortunately such self-deception is almost inevitable if we do not know our subjects. We always measure performance in experiments. Sometimes it reflects "nature," not nurture. It is a truly wise experimenter who knows when he is observing one and not the other.

Differences within species. So far we have considered only the matter of species differences or differences between breeds. Even

---

[7] The fact that cats can be *trained* to live with mice does not bear on the question of what they would do naturally without the training.

within the same general animal type, great differences may develop as a consequence of various environmental factors or breeding practices. The now famous experiments of Tryon (1942) in developing so-called bright and dull strains of rats by mating good maze learners together and poor maze learners together are only a laboratory illustration of what might happen quite normally in nature. Since later experiments (Searle, 1949) have shown Tryon's rats not to be bright or dull but rather aggressive and timid or equipped with some other temperamental characteristics, it is possible for groups of animals living under certain conditions of climate, nutrition, or natural dangers to develop temperamental features which are useful for survival. Individuals possessing suitable temperaments may, therefore, have a higher probability of survival and of procreation. The transmission of some temperamental factors appears to be satisfactorily established (Hall, 1951), and unless the genetic background of groups and individuals is adequately known, a learning performance may be grossly misinterpreted. Anthropologists who study isolated tribal groups and emphasize the role of culture in creating personality differences might have to reverse their interpretations if it turns out that a rigorous climate and precarious existence result in the genetic development of a group which finds expression for the basic personality traits in cultural practices that differ from those enjoyed by a group living under radically different conditions. Whatever germs of truth may be reflected in our stereotypes of various racial and national groups may represent just such inherited temperamental strains that derive from selective factors within a given environment.

Individual differences. In his presidential address to the American Psychological Association, Tolman (1938a) introduced the term "intervening variable" to represent inferences about the relationship between certain independent and dependent variables. In considering the kinds of independent variables which need to be considered in the development of a behavior theory, Tolman presented a list of environmental variables such as "goal objects," "maintenance schedule," types of stimuli, and so on. We will consider these in due course and need not tarry over them now. In another category of "individual difference variables," Tolman recognized the significance of such individual differences in learning experiments and the degree to which they complicate the story of learning and behavior. As a convenient framework, Tolman summarized what he regarded as perhaps the most important individual difference features by terming them the

H.A.T.E. variables. Perhaps the choice of initials was deliberate, for the psychologist might well have reason to hate them for the trouble they cause. Consideration of the H.A.T.E. variables may serve as our best introduction to the problem.

THE H.A.T.E. VARIABLES

The initials stand for heredity, age, previous training, and special endocrine, drug, or vitamin conditions. Tolman himself does not speculate on these variables nor refer to any related studies; perhaps no extensive support is necessary to substantiate their importance. In any case, a brief look at the variables may not be amiss.

Heredity. We have already discussed this factor sufficiently above. For those who suspect that learning psychologists undervalue the contribution of heredity to behavior it is appropriate to quote from C. L. Hull on this problem. The following remarks seem especially apposite since Hull and Tolman were, and considered themselves, friendly opponents in the battle of learning theory. Hull (1945) stated:

> There is much reason to believe . . . that even if organisms could be subjected to identical environmental conditions from the moment of conception, great differences would still be displayed in the behavior of different species as a whole and in the behavior of the individual organisms of each species. Such differences must presumably be regarded as dependent upon, i.e., derived from, differences in the innate or original nature and constitution of the individual organism. We shall accordingly call them *innate* differences.

Certainly if such "great differences" in behavior can be expected on a hereditary basis, learning theory, however correctly worked out, will have to be heavily dependent upon support from genetic findings for the understanding of not only individual behavior but even that of entire species. Any attempt to understand behavior without an appreciation of biological backgrounds would seem doomed to failure, and this according to the outstanding figure in learning theory in our time. As if this were not enough of a headache, there are still other variables to consider.

Age. The variable of age is not a simple matter of counting days or years and introducing an age factor into a formula. Age complicates the picture in at least three ways:

1. Maturation and growth. The processes of maturation and growth occur within the dimension of age. Such growth or development has its own pace in each individual and we have now become accustomed to thinking in terms of "physiological" age rather than the chronological measure. Estimates of physiological age, however, are understandably complicated and to find mathematical units is still a task for the future. The host of maturational studies which have become part of the background of psychology force us to consider such proposals as "learning readiness," "reading readiness," "arithmetic readiness," and a score of other "readinesses." The discrimination between the effects of practice on learning and the effects of maturation is sometimes difficult, if not impossible to make. Wheeler (1940) promotes this concept in his "organismic" psychology. Experiments in which the passage of time alone seems to be as useful as practice appear to support some of Wheeler's notions, particularly that of stimulus-induced maturation. Doré and Hilgard (1937) and Hilgard and Smith (1942) found such an interesting result with pursuit-rotor learning. Snoddy (1945) obtained similar results in mirror-drawing wherein one group, practicing only once a day did as well as another group which practiced 10 trials per session and every other day. At the end of a week, the 7-trial group was doing as well as the 31-trial group. A simple interpretation of such results amounts to stating that learning consists of exposing a subject to some situation and waiting for the effects to take place through a process of growth. Perhaps some things are learned in this way. We will have to see if any other than perceptual-motor skills are helped by the passage of time.

2. Learning ability. In the second place, the age factor is of concern in terms of the curves of growth and decline of learning ability. We now know that human subjects appear to reach a peak in capacity to learn verbal and symbolic materials somewhere in the mid-twenties and undergo some decline with the passing years. Thorndike et al. (1928) and Miles (1933) have investigated the learning abilities of the aged and have pointed out the importance of motivation in the learning of our "senior citizens." We can hardly expect an octogenerian to whip up any great interest in mastering a list of nonsense syllables. If there are differences in the learning capacities and in the relative importance of different variables at different ages, we must be careful in evaluating experiments in which the age factor is not adequately appraised. As a general proposition we can presume that

the examination of the infants and children is unlikely to provide principles that describe the learning of adults. The use of a standard age population is of not much help. Psychologists frequently use rats between 2 or 3 months of age. The generalizations drawn from studies employing such subjects might require considerable modification and augmentation if they are to apply to year-old rats, to say nothing of other species. Since most studies of human learning are done with college students, we must again be careful in extrapolating in either age direction from the findings with postadolescent groups.

3. PREVIOUS TRAINING. The variable of previous training is intimately related and interwound with that of age. We can discuss the third aspect of the age factor in connection with previous background. Age provides the opportunity for experience and practice effects to enter in a fashion that is difficult to evaluate or control. Only by the sheerest chance could one expect even two college students to have had *similar* training even if they were boon companions from kindergarten until they appear to serve as subjects in a learning experiment. As we shall discover later (if it is not already quite clear) "experience" can work in diverse fashions. One kind of past experience facilitates the learning of something new; another hinders and hampers the learning of a new idea or technique. Although "It's never too late to learn," "you can't teach an old dog new tricks." Learning to touch type on a "scientifically" designed typewriter (Dvorak *et al.*, 1936) is difficult for even experts with a standard keyboard. Illustrations are superfluous at this point. In a later chapter (see Chap. 13) we will consider how previous training affects the acquisition of new patterns. For the present we might examine another, less obvious effect of past experience. Certain kinds of activity, for example, memorizing poetry or simple arithmetic exercises may be so highly practiced in childhood as to have reached the peak of practice and be at such a level for any given individual as to resist improvement in experiments designed to test the efficacy of some training technique. Thus William James (1890) found that practice did not improve his "memory." As Hebb points out (1949), James ignored a previous lifetime of practice and could hardly expect any change from what, in effect, was a minor effort even though it appears heroic (memorizing "Paradise Lost"). The moral is clear. The experimenter must exert the greatest care in evaluating the effects of what we so glibly summarize by "past experience." If he does not, his efforts may not only be unrewarding, but even misleading.

Special endocrine, drug, or vitamin conditions. In listing the variables of endocrine, drug, or vitamin influences on behavior, Tolman is referring to what psychologists and physiologists have come to refer to as "the internal environment." Presumably the effects of such chemical factors are expressed in and through the nervous system, and to a large extent may be significant determinants of what we refer to as temperament, mood, sentiments, and sometimes, "personality." While we can readily accept the specified factors as of significance for behavior, there has been but little attention paid to their role in *learning*.

We could not hope to cover the enormous literature dealing with internal chemical influences on behavior. The studies that are relevant for *learning* have not been systematic and have been more or less confined to drugs and such personality traits as "anxiety." For the present we can content ourselves with reference to some illustrative studies which may point up the methodological difficulties in this field.

In the area of investigation of drug effects on learning we have to deal with, in general, two types of drugs, the stimulants and depressants (in terms of nervous system effects). Further, we note that we have two aspects of learning to consider, acquisition and retention (or its opposite, extinction). Hilgard and Marquis (1940) summarized the general effect of drugs in this way: "Sodium bromide and other drugs of a depressant character retard the rate of conditioning, but accelerate the rate of extinction. Excitants such as caffeine and benzedrine have been found to increase the strength of conditioned responses but to decrease the rate of extinction." While these conclusions appear to be based on the net effects of such drugs on activity level, Hilgard and Marquis believe that there are additional effects over and above general behavioral levels which bear more specifically on learning in some still unknown fashion. The use of drugs has been limited to simple conditioning situations (Switzer, 1935) and we know little of the influence of drugs on the learning of "higher" level responses.

The study of the influence of various vitamins on learning has not been very fruitful in terms of positive results. In most cases only tendencies have been observed without convincing or reliable statistical differences. The general pattern of experiments is to withhold vitamins from the diet of subjects or supply more than normal amounts and to compare groups in some learning task. Bernhardt and Herbart (1937) studied the effects of vitamin B deficiency in rats which were later trained to escape from a water maze. They found a tendency for rats which had been deprived early in life to be more retarded than those deprived later. Stevens (1937) found no differences between a vitamin B-1 deprived group and a normal group in maze learning. O'Neil (1949) found that rats with less than 3 micrograms of thiamine in their daily diet learned water mazes poorly. Over 100 micrograms resulted in better than normal learning. In an experiment with children, Harrell (1947) found that supplementing the diet of one group with 2 micrograms of thiamine daily resulted in improvement in 18 different tasks as compared with a matched group of controls. The improvement ranged from 7 to 87 percent. For the present it is difficult to evaluate the small amount of work done in this area. The experiments have differed too widely and have not been designed in terms of theoretical expectancies of any kind beyond the simple notion of "let's see what effects can be found if this vitamin is withheld or oversupplied." The individual physiological variables might be presumed to be of the greatest significance. The effects of deprivation might well be of a long-term variety or of such a nature that we have not yet even begun to suspect. For the present, then, we might more profitably turn to another of Tolman's special factors, one which he himself does not specify but which we can presume he would have, had the work been done at the time of his writing. It is one of what might be many intrinsic "personality" variables, that of "anxiety."

Child (1954) has summarized the studies dealing with the effects of anxiety on learning. In recent years such experiments have become increasingly popular. In general they follow this formula: subjects are first given personality tests of "neurotic inventories." Those that turn out to merit the label "anxious" are then compared in a learning situation with those who appear to merit a clean bill of mental health. In the typical experiment, like that of Spence and Taylor (1951) for example, high-anxious subjects were found to develop conditioned eyelid responses more readily than low-anxious subjects. Spence and Taylor (1953) found that anxious subjects not only conditioned more readily but also took longer to extinguish the conditioned eyelid response. Hilgard et al. (1951) found no differences between anxious and nonanxious subjects in simple conditioning (eyelid blink) but did find a difference in discriminated conditioned responses. Anxious subjects were less able to form such discriminations. Warren and Grant (1955) found psychopathic deviates (measured by the MMPI) similarly unable to form discriminated conditioned responses.

When subjects are asked to learn more complex tasks, for example, mazes, nonsense syllables, and so on, the findings become somewhat confusing. Farber and Spence (1953) predicted that the more anxious subjects would suffer confusion and interference and consequently learn less well than do low-anxious subjects. They found this to be so in an experiment employing stylus mazes. Montague (1953) found similar results with nonsense syllable lists. The more difficult lists could not be learned so well by the high-anxious subjects. On the other hand, Deese *et al.* (1953) found no significant differences between high- and low-anxious subjects learning nonsense syllables unless the subjects were shocked. With shocks given for errors, the low-anxious subjects began to break down or suffer some confusion and their scores became so poor that Deese speaks of "strikingly large" differences in favor of the anxious group.

Neither facts nor theory are settled in this area of investigation. Farber and Spence (1953) offer a theory based on the assumption that "anxiety" (measured as a personality characteristic) also functions as a "drive." It is suggested that the anxious subjects are "driven" toward acquiring or performing a response which is different from that toward which "normals" are "driven." Until they give up the "goal" of the anxiety drive, they cannot learn well. This interpretation need not concern us at the moment. We are now interested only in pointing out that the personality of the learner may be a significant variable and, as in the illustrations given, personality variables may work in opposite directions with different kinds of learning assignments. We cannot begin to appreciate the extent to which the hundreds of experiments done in only the two areas of eyelid conditioning and memorization of nonsense syllables have been contaminated by "personality" factors, to say nothing of other sources of contamination.

Are the H.A.T.E. variables the only ones that count? Did Tolman believe that they more or less cover the range of individual difference and species variables? Are there any others that might properly be included? What about "intelligence," sex differences, medical history? It is easy enough to make out a case for the incorporation of these within the H.A.T.E. group. Intelligence, for example, might be presumed to fit in with age, heredity, and experience, and, for that matter, with the special endocrine, drug, or vitamin condition. What we must not lose sight of is that none of the H.A.T.E. variables is a simple factor in itself but includes a multitude of specifics. "Endocrine condition" covers all the glandular functions in all their variations, normal, hyper-, and hypoactivity. It includes sex differences in all degrees. There are many varieties of drugs and vitamins. The influence of each must be adequately evaluated. We must appreciate that Tolman is offering us a program, not an answer, and the program is awesome, if not frightening, in scope. We should also note that this program is only the first step; a step that presumably should be taken *before* we begin to consider environmental variables. If we can consider the H.A.T.E. variables the horse and environmental variables the cart, then we must conclude that psychologists have put the cart far ahead of the horse and we may have to wait for the horse to catch up before we can do a scientific piece of work.

THE SIGNIFICANCE OF INDIVIDUAL DIFFERENCES

The present chapter has been concerned with the influence of "nature" on the learning process. There has been but little research in this vital area but we can begin to look for much more if current trends are any indication. Psychology has, perhaps, come of age and can now afford to step outside its S-R shackles. A more mature point of view is replacing the earlier enthusiasm for and dependence upon the "environment." The trickle of research and the lip-service to "individual differences" is being transformed into a genuine preoccupation with personality variables of all kinds. In this chapter we mentioned the new concern with the nervous system, and the H.A.T.E. variables of Tolman. The research in recent years in connection with only one of these, personality, is already enormous in quantity. While contradictions are found, the interest in this area is encouraging and we can look forward to similar intensive studies in the problems of vitamin and other chemical factors. Developmental and genetic studies are also increasing and psychologists no longer get upset at hearing a formerly nasty word, "instinct." Physiological psychologists are making their influence increasingly felt. We can summarize the trend with a statement of Warren and Grant (1955): "Present day investigators are no longer content with the broad statement that individual differences exist or with the typological approach proposed by Pavlov; instead they tend toward more analytic approaches." Such analytical approaches as are noted in connection with the "anxiety" studies represent the "new look" in learning psychology and we can look forward to an even greater volume of researches designed to determine the relationship of biological, physiological, and personality factors to the learning process.

THE NATURE OF THE TEACHER

We cannot conclude our examination of the nature of the learner without some attention to the nature of the teacher, or, more appropriately in our context, the nature of the theorist or experimenter. It is by now almost a truism that experiments done in California do not work out in the same fashion at Yale or at Iowa. When a representative of one point of view or one learning theory does not verify the observations of a representative of another learning theory the bystanding student is at a loss. He frequently chooses sides upon other and completely extraneous grounds and joins in the argument. Sometimes the facts or observations themselves are not questioned, but the interpretations of the facts are cut and fitted or tailored to meet the theory. Rarely is the basic theoretical orientation itself altered to make room for new facts although every theorist will stoutly announce that his theory is open to modification as the facts come up to challenge the theory.

What are the reasons for the disagreements? We can probably dismiss any naive notion that the experimenters are deliberately distorting the evidence or that the theorists are self-aggrandizing blackguards. We can afford to consider them "all honorable men" who happen to be working in a difficult area with different tools and procedures, sometimes with different kinds of subjects, and most frequently with different kinds of specific problems. Considering the complexities of the situation, and the rest of our study will be concerned with these complexities, it would be a little surprising if there were any more agreement among the researchers than now exists. We shall try to work out an explanation of specific differences in connection with the several aspects of learning as we come to them. The student who might have been asking himself why learning theorists do not agree appears to believe that it is only a question of personalities or opinion. The issues of learning theory cannot be settled by democratic vote or dictatorial edict. They can be settled only by patient inquiry coupled with a modest regard for the principles of logic. Instead of asking for agreement, then, our job is to find out why none exists, and, if necessary, prevent agreement based on jolly good fellowship.

We can now conclude the consideration of the influence of the learner on the learning process and turn to the process itself. The reader is urged to keep the present reflections constantly before him as we proceed. It is easy for the student of learning to forget that there is an organism between the S and the R.

Chapter

4 Are There Several Kinds of Learning?

Among the many issues and disputes that divide the several camps of learning theorists and experimenters there are three general controversial questions that must be considered before we can begin to make much progress in the area of learning fact and learning fancy. These three questions are:

1. Is learning a single, a unitary process, the same sort of affair regardless of who is doing the learning or what is being learned, or are there several kinds of learning to be distinguished? This question is confounded by the fact that organisms learn many *kinds of responses or behavior patterns* and different levels of analysis may appear to require different explanations of what is going on.

2. The second question is really an elaboration of the first in that any conclusion to the effect that one kind of learning differs from another automatically calls for a different principle or principles to explain the learning. Here the problem becomes confused because of the insistence of different students that their particular principles can account for any and all alleged types of learning. If the principles of each theorist are in fact different from those of other theorists, then it becomes obvious that somebody is wrong when these principles are applied to the same phenomena. If there are four explanations, all different, for any set of observations, it is likely that at least three are incorrect and perhaps all four are. Hull (1935) has pointed out that when we already have 12 different learning theories, a thirteenth entry which challenges all the rest is not more likely to be correct than any of the previous 12. One solution of the problem on a diplomatic

level is to divide up the allegedly different kinds of learning among the several theorists allowing each to enjoy the privilege of explaining one or a few kinds of learning (assuming there really are a variety to pick from). Psychologists, however, are not necessarily diplomatic, and in the learning area each theorist has tried to keep the entire pie for himself.

3. The third question also interlocks with the other two: it is the question of "what is learned?" If there are several kinds of learning, and several kinds of explanatory principles, then it is possible that each theorist is referring to the learning of different "things." One might be referring to the learning of "stimulus-response" bonds, another the association of ideas, another to neural connections, still another to "conditioned reflexes," "insight," and so on. It is awkward to discuss these three questions in isolation but even more awkward to attempt to handle them at the same time, and so we will devote the next two chapters to them. The present chapter will deal with the first two questions: Are there different kinds of learning and are different kinds of explanatory principles involved? The next chapter will deal with the third question: What is learned?

PAVLOV AND THORNDIKE

The dog and cat again. The work of Pavlov, even though he always considered himself a strictly physiological student of the higher nervous centers, had a tremendous impact on American psychology because Watson (1924) adopted the conditioned reflex as the unit of habit, his basic structural unit of behavior. According to Watson, complex adult behavior consisted of elaborations of conditioned responses which were compounded of original reflex movements and their acquired conditioned initiators or conditioned stimuli. The term "conditioned" crept into, and in some circles, swept over, the language to the point where psychologists of Watsonian leanings were accounting for all acquired behavior as "nothing but" conditioning. Pavlov himself gradually developed the same views and came to regard conditioning as the means by which not only normal behavior could be studied but also as a basis for explaining and treating abnormal behavior (Pavlov, 1942).

The basic principle of "association by contiguity" on which conditioning theory is based was adopted by numerous psychologists, as a sufficient explanation of all behavior that could not be shown to be innate.[1] Guthrie (1935), although disagreeing with Pavlov on details, based his systematic thinking on the postulate of association by contiguity and added the strength of his persuasive talents to the growing acceptance of conditioning as a basic principle of learning.

In the meantime, Thorndike (1898) had been developing his own lines of reasoning about learning in a somewhat different direction. It will be recalled that Thorndike had hit upon the "problem box" as an experimental device. In this box, cats were provided with the means of escape and would have access to food if they made use of the means and escaped. The means consisted of pulling strings, depressing latches, or operating other simple mechanisms such as stepping on a pedal. Thorndike did not, as did Pavlov, force the cats to do anything. He waited until the subject did something, which Thorndike thought appropriate or had previously arranged to be appropriate. In a *tour de force*, Thorndike once decided to open the problem box if the cat scratched his left ear. When the cat scratched in the manner Thorndike had decreed, the door opened and food was available. Since no stimulus had been applied by the experimenter, the response could be considered in various ways as, for example, a "voluntary" response, or a spontaneous movement, a random act, or, in Thorndike's objective language, a "trial." We can note, parenthetically, that although Thorndike himself did not irritate the cat's ear in any fashion, something might be presumed to have done so, and if Thorndike wanted to have the learning occur a bit faster he could have arranged to irritate the ear, provoking the scratch, and in this fashion getting the cat to perform the proper movements. Since there is no apparent connection for the cat between scratching ears and opening doors, we can imagine that it would be some time before the cat would get out. The college student, with his ear-pulling tendencies when caught in problem situations, might get out sooner, but he would probably be more astonished than the cat was likely to be. In the case of either the cat or the collegian, the response of scratching an ear would come to be made more and more readily with succeeding trials, regardless of the lack of any "logical" connection between the behavior of the subject and that of the door. According to Thorndike the connection will have been "stamped in" or learned.

---

[1] The early behaviorist psychologists tried to put the burden of proof on others. They freely assumed behavior to consist of bundles of conditioned reflexes.

This kind of blind, mechanical behavior is the basis, according to Skinner (1948b) for superstition.

For the present we will ignore the feature of the food outside the box and observe only that for Thorndike the acquisition of the connections went on more or less blindly and stupidly, automatically, with no particular credit to the cat (or college student if one could be used) for acquiring the habit of "connection." In later years Thorndike modified his position to include various subprinciples which facilitated the acquisition of connections, but we can consider these later. The learning which both Pavlov and Thorndike described was basically a mechanical acquisition of connections, which left no direct room for any "subjective" possibilities such as insight, understanding, intelligence, and so on. Guthrie (1935) emphasizes that bad habits are learned in exactly the same way as good ones and bright habits just like dull ones. For both Thorndike and Pavlov, learning was a blind business, the only difference between their procedures which concerns us at the moment is that Pavlov deliberately provoked the animal to respond, whereas Thorndike did not. Whether or not Thorndike provoked the animal to respond, we can be sure that he would not employ a procedure to study learning where learning was unlikely to occur. That is, the response to be made by the subject must be one that would be made in that situation, sooner or later, preferably for Thorndike a little later. If the cat on introduction to the chamber proceeded to scratch his left ear, Thorndike would certainly switch the problem to the right ear, as a minimum. In other words, Thorndike's experiments were conceived in such a way as to employ a response that the organism would make, *but not immediately.* Pavlov's arrangement, on the other hand, called for an immediate response to his "unconditioned" stimulus.

The bare question that confronts us now is: did Thorndike evoke, provoke, or elicit the behavior he had decided to require of his cat or did this behavior, in fact, come about as a random, unprovoked reaction? We can immediately assume that cats do not scratch their ears without cause. We are in no position to determine the stimulus or stimuli which initiate, precede, or accompany this behavior in this situation, and perhaps never may be. In line with the ordinary assumption made by psychologists, however, it is unlikely that there will be any disagreement on the answer: stimuli for ear scratching must have been present. The experimenter had merely arranged things to prevent such stimuli from being the most active and immediate stimuli in the situation. Had they been so, he would have chosen another response.

In the light of these comments it seems justifiable to conclude that the Thorndikian experimenter is taking pains to delay the appearance of the "unconditioned" stimulus, while the Pavlovian experimenter is equally anxious to prevent such delay. Whether this difference is enough to make a difference is a question that has harassed learning theory for some time. It has been stated in many other ways, some of which tend to confuse the issue in devious and complex directions. When stated as above, it seems that the difference is as trivial as it could possibly be and has no connection with the behavior of the animal but only with that of the experimenter who, in some instances, appears to have put the blindfold on himself instead of on the subject.

If the Thorndike and Pavlov procedures are really examples of different kinds of learning, we might expect to find some different kinds of principles operating in the two types. Any search for systematic differences in learning principles between the two types will prove extremely unrewarding, as we shall see from the remainder of the text. On the contrary, the same principles which Pavlov established in his 50 years of research have been found to apply consistently to the Thorndikian method (Youtz, 1938a, 1938b) and vice versa (Sheffield, 1948). The same terminology is used frequently by experimenters using either technique. Nothing has been gained, and probably much has been lost in developing and maintaining the dichotomy between the two procedures. The only gain, if it can be called that, is that one can identify the procedures of the experimenter more readily if he knows that the procedure was Pavlovian or Thorndikian. It is quite certain that the procedures of the cat or dog are not made one bit more understandable by the distinction.

It is not enough for us to dismiss the controversy with a passing analysis of its origin and apparent irrelevance. The controversy has grown into a major issue and the student of learning must become familiar with the historical developments of current situations if he is to understand them. We must get down to a more minute scrutiny of the underlying currents of psychological thinking in the past decades if we are to arrive at a critical appreciation of the learning problem.

Thorndike continued with his cats and monkeys until he had developed what for him was an adequate analysis of learning. He then turned to problems of education and became an outstanding figure in that field. He continued his experiments with college students, using the principles derived from cat experiments (Thorndike, 1931, 1932). Whatever his authority in educational circles, it was not equally strong among psychologists. His principles became centers of controversy instead of application and his dismissal of Pavlovian conditioning as a curious and interesting laboratory phenomenon did not find universal acceptance. On one or another ground Watsonians, Guthrians, Tolmanians, among others, found occasion to disagree. The Thorndikian principles needed revamping, modification, or elimination, depending upon the point of view.[2] In various ways camps of contending theorists grew, each favoring a point of view which was alleged to be different and correct. Some favored one kind of learning, some another. Some settled for one kind, others for two, others for three, four or, in one of the latest attempts (Tolman, 1949), six. It will repay us handsomely to examine these suggestions as a general introduction to our *dramatis personae* as well as to highlight some of the issues on which learning theory is developing. We will not be able to stop to examine each aspect of controversy that divides the numerous camps, but we can uncover the questions on which they part company.

CLASSICAL AND INSTRUMENTAL LEARNING

The distinction between Pavlovian and Thorndikian learning has been more or less formalized by Hilgard and Marquis (1940) in their text, *Conditioning and Learning*, where they classify the Pavlovian technique as dealing with some type of *substitution* learning. They identify the work of Pavlov on conditioned reflexes as illustrative of "classical" learning. They offer no particular justification for the term but it caught on and whenever the term "classical" is applied to a learning situation we are supposed to think of a typical Pavlovian conditioning experiment. Thorndikian learning is classified as "instrumental" learning. "Substitution" refers to learning in which some new stimulus acquires the capacity to arouse a response which was formerly evoked by some other stimulus (the unconditioned stimulus). "Instrumental" learning covers all other types. It is called "in-

---

[2] Postman (1947) has described the various changes in Thorndike's views in a very useful review.

strumental" because the organism is learning how to affect its environment to bring about some change, which presumably is of an adaptive nature, for example doing something which will result in food for a hungry animal. The learned behavior is *instrumental* in bringing about a change in the environment. There are other alleged differences between Pavlovian and instrumental learning but these will be examined later. For the present a more detailed picture of instrumental learning is in order.

Types of instrumental learning. According to Hilgard and Marquis, there are four classes or types of instrumental learning: (a) escape, (b) avoidance, (c) reward, and (d) secondary reward. We can illustrate each of these briefly and then consider the possible differences and similarities.

Escape. This category of learning includes all those instances wherein the organism encounters or is placed in a painful situation (or otherwise unpleasant circumstances) and by engaging in some specific behavior reduces the time of such exposure. The point to be noted about such learning is that some degree of discomfort is generated in the situation. The organism, through learning, reduces the time of unpleasant stimulation. The only example cited by Hilgard and Marquis (and this specific type of experimentation is rather rare) is one in which Mowrer (1940a) placed rats in a situation where electric shock would be introduced gradually and build up in intensity during a 2-minute period. At any time the animal could turn off the shock by pushing against a pedal. Pedal-pushing would terminate the shock momentarily and it would start to build up in intensity again. For the first minute or so, the shock would approach threshold strength; after that the rats would exhibit progressively greater agitation. The learning consisted in reducing the exposure to shock from approximately 6 minutes on the first trial to about 1 minute in the course of training. The student will note that the situation provides only meager opportunities for adjustment. The rat can do nothing about the shock until it is of threshold strength, at least. The rat can only learn to turn it off, which it does, with reasonable promptness, considering its lack of familiarity with switches and the unratlike nature of the behavior which is called for by the experimenter.

Mowrer would have us believe that pressing the pedal was not "evoked" by the shock, but we can note that he arranged the pedal in an upright position at one end of the box so that whenever a rat leaned against it the shock would be terminated. Since rats characteristically move about when shocked, and usually manifest behavior which could be interpreted as "leaving the field," they will soon enough be provoked into heading for the end of the box where the wall is sufficient to give them pause. Since rats also characteristically get up on their hind feet when shocked the probability of the pedal being depressed is, of course, high. Mowrer surely knew this and chose the situation so that the pedal would be depressed in some reasonable interval for the experimenter.

It seems fair enough to conclude that in this experiment the rat was in a situation where, considering the nature of the beast, it was forced to press the pedal. This is our main concern at the moment, but we cannot avoid the additional factor that cessation of the shock presumably brought some relief to the subject. This relief is interpreted by almost everyone concerned to have the status of a reward or *reinforcement*. The exact nature of this reinforcement is subject to argument and will be examined later. In this situation, in any event, it is clear that the rats come to press the pedal sooner and sooner as the trials continue. It should be pointed out at once, lest we overlook it, that the same phenomenon is observed in the Pavlovian experiment, where the dog salivates sooner and sooner as the trials continue unless special training is undertaken to delay salivation.

We have already described Hull's "demonstration experiment" (see p. 13). It will be recalled that the experimenter makes use of a box with a grid floor and a dividing panel in the middle. Either side can be electrified. A rat dropped into the box on one side can be shocked until it jumps over the partition. The time before it jumps will be a function of such factors as strength of shock, height of barrier, and any nonjumping behavior in which it might indulge. Here again we have a situation wherein the animal comes to jump over the barrier and escape the shock sooner and sooner. To make a learning situation out of it, we have to make the barrier high enough so that the first tingle of shock does not propel the rat over the fence. As long as the animal gets shocked first and then gets away from it, we can speak of escape behavior. Whether this behavior is actually different in kind from any tropistic behavior, such as an organism might engage in when the light and heat of the sun prove uncomfortable and provoke retirement into the shade, is a question. Removing the hand from a bowl of hot water is not essentially different, and experimentally it would not be different if some ingenious experimenter arranged our arms in some fashion so that a normal direct withdrawal was ineffective.

When Pavlov introduced some acid substance in the dog's mouth and the dog then salivated "defensively," the question of escape behavior might also be raised. Simple struggle and withdrawal are out of the question for the harnessed dog. The reflex behavior of salivation happens to be appropriate; it also happens to be the first behavior to emerge. The probability that the dog will learn something if it is repeatedly stimulated with acid is high. What it will learn might be such a variety of responses that we might overlook the additional learned activities in our concentration on the reflex salivation which could scarcely improve in time or amount. But even these parameters should be investigated. If the psychologist knew how to manipulate the shock and the animal (it would have to be a joint affair) he could probably get the rat to jump a fence or press a pedal as soon as the shock came on. The possibility exists, then, that the only difference between Pavlovian and instrumental escape learning is the ignorance of the experimenter or (to be less caustic on the experimenter, although, as in the law, ignorance should be no excuse) the complexity of the behavior of pedal pressing as compared with salivation, a difference which certainly involves the relative number of behavioral components involved.

AVOIDANCE LEARNING. Recall now Hull's demonstration experiment B (p. 13). In this experiment, a buzzer is introduced just prior to the shock. At first the behavior of the rat is not different from the situation without a buzzer, but after a number of trials, the animal begins to get over the barrier after the buzzer has sounded but *before* the shock is turned on. Hull describes this behavior as an instance of a response (jumping) becoming associated with a signal or stimulus (buzzer) because of the diminution or reduction of pain normally accompanying the shock. Regardless of the possible effect on the animal of getting away from pain, we note here again the antedating tendency of the response in its moving forward in time so that eventually it occurs prior to the shock.

At that time, Hull (1943) did not recognize any such categories as "escape" or "avoidance" learning. For him, both categories were easily incorporated within a broader "reinforcement" view. In escape learning, a drive (pain) is reduced and the reduction of this drive is considered the reinforcement. In the avoidance variety we have only an additional stimulus thrown in which becomes associated with the response which is followed by drive reduction. Even the Pavlovian bell-food experiment is reduced to reinforcement theory and is considered a special case. The explanation is simple: the dog is hungry. Food reduces the hunger drive. Salivation is followed by drive reduction and is, therefore, learned. It is a special case because it is only a laboratory accident that food is used to initiate the salivation and serves, thus, as both unconditioned stimulus and reinforcing agent.

Hilgard and Marquis (1940) take a radically different point of view in their text. They take as their illustration of avoidance learning an experiment by Brogden, Lipman, and Culler (1938) in which two sets of guinea pigs were trained to run in a revolving cage when a tone-and-shock combination were used. For one set of guinea pigs this shock occurred whether the animals ran or not (this is described as Pavlovian procedure). For the other guinea pigs, no shock was given if the animals moved a minimal criterion distance. In the early phases of training no differences appeared, but after three days of training the guinea pigs which were not shocked if they ran began to run more and more frequently to the tone alone, whereas the other animals showed less tendency to run. In eight days the "avoidance" animals gave 100 percent running responses, where the shocked guinea pigs, even after 20 days, gave only 20 percent.

Hilgard and Marquis make a great deal of this experiment. It is assumed that the learning is "based in a real sense on the avoidance of the shock" (p. 58). The new response is said to be "strengthened in the absence of any such stimulus; indeed it is strengthened because of the absence of such a stimulus." Later (p. 60) it is stated in connection with another of Brogden's experiments that "Omission of the shock on trials in which the conditioned flexion occurs does not produce extinction but instead strengthens the conditioned response." By means of Brogden, Lipman, and Culler's experiment, Hilgard and Marquis introduce the concept of *expectancy* as a possible principle in learning. In brief, in this instance it is assumed that the tone in some fashion sets up an "expectancy" that shock will follow. The animal, then, presumably after some inappropriate responses, happens upon one that works in the sense that the shock is not encountered. A more positive expectancy might be presumed to operate within the animal to the net effect that if the animal runs, no shock will be experienced. The animal runs, the expectancy is "confirmed," and in Hilgard and Marquis' language, the response is strengthened. The crucial point for Hilgard and Marquis seems to be that this kind of behavior is different in kind from other types of training in which "the conditioned response is followed by a definite stimulus change—food or the cessation of shock." The expectancy hypothesis is equated with Tolman's (1938a) general principles of learning which can be briefly summarized at this time in this way: according to Tolman, what we have called "conditioned stimuli" might better be described as "signs." In a typical learning situation such signs are normally followed by other (unconditioned) stimuli which are of some importance to the organism. Such stimuli or circumstances might be labeled "significates." The signs precede the significates or *lead* to them via some action on the part of the organism. The action might merely be that of waiting, or it might involve movement on the part of the learner. Thus, in the Hull shock box, the animal learns that the buzzer (sign) will be followed by a shock (significate) if the animal sits around and waits. In a maze a rat learns that a given turn (sign) will be followed by food (significate) if it makes the turn. Waiting or moving are considered "behavior routes" and the whole picture is formalized by the statement: Signs lead to significates via behavior routes. The whole pattern is considered a *sign Gestalt* or *sign-Gestalt expectancy*, or more simply in Hilgard and Marquis' language, as an "expectancy." It should be observed that the animal acquires "knowledge" and not "habits." It learns what is going to happen if it follows a given behavior route but whether it follows the route or not is due to other factors and is not a learning matter.

It should be noted that all "avoidance" training starts out as "escape" learning. Since we have already taken some pains to point out that conditioned responses tend to come forward in time, it is obvious that for *escape training* to be transformed into *avoidance training*, all that need be done is to provide for a time interval between the conditioned stimulus and the unconditioned stimulus sufficient for the response to occur. If this explanation should prove adequate no other assumptions are necessary to account for the avoidance behavior. It would not be avoidance behavior in any but a temporal sense and nothing need be said or implied about expectancy or its confirmation or strengthening. Since the reasoning about avoidance behavior appears to be based on the Brogden, Lipman, and Culler experiment, it perhaps deserves closer scrutiny.

Such closer scrutiny has already been given by Sheffield (1948), a student of Guthrie, who repeated the experiment with a reasonable facsimile, although some details varied. Sheffield challenged the notion that the animals were in fact strengthening the running behavior through the avoidance procedure. He found, in the first place, that running was not necessarily the unconditioned response to shock; in fact, running was incompatible with the unconditioned responses to the shock for some animals. Secondly, Sheffield points out, by carefully measuring the time of running and the distance run, the alleged avoidance animals were, in fact, extinguishing the behavior of running all along, instead of strengthening it. With successive trials they ran less and took longer to get started. When measured by number of runs (moving the wheel 1 inch or more) the avoidance behavior appeared to be learned readily; yet, when scrutinized closely, it showed the same characteristics as any Pavlovian response and was undergoing extinction. Sheffield concludes: "The results are interpreted as showing that omission of shock has no strengthening effect and that the results obtained by Brogden, Lipman, and Culler are consistent with the contiguity theory of learning."

The notion that the response is strengthened by omission of the shock as suggested by Hilgard and Marquis implies that the response should more or less continue indefinitely and get stronger right along. This would mean, in practice, that avoidance responses should not extinguish. There is no evidence that such is actually the case although some reports of very long extinction training have appeared. Miller (1948), for example, found that in his white-black box, the rats continued to turn the wheel for as many as 600 trials in some instances. Solomon and Wynne (1953) also report that many trials for dogs in a shuttle box (a two-compartment enclosure divided by a hurdle which the animal must jump). Brogden (1949), on the other hand, compiling results for 30 dogs trained to give a leg-withdrawal response, found that while it took an average of 11 days of 20 daily trials to establish the response, only 4 days were required to extinguish. Woodward (1954) found with 20 daily trials for albino rats that both acquisition and extinction of a hurdle-jumping response took approximately 3 days to a criterion of 20 successive jumps and 3 more days for 20 successive failures. Woodward also found that the habit was strongly controlled by the time interval between the conditioned and unconditioned stimuli and the height of the hurdle. (See Fig. 4.1). The response can actually be extinguished in 1 trial if the animal is restrained from making the response to the conditioned stimulus for as long as 1 minute. The writer found that a strong avoidance reaction was easily eliminated by simply blocking

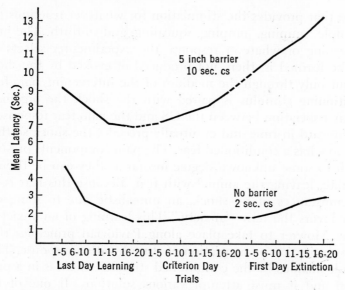

FIG. 4.1. The effect of time interval and barrier height on an avoidance response. Notice that a 5-inch barrier retards learning and hastens extinction. With no barrier and a short time interval (2 seconds) between CS (light) and UncS (shock) learning is rapid and extinction delayed. (After Woodward, 1954.)

off the entry to the other side of a shuttle box and sounding a buzzer for 1 minute. Removal of the barrier after such continuous stimulation left the animal apparently indifferent to ordinary presentations of the CS. Hurdle jumping in rats is easily extinguished even after a severe criterion such as 20 responses in succession to the CS. There is strong reason, then, to question the acceptability of the notion that the response is somehow self-strengthening.

Mowrer (1950) and Miller (1951) have made the greatest theoretical use of the avoidance type of response. Both consider the avoidance situation as illustrative of acquired drives. We shall examine the concept of acquired drives later and for the moment we note only the Mowrer view, to take the one that has been made most explicit (Miller has refrained from taking a position on the nature of the learning process involved). According to Mowrer, the following sequence of events is alleged to take place in avoidance training: when an animal is shocked it experiences some degree of pain. Such pain is more or less innately strongly associated with fear. It is this pain-fear response that provides the stimulation for whatever reactions follow, for example, running, jumping, squealing, and so forth. The jump or wheel-turning or whatever response the experimenter selects as the one to be learned is, then, not produced or evoked by the shock directly but only through the medium of the intervening pain-fear. As a conditioning stimulus is paired with the shock the organism acquires an association between the CS and the pain-fear response. This moves forward in time and eventually precedes the shock so that the animal now has a conditioned fear. The pain components presumably diminish to some unknown degree insofar as they can be thought of as separate, leaving the animal with fear. Because this fear is, under the circumstances of no shock, an unrealistic one to some degree, Mowrer favors the term "anxiety." This learning of an anxiety is alleged by Mowrer to take place along Pavlovian principles through simple substitution or association of stimuli with a response. The animal made anxious by the conditioned stimulus, then, is in a problem situation and it must attempt various solutions. If one of the responses removes it from the presence of the conditioned stimulus, the anxiety is diminished and the response is then strengthened in the Thorndikian sense. (See Fig. 4.2.) Recently, Mowrer (1953), who originally considered his views as comprising a two-factor theory (1947), has come to the conclusion that actually only one kind of learning (the Pavlovian) type is involved, at least in avoidance behavior, and that the resultant behavior initiated by the acquired drive is really more akin to "voluntary behavior." He does not make clear precisely what he means in this connection. We can reexamine his latest views at a more appropriate time.

In spite of the authority of Mowrer and Miller regarding the acquired-drive nature of avoidance learning, there are numerous difficulties with the view that it represents a separate kind of learning. The heuristic value of the hypothesis of acquired drives has been amply demonstrated. On the other hand, one should not accept the hypothesis solely because of heuristic value. It has already been indicated that Hull [3] analyzed the situation as one in which the response became antedating in form and that, in effect, avoidance behavior was a more or less necessary artifact of the training procedure in which the CS is allowed to precede the UncS. If avoidance is, in fact, a necessary artifact of escape training, there is hardly any point to

[3] Later (1951) Hull adopted a postulate which included the concept of "acquired drives."

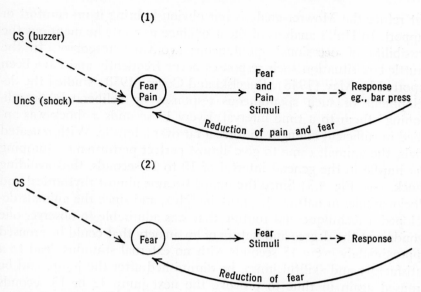

FIG. 4.2. The Mowrer interpretation of avoidance learning. In (1) the CS becomes associated with the UncS by Pavlovian conditioning. The stimuli from the pain-fear compound lead to the instrumental avoidance response which is reinforced by the reduction of the drive stimuli. In (2) the fear, now serving as an acquired drive, leads to the response which is still being strengthened by acquired-drive reduction. Solid lines represent natural tendencies. Dashed lines represent learned reactions.

magnifying it into a special type of learning. If no time interval prevailed between the CS and UncS avoidance training would be theoretically impossible, because it is necessary, according to Mowrer, for the CS to arouse fear first, and for fear then to initiate in some fashion the avoidance response. The experiment called for is virtually impossible of achievement in an avoidance situation because there will always be some time during which the CS and the UncS overlap before the avoidance response is given. Woodward (1954), however, did find that rats learned to jump a hurdle when a light-shock combination was presented simultaneously and that such learning was as strong (when measured by trials to extinction) as that acquired when a time interval separated the onset of the two stimuli. Further, he found that when the conditioned stimulus was presented at 5 seconds before the shock, the learning was poorer than when only 2 seconds separated the stimuli. A 10-second interval resulted in even poorer learning. The avoidance hypothesis would be strongly supported if the reverse kind of results had been obtained. The actual findings do not refute the Mowrer analysis but obviously bring it no comfort or support. In Hull's analysis of the avoidance response he mentions the possibility of occasional spontaneous avoidance responses. In the shuttle-box situation such responses occur frequently and have been reported by May (1948). Bugelski and Coyer (1950) studied the development of such spontaneous responses by deliberately "conditioning" them to a time interval. Every 15 seconds a shock was applied in sufficient strength to force a rat over a hurdle. With repeated trials, the animals came to give almost perfect performance, jumping the hurdle in the general interval of 10 to 15 seconds, thus avoiding shock. (see Fig. 4.3) Since the jumps became almost rhythmical and clockworklike in nature (to speak loosely), and since the animals developed a technique and routine that was admirable to observe, one wonders at the degree and nature of an anxiety that could be aroused approximately every 15 seconds with no external stimulus, lead to a satisfactory and skillful jump, be diminished after the jump, and be aroused again in time to provoke the next jump 12 or 13 seconds later. Certainly on observational grounds there would be no basis for introducing an intervening anxiety. This, of course, does not preclude there having been some; but, at least, it suggests that some more direct measures of the anxiety must be made if the hypothesis is to stand. To suggest that anxiety must have been there to begin with, but that it later disappeared and the behavior became irrationally compulsive and autonomous, is, of course, begging the question.

We have devoted so much comment to the avoidance category because of the great applications that have been made of it both to an analysis of abnormal behavior and to the analysis of learning presented by Tolman in his use of expectancies. We will return to it later in considering the question of reinforcement. It is to this question that we turn now, not with the view of analyzing the *construct* of reinforcement but rather to illustrate further the categories of learning advanced by Hilgard and Marquis.

REWARD LEARNING. Reward learning is by far the most common type of learning studied by contemporary learning psychologists. For Hilgard and Marquis it represents the type of learning most prominent in the behavior of organisms. Skinner (1938) and Mowrer (1947) emphasize the breadth of this type of behavior as against the Pavlovian type which they, more or less, with Thorndike, relegate to the area of laboratory curiosities. For Mowrer and Skinner, Pavlov might account satisfactorily for the learning of autonomic nervous

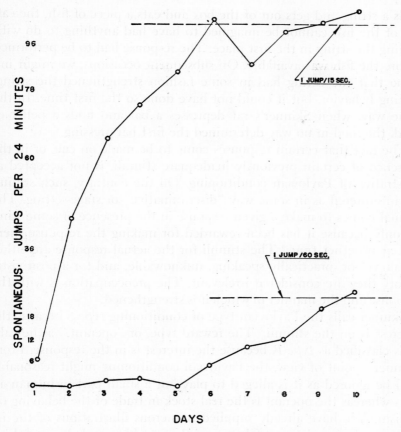

FIG. 4.3. The acquisition of "spontaneous" avoidance responses. Rats (10 in each group) were shocked every 15 seconds or every 60 seconds if they did not jump an 8-inch barrier in a shuttle box before the time was up. No other stimuli of any kind were given. The training trials lasted 24 minutes per day. The 15-second group learned to avoid the shock by the sixth day, the 60-second group required 10 days to learn to jump at 60-second intervals.

system responses, including such matters as emotion and its manifestations and perhaps for some limited number of primitive reflexes like the knee jerk or the eyelid reflex, but for any behavior involving essentially the whole organism, some kind of reward learning is presumed.

The category of reward learning covers any kind of response learning wherein the resulting change in the environment had nothing to do with bringing about that change. Thus, when Thorndike's cat pulls a string and gets out of the box and eats a piece of fish, the eating of the fish cannot be imagined to have had anything to do with pulling the string in the first place. The response had to be performed before the fish was available. On subsequent occasions, we might imagine that the eating had in some fashion strengthened the string-pulling behavior, but it could not have done so the first time. In the same way, when Skinner's rat depresses a bar and finds a pellet of food, the food in no way determined the first bar-pressing.

The fact that certain responses come to be made on cue, or in the presence of certain previously inadequate stimuli, is not accepted as illustrative of Pavlovian conditioning. On the contrary, such stimuli are interpreted as in some way "discriminative" or stage-setting. The animal comes to make a given response in the presence of some stimuli only because it has been rewarded for making the response then, and at no other time.[4] The stimuli for the actual response are either unknown, or, practically speaking, unknowable, and for a positivistic theory they are considered irrelevant. The preoccupation is with the response and the manner in which it is strengthened.

Skinner calls the Pavlovian type of conditioning *type S* because the interest is on the stimuli.[5] The reward type, or "operant," as he calls it, is classified as *type R* because the interest is in the response. From Skinner's point of view, the Pavlovian conditioning might reasonably well be ignored as it is alleged to play but a small part in human affairs whereas the operant is the real stock in trade of the behaving organism. We have already supplied numerous illustrations of the instrumental reward type of learning. Presumably any behavior which is *emitted* by the organism can be so classified if it is strengthened by the succeeding change in the environment. Any verbal or motor learning, language acquisition itself, maze learning, problem-solving situations, skills of any type, the whole gamut of personal and social adjustive responses are presumed to illustrate reward learning. When a dog learns to roll over or play dead he illustrates reward learning. Sometimes the reward is difficult to identify. It is reasonably clear that some hamburger meat for a hungry dog might play the reward role, and ice cream for a child might also be readily accepted as illustrating a more or less natural reward. Because of the apparent reward value of such things as a pat on the head, those psychologists

---

[4] See the report of Schoenfeld *et al.* (1950).
[5] Another name for this type of conditioning is "respondent." Skinner uses this term in contrast to "operant."

who favor a reward interpretation for much, if not all, learning, have been forced to devise a category of acquired rewards, or secondary rewards. This brings us to the last category offered by Hilgard and Marquis.

SECONDARY REWARD LEARNING. As indicated above, most learned behavior that can be observed among humans occurs in the absence of any direct and "objective" rewards. Even when rewards are given they are often long removed from the learning which has occurred. Psychologists who make reward of some type central to their views have to account for learning in the absence of food, ice cream, or other physical gratification. (Such physical gratification has a centuries-old identification with the concept of reward.) The obvious line of search for such substitute rewards is to pick out some items among the immediate consequences of the learned response and examine them for possible reward characteristics. This obvious line of research did not actually occur to psychologists until about 1935, but since then a flourishing literature has grown describing the function of alleged secondary rewards or learned rewards. For the moment we will content ourselves with one example of how secondary rewards are supposed to be acquired and how they presumably operate.

In some interesting experiments with chimpanzees, Cowles (1937) induced them to operate a slot machine device labeled a "chimpomat." After using poker chips as coins in operating the vending machine, the chimpanzees would prize the chips themselves, would work for them, and would even discriminate among them in terms of values Cowles assigned. A brass chip, for example, might be worthless. Inserting it in the machine produced nothing. Different colored chips would produce other colored chips which would produce grapes and tidbits of fruit. The chips which produced fruit would be valued more highly than the ones which merely produced the chips. Brass chips would be rejected. On the basis of these observations, Cowles suggested that the chips had acquired their reward characteristics or values through association with actual rewards and played a more or less symbolic role of representing the genuine rewards. Such rewards might in time come to be valued for their own sake alone.

In the same fashion, it is assumed that anything that accompanies a primary reward, any sound, any visually perceived object, any smell, even a pain of some modest degree might acquire secondary reward value and serve to reinforce or strengthen some learned behavior later on in another connection.

The concept of secondary reward is presumably strongly allied to secondary or acquired drives as a means for accounting for adult learning. The college student when he learns something does so because, according to Dollard and Miller (1950), he is operating under the influence of an acquired drive of anxiety, however mild it may be. By performing responses which reduce this anxiety and/or by obtaining secondary rewards for the performance, the new behavior is strengthened and has a higher probability of emerging on a future instance of the repetition of the problem situation. Hilgard and Marquis strongly suggest that secondary rewards function like "expectancies" and favor the Tolman interpretation of this type of learning.

CAN WE SUBDIVIDE LEARNING INTO TYPES?

We will leave the categories of Hilgard and Marquis for the present and turn to some other points of view on the subject of types of learning. Before doing so, we should note that Hilgard and Marquis appear to believe that the four instrumental types and the classical Pavlovian type adequately take care of the claims of the various theorists with due credit all around. If each theorist were content with being able to explain only a part of learning phenomena (instead of trying to make one principle account for everything) then everything would be nicely arranged. Thus, Pavlov and Guthrie could account for substitution learning. Hull could take care of reward learning (and some escape) and Tolman could handle avoidance learning and any situations in which expectancies appeared to operate, such as secondary reward learning. The only trouble is that the theorists themselves do not welcome this distribution of spoils and continue trying to make a single principle do.

The question of the variety or number of kinds of learning appears to be a pseudo-question. It actually deals not with kinds of learning but with kinds of experimental procedure and, if taken seriously, results in the kind of difficulty we have just encountered in the various speculative solutions offered, with different speculators offering one, two, five, or six categories of learning where parsimony requires a more intimate examination of the question as to whether or not one type might do. Once the door is opened to raising the question of number, speculators will develop as many kinds as are convenient, regardless of whether or not they are required.

Consider the several kinds of learning that have been suggested and what we find. In Pavlovian conditioning an organism appears to respond to a stimulus which previously was ineffective to arouse the response that does actually occur. Whether or not this is the same response as to the "unconditioned" stimulus may prove to be another pseudo-question. In other words, on the first occasion of presentation of the conditioned stimulus, the organism does not respond in the way it will come to eventually. Does this differ in any essential fashion from the behavior of the rat in the Skinner box? Or the chimpanzee with the chip? Or Miller's rats in the dual compartment box? It is interesting to note that although Hilgard and Marquis used Brogden's work to support the division of learning into types, in Brogden's own opinion (1951, p. 571), "The distinction of four varieties of instrumental training is based primarily upon the lack of control exercised by the experimenter over the conditions under which the acquisition takes place and the time at which responses occur." This conclusion can be expanded to cover the Pavlovian type of conditioning which differs only in the relatively greater ease of control over conditions and time of response.

Even if we allow the distinction urged by Mowrer, that some intervening activity such as anxiety operates prior to the occurrence of an avoidant response, the same single general description of what does go on can be permitted, with the extension, perhaps, of the description to cover the learning of two different responses. The fact that there are two different responses which closely follow one another is certainly not unique to avoidance learning, but on the contrary illustrates the most common feature of behavior, namely its sequential and continuous character. There is not a necessary difference in kind between learning to be afraid in the presence of one stimulus and learning to open a door in the presence of another. The *kinds of behavior* differ, the muscles or effectors are different, there may be levels of complexity and integration involving more or less of the total organism, but the basic generalization that a response occurs in the presence of a previously ineffective stimulus still prevails.

In his original approach to the question of the nature of learning, Tolman (1932) proposed his sign-Gestalt hypothesis which we have already described. Later, however, Tolman (1949) decided that there are at least six different kinds of learning. These he described as: cathexes, equivalence beliefs, field expectancies, field modes, drive discriminations, and, finally, motor patterns. We shall not examine these alleged kinds of learning except to indicate that Tolman's major emphasis seems to be that somehow all the categories he advances except the last are central phenomena. The last must be by exclusion, some noncentral or peripheral phenomenon. Here Tolman must find himself in an awkward position because Hull, for one, has long insisted that even motor patterns are central phenomena; in fact, that all learning is central and functions through the modification of the nervous system. It is time to consider the nature of the central phenomena involved in learning. For the present we will do so only superficially to indicate the general nature of the orientation. In later chapters, we shall have to come to closer grips with the problem.

It is true that students might get the impression from even careful reading of learning experiments that the theorists involved are talking about associations or connections being formed between stimuli and responses. The talk is consistently about lights, bells, buzzers, and movements of leg or arm, or discharge of gland or electrical property. It is also true that some psychologists, like Skinner, and to some extent Guthrie, speak almost exclusively of the external response or the external situation as a stimulus pattern or stimulus situation. The conclusion might easily be drawn that associations are made between such externally observable events as lights and leg withdrawals. Even a momentary consideration of the situation, however, reveals the necessary impossibility of such associations. The "associations" (and, for the present purpose we will not concern ourselves too closely with their nature) must be formed within the organism. If this is what Tolman means by central phenomena, he is no different from any other psychologist. Of necessity, they must all deal with the organism. Some may take the position, as does Skinner, that the internal events in the organism do not concern him to any practical extent, that in any event he must always deal with an external environment and record an externally observable event, but this by no means indicates that the animal can be dispensed with. The organism is not expendable.

Other psychologists like Hull (1943) and Hebb (1949) spell out to varying degrees the nature of the internal events that might be assumed to be taking place. Hull, for example, emphasizes that the external stimulus or S of the typical formula, is of little or no consequence, that its only function is to initiate a nervous impulse in an afferent nerve or system (this is labeled s). In the same way, the external response need not even occur (for example, salivation might be physically blocked by a drug so that the animal could not salivate to any measurable degree; all that is required for learning to take place is that a motor impulse (r) be initiated in the *central nervous system*). The learning or association then, if any takes place, consists of a *connection* (in Hull's language) between s and r and not between S and R. Although Hull is usually considered to be a "peripheralist," he might well claim that he is even more "central" than Tolman in that, for Hull, the motor pattern type of learning, or rather the type of behavior that might be categorized by that expression, is also a central phenomenon. How Tolman imagines that motor responses are learned he does not indicate. In fairness to Guthrie, mentioned above, it should be pointed out that he makes much use of what he calls "movement-produced stimuli" in his explanations of much serial behavior. Such stimuli might be considered "central," and the association might very well be made between stimuli that the experimenter could not observe in any currently available fashion and responses that might well be only the instigators of the final observable response.

Before leaving the topic of the central nature of learning phenomena we should point out the contribution made by Hebb (1949) in this connection. Hebb suggests that any limitation of the term "response" to some externally observable and gross activity of muscle or gland is not only unwise but improper. There is no reason why the activity of neural elements should not be included in the term and long tradition certainly justifies the usage of speaking of "neural responses." When a nerve is stimulated, it reacts or responds, assuming normal conditions. Such responses are not different in kind from any other responses in the ordinary or common meaning of response to convey the general impression of a "reaction." While muscle and gland may respond in terms of different chemical and physical activities from those in a nerve, the similarities might well outweigh the differences and there is every logical justification for using the term "response" to cover neural action. In Hebb's view then, neural responses are just as important, just as genuine, and just as much involved, if not more so, than responses of the effector units. For other reasons, also, it is ordinarily assumed, and explicitly so by Hebb, that whatever learning goes on will be in the nature of a modification of the neural activity and probably its structure. In any case, the learning will represent the association between neural responses and not between stimuli like bells and responses like raising a leg. A more detailed account of Hebb's views on association is presented later (see p. 113).

Early and late learning. There is one distinction between kinds of learning that may have some merit. It is the distinction advanced by Hebb (1949) between learning that occurs in infancy or early development and learning that takes place in later life. The implication of the distinction is that learning that takes place in a naïve organism may be quite different in nature from the learning of experienced or sophisticated subjects. We have already commented (see Chap. 3) on the factors of age and past experience and, indeed, this will be a recurrent topic. The present point, however, is that whereas early learning might follow one set of rules or principles and give the appearance of being a gradual, step-by-step process, the learning of later years might provide a completely different picture, one of rapidity and one-trial perfection. Learning from books or lectures might differ considerably from learning by experience. Not only might the external features differ grossly but we might expect radically different action in the nervous system. In infancy certain specific areas of the brain might be involved in some learning activity. In later life these areas might be almost completely unimportant, even if involved. Hebb (1942) reports, for example, that remarkable intellectual performances are possible even when the frontal lobes are removed in adults. Such operations in infancy might prove disastrous. We shall consider this distinction again in the following chapter and again in Chapter 13. For the present we do not wish to dismiss the question of how many kinds of learning there might be, even if parsimony suggests that one kind would give us enough difficulty. A distinction between early and late learning, however, would be based on different reasons from those offered in connection with other distinctions examined earlier. We would not necessarily be searching for new principles but rather be taking account of the changes occurring in the organism because of past experience.

An immediate difficulty arises in attempting to distinguish between "early" and "late." If we consider the experiences of an organism to be cumulative or have some cumulative effect, then "early" learning might be limited to the first moments of life or the first moments of exposure to certain conditions. All other experiences, then, would be relatively "late." There appears to be evidence that we must all learn to use our sense organs, that is, that we must learn to see (Riesen, 1947; Senden, 1932), and feel (Nissen, Chow, and Semmes, 1951), and presumably to hear and smell and use all the rest of our sensory equipment. The later exposure would benefit from or be hampered by the results or consequences of the earlier exposures. The distinction between early and late learning might prove of great value if it can be translated into other frames of reference. We might identify early learning with some kinds of primitive, naive, or first experiences and "late" with the more involved, more complex, or more sophisticated levels. Thus, learning to read the letters of the alphabet as individual letters might be a form of primitive experience or a type of "early" learning; reading words, then phrases and sentences might be considered "late" learning. In other frames of reference, learning one skill or maneuver, such as a maze, for the first time, might be called "early" learning; learning a second maze, which we can readily assume to be a somewhat different performance, might be an example of "late" learning. Hebb points out how easy it is to memorize a "meaningful" sentence and how difficult it is to learn the same verbal material if it is broken up into nonsense—syllable form. Learning the nonsense syllables might take 12 trials and learning the sentence only one. It may be that the learning of nonsense syllables amounts to something like "early" learning. Individual reactions usually are quite meaningless in their original form. Learning sentences *after the words* have been learned previously might illustrate "late" learning. How valuable the distinction will prove to be, we can leave for the subsequent chapters to determine.

Chapter

5   *What Is Learned?*

We have examined the question of how many different kinds of learning there are and have found no necessary or sufficient reasons for deciding that there is more than one kind. Instead, we have found that in all of the alleged kinds what was considered a kind of learning might really be a kind of behavior. Different kinds of behavior are learned. On this there can be little question. And it also appears that different kinds of psychologists favor the study of one kind of behavior over another. The question to be dealt with now is, therefore, the question of what kinds of behavior there are. This question does not call for a classification or enumeration of all the separate kinds of things that organisms do, such as baking pies or playing pinochle or square dancing. Rather, it is concerned with the analysis of these and thousands of other activities into their basic components so that significant aspects of the learning process may be brought under observation. Different kinds of behavior are presumably only the *content* in which the activity of learning takes place. By analogy, we might presume to study reading as a process without being too concerned about the content of the printed page as such.

To begin the analysis, we recognize that psychologists typically concern themselves with stimuli (S) and responses (R). Neither of these terms is at all carefully described by any learning theorist. Whatever efforts they have made to do so have proved unsatisfactory to critics (Estes *et al.*, 1954) and it would take us too far afield to get involved in this problem now. It is also usually assumed by learning psychologists that the S represents some sort of peripheral agitation of sense organs which is followed by a "sensory event" of some kind; such sensory events are frequently referred to as "central" and with no attempt at further amplification. These alleged events are located in, or rather, buried and forgotten in the CNS. The nature of such sensory events is never spelled out and a conspiracy of silence seems to exist among behavioristic psychologists lest some form of mind-body problem arise. Because the nature of this sensory reaction is not presented for inspection, we must leave it as we find it. Some psychologists, like Hull (1943), equate sensory with "afferent neural action"; others, like Tolman (1932), equate it with "signs" or "cues." In Tolman's case (as we have already seen) the "significate" in an expectancy is another form of sensory action. Taking the terms S and Sensory and R and Reaction with all their vague and unspecified implications, we can attempt a preliminary breakdown of what learning theorists have haggled over. Spence (1942a), in a sense, started one of the persistent controversies in learning theory when he chose to raise the question of what is learned and answered it to his own satisfaction by setting up three distinct approaches, two of which he chose not to favor.

THE S-R VERSUS S-S CONTROVERSY

According to Spence, it is desirable to think of learning as amounting to the formation of bonds, connections, or associations between stimuli and responses. Those who hold this view can be referred to as S-R psychologists. They may differ among themselves as to such matters as why a given association is formed (that is, they can disagree on the laws of association). Since Spence himself regards a *reinforcement* principle as a basic law of association, it is convenient for him to divide S-R psychologists into an S-R + reinforcement group and an S-R without reinforcement group.

The only other alternative Spence considers is the association between stimuli (or their immediate consequences in the form of "sensory events"). Tolman is regarded as the chief proponent of the S-S view. Any psychologists concerning themselves with associations among stimuli would be included in the Tolman camp. Since Tolman disclaimed interest in reinforcement (of the Hull-Thorndike variety) and favored a "frequency" principle of learning, another difference between the S-R and S-S psychologists was emphasized by Spence. Actually, since Tolman made use of a principle of "confirmation" of expectancies, a case could be made out to include him in a reinforcement camp but neither side cared to make the attempt. Instead, for over two decades reinforcement theorists (primarily Hull and his students) fought skirmishes in the journals against nonreinforcement theorists (Tolman and Guthrie) [1]. Attack was met by strategic retreats and counterattacks on both sides. The contradictory experimental findings led only to further contradictions. The "latent learning" [2] experiment has been reported at least 19 times in respectable journals with about 11 positive sets of results and 8 negative sets. (Reynolds, 1945b, Thislethwaite, 1951; Blodgett, 1929.) Anyone who asks for the facts in the matter is asking the wrong question.

Spence (1951) apparently began to appreciate that the battle was getting nowhere and suggested that the S-R versus S-S controversy was a futile one and should be abandoned. (He does not remind the reader that he started it, in good measure.) Spence proposes that a closer analysis be attempted of what is going on in the learning situation. His suggestion brings the problem back to where we started, that is, the question of what is learned.

INTERVENING VARIABLES AND HYPOTHETICAL CONSTRUCTS

In trying to answer the question of what is learned Tolman (1932, 1936, and 1938a) introduced the term "intervening variable" to psychology. At about the same time Hull (1935) was talking about "hypothetical constructs." These two terms have been responsible for considerable argument and abuse among psychologists and an appreciation of them is very much in order in connection with the question of what is learned. If Kendler (1952) is correct, the entire question is a pseudo-question and has no possible answer because learning psychologists have not appreciated the differences between hypothetical constructs and intervening variables; if they did, they would stop talking about what is learned (and about most of their activity) and begin their proper work, that of determining the number and nature of interactions of the intervening variables in behavior.

To appreciate the controversy we must first appreciate the alleged distinction between hypothetical constructs and intervening variables. If we notice a child solving an arithmetic problem we are prone to

---

[1] Guthrie was catalogued by Spence as an S-R nonreinforcement psychologist.
[2] We have seen an example of "latent learning" in Chap. 2, p. 21. We shall meet it again, p. 249.

infer that there is something in the child that worked the problem for him. Our inferences are limited only by our fancy, but in the illustration at hand, we are inclined to infer "intelligence" in the child when he solves the problem. Sometimes we infer "stupidity" in the same child when another problem proves too much for him. What do terms like "intelligence" and "stupidity" mean? Do they not basically refer to the fact that problems are solved or not solved and that the problems are of such a level of difficulty that a given child might have been expected to solve them? Breaking this situation down in S-R terms, we have the problem, S, the solution, R, and something alleged or assumed in between (intelligence). We may all have vague and hazy notions of what "intelligence" means but the fact is that psychologists have found it impossible to agree upon a definition. Even if it were defined in an agreeable fashion, there would still be little we could do with it scientifically. It was not until Stern (1914) devised the formula of $MA/CA = IQ$ that psychologists were able to make any extensive use of "intelligence." IQ, of course, does not equal intelligence, but stands for "intelligence quotient." The important point about "intelligence quotient" is that it does not mean anything beyond IQ which in turn means only MA/CA. No matter what we think or say about IQ we can put no meat on its bones. It remains a mathematical figure or formula. Such a formula or mathematical relationship is called, by Tolman, an "intervening variable." Those who believe there is some *thing*, some entity, or physical structure or process behind (or some place) the IQ and would perhaps prefer to talk about "intelligence" as something we will someday be able to see, feel, palpate, or sense in some other way, are using a "hypothetical construct."

Getting back to our own area, in the field of learning hypothetical constructs abound in great numbers. Hardly anyone questions the essential reality of such "things" as drives, motives, habits, reflexes, conditioned reflexes, reinforcement, inhibitions, synapses, fatigue, and a host of others we will come to in due course. A moment's reflection will convince the reader that he has never seen a habit or a drive, for example. If he arrived at such "constructs" by himself, he must have *inferred* them from observing some situation (S) and some behavior (R) and put the concept in between by and for himself. Such an inserted inference is an intervening variable, that is, a variable that is interposed between an independent and dependent variable. If this intervening variable is presumed to be something "real" and perhaps possessed of other characteristics, it is called a "construct." If, on the other hand, *nothing* is implied beyond the fact that some determinable (mathematical) relationship holds between the S and the R, then the term "intervening variable" is recommended by Kendler (1952) and MacCorquodale and Meehl (1948).[3] Kendler goes further than merely recommending the use of the "pure" intervening variable. He suggests that the use of hypothetical constructs is misleading and futile in the pursuit of learning about learning. Learning itself is an intervening variable and any attempt to talk about *what* is learned is, therefore, silly. The question of *what* is learned is pointless and unanswerable because, says Kendler, science does not deal with hypothetical constructs but only with intervening variables. What we should do, according to Kendler, is to start finding the mathematical relationships between S's and R's and waste no more time on hypothetical constructs. Actually, this is what Tolman (1938a) suggested as a program for psychologists long ago although he did not carry it out in the intervening years and instead started a program of investigating his own favorite hypothetical constructs like "expectancies" and "cognitive maps." While this is not the place to argue what "science" studies, it is unlikely that Kendler could establish that the history of science is even remotely the story of working with pure intervening variables. Such formulae as those for gravity or atomic fusion or fission, or even Einstein's $MC^2 = E$ are the results of hundreds of years of toil by scientists who patiently nursed their hypothetical constructs like ether, phlogiston, and atoms, neutrons, protons, and so on until some of them could be disposed of as convenient fictions. It is doubtful if psychologists will drop their hypothetical constructs as quickly as Kendler might hope and about as doubtful that they will make much progress with the intervening variables if they cannot even get settled on the matter of the number and nature of independent and dependent variables. It is unfortunately true that there is no agreement yet on the meaning of the term, "stimulus." It is usually defined in terms of a response, as: a stimulus is that which causes (or is followed by) a response. There might be some meaning to this if we could state what we mean by a response, but there we are, perhaps even worse off. Sherrington .(1906) has called the "reflex" a convenient abstraction. A conditioned reflex is also convenient but a bit

---

[3] Bergmann (1953) offers a philosophically sophisticated treatment of this problem.

more of an abstraction. When we ask psychologists to identify responses they are strangely uninformative if we mean business. If we are merely asking, they will talk about bar-pressing, maze-running, reciting nonsense syllables, choosing left rather than right turns on a T-maze, or going to certain "places" rather than to others. To what degree the world of science is going to equate a bar-press with a "response" remains to be seen.

It is not our problem to advocate the choice of intervening variables over hypothetical constructs. Critics of the thinking of learning psychologists like Bergmann (1953) and Adams (1954) and the Dartmouth group (Estes *et al.*, 1954) do not agree that the distinction is a real one and there is no indication in current trends that all or even a majority of psychologists are going to follow one interpretation of how science should (or does) operate. The likelihood is that for many years to come supporters of an inductive empiricism will continue to wrestle with the same problems that others are trying to approach through a hypothetical-deductive [4] procedure. Positivists and operationists will find other psychologists who are willing to indulge in looser thinking for the benefit of backing up their "insights." Our problem is rather that of seeing what the learning psychologists have been doing and what they say they have been thinking about. To a considerable extent they have been thinking about what is learned whether or not the question is legitimate and meaningful. That they will continue to think about it for years to come is certain. It is time to return to these thoughts and attempt some evaluation.

We have already seen how Tolman is alleged to favor the view that signs and significates are associated, whereas Hull and Guthrie favor the view that stimuli and responses are associated. We have also noted that Hull openly assumes that the nervous system is the mediator of learning, that is, what learning goes on, occurs between neural processes and not between external events. The others would also agree to this proposition, even those who, like Skinner, assume that the study of external events will be the more rewarding occupation, if not, indeed, the only one available to the psychologist. Hull (1952) and Spence (1951) also claim to operate in terms of external events,

---

[4] The hypothetico-deductive method refers to Hull's (primarily) interpretation of the nature of science. In using this method, the theorist decides on a minimal number of postulates or assumptions and proceeds to deduce *theorems* by logically following through the implications of the postulates.

their "intervening variables" being only aids to theorizing and not entities for which physiological data must be obtained before progress can be made on the behavioral level.

WHAT IS LEARNED? MOVEMENTS OR ACTS?

Looking at the behavioral level for the moment, what are the kinds of behavior that the psychologist thinks of as learned? It might be best to start with Guthrie, who favors a distinction of kind that might serve as a background against which to examine the others. According to Guthrie (1935), we learn to make specific movements to specific stimulus patterns. A given pattern of muscular contractions and relaxations occurs when a given stimulus pattern affects us. Thus, we do not learn to open a door, rather, we learn to grasp and twist a particular knob and pull backward or push forward, depending on the door. In a lifetime of experience with doors we meet doors in all kinds of stimulus patterns and settings. Sometimes we are moving slowly. On other occasions we are running. Sometimes our hands are occupied with books or bundles. We encounter doors with knobs on the right, on the left, with latches, keys, electric eyes, and so on. We crawl up against doors as babies and have doors opened for us as we get older. We find doors ajar, half open, locked, and so on. Sometimes we nudge doors with our elbows, shoulders, hands, or kick them with our feet or knees. We have thousands of practice sessions with doors and learn thousands of different responses to the thousands of stimulus patterns. Under ordinary circumstances there is a response available for almost any door situation we are likely to meet. When we approach a particular closed door it is presumed by Guthrie that the pattern of stimulation which operates on us at the moment determines the reaction we make. Whether or not the door opens belongs to the psychology of doors, not people. In the same sense, we do not learn to shoot the enemy—we learn to focus our eyes on a given target and squeeze with our trigger fingers while holding our weapon in a particular manner. Again, we do not learn to dance the tango or any other "step." Rather, we learn to make series of steps—in the tango we must move, in the words of the dance instructor, "slow, slow, quick, quick, quick." The fox trot and waltz require different movements at different time intervals (rhythms). In fact, regardless of the activity we familiarly speak of as having learned, it always resolves itself into a series of movements and not *acts*. Acts are equated with changes in the environment. They are *results* or achievements of behavior, and not behavior itself. When we have learned all possible responses to all possible stimulus patterns in some area then we can speak, for conversational purposes, of having learned to do something, say, eat, be polite, type, or play the piano, but behaviorally we have only done what was indicated above, namely, learned the movements to the stimuli involved. Any attempt to view the problem otherwise sends the psychologist off into what must be, according to Guthrie, a blind alley from which he will emerge with a variety of grand but worthless principles or laws of behavior which will apply to objects like food, saxophones, or chessmen, but not to people.

One possible interpretation of the Guthrie view might be that if you learn to do something in a certain way, you will continue to perform in the same fashion regardless of the possibly altered propriety of the behavior. In other words, behavior indulged in once should be repeated on the presentation of the same stimulus pattern and variability should be minimal. This is exactly what Guthrie predicts with careful emphasis on the necessity that the same stimuli be repeated. Since Guthrie and everyone else admits that the likelihood of the same stimulus pattern ever repeating itself is small, there seems to be little to be concluded from the argument. When the behavior is the same we can conclude, in reverse, that the stimulus pattern must have been the same as on the occasion when the behavior was learned; if the behavior is different, the stimulus pattern must have changed. Such a situation is hopeless of reduction to anything like scientific proof and although there are several experiments that demonstrate the astonishing degree of stereotypy in behavior, notably that of Guthrie and Horton (1946) with cats, nothing is actually proved by them and they hardly merit comment. A homely example is as good proof or lack of it as the most refined experiment. The writer, for example, like everyone else, acquired a certain manner of emerging from his car. When cold weather arrived and an overcoat was indicated it turned out that the ordinary manner of getting out of the car resulted in a heel being caught in the lining of the coat, producing a tear. The tear was enlarged on the next debarking. A repair was only good enough to last until the next occasion, for on leaving the car the tear was reopened. This ridiculous behavior persisted more or less through the winter with some rare occasions when self-admonishment and "determination" resulted in a different manner of leaving. The real cure came about in the spring when the overcoat was discarded. The following year with a different car, calling for different movements, was a complete success. Numerous other examples can be offered of the stereotyping of behavior, but as indicated above, they prove nothing. Later, they may turn out to be suggestive for a consideration of habit breaking, but for the moment we can leave them without regret.

WHAT IS LEARNED? HABITS OR RESPONSES?

The learning versus performance controversy. Although Hull does not take time out to agree specifically with Guthrie in this approach, he sometimes (1943, p. 25) writes just like Guthrie and he may be counted as sharing Guthrie's view in this analysis. Hull talks about the associations that are formed as formed between stimuli and responses in the nervous system and this presumably refers to specific stimuli and specific responses. When the Guthrie view leads to superficially difficult situations, Hull has ready means for avoiding what seems to be too narrow an approach to the problem, but on the whole the views cannot be said to differ. Whereas Guthrie speaks in general terms about associations between stimulus patterns and movements, he does not specify for any case or illustration just what the particular stimuli are. To speak of "the sight of the door" or a "jab with a pitchfork" as stimuli leaves much to be said. Hull tries to be more specific, at least on a theoretical level, and for him the association involved in any learning is represented in terms of a hypothetical construct of a habit. A learned S-R connection is thought of as $_sH_R$, a symbolic notation for habit. The obligation of the theorist is to specify the S and the R in precise operations of the experimenter. It is further specified (1952) that $_sH_R$ is a function of the number of times a selected R has been reinforced. This is a problem for later consideration (see p. 256).

For the present, one further distinction between Hull and Guthrie is important. For Guthrie, there is no such thing as learning unless there is evidence in terms of doing or performance. Given stimuli always bring out a particular response. There is no logical way to prove or disprove this assertion as should be quite apparent. If an expected response fails to materialize, Guthrie can always claim that some part (unspecified) of the stimulus pattern was missing.

Hull chooses another method for handling the question of whether or not a given habit will work. He postulates a concept of "excitatory potential" or $_sE_R$. $_sE_R$ is the real *behavioral* unit in Hull's systematic thinking. $_sE_R$ is designed to account for the occurrence or nonoccurrence of a response. It includes $_sH_R$, or habit, as one component but also a variety of others. Thus, at one time Hull (1943) described the formula for $_sE_R$ as $_sH_R \times D$, or drive. If some drive strength is present there will be some degree of response. If $D = 0$, there can be no behavior. It is particularly important to note this distinction between $_sH_R$ and $_sE_R$ as they represent respectively learning and performance, and Hull has sometimes been criticized for not paying attention to this distinction. As a matter of fact, Hull was more concerned with $_sE_R$ than with $_sH_R$ as he hoped to develop not only a theory of learning but a theory of behavior, and the larger interest occupied him far more than the lesser.

WHAT IS LEARNED? EXPECTANCIES?

Knowledge versus performance. The cognitive map. In his own interpretation of what is learned, Tolman (1938a) takes the view that the Guthrie and Hull propositions emphasize unduly and unnecessarily the *performance* of responses which are to be learned, whereas his own position leads directly to what might be contrasted with performance, namely, *knowledge*. Basing his argument on certain experiments of Blodgett (1929), Tolman arrived at the conclusion that organisms learn what might be called "general orientations" or appreciations of situations; that they learn, in some fashion, certain relationships between stimuli, of the nature of what leads to what. The specific activity that might be engaged in to achieve certain ends or goals is somewhat irrelevant to the situation. Thus, in the Blodgett experiment, rats were placed in a maze and allowed to run about more or less freely. When they made what Blodgett called "correct" turns, doors were closed behind them until eventually they arrived at the last compartment of the maze, whereupon they were removed and not fed until some time later. These rats showed no apparent signs of learning for seven days. On that day they were fed in the maze when they reached the end compartment. On the eighth day, their performances changed radically and they ran through the maze almost as well as rats that had been rewarded from the first and had displayed a gradual learning of the maze. From Tolman's viewpoint, the behavior of the animals is clearly explained: the rats were learning continually although they did not show it because there was no need to demonstrate the learning. While wandering around in the maze they were learning what leads to what, they became familiar with the location and *meaning* of all the turns. They were building up a series of expectancies. Later when it proved desirable to get to the end as quickly as possible, the rats were fully equipped for such a behavior pattern. Thus, the animals are alleged to have acquired what Tolman now (1948) calls a "cognitive map" of the maze and could make use of it in any desired way. Presumably they could have started from any point in the maze and gone to any point. They could start at the goal end and get back to the starting end if the experimenter chose to switch food places. Tolman has devoted much of his experimental practice to establishing his views in numerous experiments designed to demonstrate that a rat learns to go to a certain "place" as opposed to learning to make a certain turn or "response." We shall have to examine some of these experiments in detail shortly (see p. 94), but for the present a more general appreciation of the problem is required.

WHAT IS LEARNED?

What Do the Learning Psychologists Learn About?

We might profit more if we return to the laboratory and examine the behavior of learning psychologists. We shall look over their shoulders while they study "learning" in two of the most popular forms of learning experiment, the Skinner bar-press situation, and the T-maze. We shall start with the Skinner box and try to find out if the rat in the box is learning movements, habits, or expectancies, or even, perhaps, something quite unlike any of these.

The Skinner box. When an animal is placed in the Skinner box it is allowed to operate a device which activates some mechanism which discharges tiny pellets of food. It might be compared with any kind of slot machine or automatic dispenser which requires that the operator do something to set it into action. It is customary, when using this apparatus, to arrange an electrical switch which operates a marker on a moving tape every time the bar is depressed. The psychologist ordinarily inserts the rat into the box and starts the moving tape.

From then on it is up to the rat and the psychologist may very well leave the scene to return an hour or so later, remove the amassed tape, and proceed to analyze it. The study of the rat's behavior then turns out to be a study of the marks on some tape. The number of reports based upon the number and distribution of marks on a tape is tremendous. How much of it reflects the behavior of the rat is a serious and grave question. Unlike Pandora, Skinner does not appear to be very curious about what goes on in the box. The student might desire a more intimate view of the rat in the process of learning, and so it is proposed to analyze, not the tape, but the behavior of the rat in this situation to determine if possible what it is that actually goes on and what the rat actually learns.

The ordinary Skinner box is rather small, and the bar is mounted above the food cup so that almost any move in an upward direction away from the food cup will bring the rat in contact with the bar. In this situation things happen so quickly that the details can hardly be observed and one might as well study the tape. The writer has constructed a box which is much larger, about 2 feet square with the bar on one side and the food cup on the other. This has the effect of exploding the pattern of behavior so that it can be scrutinized a bit more closely. At the same time, it has the effect of making the bar-pressing behavior more difficult to learn and by delaying the learning it makes possible more observations. The box has a glass front so that the rat can be watched and photographed. How does a rat learn in such a situation? It will become apparent in later discussions, but we can note now the observation that in most serial or sequential responses or chains of responses, the first thing learned is the last operation performed in the sequence. In the Skinner box, the first thing the rat learns is to eat the food that is supplied. This is frequently a problem if the rats have not been fed such pellets in their ordinary rations. Having learned to eat at the cup, the next phase in the sequence that is to be established is to learn to come to the cup. This can only be done if the rat leaves the food area in the first place. The second step in the training consists of "teaching" the rat to come to the cup, eat a pellet, and leave the cup area. The rat appears "reluctant" to leave the feeding station and the experimenter simply waits until it does so. To facilitate this phase of the training, the experimenter takes advantage of the fact that the food dispensing mechanism is somewhat noisy and its operation provides a definite auditory stimulus or click. The sound of the pellet dropping into the metal cup

is an additional such stimulus and can be seen to be effective in arousing food-cup approaches on the part of the rat. After each departure
from the cup the experimenter activates the feeder and waits for the
rat to return. Within a few trials the pattern of eating and leaving the
cup is fairly well established. The problem now is to get the rat to
depart for greater and greater distances until it is near the far wall
where the bar will be inserted later. By waiting and watching, the
experimenter gradually builds up the departure distance until the rat
comes promptly when the mechanism sounds, eats, and leaves the
cup, going all the way across the compartment to the far wall. Twenty
trials of such a nature are usually sufficient to ensure that the rat will
waste no time at the empty food cup but will stay in the vicinity of
the far wall until the food is dropped into the cup. This represents
the second stage of the learning, and is the second-to-the-last thing to
be done in the bar-press operation.

Later, and usually the next day, the animal is returned to the box.
A bar is now present, protruding through the rear wall. The typical
animal will sniff about the food box and then leave for the far
wall. It will remain there, generally speaking, indefinitely if strongly
trained, and again, generally, it will not approach the food cup with
any great frequency. In moving about in the rear-wall area it will inevitably come upon the bar and duck under or crawl over it. Contact
with the bar will generally activate the dispensing mechanism and the
click of the apparatus will usually be followed by a prompt food-cup
approach. Although Skinner intimates that one such "reinforcement"
is quickly followed by an increase in bar-pressing, in the situation under consideration the experimenter may have to wait for a long interval before the next bar press. It should be remembered that the rat
has learned to do other things at the far wall and it will return to
such activities. The longer it takes to go through these other activities,
the longer it is before the bar is pressed again. Eventually, however,
the bar is activated again, the click sounds, and the animal goes to the
cup. The time between successive bar-presses now gradually drops and
a witness brought in at this stage might feel inclined to describe the
behavior as consisting of these steps: (1) press the bar, (2) run to
the cup, (3) eat. Actually, the pattern is more suitably described as:
sniff in cup, eat if anything is present, leave the cup, activate the bar,
run after the mechanism clicks, and eat. At this point the whole cycle
is repeated. The important point to observe is that the cycle starts
with eating and not with bar-pressing. The behavior tends to become

stereotyped (see p. 16), and the pattern followed by an individual rat can be fairly well predicted. Some rats "eat and run"; others take their time about the whole routine and settle down to eat, visit a water source, perhaps sweep the food cup with their whiskers again before returning to the bar, and so on. These additions to the eat-run-press pattern appear quite ritualistic and probably serve to provide cues for each successive stage in the sequence as any interference with the pattern results in a delay of the sequence.

We now turn our attention to the click and its role in the situation. In Chapter 2 we promised to give a fuller account of this stimulus. What kind of a stimulus is it? Skinner (1938) regards such a stimulus which follows the bar-press as a reinforcer if it strengthens the bar-press behavior. Skinner and others (Estes, 1949b) have demonstrated that a rat will press the bar for no other reward than the occurrence of the click if the click has been associated with food previously. The click in such an event is called a "secondary reinforcer." Is the role of the click really that of a secondary reinforcer or does it have some other function? One of the writer's students, R. T. White (1953), designed an experiment to discover the possible role of the click in the Skinner box. He trained several groups of rats in the manner previously described so that they were efficient bar-pressers. When all the rats were trained they were given different *pre-extinction* training. Some rats were placed in the box without a bar present and were presented with a click at an average interval of 30 seconds. The click was followed ordinarily by an approach to the food cup, now empty. As the clicks continued the fruitless trips began to decline until they stopped altogether (usually within a period of 30 clicks). It would appear that the food-cup approach was extinguished as far as the click was concerned. The next day the rats were replaced in the box with the bar present and underwent ordinary extinction (that is, no food was dropped to them after the bar-presses). Allowing for "spontaneous recovery" (see p. 353) and for the probable short-circuiting of the behavior so that the click might not be particularly important if food was present, we could expect the rats to make some food-cup approaches, which they did. However, an interesting chain of events began to unfold. The rats began to cut down the number of trips to the food cup after bar-pressing, compared with a normal (nonpre-extinguished) group. Their behavior toward the food cup became less regular, frequently they failed to reach it at all, and frequently they failed to "search" it for food. (See Fig. 5.1.) As the food cup behavior

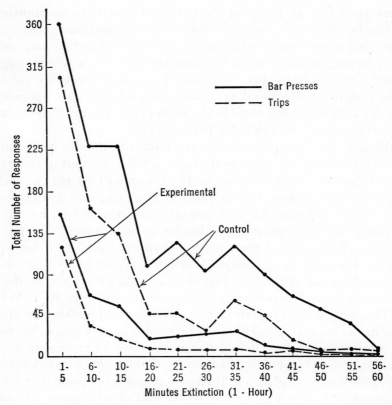

FIG. 5.1. Extinction behavior in a Skinner box. The number of bar presses and trips to the food cup in 5-minute intervals in a 1-hour extinction period. Totals for 12 rats in each group. The experimental group had a pre-extinction period of 30 minutes in the box with the sound presented at 1-minute intervals, on the average. No bar was present. The control rats were also in the box for 30 minutes but no sound cue was presented. Note that bar presses always exceed cup responses. Note also how the pre-extinction experience has depressed the rate of both bar presses and trips to the food cup. (White, 1953)

began to break down, the entire pattern of return to the bar also weakened and broke down. Now the rat did not get to the bar and consequently could not press it. When it did get around to the bar and pressed, it failed to go to the cup, and consequently spent more time in the bar area. Spending more time in the bar area permitted a few more bar-presses than might be ordinary, but even that behavior began to weaken. The pre-extinguished rats met an extinction criterion sooner than did the control animals. From the description of the behavior of the rats it would appear that rather than talking about secondary reinforcement we might more logically conceive the click to be a stimulus which happens to become associated with one segment of a chain of responses, namely, that part of the pattern which we can label "going to the food cup." This behavior will go on anyway (because of antedating? or short-circuiting?) and so long as food is present, the click merely is one of numerous stimuli which are associated with turning to the cup. Being such a stimulus, however, it plays its role in the pattern and helps to keep the behavior going. When it is dropped out of the picture, the pattern is to that extent weakened or altered so that the behavior is less likely to occur and will be eliminated more rapidly as the rest of the pattern gets extinguished. The click is not, then, a secondary reinforcer in any sense, particularly that of a reward or subgoal; it is not a discriminated stimulus as suggested by Schoenfeld, Antonitis, and Birch (1950). It is rather a part of a pattern that *evokes* a particular response. Every part of the bar-press behavior is controlled by stimuli of a direct or unconditioned nature or by conditioned stimuli. The click is such a conditioned stimulus. To talk about "operants" is a futile business if we are to arrive at any understanding of behavior. To infer the laws of behavior from what the experimenter is doing instead of from what the subject is doing is equally futile. Observing the rat instead of the kymograph or tape shows us that the rat is forced by the construction of the box (usually the bar protrudes through an air hole or opening in which rats appear to show an interest) to come to the bar area. Once in the bar area, the location and construction of the bar virtually provokes one or another kind of manipulation. To what extent the rat's prior history with isolated objects in his living cage enters we cannot state, but we can presume that in an otherwise empty box a movable object may have some stimulus value of a "conditioned" if not an unconditioned nature. Without more direct knowledge of what rats do with bars naturally, we are obligated to assume a burden of proof when we begin talking about operants rather than respondents. Once the bar is moved, the previously established habit of going to the cup is quickly initiated by the noise of the food mechanism.[5]

---

[5] The writer once trained a pigeon to peck at a target placed at a distance from a food cup. The pigeon quickly learned to stay at the target until the sound of the kernel of corn could be heard. After each peck the pigeon cocked its head. If no corn was dropped, another peck occurred.

There appears to be little reason to consider the possibility that the rat "knows" what it is doing or that it has an expectancy that pressing the bar will be followed by food unless we define an expectancy in some way that denudes it of any conventional implications. When rats in other adjacent boxes manipulate the bars in their boxes, a rat that has not pressed the bar in its box may run to the food tray. Frequently the short-circuiting (antedating) features in the circuit may bring the rat back to the food cup after it has merely approached the bar area and done nothing in the nature of pressing or even waving at the bar. It is likely that if the bar were moved to a side of the box from its original location that the rat would continue to press away at a nonexistent bar on the rear wall until it learned a new sequence of responses in connection with the new location. Thorndike's and Guthrie's observations on their cats would certainly support such an expectation.

Has our somewhat protracted observation of the rat in a Skinner box thrown any light on what is learned? Of the three views we are considering at the moment (Hull, Guthrie, and Tolman) none can be considered eliminated. Each could easily incorporate the findings, although the student may be picking a favorite. It may be that all three are correct, perhaps only in part, and from different levels of observation. We might consider Guthrie's view a "molecular" picture and Tolman's a "molar" [6] picture with Hull somewhere in between. Is the behavior of the rat something we are ready to discuss in terms of "pure" intervening variables or must we still resort to "hypothetical constructs?" Before we can consider a decision we need more observations, and we may find our time profitably spent by looking at some of Tolman's work on "place" learning. After all, Skinner's box may prove too limited a source for comprehending the complexities of what goes on in "learning."

"Place" versus "Response" Learning

In one way or another most of Tolman's experimental ventures have been designed to determine to what extent an animal operates in terms of familiarity with some location. Tolman likes to talk about

---

[6] Psychologists frequently use the term "molar" to refer to behavior of a more general nature, involving the whole organism. The term "molecular" is used, in contrast, to refer to finer, more specific, often physiological, units. Guthrie's distinction between "Act" and "Movement" might illustrate the contrast.

"cognitive maps" and maps necessarily apply to spatial and location propositions. In a general way, Tolman is concerned with finding out if animals "know" something about where they are and where other items like food might be. Such knowledge they could possess whether or not they were hungry or even bothered to make the effort of getting to the location. If he could demonstrate that an organism could get to a presumably desired place regardless of how it got there, especially by some new route for which no prior habit or response system had been built, he would conclude that just such things as "cognitive maps" had somehow been employed.

Tolman has attempted to establish the verity of cognitive maps in numerous ways, some of which we will discuss in other connections (see discussion of incidental learning, p. 225, and learning with irrelevant drives, p. 226), but his most commonly employed experimental design is to use a T-maze so constructed that the starting place can be changed from one side of the crossarm to the other (see Fig. 5.2). With such a maze, Tolman and his students have run a series of studies[7] in which rats are compared for efficiency of learning when one group learns to get to a certain place (the west side of the maze) while the other learns to make a certain response, a right turn. (In actual practice other groups are trained to "go east" and to make left turns. We shall ignore these for ease of treatment.)

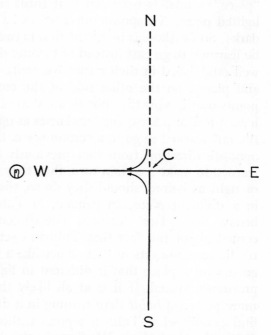

FIG. 5.2. A T-maze with a movable starting runway. Rats trained to run West from South, making a left turn at the choice point (C), will turn right when started from the North point if they have learned to go to a "place." If they have learned only to make a left turn, they will turn left and wind up at East and would be called "response" rats by Tolman.

[7] See Tolman, Ritchie, and Kalish (1947), the fifth of such a series.

In a typical experiment the maze is set up so that the starting leg points south and the arms east and west, as far as the floor plan of a room might be concerned. At the west end a light bulb is mounted so that the west end is illuminated; the east end is relatively dark. A "place" animal is rewarded if it turns left and gets to the west, a lighted place. A response rat is rewarded for *turning right* (into the dark). So far there is no distinction between the groups as one might be learning to go east instead of turning right. When both groups are well established in their respective turns, the starting leg is detached and placed on the other side of the cross member so that now it points north. Now the animals are started from the north end and we have a test of place-going tendencies as opposed to response habits. If the rats learned to go to a certain place, then they should turn in the opposite direction from that previously followed. If, however, they learned to make a certain turn, then they should continue to turn left or right as before; should they do so, they would, of course, end up in a different *place*. In general, in Tolman's experiments the rats behave like "place" learners. The student might be somewhat concerned about the fact that Tolman's setup seems somewhat unfair to the response rats in that to act like a response rat the beast must go toward a place that is different in light characteristics from that previously visited. If it is at all likely that approaching a light is a more powerful *habit* than turning in a different direction, we would find exactly what Tolman reports without having a justification of Tolman's conclusions. We have in this kind of experiment the possibility of two simultaneously operating intervening variables (that is, the rats may have learned to go toward a light or they may have learned to turn left) and there is no way to decide from Tolman's experiment if the rats were really going to a certain place or merely following the path of least resistance as far as habits are concerned. In the study by Scharlock (1954) an attempt was made to provide a more definite test of place versus response learning. Scharlock placed lights at each end of the crossarm. Now if rats are concerned about getting to a certain place (west) they have to turn in the opposite direction when the starting leg is rotated. In Scharlock's experiment the "response" rats won the contest with hardly a struggle. There was now no difficulty about turning in the same direction. The rats appeared to have little or no place-going tendencies and Scharlock concluded that Tolman's place-turning rats were merely engaged in light-approach habits rather than going to a certain location.

To talk about light-approaching habits may sound a bit vague, but what is meant by the expression is that the light serves as a stimulus which is associated with running, and, even more, the different illumination strengths are associated with different running speeds so that the rat runs somewhat more rapidly as the light affecting it grows stronger (that is, as it approaches the light). We will have occasion later to talk about this under the heading of "the goal gradient." That this is no sheer fancy was demonstrated even more clearly in another experiment by Scharlock (1954). In this study 10 rats were trained to run on a T-maze and turn left toward a lighted end. The light was placed 6 inches from the food end of the cross member. When the rats were thoroughly trained, the light was moved back 6 more inches, making a total distance of 1 foot. On the first test run with the light at the new distance 9 of the 10 rats fell off the end of the T and the tenth barely saved himself the fall by hanging on to the food cup. Clearly, the behavior of the rats was controlled by the light and their running and stopping was determined by an illumination gradient. To speak of their "going west" seems highly superfluous.

Other experiments of Tolman have not fared too well when repeated by supporters of other points of view. The best that can be said for them is that they can bring Tolman only mild comfort and support. The situation which we find amounts to a series of charges and countercharges of criticisms and rebuttals. This may be a sad commentary on the state of affairs or indicate a healthy growth of a stripling science. We will have to await the verdict of the future.

To round out our excursion into expectancy theory we should call attention to a brief paper by Thorndike (1946) in which he challenged Tolman to see what would happen in four situations that Thorndike thought suitable tests of the "expectancy" view. Two of the situations were briefly: (a) ride a rat through a maze, giving him a chance to observe the proper path, and check later to see if the rat had benefited from the sight-seeing tours; (b) carry rats by hand alongside a ladder to a platform mounted on a pole, feed them on the platform, check to see if they had learned anything about the necessity of going up the ladder. The remaining proposals were similar in nature, employing other apparatus and movements. Bugelski, Coyer, and Rogers (1952) checked all the suggestions and found nothing to support an expectancy view (as Thorndike probably had done also before issuing his challenge). Tolman could argue that the tests are unfair. If they are unfair then we must conclude that Tolman has not

described his construct of "expectancy" clearly enough so that Thorndike could understand it.

Mediated Behavior

Up to now we have been talking about stimuli and responses that
were, to some degree, observable. But much of our behavior appears
to us to be internal, private, unavailable to outsiders, and difficult
to describe, much less measure. We think, or at least we think we do;
we sometimes claim foresight, make plans, decisions, get "ideas," and
so on. Is this kind of behavior independent of learning? What kinds
of responses are being learned? What is responding? Can a psychology of learning that deals with stimuli and responses make much
sense in explaining behavior that is unobservable directly?

We have already alluded to certain alleged internal events. Guthrie
spoke of movement-produced stimuli. Such largely proprioceptive
stimuli have not been observed by Guthrie but are inferred from our
knowledge of the physiology of movement. Such stimuli do occur
with every muscular contraction. When glands secrete we might
imagine that the presence of their substances (tears, saliva, hormones,
and so on) serve as stimuli—a dog with a watering mouth certainly is
in a changed situation which technically qualifies as a "stimulus."
Such stimuli are just as significant and important, if not more so, as
external world changes such as lights or buzzers. They offer us, because they are internal, an entry into "internal" events.

Let us examine some examples of internal behavior and attempt
to evaluate the role of internal stimuli in the production or development of the aspects of behavior that are more in keeping with the
obvious complexity of adult human behavior. But before we get to
the human, let us take another look at Pavlov's dog. You recall that
Pavlov took certain precautions to keep the dog in a relatively fixed
position. The dog was strapped to a frame which prevented any
movement of any real extent. As the dog undergoes successive trials
of paired stimulation we can observe the gradual development of the
conditioned response—the dog salivates to the conditioning stimulus.
At this point, Pavlov loses interest in what the dog might do in addition to salivation and proceeds to speculate about the significance of
the number of drops. Had Pavlov cared to buzz his buzzer sometime
without tying up the dog he would have seen the animal rush to the
feeding station just as any house pet runs to the kitchen at the rattle

of the food dish on the floor or as farm animals come to the barn at various signals or calls. It appears that Pavlov cut his observations short for the, perhaps in this case, questionable quantitative values. We must not be too hasty in our judgment, however; the saliva may prove of greatest interest after all, not for Pavlov's reasons, but for purposes of explaining why the dog caller is successful. The really important question may be: Why does the animal come to the food dish even if we have spent half a century learning why it salivates?

What we are concerned about may be more easily illustrated by another common form of experimental observation. Rats are frequently "trained" to run down an alley or along some platform to a "goal" end where they are fed. They usually learn a simple routine of this sort in relatively few trials. In 10 trials they will run speedily down a stretch of 6 feet or so. The layman has no problem accounting for the speed or the run. Why does the rat run from one end to the other? Because it "knows" that it will find food there. But is not this the question with which we are concerned, rather than the answer? How does the rat "know" about the location of the food? What is this knowledge? Certainly we have no basis for assuming that the rat "knows" anything. We make this judgment on only the most dubious sort of analogy based on what we believe to be true of ourselves.

Behavior of this sort exemplifies what we usually mean by foresight or purpose. It involves the difficult problem of having a future event determine the present. Such a state of affairs is normally repugnant to the scientists. It represents something like "action at a distance." Psychologists are usually attracted to, or more favorably disposed toward, any explanation wherein it can be shown that the past influences the future, or if necessary, that the present determines the present. The problem for the psychologist is to bring the future, the food, into the present in some manner. To do this is not so difficult as it might appear. It is only necessary to postulate some present activity which is related in some fashion to the future activity. In the kinds of illustrations we have considered the activity that must be assumed can also be seen and even measured; it is, in fact, the salivation that Pavlov studied. We have already seen how a conditioned response comes forward in time; in effect, the future becomes less future or more present. If the conditioned response comes forward enough, it can provide the necessary stimuli for taking the next steps forward in time. We must note that nothing has been said about the "meaning" of salivation or what the dog "knows." It does not need to know anything. All it needs to do is salivate, and the resulting stimuli will take care of the next move. It is not the "meaning" of the salivation that is involved here. It is the meaning of the food. And the "meaning" of food, insofar as we need concern ourselves with it, is the response of salivating with the resultant stimuli that it generates.

The fractional anticipatory goal response (rg). On the basis of the antedating nature of the conditioned response Hull (1930a) has built up a schematic analysis of foresight, knowledge, and purpose. He notes, in particular, that any situation which merits the term "purpose" or "knowledge" implies that no immediate action is necessarily involved. The action will take place *later*. That is the defining sign of "purpose." For Hull, this means that we must search for *action* which is actually in progress but which may be hidden because our attention is misdirected, as by a magician, to the action which will take place later. He finds this present action in the antedating aspects of the conditioned response. If we recognize that a dog free to roam around would make a consummatory response of eating if food were present or that it would go to a feeding station and indulge in exploratory behavior, we can recognize also that salivation is not the important response as far as the dog is concerned and that it is but a fraction, a preparatory or anticipatory (in the temporal sense) response. Salivation is only part of the picture. Hull calls such fractional antedating aspects of a consummatory response "rg" (little argy). These rg's and the stimuli they generate are Hull's means of accounting for both knowledge and purpose.

Let us return now to the rat on the starting platform of a runway with food 6 feet away. The consummatory response of eating has been conditioned or learned in association with stimuli at the end of the runway. The eating "response" or complete behavior pattern we call eating can go on only at the food end of the runway. Yet we know from many experimental studies that the learned reaction tends to become anticipatory, that is, come forward in time, and so we should expect the animal to start eating as soon as the conditioned stimuli begin to impinge upon it. Since the beginning of the runway is similar to the end, we can think of stimuli at the beginning as equivalent or similar to the conditioned stimuli at the end of the runway and so we can expect the animal to start eating at the beginning of the runway or at least sometime *before* he gets to the food. Obviously "real" eating is impossible in the absence of material substance in the mouth. Eating, however, is a complicated business of salivating, chewing, swallowing, lip-licking, and other components. Some of these parts or "fractions" of the total response can occur in the absence of food. The rat can begin to salivate well in advance of food and perhaps even engage in some sort of chewing or other adjustive behavior which is appropriate for the intake of a particular food substance. If the salivary reaction comes forward in time we can speak of a "fractional anticipatory goal response" occurring. Such a reaction does not occur without its own consequences, namely, stimuli generated by the reaction. We now have to deal with such stimuli from the rg and, for convenience, we can label them $S_{(rg)}$. These $S_{(rg)}$ can be presumed to function like any other stimuli, to provoke other reactions, to become conditioned stimuli for still other reactions, and so on.

The $S_{(rg)}$ represents one type of internal stimulation, similar to "movement-produced stimuli" (the MPS of Guthrie) which go on for the most part unobserved and which can be used to explain the continuation of a serial response or persistence of behavior in a given direction. They are "manufactured" stimuli which, if not taken into account, leave us without an explanation for how a distant goal (in time or space) can affect present behavior which eventuates in that goal.

The rg or fractional response, since it comes between some external S and some subsequent goal response, R, can be considered an intervening variable of the hypothetical construct variety. In this capacity of intervening variable, it serves as a "mediator" or intermediary between a stimulus and a response, and if there are several responses in a series or chain, the rg can serve through its stimulus-producing capacity as a source for stimulation of consequent movements or responses, either directly or through conditioning.

Lest the student come to think of rg as something peculiar to eating behavior it should be emphasized that the construct is presumed to have broad application to any situation where any goal reaction can be identified. When a driver of an automobile is about to stop, for example, there will be preliminary movements of the feet involving stepping on the clutch and brake sometime before it is necessary. If he is about to make a left turn he will begin to veer toward the middle of the road long before it is really necessary to do so. The child learning to catch a ball may close the hands too soon. Passengers waiting for a bus will finger their change and, in a sense, board the bus and pay the fare before the bus arrives. The mistakes we make in speech or typing frequently illustrate the coming forward in time of fractional goal responses. Hull suggests an obvious example in sexual tumescence.

A few examples of how the rg is used in theoretical accounts of experimental findings may be appropriate for the student to form a judgment of the usefulness of the rg. We can start with an experiment by Tolman (1933) who trained rats to run down an alley to a goal box. When the animals were running well he detached the goal box and shocked the rats in it. Now when the rats were placed in the alley Tolman expected them to hesitate in running if not actually refuse to run down to the goal box. At the same time he stated that Hull would have to predict that the rats would run on down without concern. To his discomfort, if not dismay, the rats all ran down to the goal box. Miller (1935) then pointed out that Hull would have predicted stopping rather than running, contrary to Tolman's opinion, and that the rats would have stopped if the goal box had been of a nature as to provide for a different reaction from that of merely running forward. Miller thereupon designed a box which required that the rat twist itself sideward and upward in order to get to the food. When rats were shocked in such a box and then replaced in the alley, they started to run down but began to slow down and stopped before entering the box. Miller explains this by invoking the rg and $S_{(rg)}$. When the animal is learning to get food in the awkward position it gradually develops the rg of twisting and turning in the direction that will have to be assumed in the box while it is still in the runway. When it is being shocked in the contorted position stimuli from the musculature involved are present and become associated with the escape movements (withdrawal) that followed the shock. When these same stimuli are activated in the runway later as the rg develops, they initiate the hesitancy, withdrawal, and stopping behavior.

In the experiment by Tolman and Gleitman (1949) described in Chapter 2, Tolman reinvestigated essentially the same problem with results to his greater satisfaction. He admits, however, that an explanation in terms of rg is also possible as against his own expectancy account. In this later experiment Tolman required the rats to go through different maneuvers while traversing the T-maze arms and thereby invited an rg explanation even more than his theory calls for. Perhaps the behavior he found is impossible without requiring different maneuvers on the part of the rat. If this is so, it strongly supports the hypothesis that the *rg* is a required element in accounting for such "foresight."

Another illustration is available from a little exercise frequently performed by the writer's students who happen to have dogs. The dog is leashed about 10 feet from a point where two paper cups are placed and while the dog it watching, one of the cups is baited with suitable food. A screen is then lowered while the experimenter goes back to release the dog. If the cups are placed about a foot or more apart, horizontally, the dog has no trouble in going directly to the correct cup after the screen is raised. If the cups are placed one behind the other and a foot apart, the dog usually pokes its nose into the first even though only the far cup is baited. What mechanism enables the dog to discriminate with ease a horizontal separation and prevents him from discriminating a front-rear relationship? Whatever may be the true explanation [8] an *rg* account is applicable. It needs only to be assumed that a dog watching the cup on the left starts off in that direction. The restraining leash prevents progress. Only *rg*'s can be made. When the screen is lifted, the *rg*'s are reinstated by sight of the cup. The stimuli from *rg* are associated with straining toward the left and if the dog is released it accomplishes the mission. Consider the front-rear situation now. In the original situation the dog can only strain forward. There is no different *rg* for front and rear available. When the screen is raised, the *rg* recurs but it is of no help since it directs only forward action.

Similar explanations of delayed reactions in other situations can be given in terms of *rg*. In Tinklepaugh's (1928) famous experiments with monkeys a similar delay procedure was used but only one cup was baited. The experimenter would place some food, for example, a piece of banana, into the cup while the monkey watched. When a screen was lowered, the banana would be replaced with orange or lettuce or some other acceptable food. When the monkey was later released and picked up the cup it would give evidence of rage, frustration, and general displeasure at the alteration of the food. How do we account for the monkey's distress? How does it "symbolize" the banana for itself? An *rg* explanation may apply. If it can be assumed that seeing a banana provokes some reaction which is peculiar to eating bananas and nothing else, then we can consider that such a re-

[8] We are assuming that the dog has a capacity for depth perception within the limits of the distance used.

action (essentially an *rg*, since the monkey is restrained and cannot actually eat) is conditioned to the sight of the cup. Later this same reaction is evoked and found to be inappropriate for eating oranges or whatever the substitute may be. Students frequently report a feeling of modest frustration when a previously promised item fails to appear on the dinner table even if the substitute is more desirable in general. It may be that we salivate in special ways or in different quantities or that we otherwise "set" ourselves for eating different foods. Whether or not the accounts are correct remains to be seen. Since the *rg* is a hypothetical construct it presumably can be investigated directly. Thus far we have no experimental measurements of *rg*'s in action. They remain inferences even though, as in the case of salivation, they are measurable. The successful "anchoring" of the *rg* construct to independent and dependent variables has not been accomplished.

We have spent so much time on the *rg* because it serves two purposes in the present discussion: (1) It serves as an introduction to the more general concept of mediation. (2) In its alleged characteristics it is a close cousin of another hypothetical construct proposed by Hebb (1949) to account for such processes as expectancy, set, and attention. It should be obvious, of course, that for Hull the *rg* is the surrogate for such concepts as "ideas" and, particularly, for Tolman's expectancy.

Other forms of mediation. The *rg* is just a special case of a more general class of mediating responses. In any serial pattern of responses, the behavior can be considered as reducible to a chain of stimuli and responses with the responses generating stimuli for the next movement which in turn provides stimulation for the next, and so on. On a simple level, the process of walking might illustrate the point (although this too is physiologically complex, involving as it does crossed-extensor reflexes, compensatory movements of the arms, balance operations, and so forth). Taking one step provides the stimuli for taking the next step. Here we have what Guthrie refers to as his "movement-produced stimuli" (MPS). Hull (1930b) was fond of accounting for serial behavior along similar lines, and we can modify one of his illustrations to suggest the kinds of stimuli and responses that serve as mediators and their several peculiarities. Suppose we try to account for the behavior of someone who is learning to type "by touch" when he taps out any word, say, "touch." At first the learner looks at the individual keys. (We can refer to these visual stimulation in Hull's language as "external world stimuli.") To each "external world stimulus" a different response is made. Thus:

External world stimuli T O U C H

Responses R_1 R_2 R_3 R_4 R_5

As each response is made, it initiates movement-produced stimuli, so

$$R_1 \to S_1, R_2 \to S_2, R_3 \to S_3, R_4 \to S_4$$

We now have the situation:

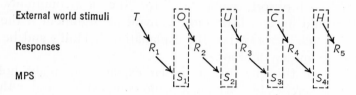

Now, since S_1, S_2, and so on, are present at the same time that external world stimuli are eliciting responses R_2, R_3, and so on, it is possible for conditioning to occur so that S_1 becomes associated with R_2, S_2 with R_3 and so on, and we now have:

$$T \searrow \quad O \searrow \quad U \searrow \quad C \searrow \quad H \searrow$$
$$R_1 \to S_1 \to R_2 \to S_2 \to R_3 \to S_3 \to R_4 \to S_4 \to R_5$$

Once this conditioning has occurred, we can remove the external world stimuli and, given R_1, the entire sequence can run off by itself.

The problem is complicated by an additional kind of stimulation that remains more or less permanent during the sequence, that from various possible sources of "motivation." Hull presumes for learning to take place that some "drive" must be present. Without going into the details at this time we can simply assume a drive and, further, stimuli from this drive (S_D) as continually present. Our diagram then becomes:

External world T O U C H

MPS

Drive stimuli

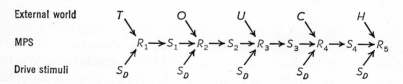

Now we have three sources of stimulation for each response. One of these, however, the S_D, is conditioned to each of the responses. If we make another assumption, with Hull, that the learning is stronger the more closely reinforcement follows a given response, then we can presume that S_D is most strongly associated with R_5. This, then, suggests that there will be continuously present a tendency to produce R_5 before its proper time. If at any moment the tendency $S_D{\rightarrow}R_5$ is stronger than any other combination for another response, then R_5 will appear. For Hull this arrangement accounts for many kinds of anticipatory errors. It is apparently true that typing errors are usually of the anticipatory sort; typing "hte" for "the" is a commonly made error. It would make a little more convincing argument if the error was of the "teh" variety, but the explanation is Hull's and he must shoulder the burden of proof.

It might be thought that a similar explanation might hold for other serial exercises like playing a piano composition, and perhaps it does for many instances. Some pianists, however, move their fingers so rapidly that there does not appear to be time for the proprioceptive stimuli (the MPS) to even get into the act (Lashley, 1917). Such performances require perhaps a different level of attack and explanation and there is no point to trying to stretch the modest illustration beyond its own explanatory range.

Two more illustrations of mediators might be enough to cover the area of application which has been attempted by speculators which we will have to scrutinize more closely later. The first is already familiar to you from Chapter 2 where we described Lumsdaine's experiment. There, you recall, a subject was first "conditioned" to blink to a light which preceded a tap on the cheek. Later the tap preceded a shock to a finger. Finally, the light was presented alone and the subject withdrew the finger. We can diagram the program so:

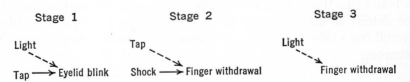

Because the light was never associated with finger withdrawal we have a problem. To account for the behavior observed by mediating responses appears to be easy enough, at least superficially. We need only assume that there are movement-produced stimuli deriving from the eye blink. Such stimuli will be present at the appropriate time to become conditioned to finger withdrawal. We can picture the situation in Stage 2 as somewhat more involved than indicated above. Thus:

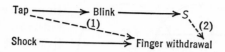

If the mediation explanation is correct, there may be two conditioned stimuli instead of one in this setup. Now, any stimulus (the light in this instance) which elicits the wink will lead via the stimuli produced by blinking to the finger withdrawal. This explanation requires that the blink actually occur in time to produce the relevant stimuli. Lumsdaine (1939) reported, however, that his records occasionally showed finger withdrawal before the blink occurred. This appears to raise a difficulty. A further assumption can easily extricate us from this apparently awkward situation although it might be too much to assume for anyone but a learning theorist, namely, that once the pattern is established, various neural components can come forward in time and short-circuit the actual blink; that is, neural responses corresponding to those initiated by blinking can become active before the blink when the light goes on. We shall try to make the assumption less incredible in the discussion of Hebb's "cell assembly" (see p. 113).

A final illustration of mediation will show an even more abstract level of application of this useful construct. In the area we are about to describe the construct appears so logically necessary that it is frequently accepted without much argument. Students who strain at the gnat of the MPS swallow the camel of the mediational "central response" without difficulty. One of the writer's experiments (Bugelski and Scharlock, 1952) can serve as the illustration. College students were asked to learn pairs of nonsense syllables. In any pair the first syllable was the stimulus, the second the response. Thus, we set up $S_1 \rightarrow R_1$. When a list of such $S_1 \rightarrow R_1$ pairs was learned, the students learned a new list. This time, however, the former R_1's became S_2's and they were paired with R_2's. When these $S_2 \rightarrow R_2$ pairs were learned the students were asked to learn $S_1 \rightarrow R_2$ combinations. Suppose we symbolize the elements involved in the three tasks as follows. S_1 can be considered as referring to some neural action A. R_1 will refer to neural action B and this will be the same as that for S_2; R_2 will refer to neural action C. In Task I some connection is established between the neural actions A and B. In Task II, the connection between B and C is formed. In Task III, A and C are to be joined. Because we already have the connections between A and B and between B and C established, it should be relatively easy to get from A to C via B. We can diagram the proposal as in Figure 5.3.

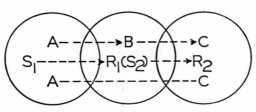

FIG. 5.3. Mediated associations A, B, and C represent neural activities initiated by the appearance of printed symbols (nonsense syllables) in the exposure device. The subject sees and says each syllable. In the mechanics of the procedure, the first syllable serves as a stimulus S_1 and the neural action associated with the seeing of this syllable is diagramed as A. When the associated syllable appears the subject says it (response—R_1). This activity B is similar to the activity when the B syllables serve as stimuli for R_2. The interlocking circles represent associations. According to the argument presented in the text, S_1 can initiate R_2 via neural activity B.

Since we are operating at the level of speculation, we can assume that an impulse originated by S_1 can arouse R_1, which in effect is also S_2, and since a connection exists between S_2 and R_2 we can get the reaction R_2 from the presentation of only S_1.

The only evidence we can offer in support of such hypothetical action comes from the data of the learning experiment. Students who have to learn the three tasks do significantly better at Task III than control subjects who learn the same amount and kind of materials where the pattern of the S-R combinations is arranged to prevent the formation of the necessary mediating connections. If we mix up the S_2R_2 combinations in such a way that they do not offer any means of transition from S_1 to R_2, the subjects do not benefit from the S_2R_2 learning. They have learned the same elements but not in a useful order. We can illustrate this by some ordinary word examples:

Experimental Group

Task I	*Task* II	*Task* III
S_1 R_1	S_2 R_2	S_1 R_2
dog-boy	boy-roof	dog-roof
fish-hat	hat-book	fish-book

Control Group

dog-boy	boy-book	dog-roof
fish-hat	hat-roof	fish-book

Inspecting the table, we find that both groups have the same material to work with, and in Task III they are required to learn exactly the same associations, but the arrangement of materials in Task II determines the ease of learning Task III. One further point should be noted. Previous experimenters, for example, Peters (1935), were unable to demonstrate any positive benefits in learning Task III assignments because they did not arrange the materials in the order $(A\text{-}B)\text{-}(B\text{-}C)\text{-}(A\text{-}C)$ as was done here. Rather, for unknown reasons, materials would be arranged as $(A\text{-}B)\text{-}(C\text{-}B)\text{-}(A\text{-}C)$ or $(A\text{-}B)\text{-}(B\text{-}C)\text{-}(C\text{-}A)$. It is the writer's contention that such arrangements are violations of what might be considered a proper temporal order. It is possible that the several variations indicated might help the final learning, but it would appear that the $(A\text{-}B)$ $(B\text{-}C)$ $(A\text{-}C)$ arrangement follows a direct sequence from stimulus to response.[9] One of the writer's students, N. Scharlock (1952), made a direct comparison of the $(A\text{-}B)\text{-}(B\text{-}C)\text{-}(A\text{-}C)$ order with the $(A\text{-}B)\text{-}(C\text{-}B)\text{-}(A\text{-}C)$ pattern and found the former significantly more effective. The temporal arrangement appears to be important.

In the above discussion we have cheerfully assumed various processes or activities in the nervous system to carry the burden of the learning. The subjects who are able to give R_2 (or C) to S_1 (or A) are presumed to enjoy the benefits of a neural process corresponding to S_2 (or B), so that when S_1 is presented, a neural sequence corresponding to $S_1 \rightarrow R_1 \rightarrow R_2$ runs off. (R_1 is also S_2.) In the experiment described above, none of the subjects reported any "conscious awareness" of the R_1 when learning $S_1 \rightarrow R_2$. The assumed intervening or mediating process was, therefore, referred to as "unconscious." Had the students been able to report the presence of R_1 a host of other types of explanations might be conjured up to account for the ease of $S_1 \rightarrow R_2$ learning and the role of the mediating process would be, perhaps, distorted from that it is alleged to have here.

The student might object that the above is only a laboratory dem-

---

[9] Whether this bears on the usual assumption about one-way transmission in the nervous system (from dendrite to axone) across synapses is, of course, undeterminable from the behavioral type of experiment we have described.

onstration dealing with nonsense syllables and not very true to real life. Another experiment, although still in the laboratory, comes a bit closer to the point being made here. It is the study of Russell and Storms (1955) who improved on the Bugelski and Scharlock experiment in two ways:

1. They had subjects learn to respond with words to nonsense syllables, for example, cef—stem, dax—memory, and so on.
2. They then assumed that normal adult subjects will have formed in their previous experience certain common associations to such words as "stem." The most common such association to stem is "flower." Now, "flower" itself as a stimulus normally elicits the response "smell" most frequently. If we think of the nonsense syllable as A, "stem" as B, "flower" as C, and "smell" as D, it is possible that a subject, having learned A-B might be able to benefit from previously acquired chains of association B-C and C-D, so that if we now asked him to learn A-D he might be able to learn such combinations readily. If such learning was indeed facilitated over control materials, we would have a demonstration of mediation working through quite remote past experience and through several stages. In outline form, then, the Russell and Storms experiment follows this pattern:

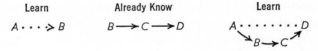

| Learn | Already Know | Learn |

The important point to note is that the intermediate step is not learned in the laboratory. Russell and Storms found that subjects did benefit from such associations even more than did the subjects in the Bugelski and Scharlock study. Again the subjects were unaware of what was going on and could not describe the intervening association items which are assumed to have been operating.

The applications of the construct of mediating responses. In considering the hypothetical construct of mediators we started out with rg in the form of a physical, measured discharge of saliva in Pavlov's dogs and easily endowed other dogs and rats with similar reactions where they were not, in fact, observed but merely assumed. Such rg's were, then, further embellished with the function of generating stimuli which could initiate action in other effector systems either directly or indirectly via the conditioning process. We found the rg to be a special case of a broad class of mediators which we define more or less generally as intervening events. These events can be responses, in the first instance, or, stimuli from such responses (the MPS of Guthrie). In the special case of such practices as reciting nonsense syllables we overlook the more molecular distinctions and refer loosely to a particular nonsense syllable, say one in the middle of a list, as both a response to the preceding syllable and a stimulus for the next. Obviously such looseness requires a more detailed analysis of the behavioral components, but for the present we can by-pass the problem.

We have found the "mediator" convenient for a preliminary analysis, if not an explanation, of such diverse phenomena as "action at a distance" in the case of Miller's rats that refused to run to the specially contrived goal box, the acquisition of serial response patterns from the basic two-component example of Lumsdaine's finger withdrawal to light, and the more involved, multiple-unit business of typing and similar "chained" behavior. Presumably the "mediator" is essential for any such tasks as running mazes, reciting verbal material in nonsense lists or, again presumably, in conversation and literary discourse. We found the mediator functioning to make learning of subsequent tasks easier (or more difficult) and if we care to project our ambitions on to a broader screen, we can hope to account for knowledge, purpose, insight, and problem solving generally by resorting to mediators as do Hull (1930a) and Hebb (1949). We shall follow some of their excursions into these broader problems as we proceed. For the moment we need to remind ourselves that the construct of the mediator has been conjured up to provide a source of stimulation in behavior that goes beyond the level of a single muscle twitch. We found it necessary, or convenient, to have such a source to explain the behavior of the rat in the Skinner box where we could perceive the role of at least one "stimulus," the noise of the feeding mechanism, as a determiner of one segment of a chain of responses. In Tolman's "place" learning we saw that the light or illumination gradient controlled the behavior of the rat and "mediated" its activity.

In all the above discussion we have been freely assuming the occurrence of events that are for the most part (at least with current technology) unavailable for direct observation. The events referred to are presumed to be primarily of a neural nature and virtually nothing is known of their actual features, or indeed, of their existence or presence. Learning theory, however, has rarely been hampered by hesitation to speculate. If we do not speculate, we might never investigate. In the next section we will consider the speculations bearing on mediation that have been offered by a theorist who is sufficiently familiar with the limitations of our knowledge, as well as with the actual positive lore that has accumulated about the nervous system, not to conjure up activities and processes in the nervous system that are known to be impossible. We refer, of course, to Hebb (1949), and his attempt to make much of the mystery of mediation intelligible.

Some neurological speculations. In this section we shall consider Hebb's attempt to account for learning in terms of neural action. It should be noted at the outset that the speculations are of a quasi-neurological nature, that they deal with a *conceptual* nervous system and not necessarily with the intricate physiological apparatus itself. Some critics will undoubtedly prefer the term "pseudo" to "conceptual." Hebb is fully aware of the hypothetical nature of his suggestions and believes that only positive assertions are likely to lead to investigation. Our responsibility as psychologists is to state the *psychological* case as precisely as we can so that the physiologist can begin to look for something that might correspond to our needs, or tell us how far off we are.

The basic problem for Hebb is to explain the mechanism of *association*. We have been using this term repeatedly in the previous chapters and, indeed, it is difficult to get along without it and still pretend to talk about learning. Insofar as learning is anything, it is *association* and an explanation of association would be a sufficient contribution to set off the twentieth century as *the* century in the history of the concept which goes back beyond Aristotle.

In his attempt to explain association, Hebb employs two neural concepts: *Cell assemblies* and *Phase sequences*. Actually, "phase sequences" are a complication and elaboration of cell assemblies and cannot be appreciated witthout an understanding of cell assemblies. Our first task then is to get acquainted with cell assemblies. Before we embark on this venture, we should note that Hebb is particularly interested in problems of "perception" and chooses his examples largely from this area. If we but recognize that as far as Hebb is concerned we have to *learn to perceive*, we will have no difficulty in relating his discussion to our own problem of learning. Awhile back we referred to the *rg* as a first cousin to one of Hebb's constructs. It should prove an intriguing problem for the student to trace out the family ties in Hebb's descriptions of cell assemblies and phase sequences. By means of these constructs Hebb hopes to account for knowledge, "ideas," expectancies, and "attention." We have already seen how rg's can be used to account for some of these "psychic" entitles on a *molar* level. Hebb's proposals can be considered a more molecular approach.

THE LEARNING OF CELL ASSEMBLIES AND PHASE SEQUENCES

The cell assembly. To introduce the argument for the construct of the cell assembly, Hebb adopts two assumptions that have long been honored in the tradition of psychology. These are: (1) Any two cells (or systems of cells) that are repeatedly active at the same time will become connected functionally and/or structurally.[10] (2) Frequent activity at the junction of two neurons will in some manner lower the "resistance" to the passage of impulses from one to the other. Without going into the neurological illustrations that Hebb employs we can appreciate

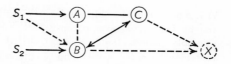

FIG. 5.4. A cell assembly (see text).

the general notion of a cell assembly by resorting to a diagram (Fig. 5.4). In the diagram, A, B, and C stand for single neural cells (or systems of cells) that happen to be close enough (in function and location and perhaps other characteristics) so that stimulation of any two of them is likely to activate the other.[11] Suppose then that a stimulus (or separate stimuli) activates A and B simultaneously. This is a condition favorable to the firing of C which is presumed to have some connections, or at least tentative connections, with A and B.

With the firing of C it is possible that impulses from C to B are set off which can reactivate B should it have become inactive for any reason. With repetition, it is assumed that connections would be formed or strengthened between A and C and C and B (among others). If this is the case, A and B would no longer be independent of each other but would or could operate in such a manner that the

---

[10] Hebb assumes that something like "neurobiataxis" (see Kappers, 1932) occurs so that neurons actually grow toward each other and/or that enlargments on nerve endings (boutons) develop as a result of use and provide contact surfaces.

[11] Hebb assumes that it is necessary for two cells to fire simultaneously in order to activate another cell, at least, on the first occasion.

firing of A alone, through the mediating action of C, would arouse B (joint action of A and C) and this, in turn, might either rearouse C, then A, or activate some completely new cells that are associated with B and C as x (see diagram).

Now all the above-described activity would occur with great rapidity and be over with in a fraction of a second. For any substantial "growth" to take place, a more enduring activity would seem to be required. To provide for such continuity of action, Hebb resorts to the principle of recurrent neural action which has been advanced by Lorente de No (1938). Assuming this principle, a more likely paradigm for a cell assembly might be pictured as in Figure 5.5. If we follow the assumed course of action in this more involved diagram (though it is still simple relative to the complexity of actual neural action), we see how neural activity might persist more or less indefinitely in what we might call a "reverberating circuit." As soon as one pathway is temporarily out of action another takes its place, and the action goes on in other pathways until the first units are ready to fire again. Such a circuit could be maintained indefinitely or at least until interrupted by other stimulation from a different source. With these considerations in mind, we can appreciate Hebb's characterization of the cell assembly as a "system inherently involving some equipotentiality, in the presence of alternate pathways each having the same function."

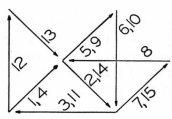

FIG. 5.5. A cell assembly which can be kept active over a considerable period. The numbers represent the order in the firing sequence of the various neurons (arrows) involved. If for any reason one pathway is blocked, another may be available for discharge. (From Hebb, 1949, p. 73.)

The phase sequence. One aspect of the cell assembly that has been ignored so far is the possibility of motor associations, at least in terms of their neural initiators. Hebb assumes that for many cell assemblies it is possible that fibers connecting with motor centers may also be included and lead to some movement when the activity becomes superliminal. The cell assembly then can operate as a link in the development of a serial or otherwise integrated response. Consider the case of a simple triangle with corners marked A, B, and C. When the observer fixates one corner, say A, a particular neural reaction begins involving numerous neural events which take place at the time of fixation. Because of anatomical connections between visual area fibers or

cells and motor centers involving eye movements, there will be tendencies, instituted by peripheral stimulation of the whole triangle, for
the eye to change fixation and move on to B or C. Such simultaneous
motor activity will become part of the total cell assembly which we
can call a. Similarly, for any fixation at B or C, there will be eye-
movement tendencies toward the other corners, producing assemblies
b and c. As the triangle is viewed on repeated occasions, the various
assemblies will be instituted frequently in sequences with the result
that looking at A will lead to, or "facilitate" looking at, one of the
corners, leading to the arousal of the next cell assembly. Such a series
of events Hebb calls a "phase sequence."

With repeated exposure to such a triangle, the several cell assemblies, a, b, and c, will be aroused in relatively rapid sequence. At first
numerous cells not essential to the eventual reaction "triangle" will
be present. For example, there will be simultaneous incoming sensory
activity, or rather afferent stimulation from many parts of the body,
from postural stimulation, auditory, olfactory, and other sense avenues; likewise there will be numerous afferent neural reactions involving body position, vocalization, and so on. Most of these will have
nothing to do with the cell assemblies that are specifically aroused by
the particular visual stimulus, and because they will vary from time
to time they will not be incorporated into any of the assemblies that
result from fixation on any one of the corners of the triangle. Any
fibers or cells that do participate for a time, but which are not of any
consistent and reliable status, will drop out or, more properly, will
not be incorporated into the assembly. At the same time, other cells
which at first may not participate at all because they are subliminally
stimulated may eventually come into participation in the cell assembly. According to Hebb, this line of reasoning accounts for the fact
that we come to see some things differently with additional experience and that our "perceptions" are always changing. It is exceedingly
unlikely, for example, that any adult reacts to some stimulus object,
say an apple, in the same way as he did at the age of ten, five, or one.
With the frequent repetition of cell-assembly activity Hebb assumes
that various components of the several assemblies that are involved in
any reaction become integrated into what Gestalt psychologists call
"wholes" or patterns. Thus, in connection with the triangle illustration, the several assemblies, a, b, and c which were assumed as basic
building blocks become integrated into a more or less super-assembly,
not in the sense of better or greater but in terms of a different or de-

rived assembly which shares some of the functions of each subassembly.

With continued exposure to or fixation on a triangle an observer might react first with one, then another of the several assemblies that are possible and gradually develop, because of temporal overlap of the activity of the separate assemblies, a totally new and distinct pattern which he would later come to describe as a "whole." Such a "total" or Gestalt would be made up of component parts of the several separate cell assemblies and represent nothing more than a new sequence of firing of such components. Just as is the case with the more restricted assemblies, the new total pattern would be set off rapidly and initiate one of the component members again, which then might set off the total pattern or another separate assembly. If we describe the new or derived pattern as "t," then a possible sequence of the neural events might run like this: *a, t, b, t, c, a, b, t, c, a,* and so on. According to this hypothesis, an observer could not long react to a pattern of visual stimuli like a triangle, for example, for any great length of time in the sense of "seeing it as a whole." In half a second or less he would presumably be reacting to one of the details such as a particular corner or angle or line, then back to the triangle as a whole, and so on. According to Hebb, this is just what happens insofar as we have introspective evidence on the subject.

Hebb refers to such a series of neural events as a "phase sequence" and proposes that it can be considered along with the cell-assembly development as a basic mechanism for learning, especially in the early periods of acquisition of any type of association. As such phase sequences develop and multiply in various behavioral areas they provide the means for ideational or "higher" levels of behavior such as thinking. Conceptual and higher orders of behavior, however, do not concern us now. For the moment we are interested in the basic learning process and the fundamental question of what kind of things, events, or activities are learned, that is, what are the components of what we call "learned" behavior. Hebb's answer is: cell assemblies and phase sequences. It is obvious that cell assemblies and phase sequences are the basis for what we have already talked about as "mediated" behavior.

It will be recalled that Hull hoped to be able to account for goals, purposes, ideas, desires, and so on, with his r_g's. Hebb similarly attempts to account for such psychic "stuff" with his cell assemblies and phase sequences. For Hebb, a phase sequence *is* an idea and an idea is *nothing more* than the neural action that occurs at the time of the existence of the "idea." We see then that the *rg* which has usually been thought of by Hull as some actual motor movement or glandular action or other chemical or circulatory disturbance is a more molar conceptualization of what Hebb is describing on a molecular (neural) level. Further, as we have pointed out before, the *rg* is really a special case of a class of mediating events which occurs between some observed external stimulus and some final, or consummatory, response. Such a restriction of mediators is unnecessary and ignores the role of other intervening actions in sequences of behavior that may be distantly removed from whatever we choose to call "goal responses."

The *rg* of Hull is related to one aspect of the action of phase sequences as Hebb pictures them. It will be recalled that in the formation of phase sequences Hebb incorporates any *motor* components that normally initiated actual muscle responses. Such motor components need not terminate in actual movements in order to play their role in the phase sequence. It is possible that they may be sidetracked and their associated movements never take place at all while a particular phase sequence runs off. Assuming, however, that the motor components do eventuate in some muscular reaction, such action will occur at a later stage in a given phase sequence. Putting it in another way, by the time some actual movement is made by an organism, the phase sequence will have entered some later stage. This later stage must be of a nature not to be confounded by the movements themselves or by stimuli feeding back from the movements. If such confusion did occur, the phase sequence would be disrupted, disorganized, and, really, no *sequence* at all.

Suppose we illustrate all this by returning to Hebb's example of the perception of a triangle. If the subject fixates on the lower left angle of an equilateral triangle, say, and the cell assembly *a* is initiated, according to Hebb, this cell assembly will include (after some repetitions) motor impulses from the peripheral stimulation of one of the other corners (or both of them). It will be recalled that Hebb spoke of the *facilitative* effect of the action of one cell assembly on the activation of others, and in the example before us, we can speak of the facilitative effect of the assembly *a* on the arousal of assembly *b*. The motor elements (in this case referring to impulses which would initiate eye movements involved in looking toward another corner) of *a* will help to initiate the assembly *b*, but this assembly depends for its successful and complete development and "run off" upon the activation of other neural elements which normally occur only when the triangle is viewed with fixation at corner B. If corner B has been removed, cut off, obscured in some fashion, then b cannot be complete; it cannot run off smoothly and a disturbance of the entire phase sequence occurs.

Whenever a phase sequence is interrupted, that is, when some sort of action is thwarted, when something fails to happen that normally does happen, we have a state of affairs that we usually refer to as "something gone wrong." But for something to go wrong means that we have some notion of what is right and what should have happened. This condition seems to meet all the requirements of any normal or casual interpretation of what is meant by the term "expectancy." We do not ordinarily go about labeling our expectancies until or unless they fail to materialize. If we are looking for a book on a shelf or some item in a drawer we might say that we "expect" the book or item to be there, but we would do this *only if someone asked*. In other words, we do not talk about and do not appear to need a concept of expectancy unless some failure of an expectancy is suffered. Any references to expectancies when some behavior sequence runs off in an orderly sequence is gratuitous and does not appear to require more than a statement of the stimuli and responses in the sequence, including, of course, all intervening stimuli and responses. To cite our laboratory illustrations again, expectancies are not required to describe the behavior of the rat pressing the bar or turning in the direction of a light. It is only when the outcome of these maneuvers fails to result in the appearance of some stimulus that normally follows upon them that we note a disturbance in the rate and invoke expectancies to account for the disturbance.

In terms of Hebb's analysis, we see that what has been passing for an expectancy is the facilitation effect of one assembly upon another due to their repetitive occurrence in sequence. One assembly sets the stage for the next. This next assembly begins to run off, but some of its elements depend upon the appearance at their own proper time of other stimulus-generated actions. If these subsequent events (components of an assembly) do not and cannot run off because their initiators are not present, the subject is distressed, frustrated, confounded, or otherwise disturbed. He is likely to express it as, "I expected this to be there, but it wasn't." Or, "I expected this to happen, but it didn't." In general, according to Hebb, an expectancy is translatable into the beginnings of action in a cell assembly that usually follows the action in another assembly. Any time we learn anything we form such expectancies. It takes a failure of an assembly's fulfillment, however, to lead us to use the term. While it is a vital and actually necessary component of the learning process, it is not something so vague and perhaps even mystical as it might appear. It is a type of event in the nervous system which has as its correlates in more molar aspects of behavior such operations as movements and their "produced" stimuli and such actions as Hull would like to include in his construct of the rg. The rg is the molar equivalent of a facilitative process in the sequence of cell-assembly actions. Other mediating responses serve the same general function.

A DEFINITION OF LEARNING

Perhaps we have come as far as we can at present in our investigation of what is learned. In general we have seen that the prevailing practice is to indicate that some kind of connection or association is formed between alleged activities in the nervous system and even between the physical structures through which or by means of which these actions take place. Whether one theorist believes that associations are made between stimuli and responses and another believes that it occurs between stimuli and stimuli (or signs and significates) it is quite clear that once stimuli enter the nervous system and initiate neural action we are no longer dealing with stimulus elements but with neural impulses or, to use the term in a broadened sense, with neural responses. The fact that one neural response can *initiate* another neural response need not disturb us, except semantically. As far as we have been able to determine, then, the association takes place between neural responses and not between buzzers and jumps, or levers and presses, and certainly not between vaguely indicated "stimulus situations" and "acts." Perhaps we are now ready to attempt a definition of learning which will include an answer to our current question of what is learned.

On the basis of Hebb's propositions, and indeed on the remarks of others previously examined, we may be ready for a definition of learning, a definition that is admittedly speculative, and for the moment, nonoperational in the sense that we cannot hope to create the phenomenon by describing the steps and specifying the procedures from which the definition is derived. The definition, however, is presumably testable eventually, in contrast to the other definitions previously examined. It is positive, and thus does not leave learning as a residual effect after consequences of fatigue, drugs, and so on, are excluded. As in other definitions, it is an inference, but all conceptual statements are inferences and this feature should not be detractive or distractive. The definition is not tied to performance, but, instead, provides for an appreciation of occasions when the learning is and is not reflected in performance.

According to the present line of speculation, then, *learning is the process of the formation* [12] *of relatively permanent neural circuits through the simultaneous activity of the elements of the circuits-to-be; such activity is of the nature of change in cell structures through growth in such a manner as to facilitate the arousal of the entire circuit when a component element is aroused or activated.* The number and location of participating elements is not limited; the presumption is held that proximity is favorable to the formation of circuits. Functional proximity (that is, similarity) may be of greater positive effectiveness than structural. While specific elements are presumed to operate in any particular circuit, the circuit itself may be modified from time to time by addition or subtraction or short-circuiting of elements and may disappear entirely as a unit through integration or incorporation into larger circuits. The circuit may be included in larger patterns or combinations where it may participate with various degrees of significance from little or almost none to relative dominance. An analogy with an electric-light bulb, while somewhat misleading, may be helpful. The bulb must have a separate circuit of its own but may be connected in series and in parallel with numerous other bulbs and switching elements so that it may be activated or not activated in a series of different, larger, or "whole" patterns.

---

[12] Circuits might already be formed but in a more or less potential state so that some use must be made of them before they can operate in the final fashion.

Chapter
6

The Characteristics
of Learned Behavior

STIMULUS AND RESPONSE CHARACTERISTICS IN LEARNING

In the present chapter we will confine ourselves to the characteristics of early or primitive learning, the basic learning that controls or modifies later learning and the adjustments of the individual to more complex situations. The characteristics of learned behavior on the latter, or higher, level are so complex as to be virtually beyond ready description in any universal terms. Studies of adult learning are too contradictory in the matter of principles involved for us to hope for any appreciation of the general laws of learning if we start from that end of the story.

Returning for the present from our conceptual neural level to a behavioral one and again facing the situation that directly confronts the learning psychologist, we find him concerned with the observation and measurement of either one or two aspects of a learning situation. If he is studying an "instrumental" situation he is observing and recording responses in one way or another; if he is engaged in a "classical" experiment he may be observing and recording not only the response but also certain aspects of a stimulus. What is it about these stimuli and responses that he does record or observe and what kinds of relations prevail between them?

Although any separation of stimuli and responses is bound to be artificial it may serve us well to look separately at the kinds of operations the psychologist performs in connection with the stimulus and response sides of the learning picture and, later, to try to bring the two together in a more integrated manner. Remembering that the instrumental psychologist is prone to slight the stimulus side except in connection with what he terms "discriminated" stimuli, we can start with the stimulus [1] in learning. Obviously our discussion is going to be "loaded" with classical references in this connection. At every point the student might raise the question as to the possible significance of the observations made on classical experiments for the instrumental type.

What is there about a stimulus that the psychologist can manipulate or vary? Reflection on the activities of the early introspectionists suggests that certain stimulus dimensions might be defined along the lines suggested by the old sensation psychology.[2] Thus, we can consider the *quality* of the stimulus (light, sound) and related subqualities (pitch, color or hue, complexity, pattern). The dimension of *intensity* is obviously related to the above and raises the question of the degree of dependence of learning on strength of stimuli. The stimulus must come into being, exist for some definite time, and terminate. Certain aspects of "duration" or temporal sequence are, therefore, to be considered. Another classic dimension is that of "clearness." This dimension is usually considered as peculiarly subjective but we will attempt to show the relevance of this dimension to the learning problem at the appropriate time. The dimensions of quality, intensity, duration, and clearness may be adequate for our purpose as numerous other special parameters can be subsumed under these four rubrics. For example, the dimensions of quality and clearness might include the subcategory of number and pattern or arrangement of stimuli and the question of the effects of similarity of stimuli (the problem of generalization and discrimination).[3] The nature of the dimensions of the stimuli involved in learning are additionally complicated by the fact that in classical experiments we are dealing with two categories of stimuli—the unconditioned stimulus and the to-be-conditioned stimulus. Our discussion must then take both types into account, and a definition of each is perhaps the first step to be taken.

The unconditioned stimulus (UncS). Before any classical learning can be observed it is necessary that a response be selected for training

---

[1] At this time we are dealing with a "stimulus" as an energy change in the environment, manipulated by an experimenter.

[2] These "subjective" terms are employed to suggest an historical continuity in the development of psychology. The same problems which were previously studied by introspective methods are still being studied, but now the methods and assumptions differ.

[3] Generalization along the intensity dimension must also be considered.

or observation that can be effectively induced or evoked with regularity and assurance. Such responses are readily available from the category of "reflexes," which, however the physiologist may debate the matter, for the psychologist generally represent any reaction of some organ or restricted system of organs that can be activated by some suitable, empirically known stimulus. Thus, a puff of air directed at the eye of any organism with eyelids usually results in a closure of the lid. Such closure is a dependable reaction for a considerable number of repetitions of the stimulus and, for the psychologists' purpose, amounts to a "given." Whether the reaction is itself learned in the prior history of the organism or not, the dependability of the reaction is the important concern of the psychologist and he takes it as a starting point. Similar "reflexes" frequently used by psychologists are knee jerks, galvanic reactions (the PGR), breathing, swallowing, salivating, temperature changes, and eye movements. Hull (1934a) has catalogued a score or more of reflex reactions reported in conditioning literature including such reactions as defensive reactions of the blood stream to invasion by infectious agents. Our present interest, however, is the definition of the unconditioned stimulus and we can return to it now and identify it as any stimulus which consistently evokes a particular reaction. The nature of this reaction is a limiting factor in this definition in that the reaction is one that is to be associated with *another* stimulus. This definition, whatever its particularizing deficiencies, has the virtue of avoiding the problems associated with defining the response characteristics beyond the fact that a special response, to be measured in some specified way, will be chosen for the association to be formed. Any stimulus which elicits the unconditioned response for the purpose at hand will be identified as the unconditioned stimulus. Thus for the eyelid blink, a puff of air, a loud sound, a blow to the cheek, an electric shock, a threatening gesture all might be used as unconditioned stimuli even though the response might differ along certain dimensions depending upon the stimulus chosen.

The conditioned stimulus (CS).[4] Any stimulus that does not at the beginning of the training procedures bring out the response selected

[4] Pavlov used the term "conditional" stimulus in this connection because it better fits his use of the stimuli in that the new stimulus would be one of the conditions on which the response would come to depend; in other words, the occurrence of the response was conditional upon the presence of the stimulus. American psychologists translated the term into its present form, giving it a more verbal form in the past tense. Whether there is a change in meaning is still a question.

for conditioning can be a conditioned stimulus. The response must not appear at the outset of training in the final form or with the final frequency proportions or other dimensions which may be employed for measurement of conditioning. It should be clear that the same physical stimulus might serve different functions in different experiments, being the unconditioned stimulus in one experiment and the conditioned stimulus in another; thus Pavlov occasionally used shock as a conditioning stimulus as have other experimenters in both instrumental and classical situations. On the other hand, shock is usually or more frequently employed as an unconditioned stimulus in escape or avoidance experiments. The reader will recall (p. 106) that a blow to the cheek was paired by Lumsdaine with a shock to the finger so that the blow (normally bringing about an eyelid reflex) was the conditioned stimulus for finger withdrawal. Shipley (1935) had previously used the same combination.

Once a conditioned stimulus has acquired the property of bringing out a response formerly not its ordinary consequent, it can be used as an unconditioned stimulus for further conditioning of the same response. Thus Finch and Culler (1934) used a tone and shock in original training for a dog being conditioned to withdraw a leg. When the tone became adequate, a light was paired with the tone. Subsequently a squirt of water on the noze was paired with the light, a bell with the light, and a fan with the bell.

In the training procedure known as second-order or higher-order conditioning, then, a previously defined conditioned stimulus comes to serve as the unconditioned stimulus in a subsequent learning operation. Normally such higher order associations are difficult to create and much of the response is lost if measured by amplitude; for example, Pavlov (1927) reports that higher orders than the third are difficult if not impossible to develop. In the illustration cited we were dealing with an avoidance type of response instead of the salivary one, and either one of these might represent a special case.

THE QUALITY OF STIMULI IN LEARNING. To return to our consideration of the dimensions of the stimuli we can begin with quality of the stimulus. Apparently there are no restrictions on the type or class, qualitatively speaking, of stimuli that can be used as conditioning stimuli, except the capacity or sensitivity of the organism. Thus animals which lack color vision cannot form associations involving color, but if the organism is capable of reacting to a given kind of energy change, it can serve the purpose. Buzzers and lights are most com-

monly used because of the relative ease of handling and their availability. Considering the great wealth of experimentation that has
been done, it would be difficult to name a class of stimuli that has not
been used. Pavlov, for example, frequently used the sound of bub-
bling water as a stimulus. This seems to be a needlessly awkward type
of stimulus and merely illustrates the point that no possible dis-
criminable stimulus need be considered unconditionable. Steady
lights, flickering lights, lights that go on and off or change colors or
change intensities have been used. In the auditory area sounds of
piano notes, trombones, klaxons, finger snaps, voice calls, and so on,
have functioned as CS's. Odors, pressures, blows, vibrators, pinches,
burning, electric shock, and so on, have found one use or another.
Stimuli of one qualitative class or another and of subclasses within the
sense modality can be used, subject only to the whim of the experimenter and his willingness to go to the trouble of extending his efforts beyond wiring up a buzzer or light bulb, the usual favorites.

Differences in sense quality as a conditioning variable. There is only
partial and very poorly controlled evidence on the question as to what
kinds of stimuli are most readily conditionable. In situations where
two different kinds of stimuli have been used there is always the question of their equation along other dimensions than the qualitative
one. If we are comparing colors or lights and sounds we have the
problem of intensity and duration equation. Sound, so far, has proved
to be easier in avoidance training (Silver and Meyer, 1954); this may
be an artifact due to the fact that sounds do not depend on fixation
points and do not vary from time to time in intensity depending upon
where we are looking as do lights. Obviously, an animal that is not
facing a light with its eyes open is going to get only partial stimulation, if any, from a light bulb; a sound, on the other hand, has easy
entry. Whether sound has any other special advantages is unknown.
Children, of course, learn to react to auditory cues in many learning
situations before visual stimuli are very meaningful. Results of tests
on adults (Elliot, 1936; Krawiec, 1946) as to whether they can learn
better through an auditory or visual channel are complicated and confused; the high sensitivity of some animals to sound (bats, rats, and
other night animals) suggests some speculation for an adaptive basis
for learning to sound cues in preference to other senses. Sight cannot
be relied on throughout the lifetime of an individual and obviously
sleep would leave the organism defenseless. Before any further idle
speculation is developed it appears that the area should be investi-

gated more thoroughly with standardized and graded stimulus values in the various modalities.

Number of stimuli functioning together (patterning). From fragmentary evidence offered by Pavlov (1927) it appears that if two or more stimuli are regularly paired as the conditioned stimulus complex, conditioning ensues somewhat more rapidly than if either of the stimuli is used alone. How far we can carry this hint is of course difficult to judge, but ordinary observation suggests that learning goes on better if a whole situation remains reasonably uniform and unchanged from one learning session to another. Children are notoriously fond of ritual and regularity in connection with certain practices and games that might well be considered as learning experiences. In such games the conditioned response will not emerge unless "everything is just so." To suggest to a three-year-old that one toy, utensil, song, or what not is just as good as another is playing with fire. Dramatic coaches frequently insist on rehearsals being conducted on the stage on which the play is to be performed, and there is even some evidence (Abernethy, 1940) that college students do better on examinations held in their own classrooms with the regular teacher as proctor than under other circumstances. Other illustrations will occur to the reader and no point is served in belaboring the suggestion.

Guthrie (1935) makes a rather important principle out of the notion of stimulus pattern or complex and insists that behavior will be varied to the extent that the pattern changes in any significant way. Of course, since there is no *a priori* way of deciding what a significant change might be, we have to wait for the behavioral change before identifying the significant element. Since this is frequently alleged to be internal as, for example, a different degree of hunger, it becomes virtually impossible to make a decision concerning significance without completely circular reasoning. Experimentally the problem offers some complications because it means, in effect, that the actual conditioning stimulus may be misidentified. If, for example, a switch is closed to activate a light bulb, the sound of the closing of the switch may be the actual conditioning stimulus and the light need not go on at all. This, of course, can be discovered only if a test is conducted and such tests are frequently out of the question, or, at least, not carried out. Razran (1940) makes a strong point of the fact that in Pavlov's situation the frame to which the animal is harnessed as well as other factors in the situation, such as postural, emotional, visual, and other environmental cues, are all part of the conditioned stimulus pattern and that to pick out one that the experimenter thinks he is manipulating in some isolated sense is to make an error which may have ramifications in other areas when interpretation of some kinds of observations is attempted.

INTENSITY FACTORS IN CONDITIONING. Both conditioned and unconditioned stimuli can vary in their intensity or amount. In the case of the unconditioned stimulus this is seen most easily in connection with such stimuli as blows, shocks, temperature changes, and so on. In the conditioned stimulus we can vary the loudness of tones or brightness of lights and get a continuum of some type from which to choose. The question under study is: how much effect is there on the eventual conditioned response from varying intensities of these stimuli? No clear-cut answers are available, although some partial suggestions appear reasonable. Before we get to the results of some limited studies we might point out that changes in the intensity of stimuli are not always pure changes in that dimension. In the area of sound, for example, a change in loudness or intensity may be accompanied and usually is so accompanied by a change in pitch or tonal value (Stevens, 1935).

Without controlling changes in other dimensions it is difficult to appraise a change in stimulus intensity. Experimental results suggest that conditioning can occur over a wide range of stimulus strengths from barely threshold levels to severe and damaging. Thus Baker (1938) reports conditioning to "unconscious" stimuli at a near-threshold strength. Cohen, Hilgard, and Wendt (1933) reported conditioning of an eyelid blink in a hysterically blind person to a low-intensity light stimulus in an obscure location that presumably functioned as part of a piece of apparatus having nothing to do with the experiment. On the other hand, Pavlov used electric shocks as conditioned stimuli for a salivary reaction and brought them gradually to such strengths that they resulted in burning the skin of the dog and were of such strengths as to have been intolerable if used at the beginning of the experiment. None of these experiments was designed to evaluate stimulus intensity factors. In using shock in avoidance experiments Miller (1948) reported failure to secure avoidance behavior when a 90-volt shock was used but success when 150-volt shocks were employed. Dunlap, Gentry, and Zeigler (1931) reported that a medium shock proved better for conditioning an avoidance response than either weak or stronger shocks. Until further work is reported we must rest with the conclusion that stimuli of both conditioned and unconditioned types need be only above threshold for conditioning to occur, but that stimuli in the medium range might be most practical. Assuming a gradient of generalization (see p. 150) to operate in the intensity dimension, then, regardless of the strength of the original training stimulus, other stimuli on the continuum would also evoke the response. The one limiting factor on the strength of the CS is that it should not be so strong as to evoke a strong defense reaction in its own right. If it is too strong, it might become an UncS and the original UncS would then serve as a CS.

Temporal factors in classical conditioning (duration). The temporal aspects of conditioning are somewhat involved in that this dimension has several facets. The stimuli must, for example, have a certain relation to each other—one can be presented before, during, or after the other. The CS can begin at any time before the UncS and last for a moment, for the entire interval until the occurrence of the UncS, or even terminate later. No CS at all need be presented and there can still be a temporal factor if the UncS is presented regularly at short intervals. One additional and most important temporal fact is that, as has been emphasized before, the conditioned response tends to come forward in time and thus antedates the unconditioned stimulus. Besides having great theoretical significance this fact is, in effect, a test of conditioning. If the response occurs before the unconditioned stimulus, it is considered learned. An additional complication is offered by Guthrie who points out that external temporal factors are relevant only in connection with the internal events to which they lead. The true conditioning stimuli might be those that arise from movements aroused either by stimuli from previous movements or by the original external events. It is possible, argues Guthrie, that the actual CS is one that is quite distantly remote in time from what the experimenter fondly regards as the CS. With this introduction, we can turn to the details.

1. Before, during, of after. It is generally regarded that presenting the CS after the UncS is unlikely to lead to conditioning. Some experimenters (Wolfle, 1932) suggest that a low degree of conditioning occurs if the CS is presented very closely following the UncS (within a matter of a second or less), but others claim such conditioning to be of only pseudo status and that what has happened is that the organism has merely been *sensitized* to almost any stimulus (Hull, 1934a; Grether, 1938). Pavlov denied the possibility of backward conditioning in his early views but later admitted that they might be formed

with difficulty. In the Wolfle study cited above, an avoidance (finger withdrawal to shock) reaction was conditioned. It is possible that the effects of shock (or the shock itself) are still present when the CS is presented so that the CS is "backward" in form only, not in fact. In hurdle-jumping reactions, a common type of avoidance experiment, the shock may be present for quite a period especially in the early trials so that any stimulus coming after the *start* of the shock might well accompany it, making it a matter of simultaneous conditioning.

Spooner and Kellogg (1947) using a buzzer CS and a finger withdrawal to shock found that any signs of backward conditioning disappeared with continual training and that any responses that appear early in training might be attributed to sensitization.

The latency of the responses to the separate stimuli may also be involved. If the response to the UncS is slow it may be that a CS, though formally presented after the UncS may be effectively activating the neural elements involved before those initiated by the UncS have begun or finished. In any event, we must think of the central neural activity initiated by the stimuli as the actual elements of the conditioning process. Hull (1943) speaks of such neural effects as *stimulus traces* and regards the conditioning process as a matter of strengthening the connection(s) between such traces and the motor elements involved.

Guthrie (1935) holds that only simultaneously active neural (or other representations) can be conditioned. With Hull's *traces* and Hebb's cell assemblies we can see agreement among all three of these students. Experimental data generally support the notion that the CS and UncS must be present (in their effects) at the same time. Results of numerous experiments point to an arrangement of the CS being presented within 1 second of the UncS as the most successful period. The actual optimum time varies with various stimuli and the latency of the UncS. A slow response such as a galvanic or vascular reaction permits more freedom in time than does a rapid response such as the eyeblink where a .45-second interval seems best. (Reynolds, 1945a, and Wolfle, 1930, found .5 seconds best for the finger-withdrawal response.)

As Hilgard and Marquis point out (1940, p. 162), "The most favorable interval appears to be somewhat greater than the latency of the conditioned response, thus permitting the conditioned response to anticipate the unconditioned stimulus."

2. DELAYED AND TRACE CONDITIONING. Pavlov introduced the ex-

perimental procedure of presenting the CS earlier and earlier in the conditioning series while keeping the UncS at some fixed point. The animal is originally trained with a CS beginning about 5 seconds before the UncS (Pavlov's favorite interval for a salivary response), and, after conditioning is under way, the CS is advanced by short intervals until as much as 4 minutes have gone by before the UncS is presented. According to Pavlov his animals generally became somnolent and inactive during the interval, but about the time that the UncS would be presented they awakened and began to give the response. If the stimulus was allowed to continue for the interval, Pavlov spoke of a "delayed" CR. If the stimulus itself was terminated shortly after it was presented, Pavlov called any ensuing conditioning a "trace" CR on the ground that the CR must have been given to a trace or some neural aftereffect of the stimulus. Because it is unlikely that a specific stimulus would leave any "trace" of itself in its own right for longer than a few seconds (Hull, 1943, sets the limit of 30 seconds) it must be assumed that some other neural elements are activated to occupy the interval and thus to "mediate" the conditioning. Hebb's suggestion has already been considered (see p. 114). Guthrie suggests that the mediation can be considered to occur on the basis of a sequence of movements, one movement leading to another and so on as long as necessary so that the actual CS for the response in question would be a movement-produced stimulus from some response that occurred just prior to the conditioned response. In general it is reported that trace conditioning is more difficult to establish than delayed conditioning. Why this should be so in the light of Hebb's or Guthrie's views is not clear, although it is easy enough to speculate about the problem.

3. SHOULD THE CS TERMINATE WITH THE CONDITIONED RESPONSE? Experiments can be arranged so that the CS can occur briefly and be followed after some time with the UncS (trace conditioning) or the CS can continue until the response is made, or finally, the CS can continue after the response has been made. Although it is not difficult to tell what is likely to happen, it is proper that our analysis be based on data. Such data have been supplied by Mowrer and Ullman (1945) who showed that the most favorable relationship is for the CS to terminate with the response. If the trace situation is used, it is possible for the animal to associate some other stimulus following the supposed CS and therefore fail to react on subsequent occasions to the CS. If the CS continues following the response there is the possi-

bility that later, undesired responses might become associated with the CS.

4. TIME INTERVALS AS CONDITIONED STIMULI. Pavlov reports briefly (1927, p. 41) some experiments in which no CS was used but in which the UncS was presented every 30 minutes. He does not present detailed data but states: "After this had gone on a little time it was found that food or acid was no longer necessary to produce the alimentary or mild defense reflex." A variation of this experiment involves presenting a stimulus of some kind along with food every 30 minutes. In this situation the response is conditioned to both time passage and the stimulus. The added stimulus produces no effect at other intervals. Pavlov adds: "Of course in the establishment of a conditioned reflex of this type any length of time interval can be employed. No experiment, however, was made with longer intervals than half an hour." Pavlov does not report any studies of shorter intervals although he implies such were made.

Experimenters who give frequent trials in one training session usually takes pains to avoid temporal conditioning. Mowrer (1940b) presented stimuli at 30 seconds, 1 minute, and 1½ minute intervals in random order to prevent temporal conditioning. The area of temporal intervals is still largely unexplored. We do not as yet know the most effective intervals for such conditioning. In the Bugelski and Coyer study (see p. 69) a 15-second interval proved better than a 1-minute or 30-second period. No intervals below 15 seconds were explored.

It is usually held that *time per se* cannot serve as a CS, but that something must be occurring within the time interval that serves as the real CS. The "something" may be of the nature of postural changes, movement-produced stimuli, or other usually unobserved events. The identification of such events would be a strong step toward explaining temporal conditioning.

THE ISOLATION OF VARIABLES IN CONDITIONING (CLEARNESS). The attribute of clearness is traditionally associated with sensory experience and is ordinarily to be talked about only in an introspective setting. However, all the other aspects of stimulation so far discussed are also derived from introspective psychology even though we were able to treat them objectively. Can the same be done for clearness?

When we considered *quality* of stimulation we, of course, had to think in terms of the organism and the sense organs involved, the limitations of various species, and so on. The same considerations hold for intensity and temporal factors. We cannot emphasize enough that events in an external world *cannot* be associated with behavior. Only neural events can be associated. If clearness is to have any value or meaning in connection with stimuli in a learning situation, it will be only as a feature of some neural events.

Before turning to the neural aspects, some behavioral features of clearness might be noted. The teacher frequently asks his students: "Is that clear?" What "that" means can hardly be specified here. Nor can the "clear." Still the teacher must feel that he is communicating and he frequently has the satisfaction of seeing nodding agreement. The students like to have "things made clear." Educators are devoted to the notion that there are ways of presenting matters clearly or in some degree of its opposite, which might be described as "confused." The problem of the teacher is to make things "stand out." Gestalt psychologists have dealt with this problem in their perceptual studies under the general heading of Figure-Ground Relationships.

The teacher, formal or otherwise, has some appreciation of the elements to be associated. The student may have none or very little. The parent teaching his child the alphabet from a picture book may find the child calling an A, "apple" or the E, "elephant." Obviously the child has learned the wrong association. Equally obviously, the situation was not a "clear" one. The child did not appreciate the problem or even, perhaps, that there was a problem. When the child begins to make some progress in naming the letters he frequently confuses some letters, perhaps because they make poor "figures" although the normal adult has little difficulty with the same figures in the situation. The parent or teacher has no better figure to look at than the child. Yet the child says X for K, or F for E, C for G, and so on. Clearly, the child is not reacting to particular features of the stimulus that it must pick out of the complex if it is eventually going to read.

An illustration from one of Hebb's (1938) experiments shows the same situation, perhaps a little more startlingly. Hebb trained rats to run from a fixed starting point across a circular table to a food position that was surrounded by a high white screen. Other low, black screens were placed at 90-degree separations along the circumference of the table. When the rats were running quickly to the high white screen the table was rotated 90 degrees so that a black low screen occupied the former food area. The rats ran directly to this low black screen, ignoring the high white one 90 degrees away. An observer, prior to the test, would have judged that the rats were "obviously trained to run to the taller white screen" which anyone could see "clearly stood out" in the situation. The test proved that what was so "clear" and obvious to the human was not so obvious to the rat. Hebb was able to show that the rats were actually ignoring the clues that were "near at hand" and were reacting to more distant cues which were probably "clearer" to them.

In one of his illustrations Hebb (1949, p. 93) describes how a rat is trained to jump from one platform to another for food. The jumping apparatus is enclosed by a framework of four doors. In the original training one of these doors is left open and provides a general, distant orientation cue. Later the food platform is moved 90 degrees and another door is left open. The rat proceeds to jump off into space in a direction that is apparently a function of the new open door. Scharlock's experiment (1954), mentioned earlier (p. 97), illustrates the same kind of control over a response by a distant orientation cue.

One more illustration before we return to the general problem. Leuba (1941) in a series of observations on hypnotized subjects was able to establish conditioning in one trial by the simple expedient of eliminating the subjects' awareness of all aspects of the situation except the factors to be associated. Thus, if a subject was to associate a buzzer with a pinprick applied to the hand, Leuba would suggest that the subject was blind, anosmic, and otherwise insensitive to everything but the buzzer and the pinprick. One pairing of the stimuli was enough to bring about a scratching of the palm when a buzzer was sounded in a posthypnotic test. The observations of Leuba fall in line, of course, with Guthrie's principle of one-trial learning. Presumably, if we want to increase learning efficiency we must have complete control of the variables which we are interested in associating. When a child fails to learn, it may not be the fault of the child but rather that of the teacher who did not recognize that the proper components were not actively present in the learning situation in such a way as to be able to enter into an association. If the child is looking at the ornamental trappings of the elephant when the parent says, "E," what is going to be learned? When the teacher is presenting the material of vital consequence to success in the fifth grade and the student is occupied with day-dreams of supermanhood and spacemanship we can hardly hope for a meeting of minds and suitable associations.

An observation of a general nature that must have already occurred to the student is that somehow we have become involved with the problem of *attention*. Generations of teachers have known how important this difficult variable is in the learning situation. They have shouted and begged that the students "pay attention" throughout the history of education. They knew or recognized without being able to specify the circumstances or the details that the attentive child learns, the inattentive does not—or it could be that the learning child creates, somehow, the impression of being attentive, however we describe this impression. We shall have more to say about the matter of attention when we deal with motivation (see p. 211). For the present our concern is with "clearness."

Razran (1940) has made the point, in connection with the Pavlovian salivary experiment, that one reason that any delays are experienced in the acquisition of the conditioning is that the situation, in spite of Pavlov's attempts at simplification, is still so complex. The dog certainly does not know what the experimenter's problem is. He may learn and unlearn a long series of associations before learning the one the experimenter has in mind. The stimulus input in any learning situation is likely to be of great complexity. As if this were not enough, we must recognize that the organism itself is also too busy just *living* to be concerned about some experimenter's designs.

Neurophysiologists since Sherrington have been pointing out how the behavior of the organism is based on *integration* of incoming and outgoing impulses. More recently, since the first reports by Berger (1929) of the rhythms of electrical activity in the brain, the physiologists have become concerned with how constant activity of the cortex modifies the incoming impulses and the resulting behavior. Hebb (1949, 1955) has persistently emphasized the point that present and recently prior activity of the cortex and lower centers plays a prominent if not all-determining role in the possibilities of associative activity. Hebb discusses the problem in terms of neural facilitation and inhibition. If prior and/or present neural activity is such as to facilitate the discharge of appropriate cells then the possibility of the development of specific cell assemblies and specific connections is favored. Should such neural background activity be unfavorable or inhibitory then cell assemblies will not be formed. "Clearness," for Hebb, would then reduce to something like readiness of neural elements for reaction. He speaks of such "central facilitation" as the equivalents of attention or "expectancy" or "set." For our present purposes we need not get involved in the neural details, especially since there is no present way in which we can control the neural action. What we can recognize, however, is that learning will depend on the complexity of the learning situation, including the temporal aspects in the sense of just prior activity as well as presently active stimuli of all kinds. This principle, of course, does not turn out to be of any ·simple practicality since complexity is relative to the learning organism and not to the teacher, and prior neural activity is also largely uncontrollable. The practicality of the principle may largely be negative. If an organism is not learning with some expected efficiency, the problem should be examined to determine if the association possibilities are being obscured by interfering biases, sets, expectancies, or stimulus properties. In human learning situations, the teacher, insofar as possible, should put himself in the place of the student quite literally both physically and temporally in terms of experience. When a teacher becomes equally familiar with all aspects of some procedure he is teaching, he might not remember that as a student he might have had difficulty with some one phase or another of the problem. The present learners may be having an equally difficult time with the same or different obstacles where the teacher now sees no problem.

Clearness, then, refers to the relative degree of isolation of the variables to be associated both in the present setting and in temporal history of the learner. It is likely that an organism is always learning something whether there is a teacher about or not. The problem is to find out what is being learned and then make the necessary changes if the learning is not of the desired material. We can close this section with reference to an experiment by Ehrenfreund (1948) who provides an unusually appropriate illustration. Ehrenfreund was critical of an experiment reported by Lashley who implied that no learning was going on in the early trials (up to 50) in a jumping-stand experiment. Rats were trained by Lashley to jump toward a card with vertical stripes rather than toward a card with horizontal stripes. The learning time proved to be unusually long for the rats and after 50 trials the animals were still jumping in a chance fashion. Ehrenfreund repeated Lashley's experiment with similar findings. He then raised the platform from which the rats jumped and learning improved noticeably. Ehrenfreund concluded that in Lashley's original situation the animals were placed so low in relation to the target that all they saw effectively was the lower portion of the cards which presumably looked the same. When the stand was raised they were able to react from a different viewpoint and for the first time had some opportunity to be affected by the features of the stimuli. The moral of the clearness attribute should need no further exposition.

RESPONSE FEATURES IN LEARNING

Although any separation of stimuli and responses is artificial we have tried in the previous sections to consider only the stimulus aspects in learning, and because of the special significance of stimulus features in classical learning, most of the illustrative material was chosen from Pavlovian conditioning. It is time to consider the response side of learning behavior, and here we will have more freedom to choose illustrations from both classical and instrumental experiments. At the same time we can consider the special role of experimenter-manipulated stimuli in the case of instrumental learning. As a first step in appreciating the response side of learning we should remind ourselves of certain distinctions between classical and instrumental learning to which we now turn.

The conditioned response in classical conditioning.

THE CONDTIONED RESPONSE. Any response which can be evoked consistently by a stimulus might be selected for conditioning. Reference has already been made to Hull's (1934a) catalogue of such responses. At this point we might illustrate the range or extremes to which researchers go to demonstrate Pavlovian principles. An interesting collection of examples of what Russian experimenters are doing in the field of conditioning is available in English from a review by Airapetyantz and Bykov (1945). These writers describe numerous studies involving various internal organs like the stomach, kidney, and spleen. Several studies are reported in which the processes of urination and defecation are brought under the control of conditioning stimuli after surgical interruption of normal bladder and intestinal outlets. Two of the experiments are described in sufficient detail to provide an appreciation of some of the procedures; since they are briefly stated we will quote in full. The first experiment follows:

By means of a rubber ballon, water at a temperature of 6–7° is admitted, in one case, into the intestinal loop, opened according to the method of Tiri-Vella, and reinforced by an electrical current administered to the paw. In the other case, water was admitted to the ballon at a temperature of 28°, but without association with an electric current. As a consequence of such a combination of stimuli in the receptors of the intestinal mucous, the dog reacted by raising his paw to the cold water only. But the dog did not react at all to the warm water; it continued to stand quietly and showed no special motor reaction.

In the second experiment, carried out in an evacuation hospital, we have this report:

During the treatment of the invalid, Comrade F, a temporary fistula was attached in the middle region of the small intestine. The experiment was as follows: Through the fistula a small rubber balloon was inserted into the bowels, filled in one case with cold water, in another case with warm. These thermal factors play the role of interoceptive unconditioned stimuli. The role of the conditioned stimulus is played by visual perceptions: the flashing of a red or blue electric light. It goes without saying that here, just as in the previously described experiments, the method and procedure were of a nature to exclude any intrusion of epidermal or acoustic components, while the visual stimuli were restricted to those intended.

It was found, first, that the cold and warm interoceptive impulses evoked sensations in F which he perceived with full adequacy, and it was significant that F was aware of peristaltic movements of the bowels. In the second place, all these feelings could easily be reproduced by way of conditioned reflexes, in consequence of several associations of light signals with them. The isolated action of the red lamp (without the balloon!) after a certain latent period elicited in F a current of emotive reactions, corresponding, for example, to the contact of the cold-water balloon with the mucous lining of the intestine.

Such experiments are, to be sure, unusual in this country. Very few American experimenters ever even try to condition the salivary response. Razran (1939d) is about the only current researcher who uses salivation as the response to be conditioned and he uses it with humans. (Cotton wads in the mouth are used to absorb saliva; weighing the wads reveals the amount of conditioned response.) Razran approves strongly of the salivary response as a useful laboratory tool but is disturbed by the difficulties involved in measurement. Other experimenters favor the galvanic and eyelid reflexes. The knee jerk is not readily conditioned although Wendt (1930) was successful in his study. Other alleged reflexes or responses are frequently complicated by "instrumental" features and do not easily fit the theoretical needs.

It is not unusual for critics of the classical conditioning procedure to speak somewhat patronizingly of conditioned reflexes as "muscle twitch" psychology and Thorndike (1931) and Mowrer (1947) have implied that CR's are so limited in their scope as to represent only laboratory curiosities and are unlikely to have much significance outside the laboratory. Mowrer, to be sure, was limiting his remarks to those experiments wherein an attempt is made to condition striated muscle responses. Many critics of the significance of Pavlov's work (including Mowrer, 1950; Skinner, 1938; Maier, 1931; Schlosberg, 1937) are willing to accept the "conditioned reflex" of Pavlov as providing a good enough account of visceral learning, of learning involving autonomic nervous system functions, or, in general, of smooth muscle and glandular activity. They regard any striated muscle conditioning as dubious, or trivial, or the result of other than Pavlovian principle at work.

Other critics (Hilgard and Marquis, 1940) like to point out that the CR is not the same thing as the unconditioned response. Actually, there appears to be no record of anyone ever having said they were identical and so the criticism might be said to be uncalled for. Numerous studies have been devoted to pointing out the differences between CR's and UncR's (Hilgard, 1936a, b; Peak, 1933) and, in general, the differences between voluntary, reflex, and conditioned responses. There is no good reason to look for identity between CR's and the UncR's on which they are based. When the UncS is omitted, we can presume that an important determinant of the nature of the response is absent and that the response will, therefore, not appear in its usual form. In fact, for the CR to be an exact duplicate of the UncR would be somewhat of a tragedy for organisms that learn as well as for learning theorists as we shall try to point out shortly (see p. 156).

Before leaving the Pavlovian CR, we should note, at least briefly, the response to the CS before it has become associated with the UncR. Usually the CS evokes some response in its own right; a light, for example, might elicit a pupillary reflex or some eye movements. A tone might involve pricking up the ears, and so on. These responses are unusually ignored because the attention of the experimenter is focused on the UncR and the UncS. It appears that in the course of conditioning the original responses to the CS gradually drop out or decrease in extent (Pavlov, 1927) as do many irrelevant responses to the UncS. Presumably, the findings are attributable to the relative strengths of the stimuli involved and there is no theoretical reason why the original response to the CS should not become the CR if the strengths of the stimuli were reversed. Pavlov states as much in his discussion of the use of electric shock as the CS. If the shock is sufficiently severe, the dog will stop salivating to food and the food becomes the CS for avoidance. The general picture of what goes on in a conditioning experiment might be described as a kind of differentiation or individuation of specific responses out of a general, mass reaction. With the growth of conditioning, there is a gradual improvement in what might be termed the important business of the occasion, and with the increase in efficiency, a dropping out of unessentials.

LEARNING UNDER INSTRUMENTAL CONDITIONS. We are already familiar with a sufficient array of illustrations of typical instrumental responses studied in the learning laboratory. We have considered such things as bar-pressing, string-pulling, target-pecking, and many others. By the process of exclusion, any response that is not a Pavlovian type is instrumental. As the term is now used it includes such behavior as talking, dressing, eating, making love, playing baseball or bridge, or voting at the polls. According to Skinner (1938, 1953), the more interesting, if not all-important, behavior is of the instrumental or operant variety.

As soon as we begin to examine instrumental learning we are struck by the importance of specifying the situation or stimuli that enable us to talk about instrumental behavior. In spite of Skinner's indifference to stimuli, we know that behavior does not take place in their absence and even his rats must be placed in special containers before they can begin to emit bar-presses. We would be hard put to describe the behavior of a ball player without at least some modest mention of the ball. It is just this problem of the relation of stimuli to responses that is of first significance in instrumental learning. Before we look at Skinner's solution of the problem we should start with some older views.

In his early work Thorndike (1898) described a learning situation as amounting to a problem. The organism was faced with a problem situation. In this situation the organism (for reasons to be examined later) makes various responses or "attempts" to solve the problem which can be thought of as "trials." If the first trial eliminates the problem, we can hardly talk about learning. In fact, unless the first attempt fails, we do not recognize it as a matter of learning but account for it as the result of instinct or intelligence or accident. The hallmark of learning, for Thorndike, was the occurrence of errors. Errors had to occur and be eliminated, the right response had to emerge from a background of mistakes. Thorndike spoke of "trial and error, and chance success."

Following in Thorndike's footsteps, Hull (1943, 1934b) rephrased the statement in somewhat the following manner: When an organism is in any stimulus situation that calls for action, it will react with the most natural response. (This is not specified in advance; whatever the organism does first, is automatically the most natural thing to do. If this does not meet the needs, that is, remove the stimulus or solve the problem, then the organism will do the second most natural thing to do, and so on.) Actually, Hull talks in terms of response strengths rather than about natural responses and he assumes that for any given stimulus there may be a series of responses ranging from strong to weak that have a probability of emergence which is proportional to their strength.

THE HABIT-FAMILY HIERARCHY. If we follow Hull's (1934b) analysis we can picture a given stimulus (S) as having a group of potential responses related to it in a decreasing order of strengths, or probabilities of occurrence, thus R_1, R_2, R_3, R_4,—R_n. When the stimulus is present R_1 will occur and continue to recur until its strength or potential is exhausted or weakened. (The process of weakening is not spelled out but we can assume that principles that account for extinction [5] pertain.) If the strength of R_1 is diminished, the potential of R_2 may be strong enough to bring it into operation. If R_2 is repeatedly performed without effect, R_3 will occur, and so on. Eventually the organism will go through its repertoire and if the appropriate response is in that repertoire, a successful trial will occur. Hull's analysis leaves us with an interesting paradox. The organism must already "know" what to do before it can learn what to do. Actually the paradox is only superficial. What is really involved is the point that organisms must be capable of making the correct responses before they can be expected to perform them rapidly, and *first* when confronted by a specific stimulus or situation. From Hull's point of view, then, learning consists of increasing the strength or raising the potential of a given response in a *hierarchy* of responses, any member of which has some probability of occurrence.

Experimenters arranging learning experiments usually pick a response that is relatively low in the hierarchy in order to prolong the learning at least long enough to permit observation of what is going on. It should be recognized that even the highest member in the hierarchy can be strengthened just like any other member if it happens to be the appropriate response. Hull assumes that there is no

---

[5] See Chap. 12. For the moment, a process like fatigue might be postulated as a weakener.

real limit to the strength of any reaction no matter how often it has been strengthened. It is possible, therefore, that even the first response to a stimulus may also be learned although it would hardly be chosen for observation by an experimenter.

So far we have just considered one part of the habit-family hierarchy. A number of other interesting relationships are postulated by Hull in his description of learning. Hull looks at any learning be-

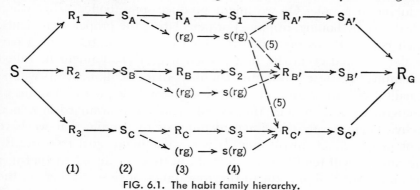

FIG. 6.1. The habit family hierarchy.

(1) Any S may evoke a variety of responses. These will emerge in order of their relative strengths and thus form a hierarchy.

(2) Each R gives rise to its own consequences as new stimuli (A, B, C, etc.) and these in turn lead directly to new responses R_A R_B, etc.

(3) With practice and learning, that is with occurrence of R_G, fractional goal responses (rg) begin to occur prior to R_G, and become associated with the various stimuli a, b, c, etc.

(4) But rg being a response also produces stimuli S_{RG} and these stimuli become conditioned to subsequent responses in the series $R_A{}^1$, $R_B{}^1$, etc.

(5) By virtue of the rg being identical in the several sequences, it is possible for S to initiate R1, this initiates S_A which may initiate (rg). At this point it is possible for the organism to make $R_B{}^1$ or $R_C{}^1$ each of which is associated with Srg.

The arrangement described provides the basis for any of a number of S's to eventuate in the same R_G. Because each member of the series is equivalent and because there is a common characteristic, rg, Hull called this proposal the "habit family hierarchy."

havior as involving some final consummatory, drive-reducing, or goal response. This he identifies as R_G. Such goal responses may be associated or have connections with a number of stimuli, as S_a, S_b, S_c, and so on. Frequently, or even typically, such stimuli for R_G will be movement-produced stimuli from prior responses so that they might represent the consequences of previous responses. We might diagram what has been described above as in Figure 6.1.

The diagram is simplified from Hull's description in that we have left out other possible intervening responses and their stimuli, but it might serve the purpose. We have, so far, a suggestion that a given stimulus (S) may result eventually in a given response (R_G) but that might occur through any of several avenues or different steps. To illustrate, we might see a cat in a tree (S) and get it to the ground by (a) climbing the tree, (b) getting a ladder, (c) inducing the cat to hold on to a pole. Or we might produce some coffee (R_G) when asked (S) by boiling, dripping, or percolating the proper ingredients. Such combinations of responses which might be initiated by a particular (S) and eventuate in a particular goal (R_G) might be called a "family." Because it is more than likely that not all members will be equally likely to occur, but rather will follow a sequence in terms of strength, we can consider the several members as arranged in a hierarchy. There is one additional member of the family that we have kept in the closet up till now. It is *rg*. The major goal response R_G presumably will tend to come forward in time to the extent that it is possible. This will amount to the appearance of *rg* somewhere in the earlier phases of the sequences. Since it is the same R_G, the *rg* will be similar regardless of the particular sequence. Stimuli from *rg* will become conditioned to any responses of any sequence and therefore be a *common* factor in the family of habits. If we wish to follow Hull's reasoning at this point, we can also postulate that because *rg* is common to any sequence, then any route which leads to R_G will be strengthened, *but,* and this is the main point, so will every other route that has the same *rg*. We now have the possibility that a route that is low in the hierarchy can benefit from practice of some other route, or that a route higher in the hierarchy benefits from the operation of a habit low in the hierarchy.

We have come somewhat far afield but this merely illustrates the difficulty of considering either stimuli or responses alone. It cannot be done effectively and we always get involved with one when discussing the other.

STIMULI IN INSTRUMENTAL LEARNING

Before going on to other characteristics of learning we should take note of the role of stimuli in instrumental learning and determine if there are any genuine differences from classical conditioning. We have already touched on this question in discussing bar-pressing behavior, but here we require a more general appraisal.

We have just seen how Hull handles stimuli in his habit-family analysis. Obviously there is no difference in his treatment of stimuli from that of Pavlov. A stimulus is some form of external energy that initiates neural activity in afferent nerves. Presumably from there the neural activity leads to some kind of effector reaction.

Now the kind of response Hull has made use of in his experimental and theoretical work has been primarily of the instrumental variety. In our presentation of the different varieties of instrumental learning situations we had occasion to mention that some theorists tend to ignore or slight the importance of stimuli in such situations and concentrate on the responses. When stimuli are introduced by experimenters they are not regarded as of direct significance in eliciting behavior but merely present the opportunity or occasion for the organism to respond. What makes the animal respond is not spelled out, and the student is left with the supposition that the organism will respond if it wants to or if it feels like it. The experimenters themselves are too sophisticated to make such remarks but speak more vaguely of motivation or deprivation conditions which somehow get the organism into action. Thus Tolman speaks of the association between stimuli (signs and significates) but does not specify any detailed machinery for getting out a response.[6] Skinner, emphasizing operants, prefers to consider stimuli as stage-setting in their effects and it is to his view that we now turn.

Discriminated stimuli (S^D). When an experimenter manipulates some feature of the environment and finds alterations in the behavior of the organism, Skinner speaks of "discriminated" stimuli. An illustration from bar-pressing behavior might be appropriate. The experimenter may choose to "reinforce" the animal only under certain conditions and not others. For example, he may elect to supply pellets for the rat when a light is turned on and cut off the supply when the light is extinguished. After some experience in pressing the bar under light and dark conditions, the rat will cease pressing in the dark and start working actively as soon as the light comes on. Skinner refers to this as a "discrimination," and the light is consequently considered a "discriminated stimulus" or S^D. Skinner prefers to think that the S^D does not elicit the responses but merely occasions them. The

---

[6] Guthrie is frequently quoted as saying, "Tolman leaves the rat in the middle of the maze, lost in thought." (See Estes *et al.*, 1954, p. 235.)

similarity to Tolman's view is striking, however much they differ in philosophy of science or other aspects of their views.

Skinner (1938) and Keller and Schoenfeld (1950) insist that the S^D does not *elicit* the response but merely sets the stage for the behavior. The curious student will inquire as to how an S^D serves this function. Skinner does not offer much help but it is quite clear that a discriminated stimulus becomes such only after learning has taken place. The usual training procedure is to present the S^D and wait for the response. As soon as the response occurs, the "reinforcement" appears and the S^D is terminated. There is no essential difference between this procedure and that of Pavlov. The animal may continue to respond in the absence of S^D but such responses are not reinforced. Gradually the S^D is followed by the response more and more quickly. It acquires control over the behavior and the animal responds as soon as it is presented. There does not appear to be any reason to differentiate Skinner's S^D from any other kind of CS. They operate in the same way. Keller and Schoenfeld (1950, p. 120) admit that for rats in a Skinner box responding without the S^D "never disappears entirely." We will see in the next section the basis for the formation of S^D's in the "method of contrasts." The conclusion appears justified that what Skinner calls an S^D amounts to saying that cues of one kind or another can control starting or stopping of certain behavior. To make this statement appear to mean something else seems more confusing than useful. It is the most obvious fact of learning. Even when an animal continues to "operate" in a Skinner box, for example, while a light is on, there is no great mystery about why it should stop when the light goes out. Bullock and Smith (1953) have demonstrated that rats can learn to stop more and more quickly with succeeding trials when food is no longer supplied after a series of responses. The elimination of the light would be only one additional cue for retiring from the bar. We can conclude that the S^D is just another name for CS and that there is no operational distinction between these terms.

Both Tolman and Skinner seem to feel that their views differ in some basic manner from those of Pavlov (or Hull) but the difference appears to be more imaginary than real and may rest on a dubious view of causation. There appears to be some reluctance on the part of Tolman and Skinner to espouse the notion that a stimulus *causes* behavior. Actually no one else speaks of "causation" either, and no more appears to be intended by the term "evoked" than that the response appears some time after the stimulus has been presented.

Whatever the philosophy of causation may be that is held by those who think of the stimulus as having some "evoking" capacity, there is no operational difference in the use of stimuli as practiced by either Hull or Skinner. The distinction does not appear to be of any genuine significance for the analysis of behavior. As far as experimental operations are concerned, stimuli are presented and responses follow. The important problem for the experimenter is to observe any relationships that develop between what he does and what the *organism* does or, more exactly, between stimulus properties and response features. We turn now to one of the more interesting (as well as strongly debated) of such relationships.

Chapter

7 *Learning and Adaptive Behavior*

Adjustment to life's problems consists of doing the right thing at the right time. That this is not always easy is readily admitted. There are always new problems to face, new obstacles or dangers to overcome. In a complex civilization there is not enough time to learn all the right answers. Yet, frequently enough, we give them without having learned them directly. How can this be done? On the answer to this question psychologists are widely divided. Some talk about "instinct" and others about "insight"; learning psychologists generally favor an approach based on potentially more observable mechanisms. In trying to show how learning or past experience is involved in producing reactions that have never been learned in their own right, we have a paradox to explain. Can we get something for nothing? Can we know something without having learned it? There are three propositions that have been advanced to solve the paradox; these are (a) the principle of generalization, (b) the principle of mediation, and (c) the habit-family hierarchy. We have already met these principles. It is time to examine them more closely and see how they solve the "something for nothing" paradox.

GENERALIZATION AND DISCRIMINATION

Among the early observations of Pavlov (1927, p. 110) was the finding that conditioned responses could be initiated by stimuli which differed to some extent in quantitative and qualitative dimensions from the original conditioning stimulus. If a dog had been trained to salivate to a touch on the flank, it was not necessary that it be touched in a precise and exact spot in order to have the CR occur. Within some range around the original spot, any point might do. Pavlov did claim, however, that if the CS was varied, then the response would vary and the dog would give less and less response (drops of saliva) as the distance from the original point increased. Presumably a touch on a distant point, for example, the head, would be entirely ineffective. Failure to give a response to a stimulus along the continuum of the original quantity of quality was termed "discrimination," while a positive reaction to such a stimulus was considered a sign of "generalization." The degree of generalization and discrimination was tested by Pavlov over a wide range of stimuli and the usefulness of the "construct" was upheld in studies involving lights, tones, tactual stimulation, and so on.

Generalization and discrimination as tests of acuity. Pavlov found that the generalization effects were strongest early in the training but that they diminished with successive reinforcements of a particular stimulus value. In order to study the process more closely he developed the *method of contrasts* which amounts to reinforcing a particular stimulus value with the UncS and omitting the reinforcement for any other value. If this is done, CR's to generalized values of the stimulus drop out (extinguish) while the original is maintained in strength. With this technique it is possible to determine the degree to which a subject can discriminate the original stimulus from any other value. If, for example, the original CR is established to a metronome beat of 100 per minute, the dog will salivate, at first, to any metronome rate. Gradually the response will become restricted to the neighborhood of 100 beats per minute. This process can be hastened by differential reinforcement and after some trials the animals will no longer respond to metronome rates in the vicinity of 90 or 110. As the training continues, the response will become more and more specifically restricted to the immediate area around 100 beats per minute and the dog will no longer respond to rates that are not close to 100. In an actual experiment with metronome rates Pavlov found that a discrimination was established between 100 and 96 beats per minute, that is, the dog would not salivate to 96 beats but would to 100. By analogy to psychophysical experiments, we could speak of a differential threshold of 4 beats for the dog and refer to the discrimination range as a j.n.d. Watson (1914), as a matter of fact, seriously considered using the *method of contrasts* as a substitute for verbal reports in determining discrimination thresholds and sensory acuity in humans in his efforts to get away from subjectivity.

Experimental neurosis. If the *method of contrasts* is pushed to the extreme limits and finer and finer "discriminations" are demanded of the subject, it is found that some animals become extremely disturbed and lose even the discriminations that have been acquired. The behavior of the disturbed animals varies greatly, but the reactions of some are so extreme as to have prompted Pavlov to describe them as "neurotic," and the term "experimental neurosis" was applied by Pavlov to the condition of the animals who "broke down" in the discrimination testing. Some animals became violently agitated and fought against being strapped into the experimental frame, others gave the appearance of complete inhibition or depression, some refused to salivate to any stimulus, others salivated to any at all, and so on. How "neurotic" such behavior is we shall try to examine in Chapter 15. For the present we are concerned only to note the fact of possible disturbance when discrimination tests are carried beyond certain limits. It might be profitable, however, for future purposes to describe an experiment leading to "experimental neurosis" and we can hardly do better than to select one of Pavlov's classical efforts. In one of the early attempts to establish discrimination limits Pavlov used a circle and an ellipse as stimuli to be discriminated. The circle was "positive," that is, always reinforced; the ellipse was negative. Starting out with an ellipse with a diameter ratio of 2:1, the discrimination was quickly established and new ellipses with closer diameter ratios were introduced. With successive discriminations established, Pavlov finally introduced an ellipse with a 9:8 ratio. This proved to be too much (or too little) for the dog and the animal began to behave in a disorganized fashion, reminding Pavlov of the behavior of animals trapped in cages in the cellar of the laboratory at the time the river Neva overflowed. The reactions of the dogs in that emergency seemed to be approximated by the behavior of the animals in the laboratory frame and merited, in Pavlov's opinion, the diagnosis of neurosis. We shall return to the problem of neurotic behavior in the laboratory. For the moment we merely paused to take note of the findings when high-level discriminations are required.

Generalization and discrimination as quantitative variables in learning theory. In his efforts to establish a quantitative theory of behavior, Hull (1943) became interested in the nature of the relationships between the degree of generalization of a response and the variation of the stimulus along some continuum. In one of his early experiments with Bass (Bass & Hull, 1934), he satisfied himself with the reality of the generalization phenomenon by finding diminishing degrees of a galvanic response to vibratory stimuli placed along the back and legs of human subjects who were shocked when a stimulus in the neck area was presented. He was not satisfied, however, with the assumption that a certain amount of skin on the upper back was equivalent to the same amount of skin on the lower back and began to search for some stimulus continuum which would provide adequate steps of known equality. The experiment of Hovland (see Chap. 2) seemed to provide the needed equal-distance scale as Hovland tested the generalization of a response (PGR) to tones that were selected as to be equally distant along a psychological scale of j.n.d.'s. Thus, Hovland used tones of 153, 468, 1000, and 1937 cycles which he considered to represent steps of 25 j.n.d.'s.[1] With one of these tones as a conditioned stimulus, it was possible to test the amout of reaction to any of the other tones. It was also possible to extinguish either the conditioned stimulus or one of the generalization stimuli and note the effect on the rest of the tones. Hovland found that generalization seemed to follow a negatively decelerating curve or gradient, both for positive generalization effects and for extinction effects; that is, the amount of extinction decreases as the separation of the stimuli from the extinguished stimulus increases. This particular finding will shortly prove of some interest (see p. 154) but for the moment we will ignore it in favor of considering the positive findings. Hull accepted Hovland's results as more or less defining the function of generalization and used the "concave" gradient (Fig. 7.1) of Hovland in most of his subsequent theorizing about generalization. It is of interest to point out that Hull used the construct of generalization as an "intervening variable" and dealt with it largely in terms of a mathematical expression without concerning himself greatly as to its possible "hypothetical construct" characteristics.

Critics of Hull are not so ready to accept the gradient of generali-

---

[1] The work of Stevens & Volkman (1940) on pitch j.n.d.'s suggests that below 1000 cycles it is possible to discriminate differences between stimuli varying by 2 or 3 cycles; this would mean that a range from 153 to 468 would contain not 25 j.n.d.'s but from 105 to 150 or so. Above 1000 cycles the j.n.d. seems to amount to about a 3 percent difference. The range between 1000 and 1937 would include roughly about 30 j.n.d.'s. The use of the j.n.d. as a measure of equal psychological distances was warmly received in the 30's and 40's but has been criticized recently (Estes *et al.*, 1954) as a departure from a *physical* basis for behavioral phenomena which Hull claimed to espouse.

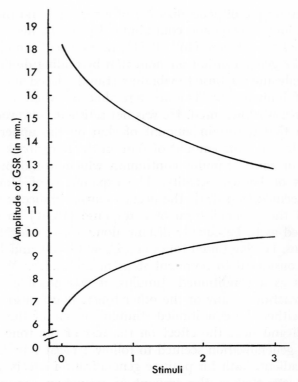

FIG. 7.1. Generalization. The galvanic skin response was conditioned in 20 subjects by pairing a tone and shock. The upper figure shows the generalized habit strength for stimuli along the pitch continuum. Only the 0 point was employed in the training. After such training subjects responded with decreasing magnitudes of the galvanic skin response to test stimuli.

In the lower figure, all points were equally reinforced and extinction was carried out at point 0. The extinction generalized to the other points. Note that there is less and less loss of conditioning as the separation from the original extinguished point is approached. (After Hovland, 1937).

zation as a significant or meaningful postulate. The criticisms come from both the laboratory and the armchair and it is alleged that the kind of finding that one obtains in the laboratory may be a limited artifact of the kinds of stimulation employed. Guthrie (1935), for example, emphasizes that we probably never know what the *actual* conditioning stimulus is. The fact that we blow a whistle or shine a light may be of importance only in setting off a particular set of muscular reactions which produce their own stimuli for new reactions, and so on. Somewhere along the line, one of the movement-produced stimuli may become associated with a response. Any generalization phenomena would then amount to initiating a movement sequence which produced the important stimulus-generating response. Concentrating on some external stimulus may result in missing the point altogether because it may play only an indirect role. In *Educational Psychology* Guthrie and Powers (1950) describe the mechanism of generalization as amounting to the arousal of a mediating response which can serve as a signal. If a child is bitten by a nonbarking dog, it may shrink in fear at the sound of a bark, in spite of the proverb, because the bark arouses a verbal association ("dog") and this verbal association has already been conditioned to the fear reaction. Any stimulation which arouses this mediating response will now be capable of arousing fear in the child, and it matters not whether this is the sight, sound, or smell of a dog even though some of these did not function in the original situation in which the child was injured. From Guthrie's viewpoint there could not be a negatively accelerated gradient in the degree of fear associated with some diminishing aspect of doghood. The response would be more of an all-or-none nature depending upon how fully the mediating response was aroused. If Pavlov's dog salivates more to a stimulus that is "close" to the original than to a more distant stimulus, this means only that the "close" stimulus more nearly activates the appropriate stimulus-producing response. Because such a response may depend on numerous other sources of stimulation and adjustment (for example, postural orientation) it is perfectly possible for the CR not to occur even to the original stimulus if the rest of the stimulation pattern is lacking. We do not expect Pavlov's dog to salivate when the bell sounds, but the dog is in its home cage instead of the laboratory. The dog must be strapped in the frame and standing in an appropriate fashion. Pavlov himself went to great extremes to secure the utmost control over the stimulus situation, thereby ensuring, according to Guthrie, that the appropriate mediating responses would occur.

Some evidence to support Guthrie's views comes from the work of Razran (1939b) who found a high level of generalization (no gradient of the Hovland variety) to patterns or combinations of stimuli. When only a single stimulus was used a gradient of diminishing response strength tended to appear, but Razran claims that the gradient is a crude thing and that generalization occurs only over a few steps of change of the stimulus with no such mathematical precision as Hull would be pleased to find. Razran (1949) also criticizes Hovland's experiment on the grounds that the reported gradients are artifacts produced by combining results of the individual subjects, none of whom, individually, showed any gradient. Osgood (1953, p. 357) points out that Hovland's experimental design was such as to preclude individual gradients from appearing and this is probably a good defense, but we are still far from being in a position of having incontrovertible evidence of generalization gradients. For theoretical purposes they would be extremely handy. Empirically, however, the question is still open.

Generalization and mediation. The possibility that the generalizing process works through some mediating mechanism has already been mentioned above in discussing Guthrie's views. For several years now the term "mediated generalization" [2] has been quite popular and a number of investigations have been conducted in which the construct is used as an explanatory device. Whenever a report appears announcing the successful demonstration of "sensory-sensory" conditioning, for example, opponents of the postulate of sensory-sensory learning attempt to account for the findings on the basis of "mediated generalization." Brogden (1939), for example, stimulated a dog with 200 paired presentations of a light and sound. Later the sound was used as a CS for a withdrawal of a leg to shock. When the CR to sound was established, the light was presented and the leg was withdrawn. In other similar experiments Brogden (1947, and Chernikoff and Brogden, 1949) paired lights and sounds for human subjects, then asked the subjects to give rapid "reaction-time" type responses to the sound. After a number of sound presentations, the light would be turned on and most of his subjects would give the response without having been told to do so. Wickens and Briggs (1951), among others, criticize this type of experiment on the supposition that in the original (sensory preconditioning) trials some response (unspecified usually) is present which is conditioned to both light and sound. Later when the light is presented alone (never having been associated with the response conditioned to the sound) it evokes the supposed

---

[2] It is doubtful that the combination of words is particularly more meaningful than the single term "mediation." The meaning of "generalization" in the combination seems to have some kind of logical or inductive properties and may confuse the issue. The writer will use only the single term "mediation" when referring to some alleged intervening process which leads eventually to some response.

intervening response; this now generates stimuli which have been conditioned to the desired CR at the time the sound stimulus was being used as a CS, and so the CR appears. Bugelski and Scharlock (1952) criticized the Wickens and Briggs experiment as inadequately designed to demonstrate their postulated mediating response, although this does not necessarily reflect on the mediation explanation. As far as the writer is concerned, sensory-sensory conditioning is valid enough and has been reasonably demonstrated (Ellson, 1942; Leuba, 1940). Its explanation in terms of mediation is still a moot point although there is every logical ground to assume some mediating process, perhaps of the type of Hebb's phase-sequence variety. It is not necessary that the mediation occur on an overt, observable, response level. A neural mediation is logically sufficient. Unless we accept some kind of mediating mechanism, we shall be unable to account for the most interesting as well as the most human behavior.

Razran (1936, 1939a) has long been concerned with what he calls "semantic generalization." In his work, human subjects are conditioned to salivate when certain word stimuli are presented. Later subjects are tested with other words which are synonyms, homonyms, or antonyms of the original CS's. If physical similarity of sounds were important, one would expect greater generalization to homonyms which sound the same as the original CS's. Actually Razran finds more generalization to synonyms which, of course, have the same meaning and none of the appearance of the CS. Razran's results, however, have been challenged by Eisen (1954) who, using the PGR, found no consistent generalization effects to any kind of verbal stimulation along the synonym-homonym-antonym range. Early Russian experimenters had satisfied themselves that meaningful generalization occurs. They based their conclusions on experiments where chocolate bars would be original conditioned stimuli and test stimuli would consist of such items as the printed word "chocolate." Assuming adequate controls, we would have here something similar to Guthrie's fear-of-the-dog kind of mediation.

The interaction of generalization effects from reinforcement and extinction. It will be recalled that Hovland reported a negative deceleration in the curve of generalization for both learning and extinction. This situation leads to some interesting paradoxes when the *method of contrasts* is employed, and this method in one form or another is commonly employed in many experiments involving discrimination training. When a rat is jumping to one stimulus card, for example, a horizontal line, and is reinforced for it, there may be a positive transfer of generalized effect to the negative card, which might be a vertical line. This effect might result in a jump toward the negative card. The failure of reinforcement here might generalize to the positive card and result in hesitation in jumping toward the correct card. In a situation such as Pavlov employed involving the use of circles and ellipses a similar cross-effect of positive and negative stimuli might confound the learning and delay a discrimination. To speak loosely, "generalization" may help acquisition of wrong habits or hinder acquisition of correct habits in discrimination situations. For the child to learn that "daddy is a man" amounts to learning that "every man is daddy." The interplay of generalization of reinforcement and extinction becomes of extreme importance in any fine discriminations and we cannot presume that a discriminated habit has any considerable strength if it has been "cut down" by negative effects of generalized extinction from nonreinforcement of closely related stimuli. To take an imaginary case, let us presume that a subject is supposed to do some particular thing in response to a red light and nothing (or something else) to an orange light. If we reinforce the red light habit 10 times we will, by generalization, be strengthening the tendency to react to the orange light, perhaps to the level of 5 reinforcement points. If, in the meantime, we follow an extinction procedure with the orange light 10 times, we may, again by generalization, weaken the habit strength of the response to the red light by 5 points. The net effect would amount to having a positive habit strength to the red light of 5 points instead of 10 and a negative value of −5 for the orange light instead of a +10 and −10 situation our procedure might be presumed to establish. We will see in Chapter 14 how such generalization effects may become important in "transposition" behavior. For the moment we content ourselves with the observation that due to generalization, every time we learn one right answer we may be learning dozens of wrong ones if the world at large has decreed that only one answer is right, and similarly, every time we are punished or not reinforced for wrong answers, we weaken any tendencies we may have to come through with right answers.

A conceptual neurological scheme to explain generalization. Pavlov (1927) attempted to account for generalization effects by postulating spreading waves of excitation and inhibition in the cortex. While it is true that stimulation effects do appear to spread over the cortex (von Bonin, Garol, and McCulloch, 1942; and McCulloch, 1944) they do not appear to follow Pavlov's neat speculation and conceptual elaborations, and so far no adequate neurological account of generalization phenomena is available. Some interesting speculations have been advanced by Wolpe who has attempted in several papers (1949, 1950, 1952a, b) to provide a plausible neural account of a number of learning phenomena. We can look at his account of generalization briefly and note especially his suggestions for an experimental (behavioral) attack on the problem.

Wolpe takes his cue from Hull who assumed that primary stimulus generalization was due to "the partial physical indentity of the stimulation compounds." If this is the case, then any generalization that occurs is due to the fact that the generalized stimulus is activating some of the same, identical, neural components that originally determined the learned response. Since these will not be likely fully to reproduce the effects of the original stimuli, the response will be of lesser magnitude or lesser complexity. Thus, when Pavlov conditions a leg withdrawal or salivation to a cutaneous stimulus on the thigh, stimulation at some other location not too remote from the original locus will bring out a lesser response because some of the original afferent fibers are stimulated along with new ones specific to the new locus. If a generalized response is given to a tone higher or lower in pitch than the original, it is because some of the fibers on the basilar membrane of the cochlea which were active in the original response are activated by the new tone. Wolpe cites anatomical evidence to support the possibility that anatomical proximity of fibers is adequate for the task. He points out that Humphreys' (1939) findings that a better or greater response is obtained from octave tones than from tones closer physically to the original is easily explained on the assumption that the octave note will excite overtones of the original tone and thus make use of the original conditioning pathways. A diagram of Wolpe's hypothesis may clarify the reasoning.

From Figure 7.2 we can assume that if S_2 is present, n_2 will be active, and to the degree that it is capable of initiating R_1 by itself, it will do so. Wolpe suggests that this will be in terms of some reduction of amplitude. Whether we need make this assumption is debatable until the evidence for reduction of amplitude is of a stronger caliber than now available. In any event, the response when it occurs makes use of a pathway that is identical with that which also participates in the original conditioning. An interesting corollary is suggested by Wolpe and it is hoped that an experimental design can be developed to test this corollary. If Wolpe is correct, then extinction of the generalized response, that is, to S_2, should have some debilitating effect on S_1 as is generally suggested by the evidence (see Spence, 1937, Hovland, 1937) but should have no effect on S_x. This is contrary to Spence's prediction which would leave S_x less affected than S_1. Wolpe implies that Spence would predict that the response to S_x should be actually stronger than to S_1 but Spence does not say this, merely indicating that the degree of impairment of S_x would be less than that of S_1. If S_1 is very strong, even if it is impaired considerably by extinction of S_2 it could still be stronger than the gen-

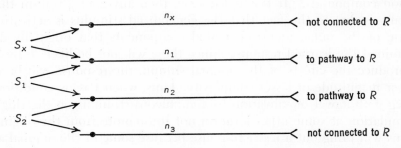

FIG. 7.2. Response R has been conditioned to stimulus S_1 which activates neurons n_1 and n_2. S_2 also activating n_2 also elicits R_1, though less strongly than S_1.

eralized response to S_x. The point, however, is that S_x should not be impaired at all according to Wolpe, since it operates only through a pathway that could not have been active at the time that S_2 was operating. We can await the findings of an experimental attack with interest. For the moment Wolpe's analysis must be considered for what it is, an attempt to offer an account of generalization through a conceptual nervous system, devised to some extent to fit empirical data. Should these data themselves prove in error, that is, should it be found that generalization is actually an all-or-none phenomenon as has been suggested above, the hypothesis or at least some of its features will have to be revised. As it stands, if Wolpe did not assume that the conditioned response to the generalized stimulus was diminished, the hypothesis might have some basic merit.

Learning and adaptation. The learning process is frequently identified with "adaptation" or "adjustment." For some writers (Hull, 1943), the unique function of learning is to permit individual adjustment to the problems of survival in a hostile environment. Hull pictured the learning process and his basic principle of learning by reinforcement as serving individual survival just as Darwin's laws of natural selection are presumed to operate in the survival and evolution of species. For Hull, the psychology of learning is an aspect of natural science with its roots or molecular principles in the general area of biological and physiological studies.

The biological orientation that underlies Hull's thinking may have prompted the inquiries which resulted in the concept of the rg, the habit-family hierarchy, and the emphasis on generalization in Hull's systematic development. Hull found these principles or constructs necessary for the simple reason that he believed that no one can learn enough habits, and learn these rapidly enough, to survive if he must learn every individual and specific response of which he is capable to every stimulus pattern that he is likely to encounter. Stating the case somewhat differently, Hull recognized that we all "know" more than we ever learned by some process of associating a specific S with a specific R. This somewhat paradoxical assertion amounts to a recognition of the failure of Watsonian Behaviorism to give an adequate account of behavior and, particularly, of learning. From Watson's point of view, learning took place as a process of conditioning one response after another to specific stimuli. This "building block" psychology did not prove satisfactory for the simple reason that it just could not be made to work. It could not account for the adjustment process which showed behavior to be far more complicated than a matter of S-R connections which were individually learned in a given organism's lifetime. Beyond the fact that students of behavior resented a theory which tried to account for behavior as a "bundle of conditioned reflexes," [3] it was quite apparent to any observer that organisms frequently react appropriately to stimuli seen for the first time. When a hungry dog is shown a bone on the opposite side of a fence and solves the problem by running around one side of the fence, the Watsonian behaviorist is stumped for an explanation if it can be proved that this dog never saw such a bone behind such a fence before. The child that spells a strange word correctly on the first occasion offers another test case. The inventor who comes up with a "new" idea, as did Watson, cannot be explained without a rather tortuous array of assumptions, speculations, and bald and unsupported allegations concerning probable past conditionings.

The view of Hull, frequently described as "neo-behaviorism" rec-

---

[3] This view is often referred to as the "bundle hypothesis."

ognizes the complexity of behavior and attempts to cope with the difficulties by determining the kinds of principles which could account for phenomena such as mentioned above without trying to tie them to a long line of conditioned reflexes which reaches back to the nursery. Hull tried to solve the problem by recognizing that "past experience" must be interpreted as more than a bundle of conditioned reflexes in the Watson sense if we are ever to account for how someone can "know" more than he has learned. His answer came in terms of showing that any conditioned response amounted to more

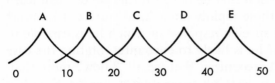

FIG. 7.3. With a practice range from some zero point to a value of 50, the learner needs to practice only at points A, B, C, D, and E. By generalization he will be able to function at the intervening values. (After Wolfle, 1951, p. 1274.)

than a specific connection between a particular S and a particular R as we have been at pains to demonstrate in the preceding discussion of generalization, mediation, and the habit-family hierarchy. In general, all three of these mechanisms or principles provide the means for endowing the organism with extra *potential* behavior without specific practice.

Let us now illustrate the basic significance of the three propositions in the light of their usefulness for accounting for "new" behavior.

Starting with the principle of generalization, and accepting its genuineness for the purpose at hand, we see at once that whatever be the actual conditioning stimulus, the reaction involved can be expected whenever a stimulus within the generalization continuum is present. It is not necessary to establish 88 conditioned responses to provide a CR to a note on the piano. The frequency range of tones involved (35–4000) could probably be covered by half a dozen well-chosen tones (see Fig. 7.3).

Hull illustrates the adaptive significance with an amusing illustration involving a monkey learning to avoid tigers. The monkey needs only one escape experience to learn to avoid the sound, smell, or sight of any tiger or any of a variety of other carnivores even remotely resembling the original threatening beast. To be required to learn to avoid each tiger in person would amount to a rapid liquidation of the monkey population. Similarly, Guthrie's once-bitten, twice-shy child avoids not only the dog that bites but also other canines and perhaps a variety of other domestic beasts. To see an otherwise stalwart lad quailing before a puppy might be discouraging to a proud parent but presumably understandable in view of past, unpleasant experience.

There is a negative aspect to the generalization principle which is of great importance. Much of our adjustment amounts to responding to specific stimuli and not to others, however "similar" or close to the original. When society or circumstance dictates that only a specific S is to be responded to in a particular manner, then any response to any variation of S may be incorrect, improper, maladjusted, or even fatal. Shooting the farmer's prize cow instead of a deer is costly. Shooting a hunting companion is even more distressing. For the monkey to rush to the top of the nearest tree at the sight of an orange and black butterfly is wasteful, and calling the milkman "daddy" may result in a domestic comedy or tragedy, depending upon the principals. The process of socializing a child is beset by difficulties which can be discussed within the framework of generalization and discrimination principles. The child must learn to eat or not to eat, depending upon circumstances. He must be vocal or quiet depending upon other, and for the child, meaningless variations in the situations. By far the greatest obstacle to child training is the conspicuously present stricture: "Do as I tell you, not as I do." Here we have a discrimination of no mean proportions to be acquired. By the time the average child acquires the equipment of habits demanded by a society geared to the survival needs of adults, he has become an adult and is starting the same routines with his own children. The two-edged sword of generalization and discrimination is often wielded carelessly by an all-powerful society, and we are hard put to judge whether it helps more than it hurts although the survival of so many of us suggests the former.

Adaptation and mediation. As in the case of generalization, the construct of the mediating response (and the stimuli which it produces) offers another means for accounting for knowledge we never learned, or even knew we possessed. It is another "something-for-nothing" device in that through the process of mediation, organisms are capable of performing responses that never had to be learned in their own specific right. The right answers may be given to questions never previously heard. Whether the answers are "right" or "wrong" depends not on the answers themselves, of course, but on what rules society has laid down. For Brogden's dog to raise a leg when the light flashes may be considered bright or stupid behavior depending on the point of view of the observer. We presume that for the dog, no values are involved and it merely reacts as it must under the circumstances. We will see later (see Chap. 14) how the mediation postulate is made to carry the burdens of insight, problem solving, and efficiency in transfer situations. For the present our purpose is merely to underscore its something-for-nothing features as significant for the adaptation process which could hardly go on if we had to learn everything "from scratch."

It should be recognized also, if Guthrie's view is correct, that the mediation postulate may also carry the full burden of the findings in "generalization" experiments. If the generalization is actually due to the all-or-none elicitation of a particular mediating response, then it allows for generalized responses to stimuli that cannot possibly be thought of as in a continuum of any kind. A child, for example, can be taught to avoid a radiator by being burned and told about "hot" things which "burn." Later the term "hot" can be used in connection with any dangerous object such as a knife or electric wire and evoke an avoidance reaction. Similarly, words like "good" or "dirty" can be used to control behavior through the typical reactions previously associated with them. Such semantic mediation would account for much of the empathetic communication that goes on in human conversation.

In connection with the role of mediators as "labels" or verbal reactions we can briefly note their operation in any kind of mathematical operation. As soon as we have mastered the multiplication table we are ready to multiply any combination of figures. A simple addition problem of 37 and 44 involves a mediated verbal symbol of "11" and a step later another of "and 1." As we proceed through any such arithmetical operation we continuously provide ourselves with stimuli for the next step. Such stimuli fit the mediation pattern as neatly as any so far discussed and again illustrate the necessary "something-for-nothing" phenomenon.

Again the negative side cannot be ignored. How frequently have we all worked a problem and found the wrong answer and only much later discovered where the error occurred. The difficulty in such discoveries is due to the fact that the error comes from a mediating reaction which frequently does not ever appear in the work sheet. Any erroneous labeling of a stimulus can be of considerable importance and adjustment can be hindered as well as helped by mediators.

A final illustration of a common difficulty and we can leave this point. In recalling a forgotten name we frequently indulge in self-stimulation consisting of mouthing the alphabet to "get a start" on the name. The procedure works often but may just as easily fail completely if we take a liking to a wrong initial letter. In this example we are considering the mediator as a mnemonic device, the crutch of memory systems. Such "conscious" use of the mediation principle is presumably a special case of the more general, presumably automatic, and quite unconscious operation of mediators such as we have been discussing heretofore. We are scarcely aware of the stimuli from movements or even of labels as we normally use them.

Adaptation and the habit-family hierarchy. We return now to the third something-for-nothing device and its role in adaptive adjustment. Because of the common family tie represented by the rg we have the possibility of arousing reactions previously conditioned to stimuli from rg in situations met for the first time. Here the something-for-nothing is perhaps more questionable as the prior learning experience (the association with rg and stimuli from rg) is required, but it is not necessary that the particular response that happens to occur be learned to the *external* stimulus situation that prevails at the time. Once a repertoire of responses has become organized into a hierarchy we can reach a given goal by running, walking, skipping, crawling, or hopping on a pogo stick, if necessary. An object can be picked up with either hand, toes, or teeth, and distant objects by attachment of a magnet to a string or chewing gum to a stick, once the different members of the family become related through rg. Sometimes such behavior is referred to as "response generalization" but the present interpretation seems to go beyond this "naming" or labeling explanation. Hebb (1949 p. 155) treats of the same problem in essentially the same way with some objection to Hull's views which appear to Hebb to involve the final use of a specific response. Actually Hull's own illustrations do not demand that the final response be identical (except in the broad sense that it be a consummatory response) and if this is so, then Hebb and Hull appear to be in strong agreement on this important adjustment mechanism. Each lays considerable stress on early training in the development of potential alternate reactions. We will return to some of these speculations later when we discuss transfer problems.

Chapter

8 *Learning and Performance. The Problem of Measurement*

In previous chapters we have from time to time referred to various features of learned behavior, but in most instances we refrained from getting down to details of measurement. The restraint was deliberate because the various ways in which learning is measured require some explanation and evaluation. Before we can draw conclusions about learning we should know if the data presented actually bear on learning or on something quite different.

Earlier we discussed various definitions of learning and pointed out how different students have indicated that learning is always an inference from performance (see p. 86). In other words, learning itself is never measured directly but amounts to some "construct" derived from measures of behavior. Since all other psychological constructs are also inferred from behavior, and since sometimes the same measures are used as a basis for inferring conclusions about different constructs, the need for caution in interpretation is obvious.

LEARNING AND PERFORMANCE

One distinction that must be drawn immediately is that between learning and *performance* itself. It is always performance that is measured, and sometimes this performance is identified with learning or with lack of learning when it may not represent either. Let us examine the latter instance first.

It is a common experience for parents with more pride than good judgment to demand a public display of their children's achievements in recitations or other artistic or intellectual displays. Frequently a child fails to perform for the visitor and instead is emotional, shy, uncomfortable and so on. The parent then explains that the performance would be regarded as beyond compare if it only could be witnessed. Similarly adults on occasion display "stage fright" or "mike fright" and acquit themselves miserably in performances that are mockeries of their before-the-mirror rehearsals. The audience, measuring the *performance*, draws its own conclusions on the degree of the learning displayed.

The failure to perform what the teacher or trainer *knows* the subject to "know" is common enough with animals as well as with humans, on the stage, in the home, and in the laboratory. A rat that has run through a maze many times without an error fails to do so on some trial. Pavlov (1927) reports his amusement at the failure of his students to demonstrate some feature of conditioning which they had reported to him with great excitement. When the master arrived to see for himself, the dog ignored the conditioned stimuli and sniffed at Pavlov.

The schoolboy, from grammar school to college, leaves in the examination room a performance record which he then announces not to reflect his true knowledge of the subject. There is no point to belaboring the issue. It is readily apparent to everyone that sometimes the performance does not match the learning.

The varieties of inhibition. How do we account for such failure to perform what is known to have been learned? It is obviously difficult to experiment with this phenomenon as one can hardly be certain that a failure will occur and arrange to observe the condition in advance. Writers on stage fright are of little help with their post-facto analyses in terms of fear and anxiety. Learning psychologists and phsyiologists have done little more. The best they have come up with are more or less circular concepts of "inhibition" and "disinhibition." We can glance at these constructs briefly.

The concept of "inhibition" has a respectable history in the physiology of reflex action where it is used to account for such phenomena as reciprocal innervation and coordinated movements involving opposed muscle systems. By using a concept of inhibition it is possible to account for the relaxation of extensor muscles which permits the flexors to operate, and vice versa. The construct is also used to account for various failures to respond to special kinds of stimuli under certain conditions. Stimulation of some nerves is supposed to result in the inhibition of activity in some organs; for example, in emotional states some visceral functions are "inhibited" while others are heightened. Some physiologists (Sherrington, 1925) have posited such mechanisms as the "Cental Inhibitory State" (C.I.S.) and have suggested various chemical mechanisms to account for observed diminution of activity in neural or muscular structures.

Pavlov (1927) took a somewhat different approach to the problem. Noticing that too rapid a rate of stimulation resulted in diminished conditioned reflex activity, he evolved a concept of inhibition which he used as a correlate of excitation and which enabled him to account for various aspects of his behavioral observations. In general Pavlov interpreted the neural effects of stimulation to amount to a dual process. First a wave of excitation was assumed to emanate from the locus of the projection area of a given stimulus. This wave of excitation would recede, and, sometimes, be followed by a similar wave of inhibition. Such a process he called "induction." The inhibition referred to here is assumed to be a basic function or feature of cortical activity. In the process of "extinction" (see Chap. 13) the formerly conditioned stimuli acquire inhibitory characteristics and initiate the inhibitory cerebral processes which prevent the response.

Pavlov distinguishes between "external" inhibition and "internal" inhibition. The latter notion is more or less confined to the process of extinction and will be considered later. The former is assumed whenever some new, exciting, unusual, or otherwise disturbing stimulus occurs. Such external inhibition is invoked by Pavlov to account for failure of some response to occur. It is a purely circular "construct" inasmuch as the occurrence of external inhibition is claimed only when the organism fails to respond and some novel aspect of the stimulus pattern can be blamed.

"Disinhibition" is a parallel concept. It refers to the inhibition of an inhibition or a negation of an inhibition. An animal that is in the waiting stage of a delayed CR may not be able to "inhibit" the response if some disturbing stimulus is introduced. Similarly, if an organism is undergoing extinction (that is, according to Pavlov, developing "internal inhibition"), such an inhibition may be disturbed by a novel stimulus and the CR will be given when we might expect it not to occur. If in a routine conditioning series the animal responds in spite of the intrusion of what might otherwise be regarded as interfering or inhibiting stimuli, then no reference is made to "external inhibition." There is no *a priori* definition of inhibitory stimuli and no way of anchoring the construct. The layman uses a similar line of reasoning, or rationalizing, in accounting for the failure of his child to recite: "He's not used to doing it in public." The more successful efforts of other people's children are attributed to boldness, lack of sensitivity, and so on.

Guthrie (1935) copes with the problem by insisting that one cannot expect the same response in situations that differ from that in which the original training took place; but Guthrie never gets around to specifying the stimuli in an original learning situation and thus easily avoids the problem of describing the important differences. His position is, again, purely *ad hoc* and circular. If no failure occurs in spite of a striking change in the stimulus situation, then, for Guthrie, the important stimuli have not changed. If a tightrope walker attempts a back flip halfway across the Grand Canyon, Guthrie can readily account for either success or failure. An insurance company would want a more specific prediction and a behavior scientist should be at least as rigorous in his standards as an underwriting agency.

The inhibition concept has been applied in many other ways to account for failures in performance when success might well be expected. Two widely used applications have been made under the labels of "proactive inhibition" and "retroactive inhibition." We shall discuss these concepts and evidence relating to their labels when we consider transfer effects (Chap. 14). For the present we will merely consider the labels and the general areas of application. "Proactive inhibition" (P.I.) is alleged to occur when learning fails to take place in what might be the expected manner and it is known that some other kind of learning had taken place in connection with stimuli involved in the new learning. Thus if some stimulus, A, had been previously associated with some response, B, then we might expect an organism to have difficulty in learning some other response, C, to stimulus A. Sometimes it is claimed that difficulty exists even if none is immediately apparent. If the organism learns A-C easily, even better than A-B, then it is held that a practice effect has facilitated the acquisition of A-C and thereby obscured or counteracted the negative, inhibitory effect of prior learning.

"Retroactive inhibition" (R.I.) refers to a failure to remember something like A-B when the learning of some other response like A-C has followed the original learning of A-B. Various explanations have been advanced for such inhibitory effects of both the proactive and retroactive inhibitions, the most popular being in terms of *interference*. The proactive and retroactive labels suggest to some critics (McGeogh and Irion, 1952) the action of mystical forces working forward or backward in time, and these labels are losing favor. The term "inhibition" itself is actually more descriptive than informative and is also losing favor. McGeogh (1942), for example, prefers to translate "retroactive inhibition" as "reproductive interference" which more clearly suggests that a failure in recall is attributable to interfering responses.

Pavlov (1927) and Hull (1943) made considerable use of inhibitory constructs in accounting not only for failures to respond, but also extended the use of such constructs to explain more positive and regular features of behavior. Thus Pavlov applied the inhibition concept to the explanation of "delayed" and "trace" CRs, and to sleep. Hull, following White (1936) and Lepley (1932), adopted the Pavlovian "inhibition of delay" to account for the manner in which nonsense syllables are learned in a serial list (see p. 189). Hovland (1936) noting, as did Pavlov, that frequent conditioning trials led sometimes (especially under conditions of rapid repetition) to a diminution of CRs proposed a construct of "inhibition of reinforcement" to account not only for the original finding but also that of reminiscence.[1]

Hull (1943) added still another kind of inhibition, I_R or reactive inhibition. This was postulated to be a negative drive state, analogous, if not similar, to fatigue which comes about as a consequence of activity. We can illustrate the effect of reactive inhibition on performance (and inferentially on learning) with a study by Ammons (1947). In this study, subjects worked continuously for 8 minutes at the task of keeping a stylus on a rotary target. The scores (amount of time on target) improved slowly over the 8 minutes but showed less and less improvement per minute toward the end of the period. After a rest period of 5 to 20 minutes, the scores for the subjects were superior to their scores at the end of the previous training. Apparently "fatigue" or "reactive inhibition" or some other consequence of massed trials had prevented the real degree of acquisition to be displayed. The in-

---

[1] Reminiscence refers to the finding that sometimes recall for learned material improves (especially with children) if a delay is interposed between the last learning trial and the recall test. Immediate testing sometimes gives poorer results (see p. 310).

terpreter of "performance" at the end of the first 8 minutes would have to admit that only a little learning had occurred. Actually the subjects had learned two or three times as much as they could demonstrate.

Reactive inhibition, in Hull's system, serves as the basis for the development of conditioned inhibition $(_sI_R)$ which, as for Pavlov, is a kind of "internal" inhibition used to account for extinction. We shall encounter these various inhibitions again as the more detailed principles of learning are examined. For the present they are mentioned only as means or attempts to account for failure of response. Our present problem is to deal with the observations made concerning positive instances of response, and to this we now return.

THE MEASUREMENT OF LEARNING

It has been stated earlier that whatever else we can say about it, learning is an inference from performance. If learning is an inference, how can we go about the business of measuring it? Measurement can only be applied to some dimensions of space and time and movement, to indicants (Stevens, 1951), not to inferences. This difficulty has resulted in considerable confusion in learning theory and our present task is to attempt to clear away some of this confusion and to see if some of the attempts to measure learning can throw any light on the process itself.

The kinds of events studied by learning psychologists have set up certain limitations on what can be measured, and in some instances the features of the events that have been measured bear little or no relationship to the process itself. Measurement for measurement's sake is of dubious merit, yet frequently the objective psychologist has recorded and recorded masses of data which only add to the confusion rather than assist the understanding of the problem. On the other hand, the process of measurement has itself sometimes revealed peculiarities in the data that suggested important principles which might otherwise be overlooked. Among such data-suggested principles are the goal-gradient hypothesis, the notion of backward elimination of blinds in maze learning, and the r_g account of goalward-pointing errors. We shall meet these and other such data-evolved concepts as we consider the several types of data that have been collected in learning researches.

What can be measured in a learning situation? Reflect over the various experimental studies that have been mentioned so far and you will acquire a promising list: We have Pavlov starting the story with a record of the number of drops of saliva as a presumed correlate of learning; with Ebbinghaus (1885) and his legion of followers, such factors as number of trials to learn a list of syllables, or the number of syllables retained after an interval, or the number of trials required to relearn a previously learned list. We have the extent of an eyelid blink, amplitude of the PGR, or the degrees of change of temperature. We have reaction time or latency, we have the number of times a rat presses a bar in a Skinner box in a given time (rate); we have the number of trials, the time per trial, and the errors per trial for various subjects to learn various multiple unit mazes; we have the percentage of conditioned responses or discriminated jumps from a Lashley stand; we have time to get out of a box or into a box, and a variety of other kinds of speed or time measures. Let us reduce these to a list phrased in more general terminology (Table 1).

A little consideration of Table 1 might suggest some interesting comparisons and conclusions. What is actually being measured by

Table 1

Measures	Examples *
Amount of response	Salivation, eyelid blink, PGR
Latency of response	Eyelid blink, escape from puzzle box, nonsense syllables
Rate, speed	Bar press, speed of running
Frequency	
a. percent of response or percent correct	Avoidance, T-maze, eyelid blink, nonsense syllables
b. cumulative	Skinner box
Time, per trial or total time	Mazes, nonsense syllables
Direction	Approach and avoidance behavior
Number of trials	Mazes, word lists
Number of errors: total and per trial	Mazes, verbal material
Extinction:	
Rate and total number or amt.	Skinner box, salivation
Location of error	Serial lists, memory material, mazes
Kind of error or kind of response	Meaningful material, nonsense syllables, semantic conditioning

* The examples in the table are only samples and many measures are frequently employed in one experiment. Listing an example is not meant to be exclusive. A great many examples of widely different kinds of behavior could be included for each measure.

these dimensions or parameters? We have just recalled the fact that learning is an inference from performance. It is extremely dangerous, however, to forget this inferential nature of learning and start *equating* learning *and or with* performance. Obviously, all performance is not learning, and, as we have previously pointed out (p. 163), under some conditions or circumstances we may get zero performance as far as the learned behavior which we wish to demonstrate is concerned, when we know very well that the learning has, in fact, occurred. Because all these measures have been used at one time or another as measures of learning, we can assume that those who use them regard them as essentially equivalent to, or at least as correlates of, the same phenomenon. It will be interesting to look at the various correlations that have been observed or computed between the several measures. If they all measure learning, the correlations should be high. If they do not correlate strongly, then presumably they do not all measure the same thing. Hull (1943), for example, would cite different studies, employing different measures like latency, amplitude, and frequency, or resistance to extinction, as all reflecting measures of learning. To what extent is such a practice justified?

Measurement and kind of performance. It would be awkward to try to discuss all the separate measures at once or even in turn, since some measures are highly specific to the material or responses being learned. Some measures apply particularly to Pavlovian CRs, others to varieties of instrumental training, still others to what has come to be called "serial learning." Serial learning usually includes the areas of nonsense syllable and other kinds of verbal behavior as well as the entire field of maze learning and acquisition of skills.[2]

Assuming that an order from simple to complex would follow the pattern indicated above, we can start with measures of Pavlovian or classical conditioning. Some kinds of measures are employed in several kinds of learning situations. Where this is the case, the discussion will be extended to the several types to avoid repetition.

Measurement in classical conditioning. The primary measures employed in classical conditioning are amount (or amplitude), latency, percentage frequency, and resistance to extinction. We can examine each of these in turn and see where they lead us.

---

[2] It has already been suggested (Chap. 4) that there are not genuinely different kinds of learning but rather varieties of experimental procedure, and, in theory, the measurements might apply to all experimental studies. Some problems might arise in the relative ease of getting at one kind of measure or another in the varieties of experimental situations that have been studied.

1. AMOUNT OR AMPLITUDE. As a measure of learning what should we expect to observe in connection with learning? Should we expect that as learning develops and improves (grows stronger) that the response should also grow in extent? For some kinds of responses, for example, salivation and the eyelid blink, this appears to be true at first, and then the response settles down to a more or less regular amount. At this point no further improvement can be observed from amount of response alone. In other response areas, like the avoidance learning situation, the original responses are quite violent and extensive and decrease in whatever we might record as an amount equivalent as learning proceeds. This is a real difficulty with amount of response as a measure of learning. In most learning situations the amount of response decreases with practice until a minimal effort is exerted. In the Skinner box, for example, the rats get more and more casual about the bar-pressing until they barely touch the bar and frequently merely make "passes" in its general direction as they become accomplished performers.

At one time Hull (1943) regarded amount of response as an indication of learning strength and cited an experiment by Gantt (1936) in which a dog was trained to salivate with three different conditioned stimuli and three separate amounts of food as the unconditioned stimuli. When the dog was fed large amounts he also salivated more copiously. Hull at first interpreted the increase in saliva as indicative of stronger learning. Later (1952) he gave up this notion and no longer related strength of learning to amount of reward. This aspect of his thinking is not the point at issue here. It appears that amount of salivation has nothing to do with learning strength. If the dog salivates differently for different conditioned stimuli, it is likely that the different amounts merely represent different CRs. The dog is responding appropriately to the specific stimuli. A large amount of saliva would certainly be out of order for a small amount of food. The amount of saliva does not then measure strength of learning after the preliminary training is over.

What does amount of response correlate with? Of several studies (Campbell, 1938; Humphreys, 1943) where attempts were made to correlate amount with other variables we find some high correlations with frequency but poor correlations with latency. Frequency and amplitude appear to reflect or measure the same thing. On the other hand, amplitude or amount and latency appear to measure separate phenomena. Until we are satisfied what each of these measures, we cannot decide about amount as a measure of learning.

2. LATENCY. Reaction time or latency is a commonly employed measure in many kinds of learning experiments. In many studies it is the only measure taken, and in some conditioning experiments it is the only measure of conditioning. In the conditioned eyelid reflex, for example, the only test of conditioning commonly made is the occurrence of the response before the UncS occurs. This is so because the usual setup for eyelid conditioning includes the presentation of the UncS. In other words, no tests of conditioning are made by withholding the UncS. If the UncS is not presented, extinction may develop and in this kind of response, with humans, extinction can occur quickly (Miller, 1939). In the course of eyelid conditioning, the CR begins to develop gradually as a more and more rapid response to the UncS until it becomes so rapid that it precedes the UncS.

We have previously had several occasions to emphasize just such decrease in reaction time as a feature of learning. In most learning situations, we use this antedating characteristic as a sign that learning has taken place. In the laboratory a subject is presumed to know a list of nonsense syllables or any particular syllable if he can "anticipate," that is, pronounce the syllables before they appear in the slot of a memory drum. On the street we know the name of a person if we can greet him by name before he or someone else mentions it. The dog "knows" that food is about to be blown into his mouth when he salivates before the food arrives. Behaviorally, this is about all we know about "knowledge." The latency of the response determines whether we decide that learning has taken place. This is not the place, however, to get involved with epistemology; all we wish to note at the moment is that, in learning, time is of the essence.

There are some situations where latency is of less import. In power tests, as opposed to speed tests, a subject is given as much time as he requires. Sometimes answers come slowly, but if they come, knowledge cannot be denied even if it is rated as less effective or efficient than the knowledge represented by rapid answers. Sometimes a certain amount of restraint is required for an appropriate performance. The delayed or trace reflex and any "temporal" conditioning are of this nature. Premature response means that the lesson has not been well learned. In these cases, it is not a question of short or long latency, but of a proper latency. When a delay is involved in the criterion of good conduct or correct learning, we cannot measure the strength of learning by the speed of the reaction, but rather by its slowness or its propriety. The different uses of temporal measures in different learning situations perhaps accounts for the usually poor correlations with other strength measures.

3. PERCENTAGE FREQUENCY. A common measure of the progress of learning is the percentage frequency. We cannot, with all classes of responses, expect a particular response on every occasion of the presentation of a CS. This is especially true of the early trials. We can presume, however, that as learning progresses the responses should occur more and more frequently when successive blocks of trials are compared. In the first 30 or 40 trials in eyelid conditioning, only a few CRs appear. As we compare later blocks of 10 trials, the CR begins to occur more and more often.

Percentage frequency is particularly important when the response could be expected by chance in some proportion. The mere occurrence of the response itself is of no significance until the chance frequency is taken into account. The statistical requirements are rather rigid in this respect and even a long run of "correct" responses may be meaningless if such a run occurs after a very long run of incorrect or chance responses. If the chance proportion is high, then a much longer run is required for convictions about learning having taken place. Hilgard (1951) has presented the criteria for conclusions about learning in chance situations when the chance frequency can be calculated. When an animal is faced with a right-left or black-white choice, for example, there must be at least 10 consecutive successes inside of 112 runs for a claim about learning to be statistically acceptable.

Even when learning is well under way we can expect occasional lapses. In learning nonsense syllables, for example, a subject may anticipate a particular syllable on one or two occasions and then lose it for a while. The question of whether the subject really knows the material becomes a matter of probability. At what point shall we claim mastery? Hull (1943) found the frequent failure to react correctly when the subject was approaching what Hull called the "threshold of learning" to be of sufficient importance to require a special postulate which he called "$_sO_R$" or "behavioral oscillation." With this postulate he could explain, or at least tolerate, a failure of occurrence of an expected response.

The use of a percentage frequency measure raises the larger question of a criterion of learning. When do we know something? Even well-learned performances are often forgotten, lost, or disturbed. The skilled athlete has a bad day or even a month's slump. The virtuoso gives an unsatisfactory (to him) performance of an overlearned composition. Actors muff lines in long-run hits, and college students rarely remember the second verse of "Jack and Jill" or "Mary Had a Little Lamb," to say nothing about last week's or even today's lecture.

How well must something be learned to be accepted as a sure thing? Most students assume that there is some sort of a physiological limit beyond which learning cannot improve. Hull (1943) suggested that learning proceeds by increments, at first large, later smaller and smaller, and presumably continues indefinitely with successive reinforcements. Most laboratory experiments hardly begin to test the limits of learning. An arbitrary criterion is set up and it is concluded that learning has taken place if the subjects give one or two "perfect" performances. Sometimes a more modest criterion is employed, such as 7 out of 10 correct responses, or 4 in a row, or whatever suits the fancy of the experimenter. There is little likelihood of agreement on the strength of learning until more attention is paid to the meaning of "percentage frequency."

4. RESISTANCE TO EXTINCTION. We shall discuss this measure in more detail in Chapter 13. For the present we list it as a technique for appraising the strength of learning. It is usually assumed that a response that resists elimination is stronger than one that drops out quickly. Within limits, there appears to be some virtue to this assumption and much use of it is made experimentally. The trouble with it as a measure of learning, however, is that it can be used only after the learning has taken place and offers no clue to the development or course of learning as it is taking place.

In many experiments extinction is the only measure of concern to the experimenter. The learning is only something to get over and done with so that extinction can be measured. Seward and Levy (1949), for instance, gave uniform training (10 runs down an alley) to groups of rats and then proceeded to extinguish them as the major concern of the experiment. Ellson (1938) similarly trained rats for a fixed number of training trials and then began extinction observations. Gibson (1941) followed the same pattern with college students learning nonsense syllables. Each subject was "exposed" to the learning material five times, and then tested for interference effects from subsequently learned material. This is a common pattern of experimentation. More frequently an attempt is made to "equate" the learning by either selecting subjects who make the same "score" in the fixed number of training trials or by extending training trails until a criterion is met. Thus, Page and Hall (1953) in an avoidance experiment shocked rats on one side of a two-chambered box until they ran into the other side three times in succession within a 2-second time limit. It is frequently assumed that uniform learning trials or meeting a standard criterion means uniform learning. The frequently found variations in extinction after uniform training trials or variability in recall after a fixed number of repetitions leaves much to be desired from the extinction measure. Having the learners "equated" on one task does not guarantee similarity in behavior on the next and is not necessarily an improvement over fixed trials. We shall meet this problem again.

Measurement in instrumental conditioning. Besides the several methods described above in connection with Pavlovian conditioning, psychologists using instrumental training techniques make frequent use of three kinds of time measures which differ from the latency measures already discussed. These measures are total time, speed, and rate. While all can be considered as variations of each other or as modifications of reaction time, the special uses to which each has been put and the special problems arising from each demand separate treatment.

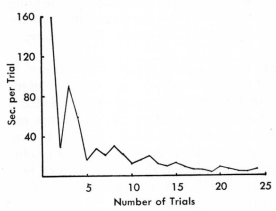

FIG. 8.1. A trial-and-error learning curve (or is it an "insight" curve?). The curve shows the decrease in time per trial for a cat to escape from a problem box. Is the dip at the early part of the curve "sudden"? Why should there be erratic rises if the cat has mastered the problem? Thorndike regarded curves such as this as demonstrating slow, blind, trial-and-error learning. (After Thorndike, 1898.)

1. TOTAL TIME. By "total time" we mean time per trial during the course of learning. This measure was the mainstay of Thorndike in his escape training of cats. The time that was spent by the cat in getting out of the box was the datum that

Thorndike recorded. Ordinarily we can expect the time per trial to drop off as the trials progress. The actual course of the drop will be discussed under the heading of Learning Curves (see p. 193) and, at present, we merely point out that as far as any individual organism is concerned we can be sure of nothing.

For the "average" organism we can estimate, after some experience with a subject population, about how much time will be required in general and about how many trials will be needed. What will happen on any particular trial will be anybody's guess in many kinds of learning. The very first trial for a cat in a puzzle box may take a minute or less while the second takes 20 minutes or more. Sooner or later, however, if the animal completes the training (that is, is not discarded for failure to learn) we can expect that it will perform within a time that the experimenter judges to be satisfactory. We can also be reasonably sure that a large percentage of the later trials will be run off in rela-tively short periods. If not, we might begin to question whether it was a learning experiment in the first place.

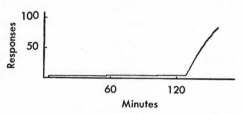

FIG. 8.2. Original conditioning. All responses to the lever were reinforced. The first three rein-forcements were apparently ineffective. The fourth is followed by a rapid increase in rate. (After Skinner, 1938.)

When the experimenter looks over curves plotted from trial data he is free, in terms of subjective judgment, to claim that the curve is "gradual" or shows "sudden drops" or pretty much what he chooses. A sudden drop might mean for one theorist that something he likes to call "insight" has occurred; for another theorist, the same drop might represent a lucky or chance success. The next erratic rise might mean a loss of insight or a more orderly state of affairs for the the-orists involved. Some experimenters looking at curves see no learning when their experimental interest is to have none appear (as in latent learning experiments); others looking at the same data see a gradual learning (see Fig. 8.2; also Fig. 10.1, p. 249).

Much of the time spent by organisms in mazes or puzzle boxes may be occupied with behavior that is apparently of no value so far as learning is concerned. When the cat goes to sleep in a puzzle box, its "learning time" is difficult to calculate or interpret. A rat washing itself in a cul-de-sac of a maze for 10 minutes may be doing a thorough grooming job. It is doubtful that it is considering the experimenter's problem. The writer once kept a record of two kinds of time while training a rat in a maze. One stopwatch kept a record of total time per trial. Another watch ran only when the rat was in motion. Two totally different learning curves resulted, the second being relatively flat and showing no dramatic gains at the end as compared with the beginning of training. It takes the rat almost as long to run the maze correctly as it does to include a chance assemblage of errors at the early stages of training. While total time may be the only measure available for some kinds of learning experiments its interpretation is difficult, especially at the beginning of training, and, to understate the case, it raises more questions than it answers.

One more illustration may be pertinent. In some kinds of experiments dealing with skilled performances, such as typing, code sending or receiving, mirror drawing, block sorting, and so on, the subject can to some degree choose to work rapidly and make a lot of mistakes or go slowly and make fewer errors. Frequently the subject is in position to appraise his own performance and may alternate speed with care. If one trial gives him a high error score he may slow down. If his error score is low, he may rush during the next trial. The plotted results represent little more than this confusion and make such tasks of little value for the theorist, whatever their value for educators who can count on an eventual drop in both errors and time even though they cannot predict from one trial to the next what will actually happen.

2. SPEED. When an experimenter selects a task which is already within the repertoire of the subject and when it is virtually impossible to make an error, then he may be able to note a change in performance only in terms of speed. The usual experiment that meets these conditions employs some kind of runway, enclosed or elevated, and all that is required of the subject is that he get from one end to the other. Rats are the most commonly employed subjects in such situations, but chickens (Grindley, 1929–30) have been similarly employed. At first the animals may move hesitantly out of a starting area or box (and may have to be forced or prodded out) and wander down the alley or runway to the "goal" end. As trials are repeated, the speed of locomotion usually increases and such an increase is regarded as reflecting learning. Learning may well have occurred, but what was learned may be a bit questionable. The running was already a well-established part of the repertoire of the organism. There is only one

place to run, that is, away from the starting box. One could say that the organism learned to run rapidly rather than slowly *in that situation*, but this does not appear to be a correlate of the *speed* measure. Since the speed of running depends to some degree on "drive" (Deese and Carpenter, 1951) and "incentive" (Crespi, 1942) even well-trained animals may move slowly; we are left with an awkward question as to just what a speed measure represents.

In experiments designed to test some other variable or hypothesis, speed may have a significance of a different nature. Hull (1932), for example, believed that responses made close to a goal would be learned better than responses made at some distance. He pictured a "gradient of reinforcement" which could be thought of as an increasing strength of conditioning as one approaches a goal. This gradient of strength could be tested in various ways, one being, presumably, the speed of running at different locations in an alley. Hull tested this "goal gradient hypothesis" by measuring the speed of running at the 5-, 10-, 15-, and 20-foot marks in a 20-foot alley. Later the alley was extended to 40 feet and similar measures of speed were taken throughout the length of the run. Early in the training, the rats did show a gradient in their running speeds, going faster and faster as they neared the goal. The gradient flattened out, however, with continued training. Bugelski and Miller (1938) used a similar measure of speed of running in observing the behavior of rats leaving an end of an alley in which they were shocked. The pattern of running speeds followed a gradient of diminishing speed with greater distance from the shock end. Such an avoidance pattern was called a "negative goal gradient."

In general, the speed measure has been of greater value in testing hypotheses on the influence of other variables than as a measure of acquisition or learning. When it is used as a measure of learning itself, it is subject to all the difficulties discussed above for time per trial. In many experimental setups, speed and time per trial are, or amount to, the same thing.

3. RATE. In his article "Are Theories of Learning Necessary," Skinner (1950) tussles with the question of the usefulness of various performance measures as indicants of learning. He recognizes that learning is an inference from certain kinds of data and wants to be sure that the proper data are used. None of the measures that are routinely used by psychologists employing maze, nonsense material, or conditioned response techniques prove suitable for Skinner and he points

out the limitations of each, much as we have done. For his own purposes Skinner finds one type of measure which he feels does not suffer
from the difficulties of others. This is the measure of *rate*. (See Fig.
8.2.) Since Skinner insists on being empirical and nontheoretical, we
must look at his own actual use of rate in an attempt to evaluate its
usefulness.

Skinner's experiments have been pretty well restricted to the use of
a bar-press response by rats or a target-pecking response by pigeons.
Pigeons apparently are capable of emitting an enormous number of
pecks and it is the distribution of pecks in time that interests Skinner as the real measure of learning. In adopting rate as a measure,
Skinner remarks: Learning is accompanied by a rise in rate, extinction
by a drop in rate. If we are concerned, then, with a measure of learning and skipping the problem of extinction for the present, we are to
watch for the rise in the rate of an emitted response. How effectively
Skinner can use a rate measure, even in his own situation, appears to
be a question. Some of his birds, he reports, peck away as rapidly as
4000 times an hour and keep this up for hours on end. This sounds
like a pretty steady rate and would suggest that no learning takes
place, since there is no rise. Obviously, the learning must already have
taken place and the question then arises, when do we look for the
rise in rate, at what stage of the training? This presumably should be
somewhere at the beginning, but Skinner does not give us any rules.
How much of a rise should be considered as indicative of learning?
Skinner, although eschewing theorizing, is forced into a bit of speculation in trying to define learning, and in his definition he makes the
assumption that learning should occur evenly and smoothly and progressively. Any measure of learning, then, should also follow a
smooth, even, and progressive course. Rate does this, says Skinner,
and none of the other kinds of measures employed do; on the contrary, the other measures are frequently erratic and show reversals,
irregularities, and are without a genuine rationale. Skinner does not
discuss or elaborate on his assumption that learning should be smooth
and regular and does not appear to recognize the possibilities of there
ever being a question about the course of learning, which like true
love, need not run smoothly. If Hull is correct, for example, in his
concepts of habit families, learning could take place long before any
change in rate or change in any other measure could be shown to be
occurring. An $_sH_R$ unit might be in the process of being learned but
be so far below threshold that it would not be discernible behavior-

ally. Even where a response does occur with increasing frequency, there is a further question as to whether or not it should reflect any smooth, steady progress. Hull (1943) makes two points in this connection: First, the effectiveness of reinforcement is incremental and in proportional units. Since this presumes some type of quantal relationship and since we are unable to specify the proportions, the question remains as to whether the course of learning will run along in a series of steps of different size or whether the steplike course is a reflection of lack of refinement of the units of reinforcement. Further, it will be recalled, Hull postulates a process of behavioral oscillation at the threshold of learning which he uses to account for the erratic nature of responses in the process of learning. This oscillation, presumably, precludes any smooth, even, and regular process.

Skinner normally arranges his apparatus to produce his subjects' performance curves automatically; that is, each response is recorded as a slight rise above the previous and a *cumulative* curve is the result which Skinner interprets. Cumulative curves have a way of obscuring deviations and losing individual reactions within the mass. Verplanck (1954) has criticized Skinner's use of such cumulative curves as completely inadequate for the purpose of analyzing learning, or in fact, any other kind of data. The most irregular and diverse data can give the appearance of smoothness and regularity when they represent, in fact, highly irregular and unrelated events. Skinner, furthermore, relies to an unexpectedly great degree on his perception of such "smoothness" as he sees in his curves. Far from picturing the course of learning, Skinner's bar-press or pigeon-peck curves are quite uninterpretable. The accumulation of cumulative curves is hardly a worthy effort when made in the name of positivistic empiricism. If such curves represent the facts of learning, then we must admit that we do not know what the facts are.

Guthrie finds little use for a rate measure since he has always insisted that learning occurs in one trial (see p. 283), and there is little use for a rate measure involving a single occurrence as Skinner himself points out. To the extent that some kinds of learning occur in one trial, Skinner's measure proves useless. Even where learning is prolonged and involved, there is little hope of using rate as a scale in situations that are unlike the restricted and circumscribed push-or-peck situations that Skinner employs. Unless we are to presume that all research on learning done outside the Skinner box has been wasted, and Skinner is prone to make this assumption, the measure of

rate appears largely indefensible as a measure of learning, however well it serves to reflect various changing circumstances in the
Skinner box. Skinner actually speaks but rarely about learning, being
more interested in conditions of reinforcement such as periodic, aperiodic, fixed ratio, and so on (see p. 350); here also he considers the
behavior during extinction sessions much more extensively and intensively than he does the behavior during learning.

It is possible to translate some other types of measure into rate by
a bit of torturous reasoning and so follow along with Skinner's
scheme; but such a procedure is indirect and most probably inappropriate at the present time. For example, one could count the number of responses per trial in a serial learning experiment or the number of errors in a maze per trial and report this as a rate. Whether this
does not raise more problems than it solves is a question.

If rate, speed, or time are not adequate measures of learning, what
have we left? Is there no other criterion of learning, nothing else we
could measure? We have just alluded to correct responses and errors.
Cannot these be used to serve as a commonly accepted measure of
learning? Certainly they are so used by everyone else outside of psychology. They represent a conception of learning as improvement in
performance.

Skinner challenges their use by raising two questions: (1) Improvement in what? (2) Improvement in whose point of view? He
leaves these questions unanswered and implies that they are unanswerable. Actually the situation is not so poor as Skinner makes out.
The concept of improvement is readily translatable into measurement
of correct responses or error reduction. "According to whom" is even
more easily settled. The experimenter (teacher, trainer, and so on) is
the determiner of what is to be learned and when it is learned. He
selects and sets the problem and the criterion of satisfactory performance. A record of correct and incorrect responses with succeeding
trials approximates as closely as anything imaginable what is normally
regarded as learning or the changes resulting from learning. Any light
dismissal of such considerations flaunts the *indicant* of learning which
has been interpreted as such for centuries. While no brief is being introduced for educational practices, certainly there is no substance behind Skinner's questions. To dismiss error scores or frequency (or percentage) of correct responses in time in favor of rate is a specious
argument. The argument against rate has already been presented and
will not be repeated. It is instead proposed that some measure of "cor-

rect" response is more likely to reflect the process of learning than almost any other. In practice, the method of counting or measuring improvement can vary from simply enumerating the presence or absence of a response to a test stimulus (Pavlov's method), to performing various mathematical operations (ratios or percentages of responses to total test presentations), or counting errors. In some situations partially correct or partially incorrect responses can be tabulated. It is also possible to measure potential errors such as Muenzinger (1938) describes in terms of his concept of vicarious trial and error, or VTE, where a subject at a choice point makes a tentative or preliminary "testing" response such as looking in one direction or another without actually committing himself to a complete response.

The advantage of success-or-error scores over other measures is that it offers a closer glimpse of what goes on at various stages of "response." There may be a variety of movements, procedures, or steps in what finally turns out to be counted. For example, a rat might make a pass at a bar in Skinner's box without actually striking it. Skinner would have no record of such a *partial success*, yet an appreciation of bar-pressing behavior certainly is improved if such partial successes are observed and counted.

In any sequential kind of learning (serial responses such as are involved in learning verbal material or mazes) or any complex habit, the location of errors and the sequence of elimination of errors is of great importance. Rate, in Skinner's sense, is useless here. We can now turn to a consideration of learning where serial responses are studied as such even though much of what has already been discussed pertains to serial learning. Unfortunately, the serial characteristics of most responses studied by psychologists have been overlooked to a great extent and our first obligation is to clarify the concept of serial learning.

Measurement in serial learning. From time to time in previous chapters we have alluded to the learning of mazes and lists of nonsense syllables without pausing to consider these learning materials in any detail. It is time to take that pause and look more closely at both these learning materials even before we consider the problems of measurement that they generate.

Tob, del, rec, bac, com, lyt, coh. How long will it take you to learn to repeat these nonsense syllables perfectly? How many times must you repeat the series? Now try this one: "I recommend the delights of tobacco heartily." One trial should suffice. Yet the sentence contains a few more sounds than does the list of syllables. What kind of material seems more normal, natural, or usual for human beings to engage themselves with, not to speak of college students who have frequently been cajoled or coerced into learning lists similar to the one above? We have taken the above example from Hebb (1949, p. 128) who suggests that the meaningful material represented by a normal sentence is readily learned and, in fact, it is the meaning of the material that is learned most readily rather than the material itself. He speaks of the central effects of sensory stimulation as being the components that enter into association rather than the simple sensory events themselves.

If this is so, why have so many psychologists spent so much time in studying serial learning, particularly with nonsense syllables and mazes? Before we can justify exposing the student of learning to the great mass of studies dealing with mazes and nonsense syllables we must be careful to examine the rationale underlying this work and adopt some basis for the selection of studies.

Usually the maze or the nonsense-syllable list is referred to as involving "serial learning." This may well be correct enough but the implication is usually also understood to be that some of the other kinds of learning are nonserial or unserial or belong to some other special class. We have been at some pains to point out in the consideration of both classical and instrumental conditioning that the responses under study were probably always only partially observed in that some of the preceeding stimulus-response elements had been overlooked or ignored and the stimulus-response sequences that followed shared the same fate. In discussing the Pavlovian experiment we noted that salivation was only a part of a total eating sequence and that Pavlov, in isolating it for special study, failed to see it as only a step in a longer, more complex, chain or pattern of behavior. Similarly, when Skinner isolates a scratch on a kymograph for scrutiny, he ignores the total chain of events that brings the successive scratches into being. Even the eyelid blink is a complicated affair of closing, resting, and then opening confounded by facilitative and/or inhibitory features from previous stimulation and activity as well as present "sets" and influences. The point made by Sherrington that the reflex is a convenient abstraction was found to be even more apposite when learning is involved.

It is probably foolhardy to attempt to discuss *nonserial* behavior in a living organism. All we can hope to do is to arrange experiments where we can more specifically examine the several components in a serial situation, or, in other words, try to exaggerate the serial nature of learning by deliberately making it more serial than it otherwise might be. Whether this will help or hinder the accumulation of knowledge is a question. If we could actually isolate the minimal number of components that are necessary and essential for an instance of learning as has been attempted by Shurrager and Shurrager (1946), we might actually make great progress. We can debate the issue later. For the present we accept the fact that many studies have been done in which serial, or rather, more serial, learning has been studied.

To some extent the exaggeration of the serial nature of the learning material is justified as much of our human adjustment, as well as that of animals in a natural environment, is of the one-thing-leads-to-another variety. When someone bakes a pie, a series of steps must be followed; it is not a single or unitary response. Even a simple purchase at a store involves dozens of separate reactions, to say nothing of the process of getting there and returning home. Going about our business is a complicated matter of making the appropriate movements at the appropriate times. The most human feature of human behavior, speech, is a matter of serial response. On the other hand, it is equally obvious that some things are learned piece by piece in isolation, in separate stages, long before the units are combined in any sequence. The baby learning to talk does not practice a series of words in sentence form, however much its babbling is representative of the serial nature of learning. Saying da-da-da-da-da is quite a different matter from saying do-re-mi-fa-sol.

In our analysis of serial learning we must take care not to get lost in a maze of our own verbiage so that we do not lose sight of the basic factors involved. When Ebbinghaus (1885) introduced the experimental procedure of memorizing nonsense syllables in lists he hoped to approximate some of the features of learning in the public schools where much of the learning was done by rote. His interest was in how rote learning could be improved and how factors that impaired rote learning could be reduced or eliminated. His concern was more with memory and forgetting than with the process of learning in a theoretical sense.

SERIAL LEARNING OF NONSENSE SYLLABLES. When the modern experimenter uses a list of nonsense syllables he should appreciate that what he has done is to have multiplied the number of units to be learned at one time and perhaps has opened the door to some variables that operate in a situation where many units are being learned in a fixed order in each learning trial. This is a highly specialized learning situation and it is unlikely that a parallel to it can be found in any normal human activity, except for memorizing the alphabet or the number system in childhood. The child does not even learn the names of the days of the week or the months of the year in serial fashion until long after he has become familiar in one way or another with individual units and separate pairs. The poetry of *Mother Goose* and other nursery classics may have some resemblance to nonsense syllable lists, but even here we cannot draw exact parallels to sequences of sounds of presumed equal difficulty and length such as are commonly employed in situations where the exposure time is controlled and repetitions follow closely for a fairly extended number of trials.

One further point should be noted closely. In learning a list of nonsense syllables, one not only has the duty of learning the order or sequence, one must also learn the syllables themselves. When such syllables are first learned in isolation, that is, when the subject has the opportunity to get acquainted with the materials, he does better than when a "cold" list of syllables is given to him to master in sequence (Hovland and Kurtz, 1952). If this is not done, the gradually increasing familiarity with the syllables introduces certain kinds of reactions which might otherwise not occur. For this, and perhaps other reasons, the subject frequently mentions a syllable at the wrong time. Ebbinghaus refers to such "intrusions" as "remote associations." We are not trying to account for such associations at this time, but rather we are pointing out that in learning a list of ten syllables, for example, a subject has the *possibility* of giving any one of nine different responses whenever a stimulus syllable appears in a memory drum. This is certainly a unique situation compared with any normal human learning assignment. Before a human subject gets involved in a situation where a sequence of ten or even five different responses is to be learned he has already had sufficient experience with the elements and some combinations to alter the relative probabilities of their occurrence. It is not likely that he will face a situation where any response out of a potential dozen or so is equally likely. Experience sets certain limits.

From the above considerations it appears that the task of learning nonsense syllables is a highly special case of learning. When the prin-

ciples of serial learning are discovered they may well be so special as
to preclude their usefulness for the understanding of anything but
the special case from which they are developed, a case that is characterized by such features as: uniform exposure time per unit, equal
time between exposures, immediate repetition of a sequence or a constant interval between trials, unfamiliar material of equal difficulty,
and opportunity for a variety of erroneous reactions. Many of the
findings resulting from the use of nonsense syllables are of great interest and these comments are not meant to be disparaging. Frequently nonsense materials are used to study the influence of variables outside the list itself, and the benefits of such experiments should
not be confused with studies devoted to rote learning *per se*. We shall
try to keep this distinction as we proceed.

SERIAL LEARNING IN THE MAZE. The multiple-unit maze is frequently thought of as paralleling, for rats, the same kind of behavior
that humans demonstrate in nonsense syllable learning. The parallel
is largely imaginary as the essential features of nonsense syllable learning are absent. In the first, and perhaps most important, place, the
maze usually provides for a choice of one out of only two possible
reactions, a left turn or right turn, instead of the dozen or so of a
nonsense list. The rat is obliged to make the same responses from
time to time at different places in the maze and these places are not
distinguishable from one another if the experimenter can help it. The
rat is faced with a 50–50 proposition, repeated as often as there are
choice points. If there are 8 blinds the rat has 1 chance in 128 of
getting through without an error. This is the rat's problem. How
"real" it is to the rat remains an open question.

In further distinction from the nonsense syllable list, the maze does
not prescribe the time per choice or any other time. The rat may
spend 95 percent of the time in one trial at the first choice point and
divide the rest unevenly among the others. Trials are not given in
rapid succession; there is an interruption for feeding, and so on, at
the goal end. There appears to be considerable question as to just
what is going on in the maze, as we have already suggested. (See p.
174 where "total time" is discussed.) When Small (1899–1900) introduced the maze into psychological experimentation in 1899, he
may not have fully realized to what arguments it would lead. Certainly, the maze, like the nonsense syllable list, is a "special case,"
unique in the experience of the learner. For humans there is no parallel except at an amusement park where a maze itself might be in-

volved. Any other kind of locomotion sequence does not involve the same kind of 50–50 choice repetition. Even in sewers there are distinguishing cues relating to the sewer and not to what the worker may have done last.

The maze in its ordinary multiple-unit form is, like the nonsense list, a special case and its use has led to the finding of specialized data, perhaps even "laws" which apply to mazes but may have little general application. It is held, for example, by Hull (1934b) that, in theory, a maze should be learned backward, that is, the goal end first, then the region near the goal, then the middle, and finally the end. Such a theorem is difficult to demonstrate and all sorts of adjustments or explanations must be made to have the data correspond with such a principle. Whether the principle comes from observations of long alleys (the source of the "goal gradient") cannot be stated with certainty. What can be stated with reasonable certainty is that one cannot be certain which blinds will be eliminated first or last by any specific rat in any specific maze, although general sequences can be predicted for groups of subjects.

Other principles which appear to be borne out by observation include such laws as: (1) The short blind alleys, in a maze with alleys of different length, will be eliminated more slowly than the long alleys (Hull, 1932). (2) Blinds located close to the goal will be eliminated more easily than the same alleys if they are located relatively more distant from the goal (Yoshioka, 1929). (3) Alleys that point toward the goal will be eliminated more slowly than alleys that point away from the goal (Spence and Shipley, 1934). The first two of these principles depend upon the fact that it takes longer to arrive at the goal if one wastes time in longer alleys or if a relatively longer delay occurs between a choice point and the goal. The third principle is based on the notion that nongoal-pointing responses will tend to extinguish more easily than goal-pointing responses.

It is possible to increase the number of choices at each choice point and thereby complicate the maze still further. In a sense this makes the maze more comparable to the nonsense syllable list with its greater variety of alternative reactions to each stimulus. When this is done, observations similar to nonsense syllable learning data are obtained. In nonsense syllable learning, for example, it is usually found that the greatest difficulty (most errors) is experienced in learning the syllables just beyond the middle of a list. Hull (1947) found similar difficulty in learning just past the middle in a modified multiple-choice maze where each choice point included four alternatives. There were four such choice points and Hull's rats had the greatest trouble in learning the correct choice at the third segment of the maze. Using a similar box Coyer (1953) found similar results. Again, the third choice point proved the most difficult.

Whether further effort should be expended in trying to make the maze more similar to the nonsense syllable list is debatable. One point is suggested by such efforts as that of Hull: The nonsense syllable list may represent only a series of odd tongue and other vocal apparatus movements and have little to do with what it is normally taken to have some bearing on, namely human speech and verbal learning. It is suggested that a human being might learn a series of otherwise meaningless movements like those in settingup exercises in about the same way that he learns nonsense syllables. If an experiment were to be done on this point, care would have to be taken that the movements selected had no "sense" or logic to them or any previously experienced relationship. It might turn out from such an experiment that nonsense syllable learning has nothing to do with *verbal* behavior but only with *vocal* behavior.

We should not overlook the possible values of using the maze as an instrument, just as the nonsense list can be used, for studying the influence of other variables like deprivation, effort required, frequency of repetitions, amount and quality of reward, and so on. For such purposes the maze might prove useful in that any technique that delays learning at the same time gives the experimenter a chance to observe some of the behavior. We emphasized this point in connection with the Skinner box (see p. 56). On the other hand, the multiple units may so confuse the issues that the wood is not seen for the trees. Tolman seems to have reacted in this way in his long-term preoccupation with the single-unit T-maze. Tolman stated (1938a) that there was difficulty enough in predicting which way a rat would turn when faced with only one choice, and judging by the arguments that abound in this area he can certainly be commended for simplifying the maze into its simplest form, the single T.

Measurement in nonsense syllable learning. We have arrived at the point where we can afford to look more directly at the performance of a subject in learning a series of nonsense syllables. What does the experimenter measure or record? The usual measures are: (a) total number of syllables correct per trial (or the converse—number of errors), (b) number of trials to reach an arbitrary criterion, (c) specific trials in which particular syllables are learned (this results in information pertaining to which syllables, that is, which position in the list, are most difficult to learn), (d) a record, sometimes kept, of which syllables are pronounced on every trial. This procedure allows some attempt at analyzing the data for intrusion, inhibitions, interferences, or "remote" associations. We can consider each of these in turn.

1. TOTAL NUMBER OF CORRECT RESPONSES PER TRIAL. This measure usually shows a rapid initial gain followed by a declining (negative acceleration) rate of acquisition as the trials continue. In learning a long list of syllables, the first few to be learned may be learned on the first or second trials and retained throughout the session while the last few may take many trials to learn. If the criterion is one of two perfect repetitions, for example, the subject may flounder around in the late trials knowing all but one or two syllables, getting the correct response on one trial and failing to respond correctly on the next trial (Hull's behavioral oscillation). In the meantime, the first-learned syllables are being overlearned to a relatively great degree. When the criterion is finally reached, it is obvious that the list is not learned uniformly well and a great deal of confusion of interpretation is inevitable if the list is then treated as a "whole" or unit. The whole process is exaggerated greatly when lists are made longer, as far more than a proportional number of trials is required to learn a list of 15 syllables than a list of 12, and so on (McGeoch, 1942). The number of units per trial is a somewhat erratic measure and when plotted for individuals shows the oscillatory ups and downs although, of course, if the criterion is met, it will slow up as a negatively accelerated curve. Its smoothness can be improved by plotting the data as a cumulative curve but this, as noted previously, merely conceals the drops.

2. THE NUMBER OF TRIALS TO REACH CRITERION. This measure varies greatly with individual subjects and makes for considerable labor when any attempt is made to group the data for purposes of studying other measures such as the first to be discussed above (number of syllables correct per trial). It is necessary to resort to Vincent curves or other artificial techniques to take advantage of the total number of subjects. It should also be noted that individuals vary from list to list as they continue practice (Ward, 1937) and show improvement for as many as 14 and more lists. (See Fig. 8.3.) Such practice effects make comparisons between effects of other variables or conditions that much more difficult.

3. SPECIFIC TRIALS IN WHICH PARTICULAR SYLLABLES ARE LEARNED. This measure gives an indication of which position in the list is most difficult to learn and the relative difficulty of all the positions. The frequently confirmed finding is that the first few syllables are usually learned first, the last few next, and the middle group with greatest difficulty. In specific experiments to determine the relative difficulty of position in a list, Hovland (1938) and Bugelski (1950) found that the syllables just past the middle were most difficult to learn. Hull (1935) had originally assumed that the middle point itself would be the most difficult to learn and tried to explain such difficulty by an assumption of accumulations of "inhibition of delay" which, according to his explanation, would be massed in the middle of a serial list. Bugelski (1950) preferred an explanation in terms of the relative strengths of remote associations or intrusions as more in keeping with the findings (greater difficulty beyond the middle) and as more demonstrable than assumed inhibitory forces. The positive nature of the intrusion evidence favors an *interference* explanation over an unsupported assumption of inhibition.

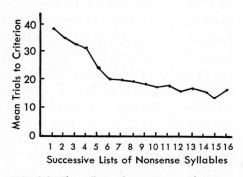

FIG. 8.3. The effect of practice on learning successive lists of nonsense syllables. Notice that improvement continues for as many as 16 trials although most of the gain occurs by the sixth or seventh list. (After Ward, 1937.)

4. OVERT RESPONSES MADE BY SUBJECTS. If a record is kept of each response given by the subjects, there is direct evidence of the kinds of associations that are being formed (and sometimes their origin can be discovered either within the list being learned or in lists previously learned). Normally subjects hesitate to pronounce erroneous syllables and wait for some degree of certainty. If subjects are requested to say something, even if in error, information is obtained which might otherwise never be considered. It is possible to obtain leads from such responses as to what is going on in the subject. Frequently he "manufactures" responses from components of other syllables. If the syllables "mig" and "por" are in a list, the subject may announce "pig" or "mor," suggesting some failure of discrimination. McGeoch (1936) has obtained data which show the relative frequency of vari-

ous degrees of "remoteness" in these erroneous, intrusive associations. Thus, a subject is more likely to respond to the first syllable with the third than with the fourth if he fails to give the correct syllable. Such a response would be considered a "first-degree remote" association. In a long list a subject might respond with the seventh or tenth syllable to the second. These would be fourth and seventh degrees of remoteness. Occasionally the subject repeats a previously exposed syllable in response to the one in the drum. This is considered by McGeoch as a "backward remote" association, although there is some question as to the reality of backward associations actually being formed as such. They could be interpreted as extremely remote forward associations in terms of the next trial, or, if the subject is practicing reciting the list, it is possible that it is a simultaneous association made on a previous trial. Failure to record the subject's individual responses obviously deprives the experimenter of much potential analytical data.

Measurement in the maze. The kinds of data obtained in mazes are similar to those obtained in serial lists. Again we have to take note of the number of trials to reach the criterion; the time per trial, the number of errors per trial, and the location and nature of the errors. There is no need to comment on the number of errors per trial or number of trials to attain an acceptable score as the comments would be similar to those made in connection with nonsense syllables.

SPEED OF RUNNING AND NUMBER OF ERRORS IN MAZE LEARNING. We have already considered speed (see p. 176) in connection with instrumental learning in runways and alleys, but special note should be taken of this measure as used in maze situations. In measuring "speed" we are, of course, measuring "performance." The question, as always, is, what is the relation of the performance to learning? We have already referred to the Deese and Carpenter (1951), and Crespi (1942) studies which show the influence of drive and incentive on runway speeds. In the maze we have a reasonable opportunity to compare speed and errors. If it can be taken for granted that errors are a sign of inadequate learning, and freedom from error is a fair indication that learning has occurred, then a comparison of speed and errors should prove fruitful. By restricting the discussion to rats and other lower organisms we can avoid reference to the awkward problem created by humans in mirror-drawing experiments where they can control the error score by reducing speed or increase speed by ignoring errors.

A study that permits such a comparison was carried out by Coyer (1953). Coyer trained rats in a multiple-unit, multiple-choice maze of the Hull type (see p. 186) and recorded both errors and speed as training went on. Using rats under different conditions of deprivation, Coyer was able to show that the speed of running was a significant function of "drive," but that errors have no relation whatever to either speed or drive. With successive trials the error score gradually decreased, but speed retained a close relationship to deprivation throughout the training. From Coyer's data it appears that speed has little or nothing to do with learning. Under a constant drive condition it might show improvement to the extent that freedom from error permits the animal to get to the goal faster. This, however, would hold only for a constant drive condition and any improvement in speed would thus be an artifact and not a real measure of learning.

THE INFLUENCE OF PAST EXPERIENCE. As with serial lists, it should be noted that successive mazes can be learned more and more easily under some conditions, and there have been several studies of such findings with "maze-wise rats." If a maze is built to require the same kind of turn at each choice point (say, all right turns) then successive turns are learned more easily. We will return to this "influence of past experience" in Chapter 14.

THE LOCATION OF ERRORS IN THE MAZE. The distinctive measures from maze studies are derived from counting the relative frequency of errors at different points in the maze. Reference has already been made to the proposition that the maze should be learned backward. This hypothesis may be derived from Hull's reinforcement theory or from Guthrie's general principle that the last response made in a given situation is the most likely to be retained. Evidence for the hypothesis, however, is far from overwhelming, and failure to verify the hypothesis can be blamed on the variations in maze designs that have been employed. To test the hypothesis adequately, a maze of uniform character (equal number of left and right turns properly distributed) would have to be employed. What "properly distributed" means, however, is a question, as the principle of backward learning may be interfered with if the blinds near the goal are in the same direction as the goal turn itself. This makes for difficulty in elimination of this late blind. We have the further complication mentioned earlier that nongoal-pointing alleys are eliminated earlier than goal-pointing. Such nongoal-pointing blinds may be quickly eliminated even if they are located early in the maze. If some way could be discovered to allocate the proper weights to such factors, the hypothesis of backward learning might be confirmed. So far that has not been done. One approach to a demonstration of the hypothesis consists of simplifying the maze into its lowest terms, that is, the use of a T-maze with a short or long starting runway and a short or long cross member. The writer has constructed such T-mazes, one of which has a runway of 1½ feet and a cross-member of 16 feet. The total distance to the goal is 9½ feet. In another maze, the runway is 8 feet and the cross-member 3 feet. Again the distance is 9½ feet to the goal. Animals trained on the runway with the long cross-member have a difficult time of it while animals with the long starting leg learn easily. The distance from a given choice point to the goal is evidently the important determiner of how well the correct response will be learned. If the distance is short, the turn is quickly learned. Such a demonstration is a simplified version of Yoshioka's finding (1929) referred to previously.

Our discussion of nonsense syllables and mazes has been limited to a consideration of the measurements employed in their use in learning experiments. It has been emphasized that both materials are primarily useful as tools for the study of other variables that are related to learning and that in themselves they represent special cases which most probably involve complex interrelations of principles that are unlikely to find easy applications in the analysis of more usual kinds of learning situations. It has not been at all intended to disparage interest in either of these fascinating learning situations. They can be considered as suitable areas for the development and testing of "miniature systems" such as Hull (1935) has advocated as profitable exercises for the student of psychological theory. Such special areas, however, cannot profit the general student interested primarily in the fundamentals of learning; preoccupation with mazes and lists of syllables may sidetrack the search for more general principles.

Before we leave the subject of measurement we should point out that we are not in position yet to discard any form of measurement. Each of the measures we have considered, including rate, plays a useful role for restricted purposes and may, in some situations, be the only one available. There is no objection to the measuring stick. The only objection is to the interpretation of the measurement. When a rat runs down an alley faster on one trial than on the previous trial, it is very doubtful if the difference can be considered to reflect some proportional increase in learning. We have already shown (Coyer's study, p. 191) that rats can run at varying speeds and make the same number of errors (or even more errors with faster speed) so that all we have is a performance difference which needs explaining rather than an explanation of a performance. Yet, such performance measures are of importance in evaluating the influence of drives and incentives or various conditions of stimulation. Psychologists are interested in the principles governing behavior and not only in an appreciation of learning. Confusion enters the picture when behavior and learning are identified. The basic obligation of the learning psychologist is to limit himself to *learning* and not to spread out into general behavior studies under the impression that he is working in a learning situation. It is of the first importance to resist the tendency to act as if we know what we are doing if in fact we do not. In the discussions to follow we shall try to observe the precaution implied in this section.

LEARNING CURVES

The plotting of learning curves is a popular psychological pastime. Data obtained in alleged learning situations are arranged in such a way that some kind of representation of a trend or change in behavior is revealed. Usually the abscissa of learning curves is described in terms of number of trials or some measure of time. The ordinate usually is represented by scores (latency, amplitude, frequency, errors, and so on). Before we proceed to call any record of change in performance a "learning curve" we should of course examine carefully the measures involved and the conditions under which they were obtained. Besides this general precaution there are a number of other considerations that should be entertained.

1. INDIVIDUAL DIFFERENCES IN LEARNING CURVES. The fact of individual differences in acquisition is so obvious from ordinary observation that one hardly need mention it. Examination of individual performances usually shows erratic and irregular variation. Assuming some zero or chance point to begin with, and requiring some level of performance above that to stand as a criterion of learning, any subject that does learn will necessarily show some rise from 0 to, say,

100, in terms of some criterion, if training is continued long enough and if the subject is not discarded because of failure to learn. The manner in which the rise occurs is the important feature. The rise might occur gradually with less and less improvement between trials (negative acceleration) or with more and more improvement per trial (positive acceleration) or with any intermediate degree of change per trial. On the other hand, the curve might show little or no improvement for some time, followed by a sudden rise to the criterion. The former, slow, gradually rising curves are supposed to be typical of trial-and-error, rote-learning situations, acquisition of skills, and motor learning generally. The latter, the sharply rising curves, are supposed to reflect "insight" or some kind of sudden solution of a problem, the realization of a significance, the perceptual reorganization of a field, and so on.

The difficulty with interpreting any curve of learning that allegedly reflects the learning of a group of subjects is that examination of the curves of individual subjects frequently shows wide variations among the subjects, some showing gradual learning, others sudden spurts, some positive acceleration, others negative, and mostly highly variable performances with numerous rises and falls of an erratic nature with frequent reversals of trends. Regardless of individual performance, combining the data from all subjects generally shows a slowly rising, negatively accelerated trend. We have already referred to Verplank's (1954) criticism of Skinner's cumulative curves (p. 179) for individual subjects. The grouping of subjects turns out to be equally suspect. Hayes (1953) has criticized the usual practice of combining individual data for purposes of plotting learning curves where the data for trial 1 are combined for all subjects, then trial 2, and so on. He has shown that regardless of individual performance, the group curve will appear negatively accelerated where not a single individual subject shows such a trend. Hayes replotted some data from an experiment in which rats learned a discrimination (brightness). By working backward from the criterion trials (actually from just before the criterion was met) Hayes found that the curves so obtained showed a steep, sudden acceleration which would commonly be accepted as an "insight" curve. Another curve, based on a visual discrimination learned by monkeys, showed somewhat more negative acceleration although, it, too, is erratic and irregular. Hayes recommends that learning curves be plotted backward rather than forward in order to show what is going on just before the criterion trials. It may well be that we are frequently deceived by the normal procedure. (See Fig. 8.4.)

Because a theoretical position may stand or fall with the determination of a formula for a curve of learning, it is extremely important that such curves be evaluated with the utmost care and that all features of the learning situation be examined prior to the plotting of the curve and its study. We shall see later (see p. 283) that one of Guthrie's basic "laws" is that learning occurs in one trial. For a given S-R relationship the learning is as complete as it ever can be after one pairing. If one-trial learning is to occur, there can be no learning curve whatsoever. All learning will then be *sudden*. What will the suddenness mean? Guthrie would be the first to object that any insight had been demonstrated. On the other hand, Hull's analysis of learning (1943) incorporates a concept of 'threshold" which suggests that learning may be going on with no possible ways of measurement because the learning is still below the

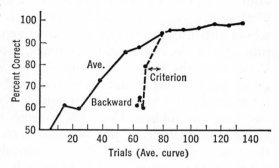

FIG. 8.4. Forward and backward learning curves. The traditional curve is shown as a solid line. Each point represents the average of 40 rats in a visual discrimination learning experiment. In the broken line curve, Hayes replotted the data backward from a point just before the criterion was met. The sudden improvement is obvious. According to Hayes, the traditional curve gives a misleading picture of slow and gradual learning when individual curves and curves plotted backward show an almost all-or-nothing learning picture. (After Hayes, 1953, p. 272.)

reaction threshold. That is, some response may be selected for training which is low in the behavioral repertoire or "hierarchy." If this response can be elicited and reinforced it will eventually rise in the hierarchy until it appears as the primary response to a given situation. The first trials may appear quite fruitless and useless. Forcing a child to say "Thank you," and reinforcing this behavior may not show any results for a long time. The response is still below threshold and any attempt to count its occurrence or measure it will consist of a series of zero scores. If these scores are plotted they will show no rise for some time along the abscissa. Once the response has reached threshold value, we can begin to observe its percentage of occurrence, treating failures now as somehow different from those when the response had no chance of occurrence because it was below threshold. Consider the same response, "Thank you," as being learned by a foreigner who is just beginning the study of English. Can the response be considered as below threshold in the same sense as for a child? We are likely to have a completely different series of points on the learning curve.

2. PRIOR EXPERIENCE IN THE LEARNING SITUATION. The position of Hull illustrates one of the problems we encounter in observing and plotting the course of learning. Where is the zero point? Do high-school girls learning to type start from zero? Is the machine and the problem, or the responses to be made, a completely novel business? What does the usual score (number of words per minute) reflect about the learning of individual students? Is the learning of a code, for example, the Morse code, a completely novel proposition to the boy scout or soldier? Does his previous experience with language, codes in general, pencil pushing, and so on have anything to do with the course of his learning? We have already discussed (Chap. 3) the nature of the learner and his previous background. Obviously background is going to affect scores. In Chapter 10 we shall consider the continuity-noncontinuity controversy which deals with just this problem of the effect of prior experience where the past experience appears to have been of no consequence, at least, on the surface. In the next chapter we shall deal with Harlow's (1949) experiments on "learning sets" in which Harlow showed that monkeys could solve relatively difficult problems in one trial after experience with 300 other similar problems. What does the learning curve for such educated monkeys mean?

3. THE MEASURES EMPLOYED. We have already examined the weakness of the several techniques or measures used in plotting learning. Changes may occur in amplitude or latency which have nothing to do with the progress of learning. Many other variables can affect the performance and each of these must be systematically and individually teased out. The learning curve, whatever measure is plotted on the ordinate, is going to be to some degree an artifact in that the subject is going to start at some level which is arbitrarily considered zero and wind up at some point that the experimenter chooses as the point at which to conclude observations. Consider the common laboratory exercise of mirror-drawing. The subject traces a star or some other pattern, watching his movements in a mirror and a record is kept of

time and errors. The time and errors in the first trial are considered zero bases. On what grounds? Obviously if the subject does not care about errors, he can go around the star as fast as physically possible on the very first trial. Similarly, if time is of no concern, he can, with considerable patience, avoid any measurable errors. With succeeding trials, his desire for speed and his reluctance level, as far as errors are concerned, are going to interact to such a degree that at no single point in the whole series of trials can the experimenter be sure of what is going on. The measures are arbitrary and any attempt to combine them in some weighting system or other is even more arbitrary. The learning curves that result are usually masterpieces of variability, although some regularity can be imposed on the subjects by instructions and usually a downward trend results for both time and errors.

4. ARE WE READY FOR LEARNING CURVES? Although learning psychologists have plotted curves of learning for years, ever since Thorndike concluded that his curves demonstrated the "trial-and-error" nature of learning (incidentally many of his published curves looks as "insightful" as could be desired), there is a real question as to the virtue of this preoccupation. In some writings, even the critical ones such as those of Hayes, the impression is created that there is *a* learning curve, or *the* learning curve. This may prove to be as baseless a postulate as the Fountain of Youth and before we can approve of the continuation of the search, we should consider the essentials of the problem a bit more closely.

The behavior to be learned must certainly be scrutinized. Should we try to plot such responses as salivating to a bell in some fashion? The criticism is that they are learned too quickly to provide enough points for a reliable curve (Hayes, 1953). Should we plot responses of a complex nature and ignore the complexity in favor of counting some simple resultant of the behavior, such as a scratch on waxed paper, without examining how that scratch came into being? Should we plot the simultaneous acquisition of numerous responses such as a maze or list of nonsense syllables involve? Should we ignore the backgrounds with which our subjects come equipped? It appears from all aspects of the situation that we should concentrate our search on the development of some single association in a naïve subject without prior experience of any kind that could conceivably affect the association in question. The observations made of the changes in the behavior of such subjects might represent the fundamental data out of which a substantial theory of learning might develop. Such observations may be extremely difficult to obtain; in fact, there may be no prospect whatever of noting any external or overt changes in the behavior of the learner. The investigation might have to be made on a molecular level and in terms of neural activity in the simplest kinds of organisms. The difficulties are not inviting, but the alternative practice of observing complex organisms learning complex behavior patterns and accumulating mountains of incomprehensible data can hardly be more attractive.

Chapter

9   *Motivation and Learning*

It can be imagined that the first parents in man's history instituted the practice of punishment, and perhaps of reward, in attempts to control the behavior of their children. A misbehaving child (one who irritates the parent) would receive a horny-handed clout and be sent spinning into a more remote recess of the cave with at least some temporary improvement in behavior, from the parents' viewpoint. The practice has not ceased as yet, although parents have become, in some instances, a bit more genteel. The clout has been replaced by more subtle tortures, some of which are even described as being "for the child's own good."

It is of interest that the early Greek philosophers and the later British Associationists did not find it necessary to relate rewards and punishments to the formation of associations. Various other laws like contiguity, similarity, frequency, recency,[1] and the like were described, but rewards and punishments did not play a prominent role in the theory of association. Equally interesting is it to note that Pavlov appeared to ignore the fact that the food he presented to his dogs might have been functioning as a reward, or the possibly equally significant fact that his dogs were hungry.

The reward and punishment problem arose in learning psychology only after the pleasure-pain views began to find favor at the end of the last century in the philosophies of Spencer (1880) and Bain (1870). The problem became a problem only with the work of

---

[1] These are discussed in Chap. 11.

Thorndike (1911) who attempted to objectify the situation and began to talk about satisfiers and annoyers instead of punishments and rewards. Our present interest, however, is not in punishments and rewards but rather in what their use implies. The implication is fairly obvious but perhaps requires some elaboration. It is simply that an organism is supposed to have a reason for doing something. Such a reason, in the present context, might be one of *wanting a reward* or *wanting to avoid punishment* and so going about the business of securing the one or avoiding the other. On the other hand, it might be imagined, and was so imagined by Thorndike and subsequently by many others, that the reward in some way operated to affect the organism in such a way that whatever the organism had been doing just prior to receiving the reward would be learned, or at least that there would be some tendency toward learning the responses that had just taken place. It is obvious, however, that a reward can serve as such only if it is in some way desirable; the same objective event or item may or may not be a reward depending upon whether the organism is interested in it. Even a little boy will look askance at the fourteenth ice-cream cone that is offered.

The introduction of speculations concerning rewards and their relations to learning automatically introduced the problem of the *state of the organism*. The organism had to want, wish for, have a need of, have an urge, a desire, or in later years, a *drive* or *motive* if learning was to take place. At first, as just implied, the necessity for a drive was predicated upon the prospective effectiveness of a reward or punishment. Later, questions were asked about the possibility that learning might be dependent upon motivation in other ways than simply in connection with an appropriate reward so that some psychologists came to view motives and drives as important for learning but not necessarily in connection with rewards. The relationships between rewards and learning will occupy us later. The present problem is that of the significance of motivation for learning.

At about the time Thorndike was beginning his experiments with cats and rewards, other investigators were becoming preoccupied with more general questions about the causes of behavior. The development of the science of biology and evolutionary theory and the consequent general implications of the animal nature of man resulted in numerous attempts at finding biological, rather than psychological, causes for the behavior of men, singly and in groups. Thus, various doctrines of instinct and tropism were developed and applied indiscriminately to man and bee and gosling. It should be noted that the attempts to relate human behavior to biological sources were not confined to the learning problem but to behavior in general and to adaptive behavior in particular. Learning is simply one of the ways in which it is possible for some organism to adapt to its environment. The speculations of philosophers, clinicians, and physiologists resulted in a great variety of proposals designed to account for behavior. We had the *élan vital*, the libido, the instinct of self-preservation, the reflex, the prepotent reflex, and so on. Psychologists were, in fact, a little slow in attaching themselves to the biological developments, perhaps because of a cultural lag or perhaps because of persistent resistance to surrendering themselves and their institutions to the inevitable and mechanical operation of forces that accounted for the behavior of poets and peasants alike with no qualitative distinctions.

The doctrine of *drives* was popularized by Dashiell (1927) in his *Fundamentals of Objective Psychology* which made the first attempts to trace the motivations of the engineer and the doctor back to stomach contractions and other "tissue conditions." Prior to his efforts, Watson had set the stage with his reflexes and their modification by conditioning, but the *drive* concept had to wait upon the demonstrations of stomach contractions and the new developments in the study of hormones as well as the experimental observations of behavior following the removal of glands or the administration of glandular extracts. The result of Dashiell's analysis started a trend which has been piously reiterated in a long succession of elementary tests in which the author starts his analysis of behavior by listing a series of drives (hunger, thirst, sex, fatigue, elimination, and whatever else seems important) as the basic "tissue conditions." From these, through learning, motives develop—motives for prestige, money, social approval, war, peace, and so on. The exact manner in which motives develop from drives has never been specified with satisfactory precision, but that is usually passed over as a detail, and the next step is to turn the motives to a practical use and make them operative in accounting for learning, perception, personality disorders and their cures, and for almost every other subject in the text. The pattern initiated by Dashiell's text is still followed. Hilgard's popular text (1953) repeats the routine with only minor changes. Hilgard talks about "incentives" as significant components of the drive→behavior sequence, but

he loses the student someplace between the hungry rat and the be-
jeweled dowager who goes to the opera because of some "social"
motive.

The attempts to account for the complex motivations of adults
have not met with much success. The logical leap from a baby's
stomach cramps to the behavior of a banker is quite a stunt. The
difficulty comes from trying to make complicated problems simple
when they are not in fact simple. The problem of motivation involves many considerations and can only be appreciated if each feature is attended to individually and if a careful guard is kept over the
various facets of motivation to keep them quite apart. In the following discussion we shall try to draw some distinctions which appear to
be necessary to at least separate the confusing lines of thought about
the problem.

BEHAVIOR AND STIMULI

The S→R formula. It is a basic assumption of present-day American psychologists that behavior can occur only if some form of stimulation is present. This is usually interpreted to mean that some kind
of energy change impinges on the organism either from the outside
as in the form of light or sound waves, pressures, temperature variations, and so on, or from inside the organism in the form of organic
changes which are presumed to initiate afferent neural impulses from
sense organs in the linings of various organs like the stomach, bladder,
intestines, and the like. The contractions of muscles and tendons and
the movements of joints also initiate proprioceptive stimuli. We have
already referred to these in connection with Guthrie's emphasis on
movement-produced stimuli.

There are several points to be made in connection with this assumption before we can proceed.

The assumption as stated above is not quite free from additional
and sometimes blithely ignored assumptions. In fact, the assumption
of the S→R formula rests on numerous other assumptions relative
to the nature and function of both stimuli and responses. We shall
try to examine these assumptions in the following sections. We can
start with the usual treatment of stimuli in psychological texts, where
the stimulus (which can be anything from a bell or light to the view
of a cathedral or a circus parade) is regarded as something which

evokes a reaction from the stimulated organism. Yet we know quite well that stimuli do not evoke behavior directly, although in the case of some "reflex" responses they appear to elicit the behavior rapidly and, for the most part, effectively. It should be understood, as previously noted, that external (or any other kinds of stimuli) must initiate afferent impulses in the central nervous system and must then be transferred to the proper motor channels before motor reactions become possible. On this ground, then, all stimuli are alike whether they are external or internal in origin. An afferent impulse, however, may or may not have ready access to some specific motor channel. In the commonly employed reflexes typical of the laboratory or the medical examiner's office only such stimuli are applied as are likely to be followed by certain specific responses; these reflexes might be thought of as "potent" or even "prepotent." Other stimuli, however, and this might be more pertinent to the organic variety, may not have readily available any specific motor pathway, particularly in the young organism. Such impulses could be expected to initiate (before much training) relatively vague, unorganized, and diffuse responses even as do many external stimuli in the neonate (Pratt, Nelson, and Sun, 1930). Since it is unlikely that organic impulses are merely dissipated without consequence, we can assume that they lead to behavior of a general, unorientated variety which might be called "restlessness." Such restlessness, however, is a complicated set of responses and as such not the *cause* of anything, except perhaps more restlessness. We must keep this point in mind later when the function of motives is being considered.

Responses as sources of stimulation. The point just made should be elaborated in connection with any stimulation that arises from any alleged "state" or "drive condition" or from *movements*. Movements are responses and must first be made before they can lead to stimuli which participate in the development of additional responses. In the same sense, a full bladder is a condition that must first be brought about by a series of prior events in the digestive tract. In other words, tissue conditions, be they stomach contractions or discharges of secretions of glands, are results or consequences of prior conditions or "stimuli" and might also be thought of as "responses." Such responses must themselves be initiated or "caused" before they produce their consequent stimuli. How specifically these stimuli initiate motor patterns is a question for which no reliable answer is available. It is quite likely, however, that no sex hormone ever initiated a direct sexual response and that stomach pangs never initiated eating behavior, to say nothing of going to work to earn the daily bread. Both eating and sex behavior require other and highly specific stimuli. Hunger pangs might make a baby cry but they might also prevent him from eating.

Spontaneous neural action. In most psychological discussions emphasis on stimulation is so strong that other sources of action are overlooked. It is only recently that some psychologists have been willing to suggest or admit that some kinds of behavior patterns, and these might represent anything from a muscular twitch to major convulsion, might be due to the characteristics of the nervous system itself. Thus, Hebb (1949 p. 8) argues that neurones will "fire" spontaneously, if they are not otherwise discharged from time to time. There is actually no reason why any action of the body or its components might not occur at one time or another under suitable, but at present, unspecifiable, conditions. Prior to the knowledge about spontaneous firing of neurones it was psychological heresy to suggest that someone might be responding to unaccountable impulses or that he might just get some "idea" without a good and sufficient series of stimulus events, which adequate analysis or introspection might reveal. From the present point of view, it appears plausible that some kinds of reactions—flight of fancy, imagination (imagery), even the response patterns of some complexity, might be quite spontaneous and free from any identifiable specific stimulus agency, external or internal.[2] It should be recognized, of course, that the spontaneity does not remove the behavior from the realm of scientific study. The behavior is still "caused" just as is the neural discharge, but the predictability that the psychologist might desire is somewhat interfered with, and the basic mechanisms are still far from appreciated. If we so desire, we can speak of "neural stimulation" to keep the S→R formula intact. This, however, should be done with caution and the distinction between various kinds of antecedent conditions (external, proprioceptive, and organic stimuli, spontaneous neural discharge, and so on) should be preserved. The confusion we started out to clear up cannot be eliminated if we lose sight of the various classes of stimuli so far mentioned. Others are yet to come.

Behavior as a function of conditioned stimuli. We have just examined the traditional S→R formula and found that it needed some

[2] See especially the complicated patterns of "imaginative" behavior that Penfield and Rasmussen (1950) report as following a single stimulation of the cortex.

elaboration if it is to prove meaningful. On the S side of the formula it is necessary to indicate more specifically than is the usual practice the nature of the afferent discharges in terms of their sources. We have also pointed out that either afferent, central, or efferent cells may spontaneously discharge and eventuate in some behavior pattern of an unpredictable nature. If such spontaneous cell action is included in the general category of stimulation then we can retain the formula and proceed to additional considerations. All of the sources of stimulation just discussed, that is, external, organic, and proprioceptive stimuli, can serve as more or less direct innervation sources for specific reactions (although in the case of many varieties of each category the specific reactions may be components of a vague general and unorganized pattern). Some of the responses will be more or less "built into" the organism in the form of reflex connections, and through maturation will be available for relatively rapid incorporation into organized patterns of reaction. Thus proprioceptive stimuli from moving one leg or arm may be available for cooperating in the activation of the other leg or arm as in walking, crawling, or other postural adjustments. As the organism matures such proprioceptive stimuli may become the only active stimuli for continuing various sequences. Once the organism is walking along, stimuli from the muscles and joints of one leg may lead to the necessary innervation of the muscles of the other and the action becomes automatic. Whether the proprioceptive stimuli in such cases should be considered *conditioned* stimuli may be arguable, but they serve to illustrate the manner in which such stimuli might serve as substitutes for original unconditioned stimuli.

In the same way, the originally undifferentiated organic stimuli which lead at first to no specifiable response can come to be conditioned to particular differentiated responses, and the organism may engage in any of a variety of responses which were made to more direct forms of afferent stimulation in the presence of such organic stimuli. Thus, the organism may engage in food-seeking behavior when hungry, look for water when thirsty (Hull, 1933b; Leeper, 1935), reach for a medicine bottle when suffering a variety of internal distress, and so on. The manner in which such sophisticated behavior develops will be examined shortly, but for the present our only concern is to indicate the possibility of the motivational features of internal stimulation through conditioning.

Under the general classification of conditioned stimuli we have already noted the possibility of any kind of external stimulus (and now we have included internal energy changes) becoming a substitute or associated stimulus for some response for which it has no innate or maturational connection. It is necessary at this point to add one more elaboration of the role of conditioned stimuli. They can come to serve as the base for the development of other stimuli as conditioners. The experiment of Frolov (see p. 11) will be recalled in this connection. The metronome Frolov used as a CS for salivation was later presented as an "unconditioned" stimulus in the presence of the black card stimulus which then acquired the capacity to elicit salivation even though never associated with food directly. Such secondary conditioned stimuli are sometimes referred to as secondary motivators. Labeling them as motivators does not clarify their role in any meaningful fashion and the practice might well be discouraged in favor of the original Pavlovian practice of treating them as secondary conditioned stimuli. This might serve to specify the procedural origin of the behavior without confusing the issue. The procedure by which a secondary conditioned stimulus becomes functional is presumably identical with the procedure in which the original conditioned stimulus does so and no point is served by introducing mystery within a mystery.

Deese (1952, p. 95), for example, in discussing the role of the poker chips in the chimpomat experiments and the function of the "click" in the Skinner box experiments (see p. 96) states that the rat continues to press the bar *for the click.* [3] If he means, and apparently he does, that the rat presses the bar in order to hear the click, that it in some way serves as a source of satisfaction or pleasure, or a secondary reward, he is obviously jumping ahead of the data and certainly beyond any necessity. We have already pointed out the role of the click in the Skinner box experiment (p. 91) as that of an added stimulus in the pattern of stimuli associated with different phases of the bar-pressing response. The click stimulates, as part of the total pattern, the behavior of approaching the food tray. The stimuli from the food-tray situation, in turn, stimulate bar-pressing activity, and so on in a circle. In the same manner, the poker chip stimulates behavior of insertion of such chips in the slot machine. The chip does serve to activate other behavior patterns as well, but the function of the chip in other situations is far from clear at present. To attach new

---

[3] My italics.

and special varieties of significance to such stimuli in the form of "rewards" or other pleasure-connotating concepts takes the matter out of the realm of scientific discourse since "reward" or other pleasure terminology cannot be used to explain behavior in any objective framework of measurement. It is rather the reward that needs explanation and reduction to physical terminology. The matter is obviously not a simple one and we will return to it shortly in discussing goal responses (see p. 215).

DRIVES

Drives as intense stimulation. In discussing intensity of conditioned stimuli (see p. 127) the point was made that intensity of stimulation on the side of either conditioned or unconditioned stimuli did not appear to bear any systematic functional relationship to conditionability. Miller and Dollard (1941) found it convenient to discuss the nature of drives in terms of intensity of stimulation. Thus, for them, any form of intense stimulation might function in the same way as a drive when the drive is first conceived as some unpleasant internal state or condition that demands satisfaction, or in more modern language, "reduction." The incorporation of any form of intense light, loud noise, strong odor, and so on into the category of drives has the obvious advantage of increasing the foundations on which behavior is elaborated. The puny results of a psychology that deals only with sex, hunger, and thirst are thus aided by the extension of original sources of action. Any strong stimulus is a drive for Miller and Dollard. As Wolpe (1950) later pointed out, this statement can be reversed to some degree with the general proposition that many drives are nothing but strong stimulation. He excludes some drives related to hormone increases which may change behavior by lowering resistance in certain synaptic connections without apparent increases in afferent stimulation. Since the concept of stimulation is already established and since strength of such stimulation is an obvious parameter along which to conduct investigations, it appears reasonable, and Wolpe so judges, to dispense with the category of "drives," replacing it with the general category of strong stimulation. This proposition has some merit but also has some deficiencies. The strength of a stimulus is a relative matter, and in quiet situations a dropped pin is traditionally noticeable. The strength of stimulation would have to be determined in the light of the total background as well as, per-haps, the constitutional factors that might be operative in a given situation. Thus, what is strong stimulation for the rested healthy in-dividual might be of modest potential for the weak, tired, and sick.

Wolpe further points out that the strength of stimulation, es-pecially of drive stimulation, is usually measured by the strength and extent of effector responses. This is an obviously indirect form of ap-praisal and is an unnecessary limitation on the possibilities of more exact measurement of the stimuli themselves as well as their central consequences.

In Wolpe's interpretation the term "drive" is usefully employed to describe an excitation in the central nervous system that intervenes between what he calls "need conditions" and effector responses. Such need conditions (typical organic drives), however, he describes as having the common characteristic of being antecedents of neuro-effector responses. These antecedents (states of the organism, for example, dryness of the mouth) generate stimulation of sense organs of various involved parts of the body such as those of the throat and mouth cavity in thirst, which, in turn, lead to the central neural ex-citation. This central neural excitation is "drive." Diagramatically we could represent this situation thus:

Tissue condition, e.g., hunger or various "needs"	stimulation of sense organ activity	central neural excitation (specific for each tissue condition)	response behavior related to needs—possibly a specific response but probably a general restlessness.

The description presented of the course of events eventuating in be-havior would not differ from that which would be offered if the tissue condition happened to be stimulation of the retina by light or the cochlea by sound waves. For this reason, Wolpe concludes that "Every sensory stimulation, therefore, has the essential characteristic of a need." This conclusion fits the position adopted by Miller and Dollard and has considerable merit in clearing the air of confusion surrounding motivation concepts. It has, however, a major limitation which we are now ready to examine.

Wolpe's analysis of drive as a "central excitation" is carried for-ward by Hebb (1955) in a paper cited previously (see p. 38). Hebb points out that sensory events (which we take to be afferent neural reactions to stimuli) have two functions: (a) a "cue function, guiding behavior" and (b) an "arousal" function. It is the latter function which interests Hebb and which he identifies as a "general drive state." This "drive" which amounts to activity in the "nonspecific or diffuse projection system of the brain stem" is conceived of as an energizer and controller of the results of stimulation. Activity in the diffuse projection system determines whether sensory impulses will reach other parts of the cortex. Hebb admits that intimate physiological information about the operation of the "arousal" system is still lacking, but, speaking in terms of a "conceptual nervous system" he pictures the cortical synaptic function as "facilitated by the diffuse bombardment of the arousal system." An important caution is raised by Hebb in his conjecture that too great an activity in the arousal system as in extreme emotion, great hunger, and so on, results in an upset of "delicate adjustments involved in cue functions" and a consequent disorganization in behavior. On the other hand, too low a level of "arousal system" activity results in loss of stimulus-response relationships because of failure of sensory impulses to get to the proper cortical areas.

The above analysis leads directly to the conception of an "optimal" degree of arousal system activity for behavior to occur. The concept of an optimal level of brain activity, in turn, leads to the notion that such an optimal activity represents the brain's normal function. Hebb subscribes to this notion and uses it to account for the fact that organisms will *seek* stimulation when otherwise unoccupied, that they will seek a moderate degree of excitement, that they will avoid inactivity and find quiet, rest, and isolation impossible to endure for any great length of time (Bexton, Heron, and Scott, 1954).

In a challenging paper Leuba (1955) comes to similar conclusions about the concept of optimal stimulation. He, too, pictures the organism as more or less constantly (when awake) striving to attain an optimal level of stimulation. If stimulation is extreme, the organism engages in activity which may reduce this high level. Contrariwise, in conditions of quiet, excitement and additional stimulation will be sought.

The importance of the views of Hebb and Leuba is that they represent a reversal of the traditional orientation which pictures the organism as pretty much of a vegetative automaton, sleeping or resting until aroused. According to this older view, the objective of life is sleep or rest and inactivity. The new approach is an attempt to account for the obvious activity of organisms where no "good reason" in the form of external stimulation or internal "tissue condition" is apparent.

Coming back to Hebb, we can now adjust the formula offered by Wolpe and Miller and Dollard where motivation is equated with stimulation, weak or strong, by adding the arousal or optimal level conception to the original formulation. It will be recalled that Hebb considered stimuli to have "cue" functions as well as the arousal function we have been discussing. The cue function is not detailed by Hebb and we are left with the notion of a sensory impulse evoking an appropriate learned response if it has the blessing of the arousal system. We may be able to adorn the framework Hebb leaves by considering another approach to the problem of motivation. Our language will be less physiological or rather more psychological now (as we have not really been talking physiology at all) as we turn to the concept of "set."

Drives as "sets." In an earlier publication (Bugelski, 1951) the writer took the position that as far as laboratory experimentation is concerned, the concept of motivation can be most usefully thought of in terms of "sets," particularly in connection with human subjects, as "instructional sets." Since much of the present problem deals with laboratory investigation it may profit us some to consider the relationship of the drive construct to the hypothesis of set. In considering Wolpe's suggestions above it was noted that he regards sensory stimulation to be of the same class of events as are drives but that reverse is not necessarily true; that is, all drives are not sensory stimuli. He illustrated this with reference to glandular changes which are not known to involve increases in afferent impulses.[4] Thus at least some kinds of drives, and perhaps all, may have another function besides that of providing stimuli. This function, as in Wolpe's illustration, may be that of "lowering" the resistance of certain nervous pathways to other stimulation. Beach (1947) is referred to as showing the increased activity noted in animals injected with testosterone in the presence of a variety of other animals of different stimulus value. Such observations suggest that some drives have the function of lowering thresholds for certain kinds of stimuli. This may also (but not necessarily) mean raising the threshold for stimuli of other varieties. Thus an animal deprived of water but supplied with dry food

---

[4] See his footnote (p. 22) and recall Hebb's "arousal system" which can be affected by internal chemistry as well as external stimulation.

may have a low threshold for water-associated stimuli but a high threshold for food-associated stimuli. In an experiment involving just such a situation, Spence and Lippit (1946) found that rats that had been given the opportunity to notice food in one goal box of a T-maze when thirsty showed no effect of such exposure when tested on a later occasion when hungry. Leeper (1948b) in criticizing this experiment suggested that the animals had not paid adequate attention to the food because they were looking for water. Numerous other experiments involving variations on the theme just described have been performed with the intent of supporting one or another theory. Since the results are contradictory and reflect various prejudgments in interpretation which cannot be resolved (such as that an animal that is fed dry food must also be hungry if deprived of water because thirsty animals cannot eat so much as they would if water were available) there is no point to discussing them at present. The position of Leeper, however, is interesting in connection with the present view. If the "drive" state can be considered as one which lowers resistance to the passage of certain impulses we have a situation which is analogous to setting a switch which permits some kind of reaction to occur smoothly and efficiently and prevents others from occurring at all, or at best with difficulty. Presumably this must be done in terms of some kind of alteration of neural states in the central nervous system as it is not readily conceivable how such control of sensory and motor thresholds could rest directly and solely in nonneural tissue. The "central neural excitation" of Wolpe appears to serve as an appropriate device to serve the functions described. It corresponds with Hebb's (1949, 1955) central facilitating and arousal states and behaviorally amounts to what has been described in the psychological literature as "sets" (Mowrer, 1938; Rees and Israel, 1935).

It should be quite clear that what we have been talking about in connection with "set" could just as easily be applied to the more psychological concept of "attention." Hebb (1949) equates attention with neural facilitation, and our concept of set amounts to such neural facilitation which permits the organism to respond readily to some stimuli and not easily, if at all, to other stimulation. The same operations that are performed to create sets are employed to create "attention." A rat is starved so that it will "attend" to food stimuli or factors associated with food. We have already treated this problem in connection with clearness (see p. 131 f) and that discussion should be consulted in connection with the current problem.

A set, behaviorally considered, amounts to preliminary or preparatory responses which have the functional characteristics of increasing the efficiency of responses to stimuli about to be presented. The postures adopted by sprint men in track events are typical examples of such sets. The literature is replete with illustrations of the influence of sets and instructions on perception, learning, and numerous performance measures. (Irion, 1948; J. Miller, 1939; Grant, 1939.) The experiment of Luchins (1946) is particularly interesting in this regard and should be enjoyed by all students. Luchins was able to make use of a procedure reminiscent of an old joke routine in which the interlocutor describes a streetcar picking up and discharging passengers at numerous stops. The listeners ordinarily and characteristically start adding and subtracting passengers, ignoring the stops, and are consequently nonplussed when asked how often the car stopped. Luchin's experiment makes use of a series of problems which can be solved in only one way. After a number of such are solved, later problems are solved in the same way even though easier methods could have been used. As in the joke situation, subjects instruct themselves to do certain things and then react in terms of their own instructions or sets.

In the present context we can restate the concepts of set and drive (in the sense of tissue condition) in terms of stimuli and responses. We have already spoken of lowered thresholds for certain classes of stimuli and possibly raised thresholds for others. Reconsider now the Spence-Lippit experiment: Rats are first deprived of water for a period of 24 hours. Meanwhile dry food is available. Hunger is presumably eliminated to some degree, thirst possibly increased by the dry food. The parched membranes of the animals' throats presumably initiate impulses which lead to restless, unorganized behavior. If the animals have previously been stimulated in the same or similar fashion, it is possible that these stimuli could have been conditioned to responses of approaching and licking at water bottles. The bottles are now absent, however, and the behavior consequently either extinguishes or cannot be performed adequately. The animals are now placed in the T-maze. The start of the maze limits the behavioral repertoire to movements of a narrow range. There is hardly anything the animal can do except move down the runway. The restlessness initiated by stimuli from the membranes of the throat and perhaps from more general regions of the body due to dehydration effects on the cells is perhaps sufficient to provoke movement along the alley.

The animal is prevented from doing anything else by the limitations of the situation. We cannot infer with any assurance based on evidence that, on the first trial, the animal is *looking* for water. It can be inferred, however, that it is not looking for anything else. The appearance of food in one goal box may not then be an effective stimulus for seizing and eating the available food. This kind of behavior has too high a threshold—the animal has eaten as much as it is going to eat before the trial, and food stimuli have lost temporary effectiveness. Since the animal does not eat, we judge the stimulus value of food to be low or nonexistent. When the rat is allowed access to the other goal box, the water as stimulus is immediately effective. We judge it to be strong in stimulus value. For the moment let us assume that drinking in the water goal box in some fashion strengthens the behavior patterns of turning toward that box when on the runway.[5] This assumption is not essential to the argument but it permits a more fluid discussion without disturbing the net outcome. The necessary essentials for creating a set are now available. As the animal drinks it makes a variety of responses the total complex of which we label "drinking behavior." This total pattern is being conditioned to whatever stimuli are effectively operating on the animal, including the traces or neural aftereffects of any recent stimulation such as proprioceptive stimulation from the recently made turn toward the water goal box and from the running behavior as well as any external cues from the goal box (visual stimuli relating to its size, shape, color, cutaneous stimuli from the floor, odors from the paint or wood, and so on).

The drinking behavior in the process of becoming a conditioned response will then tend to come forward in time, that is, antedate the unconditioned stimulus (in this instance, the water). Such antedating can be only partly successful since certain features of the response depend on actual water contact. The parts of the behavior that can come forward, then, are only those that do not depend on water in the mouth or on the tongue and comprise what we have already described previously (see p. 100) as fractional anticipatory goal responses, or "r_g's." These partial responses come to be made earlier and earlier in the total temporal sequence from being placed in the starting position to arrival in the goal box. The animal is thus preparing for drinking even before it gets to the water. Such preparatory re-

---

[5] This assumption will be examined in detail in the next chapter.

sponses, when they are being made, serve the purpose of lowering the threshold for water stimuli and raise it for any other kind. If this is accomplished, we have what we have talked about as a "set."

Whenever such a set is operating we loosely speak of the animal as "wanting," "wishing for," "desiring," some object. Searching behavior or "looking for" something is presumably the combined result of external stimulation initiating some form of directed running or movement and such set reactions. The set responses themselves are sources of additional stimuli and may become conditioned to a variety of responses once the set is provoked. Thus when we "want something to eat" we go through whatever repertoire of responses that might have become conditioned to the stimuli resulting from the appropriate set. The implications of this set reaction must now be detailed in the various ramifications:

1. WANTS AS RESPONSES TO OTHER STIMULI. It is inherent in such an analysis as has just been presented that wants, wishes, desires, and the like, are not primary motivators; rather these are themselves responses to other stimuli. Their motivation potential resides in the stimuli which are generated by such responses. These stimuli ordinarily are ineffective for initiating any coordinated or specific responses on the first occasions of their occurrence but come to do so after being conditioned to such specific responses. In the case of species displaying what passes for instinctive patterns of behavior, the stimuli generated from the set responses may be more specific than in species where behavior appears to be more modifiable. Thus sex behavior patterns may be relatively more adequate in so-called lower vertebrates than in man. Sex reactions in man may serve as an appropriate illustration of the point. The tumescence of various organs in both male and female which occur prior to actual sexual intercourse (see Kinsey *et al.*, 1948) generate stimulation enough. The reactions of novice sex partners, however, are frequently inadequate. Nissen (1954) reports that mature but inexperienced chimpanzees prove inadequate for sexual behavior unless taught or assisted by more experienced partners. The naïveté of the chimpanzees might offer some support for damaged human egos.

2. GOALS OR CONSUMMATORY RESPONSES. A further implication is that until some kind of response which, for the present, we can refer to as a goal or consummatory response has been performed in connection with various sets, there can be no wants or desires. A girl who asserts that she "wants to get married" cannot be referring to any-

thing concrete or specific if she has not been married before. She is just making noises, since marriage is not a thing or entity that can have any behavioral meaning to her. She may, of course, want or desire a great variety of objects or conditions that have been associated with the term "marriage" for her, but these may or may not have any realistic relationship to the wedded state. There is no question about her wanting *something*—there is considerable question, however, about what that something is. The actual legal process of marriage may, in fact, be unpleasant or undesirable as may a host of other facets of marriage. After marriage she may ruefully assert that "If I knew what it was like, I would never have gotten married." In the same way anyone who has not engaged in skiing cannot properly say he wants to ski. He may want to relax by the roaring fire in a mountain lodge as pictured in movies and popular magazines. He may even want to be acclaimed for his natural gifts and athletic prowess, but once he is on skis at the top of a hill he may be very dubious about what his wants are. The same argument can be advanced about any assertions of wants for previously unexperienced goal-objects or events. To the extent that rg's can be made in connection with any goal, to that extent can one speak of wishes—otherwise the assertions are probably related to other goals which have been experienced. Most alleged wants are of a verbal, literary nature and have little to do with reality. The person who is continually talking about wanting to go to Europe might very well refuse a free passage because his "real" wants do not include any rg's for travel. A girl who won a free trip to Switzerland was hilariously happy until it was time to go. Then she took a cash equivalent.

3. PROVOCATION OF APPROPRIATE RG'S. Wants can be initiated anytime that appropriate rg's are provoked. Thus, an organism can be made hungry or thirsty or what not, to some extent, by stimuli associated with rg's. On arrival at the goal it may turn out that the actual goal object is not really "wanted" because other conditions are not present. For example, a person may accept a cigarette or a drink and start to consume it even though he is not "in need" of the object. The lack of basic "wants" shows up the rg as superficial and the person says, "Why did I take that? I didn't really want it." or "That's not what I want." Sometimes, on the other hand, the "want" develops in a more intense degree (see Hebb's discussion, 1949, p. 199, of the "salted-nut phenomenon").

Recall now the Spence-Lippit experiment. The hungry animals

kept turning to the water side of the *T*. Presumably the stimuli of the starting box and runway initiated the *rg*'s for water and stimuli from these *rg*'s in turn provoked the succeeding aspects of the response pattern of turning toward and entering the water goal box. Here the animals even go through what is essentially a farce and take a drink before giving up the behavior which is obviously inappropriate.

4. Rg's as motivation and reinforcement. In his analysis of the function of *rg*'s, Osgood (1953) has complicated the problem even beyond the present measure of difficulty. He assumes that *rg*'s operate pretty much as has been outlined above by means of the stimuli they produce. These stimuli he calls "secondary motivators." "According to the present analysis, this reaction-produced stimulation *is* [6] the secondary drive and its reduction is secondary reinforcement." Later (p. 443) he states: "The anticipatory goal reaction is assumed to function simultaneously as drive and as reinforcement." The reinforcement function is conceived to be somehow mediated by conditioning of some components of the goal response to stimuli from *rg*'s. He suggests as one possibility that such stimuli could, through conditioning, come to release hormones or elicit other reactions which by their nature are parts of a reinforcement pattern. A hormone that is secreted when food is ingested might serve to reduce the drive condition and the *rg* too might thereby be eliminated.

Osgood finds himself with a paradox in this analysis. An organism about to arrive at a goal may find the drive so reduced that further progress toward the goal is unattractive or undesirable and all the effort expended in arriving at that point appears wasted or foolish. Osgood's own illustration of a channel swimmer arriving within striking distance of the shore and then finding himself without the drive to continue seems a bit farfetched as an excuse for failure. It certainly does not account for successful swims. If we take the Osgood notion seriously and find support for it, we may have explanations for such items of ancient wisdom as "Virtue is its own reward" and "Anticipation is the greater part of the pleasure." We are not inclined to argue with Osgood's analysis of the possible operation of *rg*'s and their stimuli. They may very well function in this way. The labeling of these functions as secondary motivators and secondary reinforcers, however, might be an unnecessary practice and only leads to confusion of interpretation when others use the same terms for other functions.

---

[6] Italics are Osgood's (p. 433).

Derived drives, secondary drives, learned drives. In recent years a great deal of labor has been directed toward the investigation of learned drives. Unfortunately, most of this work has been restricted to only one form of such learned drives, that of fear. Actually, of course, it is ordinarily assumed that the fear itself is not learned but that fear, as such, is one of the basic, native, reaction patterns to a limited number of adequate stimuli such as loud noises, loss of support (Watson, 1925), or any sudden or unexpected stimulus. While Watson and other earlier psychologists did not include pain-producing stimuli among the natural excitors of fear, it is actually pain stimulation that is most commonly favored by students of derived drives. We have already discussed this procedure (see p. 61 f) but a brief review might be helpful in the present frame of reference. Ordinarily, shock is administered to the subject who then presumably suffers pain and the pain is assumed to be accompanied by fear. If another stimulus, for example, light, is presented just before the shock, then, in Pavlovian terms, the new or conditioned stimulus can become associated with the reactions evoked by the shock. If fear is among these reactions, then the fear component will be learned along with the other responses. The learning involved is, of course, that of associating a stimulus with the fear. The fear itself is part of the unconditioned response and requires no learning to occur. Later the conditioned stimulus will evoke the fear just as any conditioned response is evoked. Usually when fear occurs in the absence of an unconditioned stimulus, it is referred to as "anxiety."

Because in the laboratory experiment involving fear numerous responses occur in the absence of the UncS, experimenters have freely, and perhaps too freely, taken over the concept of anxiety from clinical literature and talked about the behavior they witness as based on anxiety. Such a translation from the clinic may give the psychologist a feeling of working with something important to mankind and lend *him* motivation. Whether the analogy is appropriate remains to be seen. We shall have more to say of this kind of anxiety later.

For the present we can accept the possibility that to the extent that emotions can be evoked by unconditioned stimuli, they can be conditioned to other stimuli. If the emotions can be thought of as motivators or tissue conditions similar to others like those we have been discussing, there is no reason to exclude them from the class of drives. Leeper (1948b) has made out a case for the motivational status of emotions and the approach of Miller (1948) and Mowrer (1940b) may prove fruitful eventually. Unfortunately, little or no work has been done on other varieties of emotion. Virtually nothing is available on the positive side. Psychologists find it difficult to deal with pleasure.

The preoccupation with anxiety or fear is well illustrated by the Nebraska Symposia on motivation wherein Brown (1953) and Farber (1954) try to make out a case for anxiety as a fundamental source of a wide variety of complicated behavior patterns. Stimulus cues signifying a lack of affection, a lack of prestige, insufficient money, and the like, are said to acquire, through learning, a potentiality for arousing a state of uneasiness or anxiety having the functional properties of a drive. The present analysis is not concerned with accounting for all behavior but rather with the learning process, and so there is no present inclination to try to reduce a wide variety of complex patterns to a postulated anxiety before other possibilities are examined more closely. Brown's analysis of the function of drives is not unlike the present picture and should be consulted for comparison. He emphasizes, as does the present account, the relative unspecificity of responses to drives prior to learning. He also emphasizes the present point of view that only stimuli, not drives as such, can initiate behavior.

Brown makes several other points concerning motivation which are of interest:

1. The distinction between drives and motives on the one hand and habits on the other must be preserved.
2. Acquired drives must be thought of first as responses (because they are learned). They are drives secondarily, because they have the capacity to act as drives, that is, provide stimuli.
3. Drives have several important functional properties among which is is the fact that they combine with existing reaction tendencies to produce overt behavior (the activating or energizing function). This implies that no overt behavior occurs in the absence of a drive, but the drive itself has no directive influence. This function of drives serves to explain such phenomena as different responses to the same stimuli at various times and such events as strong reactions to physically mild stimuli.

Brown discusses other functional properties of drives in connection with *drive reduction*. We shall return to this problem when we look into reinforcement theory in our next chapter. For the moment we can readily appreciate the close affinity between the views advanced by Brown and those presented here. We cannot, however, endorse the general use of an anxiety drive as a universal explanation of behavior in the way Brown and Farber use it. The reliance on anxiety is quite unnecessary to develop equally plausible accounts of motivation. In fact, the whole question of learned drives needs the closest scrutiny and re-examination. As we have already noted (p. 68), the evidence for such learned drives is more logical or theoretical than empirical. In a moment we will note Harlow's (1953) suggestion that other (nonlearned) drives should be considered as alternate accounts in place of derived drives. Before we jump into the controversial lake of opinion about derived drives we had better continue our analysis of the nature of the drive concept. It may turn out that no derived drives are necessary. It should be remembered that the basic reason for postulating derived drives is so that learning can be explained by drive reduction. The general argument runs as follows: If learning occurs, a drive has been reduced. If a basic drive cannot be plausibly assumed, a derived drive must have been present. This circular argument is actually used by Farber as one of his criteria for the presence of a drive. The whole edifice of derived drives will fall if drive reduction proves unnecessary for learning.

Before we can appreciate drive-reduction controversies there are many other aspects of the motivation-learning situation for us to examine. Thus far we have been dealing with the general nature of motivation and have only indirectly and incidentally touched on the relation of motivation to learning itself. Some confusion may have been experienced because of the fact that certain kinds of motives ("sets") are themselves learned and subsequently function in the learning of new associations. If the various facets of motivation can be discriminated we can save some confusion by not becoming involved in the problem of drive reduction or reinforcement at this time, even though we must eventually come to grips with this problem. Our justification, if indeed there is any, is that motivation comes before the learning, at least in most attempts at analysis so far presented, and for the present we can look at this preliminary aspect of learning.

HOW DOES MOTIVATION FUNCTION IN LEARNING?

There is a general impression in learning theory that the relationship between motivation and learning is of primary importance. We have already quoted from Guthrie's (1946a) presidential address to the American Psychological Association (see p. 3) and we have also mentioned the suggestion of Hilgard (1953, p. 238) in his elementary text that understanding motivation is perhaps even more imperative than understanding learning itself: "If we had perfect control of motivation learning would just about take care of itself, that is, the role of motivation is so central that it is far more important than conditions of practice, special teaching aids, and so on." Hull (1943) at first postulated that learning was a function of motivation or drive but later (Hull, 1951) he apparently changed his views and decided that learning was independent of motivation but performance was not. Taking Hilgard and Hull together we have an intriguing paradox. Is motivation both necessary and essential for learning and at the same time independent of it? The views of Guthrie, Hilgard, and Hull are typical of the attitudes of most learning psychologists. The role of motivation is regarded as crucial in learning but on the nature of this role there has been little agreement. Lately, there appears to be some prospect of integration of the views of various theorists, especially as more and more soul searching goes on. A fine example of such soul searching is found in a theoretical paper by Harlow (1953) wherein he finds himself unable to reconcile the tissue-condition approach to motivation with his observations on monkeys and children. Incidentally, we might note that many psychologists change their views about drives and the predictability of behavior when they become parents. Children are notoriously hard on theorists.

To determine how motivation works in learning, we might start by asking some questions that appear pertinent. The answers to these questions might be of some steering value. The questions virtually ask themselves if we stop to look at the problem logically. The first question, which we will shortly ask again, is:

Is motivation essential to learning? If the answer turns out to be no, then the problem, in effect, disappears or at least takes a different direction. Let us try to answer this question in general terms now and then look for more specific answers to the ramification of the question. But what does the question itself mean? Can it be given an operational statement? Is there any prospect of developing an experimental attack? Unless we know how to create motivation we are not even in position to decide if it is present at any time, including a time during which learning is occurring. Suppose the experimenter takes no step to motivate a subject and the subject learns. What is to prevent someone from positing some unknown type of motivation being present? Obviously in such an instance the burden of proof is on the side of the claimant, but frequently the details of support for such claims are unsatisfactory.

It is easy enough to deny motivation in certain types of learning situations if one restricts the general concept to such commonly used experimental drives as "hunger," for example. Harlow (1953) in the above-mentioned Nebraska symposium shows that hungry animals do not necessarily learn better, or at least do not persist in solving certain kinds of manipulative puzzles as well as animals who cannot be said to be hungry and do not receive food for solutions. In a discrimination learning situation, Harlow points out, animals continue to learn correct responses even though they are not hungry and eat after both correct and incorrect responses. Harlow is interested, in this paper, in pointing out that tissue needs are of less significance than other motivation sources such as curiosity, some type of manipulating drive, or simply external stimuli, at least for the kinds of problems his monkeys were exposed to.

In his own paper in the Nebraska symposium, Harlow (1953) criticizes Brown and the psychologists he represents who try to base their notion of man's complex behavior on "homeostatic" drives. For Harlow, behavior of adult organisms is based less on such factors as pain, hunger, anxiety, and so on, than it is on nonemotional or mildly pleasurable stimuli. Harlow emphasizes that external stimulation is at least as basic and important as biological drives. The important point is that any source of stimulation leads to the same effect, an activation of brain centers. To emphasize one source at the expense of others is misleading and likely to prove a shortsighted policy.

In pointing out the shortcomings of earlier views Harlow raises a number of objections to traditional drive views:

1. Learning may occur in spite of and not because of pain, hunger, and so on.
2. Some problems are solved which only bring about pain and which have little or no apparent utility.
3. Organic or derived drives are frequently highly intense and disruptive and inimical to serious learning—goal reactions to drives lead to rapid satiation rather than prolonged intellectual effort.

How completely we can accept these suggestions cannot now be determined. Brown (1953) objects to them, but no direct refutation or confirmation is possible at present. Hebb (1955) and Leuba (1955) have no difficulty with Harlow's findings (see p. 209).

On the positive side Harlow suggests that more studies be made of the role of external stimulation which provokes such responses as might be labeled "exploratory" or "manipulatory" reactions. He cites numerous examples of experiments conducted at Wisconsin, employing monkeys in situations where the emphasis is on external stimulation. In one of these, rhesus monkeys are offered mechanical "puzzles" which involve a number of sequential movements if the gadgets are to be disassembled. The animals were observed to operate the puzzle arrangement for trial after trial with no rewards other than the performance itself offered. Harlow sees no homeostatic drive operating here. The monkeys appear to have a sport-for-sport's-sake attitude.

In another experiment, monkeys were placed in an opaque box. If they made a correct selection from a pair of visual cues they were allowed to look through an opening in the wall of the box for 30 seconds. The animals learned the discrimination effectively. Harlow identifies this kind of learning as typical Pavlovian or Guthrian contiguity learning although the procedure far more closely approaches an instrumental sequence. There is some confusion here, as Brown points out in the identification of the nature of the variables. For Harlow, apparently, looking out of the box is some sort of unconditioned stimulus. The 30-second look is described as a visual stimulus, a visual activator, a visual reward. The animal is referred to as having a visual exploration motive. This motive appears to be quite insatiable and appears functionally stronger than many other kinds of motives used in ordinary learning situations. Harlow suggests that visual exploration is a prominent determiner of much of the behavior of children and other higher organisms. He goes on to interpret his researches as having demonstrated "that exteroceptive stimuli may motivate a monkey as strongly and at least as persistently as any described source of internal stimuli." Visual exploration is regarded as only one of the possible many complex types of motivation which activate higher organisms. Presumably other senses are equally susceptible to exploratory motivation.

Brown (1953) and Postman (1953) feel that Harlow is confusing the picture to some degree by denying any homeostatic or derived base for his visual exploration. As Brown points out, Harlow appears to make a motive operate after a response rather than before it is made since it appears from Harlow's statements that the visual discrimination is motivated by the external visual exploration that follows a correct choice.

In commenting on the papers of Brown and Harlow, Postman (1953) is almost ready to dispense with the concept of motivation entirely. He sees no reason for retaining Brown's distinction between motives or drives as energizers and as stimuli. Drives as stimuli might be enough. The energizing function is alleged by Brown to have several functions: (a) It explains the disproportion between the stimulus energy and the response energy. Postman regards this as involving an unnecessary assumption of conservation of energy. Refusal of the assumption eliminates the argument. (b) The second argument for an energizing function of drives is the fact of variability of behavior with learning constant. Postman, however, finds it unnecessary to put the burden of explaining such variability on the basis of drive changes since an explanation in terms of factors responsible for *drive stimulus* is sufficient. In summing up his position, Postman is not so sure that we might not get along better with a simple associative principle of stimulus and response, with all stimuli thought of as motivators. For Postman, "the observed motivational selectivity becomes a consequence rather than a direct determinant of such dispositions" (1953, p. 58).

In the next Nebraska symposium, Nissen (1954) continued this line of attack. He favors the view that all drives, if there are such things, are homeostatic, or at least biological. Unless we are dealing with biological properties we are in constant danger of getting sidetracked into some kind of psychogenics. For Nissen, the visual exploration drive would be just as homeostatic or biological as hunger, thirst, and the other commonly studied drives. Nissen even suggests that the several senses have their own drives or needs. The eye, he suggests, needs to see and the ear to hear. The senses must be thought of, argues Nissen, as having demands of their own which will not be denied. Likewise, the brain as a master organ may have its own drives or needs to function. It should not be thought of only as a servant or slave of other organs. Nissen's argument is not supported by any facts not already available to Harlow and those others who argue against homeostatic drives as a basis for behavior. It is simply an argument and may attract considerable support. Recent experiments by Hebb, Heath, and Stuart (1954) and his students (Bexton, Heron, and Scott, 1954) on temporary restriction of human sense activity do show the marked irritation that develops when subjects cannot hear, feel, or see, and so on. Whether this represents a frustration of learned reactions or whether something more basic is involved we cannot yet say. The behavior of some formerly blind people whose visual capacity was restored (see Senden, 1932) or Hebb (1949, p. 18) suggests a powerful influence of learning. Some people refused to learn to see even when it became possible. Does this observation refute a "visual need"?

Up to now we have been considering the problem of motivation more or less logically and theoretically. Only a few reports have been cited, and those only to illustrate logical arguments. All this talk, however, has been necessary in order to appraise effectively the central problems of modern learning theory. We may now be ready to ask a few pertinent questions concerning the relation of motivation and learning in a clearer fashion than we could have before. We are also in a position to decide whether studies purporting to demonstrate one kind of relationship or another actually bear on the issues. The ability to ask questions does not necessarily correlate with any capacity to provide answers and we need not expect too definitive a result. What are the pertinent questions to be asked at this time? There appears to be at least these: (1) Is motivation necessary for learning? (2) If so, and even if not, how does motivation affect learning, if it does; that is, how does motivation operate in a learning situation? (3) What is the relationship of different quantities or degrees of motivation to learning? And how does the nature or quality of a motive affect learning?

Perhaps these are all the same question. A further question deals with the relation of motivation to such factors as incentives, rewards, and reinforcements, both positive and negative. These relations require a separate discussion (see Chap. 10).

1. IS MOTIVATION NECESSARY FOR LEARNING? We have just finished looking at this question in general terms. Now we must take a closer and more detailed look. The answer to this question, of course, depends on the definition of motivation. If it is accepted that motivation amounts to stimulation and, perhaps, some kind of energizing, and if learning amounts to associating stimuli with responses, then motivation is necessary. The question, however, usually refers to some assumed needs, wishes, homeostatic drives, or other states, and we cannot ignore these assumed agencies if some theorists choose to insist on them. As was mentioned earlier, the only way to answer the question would be to demonstrate that some kind of learning went on in the absence of any and all such conditions. When one considers all the candidates that have been entered as possible motiva-

tional agencies (including the ubiquitous anxiety and other derived drives and Nissen's sense organ needs) it is difficult to deny that one of them might be present especially if the claimant insists that it is and feels no burden to specify it beyond the statement that it is there as an intervening variable inferred from the behavior and the preceding situation. When theorists argue in this way, it is even difficult to say that a man is not hungry after a turkey dinner, especially if he eats desserts.

Experimental attempts to demonstrate learning without motivation have all proved equivocal. At least those who insist on motivated learning have proved strongly vocal in their attacks on any alleged demonstrations. The usual experiment to test the hypothesis is designed to prove either (a) that the learner had no business learning some material but learned it anyhow, or (b) that the learner learned without knowing that he had learned and without caring whether he learned or not. The first type usually goes under the heading of "incidental learning" and the second as "learning without awareness." It is apparent that such experiments are likely to make use of human subjects and this does not help much to eliminate confusion. We can look at a few examples.

a. *Incidental learning.* Postman and Senders (1946) had different subjects read a short story under a variety of instructions. Some were told to proofread the material, others to read for detail, others for the general ideas involved. A test was then given involving questions covering all aspects of the several instructions. The results showed that, while the subjects did better on features they had been instructed to observe, they also answered questions based on the other instructions. Such gratuitous learning may be considered incidental. The usual criticism is that the subjects instructed themselves (were motivated) to learn the other material also.

Jenkins (1933) had subjects work as experimenters with other subjects who were learning nonsense syllables. The "experimenters" read lists of 20 syllables over and over for the subjects. The next day both subjects and experimenters were tested and the latter were found to have learned, not so well as the "subjects" but certainly not insignificantly. Osgood (1953, p. 414) in commenting on this study asks: "How do we know they (the experimenters) were completely lacking motivation?" It should be pointed out that some experimenters admitted trying to learn.

Saltzman (1953) hoped to avoid obvious pitfalls in the incidental learning procedure by instructing subjects to check off numbers in a random matrix as they appeared in a memory drum. It was assumed that this "orienting" task would prevent an "incidental learning group" from learning. The incidental group learned a good deal anyhow, probably because the subjects had to memorize the numbers to facilitate the business of locating them in the matrix. The subjects might readily assign themselves the duty of learning in order to perform the job assigned by the experimenter. There seems to be no way to control such private motivation in so-called incidental learning experiments.

b. *Learning without awareness.* Thorndike and Rock (1934), Irwin *et al.* (1934), and Postman and Jarrett (1952) have all tried to determine if subjects could learn to respond to concepts without knowing what the concepts were. Hull (1920) had originally indicated that such results could be obtained. In the Thorndike type of experiment the subjects are, perhaps, motivated to learn *something* but they do not at first, at least, know what that is. Perhaps this type of experiment belongs under a later heading (see below, under Irrelevant Drives) but we include it here because it is an experimental attempt to demonstrate what is said to occur in nonmotivational situations in everyday life. The experimental procedure amounts to asking subjects to respond to stimulus words with the first word thought of. The response is announced to be right if it fits a preselected concept. In Postman and Jarrett's experiment 12 blocks of 20 words were presented in succession. If the subject starts giving correct answers without knowing why, learning without awareness is alleged to take place. Weiss (1955) has criticized such experiments on the grounds that the concepts chosen are extremely vague and difficult to score; when subjects are given information about the concept they still cannot use it because the instructions emphasize speed of response; the operant levels of chance associations have not been determined and, in general, no actual evidence is available to support Thorndike's conclusion that such learning is possible. When concepts are employed that the subject can work with, the learning curves are extremely different from Thorndike's and amount to "insight" curves.

c. *Irrelevant drives.* A third approach to the problem is that of using what are called "irrelevant drives." In this type of experiment, an animal is given all the food it will eat but no water, or vice versa, and is then observed to see if it will learn something appropriate to the irrelevant drive. Thus Kendler (1947), repeating an experiment previously described (see p. 211 for the Spence and Lippit experiment), gave thirsty animals a chance to find food (undesired and uneaten) in one side of a T-maze. When tested under hunger, the animals continued going to the water side where they had found water when thirsty. Various arguments arise concerning such experiments, depending on who does them and the views he chooses to support. Thus, if one favors the notion that motivation is necessary and specific he argues one way. If he favors the notion that motivation is irrelevant he argues appropriately to his point. Some of Tolman's supporters, like Leeper (1948b), attacked Spence and Kendler on the grounds that the animals had not been given a chance to notice the food. According to Leeper all that is required for learning is that an opportunity be given for *perceiving* certain sign relationships. None of these experiments actually bear on the basic issue because they all employ some kind of deprivation technique (the animals are hungry or thirsty or both) and as we have seen earlier, it is frequently argued, if the results of the opposition are unattractive, that one cannot deprive an animal of water without making him hungry at the same time (he would eat more if given water) and vice versa.

d. *Learning during sleep.* In the last few years a number of studies have appeared which are somewhat exciting if not alarming in their possibilities and prospects and bring the Brave New World a step nearer to realization. Should these studies prove valid, they will also prove disturbing to theoreticians in learning. In one report, Leuba and Bateman (1952) found that a sleeping subject learned a song that was played on a phonograph. In a second experiment by Fox and Robbins (1952) an extensive investigation was conducted involving 30 subjects divided into three groupings of 10 each. The subjects all learned lists of Chinese-English equivalents on the morning following a night's sleep during which for 30 minutes a tape recorder presented one or another kind of stimulation through a pillow speaker. The control group had music only. One experimental group was given repetitions of the list to be learned the next day while the second experimental group was given a mixed up version of this list such that learning it would be confusing later. The group results the next morning were averages of 7.7 trials for the controls, 5.6 for the facilitative group, and 11.1 for the interference group. These results were all statistically significant and are a little too horrible to contemplate. The editor of the journal chose to comment on the fact that the subjects were not observed during sleep but the experimenters are satisfied that all data reported are uncontaminated. In a critical review of learning literature Underwood (1953) views the study just reported with "skepticism and distrust." He is unable to find any procedural faults and concludes with the comment that if the study is valid "some of us will need to revise our thinking concerning the roles of motivation and reinforcement in human learning." Simon and Emmons (1955) criticize all sleep-learning experiments as not demonstrating positive control over the sleep state. They are not ready to accept sleep-learning.

2. How DOES MOTIVATION OPERATE IN A LEARNING SITUATION? At this time we shall offer only the traditional or common answer to this question. Later we shall suggest a new interpretation of the role of motivation in learning. The ordinary answer is, of course, that motivation or "drive" sets the organism into action, it forces him to move about, to try and to err and eventually to succeed (if success is arranged by the experimenter or at least a likely possibility). This view carries the implication that "no drive" equals "no action," or that an animal merely sleeps or rests or is otherwise quiescent unless under the pressure of some drive. Since the same theorists who favor this view also make "fatigue" a drive and sleep or quiescence a solution to problems aroused by overactivity, we come full circle and wind up where we started. Since a normal organism spends but a fraction of its life asleep or resting, we are asked to assume a succession of drives that keep it awake and operating. Such an explanation explains too much too easily and offers little to account for the wide varieties of responses that fill our waking lives. The reason the view has enjoyed such a long life is that it is virtually irrefutable even if it does not help much. It permits the wholesale multiplication of drives to the point of including a drive for activity based on good health or a condition of euphoria, and, as we have seen, Nissen extends this exercise drive to the sense organs and brain. Since nothing is ever done about quantifying or analyzing these additional drives (to say nothing of social drives and various other propulsive forces hypothesized by Freudian clinicians, such as life and death instincts along with a host of defense mechanisms that seem to qualify as drives) we might well dismiss the lot as of little value to an objective psychology.

There is a second aspect to the role of drive in learning, and this we have already alluded to on several occasions. It is argued by followers of Hull, particularly, that eliminating or "reducing" the drive in some manner serves to strengthen bonds between S's and R's. This is the reinforcement function of drives and we will examine this in detail in the next chapter and so will say no more about it here. The role of drive in extinction will also be considered at the appropriate time (see Chap. 13).

3. QUALITY AND QUANTITIES OF MOTIVATION AS RELATED TO LEARN-ING. In spite of the imposing list of drives that can be conjured up by the drive-minded, it is rare indeed that any drives other than hunger and thirst are employed in learning situations. There are studies, of course, where sex and temperature drives have been employed (Sheffield et al., 1951; Roessler and Brogden, 1943) but these are in an extremely small minority. Other drive states like "fatigue" or energy expenditure are occasionally studied (see Solomon's review, 1948a) but more for other purposes than a direct examination of the role of drive in learning. Sometimes specific hungers (for vitamins, Harris et al., 1933, or sweets, Young, 1948; Sheffield and Roby, 1950) are established and their effect on learning examined, but again the purposes of the studies vary with the experimenter and we lack good comparative data. The use of pain and its presumed associate of anxiety have become popular substitutes for hunger in recent years. Adequate comparative studies are difficult to conduct because as yet we have no good techniques for equating "amounts of drive." How much thirst equals how much hunger? Or how much fatigue equals how much sex drive? Actually we have no units for measuring any drive in any direct fashion. Drives are presumed to be hypothetical constructs and the procedure for creating drives consists in some cases of depriving an organism of some object like food for a number of hours, administering different strengths or numbers of shocks, or forcing some amount of work out of the organism. How many shocks equal how many hours without food? Measurement on the behavioral side again varies from speed of running through mazes to number of bar presses per unit time, and so on. A standardizing experiment is greatly needed. In an early attempt to measure drives, Warden (1931) employed a technique of counting the number of times a rat would cross a charged grid to some incentive. Here we complicate the problem of measuring drives with the problem of measuring incentives. Incidentally, the Warden technique has an awkward time of it in measuring pain drives because it depends on finding out how much pain the rat will take to avoid pain. Because the present state of

our knowledge is so limited in this area it is best to leave the subject and go on to a consideration of some quantitative findings with a limited number of drives.

Psychologists using hungry animals usually find it convenient to starve the animals for 24 hours. This enables the experimenter to give his animals daily trials at the same hour. Whether it is a good interval for the rats has only rarely been questioned. One point is immediately obvious and that is that the changes that go on in the rat are not a simple arithmetical function of the number of hours of food deprivation. While a 1-day hungry rat may run faster than a 1-hour hungry rat, a 7-day hungry rat is dead. How does learning behavior vary with deprivation? We have already mentioned Harlow's monkeys who learn better when well fed. Some early results of Finan (1940) suggest that rats that are 12-hours hungry learn better than 24-hour hungry rats. In recent years a number of studies by Crespi (1942), Zeaman (1949), and others (Deese and Carpenter, 1951) indicate that *performance* measures seem to follow hours of deprivation, within limits, but learning is quite independent of such deprivation schedules. Coyer (1953) for example, found his rats ran much faster when deprived of water for 24 hours than when deprived for only 1 hour or 4 hours. They all learned equally well, however. Woodworth and Schlosberg (1954) have summarized the literature on this subject and arrived at the same conclusion. Motivation has a great deal to do with performance but little or nothing to do with learning as far as differences in deprivation schedules can be equated with motivation. There are numerous ramifications of this problem which we will have to consider again (and some of which we have already noted in earlier chapters, see p. 162). For the present we can rest on the above conclusion and return to the more general discussion.

EVALUATION OF THE MOTIVATION CONCEPT

Our review of the thinking about motivation has not been very fruitful of positive statements. In the two Nebraska symposia the several experts found themselves in more disagreement than agreement. While this may reflect the way in which science advances, as Nissen suggested, it does not help the student seeking "closure." Not only is there argument on a theoretical level, but also experimenters seem to find contradictory results and then engage in caustic polemics.

We have noticed the concern of Underwood about the Fox and Robbins experiment. A while ago we noted Postman's uneasiness about the retention of the concept of motivation at all. Why is the concept retained? What purpose does it serve in a scientific appreciation of behavior? We have seen that wherever the concept is introduced it must be defined and redefined in various ways to cover the events or procedures involved in its use. We have seen it treated as a mild stimulus, a strong stimulus, an internal stimulus, an external stimulus, an overt response, an internal response, a central nervous state, a tissue condition, a fractional anticipatory goal response, and even as simultaneously an instigator and satisfier of behavior—in short, as simultaneous cause and effect. In addition to these, we have seen it described as a tissue condition or brain activity giving rise to strivings, energizing behavior, directing behavior, and mediating behavior. We have seen it described as a "set" or preparatory response and have seen it looked at in connection with conscious and unconscious functioning. Later (Chap. 15) we will even see motives in conflict.

We can hardly expect a concept with so many facets to be clearly understood and universally appreciated as representing any unitary process or event. The contradictory aspects (energizing versus directive—stimulus versus response) that have been advanced as features of motivation suggest that there is little hope that the concept can be reduced to a meaningful or operational status. Consider how the concept is used and the endless difficulties involved in trying to bring it into effective functioning. We will ignore those loose usages of the general texts which account for all kinds of perceptual reactions and personality features as due to some vaguely suggested and operationally unspecified "motivation." Postman (1953) has effectively laid this ghost. Instead, let us look at how one of the most rigorous and tough-minded psychologists employed the concept. This exercise can provide a summary object lesson for us.

Professor Hull (1943) thought of motivation as a vital and basic component in *any* behavior at all. Whether or not a response of any kind occurs was believed by Hull to be dependent upon a motivational factor. The prospect of any response was represented by him with the symbol $_sE_R$ (excitatory potential). $_sE_R$ was determined by a multiplicative function of Habit ($_sH_R$) and Drive (D). *Thus,* $_sE_R = {}_sH_R \times D$. If this formula is to hold, then, if the drive is of zero strength, any multiplication will also result in zero. We recognize that for any behavior potential to be evaluated we must have a measure of strength of the drive. This might feasibly be estimated for hunger in a rat in terms of hours of deprivation, but consider the problem involved in calculating the drive strength of a manipulation or exploratory or "love" motive to say nothing of a "sex" motive. The complicated motivation of the human female sex behavior reported by Kinsey et al. (1953) suggests that a numerical value for D in such a situation is not readily available at the moment. Look for values of D for security, prestige, money, and so on. The difficulties of this approach are obvious. It is not implied here that Hull was unaware of the difficulties. He considered his theoretical formulations only a program for research. But we can ask, legitimately, if the program is promising if it includes a motivational concept which is defined as D and refers to only one facet of the concept as understood by other writers. Hull uses, basically, the "tissue condition" type of drive definition and an operational approach which depends on a deprivation procedure. Can we deprive an organism of a measured amount of love, peace, and security? Obviously such terms are not words of scientific usefulness and to become useful the conditions they represent must be reduced to measurable variables. The prospect of such reduction is extremely dim at present. As soon as we leave the realm of inner D's related to tissue conditions, the prospects for implementing the $_sE_R$ formula become even dimmer. Then we are dealing with some kinds of alleged secondary motives whose origins and strengths are difficult to specify. Actually only the skimpiest experimental observations are available about such secondary motives. With the exception of studies of acquired fears (and those have yet to demonstrate their relationship to the motivational problem) there is extremely little information about acquired drives or motives. Brown (1953) points out the paucity of such studies in a list submitted by Miller (1951) where no other kinds of secondary motives are mentioned except fear. Myers and Miller (1954) failed to develop learned drives based on hunger. Brown himself tries to do the best he can with "anxiety" and makes it a universal secondary motive accounting for practically all other important kinds of goal behavior. Harlow (1953) mocks him for this and suggests that the view is difficult to swallow except by "anxiety ridden psychologists."

Instead of plunging along into what appears an endless series of cul-de-sacs such as we might offer a rat to explore, it might prove more useful to re-examine the entire question of the motivation proposi-

tion. Why do we talk about it at all? What question does a postulated motivation serve to answer? It appears to operate only in attempts to account for questions beginning with "why." The chapter
on motivation in the elementary text promises to explain *why* we behave as we do. Yet the "why" type of question has long ago dropped
out of the other sciences where the investigators are concerned only
with "what" and "how." Why are psychologists willing to continue
asking this question when they otherwise pride themselves on their
scientific status? In view of the corrupt situation in the field of motivation (and the Nebraska Symposia are Exhibit A and B) are we not
justified in going beyond Postman and denying the legitimacy of the
concept of motivation altogether? If the efforts of psychologists are a
misguided attempt to retain in their discipline an undisciplined concept, it is time they recognized its illegitimacy and disowned it.
Scientific psychologists have no business dealing with any approach
to motivation which conceals a conscious or unconscious preoccupation with a metaphysical concept. The only way for psychologists to
deal with behavior is in terms of stimuli and responses. These are
complicated enough for the present. When intervening variables are
introduced, they must be rigidly defined in such detail as to leave no
doubt as to the mechanisms or relations that are allegedly being presented. The intervening variable of "drive" has never been so defined
(see Hull, 1943, and Koch, 1954) and no indication is given of the
specific "anchoring" observations that would apply to any "motivation" state besides hunger and thirst. These remarks are not meant to
be an indictment of the practice of starving rats which are to be
placed in a learning situation (even though Harlow suggests we can
do better observing well-fed monkeys and children). When we do
starve a rat, however, we should simply say so and indicate the various
features of the starvation program so that the observations can be
evaluated in terms of the conditions that prevailed. Any procedure
that retains the meaningless concept of causation appears to be
doomed to scientific sterility no matter what its popular appeal may
suggest and no matter how many problems of psychotherapy it may
appear to solve.

Thus far our considerations have been largely critical and mostly
negative. It is time to turn to a more positive approach. The suggestions about to be advanced while promising and positive are highly
speculative and based on physiological discoveries within the last two
decades. While they offer no hope of any immediate application to

practical problems or even to a detailed appreciation of "motivation" and learning, they do offer a framework for the understanding of much of the material we have discussed and much of which remains.

A PHYSIOLOGICAL APPROACH TO MOTIVATION

The approach we are about to describe represents a relatively new trend in psychology; a trend which can largely be attributed to Hebb (1949, 1955). In a sense this trend represents a turn of the wheel of psychological history which has had previous periods of physiological orientation. The earlier physiological psychologies served their purposes at their own times, but in the past few years they lost favor among many students who sensed the limitations of the physiology of the 1920's and turned to one degree or another of a nonphysiological approach, culminating in Skinner's (1938) strictly behavioral psychology. Perhaps the new physiological emphasis is just another phase in the sequence of psychological fashion and will again be set aside after it makes its contribution; in any event, it is desirable to see what physiology has made available for psychologists to speculate over since 1935.

The basic discoveries of the last few decades are in the area of the electrical activity of the nervous system. The fact that the nervous system is sensitive to electrical stimulation is an ancient one, known to Volta and Galvani in 1793. But for the average psychologist of the thirties the electrical properties of nervous action were not very important. If anything they supported the "telephone switchboard" concept of the nervous system which was generally held (see p. 36). It was known that the passage of a nervous impulse along a nerve either consisted of or was accompanied by a change in electrical potential along a nerve but this information bore no import for theoretical psychology. The discovery of action currents in various members of the body during such operations as thinking were quickly adopted into psychological literature as additional evidence of the behavioral nature of the formerly troublesome and subjective business of "thinking" (see Jacobsen, 1932). The discovery that action currents could be recorded from the motionless arm of a subject instructed to think of throwing a baseball or hammering a nail, while interesting, if not even exciting, leads no place. It is an isolated fact which could not be made to fit into any theory of thought and consequently it was included in the texts but was never tied into the rest of the chapter on thinking.

In 1929, Berger presented his first description of a different type of neural electrical phenomenon. It was the first account of the discovery that if electrodes were placed on any two portions of the skull, electrical potentials could be recorded with suitable amplification. These potentials appear in the form of waves or rhythmic patterns, hence the popular description as "brain waves" or "Berger Rhythms." The electroencephalograms, as they are more properly called, or EEG's, appear in patterns consisting of waves of different frequency, amplitude, and regularity. A large, slow type of wave, the alpha rhythm, is prominently observable in records taken from people who are quietly relaxing, with eyes closed, under instructions to "make your mind blank." The varieties of and changes in brain wave patterns are described interestingly in popular form in *The Living Brain* (Walter, 1953) and more technically in *Electroencephalography* by Hill and Parr (1950).

At first the EEG attracted little attention because inadequate methods of amplification and recording permitted very little in the way of accumulating reliable information. The task of tracing some meaning out of the patterns was extremely tedious and difficult and the business of classifying and studying EEG's became a highly specialized occupation of a technological nature. Theoretical interest suffered somewhat from the discovery of some diagnostic value of the EEG's in the EEG patterns of epileptic patients. The use of the EEG became a surgical aid and received little attention from psychologists.

The possibilities in the EEG as a theoretical tool for appreciating typically psychological problems were first recognized in England. The researches of Adrian (1947), Walter (1953), Young (1951), and others have opened new vistas to an understanding of behavior. Walter, for example, has wrestled with the problem of learning as basically an electronic problem and has gone so far as to build automats which demonstrate some feature of learned behavior. Walter is concerned with principles that derive from the area of logical speculation currently known as "Cybernetics." In common with American speculators in this area like Wiener (1948), Walter regards the brain as analogous in its operations to a giant electronic calculator. The analogy to such electronic brains is considered reasonable by Young who also uses it in his attempts to describe some behavioral phenomena.

Our present interest, however, is not to detail this analogy but to pause and consider the main and outstanding feature of the electrical activity of the brain. So outstanding is this fact that one can lose sight of it once we get involved in the details of electronic calculators. The outstanding fact is the simple first observation mentioned above: the brain is constantly, continuously, and "spontaneously" active at all times whether it is being stimulated or not in the sense of environmental changes going on about a person. Certain changes in brain patterns go on from time to time with cyclical changes in the routines of living, particularly in the processes of going to sleep and waking. The fact that the pattern normally changes when the eyes open suggests another key proposition: when external stimulation is introduced, any activity that is initiated enters an already active brain and must take its chances, so to speak, of having any influence on behavior. The probability that any particular sensory stimulus will have any significant effect on the already ongoing pattern cannot be determined physiologically, at present. The situation is analogous to the entrance of an individual person into a crowded room of people milling around in cocktail-hour fashion. Some people get recognized immediately; perhaps they are expected, they may be guests of honor, or they may have an air about them which cannot be denied. Others are relatively unnoticed throughout the affair and might have a hard time proving they were there at some future date.

The general effect of any stimulation is to break up the existent pattern or to blend with it. In the latter case, no change occurs in behavior to any significant degree. During sleep, thousands of stimuli might reach the brain but if they are not sufficiently intense or unusual the sleeper does not awaken. As the intensity or quality difference increases, the sleeper may mumble, stir, turn over, develop dreams around the new inputs, or awaken. In waking states the situation is the same. So long as the inputs are mild, routine, ordinary, they fit into the pattern and they are ineffective and provoke no great changes. Stimuli from clothing, walking, sitting, and the like, are constantly with us as are a host of internal stimuli related to breathing, digestion, circulation, temperature control, and so forth. So long as they are of normal strength and type, they are taken in stride and brain patterns are largely unaffected. Let the breathing be interrupted momentarily and the pattern changes.

The effect of strong, irregular, and persistent stimuli is to alter the pattern of brain waves from the normal, vegetative state to one of relative disorderliness. The nature of such disorderliness is not under-stood at present; about the only thing that can be said about it is that it will not remain so, but that as the stimuli diminish or disappear, the normal patterns will return. This is not to say that the brain is in-terested in retaining or preserving any particular pattern. If the brain has a "purpose," a drive, or a goal, we are in no position to know about it from a study of the patterns. It can be inferred, however, from the facts that the normal patterns do recur following elimina-tion of the stimulating conditions, that the disruption of patterns can be described as something akin to a maladjustment and the re-turn of the normal pattern as representing a more adjusted state. With the repetition of disruptive stimulation, the behavioral evidence itself suggests that the unusual stimulation is attended to, or taken care of more and more readily and efficiently with less all-around dis-organization. It might be inferred that the brain pattern is also less disorganized in such cases and that the new stimulation is becoming integrated with the ongoing major patterns. The disruption will tend to become more and more local in the sense of only part of the brain being disturbed and this for shorter periods. The brain pattern will itself change, in part or whole, on the occurrence of particular stimuli and, with continued repetition from particular sources, we can sup-pose that each new stimulus acquires its own special type of pattern with its own motor elements which lead to smoother and smoother and more effective action.

An experimental illustration might elucidate the situation some-what. If a subject is instructed to gaze at a flickering light the normal rhythms are at first disrupted, then gradually take on the frequencies of the flickering light (Walter, 1953, p. 83). This is known as "photic driving." Such externally controlled rates can occasionally be imposed on travelers gazing from the windows of trains or automobiles just as easily as they are in the laboratory. It is of incidental interest to us that they also appear to be related to patterns that are related to epi-lepsy, and that occasionally a laboratory subject becomes nauseated and seriously disturbed in the situation just as some passengers get car sick. Walter supplies an anecdotal illustration of a traveler who regu-larly became nauseated when driving down a road which was bor-dered by columns of trees. The flickering pattern of lights and shades was enough to indispose the gentleman seriously.

If we recognize that flickering light can also serve as a conditioned stimulus, we are saying, in effect, that a particular brain pattern is so serving and that it becomes incorporated or integrated with a more general pattern initiated ordinarily by some unconditioned stimulus. The net result will be that a stimulus initiates a specific pattern along with its motor components, of such a nature that a particular response occurs, behaviorally speaking.

Before expanding our theme any further, it may be profitable to reduce the breadth of our speculations and limit ourselves more to laboratory investigations. Such investigations are extremely limited in number at the present time, however, and amount to preliminary observations out of which theoretical speculations emerge from which further and more refined observations will be made. It should be recognized that the brain patterns of adults are likely to be so complicated that very little of a comprehensible nature will emerge by observations made at that level. It is necessary to limit the speculations we are making to simple and young organisms, particularly to organisms experiencing stimulation of some kind for the first time. Animals raised in the dark would be ideal subjects for studies involving what happens to the patterns involved in vision. Infants are the next best type of subject. Consider for the moment the following suggestive speculations of Young (1951).

Motivation and brain functions. The feedback principle. The recently developed electronic computors and control mechanisms that depend on feedback devices provide an analogy for learned behavior that may prove fruitful. The human brain, if considered for the moment as comparable to an electronic calculator, has characteristics and structures which offer in principle, if not in detail, an account of the learning process.

Consider an example of learning in a simpler organism for the present. Young and Boycott (see Young, 1951, p. 28) describe some observations on the behavior of an octopus which are typical enough of common learning studies to serve as a general illustration. In their study they presented a crab to the octopus which quickly left its lair and seized it. The next crab was presented along with a white plate. When the octopus seized the crab, it was shocked. On the next trial with white plate plus crab the octopus emerged slowly and "hesitantly." In a few more trials, it failed to come out at all, evincing, instead, a typical avoidance pattern characteristic of the octopus.

How is such behavior interpreted by the man in the street? The remarks of Young seem to cover the likely reactions and summarize the usual view: "It *wants* the food," "It *feels* the shock," "It *fears* the square," "It *remembers* its pain," and so on. This view of the non-psychologist does not differ, really, except in degrees of refinement of language from the views of those psychologists who make use of anxiety drives in their speculations.

How does Young interpret the same behavior? He first makes a number of assumptions about nervous action which he finds necessary: (1) Incoming impulses set up chains of activity so that a series of different cells (or groups of cells) is activated in sequence. It is as if, he states, a telegram (consisting of dots and dashes) was sent from London to Bristol, from Bristol to Birmingham, Birmingham to Edinburgh, Edinburgh to York, York back to London, and then on to Bristol again, and so on and on. It will be recalled (see p. 112) that Hebb makes a similar assumption in describing his "cell assemblies." (2) The second assumption (Young, 1951, p. 36) is that every time a cell is stimulated into action "a mark is left in the brain. There is evidence that the cells of our brains literally develop and grow bigger with use, and atrophy or waste away with disuse." This second assumption provides for a relatively permanent change in the brain structure. (3) A third assumption concerns the possibility that the brain, like an electronic calculator, makes self-corrective adjustments based on the principle of feedback. Thus an automatically guided airplane or missile can be set on a course and any deviation from such a course is reflected by an input change which sets into action the necessary degree of correction. A simple house-heating thermostat reflects the same principle. Is it too wild a speculation to presume that a living brain is able to perform, with much more complicated possibilities of manifold connections, what a thermostat can do? As a matter of fact, the brain even contains a "thermostat" or heat-control center for the body and arranges for sweating or shivering as the need applies. With the feedback assumption in mind we can turn back to our octopus. Stimulation of retinal cells by the appearance of the crab sets off muscle movements and jet action designed to bring the octopus "on target." Evasive action on the part of the crab brings out corresponding changes in the octopus brain and, because of its advantage in speed and maneuverability, it grasps the crab.

When the white plate accompanies the crab, the octopus again darts out. The shock sets up stimuli leading to retreat just as the crab elicits approach. (The actual selection mechanism is not known and must be taken for granted just as we take for granted the reflex withdrawal of the hand from a hot object.)

In both instances of approach and retreat, chains of neural action were set up by the stimuli present. Approach would involve a chain of cells in the optic and motor areas with activation of numerous other cells in what, for convenience, we can call an "association area." (Young speaks of a "memory lobe" in the octopus.) When the animal is shocked in the presence of the crab and plate, chains would be set up involving impulses in cutaneous areas and visual areas as well as the motor areas concerned with the retreat reaction. Simultaneously impulses from the optic and cutaneous areas would fire cells in the appropriate association areas. The cycle involved would run something like the following: The visual stimulus of crab and cutaneous stimulus of shock lead to activation of cells, (a) in touch and vision centers, (b) in corresponding association areas which we can speculatively call a touch-vision mixing area, (c) in motor areas activating retreat, (d) in a broader association area, and back to (a) again. With the repetition of the pattern we can expect to have the entire cycle reactivated by any component. In the case at hand, stimulation of the visual area by the white plate is enough to start the chain going again, and the animal retreats without shock.

Later we will go over available information on the action of the various neural factors in learning (see p. 260 f). Right now, we can conclude with the observation that the approach offered above made no reference to motivation in any form, nor to any needs, fears, anxieties, or reduction of any of these. Since we are unlikely to know or ever discover how the octopus *feels* it might be best for scientists to dismiss consideration of its feelings as irrelevant and animistic and to observe the same restrictions on animistic forces attributed to other organisms, including man.

MOTIVATION: A SUMMARY STATEMENT

With these observations we can conclude our inquiry into motivation for the present. We cannot pretend to have solved the problem of *"why* do we behave as we do?" Perhaps, like many other *why* questions which other scientists have discarded, this is also a psuedo-scientific question. The search for drives and motives has taken us around and about but always we have been led back to observations of stimuli and responses and the conditions which prevailed when the stimuli were being presented. Skinner (1938) recognized this situation long ago and set about developing a purely empirical psychology. The physiological advances of recent years, especially in connection with the EEG and the reticular system (the diffuse projection or "arousal" system of Hebb), suggest that the pure empiricism of Skinner, in terms of restricting observations to external factors, is not quite adequate an approach if we are to appreciate more fully and more intimately the contributions of the organism to its own behavior. We have seen how difficult it is to "deprive" an organism (Skinner's major operating condition in addition to reinforcement) of various alleged reinforcers. When an organism engages in behavior without any known deprivation we find ourselves embarrassed by positing one vague and undefined drive after another.

The approach of Miller and Dollard (1941) in terms of motivation as stimulation seems to get us off on a reasonable start. When we modify their views in terms of Wolpe's criticism and Hebb's addenda we emerge with a picture of motivation which helps us understand the behavior under observation. We are left with a concept of motivation which describes a *situation* instead of the traditional and mysterious biological urges, choices, needs, forces, yens, and impulses. When we add to the concept of motivation as above described the concepts of "set" and "feedback" we may be adding confusion and vagueness but at the same time we may be avoiding the greater fault of creating an entity or "construct" which in Skinner's terms might be a "linguistic fiction."

The argument presented in this chapter can be finally summarized by quoting Hebb's definition of motivation which, it should be quite apparent, does not define *anything* but rather describes an area of discourse:

"Motivation," says Hebb (1955, p. 244), "refers here in a rather general sense to the energizing of behavior, and especially to the sources of energy in a particular set of responses that keep them temporarily dominant over others and account for continuity and direction in behavior."

This is obviously not a definition but a statement about the subject matter we have been discussing. It is perhaps equally obvious that no other definition is required if we have learned that "motivation" is not an entity or a "force" but an expression referring to a wide variety of conditions which alter stimulus-response relationships.

A last word about motivation and learning is in order before we leave the subject. We do not pretend that we have accounted for the

mechanism of learning. That will take longer. The neurological speculations advanced here have persistently encroached on the learning
problem, however, and we can appreciate now why learning psychologists have been so preoccupied with motivation. They find that they
cannot talk about either concept without the other intruding itself.
In the next chapter we will find that motivational questions will also
prove obnoxiously intrusive.

10 The Principle of Reinforcement

For years controversies in learning theory have stormed about the question of reinforcement. The position taken on reinforcement serves to divide the warring theoretical camps as the burning issue. In this chapter we will review the history of the problem, compare and evaluate the positions taken by the adversaries, and finally attempt to evaluate the evidence and perhaps reach some reasonable integration. Like the problem of motivation, that of reinforcement has numerous ramifications and cannot be appreciated without study. We will have to dig.

THE LAW OF EFFECT

The concept of reinforcement, as we think of it today, was introduced by Thorndike (1931). In the last chapter we saw how this problem arose in connection with the concept of motivation. Following his experiments in puzzle-box learning Thorndike announced what he called "the Law of Effect" as a basic principle of learning. The announcement of a law does not establish it, however. Whether Thorndike developed his law from his observations or made his observation to satisfy his preconceptions is not determinable. In any event we can assume that the original observations were not complete and unequivocal because the law underwent numerous restatements and changes with the years. Postman (1947) has provided a comprehensive history of the Law of Effect and this should be considered required reading for the serious student. We can only note the salient changes. The original law proclaimed that learning was a function of its consequences. Stating it so barely one would expect it to receive short shrift from the critics. It was not barely stated, however, and appealed so strongly to common practice that it was received with open arms by American educators and has remained a key principle in elementary and secondary education.

To avoid bickering about minor problems which disappeared in the course of time, we can start with Thorndike's (1931) statement of his law: "Acts followed by a state of affairs which the individual does not avoid, and which he often tries to preserve or attain, are selected and fixated, while acts followed by states of affairs which the individual avoids or attempts to change are eliminated." The first class of affairs was usually called "satisfiers," and the second class was called "annoyers." In the very next year, Thorndide (1932) dropped the latter section dealing with elimination of acts and so we will not concern ourselves with it at this time.

From the nature of Thorndike's language it is clear that he was trying to be objective to what might be considered an extreme, if not a fault, about a subjective proposition. Whatever his intentions, the law has ordinarily been translated to mean that when responses are followed by "rewards" they are learned. The implied negative corollary is usually interpreted to mean that if no reward follows, there will be no learning.

The law itself does not include any statement of how the rewards operate to fixate the "bond" between stimulus and response although Thorndike was not adverse to some modest neurological speculation and at one time assumed that what he called a "satisfying state of affairs" somehow permitted the development of synaptic changes which strengthened the bonds.

The Law of Effect immediately raises two questions about which reams of controversial polemics have been written: (1) What is a state of affairs which the individual does nothing to avoid and often tries to preserve or attain, that is, what is a "reward," or "reinforcement" as it has come to be called? (2) How does it work?

In answering the first question, it is evident that no one can specify in advance the state of affairs which will be effective in fulfilling the Law of Effect in any particular case, considering the variables of the organism, its momentary condition and prior history, and the response involved. One must first study the organism and its reaction to various "states of affairs" to see if it will avoid or preserve or attain them. Knowing this much we proceed to a learning situation and note whether a given state of affairs will strengthen some selected behavior. We now have a test of the Law of Effect. If it works, we assume it helps to fixate the preceding acts. If not, we are stuck for explanations and begin the alibis. We are left with the conclusion that the nature of reinforcement is a circular proposition. Meehl (1950) attempted to get around the difficulty after recognizing the circularity in any particular learning situation by offering what he calls a "strong" Law of Effect which amounts to a statement that if some state of affairs or objective item serves as a strengthener in one situation, then it can be tried in others. If it also works in other situations, we have a "trans-situational reinforcer" and have avoided circularity. Thus, we can generally depend on an animal's usual food supply to serve as a reinforcer if it has been deprived of food for some time.

Hull and the Law of Effect. The Law of Primary Reinforcement. The answer to the second question is not so simple. How does the Law of Effect work? The original Thorndike statement was usually interpreted to mean that the *satisfaction* that followed the correct response somehow strengthened the behavior. "Satisfiers strengthen, annoyers weaken." Hull tried to remove the element of subjectivity and pleasure reference by translating the law into his own *Law of Primary Reinforcement* which reads as follows: (1943, p. 71) "Whenever a reaction (R) takes place in temporal contiguity with an afferent receptor impulse $(\dot{s})$ resulting from the impact upon a receptor of stimulus energy $(\dot{S})$, and this conjunction is followed closely by the diminution in a need (and the associated diminution in the drive (D), and in the drive receptor discharge (s_D), there will result an increment, $\Delta(\dot{s}\text{———}R)$, in the tendency for that stimulus on subsequent occasions to evoke that reaction."

It is clear that for Hull primary reinforcement (whatever be the means) amounts to drive reduction. Whenever a drive is diminished an increment in the strength of a bond occurs. If the drive is diminished, the drive stimuli are also presumably reduced in intensity and perhaps frequency. Hull does not specify.

It is obvious that both the Law of Effect and the Law of Primary Reinforcement might be more or less easily applied to the learning behavior of some hungry or thirsty animals, unless they were too hungry or thirsty (see Harlow, 1953). If hunger is allowed to continue for several days, indications from activity records suggest that some kind of depletion or deterioration sets in which makes learning or any other behavior improbable. The drive reduction principle must, then, restrict itself to certain limits. Thorndike fares a little better than Hull in this connection as he was willing to include any kind of after-effect as a reinforcer if it met his definition. Thus he has no problem with the learning of verbal material by grammar-school children or college students. If the teacher says "right" or rewards the pupils with gold stars or medals, the definitional requirements are met. For Hull, it becomes necessary to either find a drive in the learner, homeostatic or derived, or to find some other way "out." The other "out" is usually supplied by "secondary reinforcers." [1] The combination of natural and derived drives, natural and secondary drive reducers or reinforcers is enough for Hull to use as a basis for explaining learning of any variety. It should be noted at the time of Hull's statement of his primary law of reinforcement he presented no evidence that drives or drive stimuli were in fact being reduced during learning. This was merely a logical inference from behavior. Thus if a dog ate, he must be reducing a hunger drive. Later we shall look over the more recent data on this problem and re-examine the question.

Guthrie and the Law of Effect. Guthrie (1935) takes a position on the Law of Effect which is simple and straightforward, leaving no awkward questions to be answered about how things work. Denying that any consequent event can have any effect on what went before (a typical anti-Law of Effect argument) [2] he concludes that rewards have nothing to do with learning. The learning, if any, has already occurred before the reward is presented, regardless of how short a time interval intervenes. Skinner (1951) in a popular article emphasizes the need for great speed in supplying at least a secondary reinforcer as soon as a desired response is made. For Guthrie such speed is meaningless since he holds that the reward has no effect at all. Guthrie paradoxically agrees that rewards should be employed, if they are found to work, but they are only necessary because we do not

---

[1] Secondary reinforcers are any stimuli that accompany drive reduction. They come in time to serve as behavior strengtheners in the absence of a drive, if such a state need be posited, since it is also possible to supply derived drives (curiosity, exploration, anxiety). How these drives are reduced is not detailed. Perhaps the answer is obvious: curiosity is satisfied by answers, exploration by moving about, anxiety by elimination of the stimuli that brought it about.

[2] Adams (1954) has recently suggested that there need be no mystery about such a process if we conceive of it as a typical feedback mechanism. Such feedback phenomena are becoming more and more apparent in physiological observations (see Young, 1951).

know how to accomplish the same net result that the reward brings about without using it. What is this net result? Only that the reward interrupts the sequence of responses to stimuli in the learning situation so that the animal stops responding to the stimuli or situation involved in learning, and turns to the food or whatever may be the "state of affairs." The reward as such has no virtues of its own. Whether the animal likes the material or hates it is irrelevant as long as he stops responding to the stimulus situation the experimenter has introduced as a learning problem. To take an experimental example: If a rat is placed in a Skinner box and fed when the bar is pressed, he learns to press the bar because doing so brings about the new stimulus of food which takes the animal away from the bar. Being away from the bar, the rat cannot perform any other responses to it as a stimulus and so he cannot acquire any later response to the bar which differs from pressing it. The same thing could be achieved by removing the bar or the rat. The latter alternative was attempted by Seward (1942) who removed the rat as soon as it pressed the bar. Such rats learned to press bars, not so well as those that found food, but they learned. Whatever procedure results in removing the learner or the stimulus from the situation *safeguards* the learning. It does nothing to strengthen it as it is already as strong as it will ever be.

Direct and unequivocal support for Guthrie's view is just not available. Even in the experiment just cited reinforcement theorists will argue that the animal was reinforced by "handling," or in some way a drive (unknown) was reduced by removal of either bar or rat. The same kind of argument is advanced whenever an experimenter finds learning to have occurred and no obvious reinforcement supplied. Guthrie and Horton (1946) point out that the cats in their puzzle box did not always eat when they left the box and take this to mean that rewards are unnecessary. The most naïve beginning student can quickly point to the possible escape motive that was reduced by leaving the box.

While there are many considerations that invite further inquiry into Guthrie's position, we will not pause over them now. We can note, however, that while superficially Guthrie appears to differ from Hull on a basic issue, the difference may not be so great as is generally imagined. Guthrie (1935) frequently refers to the removal of "persistent" stimuli as those that must be eliminated. We can recognize that from Hull's point of view drive stimuli are eminently qualified for the distinction of "persistent." If these are removed, according to Guthrie, they are also "reduced," according to Hull. The net effect is the same—certain stimuli are eliminated. If we add the Miller-Dollard category of strong stimulus drives, the resemblance between Hull and Guthrie increases. Actually, however, Hull insists on some kind of positive, and presumably, physiological effect from the drive reduction on the neural factors in learning and here Guthrie parts company with Hull since, in Guthrie's view, the learning is already past history and cannot be affected. It should also be noted that Guthrie has no use for secondary reinforcers which for Hull must play the major role in human learning.

Tolman and the Law of Effect. A third view must now be considered. Tolman (1938b) has little use for either Hull or Guthrie in their positions on reinforcement. There are superficial similarities but the real differences are strong. For Tolman, as for Guthrie, learning takes place before rewards. The learning, however, consists of associations between signs and meanings or significants. The appearance of a reinforcing agent simply *confirms* the "expectancy" aroused by the sign. For Tolman, rewards represent only some kind of objective indications that some signs are followed by certain special meanings —when no rewards are used by the experimenter, the animal learns that none can be expected in the presence of certain signs. We have already discussed (p. 80) the latent learning experiments of which Tolman is fond and which clearly bring out his concept of the effect of reinforcement. According to these experiments, animals that were allowed to explore a maze without any rewards in the goal box learned to take the correct route to the goal box almost immediately after they found food in the goal compartment. Tolman interprets this as showing that the animals knew the correct path (as well as numerous incorrect ones) as a result of their explorations. They had learned "what leads to what." When it became useful to take one path rather than another, they merely selected the correct (shortest) path to the goal. Rewards have nothing to do with learning; they merely serve to confirm certain expectancies in situations where rewards are used.

The suggestion that learning occurs because expectancies are confirmed suffers from lack of direct proof. Such proof can hardly come from animal experimentation with which Tolman is more or less preoccupied. Subjective reports on this question from humans usually receive little attention from reinforcement psychologists (see Fig. 10.1). They will quickly point to the possible reduction of anxiety in human behavior as the real basis for learning. The inferences drawn from latent learning experiments are always denounced by reinforcement theorists. The reinforcement position seems to be either (a) there is no such thing as latent learning in the first place (and this is supported by numerous studies (see p. 80), or (b) when latent learning appears to have occurred, it really happened by drive reduction. Thus it is possible that animals reduce exploratory drives, they enjoy the effects of handling when removed from the maze, they may have a delayed food reinforcement (even though an hour or more elapses since the training session), or there are intra-maze factors which provide drive stimuli which can be reduced. In this connection MacCorquodale and Meehl (1951) were able to show that animals learned to avoid narrow cul-de-sacs with little turning space and were less successful in eliminating

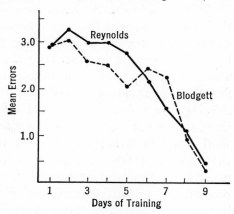

FIG. 10.1. Did latent learning occur? From these two experiments one experimenter, Blodgett, argues that there are no signs of learning until after food was introduced on the seventh day. Because of the drop in errors on the eighth day, Blodgett claims the previous learning was "latent." Reynolds argues for gradual learning even without a food reward. Does Blodgett's curve show gradual learning? (After Blodgett, 1929, and Reynolds, 1945b.)

wide culs. They argued from this experiment that animals were learning to avoid the culs (the reinforcing feature was the freedom from the annoyance of turning about in cramped quarters). Tolman and his students have tried to approach the problem from the opposite or negative end; that is, experiments are set up which purport to show how behavior changes as a consequence of fulfillment of a negative expectancy. Thus, Seward and Levy (1949) tried to demonstrate that if a rat could be shown that there was no food in an accustomed place it would then refuse to go to this place when put in position to do so. They found their rats quickly learned to just sit the test trials out. Bugelski, Coyer, and Rogers (1952) criticized the experimental design of Seward and Levy and in a repetition of the experiment failed to find evidence of such negative goal learning.

The need for an integration of reinforcement theory. Here we have three prominent psychologists of unquestionable integrity and of high intellectual stature, with broad experience of many years of coping with learning problems, disagreeing on a basic issue. Is it likely that only one is correct, that two are totally and helplessly confused? Are all three wrong and wrong because the problem is beyond us? Or is it possible that all three are correct in one or several features of their views and that like the seven blind men and the elephant they are perfectly correct in what they are saying without any of them being fully correct in describing the total situation? To the present writer the last possibility has the greatest appeal as it appears incredible that their years of observations can be dismissed as incorrect, considering the volume of mutual criticism and self-correction. If it should turn out that all three views are correct in substance then we shall either find that learning is a much more complicated business than heretofore even imagined or we may find, as has happened in other areas, that a more general view can accommodate all three approaches in a broad integration. The nature of such an integration has been suggested in the previous chapter, but before we consider it, the several views about reinforcement deserve a fuller examination. We must first discover what must be integrated. There is no point in trying to integrate unmanageable material. Our concern is no longer with the Law of Effect which deals with rewards as actual objects, events, or "states of affairs." There is no question but that rewards "work." Everyone uses them in practical pedagogy. Every theorist has rationalized their use in one way or another: for Hull they reduce drives; for Guthrie they end learning sessions; for Tolman they confirm expectancies.

Our real concern is to examine the principle of reinforcement and find out what we must accept and what can be rejected, to find the irreducible minimum that must be explained, and perhaps to find a factor that is common to drive reduction, ending of stimulation, and confirmation of expectancies. To do this we shall have to examine some of the evidence on which the various claims about reinforcement are based.

REINFORCEMENT AND THE PRINCIPLE OF DRIVE REDUCTION

The various problems that arise from the consideration of reinforcement stem almost directly from the work of Hull, and we must begin our appreciation of these problems with his analysis. Hull's basic proposals are that learning occurs when an organism, under the influence of a drive, does something which is followed by reduction or diminution of the stimulation from the drive. Whatever responses occur just prior to such drive reduction are learned. Whatever stimuli are present are associated with these responses. In those instances where no drive reduction can be readily presumed because no primary goal has been attained, secondary reinforcers are assumed to be present and their appearance is assumed to strengthen bonds just as primary reinforcers do. Hull does not indicate what happens to the drives when only secondary reinforcers are present. Anyone is free to speculate about possible results to the organism. We have already noted Osgood's speculation (see p. 216).

Support for Hull's theory of reinforcement has been offered in various experimental approaches which deal with one phase or another of his theory. A direct verification of the principle of primary reinforcement is not available for reasons of obvious difficulty. To verify the principle it would have to be shown that learning occurs (in increments) as the drive is reduced or diminished. Since an increment of learning cannot be observed but only inferred, we have one immediate source of trouble. To observe the diminution of a drive is also impossible and will remain so until we can identify the drive stimuli and watch them become "diminished." Only indirect and inferential approaches are available and these have taken various forms and degrees of remoteness from the physiological phrasing of the principle. We can look at some recent attempts to support the drive reduction postulate in relatively direct fashion.

The first experiment to be considered is one by Hull et al. (1951) and is reminiscent of an old Pavlovian experiment. A mongrel dog was subjected to surgery during which the esophagus was cut and the two cut ends brought to the skin surface where they healed to form fistulas in the throat. Any food taken by mouth would pass out through the upper fistula and could be collected and weighed. The animal could be fed by inserting food into the lower fistula directly. By inserting a coupling between the fistulas the dog could eat more or less normally, the food taking a slightly longer route than usual. With such a preparation Hull was able to make a number of observations of great interest. In the first place, it was found that in "sham" feeding (the food all passing out of the upper fistula) the dog would eat for long periods, at first eating almost as much as his own weight. In eight days he gave up this type of jaw exercise and refused to eat at all in the "sham" fashion. Hull hesitates to label this extinction

because of the extreme fatigue from long periods of eating and because there were no tests of spontaneous recovery. In another observation, the animal readily learned to select one alley of a two-choice
discrimination box when he was really able to eat by means of the
esophageal link. Choice of the wrong alley was followed only by sham
feeding. A third experiment compared sham feeding with no feeding
at all and resulted in a distinct advantage for the sham feeding—an
indication for Hull of the eating process itself as a secondary reinforcer. In a final test, the animal learned to select the correct alley
when fed directly (lower fistula). The wrong choice was followed by
pseudo-esophageal feeding (that is, a catheter was inserted, just as in
regular esophageal feeding, but no food was delivered). Hull comments cautiously about the data because of various limitations of the
experiment. It is safe to conclude, however, that as far as learning is
concerned, giving a hungry dog food is a better practice to initiate
learning than not giving food. This holds true whether the animal
gets the food by eating it or by having it dropped into his stomach.
The process of chewing and swallowing (sham feeding) is better
than not eating. Whether drives are reduced in either case cannot be
determined. The inferences, of course, are that the food in the stomach directly reduces the drive. Food in the mouth is presumably a
secondary type of reinforcement that must have been learned and
established by some type of reinforcement gradient (see p. 177).

Another experiment of a related nature has been reported by
Berkun et al. (1952). In this instance albino rats underwent surgery
during which plastic fistulas were arranged to join the stomach to the
abdominal skin. The rats could now be fed normally by mouth or
directly by fistula. Saline could be substituted for a food formula as
a control for direct feeding. The animals were "reinforced" in three
ways on arriving at the goal compartment of a maze. The three
methods showed the following differences: (a) Normal mouth feeding was superior to fistula feeding (a combination of primary and secondary reinforcement). (b) Direct feeding, by fistula, was superior to
the control condition (saline through fistula).

Coppock and Chambers (1954) attempted an even more direct
test of drive-reduction theory. They arranged for a flow of a glucose
solution directly into a rat's blood stream (through a needle inserted
into the caudal vein) whenever the rat's head was turned to an originally nonpreferred side as the rat lay strapped in a confinement apparatus. Control rats received normal saline for the same kind of head

movement. The glucose-supplied rats appeared to learn to keep their heads on the reinforced side as far as relative time spent is concerned. Coppock and Chambers concluded that their findings were "consistent with the hypothesis that reduction of a physiological need is sufficient for reinforcing a habit." It should be noted in connection with this experiment that "consummatory behavior" seems to be held to a minimum.

Other studies designed to support the drive-reduction principle are of greater remoteness and it is questionable as to what they actually demonstrate beyond the fact that hungry animals learn when given food for correct responses. Whether this involved actual drive reduction or secondary reinforcement or the operation of some entirely different principle such as Guthrie's or Tolman's cannot be determined. Hull's supporters are inclined toward accepting the general view that most learning, even that involving food-type reinforcers, is due to secondary reinforcement (see above and p. 270), because actual drive reduction is considered to take too long to account for the rapidity of learning in some instances. It might be useful to point out that Hull recognized that even in the classical Pavlovian experiment the food powder blown into the dog's mouth would serve as a secondary reinforcer and would not qualify as a "pure" primary reinforcer.

The manner in which food or eating and chewing behavior comes to serve as a secondary reinforcer has not been detailed by anyone. According to Hull, a stimulus acquires secondary reinforcing power only if it accompanies drive reduction. This would mean that some food should be available to serve as an external stimulus at the same time that some drive stimulation is diminished. The condition is presumably met, and very strikingly so, in infancy where feeding is prolonged and digestion and assimilation fairly rapid. The sight of a nipple or feeding bottle thus might become secondarily reinforcing. The fact that even the youngest baby begins to suck as soon as the lips feel the nipple and before milk has entered the mouth might leave a little doubt about this suggestion. In any event we have no other.

Attacks on the drive reduction principle. Although Hull postulates drive reduction as the basis for learning, his theoretical system (1943, 1952) does not specify any operations by which drive reduction can be measured or otherwise observed. Instead, he translates the postulate of drive reduction into a statement which makes habit formation a function of *number of reinforcements*. This dependence on a frequency of reinforcement position is forced upon him inasmuch as he never defines "drive" according to his own rules (that is, he does not show how drive as an intervening variable is "securely anchored" at both ends of an S-R chain).[3] Making learning or habit formation a function of frequency of reinforcement introduces new difficulties and controversies such as those involved with one-trial learning, sensory-sensory conditioning, unmotivated learning, the continuity-discontinuity problem, and others we have examined in discussing "frequency" as a measure of learning (see p. 172). Changing to a frequency of reinforcement principle enabled Hull to escape the criticism coming from the more or less logical conclusion that if learning depended upon drive reduction, then the more the drive was reduced, the more learning should take place. Evidence for such a conclusion has never been obtained. (The evidence appears to support the notion that greater incentives, that is, greater rewards, increase performance but not learning. See Chap. 9, p. 230.) We are left with no basis for dealing with the relationship between amount of reward (or amount of drive reduction) and learning. All we can conclude from Hull's presentation is that learning is a function of frequency of reinforcements but we know nothing about *how much* reinforcement to provide. When a small reinforcement is equal to a large one as far as learning is concerned (see Coyer, 1953; Reynolds, 1950; and Furchgott and Rubin, 1953) then we are left puzzled. When no reinforcement is provided, as Harlow (1953) insists, and learning still occurs, we are even more puzzled. Are we to resort then to new drives and new unmeasurable kinds of reinforcers of these new drives, primary and secondary, or is it better to give up the whole concept?

Consummatory responses versus drive reduction. As we saw earlier, Guthrie's position on rewards was largely negative, consisting of statements that rewards are unnecessary and only useful as expedient ways of ending stimulation from the sources involved in the learning. Some of Guthrie's students, however, have gone beyond his position and tried to demonstrate that the kind of behavior engaged in at the conclusion of some S→R chains might be more relevant to learning than the ultimate consequences of such behavior. In the usual training situation, for example, the deprived organism is allowed to eat or drink. Such consummatory behavior is regarded as the effective agent in learning. According to this view, eating or drinking are the important factors, not food or water. Sheffield has been one of the leading

---

[3] See Koch (1954), pp. 107–8.

sponsors of this approach and in several experiments with his collaborators (Sheffield and Roby, 1950) he has been able to show that animals rewarded with saccharin learned more effectively than animals rewarded with glucose. The amount of consummatory behavior is regarded as the significant factor. In the saccharine experiments the taste is obviously a variable of consequence and proves to be more effective than a nutrient like glucose. In another experiment (Sheffield, Wulff, and Backer, 1951) with a sex partner as an incentive, rats learned just as effectively if they were able to mount the sex partners even though they were removed without opportunity to complete the sex act. The animals presumably could not have reduced a primary drive but they learned anyhow. Drive reductionists invoke secondary reinforcement propositions to account for such learning. Hull's own experiment with the esophageal dog will be recalled in this connection. It is not likely that the Sheffield type of experiment will cause any changing of sides in the controversy over drive reduction.[4]

FREQUENCY OF REINFORCEMENT AND RATE OF LEARNING

Partial reinforcement. As we have seen (p. 253), Hull makes habit acquisition depend on frequency of reinforcement and the logical inference is that the more some habit has been reinforced, the stronger it will be. While this appears to be what common sense would expect, many psychologists have chosen to question this conclusion and claim that stronger learning results from offering reinforcements for less than 100 percent of the trials. This procedure, which is known as "partial reinforcement," amounts to following some "schedule" of reinforcement such that responses are reinforced only every so often or after a certain amount of time has elapsed. Such reinforcement schedules are known as "reinforcement at a fixed ratio" and "periodic reinforcement." We shall have more to say about these schedules in Chapter 13 where their relationship to extinction is discussed. At the moment we are concerned only with the general problem of reinforcement in acquisition and will consider partial reinforcement only in general terms.

If we accept for the moment that learning might conceivably be

---

[4] Saccharine does not act as a secondary reinforcer; it does not appear to "extinguish" (see Sheffield and Roby, 1950).

better if reinforcement is withheld on some trials, does this mean that the Hullian concept is incorrect? Suppose that rats are trained on a T-maze to turn left for food but do not find food on some occasions. Is their learning going to suffer? Offhand it might appear so and the Hull position might appear to be in jeopardy. There is an easy answer, however, which might save the situation for Hull, and that is, of course, the ubiquitous secondary reinforcement. Denny (1946) showed that learning was indeed poorer in a T-maze situation if, on the nonrewarded trials, new and different goal boxes were placed at the ends of the maze. When the old, original, boxes remained, getting into such boxes was found to be sufficient reinforcement for the rats and they learned equally well compared with a 100 percent reinforcement group. So long as the argument from secondary reinforcement is available, the "partial reinforcement" findings are not particularly disturbing to Hull's views. In a later chapter (see p. 349) we will consider other aspects of partial reinforcement training procedures that may account for the usual findings in favor of partial reinforcement when subjects undergo extinction.

The continuity problem and reinforcement. At this time we will merely remind the reader of the continuity-discontinuity controversy. We have already considered it (see p. 135) and will refer to it again in the next chapter. For the present it is enough to remember that reinforcement is alleged to work incrementally on every occasion that it is present even though no behavioral changes are observable at first. A response low in the hierarchy may need considerable reinforcement before it even attains threshold level, according to Hull. We are probably not in position yet to derive a verdict from the limited and controversial studies now available.

Sensory-sensory conditioning. One form of attack on reinforcement theory was launched via the hypothesis that sensory events themselves could be associated. If an organism did nothing but sit more or less idly by while stimuli were presented in pairs, and if later one such sensory event could be shown to bring about the other, it would justify the conclusion that nothing had to be done by the organism for learning to take place. If no response occurred, none could be reinforced, and, therefore, reinforcement could be ignored as a principle of learning. Birch and Bitterman (1949) presented the strongest theoretical orientation favoring a sensory-sensory foundation for learning. We have already reviewed some samples of the experimental literature dealing with sensory-sensory conditioning and will not repeat the discussion here (see Chap. 5, p. 152). Because there is no obvious reinforcement presented in sensory-sensory experiments, reinforcement theorists are reluctant to accept the findings. The usual interpretation is that some *reaction* does take place to which the separate stimuli are conditioned. In Brogden's (1939) light-bell experiment with the dog, for example, the bell might have aroused some sort of startle response (this would have had to be extremely modest since Brogden did not report observing any such response) and the stimuli from this response are the real conditioned stimuli. Such an explanation takes advantage of the concept of mediation (see p. 152) and makes the assumed implicit response function as a mediator of the response in both conditioning and test phases. Wickens and Briggs (1951) apply the same sort of reasoning to the reaction-time experiments of Brogden.

Wickens and Briggs demonstrated how results like those from sensory-sensory conditioning experiments could be obtained without ever pairing the two sensory stimuli with each other. Instead of pairing a light with a tone, they had subjects say "now" when either a light or tone sounded. Later, the subjects responded to a tone in a typical finger-withdrawal experiment. Following a number of such trials, a light was presented and subjects were found to respond to the light as frequently as a sensory-sensory control group. They interpreted their findings as demonstrating the mediation role of the verbal response: "Now." Whether such mediating responses are actually required is still a question. There is, physiologically speaking, no good reason why sensory activities in the nervous system cannot become associated or why responses cannot be short-circuited out of the pattern as Hebb has suggested.

A recent experiment by Silver and Meyer (1954) in which rats were trained to make an avoidance response after light-tone preconditioning seems to demonstrate the reality of sensory-sensory conditioning. At present we are not sufficiently acquainted with the technique of sensory-sensory conditioning to form any but tentative conclusions. Long experience with S-R conditioning has familiarized us with the details of controlling the behavior of animals in response patterns. In the sensory-sensory procedure we have no great background of experience and hardly know what to look for. We do not know for example, how many preconditioning trials to employ for best results, how the trials should be spaced, what intensities and durations to use, how much overlap, if any, there should be between stimuli, whether the stimuli must follow each other in an A-B order, or whether a B-A order would also work. These are only a few of the questions that need further investigation.

There seems to be less reluctance at present among S-R psychologists to accept S-S conditioning. (See p. 80 where Spence is quoted as no longer interested in perpetuating the original controversy.) If the actuality of sensory-sensory conditioning is ever demonstrated in some satisfactory detail, and if no response can be specified, then a strict drive-reduction view will hardly be tenable since this is tied to response learning in its original statement. Leuba's (1941) experiments in hypnosis and conditioning should be consulted in connection with the sensory-sensory controversy. Leuba reports conditioning subjects to report itches or odors and thereby raises the difficult question of what is meant by the term "reaction." The issue of sensory-sensory conditioning will prove somewhat irrelevant in our subsequent evaluation of reinforcement theory where we will concern ourselves with the neural factors involved in conditioning rather than with muscle or organ responses, overt or covert.

Conditioning of emotional responses. In an earlier chapter, we were much concerned with avoidance learning (see p. 65). At that time we considered the distinction between instrumental and classical learning and noted that some theorists, for example, Mowrer, regard the acquisition of fear to be a form of learning wherein no reinforcement can be observed. Thus far, no reinforcement theorist has come up with a satisfactory argument which would account for the learning of fear in terms of drive reduction. Miller (1946) does attempt an argument from analogy, using some data of Sullivan (1950) to show that the acquisition of a fear response follows the same pattern of development as does the learning of other responses where drive reduction can be presumed more readily.

It might be argued that fear *is* drive reducing in itself, that it eases pain, even though superficially and subjectively the opposite seems to be the case. Hebb's (1949) analysis of pain suggests some possibilities in this connection and we might consider at least that neither pain nor fear are the same without each other. The occurrence of fear along with pain may have definite survival value (see Cannon's 1929 emergency theory) in preparing an organism for greater energy exertion through release of sugar, for more rapid coagulation of blood in case of wounds, and so on. Such survival value may be an inherent reinforcement and as such could be an answer to those who insist on the nonreinforced nature of fear learning.

Incidental learning and learning under irrelevant drives. We have already discussed alleged instances of learning without motivation and, therefore, by implication, learning without reinforcement (see p. 225). Since the evidence for nonmotivated learning is dubious or at least debatable, it is not particularly disturbing to reinforcement theory. It is mentioned here only to fill out the pattern. Irrelevant drive learning is equally equivocal since reinforcement theorists appear to be quite as nimble in finding sources of reinforcement as non-reinforcement theorists are in pointing out the lack of suitable reinforcers (see p. 226).

In summary, it is just about as impossible to prove that reinforcement works in any of the ways proposed by Hull, Guthrie, or Tolman as it is to prove that motivation is or is not required for learning (see previous chapter). The problem is either unsolvable with present techniques and theoretical phrasing or it is a pseudo-problem created by the semantic difficulties we have spent so long in creating for ourselves in trying to deal with scientific questions concerning living beings in an unscientific way.

Before turning to any attempts to view the problem from a neurophysiological point of view, mention should be made of what is in a sense a defeatist solution of the problem. McGeoch (1942), finding the situation as unresolvable as we have just indicated, decided to accept the wealth of empirical observations that testify to the advisability of reinforcing the learner for his efforts. Everyone either claims or admits that rewarding desired responses is the practical thing to do regardless of how it works. McGeoch restated this in what he called the "Empirical Law of Effect," a term he took over from Carr (1925). According to the Empirical Law of Effect, acts are fixated and eliminated as functions of their effects; any attempt to go beyond this statement involves us in the theoretical disputes we have just reviewed. Perhaps the empirical law has found favor with some psychologists but few have announced themselves as in strong agreement. Skinner (1950), denouncing all theoretical attempts at this stage in the development of psychology, proposes that a more empirical orientation be adopted but he finds himself pretty much alone and undeservedly ignored by the theory-minded operators. For Skinner, anything that reinforces is a reinforcer, and the problem is to describe the conditions under which a reinforcer affects the rate of a selected behavior unit. This is enough of a task for the present. Skinner's empirical position is not favored by anyone with strong theoretical urges but it may attract followers from disappointed or disenchanted supporters of the old guard. The rebound may prove an undesirable basis for an analysis of the work psychologists have cut out for themselves. Before we go completely empirical it might be worthwhile to look at still another view concerning reinforcement.

LEARNING AND NEURAL ACTION

In the last chapter we considered the action of the brain in connection with motivation and concluded with the suggestion that what is normally referred to as motivation in behavioral terms can perhaps be more readily appreciated as a disturbance of the normal rhythms of the brain. The hypothesis was elaborated to cover the several varieties of alleged motivation processes. When the brain patterns are disturbed and altered from a normal pattern, the owner of the brain is motivated. No other meaning of the term has received general acceptance. Perhaps the meaning offered here will.

What kind of verbal magic can we now employ on the term "reinforcement"? The necessary steps are quite obvious. When the neural disturbance is terminated the motivation disappears, and whenever motivation is eliminated we have reinforcement. Reinforcement then amounts to eliminating disorganization or disturbance of neural function.

The general picture of how the neural reinforcement principle operates has been described by Young (1951) and we cannot do better than to quote from him (pp. 66–67):

These ways of acting that we learn give us a rhythm of behavior. The brain of course is not a passive mass of tissue, through all waking life it drives along. Awoken in the morning by some stimulus, it immediately begins to run through sequences of activities, according to the rules that it has learned. These sequences produce the actions by which the body lives. They are partly touched off by outside stimuli, but once started, they may run by themselves as independent trains in the brain, each combination starting another one.

The life of the new-born child consists largely of sleep, of periods, that is, in which numerous brain cells are firing in unison. We know this because electrical records show that in a baby there are very large and regular brain waves. This unison or synchrony becomes broken up by the nerve impulses arising from the receptor organs, internal or external. The receptors are so arranged as to alert the organism that its needs are not satisfied; it must be up and doing! The hungry baby wakes and cries, giving the sign stimulus that brings the mother's attention. At first it kicks and clutches at random, until it obtains the milk. When the stomach is filled, the hunger impulses from it stop, the brain returns to its simple synchronous activity, and the baby goes to sleep. But in the course of each waking episode there are changes going on in the brain. Actions, at first random, develop into little sequences, according to patterns developed during previous wakings, and these become printed or otherwise recorded in the brain.

Meanwhile the world does not stand still. The mother becomes gradually less co-operative and the child has to learn to get what it needs by ways other than crying. The eye movements are used to discriminate between faces, cups, and other objects, so that the output of the brain leads to the making of appropriate noises, the giving of names that produce satisfactory action by others—that establish communication. The effect of stimulations, external or internal, is to break up the unison of action of some part or the whole of the brain. A speculative suggestion is that the disturbance in some way breaks the unity of the actual pattern that has been previously built up in the brain. The brain then selects those features from the input that tend to repair the model and to return the cells to their regular synchronous beating. I cannot pretend to be able to develop this idea of models in our brain in detail, but it has great possibilities in showing how we tend to fit ourselves to the world and the world to ourselves. . . . In some way the brain initiates sequences of actions that tend to return it to its rhythmic pattern, this return being the act of consummation, or completion. If the first action performed fails to do this, fails, that is, to stop the original disturbance, then other sequences may be tried. The brain runs through its rules one after another, matching the input with its various models until somehow unison is achieved. This may perhaps only be after strenuous, varied, and prolonged searching. During this random activity further connections and action patterns are formed and they in turn will determine future sequences.*

The neural learning hypothesis. In the last 10 years considerable information has been accumulated about how the brain works, with the promise of a great deal more to come. The brain physiologists have not had the time to become specialists in the behavioral side of learning and when they begin to speculate about the role of the brain in learning they are liable to go astray. The learning psychologist has not had the benefit of experience in neural physiology and his speculations are equally likely to be awry. It is probably dangerous for a scientific appreciation if the two disciplines go their separate ways if, as it appears, they have much to contribute one to the other. The psychologist, fortified by some elementary brain physiology, is in the

---

* Quoted with permission of the Oxford University Press.

position now of being able to tell the physiologist a little better than in the past what the brain must be like in its action to accommodate learning data. We can invite the physiologist to look for and identify certain key operations that findings from learning experiments dictate. This can be done, however, only if we do not take a strong position, based on sentimental loyalties, to the effect that only one theorist is right. We must allow, for example, for not only one-trial learning but also for the effects of repetition. We must allow for so-called sensory-sensory as well as sensory-motor conditioning. Any theoretical partisanship at the present time is intellectual suicide.

An intelligent savage who has never seen an automobile before might be asked to tell us what is under the hood. His answers might be interesting, and depending upon his experience with the kinds of components involved, there might be a fair approximation to some general principles. The average housewife who turns on her television set might not do better in describing what goes on behind the knobs. How much better prepared are we to state what goes on in the brain when we learn? Walter (1953) suggests that in our present state of knowledge we are still pretty much in the position of the engineer and the problem of the Black Box. Wires come into and go out of the Black Box. There are keys that connect with the incoming wires and there are gadgets attached to the outgoing wires. Pressing a key results in a gadget performing some routine. The problem for the engineer is to describe what is in, and what goes on, in the Black Box.

If the number of wires is not great and the kinds of performances not too complicated, an engineer might give us a reasonable approximation of what the box contains. He can do this because he has some background from which to evaluate the possibilities. Our background in relation to brain operations is still extremely limited and we must proceed slowly and carefully with the brain-box problem. What do we know about it that can be of help?

Much of the knowledge that exists concerning the brain is, unfortunately, of little value for learning theory and what will be detailed now will appear as an extremely poor harvest. If we recognize that this information has been accumulated only recently by a handful of men we might feel a little better about it and hope for more in the near future. Here are some facts that appear pertinent:

1. The brain develops small charges of energy which, when properly amplified, recorded, and analyzed, appear to occur as relatively continuous wave forms of varying amplitude and frequency.

2. Different frequencies can be shown to be prominent in different parts of the brain.

3. The difficulties of analysis make recognition of all possible waves an unsolved problem at present. But four prominent types of waves are sufficiently common and easily identified to merit labeling; these are Alpha (8–13 cps), Beta (6–9 cps), Theta (4–7 cps), and Delta (0–4 cps) waves.

4. Delta waves are characteristic of babies and young children. Alpha waves do not become normally prominent until adolescence in most people.

5. Delta waves have been identified as prominent in certain personality types; for example, juvenile delinquents have been shown to have a higher proportion of Delta wave records than nondelinquents.

6. It used to be believed, but it is not true, that Alpha waves disappear when the eyes are open. This is generally true but not in all cases. There are different types of adult brain patterns—some show prominent Alpha rhythms and some do not. Some people lose Alpha rhythms when eyes are opened, some do not. Some lose them if they "visualize" and some do not. In some cases, people can even read without loss of Alpha rhythms.

7. Theta rhythms appear to be related to thalamic activity. They appear frequently in one or the other of the following conditions: (a) if some disagreeable stimulus is presented, or (b) if some pleasant stimulation is withdrawn.

8. Brain patterns are highly individual, like fingerprints, and show changes with growth from infancy on. After adult states are reached they tend to be fairly stable.

9. As one gets drowsy and begins to fall asleep the amount of activity in the brain seems to dwindle, and slow, large (Delta-type) waves appear. Stimulation of a sleeper results in an immediate change of pattern which will return to a normal sleep pattern if stimulation ceases.

10. Introduction of a flickering stimulus (about 8–12 flashes per second) can force a brain rhythm of the same frequency into existence (sometimes with disturbing results).

11. Introduction of any stimulus can be assumed to affect one or another rhythm although this may be difficult to demonstrate for brief and modest stimuli.

12. Strong stimulation, as in shock treatment, provokes violent disturbances in brain rhythms.

13. The brain is continuously active although the pattern varies from moment to moment as well as in longer cycles like the sleep-wake cycle.

14. Measures of variability of rhythms suggest that variability is greater in persons of higher intellectual attainment.

Do these statements suggest any theoretical formulations that can be matched with learning processes? What kind of contents do they suggest for the Black Box?

The speculations of Young (1951) are interesting in this connection. Young presumes, as does Hebb (1949), that the process of learning must take place somewhat as follows:

1. Learning is a more or less continuous process starting before birth and ending with death. The learning in infancy is of vital importance and sets the stage for future learning. Each bit of learning modifies the brain so that future learning finds the way smooth or difficult, depending upon the prior patterns imposed on the brain. In adulthood, learning new ways of behaving to situations which have previously established their own patterns will be increasingly difficult.

2. In early stages of life, some patterns can be learned readily. The charming story told by Lorenz (see Beach, 1951, p. 426) of the gosling that becomes attached to any moving stimulus it sees at birth and behaves toward it as toward a mother is a case in point.

3. The learning of any kind of association between external events (whether these be stimuli or responses) amounts to a connection being formed between neural elements (nerve cells and their ramifications). Such a connection is formed, not in an idle brain, but in a complex of activity which must necessarily be modified if a new connection is to result. We can presume with Hebb that these associations function in a manner he describes as cell assemblies and phase sequences (p. 112).

4. The introduction of any stimuli alters the ongoing pattern, such alteration persisting until either (a) the stimulus ceases acting with little or no effect on the pattern which remains; or (b) if the stimuli persist for some time (or are frequently repeated) they may alter the pattern more or less permanently. Such alteration may not be readily, if ever, identified because the number of component elements in the new association may be insignificant compared to the 15,000,000,000 neural cells.

5. The alteration of pattern is of such a nature as to facilitate the

accommodation and elimination of future stimuli of the same type so that the period of disturbance will be minimal (see 7).

6. Although Young appears to favor a homeostatic principle in the operation of the brain, this appears to be gratuitous, and for the present, unnecessary. The appearance of novel stimuli or novel combinations will not permit the normal state of affairs to remain, to be sure, but there is no need to presume any "need" for the brain to seek any return to "normal." The brain "adjusts" to the new stimulation if it can do so (meaning if it has channels for ready accommodation of such processes). If it cannot adjust to them it must incorporate them if it is to continue a normal existence.

7. The function of some of the rhythms appears to be that of "scanning" for certain types of stimulus processes, comparable to the scanning process in a television camera which "scans" for light and shadow patterns or signals. When such stimulus processes or "signals" are present, there is an end to the scanning and the rhythm temporarily ceases. With an end to the stimulation, the scanning resumes.

Applying the above account to learning, we can picture the idle organism with an active brain "scanning" or "looking for," waiting, or otherwise ready (except when sleeping) for stimulation. When stimulation related to one of the rhythms occurs, that rhythm is momentarily disturbed or eliminated and a new pattern imposed. The stimulation in the normal course of events (say a conditioning experiment) will last a matter of seconds and is gone. If some other source of stimulation is simultaneously present the two processes will jointly be incorporated to produce a different change in the rhythms from that either would produce singly. Subsequently either stimulus may bring on the changed pattern. With the elimination of the stimulation the rhythm will return, now somewhat modified and a little readier to handle the combination just previously present.

The description of the learning process suggested above is about as far as we dare go within the limits of the available knowledge of brain action. Perhaps we have already gone too far, as much of the information on which the suggestions rest is of a tentative nature, still in need of confirmation and additional support. Our picture of the Black Box may be far from accurate whenever we have intimated any detail. But the general principles of operation may be like those mentioned. The general picture described here will be referred to in subsequent sections as the "neural learning hypothesis."

Application of the neural learning hypothesis to reinforcement theory. If we look again at the three reinforcement theories we discussed awhile back, it may be possible to fit them into the neural hypothesis without stretching our imaginations beyond repair. Professors Hull and Guthrie give us no real trouble. We have already pointed out some resemblances between them and the views of both are more than superficially adaptable to a neural restatement. When strong or persistent stimuli are affecting an organism the organism responds in one way or another. Whether these stimuli are internal or external is irrelevant. The response cannot be made without first being "processed" by the brain. A response which readily and easily removes the stimulus restores the brain to normal activity patterns. We cannot presume learning to have taken place in such a case. If the response is not successful in eliminating the stimuli, the brain disturbance also persists. The brain must process more responses. Let us assume a relatively difficult trial and error situation with continuous brain disturbance. The responses follow upon one another, each setting up neural chains which persist for a while. The repetition of neural cycles results in the repeating of unsuccessful responses so characteristic of trial-and-error learning. The correct response, when it occurs, also sets up its neural linkages. Since it is the last response to the particular stimulus pattern present it is going to have the last neural pattern also, which, if it persists for a while, will have a chance to "grow" into a relatively permanent cycle. In the future, the brain disorganization will therefore be somewhat less extensive and less prolonged because at least some portions of it will be operating in a systematic manner within the larger disturbed pattern. On the next occasion that the same stimulus pattern is present, the likelihood of a particular cycle being set into action will be increased and the disorganization will be of briefer duration. With repetition, the time for the correct response to be made will decrease to virtual "reaction time speeds" and the disturbance of the total pattern will become minimal. An automatic habit is now established.

Before we proceed to an attempted incorporation of Tolman's views within this hypothesis, let us pause to review some evidence (mostly of a behavioral nature) which supports the hypothesis to some degree.

1. The view that some kind of neural events persist following stimulation is by no means novel. Müller and Pilzecker (see Woodworth, 1938, and McGeoch, 1942) posited such hardening processes as far

back as 1900. Apparent contradictions from retroactive inhibition studies are only that, apparent, and will be discussed later (see p. 321).

2. Hull bases much of his own speculations on an assumed neural aftereffect, the "stimulus trace." This is a persisting neural activity which follows stimulation and dissipates with time. Behavioral and neural evidence seems sufficient to support this assumption.

3. The evidence is conclusive that spacing learning is superior to massing when we are dealing with short intervals (under a minute). Thus nonsense syllables are learned better under 4-second rates of presentation than at any other shorter intervals (Hovland, 1938b).

4. When material is learned in temporal isolation from other material or stimulation it is readily learned. Thus, if we provide a situation where no other stimuli are effectively present (Leuba, 1941) learning is immediate and substantial.

5. The difficulties that seem to prevail in the learning of some laboratory problems may well be due to the failure of the responses to effectively remove the stimuli. This would account for the fact that voracious and starving animals cannot learn so well as mildly hungry ones and that well-fed animals learn easily (Harlow, 1953).

Coming back to Tolman now, we need no new assumptions to find his views compatible with the neural learning postulate. Only a modest measure of translation is required to reduce his language to neural terms. Hull (see Hull *et al.*, 1951) has already reduced Tolman's "expectancies" to *rg*'s—we have merely to reduce *rg*'s to their neural surrogates. Hebb has already done this in his description of cell assemblies and phase sequences, but even without his language we can appreciate what Tolman is talking about. When an animal is exposed to a sequence of stimulation (whether or not he makes overt reactions of gross muscles such as running places or pressing levers) the neural cycles like those we described in connection with the octopus and the crab (see p. 240) are set up so that a chain of activity is established and operates on a sequence basis which can be described simply as one thing leading to another. As the sequence unfolds each step generates the next just as the guided missile homes in on its target. There is no problem of "expectancies" unless the missile fails to make the necessary adjustments as the various circumstances arise. So, for the rat on the T-maze there is no problem of "expectancies"—he merely does what the stimuli dictate and each step leads to new stimuli which the brain is already preparing to receive because the cycle initiated by the first step is already in action. This is what "expectancy" means. The performance of a "correct" response allows the normal chain to complete itself or to "run off" because it depends on the stimulation from the reward to complete itself. Failure of appearance of stimulation of any kind for which the brain is "prepared," or "ready," likewise prevents the completion of the cycle. To illustrate from some simple sensory experiment: If a light normally precedes a sound, then a light-sound neural sequence will be established. The appearance of the light will herald the onset of the sound and the brain is "set" or ready for it. When the sound occurs the sequence runs off and normal rhythm is restored. Failure of the sound to occur results in the cycle running off only in part and without the normal facilitation from the *actual* sound which is required to complete the cycle and initiate the "return to normalcy." Such failure to return to normal is reported subjectively as disappointment, frustration, or lack of fulfillment of an expectancy. By projection we attribute such "expectancies" to animal subjects. Whether we gain or lose by such a projection is debatable. In any event, we find Tolman's "confirmation of an expectancy" to be in harmony with the neural hypothesis we have advanced and by no means at odds with a neural reduction of the Hull or Guthrie views.

An integration of conflicting views on reinforcement. It should be appreciated that the controversy between Tolman and reinforcement theorists has been obscured by the failure to pick apart the issues on which there is real disagreement and those upon which agreement is potentially possible. For example, the reinforcement theorists had for years slighted the notion of "expectancy" as mentalistic and inadmissible in a scientific analysis of behavior. Hebb (1949) has shown how such a concept can be introduced in an objective framework, and Hull himself used the term without quotation marks in his report on the eosophogeal dog (see p. 251). In Hull's thinking, expectancies have become more or less synonymous with rg, the fractional antedating goal response. Tolman is apparently not in violent disagreement with this interpretation (Tolman, 1949) and seems willing to concede that the Tolman-Gleitman (1949) experiment can be interpreted in such terms. Assuming that some general agreement can be reached on a translation of expectancy into rg or into Hebb's neural account of expectancy as a central facilitation for setting up of phase sequences for stimuli about to come, one of the issues can be considered as resolved.

The resolution of this issue, however, leads directly to a new consideration. Expectancies, rg's, or central facilitations can only function after some experience, that is, after learning has taken place. They are the results of learning, not the causes, certainly, and not the basic operators in the formation of learned associations—they are the associations themselves, mostly of a partial or fractional or fragmentary nature, but associations nevertheless. Appreciating this point, we recognize then that Tolman is talking about postlearning events and there is no reason whatsoever for any agreement on the issues involved when the theorists are not talking about the same thing.

Consider the kinds of experimental work in which Tolman has engaged. He has emphasized the studies in latent learning, spatial learning, sign-significate (corresponding somewhat to sensory-sensory) learning. In each and all of these experimental setups, learning itself is not observed during the acquisition period, but rather, *it is tested for* after the alleged learning has occurred. The Tolman-Gleitman (1949) experiment is a most informative example. In that experiment, it will be remembered (see p. 21), animals were given equal exposure to both sides of a T-maze (no attention to learning) and then shocked in one goal box detached from the T. Later a test (one trial) was given to determine if the animals had acquired any expectancy of shock in the appropriate goal box. The Seward and Levy (1949) experiment is another typical example. Animals were given a uniform number (10) of runs down an alley (no attention to learning); then they were given uniform exposure to the now foodless goal platform; finally, they were tested for the presumably acquired expectancy of "no food." It is true that several trials of this "extinction" were given, but no data of any type were reported on the acquisition of the expectancy. In the latent learning experiments, if we take the Blodgett experiment as gospel, learning was observed *not* taking place, although expectancies were somehow being formed. Again, the test of expectancy is the only measure of interest to Tolman.

It should now be clear that to reconcile the opposing views of Hull and Tolman would be impossible if they were actually talking about the same phenomena, but since they are not, there is no real difficulty. Hull admits, if that is the correct expression, that animals or anyone else can have expectancies (if we call them rg's) and Tolman has no objection to rg's. The only problem that remains is to fit the *acquisition* of expectancies into the general framework. Hull has already accounted for their acquisition on a reinforcement basis and his account is not at real variance with the hypothesis proposed here. Tolman (1938a) considers that the acquisition of expectancies is a function of "frequency" alone (although he does admit that the nature of the incentive objects may have some bearing on the relative intensity of the associative components). Since "frequency" alone will be seen to be inadequate as a sole principle (see Chap. 11), something else must be added to Tolman's views to account for acquisition. That something can readily be the reinterpreted account of reinforcement suggested earlier, namely, the termination of the neural disturbance aroused by the action of the stimuli which initiate the neural processes which are to be associated.

We can terminate the present section, then, with the conclusion that there is no basis for a controversy between the three major interpretations of reinforcement. To presume that Hull is right and Tolman wrong is to misunderstand the real problem. They are both correct, as is Guthrie, in describing their observations. They are all talking at different levels of interpretation and emphasizing different aspects of their observations in quite different experimental settings. There is considerable merit to broadening the scope of observations and trying out numerous experimental procedures. Had this been done more commonly, much controversy might have been avoided. The preoccupation with one type of experimental observation or one level of interpretation has resulted, apparently, in some type of "vested interest" which has led to controversy and shortsighted criticism of the adversary. If the views advanced here are accepted, we can write off the reinforcement controversy and start afresh in evaluating experimental findings in terms of the conditions under which they were obtained, regardless of the theoretical orientation of the experimenter.

Secondary reinforcement. The concept of secondary reinforcement was introduced by Skinner (1938) and in different terms by Bugelski (1938), Wolfe (1936), and Cowles (1937). Since Skinner's experiment appears to be the most pertinent to later developments we can describe it for illustrative purposes: Skinner first fed a rat in an empty box by dropping food pellets into a food dish by means of a mechanism that made a clicking sound when it worked. After a number of such presentations of food plus sound, Skinner inserted a lever into the box. The food magazine was now empty. Skinner observed that the animal now began to press the bar in a manner similar to that in which a rat that had been "reinforced" for pressing would operate the bar if no food were given. Bugelski found that a group of rats would continue to press a bar longer if the click sounded than would another group of rats for which a press was followed by silence, even though neither group received food. Wolfe and Cowles trained chimpanzees to use poker chips in a slot machine and then found that chimpanzees would work for poker chips and would solve problems when the reward consisted only of such chips. Estes (1949a), in a variation of Skinner's experiment, found that thirsty rats would press a bar if a click sounded when their previous experience in the situation consisted of being fed when the click sounded. Saltzman (1949) trained rats to run down a runway to goal boxes which differed from trial to trial. One box would contain food and a different box would not. The goal boxes were then attached to the ends of a U-maze, and Saltzman found that the rats would choose the side of a U-maze which led to a goal box in which they had previously been fed even though it now contained no food and had no other advantage over the goal box at the other end of the U.

The kinds of experiments mentioned above are the basis for all speculation about the role of secondary reinforcement in human learning. Gold stars and kind words are considered secondary reinforcers as might be coins, checks, smiles, or pats on the head. We have already indicated the way in which some of these so-called reinforcers might work (see p. 93). To review briefly, the click in the Skinner box is but one of a total pattern of stimuli associated with one phase of what is, contrary to usual opinion, a complicated serial response rather than a simple or elementary behavioral unit. The click is part of the stimulation that is associated with approaching the food cup which automatically puts the animal in position for pressing the bar. To select out the click and glamorize it into a "secondary reinforcer" is totally unnecessary, gratuitous, and theoretically harmful. If anything, such a stimulus might better be called a "secondary motivator" if there were any point in distinguishing it as either "secondary" or as a "motivator." It is not even so secondary a motivator as the metronome in Frolov's experiment on higher-order conditioning (see p. 11).

The size, shape, and decor of a goal box in the same way are stimulus features associated with eating and arouse appropriate eating responses which are frustrated by removal from the box as well as nonpresence of food. They probably serve to "strengthen" (that is, add to the stimulus pattern) food-approach responses if these are permitted. If the animal is immediately replaced on the starting leg of a T-maze, it may thus be more strongly "motivated" to choose the "good" goal box rather than the other. A direct experimental test of this interpretation is possible by delaying trials for 24 hours or some period longer than that used by Saltzman.

The secondary reinforcement value of tokens or other stimuli is not great in a new learning situation. Osgood (1953) points out how quickly they extinguish in experimental situations. Contrast this to the apparently strong value of grades in school and money in employment situations and it becomes clear that we are a long way from approaching "real life" behavior with the laboratory study of secondary reinforcement. It is possible that in new situations a secondary reinforcer functions as a mediator (see p. 98 f) between the stages in a phase sequence initiated by the response and those normally initiated by or accompanying a primary reward. It functions, in other words, as a substitute (neurally speaking) in the operations described earlier (see p. 118) for an expectancy. On the adult human level we can picture this possibility readily enough in terms of the operation of promises. A promise is a substitute for some present reality. Without the present reality, a phase sequence cannot run off appropriately. The promise (money, token, check, verbal assurance) comes to function, through learning, as a suitable phase sequence terminator, perhaps through arousing new phase sequences, allowing the original to run off.

On a lower level we find such "promises" as "clicks" or "white paint in a goal box" to operate also as sequence terminators to a more limited degree. With them present a sequence can begin to run its course. Without them, some frustration is experienced and the behavior begins to break down.

The neurophysiological view described above is broad enough to include the possible action of secondary reinforcers if such there be. They are, as Hilgard and Marquis (1940) proposed, most closely allied to Tolman's expectancies. If expectancies work as described earlier (p. 118) then they amount to external facilitative effects of stimuli on on-going neural cycles built up in the earlier presence of such stimulation. Presence of the "secondary reinforcer" allows the cycle to run off as it normally would. Its absence would result in the disruption of the pattern and consequent development of new cycles with other externally observed behavior patterns.

Until more evidence is available than we already have, there is no point to raising the question left unanswered by Hull as to how secondary reinforcement works. Some students (Osgood, 1953) like to believe that a secondary reinforcer might promote some suitable hormonal discharge which in some way reduces the drive present. Such speculation at this time, while justifiable when clearly labeled as speculation, seems much more powerful magic than our own brain-wave-pattern view and deserves little attention until some evidence is available. In Hull's system, no mechanism was offered for accounting for the operation of secondary reinforcers. They just rein-forced. This is equivalent to an "empirical law of secondary reinforcement" and can be used for what it is worth. It does not help the theory in any way and may be harmful in misleading research.

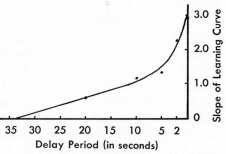

FIG. 10.2. The gradient of reinforcement. Groups of rats learned to press a Skinner bar in a nonpreferred direction. Errors could thus be counted and learning curves plotted. For each group of subjects the food reinforcement was delayed for a different interval from 0–30 seconds. The slopes of the learning curves of each group are plotted in the figure as solid dots. Note that with increasing delay of reinforcement learning is slower and slower. A delay of 34 seconds should result in no learning at all. (After Hull, 1943, p. 139.)

In recent years the role of the secondary reinforcer has grown very powerful; so powerful, in fact, that it has virtually replaced primary reinforcement. Following experiments by Perin (1943) which demonstrated that primary reinforcement did not work if the reinforcement was delayed for more that 5 seconds, Hull's system was hard put to account for learning any sequence which lasted longer than 5 seconds, such, for example, as a maze. (See Fig. 10.2.) Spence (1947) came to the rescue with the flexible explanation that any such learning took place as a consequence of a series of segmental learnings each reinforced by a secondary reinforcer. In learning a 4-choice maze, for example, the last choice might be reinforced by food (primary), the next to the last by a secondary reinforcer, the second choice by a lesser value of secondary, and the first by a still lower value of secondary reinforcer. This means of course that the first choice would be most poorly learned, and so on. Since this does not correspond to the facts,[5] other reasons are advanced to account for divergences.

[5] Hull (1947) reports that the third choice (next to the last) is most difficult.

The use of secondary reinforcement (itself in need of explanation) to account for failures of primary reinforcement to work shows the degree of facility of theoretical speculators although it attests to the sad state of such theory at the same time. As a sort of *reductio ad absurdum* we note that children sometimes have to be secondarily reinforced to indulge in eating! When an infant must be encouraged to eat by other devices, one begins to wonder about the means by which the secondary reinforcer comes into being. It appears to be already there.

Negative reinforcement, punishment. By and large reinforcement psychologists advocate the principle that "you can catch more flies with sugar." What about "spare the rod and spoil the child"? Science usually does not develop by collecting adages. Thorndike originally included a negative aspect in his Law of Effect (see p. 244) which, in effect, amounts to a statement that punishment following an act weakens the bond between the stimulus and response. Thorndike retained his views until 1932 when he decided that the negative side was not working out in experiments in which he "punished" college students by saying "wrong" when they made incorrect choices in word-matching. Saying "wrong" instead of eliminating the particular choice made it a more likely candidate on a repeat run. Thorndike concluded that punishment strengthens bonds, if anything. This view was rapidly adopted by newspaper psychologists and progressive educators and became part of the merry-go-round of child-rearing practices.

Other kinds of experimentation supported the general view that punishment fixates or at least does not weaken bonds. Tolman, Hall, and Brenall (1932) reported that shocking a human subject for selecting the correct turns in a maze led to rapid mastery. Obviously it can be argued that, in this case, the shock can hardly be considered a punishment. Muenzinger (1934) likewise showed that rats could make use of mild shocks as cues for correct turns. Pavlov (1927) had long ago reported that by starting with a mild shock paired with food, a salivary response could be conditioned to such a strong shock that the skin was damaged. The same argument applies as above.

In a series of experiments by Estes (1944) a typical Skinner box bar-pressing response was established in rats. The rats were then shocked if they touched the bar. The behavior of bar-pressing was at first "inhibited," that is, the rats would not approach the bar. If a period of rest intervened, the rats would again approach and behaved just like rats who had not been shocked. Longer waits were necessary for the stronger shocks. Weaker habits were more affected than strong habits. In effect, punishment did not weaken the bonds, it simply "suppressed" the response temporarily.

The purport of the experiments mentioned above appears to be to demonstrate that punishment is ineffective in eliminating behavior. This conclusion appears to win favor with various sentimentalists as well as with such theorists as Guthrie who, finding no special use for positive reinforcement, finds none for negative either. For Guthrie, if an act is performed, that does it. It is learned, regardless of whether it is good or bad for the organism or its parents. His example (1935) of the friend who was unable to enter his garage without suffering a powerful blow from a swinging weight which could not be seen until the door was opened is supposed to illustrate the point that negative aftereffects are ineffective.

The general conclusion that punishment does not eliminate behavior may be found acceptable if we recognize the complexity of the problem and introduce various modifiers. After all, the burnt child does shun the flame. Why should it? Dollard and Miller (1950) offer an account which might resolve the paradox. They suggest that punishment, if sufficiently severe and if applied at the time that the stimuli for the response are present, will result in the arousal of fear which can be conditioned to the stimuli which formerly aroused the now-punished response. The organism now engages in avoidance behavior which removes it from the scene of the stimuli. The withdrawal then reduces the anxiety (this is gratuitous, but may be acceptable on some other basis than the simple statement) and the reduction of anxiety reinforces the behavior of withdrawal. It is possible that while the organism is engaged in avoidance behavior some particular kind of avoidance response is performed. A new learned response may result. This situation is not simple because the original behavior presumably is reinforced positively on enough occasions to acquire some strength, and the punishment may be irregular, erratic, inconsistent, administered in the absence of the necessary stimuli, or be reinforcing in itself (the last involves various notions about children requiring and seeking attention at any cost).

Whether the aftereffects be positive or negative makes no difference to the neurophysiological hypothesis. Young's illustration of the octopus and the crab (see p. 238) represented a negative reinforcement. It should serve as a general example of adjustment to the negative stimulus. The shocked animal does what is appropriate to shock and in the presence of other stimuli will learn to do the same things when they are present alone. The assumption of anxiety is superfluous.

The problem of punishment cannot be dismissed so easily, however. We must note that as with positive reinforcements we have no real, working definitions of punishment. The term includes a wide variety of operations from extreme physical abuse of various kinds to such symbolic affairs as a frown or even the absence of a smile. Do we have any continuum here? We have not learned yet how to measure punishment and, until we do, we can only expect difficulty with the concept. When Pavlov and Tolman show us that electric shocks can be used as *positive* stimuli, either as conditioned stimuli or as reinforcers of correct responses and Mowrer and Miller show us that similar shocks are proper stimuli for escape and avoidance behavior we are at least faced with a mild paradox.

In ordinary everyday contexts we conceive of punishment as something unpleasant, something which, if made strong enough (and we have no genuine measures here) results in cessation of what is going on or in some attempt at evasion or escape. The significant event in a punishment situation is the cessation of the just prior activity. We have seen Estes (p. 274) describe this as suppression and Dollard and Miller (1950) think of it as due to anxiety. Hebb (1955) would agree that both inactivity and emotional disturbance are probably to be considered. From his point of view, the "arousal system" (see p. 209) has been overtaxed and coordinated, adjusted behavior is impossible. The degree of disorganization is related to the degree of overactivity of the arousal system. Until the arousal system resumes its normal state we can expect disorganized behavior. Since the arousal system itself can be activated by cortical activity, the function of this system can be initiated by other stimuli and organisms can learn to become disturbed by stimuli associated with activation of the arousal system. We can expect then that "punishment" will result, depending upon its severity, in various degrees of upset, disorganization, and distress up to and including paralytic states. Such emotional distress will obviously interfere with the on-going activity and result in "suppression." If at the same time new activity can be forced onto the organism by internal or external sources, new responses can be learned as Dollard and Miller suggest. These responses can then become anticipatory in nature and an "avoidance" pattern results, whether the avoidance itself is a positive affair or merely an artifact of the interfering response. A crying child, upset by pain (and presumably fear) can be made to laugh by tickling if the degree of distress is not too great. It can learn to laugh at thunder instead of shrink and run for mother.

We can think of punishment then as a process whereby a selected behavior pattern can be interrupted. Such interruption can be brief and temporary as Estes (1944) found or more prolonged (if learning occurs) so that the "emotional" distress is rearoused by components of the punishment stimulus pattern. We can assume that "extinction" of such learning can also occur so that punishment effects are not necessarily permanent. If a new response is developed by appropriate training, the "avoidance" of the original response may be permanent. If "punishment" does not operate as described above (witness Thorndike's failure to find avoidance when he pronounced responses "wrong") we can only conclude that the punishment was not genuine but merely assumed. In view of the failures of many alleged punishing maneuvers (for example, imprisonment) we must conclude that our understanding of the meaning and operation of punishment is still very limited.

Chapter

11 *Other General Principles of Learning*

THE LAWS OF ASSOCIATION

The ancients pondered the problem of why one thing seemed to lead to another—how one idea begot another. Their answer came in the form of Laws of Association. Such laws were laws of memory or thought and not, strictly speaking, laws of learning. They consisted of a variety of formulations, depending on the individual philosopher, but collectively comprised the laws of contiguity, frequency, recency, similarity, and contrast, with contiguity in space and/or time the basic principle.

The Laws of Association were described for us by a succession of philosophers starting with Aristotle and reaching their final development with the British Empiricists who are, in fact, frequently identified as the British Associationists (see Burtt, 1939). Perhaps the most detailed discussion of the classical Laws of Association is found in the work of Brown (1820) who organized and amplified the number of laws of association. As was mentioned above, these laws were meant to explain the workings of the mind in thinking, and, generally, in recalling past events, or in accounting as did Bishop Berkeley (1709) for our conceptions or ideas of anything, either concrete or abstract.

While most of the philosophic writings do concern themselves with associations among ideas, images, feelings, and other "subjective" states or events, occasionally a philosopher would drop a hint which suggested that a broader application of associative principles might be explored. Thus, Hull (1934a) points out that John Locke considered the problem of associating certain movements involved in dancing with the physical surroundings in which the dancing was being practiced. According to Babkin (1949), Pavlov credits Sechenov's discussion of association between feelings of fatigue and certain reflections about Chinese history with the development of his own ideas about associations in conditioning experiments. Hayek (1952) discovered in Montaigne's *Essays* a reference to a gentleman who came to associate the eliminative function with the appearance of an enema apparatus. This note of Montaigne's anticipated by 400 years the modern Russian experiments in which bladder and bowel responses are conditioned (see p. 136). We should note, in passing, two modern extensions of the Laws of Association, one in a clinical situation where "free association" is practiced by a patient while the therapist observes, and the other in the laboratory where "association values" of nonsense syllables are studied in the selection of suitable materials for learning experiments.

Actually, while we speak freely of the Laws of Association, there is no formal body or "constitution" of such laws. The most complete collection in modern times and terms is probably that of Robinson (1932) in *Association Theory Today*. Robinson discusses in addition to what he considers the basic law (that of contiguity), the laws of assimilation, frequency, intensity, duration, context, acquaintance, composition, and individual differences. Other lists may exclude some of these or translate some into different terms. We might find intensity treated as "vividness," acquaintance as "belongingness," assimilation as "redintegration." Some writers include "recency" and "primacy." Robinson eliminates these as of no material relevance in the process of acquisition even though they may be of some moment in recall. He says (1932, p. 69), "Neither factor can have any meaning until after a fixation process has taken place." According to Robinson, these laws deal with the problem of recall and what kinds of events (or lengths of time intervals) intervene between fixation and reinstatement. We shall see later how Guthrie tries to bring recency into the acquisition picture as his basic law.

Most discussions of the Laws of Association are devoted to identifying and classifying the laws as basic or primary and secondary, qualitative or quantitative, related to acquisition or retention, and so on. We shall not attempt such a formal treatment here but rather consider the principles of learning to which some of these classical laws have been adapted. These adaptations have been made more or less freely by translating the subjective language of sensation, image, and idea into behavioral terms. The modern learning theorist deals with "bonds" between stimuli and responses, and the laws of association become the laws of learning. We have already dealt with the factors of intensity (p. 127), duration (p. 130), similarity (p. 131), and to some extent with individual differences (p. 50) although in somewhat differing contexts. In this chapter we will deal with those "laws" that one or another psychologist has made prominent as a more or less primary if not inclusive principle in his attempt to harness the facts of learning to some unifying operation of a lawful nature.

The principle of contiguity. This principle appears to be universally adopted and acceptable to all learning psychologists. Without exception, contiguity in time (and this generally includes spatial contiguity in the environment) is presupposed as a basis for learning. We noted in the past how Hull assumes contiguity of response and reinforcer, Guthrie assumes contiguity of stimulus and response, and Tolman, contiguity of sign and significate. While they all differ on what events are contiguous, on contiguity they agree. It should be clear from the neural postulate we have been favoring that all these reduce to a neural contiguity of simultaneous activities in the brain which set up neural cycles. This assumption eliminates the controversy about what is associated by denying the significance of the behavioral or "mental" events and by calling attention to what must necessarily be the only way in which contiguity can function. When we recognize the evidence of Lorente de No (1938) that continguity of two impulses, that is the simultaneous firing of two cells, is necessary to initiate an impulse in another we come as close as we can, at present, to the real operation of contiguity (see p. 297).

The principle of contiguity reduces to the problem of time interval. We have already discussed this problem (see p. 128) and nothing further need be said at this point except to recall the almost universal agreement of experimenters that the most favorable interval for conditioning is the very close (about ½ second) succession of conditioned and unconditioned stimuli. This interval has been found to be most effective in so many varieties of experiment that it suggests some basic kind of neural operation.

The reinforcement theorists have introduced another aspect of contiguity, that of temporal relations between the response and the presentation of the reinforcement. In classical conditioning experiments, the reinforcer is also the unconditioned stimulus and so the remarks in the previous paragraph apply. In instrumental learning and in many human learning situations like going through a chapter in a text, or solving a problem which an instructor will evaluate later, there may be a considerable interval between the occurrence of the response and the appearance of the reinforcer. We have already considered Spence's solution to this difficulty via secondary reinforcers (see p. 273). There is another solution to the problem of delayed reinforcement that has, perhaps, only historical interest today, but it deserves notice as it may enjoy a revival. This solution was suggested by Thorndike as his principle of "the Spread of Effect." We can examine this proposal briefly at this time.

TEMPORAL AND SPATIAL FACTORS IN "CONTIGUITY." In the last chapter we noted how Spence (1947) tried to rescue Hull from the trap involved in the learning of some series of responses which would extend over a time interval lasting more than 5 seconds. Spence simply substituted a series of secondary reinforcers each deriving its strength from the next succeeding reinforcer until the final response brought about the primary reinforcer, if any. At one time, Hull (see p. 97) had made use of what he called the "goal gradient" principle to account for such learning. According to this principle, a reinforcer would reinforce not only the immediately preceding response but would also strengthen other responses both before and after the so-called goal response. The reinforcing effect would diminish in time in both directions with a peak of strength at the time of the goal response. With the help of this principle, then, it was possible to explain how an organism might learn to perform the earlier responses in a series although rewarded only for the last. As a typical illustration of the goal gradient in action we might observe a rat in a long runway (Hull, 1932), and note that, fairly early in the training, the rat would start out slowly, gain speed as he progressed, and run faster and faster as he neared the goal end. According to Hull, this represented the operation of the gradient of reinforcement—the later stages of running being more strongly reinforced than the earlier ones. By use of the goal gradient principle Hull could account for the learning of mazes. The correct path would always prove to be shorter, take less time, and therefore each stage would be more strongly reinforced than any path that included errors. Bugelski and Miller (1938) showed a similar behavior pattern in avoidance situations. A rat shocked at one end of an alley would retreat from that end if placed there with a negatively accelerated gradient of running. It would start out rapidly but would run more and more slowly with distance from the negative end. Hull became dubious about the validity of his goal gradient as a general principle and adopted Spence's suggestions later so that the goal gradient no longer played an important role in his system.

Bugelski and Woodward (1951) cast further doubt on the nature of the mechanism operating in such gradient situations by showing that the retreat from a negative end in an alley was a function of the degree of discriminability of the stimuli involved. In substituting a cardboard floor for the grill, they found that the rats would not retreat from the negative goal as frequently as they would on a grill floor. By making the starting end more distinctive from the rest of the alley they found that rats would barely bother to run after stepping out of the starting box. The behavior of the rats is comparable to that of spectators at a zoo who do not run from lions that are only a few feet away so long as the bars separating the lions from the visitors are in place.

THORNDIKE AND THE "SPREAD OF EFFECT." The whole idea of the gradient of reinforcement is related to Thorndike's (1933) principle of "the spread of effect" which is another way of talking about it. Thorndike believed that he had evidence that rewarding a subject for making a given response in his word-matching experiments would tend to strengthen other responses made to just-preceding and just-following stimuli. His "spread of effect" was generally accepted until quite recently when several experimenters (Jenkins and Sheffield, 1946; Smith, 1949) were able to show, apparently quite definitely, that Thorndike's observations were based on nothing more than guessing habits and favorite number sequences. It is apparently a fact that people learn or favor repeating certain sequences of numbers. Number repetition is not done at random. Most people when asked to choose, will not say 1, 2, 3, 4, 5 in that order. Thus if a subject happens to have a tendency to choose numbers between 1 and 5 in the sequence, 2, 4, 1, 3, 5, he would tend to repeat such a sequence, rewarded or not. If Thorndike rewarded the response "1," he could then find on the next trial that the subject would be likely to say "2" and "4" before the "1" and "3" and "5" after the "1." Such responses would be attributed by Thorndike to a "spread of effect," when, in fact, effect had nothing to do with the response pattern. The subject might merely be indulging himself in repeating a more or less favorite sequence.

At present, neither the "goal gradient" nor the "spread of effect" is mentioned frequently. The principles, if correct, and they may have some merit which has not been fully developed experimentally, would tend to explain some interesting learning phenomena. For example, we might note from the spread of effect that the correct response is not learned in a pure state or in a vacuum. Other undesirable, or incorrect, responses might also be learned because of some spread. The subject might then appear to be learning more slowly or awkwardly than he should because wrong responses made closely in time with the correct ones would also be learned. Rats frequently retain a particular wrong alley in their runs of a maze, especially if the wrong alley is close to the goal. Humans too frequently include unnecessary responses in a serial performance that eventuates in a goal. Whether a principle of gradients or spread is needed is questionable. The neural learning hypothesis does not need it as it also provided for including wrong responses in a pattern if their neural surrogates are active at the time of making the correct response.

The principle of frequency. Before the influence of the reinforcement psychologists was felt, it was generally held that frequently performed acts, habits, or responses were learned better than those infrequently practiced. The old saw of "Practice makes perfect" is commonly quoted. Watson (1919) and Pavlov (1927) regarded it as basic and in one way or another most students regard frequency of some importance. Tolman does not emphasize frequency but presumes that, in general, the more frequently an expectancy is confirmed, the stronger it becomes. It should be noted at once that frequency presupposes contiguity. Whatever is happening frequently also involves the contiguous association of stimuli and responses or responses and reinforcers. The reinforcers might conceivably be withheld but the elements that enter into an association must necessarily be present about the same time or we are left without any learning to consider. Guthrie, of course, represents the outstanding opposition to a frequency principle with his insistence on one-trial learning. Guthrie stands pretty much alone in this view, but the paradoxical suggestion does have an appeal for students. Before getting further involved, we had best expound Guthrie's point of view at this time.

According to Guthrie, any response that is made is immediately learned to whatever stimuli are present. The average observer, Guthrie claims, does not consider the complexity of the stimulus pattern and pays attention only to those stimuli that he considers important. This, says Guthrie, is wrong, because the response is conditioned to a pattern and cannot be expected to recur if the pattern does not recur. The components of a pattern may include all sorts of environmental, postural, and internal stimuli. Whenever a response fails to occur, Guthrie can claim that some of the components of the stimulus pattern are missing or altered. While this interpretation has a certain degree of logical force, it is obviously an untestable hypothesis and as such has little value for a scientific interpretation of behavior. Any proposal that offers no possibility of disproof is unacceptable as a scientific proposition. Since we can do nothing to support or deny Guthrie here, we might best return to other opinions and researches.

A major objection to frequency as a principle came from effect theorists who were anxious about establishing the importance of reinforcement. They pointed out that in many learning situations the wrong responses are performed more frequently than the right ones, at least up to some point when the response is considered learned. This could be true, for example, in a maze-learning program. An animal might have a persistent habit of making some particular error and make it many times in one trial whereas the correct response can only be performed once. How seriously we can consider this possibility is questionable as it does not operate so obviously in other learning situations. The fact that a wrong motion is made is to some extent a value judgment made by the experimenter. As far as the animal is concerned, there may be nothing "wrong" about an error. The learner may learn bad habits as well as good ones, as Guthrie continually emphasizes, and there is no simple accounting for why a series of errors cannot be incorporated into an over-all pattern that ends up with the goal response. The goal gradient explanation does help some, but we have seen its limitations (p. 282). Many human operators include in some of their routines a series of movements which the efficiency engineer may denounce as useless and inefficient. In any event there is no conclusive evidence that sheer frequency can result in learning because there is no such thing as sheer frequency. There are always complicating factors.

In an attempt to show that frequency alone would not produce learning, Loucks (1935) attempted to condition a leg-withdrawal response to an external stimulus by evoking the response through direct stimulation of the motor cortex. No conditioning resulted. When, however, food was supplied, the leg withdrawal was promptly learned. Spence (1951) makes much of this experiment as support for reinforcement theory. There is actually no reason to consider that Loucks demonstrated anything but a failure to condition an animal by evoking the response directly through motor cortex stimulations. As far as is known, no one ever assumed such could be done. On the contrary, it is generally assumed that the motor impulses must be centrally aroused through the action of neural elements, and so only failure should have been anticipated. Introduction of the food reinforcement altered the experiment to an ordinary reward-training exercise and the leg withdrawal can be presumed to have been centrally mediated.

Thorndike (1932) attempted a sort of *reductio ad absurdum* of the frequency principle with an experiment whose outcome might well be presumed from the start. Thorndike had subjects wearing blindfolds attempt to draw 3-inch lines. The subjects repeated the response continuously for hundreds of trials but were given no information about the performance. No improvement resulted. As soon as Thorndike began to reinforce responses that met the criteria by saying, "Right," the subjects began to improve. Thorndike felt that this demonstration clearly laid the ghost of frequency as a separate principle of learning. Frequency alone is of no value. According to Thorndike, the subjects did not even strengthen the originally most frequent responses as trials continued.

As might be inferred, the effect theorists regard frequency as only a means of multiplying the opportunities for effect to work. They assume that the more often a drive is reduced, the stronger becomes the habit that is being acquired. Since there is no way of deciding in advance how many reinforcements are necessary to develop or establish any particular habit, about the only statement that can be made by reinforcement theorists is that the greater the number of reinforcements, the stronger the habit. After some reasonably large number of reinforcements, say 90, in a Skinner box (Hull, 1943), it becomes difficult to demonstrate any superiority of one habit over another even if the reinforcements run up into the hundreds. There appears to be a limit to the reinforcement possibilities.

Hull (1943) does not recognize any theoretical limit to habit strength as a function of number of reinforcements. By an ingenious assumption that each reinforcement adds some percentage of the total possible remaining habit strength, Hull concludes that there is always room for improvement. Thus, the first reinforcement might contribute 10 percent of the total possible strength. That would leave 90 percent to be acquired. The second reinforcement would add 10 percent of that or 9 percent, leaving 81 percent. This process goes on so that there is always some, even if infinitesimal, habit strength to be acquired. Since one cannot specify the percentages for any kind of habit or reinforcement, this idea remains ingenious, but impractical. A particular habit may be strengthened 90 percent by the first reinforcement, the second reinforcement would add 9 more percentage points, and so on. A habit that was strengthened 90 percent by one reinforcement might be so strong as to give the appearance of one-trial learning since so little learning is left to be acquired (see Fig. 11.1).

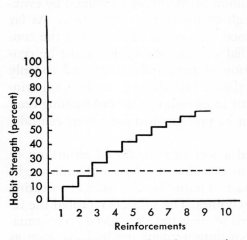

FIG. 11.1. Hull's incremental reinforcement hypothesis. With each reinforcement a fraction (here taken as 10 percent) of the total remaining potential habit strength accrues. Each reinforcement, then, provides a smaller, *absolute* gain in habit strength. According to this hypothesis, learning is never complete although only infinitesimal values are gained after the curve begins to flatten out. (After Hull, 1943.)

In all discussions of number of reinforcements there is never any indication of what a "reinforcement" amounts to. Hull talks of a reinforcement as something which diminishes a drive or drive stimuli, but it is not indicated that the drive must be completely reduced or eliminated. If that was to happen, only one trial could be given and then the experimenter would have to set up the drive state again before he could use a "reinforcer." If the drive were hunger or thirst, this would obviously take a relatively long time. Common experimental practice does not follow this procedure. From the definition of reinforcement as diminution of drive stimuli we are unable to deal with the actual value of different kinds or amounts of reinforcers. The frequency proposition treats each reinforcer as equal to every other. This is patently unlikely and offers no aid for applying Hull's learning curve to any actual situation either before or after the learning takes place. Hull's only attempt to quantify reinforcers has been in terms of weight of food (1952). No indication is given how weight of food can be translated into any other form of reinforcement. The fact that as trials continue we cannot consider drive to remain constant introduces another difficulty. Even a great amount of food is of little interest to the satiated animal.

Under certain conditions, reinforcement can be overdone. Hovland (1936) has demonstrated what he called "inhibition of reinforcement" which amounts to the finding that if reinforcements come too rapidly (massing of trials) less improvement is noted than can be achieved with fewer reinforcements at more appropriately spaced trials. Robinson (1932) had earlier called attention to the fact that frequency has a negative aspect such that even though improvement is observed in some performance for some time, there will eventually occur a decrement in performance if the response is repeatedly elicited or performed. Such a change is commonly observed in fatigue or work decrement experiments. In rotary pursuit studies a naïve subject improves rapidly at first even with massed practice, but as the practice continues he soon begins to deteriorate and loses most if not all of his recently acquired skill. Such negative effects can be eliminated by proper spacing of trials as shown by Denny, Frisbey, and Weaver (1955). It is obvious that frequency is an important determinant of behavior but only in conjunction with other factors and conditions. These factors can themselves counteract the effects of reinforcement and the benefits of repetition. There is no simple law of frequency. If frequency is to be considered at all, it must be within a context of other variables.

FREQUENCY AND THE CONTINUITY VERSUS NONCONTINUITY PROBLEM. A special problem in evaluating "frequency" and its relation to reinforcement comes up in connection with the observation of organisms learning correct responses in situations that are extremely difficult, and probably unnatural for them. When rats are required to jump at one of two targets in a Lashley jumping stand, they may have a difficult time in learning which target is appropriate, especially if the targets differ in design but not brightness. In the first 100 trials, for example, the rats may show little if any learning. This situation led to a controversy which has not been settled to everyone's satisfaction as yet, the controversy of "continuity" in learning. Lashley (1942), particularly, believed that learning occurs pretty much as a consequence of some kind of perceptual reorganization. An animal jumping at a target learns nothing, argues Lashley, if it does not *perceive* the significant and relevant variables. Once such perception occurs, learning proceeds rapidly, according to Lashley. Reinforcement theorists, on the other hand, argue that every reinforcement counts so long as the relevant variables are functioning, even though the learning cannot be proved to be taking place in a difficult problem. One way to demonstrate learning in such a situation, says Spence (1945), is to change the values of the two target cards before learning is apparent. Thus, if a horizontal line is positive at the start of the experiment and a vertical line negative, the training can be allowed to continue for, say, 50 trials. At this time the jump will still appear as a chance affair. Now the targets can be reversed in value. If Lashley is correct, such reversal should have no effect on the acquisition of the new response, because the animal has not perceived the relevant variable. On the other hand, if every reinforcement counts, then the animals should take longer to learn than a control group would.

Lashley found results confirming his views in an experiment where rats were trained to jump toward doors marked by triangles (upright and inverted). Ehrenfreund (1948) argued that Lashley's rats were not able to be affected by the proper stimulus features in the apparatus Lashley used. Ehrenfreund arranged the jumping stand so that the rats could be differentially stimulated and found that when the cues were reversed in value, the rats suffered a setback in their learning even though they had not shown any signs of learning before the reversal took place.

Another way to test the hypothesis of continuity (that is, that every reinforcement counts) is to compare learning when subjects are presented stimuli to be discriminated either (a) simultaneously or (b) successively. When a pair of stimuli is present together, the learner can presumably examine each and react to possible differences between them. This arrangement, according to the Lashley view, should permit more rapid learning than when only one stimulus is present at a time. In the latter case, if the stimulus is positive and a response is made, reinforcement follows. Response to a negative stimulus is not reinforced. An experiment embodying the above elements was performed by Grice (1949). Rats were trained to approach a door at the end of a runway marked by a small circle and to avoid a doorway marked with a larger circle. Rats with both circles present showed no advantage in learning over rats that were presented with only one circle at a time.

The question of continuity versus noncontinuity is a fascinating one because it presents a crucial problem on which theorists become divided. If an appropriate experiment could be designed to test the hypothesis adequately, we might be able to speak with more confidence about reinforcement not only theoretically but practically. On the practical side, for example, the continuity position approves the practice of rewarding the learner for every correct response regardless of the fact that he does not appear to "know" what he is doing. A small child, for example, might be rewarded for polite behavior on every occasion even if the "please" or "thank you" is dragged out of the tot, and little or no signs of progress are noted. In the long run, say the continuity supporters, every reward counts.

An interesting development of the continuity problem arises in connection with partial reinforcement (see p. 255). As Skinner (1938, 1953) points out, it is not always possible to reinforce on every occasion. What happens to the learning if a response is not followed by a reinforcer? We have already seen how Hull handled the problem (p. 256) and later (Chap. 13) we will reconsider the question. For the present we can leave the matter with the observation that most experimental data (see Osgood, 1953, p. 450) seem to be in favor of a continuity hypothesis. The Lashley view does not lend itself to confirmation by unequivocal experiments.

For the neural hypothesis "frequency" is difficult to evaluate because it is obvious that a wide variety of frequencies can be observed in the learning of different kinds of responses. Some "habits" are learned, as Guthrie says, in one trial. Others require only a few trials, while some kinds of behavior appear unlearnable regardless of trials for some subjects. Obviously certain kinds of connections are neurally favored while others are less so. The observations reported by Young (1951) suggest that frequency is important for growth of neural buds and for neurones themselves. We tentatively conclude that "frequency" as a principle of learning is important for some kinds of learning and not for others. Obviously this conclusion is of little empirical value and rests on the circular reasoning that some habits require much practice and others little. We cannot continue mouthing the proverbial "Practice makes perfect." Some things require no practice, and some kinds of practices make perfect idiots.

The principle of recency. While Robinson (1932) considered recency a factor only in memory and recall, the principle has been applied to the acquisition phase, especially by Guthrie for whom it becomes a primary, if not *the* primary principle of learning. The meaning Guthrie attaches to the term requires some elucidation. It does not refer to recent events, as one might gather from reading the old Associationists who were trying to account for various ideas that might occur to you. When so considered, recency might be invoked to explain why someone thinks of a particular person or book and so on. In learning theory, recency may have quite another function. Suppose that we consider some trial-and-error situation where an organism might try various responses, say A, B, C, D, in succession. Let us assume D is correct. Since D is the last response made it terminates the trial. On the next occasion D might occur as the first attempt at solution. In any series of learning trials that terminate with a correct response, the correct response is obviously, and must necessarily be, the most recent response made in the situation. What is the significance of this "lastness" for learning?

Guthrie holds that this function is a sufficient and adequate explanation of learning. He states that all learning situations are basically the same in the respect that they have to terminate with some response. If this response is arranged by the teacher or experimenter to be "correct," then on the next occasion we can expect the organism to repeat what it did last (that is, most recently) in the situation. If the learning situation is such as to terminate with an incorrect response, then we can expect an incorrect response on the next trial. In a T-maze situation or Lashley jumping stand, an animal can be expected to repeat the error. At first glance this might be somewhat disturbing to the reader as it seems to indicate that an animal might never learn if it "goes wrong" on the first trial and continues to repeat the incorrect response. On the other hand, it might help account for the delay in learning such simple responses which frequently take many trials. In some of Tolman's (see Tolman, Ritchie, and Kalish, 1947) studies, for example, animals require 4 daily trials for 7 days, a total of 28, before they attain a criterion of learning in a simple T-maze setup. The difficulty of learning a Lashley jump discrimination has already been alluded to (see p. 287). In many experiments animals adopt so-called position habits which in effect amount to persisting in repeating the same response that may be sometimes correct, sometimes incorrect. An animal might keep taking a left turn over and over again until the experimenter gets tired of watching it and discards it for having developed a "position habit." For Guthrie such position habits are simply illustrations of recency at work.

To get back to the original problem, how can an organism ever learn if it once gets off on the wrong track? The only answer is that for one reason or another, due to changes in the situation which the experimenter is not always keen enough to note, the animal does happen to make the correct response. This response will then be retained, says Guthrie, barring some change in the stimulus situation which would invite the former or another response.

From Hull's point of view, recency only works because it normally characterizes the response which was also rewarded, or reinforced. By itself recency would have no effect on learning. Since it is difficult to separate recency from reinforcement in many trial-and-error learning experiments the argument can be carried on with as much fervor as the debators can muster.

In Guthrie's own works (1935, 1952) he cites numerous anecdotal illustrations of the operation of recency in spite of reinforcement or in cases where he argues its absence. The apparent or face-validity of recency can be observed by the average parent of young children who can pretty well rely on a child's repeating various seemingly meaningless, ritualistic, and otherwise "unrewarding" behavior patterns. Once a child hits on some new way of eating, drinking, going to bed, and so on, the parent might well expect the child to demand the new way on the next occasion. Anecdotes and casual observation are not evidence, however, and more careful data are required. One of Guthrie's students, Voecks (1948), has offered one of the relatively few positive experimental contributions supporting the Guthrie view.

RECENCY AS POSTREMITY. In the Voeks experiment, subjects learned a punchboard stylus maze and a raised wire maze to a criterion of 3 perfect trials. Both types of mazes offered a series of 30 choice points. Stylus mazes were learned by one group under instructions to insert the point of the stylus through one of the holes; another group screwed the stylus into a threaded hole. After the first trial, Voeks was in position to notice if the subject repeated the choices of the first trial or if he varied. As trials continued, it was possible to notice whether the subject chose that alternative which he chose on the just preceding trial or if he chose the alternative that he had chosen most frequently up to that time. Accordingly, two kinds of prediction could be made, one based on recency, or as Voeks calls it, "postremity" (the last response made in the same situation), and another based on frequency. According to the data, predictions based on postremity were much more frequently verified than were predictions based on frequency. This was true for all three groups, for individuals, for cases where both frequency and postremity predicted the same response, and where postremity and frequency were in conflict. Postremity predictions were verified about 70 percent of the time even when frequency favored the opposite choice.

Unfortunately Voeks did not run a corresponding analysis of the prediction possibilities based on whether or not the last response was correct (and therefore, possibly "rewarded"). It is obvious that if the subject ever does learn a maze to a criterion of three perfect trials he will have to reach the point where he, of necessity, does the thing he did last at every choice point on at least the last two criterion trials. At the same time he will be performing the responses that were rewarded on each of these trials. Voeks does not present any data on number of trials to learn or on the course of the development of the accuracy of the predictions. It might be guessed that as the trials go on, predictions based on postremity must increase, approaching 100 percent as learning is completed. So long as any errors at all were made, frequency is bound to lose out in such a comparison. Inevitably, if a learned performance is repeated and is always reinforced, the time will come when all three factors, postremity, frequency, and reinforcement, will predict the same outcome on a future trial. From this consideration, Voeks cannot be considered to have established the primacy of postremity over either frequency or reinforcement.

Voeks does offer ingenious Guthrian solutions for the elimination of errors without recourse to any reinforcement language. The basic explanation (on a human level) consists of the notion that when a human subject makes an error at one of the choice points which he previously identifies by announcing its number, like "eight," he will say to himself, "Eight, left." Trying "left" he then says to himself, "Oops, wrong, eight left is wrong." This is the last response he makes to eight. On the next occasion, he again repeats, "Eight-left, no, eight-left is wrong," and then acts appropriately. Thus, the last thing done in connection with "eight" was to announce its wrongness and this response deters the subject from making the error. Why this should work is not explained. Animals learning a maze presumably must make use of some analogous mechanism. In a correction procedure [1] in learning a T-maze, the rat facing a choice point and making an error in association with the stimuli at the choice point finds himself

---

[1] The "correction" method describes the situation where the learner is allowed to correct an error. In the noncorrection method, the experimenter stops the trial as soon as an error is made and starts another trial.

passing the choice point again on his return trip from the wrong end of the maze. If this was the result of a left turn, then on passing the choice point he finds himself headed right. On the next trial, the possibility exists that the stimuli from the choice point can be effective in evoking a right turn since that is what the rat did the last time it was at the choice point. At the same time, some of the stimuli for making the wrong response are "detached" from the wrong response because they are still present when the animal is going away from the wrong end. This explanation may operate reasonably well in a correction procedure. Voeks does not touch on how errors are eliminated in a noncorrection procedure. Since other explanations (see p. 281) can also account for the elimination of errors in a correction procedure or noncorrection on the basis of delayed reinforcement, we cannot assume that the story is complete.

The postremity principle might be shown to be unimportant or of only indirect significance if it could be shown that the introduction of delays in removal or elimination of the stimuli associated with the responses, after the responses were made, did not affect the learning. Thus, if a buzzer is paired with a shock to the paw of a dog and the buzzer is allowed to continue afer the dog raises his leg and replaces it, the last response made would be one of replacing the paw, not of withdrawing it. Osgood (1953, p. 372) suggests such an experiment and then points out that it would not be conclusive as Guthrie could argue that the real conditioning stimuli were probably from postural and "attention" responses initiated by the buzzer. Once these stimuli occurred and the response was initiated the presence of additional buzzing would be irrelevant.

In an attempt to refute the Guthrie view on recency, O'Connor (1946) argued from an experiment by Roberts (1930) in which rats displaced a pendulum to escape confinement in a box. The door would open after various periods of delay from 0 to 30 seconds. O'Connor assumed that with long delays the rats would fail to learn because other responses would occur in the situation which involved a delay. Actually the rats learned with any period of delay, although learning was poorer with the longer delays. While this is what Hull would predict on the basis of a gradient of reinforcement, Guthrie (1946b) finds nothing awkward about it since it would be what he would also predict.

A neural model of learning. We have now considered three of the more commonly accepted laws or principles of association, contiguity, frequency, and recency or postremity if the latter term is preferred. It is obvious that these principles have an immediate kind of objectivity about them not shared by other principles like "context," "assimilation," vividness, or even reinforcement. The more objective principles have an easier entry into physiological thought and many attempts have been made by the physiologically-minded to construct both actual models (robots that learn) and theoretical models purporting to show what goes on in the nervous system when an organism learns. W. G. Walter (1953) discusses the variety of electrical, mechanical, and chemical "creatures" that have been built in laboratories and which simulate some simple learning phenomena. Walter's own "creatures" go through rather complex maneuvers, "learning" to find their way to "food" (battery chargers) when their batteries "need" charging. While these little mechanical monsters are interesting to observe it is hardly necessary to point out that they are built in accordance with the creator's own interpretation of how learning occurs, so that far from clarifying a learning process, they merely illustrate in symbolic form some aspects of *external* behavior which in a very modest way mimic what can be seen from the *outside* of a real rat, dog, or turtle. It is doubtful that examination of the insides of a robot will prove helpful for the comprehension of learning. It can only contain the biases and views of the manufacturer. Since these biases are implemented via wheels, gears, photoelectric cells, batteries, and motors, we are unlikely to learn much about learning from them. Rats, unfortunately, do not contain gears or photoelectric cells.

The manufacturer of mechanical creatures should not be dismissed too quickly. The effort involved in such an enterprise calls on the inventor for the most careful analysis of what is involved in learning, the description of minimal essentials, the elimination of contradictions of fact, and so on. In the effort to simulate learning, the inventor may stumble on mechanisms that may suggest analogies as to how the nervous system may work. The analogy can then be tested in living tissue. If some valuable principles are discovered by such analogies, it will certainly not be the first such event in the history of science. The only danger involved in such mechanical implementation of behavioral events comes from the tendency to be satisfied too easily. Popular reference to "electronic brains" does more harm than good to an understanding of nervous physiology. Complex electronic computors are not brains, they are electronic computors, elaborated adding machines. They do what is built into them to do, and far better than people can. The operation of such devices is hardly to be compared with the kinds of operations that go on in the brain except superficially and analogously. Since analogies are hardly proof, we cannot rest with them but take the more difficult step and attempt a more direct analysis of neural action.

Over the years many physiologists, and, in a more general and perhaps superficial sense, psychologists, have attempted to describe what must go on in the brain when learning occurs. From William James (1890) on, a chapter on the nervous system commonly appeared in elementary texts on psychology even though little use was made of this chapter in the rest of the book. One psychologist (Ruch, 1937) offered a text which contained no physiological material. His reason was that there was no point in having such a chapter if the rest of the text could not be integrated with physiological principles. In spite of the validity of his argument, a revised edition included a chapter on the nervous system because of popular demand. Whether they like it or not, psychologists find themselves involved with physiology in one way or another, however much they may insist that they are not concerned, or however unready they feel to make contact with the sister science of physiology. The physiologists likewise cannot avoid contact with psychological problems and we find occasional ones who are willing to speculate about nervous functions and behavioral phenomena.

Because there is little agreement among the physiologists about how learning might be described in neural terms there is little point to describing the variety of views that have been offered by Pavlov (1927), Konorski (1948), and numerous others. Hilgard and Marquis (1940) summarize the literature prior to 1940 and offer their own interpretation about some possible neural operations in learning. We have already looked at Hebb's (1949) interpretation of how cell assemblies and phase sequences are formed (see p. 112). Instead of describing the several views, each of which has been found wanting in some respect, it appears more profitable to consider the latest current interpretation by a physiologist who presents his views in full knowledge of prior efforts and who states that his own picture of learning at least does not do violence to any known facts of physiology. This is the picture offered by Eccles (1953). Before we look at Eccles' position, we should note that Eccles is attempting to give an account of what he considers the simplest kind of learning, namely, Pavlovian conditioning. Actually no other physiological explanation, with the possible exception of Hebb, has been any more ambitious. There may be some question as to whether Pavlovian conditioning is, in fact, the simplest kind of learning. For the present, however, we have only an attempted explanation of this kind of learning and must content ourselves with it.

Eccles' account of Pavlovian conditioning. In general all physiological explanations of learning attempt to account for relatively permanent changes in what is regarded as, to some degree, a "plastic" nervous system. The changes are presumed to take place at points where nerve processes come into anatomical or functional contact, the synapses, and the general problem reduces to explaining how a synapse that at first offers some "resistance" to the passage of an impulse comes to permit such passage more readily later. The additional impulse originating from the CS which originally has no capacity for arousing impulses that terminate in the unconditioned response later comes to do so. Most modern accounts of neural learning take advantage of new knowledge concerning activities at actual synapses. Lorente de No (1938) found that at least two sources of stimulation are required for firing a neurone, and Eccles demonstrated that recurrent chains of neural activity can be set in action and last as long as 4½ hours, giving an opportunity for what Eccles calls "prolonged plastic changes" (see Eccles, 1953, p. 219).

The following description of Eccles' model of conditioning is simplified from what he calls a "simplified description." To appreciate his analysis we must first note the following points:

1. The model is an abstraction or simplification. Where one neurone is mentioned, it must be understood to stand for many neurones operating as a network.
2. To initiate an impulse across a synapse, at least two sources of stimulation (active neural knobs) are required.
3. A response is initiated by the arrival of impulses at what Eccles calls a "Receiving Center" (RC) (see Fig. 11.2).
4. A point or location where neurones or their collaterals activated by different sources come together is called a "Convergence Center" (CC).

The formation of a conditioned response, then, takes place when impulses from collaterals of the neurones involved in initiating an unconditioned response summate with impulses from neurones activated by the conditioning stimulus in the Convergence Center. The newly energized impulses from the Convergence Center are now able to go out over various pathways through a Neuronal Network (NN) and, presumably, find an outlet in some response. Because the excitation at the Convergence Center is partially due to collaterals from the afferent nerves activated by the unconditioned stimulus, Eccles believes that the impulses from the Convergence Center might well be expected to discharge onto the same Receiving Center that is activated more directly by the afferents excited by the unconditioned stimulus.

In Figure 11.2, taken from Eccles (1953, p. 220), we have a schematic representation of the above discussion. The development of conditioning depends, says Eccles, on the arrival of impulses at CC at about the same time, "in close temporal sequence"; the activity at CC can be prolonged for some time without further external stimulation (up to perhaps 4½ hours). Here we

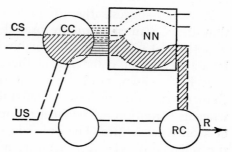

FIG. 11.2. An explanation of Pavlovian conditioning in neural terms (see text). In the diagram, CS and US are conditioned and unconditioned stimuli, R represents the response. Nervous pathways are shown as broad bands. NN is a neuronal network. CC is a convergence center where impulses from several inputs can summate and become mutually supportive. RC is a receiving center for impulses leading to the final response. (After Eccles, 1953, p. 220.)

might consider the factors of Recency and Contiguity. ". . . With an adequate number of repetitions, the increase in synaptic efficacy in the hatched zone both in the Convergence Center (CC) and in the Neuronal Network (NN) will cause impulses from CS alone to be effective in evoking a pattern of impulses in NN that leads to the response R, i.e., a conditioned reflex has been set up." Here we have added the factor of frequency to complete the story.

This analysis of Eccles' is a sample of our limited knowledge of conditioning in neural terms. It is obviously an abstraction and simplification. No real neurones are identified, no actual synapses are described, no Convergence Centers or Receiving Centers are located even in general terms. No reason is given, beyond an unsupported statement, for why impulses from the CC should end up in the appropriate RC. Yet, the description by Eccles is the best that we have at the present. There are a number of aspects of the Eccles' description that should be noted before we leave this conceptual model.

1. The model is consistent with the fact that the CR is not exactly the same as the UncR. The input at RC, developed by impulses originating only from the CS, could not have the same spatio-temporal pattern as would the input at RC from the combined sources of stimulation or from UncS alone.

2. Eccles suggests that there may be an explanation for the fact that the CS must normally precede the UncS because the pattern of activity at CC would presumably be quite different if first initiated by activity in the collaterals of the afferent system of the UncS.

3. Eccles own word (1949, 1951) has shown that in order to change synaptic efficiency, thousands of stimulations are required, whereas conditioning, when it occurs, is relatively rapid, occasionally of a one-trial nature. The only suggested solution for this problem is the reliance on the reverberatory activity in neural networks which may provide thousands of stimulus sequences.

4. Eccles believes extinction to be a matter of *disuse*. He assumes that disuse of the pathways involved will result in regression of whatever structural changes have occurred. Since experimental extinction usually involves only disuse of the UncS pathways, this raises a problem for Eccles. He has to explain how repeated use of the CS will operate to bring about extinction as a result of disuse. He does this by suggesting that when the CS is active alone there is less of a discharge from CC and that this lessened discharge is progressive through NN and RC. Without the UncS contribution there will be fewer synaptic knobs activated, and there will be a gradual lessening of synaptic efficiency throughout the system with a consequent regression and eventual extinction. We shall have more to say about disuse later when we study extinction.

OTHER ASSOCIATIVE PRINCIPLES

The principles discussed so far (contiguity, frequency, and recency) represent those on which experimental work has been done in sufficient quantity to get some reasonably adequate notion of what the principles mean. There are other alleged laws of association on which we have but fragmentary and subjective evaluations for the most part, and little or no experimental evidence. Such, for example, is the suggestion of Hollingworth (1928) based on Sir William Hamilton's earlier description of a "principle of redintegration." The principle is illustrated by such observations as are sometimes made in clinical cases where some one aspect of a situation vividly revives a whole previous experience. The victim of air raids is supposed to undergo a complete panic reaction from the sound of an airplane motor; or, the scent of laundry soap revives some old experience involving some unpleasantness incurred in a clothes-washing experience. The principle is more of an interpretation than a law and not readily reducible to experimental study.

The principle of assimilation. Thorndike (1914) recognized the problem which we have already considered (see p. 146) in connection with the discussion of generalization, mediation, and fractional anticipatory responses. This is the problem of explaining how an organism comes to respond more or less appropriately in new situations. When a suitable response is made and it can be shown that the history of the organism was devoid of the specific experience, the learning psychologist has a case to prove if he wishes to attribute the response to prior experience. Gestalt psychologists (see Kohler, 1929) characteristically solve the problem by postulation of some inherent capacity to have "insight." As Robinson (1932) points out, this is no solution but a simple avoidance of the problem, or question-begging. Thorndike solved the problem by the *Law of Assimilation*, which he put in the following fashion:

"To any new situation man responds as he would to some situation like it, or like some element of it. In default of any bonds with it itself, bonds that he has acquired with situations resembling it, act." Postulating such a law is little better than the Gestalt approach and we have already attempted to show the possible mechanisms which operate in such cases of "novel" solutions. Thorndike, and Robinson after him, did little with the Law of Assimilation beyond stating it and thereby showing that a problem area was recognized. To Robinson's credit, it must be stated that he viewed the Law of Assimilation as a problem area more than an answer. For our own purposes, it would be unnecessary to consider the Law of Assimilation at all except as we might recognize it as a general expression covering the operation of what we previously described as mediation. It may prove a more satisfactory general term to cover not only mediation, generalization, and fractional antedating responses but may be considered to include such phenomena as pseudo-conditioning and sensitization. The statement of the Law of Assimilation by Robinson may prove satisfactory as a general label for the phenomena indicated above.

Robinson's modification of Thorndike's law reads as follows (1932, p. 86):

"Whenever an associative connection is so established that an activity, A, becomes capable of instigating an activity, B, activities other than A also undergo an increase or decrease in their capacity to instigate B."

This verbalization has the merit of summarizing the problem of how new stimuli come to evoke responses without having been specifically associated with them. So long as we recognize the statement for what it obviously is and do not take it as an explanatory proposition, no harm results. It may prove convenient as a reference point to classify phenomena. The Law of Association neatly fits the situation described by Grether (1938) as pseudo-conditioning. Grether frightened some monkeys by igniting powder flashes. Later he found that the monkeys would show the same type of fear reaction when he would sound a bell even though the bell had never been associated with the flashes and ordinarily brought out no response of a fear type. Sometimes such findings are described as sensitization (see Hilgard and Marquis, 1940).

One last point should be made in connection with the Law of Assimilation. It is sometimes confused with the functioning of "similarity." Since this term is impossible of definition without specifying a reaction, it is of no particular value. To the extent that it covers such circumstances as one tone sounding like another (on a generalization continuum) or one man resembling another, the Law of Assimilation does pretend to cover the similarity situation. It goes beyond physical stimulus similarity as far as individual stimuli are concerned. Certainly a bell and a flash of burning powder are not alike. There may be elements of a *functional* similarity, for example, they may both be sudden, unusual, unexpected, presented in the same room or roughly the same circumstances, by the same experimenter, after the same kind of general preparation, and so on. Thorndike would favor an explanation in terms of some *identical* elements even though we were forced to look for the identity someplace in the nervous system. A horse and a fish may be considered far from similar as physical objects. As soon as a mediating response of "animal" is made, they become, in one sense, identical. We have spent enough time on the Law of Assimilation, considering the discussion in Chapters 5 and 9 and the fact that similar problems will vex us in Chapters 12 and 14. We can turn to another law.

The principle of vividness. The principle of "vividness" offers little in the way of experimental observation. It is difficult to decide just what vividness refers to. Sometimes discussions appear to deal with intensity of stimulation, either of CS or UncS (see p. 127). More frequently reference is made to intensity of feeling or emotional distress or excitement. There are no scales by which to measure "vividness" and one must be content with casual reports of how one exciting or "emotional" experience can be long remembered. Situations that prove embarrassing or in which one is the center of attention likewise appear to be better remembered than less "ego-involved" experiences. The student who asks a question may remember better than the rest of the class for this reason. Here we have nothing to offer by way of proof. Extensions of this principle have been attempted in studies of recall of "pleasant" and "unpleasant" memories (Ratliffe, 1938). Such studies turn out to be so contradictory and to involve so many variables that no reliable conclusions can be drawn. Recently Solomon and Wynne (1953) have described the long and all-but-permanent nature of avoidance reactions in dogs that have been severely shocked with shocks of such strength as to be just below tetanizing levels. They refer to these high-level shocks as "traumatizing." From their experimental work it appears to them that traumatic stimulation leaves relatively permanent effects. We shall return to their views is discussing extinction (see p. 345). We shall also consider other emotional effects in Chapter 15.

The law of belongingness. Another suggested principle merits a bit of comment; it is Thorndike's (1932) principle of "belongingness." This principle is vaguely defined by Thorndike as a notion of "what goes with what." What he apparently means by this is that some combinations of stimuli and responses are more readily learned than are others. First and last names, for example, appear to "go together" and may be better learned than a series of pairs of first names. Subjects and predicates go together. Whether this is to be considered as a principle of learning or a result of learning is a question. It will of course be helpful in learning some relatively new material if some advantage from previous experience with similar combinations, methods, sets, and so on, can be brought to bear on the material to be learned. For a beginner (or for basic learning of something entirely new) there appears to be no point to raising an issue of belongingness. We might easily drop into circularity if we posit belongingness whenever easy learning is observed. It has already been pointed out (see p. 125) that some stimuli are more effective in association with some kinds of responses than are others. Thus a light is not so effective as a buzzer (in ordinary strengths) in conditioning an avoidance reaction. For the present, we cannot make use of the principle of "belongingness" beyond what empirical observation might suggest although the possibilities for improving educational techniques with young children are perhaps a function of the degree to which we can take advantage of the belongingness of some materials with each other. It is alleged that children show more facility, for example, in learning division by solving problems involving batting averages than by using yards of goods as problem data. It is questionable at present whether belongingness can be related to initial learning as a basic principle. Its usefulness probably lies in the sphere of learning some kinds of new combinations of already familiar components.

With the above discussion we can conclude our consideration of the Laws of Association. More details concerning each of these as well as various other proposed laws are available in Robinson's (1932) *Association Theory Today* and in McGeoch and Irion (1952) *The Psychology of Human Learning*. Most of the other "laws," like *Duration, Context, Composition* can be reduced to those already discussed and we would benefit but little in worrying through them now. Nothing in any of the several principles we discussed is out of line with the neural hypothesis presented earlier; on the contrary, with every suggested principle obvious lines of support for the neural view appear. Contiguity is a basic assumption. Frequency is required for some kinds of learning, not for others. Recency permits the consolidation of new traces. Vividness allows for strong stimulation and suggests again the possible role of Theta rhythms. "Belongingness" reflects the consequences of prior associations and in Hebb's language would represent pairs of cell-assemblies or phase-sequences which had additional neural connections in common and needed only a few contiguous repetitions to become organized phase sequences.

With this discussion of the Laws of Association we bring to a close the consideration of the principles involved in learning in the sense of acquisition. We still have a number of problems before us which are part of the learning story. We must examine the thinking and experimentation dealing with retention or lack thereof, the nature of extinction and forgetting, and finally the broader applications to emotional and educational problems.

Chapter
12 The Retention of Learned Behavior

The past few chapters have been concerned with the acquisition of new responses. This is but a part of the story. The organism that has learned something may have fulfilled its laboratory duties but many questions remain to be considered about what happens now. It is obvious to human learners that material that was once learned is not always available for use. Even material that was well learned sometimes escapes us: the name of a friend, a frequently dialed telephone number, an anniversary. The fact of forgetting is so obvious that we come to live with it and do not expect to remember what we learn today for the rest of our lives, however much we would like to. We are hardly at all affected by the realization that we cannot recall the incidents of our childhood, the names of our grammar-school teachers, the contents of books we read or poems memorized. It is customary to forget. No one is expected to remember everything, and anyone can be expected to forget something. Social acceptance of forgetting, however, does not exclude it from the necessity of being scrutinized by the learning psychologist, and it is interesting to note that the first learning psychologist, Ebbinghaus (1885), was more interested in forgetting than in learning and entitled his major work *Memory*. Ever since, psychologists have been concerned with the problem of forgetting and they have tried to find out something about the causes, course, and nature of forgetting, as much, if not more than, they have tried to study acquisition. It is a question as to which topic is better represented in the psychological literature.

EXTINCTION AND FORGETTING

Remembering versus forgetting. For some years now, psychologists have felt that an attack on the problem of remembering or its opposite aspect, forgetting, can be more appropriately mounted in terms of a positive approach, of trying to find out the conditions under which material is remembered and the conditions under which it is less well remembered. It may be that we have two sides of a coin here, but one approach emphasizes the learning side, the other the forgetting side.

Extinction and forgetting. In the next chapter we will deal with the problem of extinction. We have already had to mention this operation frequently in the past but have not taken time out to consider it fully. For the present we can note that, as the term implies, a response "extinguishes," dies out, is eliminated, and that this happens in the process of presenting conditioned stimuli or otherwise getting the response to occur in the absence of the unconditioned stimuli. In the case of operant behavior we could talk about arranging for the response to occur without reinforcement. The essential point is that in extinction the response weakens and drops out in the course of occurring. There appears to be evidence that unless the response is brought out it will not extinguish with the passage of time (see Hilgard and Marquis, 1940). In forgetting, on the other hand, a response appears to weaken or die out during the passage of time when the response is not exercised in some way. In the one case then, we deliberately arrange to have the response occur, and in the other we presume that the response has not occurred. Can we, or need we, expect to find any similar principles operating in two such apparently different situations?

Hilgard and Marquis (1940), McGeoch (1942), and Woodworth (1938) all regard the two processes as somehow different. Yet so many of the same factors seem to play a role in both that we should not arrive at a hasty decision. While in what follows we could in almost every instance talk about both extinction and forgetting, it will be more convenient to take one process at a time. Actually, most of the material on forgetting deals with human verbal learning while most of the studies of extinction deal with other kinds of responses. By keeping the two kinds of studies apart we may be able to discern why they seem to be different.

FORGETTING AND THE PASSAGE OF TIME

When we reduce the problem of forgetting to its barest terms we find that we have a situation in which some amount of time has intervened between the last trial or occasion on which some learner had given evidence of some habit or had met some criterion of learning and the present occasion when we are testing for this same response, habit, or evidence of learning. We, in short, expect the subject to come through with the response or some reasonable facsimile, although for one reason or another we are willing to compromise our expectancies in accordance with our vague and unverbalized appreciation of the common cultural finding that there are frequent failures in such situations.

Short- and long-term retention. The criterion of learning. Viewed in this manner, the problem becomes one of appraising the nature and role of the possible variables that can operate in time between the last known occasion of the response and the present test situation. Since this interval can range from a few seconds to several years or even decades, the problem is obviously a complex one because we may find several different variables or principles operating differently at different time intervals. Some variables may prove to be of significance in short-range retention, others may operate over a longer interval.

One view of forgetting (see p. 297) is based on the now familiar proposition that right after some learning experience there is a perseveration of neural activity which must be allowed to go on for some time. Any interference with such perseveration may be destructive of retention. Similar interference at a later time might have no effect. Why do we fail to remember telephone numbers that we look up and immediately dial? Because *we immediately dial* might be the answer. If we refrained from dialing (or anything else) we might find that we remembered the number forever. It is unlikely that we will ever remember telephone numbers if we always go through the routine of looking them up and dialing at once.

The example of looking up telephone numbers can serve as an illustration of short-term retention or, perhaps more properly, of "memory span." When an immediate test of retention of material presented only once is given, we are hardly dealing with learning. In Robinson's (1927) famous experiments on the effect of similarity of interpolated materials on prior learning, he made use of short series of responses (lists of eight consonants) in what amounted to tests of memory span. While he found different retention scores with different arrangements of the materials, we should raise the question as to whether he was really dealing with learning. Robinson observed the effect produced on the retention of the first four letters by the addition of variations in the second four letters. He actually had no measure of how well the first four were learned before the next four were presented.

In many ordinary experiences we similarly confound the interpretation of our retention without recognizing that we have never checked the degree of original learning. If we complain of poor memory for names, we rarely consider the possibility that we never learned the names in the first place. Hearing something once, especially when we are not particularly interested, is no proof that learning occurred. The long-time retention of some experiences or skills or information suggests that these might have been learned to a high degree. Most adults can repeat the Pledge of Allegiance to the Flag even though they may not have rehearsed it for years. When people become parents they find themselves fairly well supplied with nursery rhymes and a lullaby or two without special research. Before we start talking about forgetting we must first determine that there was something to forget. The degree of learning, we will find, is extremely important. In this connection we should appreciate that for various reasons learning psychologists do not frequently provide their subjects with great amounts of practice or permit a great deal of "overlearning." Nor do they wait for any great lengths of time to observe forgetting. To get data on forgetting in a hurry, experiments are frequently designed so that there will be some forgetting to observe. This is usually arranged by limiting the degree of learning. As a consequence, the experimental work usually is confined to short-term intervals and poorly learned materials. We must keep these considerations before us as we examine the variables in forgetting.

The variables in forgetting. What are the variables that operate in time to influence the probability of a given response? This question can be the theme of the chapter. It is, unfortunately, not an easy one to answer and we will be ranging far afield before we can feel any satisfaction about its resolution. The simple report of the school child, "I forgot," will have to be recognized as a cover for a multitude of factors, many of which are of such an intangible nature as to give us considerable trouble, not only for evaluating, but even for stating in a comprehensible way.

VARIABLES RELATED TO REMEMBERING

To organize the discussion to follow, a listing of the major variables might be in order. Some of these might appear to have little relevance or meaning at the moment, but they appear to play roles of some significance and we can evaluate them as we proceed. The following have been selected for examination:

1. Time, and what occurs in time. The question of disuse or interference
2. The stimulus situation during learning and testing
    a. The criterion of learning
    b. The role of set
3. The nature of the responses learned
4. The nature of the test of remembering
5. The effect of intervening activities
    a. Relative inactivity
    b. Other learning experiences
6. The affective character of the material
    a. Pleasant and unpleasant material
    b. Ego-involvement
    c. Traumatic experiences

The variables listed above represent only a gross division of factors related to remembering. As we proceed with the discussion we will have to include consideration of the ramifications of each. Before we embark on this task, we might recognize that the list is only an expansion of what McGeoch (1942) described as the three "psychological conditions of forgetting." McGeoch believed that the factors of set, interference, and the stimulation circumstances could pretty well account for much of the success or failure of retention. To somewhat exaggerate his view, we might say that if one learned with an appropriate set (intending to remember and aware of the possibility of interference), if no other learning related to the original took place, and if the proper stimulation could be presented, then there would be no forgetting. Since the requirements of this formula are unlikely to be met, we can expect failure to remember to the degree to which the three factors are violated. In the subsequent discussion we shall try to spell out in some detail the significance of the McGeoch three-factor view. We cannot hope to consider any great number of the studies dealing with the problems of memory and forgetting. Excellent summaries are already available (Osgood, 1953; Woodworth and Schlosberg, 1954), and there is little point to going over the same ground. We shall try to appreciate the logic of the problem rather than worry over frequently contradictory reports.

Time and forgetting. It is commonly assumed that we forget events or material learned as time goes on. The father blames his inability to assist his son with the arithmetic homework on the many years that have passed since he last studied the subject. At the same time he keeps telling the son about how tough things were "when I was your age." Most of us, as a matter of fact, are unable to recall with any detail the events of our childhood and we are quite unwilling to take seriously the claim of one psychiatrist that he personally recalls being born, however important an event that was. Those events or items of information that we do remember we attribute to practice. The accountant can help with his child's arithmetic but is "a little rusty" in history or geography. In addition, then, to assuming that the passage of time is important in forgetting, we are prone to assume that *not using* the materials is also involved. Somehow things are supposed to become "a little rusty" if they are not used.

The layman's interpretation when dressed up as the "theory of disuse" has a long and turbulent history in psychology, and at the present time, very few active supporters. The theory of disuse rests on the assumption that neural elements involved in a learning experience somehow grow and develop or show other kinds of physical changes (synaptic knobs, for example) and when these neural processes are not activated, there is a regression or reversal of some kind, a decrease in size or efficiency. Until the anatomical descriptions of such neuronal knobs was available, there was not much support for a disuse hypothesis. Since that physiological information has been obtained, a number of students (Hebb, 1949; Eccles, 1953) have come out for a disuse principle as at least partially involved.

McGeoch (1942), on the other hand, finds little meaning to the notion that time, by itself, can affect the strength of learning or for such a negative [1] view as the disuse hypothesis. For McGeoch, even

---

[1] In the next chapter we shall consider Eccles' interpretation of disuse (see p. 362) where he describes it as a result of positive stimulation.

getting "a little rusty" involves an active process of some kind and, of course, even a little rust does not accumulate by itself but in the chemical world amounts to an active oxidizing process. Analogously, no forgetting will occur if the organism is kept in a vacuum. It is not time that is important but *what happens* in time. We can anticipate the general argument (see pp. 319 f) by indicating that, for McGeoch, most, if not really all, forgetting is due to interference from subsequent experiences or later learning. Our problem at this time is to consider what kinds of events do occur in time which affect the retention of learned responses.

Maturation and forgetting. In recent years (see Beach and Jaynes, 1954) we have become increasingly aware of changes that occur as apparent concomitants of growth and development. The layman recognizes this with the expression, "He'll grow out of it," when some undesirable behavior is observed in a child. Whether the original response involved is learned or "natural" cannot always be determined, but there is no question but that as children grow they do give up childish ways. So far we have not collected a catalogue of the kinds of behavior which we "grow out of." The learning psychologist, of course, is concerned primarily with behavior that has been learned. Controlled observations have rarely been made on "growing out of" behavior known to have been learned. Is thumb sucking learned? Sometimes behavior appears to have been learned at least in part and lost with growth and further development. Gesell (1943), for example, points out that an infant may begin to show some control [2] over bladder and bowel functions before one year of age. The proud parents then find that at about thirteen months the control seems to disappear. Gesell attributes this loss to a change in the growth patterns of the neural supply of the elimination apparatus which occurs at about this time. The infantile swimming behavior described by McGraw (1935) is also lost in a few months unless special efforts are made to keep up swimming exercises. Similarly, the tonic neck reflex of the infant (see Gesell and Amatruda, 1947) is lost with growth and further development. The negativism of the two-year-old usually disappears, sometimes even at three. The behavioral changes accompanying adolescence strikingly illustrate how the earlier patterns of behavior are altered. Habits of personal care, games, speech, giggling, eating, and almost all social practices undergo marked

---

[2] He cooperates when placed in the proper position at appropriate times.

changes. The child has become a man. The question still remains, however, as to how much he has forgotten about previous practices.

Improvement without practice. There are a number of interesting contradictions of the general notion that there is a loss of retention with time. One of them, the phenomenon of "spontaneous recovery" will be discussed in the next chapter. Another is the frequently reported occurrence of "reminiscence," a finding that some subjects, especially children, seem to do better on a test of recently learned material if they are given a short rest immediately after the learning session.

Reminiscence. Reminiscence has been a popular research concept for learning psychologists, since before World War I when it was first introduced by Ballard (1913). It enjoyed a revival of interest in the pre-World War II era but now appears to be losing its original something-for-nothing fascination. Ballard found that young children seemed to remember more poetry a day or two after the last learning period than when tested immediately after a learning session. This gain in ability to recall after the passage of time seems somewhat mysterious. Other investigators (Williams, 1926) confirmed Ballard's results and the phenomenon is usually referred to as the "Ballard-Williams effect" when reminiscence is found with fairly long delays. Ward (1937) and Hovland (1938a, 1939) investigated a shorter term influence and they also found evidence for improved recall with 2–10 minute delays. The short-term reminiscence is now identified as the "Ward-Hovland phenomenon."

Other early studies (Melton and Stone, 1942) and McGeoch (1935), designed to prevent the possibility of rehearsal, showed no reminiscence. In the Melton-Stone experiment subjects had to name colors during the delay period. Hovland (1951) suggests that any such interpolated activity may prevent the operations that develop as "reminiscence." Mrs. McGeoch in the earlier study found that 84 percent of a group of young subjects admitted rehearsing during the interpolated period. Such rehearsal seems to account for some of the "reminiscence" reported.

We have already seen (p. 166) that in some tasks where "fatigue" might enter as a variable, a rest period might bring about improved performance. Such a gain presumably fits the facts of reminiscence but may not be the basic operation when reminiscence effects occur with material calling only for mild exertions. Hovland (1951) analyzes the variables and necessary experimental controls that must be in effect before reminiscence can be considered a genuine phenomenon. As Hovland points out, the controls involved are difficult to enforce and the perfect "reminiscence" experiment is still to be performed.

How real reminiscence is has been questioned by Underwood (1953) in a review of the literature. Underwood calls it a prewar phenomenon. We will not consider these studies further except to indicate that if they ever show substantial value, then time must sometimes be thought of as helping rather than hindering retention.

The forgetting curve. One of the best known findings of Ebbinghaus is his famous forgetting curve (see Fig. 12.1). According to the curve, most of what we learn is rapidly forgotten and a small remainder of learned material slowly dwindles away as time goes by. Unfortunately, we also forget that Ebbinghaus drew his curve on the basis of findings from relatively poorly learned nonsense syllables. The facts that Ebbing-

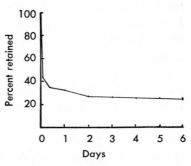

FIG. 12.1. The classical curve of forgetting. According to this widely publicized figure, most of the learned material is lost very rapidly and the rest more and more slowly. The curve represents the retention of nonsense syllable lists by one adult. See text for comment. (After Ebbinghaus, 1885.)

haus, a mature adult, was his own subject, learned the syllables by a particular process of reading through a list, and tested himself by the savings method (see p. 318) should make us pause and reflect before we accept the curve as a general law of forgetting. All the factors mentioned and many more must be evaluated before we can generalize about forgetting curves. We have already questioned the suitability of a *series* of nonsense syllables learned at one sitting as appropriate material for studying learning (see p. 181). When we examine forgetting curves for other kinds of material, for example, mazes, we find little similarity with Ebbinghaus's curve. Actually the time scale in most experiments is rather short, and we know little about any long-range retention from laboratory studies. We will do better to start examining the factors involved in retention than searching for what may be an illusion. There is no more likelihood that a particular curve can be found to qualify as *the* forgetting curve than we found in connection with the search for *the* learning curve.

The stimulus situation during learning. The first of McGeoch's (1942) psychological factors in forgetting is concerned with the nature of the stimulus situation. Here McGeoch argues that if learning occurs and is to be retained, the stimulus pattern operating at the time of the learning must also be present at the time of retention testing. No one is really surprised if the school child "forgets" his speech on the stage if his learning sessions were confined to his home. Even with some stage practice it frequently turns out that an audience makes a difference. The way in which questions are asked in examinations may differ from the way they were asked in learning, and a poor mark results when a different phrasing of a question might have called out a better answer. What factors comprise a stimulus situation? If we consider Guthrie, then almost any conceivable factor in the external learning environment, as well as any kind of internal activity which produces stimuli, might be important in a pattern of stimulation. From this point of view, we should not be surprised if we forget. Quite the contrary, we should be surprised if we ever remember anything as it is unlikely that any pattern of stimulation will ever be repeated. Here we have an untestable hypothesis as has already been indicated (see p. 284). If we forget, the stimulus pattern was sufficiently different. If we remember, the missing elements in the pattern are unimportant. Since there is no way to decide in advance about the importance of any factor, all we can do is try to reproduce the original learning situation as fully as possible if we wish to ensure the best possible performance. The other alternative is to vary all the readily controllable factors in the learning trials so that the learner learns under almost all likely combinations of circumstances.

The experimental literature in this area is sparse and poorly controlled. We have one interesting study by Bilodeau and Schlosberg (1951) in which they found that the learning situation made quite a difference in retention. Actually, Bilodeau and Schlosberg were concerned with retroactive inhibition (see p. 320), but their study bears on the present question although indirectly, and so we report it here. Subjects learned pairs of adjectives in one room while sitting before a memory drum. After the material was learned to a criterion, they went to another, very different kind of room and learned another set of materials while standing; the material in this case being presented on cards that were flipped by the experimenter. They then went back to the original situation for a retention and relearning session. Control subjects learned new material in the original situation. It was found that when new material was learned in a different environment, in a different posture, and by a different method of presentation, there was only half as much interference with the retention of the original as there was when new material was learned in the same circumstances. A previous study by Nagge (1935) found no such difference in the retention of nonsense syllables learned in a different room. We do not know from the Bilodeau and Schlosberg results which of the three factors (room, posture, or presentation method) were the significant ones, but their data indicate that the stimulus situation must be taken into serious account in measuring retention.

We could hardly expect much research in this area since most experimenters try to reproduce the learning circumstances rather than deliberately introduce changes. Other studies bearing on this issue are cited in McGeoch (1942).

The influence of "set" under which learning takes place. The second psychological condition of forgetting is that of set. The average student seems to appreciate this factor intuitively. Upon the announcement by an instructor that a test is to be given, the students want to know whether it is to be "objective" or "essay." When the instructor asks what difference it makes, the students insist it helps them in preparing. Somehow the students learn to use more or less the same material for different purposes, at least they believe this is possible.

We have already reviewed the experiment of Lester (1932) on set (see p. 23) and have observed how knowledge of a future test, of future learning, and of information about interference all help the retention of learning even though the precise mechanisms or learning techniques by which this is accomplished are still to be discovered. The numerous experiments on incidental learning point to the relative paucity of learning when no set has been established for either learning or retaining certain kinds of material. Actually the role of set as a determiner of retention is still largely a speculative affair, and much remains to be done with the problem. Most studies of set have been directed into other channels, such as perception and motivation. For McGeoch's interpretation we have only suggestive support.

Interference and forgetting. McGeoch's third psychological condition of forgetting is the operation of interference from new learning. This is currently so prominent a factor in experimental studies that we must consider it at full length. In order to do so, however, we must first examine some more mechanical aspects of forgetting studies, discussion of which would lead us away from the point if we stopped to criticize details in connection with the interference hypothesis. We will turn instead to a consideration of the kinds of responses that have been learned and the methods of testing the retention as the next step in our inquiry.

Retention as a function of the type of materials learned. It is commonly observed that we remember differentially. Some things are retained for long periods while others are forgotten almost as soon as they have served their purpose. Many people "have no head" for figures. Others complain that names elude them while faces do not. We have already noted that what is never learned cannot be retained, and the casual way in which people attend to names of strangers is sufficient reason for failure of retention. Too often it is merely a case of not learning in the first place. For any serious consideration of types of materials we must first determine the adequacy of the learning. Not much is known about how well different types of materials can be learned—we have met this problem before (see Chap. 4, "Kinds of Learning") but we can look at some of the types of learning that have been studied in terms of retention.

1. CONDITIONED REFLEXES. Studies of retention of classical conditioning are rare. Gantt (see Liddell, below) made extensive observations on one "neurotic" dog which gave evidence of retaining certain abnormal sexual reactions over a long time. Liddell (1944) cites cases of neurotic sheep that retain conditioned flexion responses for as long as 14 years. Hilgard and Marquis (1940) report a conditioned eyelid blink in a dog after a 16-month interval. A conditioned flexion reflex in dogs was observed by Wendt (1937) after 2½ years. Razran (1939c) noted conditioned salivation in man after 16 weeks. Hilgard and Marquis regard the conditioned response as more or less permanent if there is no attempt at extinction. Not many studies have been reported on the retention of instrumental responses. Skinner (1950) reports relatively strong retention (in terms of extinction) of a pecking response in pigeons. Pecking at a target appears to be retained for periods of 4½ years and, presumably, even longer. The life span of the organisms used must always be weighed. A month in the life of a rat may be equivalent to two or more years in a human.

2. MOTOR SKILLS. Everyone is familiar with the classical illustration of long-term retention of motor skills. Once we learn how to swim we never forget, or if we do we do not testify otherwise. So

with dancing and skating and other skills picked up in childhood—catching a baseball, playing billiards, and so on. A daily newspaper once pictured an elderly gentleman of eighty or so who set out on a skating pond and claimed he had not forgotten a thing about skating since the last time on skates at the age of twelve. Such evidence is, of course, subject to considerable skepticism. There is usually little or no record of past performances. Any weakness shown in later life is put down to "stiffness," sense organ weaknesses, and so on.

Laboratory exercises involving motor skills usually involve such tasks as tracking (pursuit rotor), typing, maze-learning, dart-throwing, and so on. None of these tasks when learned or practiced by human subjects can be considered purely "motor." There are obvious verbal components in any acquisition of motor skills and to speak of purely motor behavior involves us in a dubious controversy. There are few carefully controlled experiments dealing with retention of motor skills. In most instances such studies deal with periods of a week or so and are done for purposes of comparison with more verbal tasks. Thus Leavitt and Schlosberg (1944) compared pursuit rotor skill with verbal material and found the motor task even better after 7 days than when practice ceased, while the verbal task was poorer.

3. SERIAL RESPONSES LEARNED BY ROTE. The retention of nonsense syllables in serial lists is relatively poor, as Ebbinghaus was the first to discover. Actually there is little that can be said conclusively in the absence of some standard criteria for amount of practice. We rarely overlearn nonsense syllables as we frequently do with so-called meaningful material. Even with relatively low criteria of learning, some aftereffects of the learning can prevail for long periods if the subjects are intensively tested. In one of the writer's classes, students learned nonsense syllables in October to a criterion of two correct repetitions of a 12-syllable list, and were tested in May of the following year. Recall scores were of a zero order with a general report that it was absurd to expect retention of such material. By placing the students in the same situation in which the learning took place, with an empty memory drum revolving before them, many of the students were able to reproduce several syllables, one student getting as many as eight, a result he insisted was completely beyond him as he claimed to be unable to recall anything about the list before he was urged into the effort.

The fact that relearning procedures (see Bunch, 1946) indicate some retention of stylus mazes after 120 days again suggests that rote material can be retained in some degree for relatively long periods if it is not disturbed by interpolated learning of similar material. Where similar responses are continually being incorporated into new patterns, as in piano compositions, we find considerable forgetting, but even here, relearning is relatively rapid. In such instances, there are many complicating variables, and controlled studies are difficult.

4. MEANINGFUL MATERIALS. When we try to study the retention of meaningful material we run into all the difficulties that made psychologists turn to nonsense syllables in the first place. Is a piece of poetry meaningful? A story? A list of words? Can we compare relative difficulties of experimental and control materials? How do we measure retention of a poem—by the number of words, lines, verses? How many details do we require in the retelling of a story to consider it perfectly remembered, well remembered, and so on? How important are different kinds of details? Studies on retention of meaningful material are pretty much limited to semiquantitative types such as Bartlett's (1932) study of story retention wherein he observed the dropping out of details, modification of plot, filling in with extraneous material designed to make sense, and so on. We have yet to work out an experimental procedure and a rationale for the study of the retention of meanings or meaningful material.

5. COMPARISONS OF TYPES OF MATERIALS. It is generally agreed that meaningful material is better retained or more readily relearned than nonsense or rote material. Ebbinghaus (1885) was able to show that relatively fewer trials were required to relearn 80-syllable stanzas of *Don Juan* than to relearn a 12-syllable nonsense list. Here we run into an immediate difficulty in that it was easier to learn the stanza of poetry in the first place. We have not yet learned to equate the degrees of difficulty of materials. The assumption that equal trials to learn to some criterion would imply equal difficulty is not necessarily valid. Retention scores would probably still favor the meaningful material if we judge by Ebbinghaus's data which showed progressive improvement in favor of the poetry with successive relearning trials.

Comparisons between nonsense syllable learning and maze learning also involve separate and largely unknown variables. We have discussed the problem earlier (see p. 181) and need not reconsider it now. Some forms of motor learning (rotor pursuit) seem to be better retained than nonsense syllable lists (Leavitt and Schlosberg, 1944). There is the possibility that the pursuit task makes some sort of sense and involves some kinds of meaningful organization.

In general there is a dearth of studies of a satisfactory nature in this area of comparative retention. The experimental design problems are highly complex and we might profit more from an analysis of other variables in retention for the present. A word of caution is in order in connection with everyday observations about the question. The fact that we recall or remember some materials effectively may be a function of their simplicity, overlearning, their incorporation into other activities, or lack of interference from competitive responses. We do not forget how to ride a bicycle because it took some time to learn, it was overlearned in all probability, and nowhere do we find ourselves in a similar stimulus situation wherein new responses might be learned.

The nature of the test and its relation to learning. When we speak of "forgetting" in its usual context, we usually refer to an inability to reproduce the learned material. Usually the stimulating circumstances are not like those involved in learning. The teacher asks a question which the student cannot answer. A restatement or rephrasing of the question may bring out some approximation of the answer. The reverse situation is also common. Students answer questions that were never asked. Here we have a situation where failure to reproduce is contaminated by a failure to discriminate or identify the relevant stimuli. The test of reproduction operates within a wide range of stimulation from direct presentation of the isolated and proper stimulus to one of relative lack of stimulation as when you try to remember the name of some childhood friend or movie favorite. In the latter case only self-stimulation is possible, and one resorts to various crutches or aids such as reciting the letters of the alphabet and testing each for sympathetic vibration.

The test by *reproduction* is usually known as the method of "recall" and is, in most studies, and with most materials, the least effective, though in ordinary life situations it is the most commonly attempted procedure. When no source of stimulation or assistance is available beyond the vague circumstances that created the need for an answer, we are left to try to bring out the response by ourselves and failures are commonly experienced. Frequently we do not know and have no way of proving if what we recall is correct. Sometimes the recall is confused by other circumstances. If we hear stories about our childhood adventures often enough, we may remember the story but not the actual incident and later claim to recall the original event. Sometimes recall is partially successful in the sense of bringing an answer to "the tip of my tongue." Without help the answer may stay there and be of little value.

The *recognition* method is sometimes used in the laboratory, but more often in a classroom in connection with so-called objective tests. In this method, the answers to questions are provided as in matching questions, or more correctly, in true-false or choice items. The student is obliged to pick out the correct answer from among a number of others or from an imaginary opposite in the case of true-false questions. The recognition method typically results in higher scores than does the recall method. It ordinarily is much less of a strain on the subject although a problem for the examiner. The general weakness of recognition tests is the difficulty of providing equally likely choices as well as a sufficiency of these to account for chance successes. In recognition testing we provide the responses or hints thereto as in prompting. In recall we operate more on the stimulus side. It is a question, then, as to whether comparisons of the two techniques are legitimate.

In studying the learning of nonsense syllables by the recall procedure, for example, we provide one as a stimulus and test for the availability of an association of that stimulus with a response. In recognition testing, we would ask the subject to pick out previously learned responses from a collection which included a number of syllables never learned before. In the second case, the subject need have no associations between stimuli and responses at all, in the ordinary sense, and yet get a perfect score. If the arrangement or pattern of the material is important, perfect recognition might be of little value. In any event, ability to recognize, while perhaps not of great practical use, demonstrates the fact that the previous experience has been retained to some degree and is not completely lost. This is the point for theory to consider (see below).

Relearning. The third common laboratory method is that of relearning. The subject may first attempt a recall and after the extent of this is determined, he starts new learning trials. If the old material is not completely lost, it may show up as an improvement in learning to the same criterion. Thus if a poem was learned in 10 repetitions at an earlier time and is now learned in 8, a *savings score* of 20 percent has been established. There is an unestimated degree of danger here, if suitable controls are not undertaken of crediting the savings to retention whereas some or all of the savings may be due to familiarity with the procedure of learning, mastery of technique, motivation, and perhaps many other variables (for example, rehearsal). The proper control might consist of learning some equivalent material and estimating the savings from the control situation.

The three methods described above are the classical methods of measuring retention. They have the common advantage of being quantitative when applied in the laboratory. Whether they have anything else in common, however, is doubtful. They do not measure the same thing certainly, as the scores are typically different and vary considerably with recognition scores usually showing the greatest values. (Recognition can be made as difficult as desired by deliberately introducing highly similar control materials.) Comparisons among the three are questionable since it is obvious, from the different scores, that different features of the original learning are being estimated. There is no sense in which recall, recognition, and relearning can be compared. It is possible to get a zero score for recall and recognition and yet a relearning score of some value might be obtained with a potential savings of some degree which may be confounded by lack of motivation, for example, into a below-zero status. Recall cannot go below zero. Recognition and relearning can.

There are a number of less quantitative methods that have been employed on material that does not lend itself readily to measurement. Such matters as stories, arguments, and general ideas can be related in various ways, and estimates of the degree of retention must be highly interpretive. Even in such matters as poetry, it is difficult to determine how to rate a subject who knows all the verses if he once gets started but needs a prompt between stanzas.

Psychologists interested in the retention of visually perceived forms employ various methods to estimate the degree of retention. Thus Hebb and Foord (1945) made use of the recognition technique by showing the original drawing as one of a group of several other similar diagrams. Another technique is that of reproduction, in which the subject attempts to draw a facsimile of the originally perceived item. Here skill at drawing might enter as a variable and should be checked. Frequently subjects in such experiments attempt to define the form for themselves in some kind of verbal fashion, and the measures of retention may represent measures of verbal learning rather than retention of perceived forms.

The effect of intervening activities. When we discuss extinction we shall see how strong a case can be built up for *interference* as a factor in the elimination of a learned response. Psychologists who have concerned themselves more with human learning and forgetting have likewise found the interference idea tempting. The general proposal of those favoring interference (McGeoch, 1942) as an explanation is that we forget what we learned only if we subsequently learn something else. The new learning in one way or another operates to bring about the forgetting. It is the question of how and why the new learning has this result that has been most commonly studied and speculated about; the general proposition itself is accepted so broadly as to amount to an empirical law.

Assuming such a proposition for the moment, why should new learning (or really, engaging in some new activity) result in some decrement in prior learning? Two basic theoretical approaches can be mentioned briefly at this time (and the argument will be detailed later): (1) When anything is learned, the neural elements involved tend to continue in activity for some time. There might be a necessity for some period of freedom from other stimulation for the just-acquired material to be securely established. The new learning must be allowed to *perseverate* for a while. If this perseveration is interfered with, the learning cannot become suitably organized and a subsequent test will show deterioration or decrement. This view is an old one and goes back to Müller and Pilzecker in 1900 (see Woodworth, 1938). (2) The other view considers the possibility that the stimuli relating to the just-learned material might become dissociated from their recently acquired response connections and become associated with any new activity. New connections are formed, so that the stimuli which should bring out the original responses now bring out the new responses, or at least they are dissociated from the old so that a test will reveal a performance loss of some degree. Both views have led to considerable experimental work and this now calls for scrutiny.

Practically all the work involved in the study of interference effects has been done with a simple appearing experimental design. The traditional name for the design is "retroactive inhibition." The general formula amounts to this: Subjects learn "something," we can call it "material A." They then learn "material B and a test of A is made. Control subjects learn A, do nothing while the experimental subjects are learning B, and are tested for A at the same time as the experimental subjects. In diagram form the usual setup is as follows:

	Original	Interpolated period	Test
Experimental group	Learn A	Learn B	Recall or relearn A
Control group	Learn A	Do nothing	Recall or relearn A

The paradigm is simple enough. Carrying out a definitive experiment, however, is another matter. There are many variables to consider in every phase of the experiment, each of which prevents an easy interpretation. We shall list some of the most significant variables first and then review some of the more widely accepted findings.

Variables in retroactive inhibition experiments.

1. Preparation of subjects for learning the type of material involved
2. The nature of the control group activity in the interpolated period
3. The nature of the materials learned in both original and interpolated sessions. This includes the question of amount of such material.
4. The temporal variable: how soon after A is learned do the subjects learn B? How soon after B does the retest follow?
5. How well the materials A and B are learned

We can now turn to each of the above variables. We are ignoring other variables common to all experiments but which operate in this type of experiment as well, such as the fact that generally groups of subjects are used and the data from individuals are combined more or less indiscriminately. Since learning experiments, in general, show wide differences among subjects on various trials, combining subjects occasionally will obscure operations which affect different subjects at different times.

1. PREPARATION OF THE SUBJECTS. Depending on the materials, it frequently happens that subjects get better in the interpolated session and sometimes in the test period after interpolation. At first glance this would invalidate any kind of interference hypothesis since all that is demonstrated is *positive* transfer. If subjects are beginners at a type of learning material, such as nonsense syllables or mazes, they might well do better as a result of practice with the materials, procedures, apparatus, and general familiarity with the experiment. We have already mentioned reminiscence effects (see p. 310) and these might also be playing a part in a test after interpolation. Subjects might do better after a session devoted to interpolated learning if they are not brought to a peak of practice prior to the beginning of the experiment. The nature of the learning materials is of greatest importance in this connection (see below). The essential control is to employ only well-trained subjects. It has been shown (Ward, 1937) that improvement in learning nonsense syllable lists, under favorable conditions, persists for as long as 14 or even more lists. Most of the improvement occurs in the first 5 or 6 lists and subjects should be practiced on at least that many lists prior to use in "retroaction" experiments if practice effects are to be avoided (Fig. 8.4, p. 195).

2. CONTROL GROUP ACTIVITY. The control group is employed to de-

termine what would be lost in retention if the interference materials were not learned. In theory, if the control subjects do absolutely nothing except to exist for the period involved, they should retain what was learned unless some deterioration can take place simply through the process of continued living. The problem of reducing the activity of a control group to a minimum is a difficult one. There are several aspects to consider:

a. The subjects may indulge in rehearsal of the learned material. Even if they do not attempt to rehearse, they may be unable to prevent some kind of involuntary reflection. We are all familiar with the experience of having a song "running through our heads." The only control over rehearsal would be to use materials which cannot be rehearsed. One might use irregular visual patterns which are difficult to verbalize, as stimuli in paired-associate lists. Even such stimuli, however, are susceptible of some degree of verbalization. Using animal subjects might help, but the essence of the *perseveration theory* is that the rehearsal does go on and would do so in animals too.

b. To prevent rehearsal, subjects might be distracted by some simple task with no requirements of learning imposed on them. Typically subjects are asked to look at cartoons in humor magazines. While they may make no effort to learn the cartoons or jokes involved, they might not be able to help doing so. In such a case, the loss suffered by the control group is used as a basis for comparison of the interference value of the interpolated material used by the experimental group. This is obviously unsatisfactory because there is no clear appreciation of what factors are responsible for the losses in each group. A control group naming colors in the interpolation period may lose a good deal by a loss in *set* for the original kind of learning, from learning features of the color situation, from fatigue effects, and so on. The experimental group might even show better retention in the test. In such a case, there is a question as to which group was the control for which.

c. Some experimenters have tried to arrange for some degree of *suspended animation* for the control group. Thus Jenkins and Dallenbach (1924) in a now famous experiment had two subjects sleep in the laboratory after learning some nonsense syllables. On different nights they would be awakened after 1, 2, 4, or 8 hours of sleep. In the morning they could learn other lists and be tested during the day with normal daily routine as the intervening activity. It was found, for both subjects, that retention dropped after 1 hour of sleep, dropped still more after 2 hours, but did not drop much beyond that. During the day the retention would fall off to a much greater degree than for corresponding sleep periods. Because of the obtained loss after 1 and 2 hours of sleep we can assume that sleep or the process of falling asleep might involve some interference features. On the other hand, it might be argued (Worchel and Marks, 1951) that the process of awakening is not a simple matter in which one becomes 100 percent effective as soon as he awakens. If the process of awakening is accompanied by various levels of fogginess and inefficiency, this inability to work at top level might account for the drop in retention. In fact it has been found that cockroaches that were put into suspended animation by freezing suffered so from either the freezing or the thawing-out process that retention was poor (Hunter, 1932). The numerous difficulties that surround the interpretation of the control group performance make the problem of getting unequivocal results from retroaction experiments even more difficult than it first appears.

3. THE INFLUENCE OF THE MATERIALS LEARNED. This is perhaps the most confusing or confounding variable. In ordinary life situations we experience forgetting of a phone number, a date, a name, or answer to a question which we could be presumed to have learned. In practically no laboratory experiment do the psychologists study the forgetting of such *single* events. In the laboratory situation a learned single event (for example, a conditioned response) is not forgotten. In order to get data on forgetting, then, the experimenter gets the subject to learn a series or collection of responses. Either the subject learns a list of words or nonsense syllables (serially or as pairs) or they learn multiple-unit mazes (never T-mazes) or some other relatively complicated performance (complicated primarily by *addition* of units rather than by difficulty of principles or separate operations). By this procedure data are obtainable. Whether such data actually can throw light on the basic problem of forgetting might be arguable. They do, of course, serve to show how lists, series, or sequences of a limited variety are remembered. They might have nothing to do with how some mathematical operation like canceling fractions is remembered or forgotten.

a. *Amount of material learned.* The loss of retention is strongly determined by how much was learned originally. If original learning is that of an 8-syllable list, more will be remembered than if the list is increased to 12. A 20-syllable list not only requires much more than twice as much practice as a 10-syllable list, but much more is lost in a test following interpolation.

Amount also operates in terms of the number of separate sets of learning materials. Thus, learning one list of interpolated materials does not cause so much loss as learning several. As more and more lists are interpolated the original material suffers more and more. If the materials are designed so as to interfere maximally, the learning of each successive list becomes poorer (Bugelski, 1942, 1948) and the subjects begin to show a progressive deterioration in their learning (proactive inhibition).

b. *Similarity and retroaction.* It is generally held by those who would explain forgetting as due to interference from new learning that any loss in retention of some previously learned responses is due to interference from learning other responses. It would also appear to be a logical inference that the more similar the interpolated learning, the more the possibilities of interference. It can be easily shown that learning a maze after learning a previous maze interferes more with the recall of the first than learning nonsense syllables, for example. McGeoch (1942) generally holds to such an interference explanation. The problem is not so simple as it might appear, however, because the problem of "similarity" has never been solved in a satisfactory fashion. To say that one material, *B*, is more similar to *A* than some other material, *C*, involves numerous questions. The various dimensions of similarity that can be called on in accounting for the experimental results are so diverse as to defy ordinary analysis. Thus two objects may be different in size but similar in color, or different in color and size but similar in shape; if they also differ in shape, it might be argued that they are made of the same material, or that they are both designs or visual stimuli, and so on. When all else fails, it can be argued that the methods of learning are similar or the drive conditions are similar. Hilgard and Marquis (1940) resolve the problem behaviorally and state that two stimuli are similar to the degree that they bring out the same response. Thus, the sound of a gong and the odor of violets can be "similar" if each brings out the same response. Such functional similarity may be a satisfactory way of viewing the problem although it precludes any predictions in advance of testing.[3]

The situation is further complicated in that ordinarily, in learning, a stimulus is associated with a response. If we symbolize an original learning situation as S_1-R_1, then in the interpolated learning, we have

---

[3] It is possible to use judges' ratings of similarity with some materials, for example, pictures and diagrams as has been done by Gibson (1941) and Hamilton (1943).

another S-R situation, and here we encounter the similarity problem in that either the S or the R may be similar to S_1 or R_1. The interpolated learning can include identical stimuli S_1, and different responses, R_2, or different stimuli, S_2, and identical responses. The identity may be decreased by various degrees in either or both stimuli and responses so that the situation can be highly complex. The number of different degrees of similarity cannot be stipulated on the basis of any data now available. Presumably we have a continuum from identity through "similarity" to some neutral point. Beyond this neutral point, we might conceive of some continuum of *dissimilarity*. Robinson (1927), Kennelly (1941), and others (Osgood, 1949) have tried to develop schema for describing a range of dissimilarity. Most of these attempts have presumed that some things like letters of the alphabet are similar to each other but dissimilar from numbers. There is no objective basis for such a decision and no impressive data have been accumulated on this basis. Some students (Osgood, 1949) try to find dissimilarity in terms of "opposites." Thus "low" is considered as dissimilar to "high." It is possible that some validity may reside in such an arrangement. There is no general principle, however, for describing dissimilarity. What, for example, is the opposite of, or greatly dissimilar to an automobile or an Eskimo? So far, we are dealing with a highly speculative proposition. However, for purposes of the usual type of experiment we can picture possibilities (always trying to remember that they are possibilities) somewhat as follows:

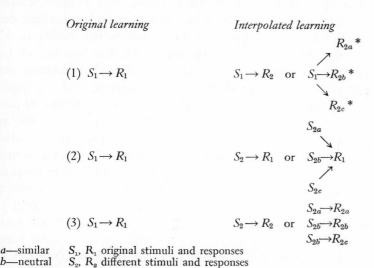

Original learning	*Interpolated learning*

(1) $S_1 \rightarrow R_1$ $S_1 \rightarrow R_2$ or $S_1 \rightarrow R_{2b}$ * $\nearrow R_{2a}$ * $\searrow R_{2c}$ *

(2) $S_1 \rightarrow R_1$ $S_2 \rightarrow R_1$ or $S_{2b} \rightarrow R_1$ with $S_{2a} \searrow$, $S_{2c} \nearrow$

(3) $S_1 \rightarrow R_1$ $S_2 \rightarrow R_2$ or $S_{2a} \rightarrow R_{2a}$ $S_{2b} \rightarrow R_{2b}$ $S_{2b} \rightarrow R_{2c}$

*a—similar S_1, R_1 original stimuli and responses
 b—neutral S_2, R_2 different stimuli and responses
 c—dissimilar

In the three situations described above we might well expect a variety of results. Taking them one at a time, let us consider the experimental and theoretical possibilities.

1. Here we have a situation in which the interpolated learning is nicely arranged to provide the greatest possible interference with both the new learning and recall of the original. If the same stimuli are operating in the interpolated learning but different responses are being learned, then we can expect to have considerable difficulty in retaining the original learning. Obviously a competitive response is being established and we have a counter-conditioning setup. To the extent that a very different kind of response is called for, we might expect more interference. To take a somewhat fantastic example, if a dog is conditioned to salivate to a bell and then conditioned to lick his lips to the bell, we might get less interference in reconditioning the original salivary response than if the interpolated learning involved foot-withdrawal to the bell. If we could arrange a hierarchy of similarity running from salivation to foot-withdrawal, we could expect progressively more interference as we departed more and more from the original response. Actually we have only meager data to support this view. Bugelski (1942) found more interference from learning new responses to old stimuli than from learning entirely new combinations of stimuli and responses. Underwood (1945) confirmed this finding in a more extensive experiment.

Osgood (1946) tried to develop a hierarchy of similarity in using words as responses to letter pairs, for example, c.m.—elated, c.m.—high, c.m.—left, c.m.—low. The learning scores of his subjects correspond to the hypothesis given above although the reality of his hierarchy is highly questionable. In any event, the findings of the several experiments add up to the net conclusion that learning new responses to old stimuli is productive of interference, and the degree of interference appears to be inversely related to the degree of similarity between the original and interpolated responses. If the responses are quite similar, there is less interference if indeed a positive transfer effect is not found. When actual positive transfer is found, we might interpret it to be in the nature of a practice effect from response generalization. Actually positive effects are unlikely so long as the stimuli are the same, and so we are limited to suggesting that an $S \rightarrow R$ association is less likely to be seriously disturbed if the R component is not drastically modified. We should expect a similar situation if the S component is not too seriously modified (see case 3, below).

Osgood (1949) expresses the above view in what he calls an "empirical law": "Where stimuli are functionally identical and responses are varied, negative transfer and retroactive interference are obtained, the magnitude of both decreasing as similarity between the responses increases."

2. If the stimulus situation is altered and the responses are the same in the interpolated and in the original learning, then instead of interference we can expect some facilitation from the interpolated learning. In effect, what we are doing is practicing the same response to a different stimulus, and if the new S is completely unrelated or highly dissimilar there is no particular reason to expect it to interfere with the learning of the association S_2-R_1. It need not help, but certainly there is no reason why it should hinder the retention of S_1-R_1. On the other hand, if S_2 is somewhat like S_1, we can actually expect a favorable influence. In the case of a dog salivating to a tuning fork, for example, any conditioning that takes place may generalize to different frequencies or intensities of auditory stimuli, particularly tuning forks near the original frequency. This would aid the interpolated learning of salivating to another fork. Likewise, if the response is now learned to the new tone, it too will generalize and may strengthen the original association through generalization to the original stimulus. No data appear to be available on just this kind of experimental design, but Hovland's (1937) generalization experiment offers some speculative grounds for the soundness of the reasoning. Hamilton (1943) arranged for three degrees of similarity of stimuli to be associated with the same response. His stimuli consisted of visual patterns which were first tested for degrees of similarity. The responses were nonsense syllables. Subjects would learn the original $S_1 \rightarrow R_1$ associations and then $S_{2a} \rightarrow R_1$ or $S_{2b} \rightarrow R_1$ where S_{2b} was less similar to S_1 than S_{2a}. Instead of interference effects when $S_1 \rightarrow R_1$ was relearned, Hamilton found facilitation. Neutral stimuli (less similar or most dissimilar) showed no facilitation, but also no negative effects.

Osgood summarizes the situation with another empirical law: "When stimuli are varied and responses are functionally identical, positive transfer and retroactive facilitation are obtained, the magnitude of both increasing as the similarity among the stimulus members increases."

3. We are ready for the last case. Here both stimuli and responses are varied in the intervening material and we can expect maximal interference as the similarity of the stimuli increases (see case 1,

above). What would happen if the responses also became more similar we will leave for the moment. Consider the experiment of Gibson (1942) with respect to the decreasing similarity of stimuli. As in Hamilton's experiment, the stimuli were geometric designs, the responses nonsense syllables. All subjects first learned $S_1 \rightarrow R_1$. Then separate groups of subjects learned $S_{2a} \rightarrow R_2$ or $S_{2b} \rightarrow R_2$ or $S_{2c} \rightarrow R_2$, where a, b, c, represent decreasing similarity of stimulus pattern. Gibson found that completely neutral patterns had practically no effect as interpolated stimuli. Subjects learning such neutral combinations recalled 7.57 responses on a retest of $S_1 \rightarrow R_1$, when their original learning had only reached a 7.91 level. Subjects learning a highly similar list, S_{2a}, recalled only 3.0 of the original 7.66 they had learned. The general findings bear out the conclusion that similar stimuli when associated with *different* responses lead to considerable interference.

Osgood has summarized the above type of finding in a third empirical law: "Where both stimulus and response members are simultaneously varied, negative transfer and retroactive interference are obtained, the magnitude of both increasing as the stimulus similarity increases."

The above material on interference effects from interpolated material seems to offer the best current picture. It should be noted, however, that Osgood's "empirical laws" are really *ad hoc* generalizations based on several different experiments, particularly those of Hamilton, Gibson, and his own. In none of these experiments was there any attempt to vary both stimuli and responses in the interpolated learning period along the similarity continuum. Since such an experiment seemed in order, the writer and one of his students (Bugelski and Cadwallader, 1956) attempted to test Osgood's laws in a rather elaborate experimental design involving 17 groups of subjects. The general design involved all subjects first learning 13 pairs of paired associates, with Gibson's diagrams serving as stimuli and Osgood's word lists as responses. Following the original learning, each group of subjects, as numbered below, learned different interpolated material as follows:

Stimuli		*Responses*			
Identical	— Similar	(1) less similar	(2), neutral	(3), opposite	(4)
Similar	— " (5)	" (6),	" (7),	" (8)	
Less similar	— " (9)	" (10)	" (11),	" (12)	
Neutral	— " (13)	" (14)	" (15),	" (16)	
Control group (17)	No interpolated learning.				

The results were both favorable and unfavorable to Osgood's laws in that the recall scores tended to confirm the first and third laws but contradicted the second law.

In Figures 12.2 and 12.3 we see the "empirical" facts plotted

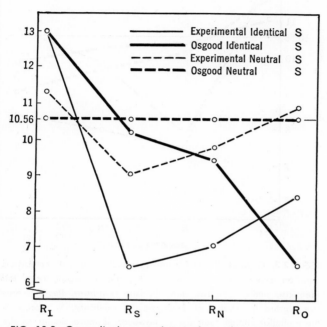

FIG. 12.2. Osgood's theoretical "transfer and retroaction surface" compared with an experimental test (Bugelski and Cadwallader, 1956). In the diagrams R_I, R_S, R_N, and R_O refer to identical, similar, neutral, and opposite kinds of responses. The control group performance (neither positive nor negative transfer) stands at 10.56 words recalled after interpolated learning with identical or neutral stimuli. The experimental, neutral stimulus curve does not deviate significantly from the control as Osgood predicts. With identical stimuli, however, there is a significant drop in recall for similar responses, contrary to Osgood's prediction (see text).

against Osgood's empirical laws as he presented them graphically in what he called the "transfer and retroactive surface" (Osgood, 1949).

The data suggest the following observations:

1. Neutral stimuli in interpolated learning do not appear to affect recall regardless of the similarity status of the response. There may be some slight benefit in learning identical responses com-

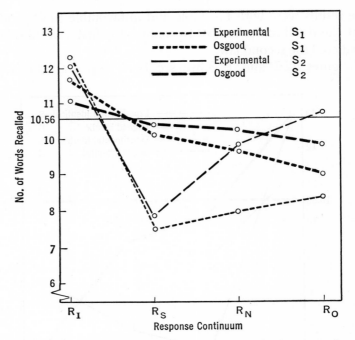

FIG. 12.3. Osgood's "transfer and retroaction surface" compared with an experimental test. R_I, R_S, R_N, and R_O again represent identical, similar, neutral, and opposite responses. Recall scores are plotted for stimuli of 2 degrees of similarity. S_I represents more similar stimuli than S_2. S_2, however, is more similar to the original than are neutral stimuli (see Fig. 12.2). In the cases of both degrees of similarity there is significant negative transfer when responses are similar, contrary to Osgood's prediction (see text for further interpretation).

pared with similar responses. This finding is in accordance with Osgood's laws.

2. When the stimuli are identical and responses allowed to vary along the similarity continuum, we find an interesting reversal of Osgood's law. The most similar responses employed had a more severe effect than neutral or opposite responses. This same pattern is repeated when stimuli are less and less similar.

In general, then, Osgood's laws appear borne out as far as stimulus relationships are concerned. On the response side, there appears to be a contradiction. Learning similar responses is troublesome when original material is recalled.

We shall have to return to these observations when we come to the problem of transfer (Chap. 14). For the present we continue with a consideration of other factors involved in an interference interpretation of retention.

4. TEMPORAL FACTORS. When material is interpolated between learning and a test, a variety of possibilities comes up. If there is any delay between learning and test, the interpolated learning can occur just after the original or at any time until just before the test. If a 16-day interval, for example, is employed as it was by Postman and Alper (1946) then the interpolated material might be learned 2, 8, 12, or more days after the original or at any of an almost unlimited number of times. Postman and Alper found that most decrement in retention came when interpolated learning was undertaken one day after the original, one day before the test, or in the middle of the 16-day period. The periods just after the learning and just before test were not so destructive of retention.

It should be noted, however, that Postman and Alper did not require any achievement of their subjects. They simply exposed lists of 20 paired associates five times in both learning and interpolated sessions and the findings can only apply to the equivocal procedure followed. Equal trials on interpolated material are unlikely to represent the same degree of learning as has been attained on the original (see below, Degree of Learning).

The experimental data on time of interpolation are so varied as to support or refute any theoretical view. Unfortunately the results are not obtained under any standardized circumstances so that, in any case, they can be held to be inconclusive. Some studies show that learning interpolated material immediately after the original is most detrimental to retention (Müller and Pilzecker, 1900); others show greatest decrement if the interpolation just precedes the test (McGeoch, 1933). Others like Postman and Alper find interference at apparently unlikely points. Bunch (1946) found an interesting result when subjects were trained on punchboard mazes and tested immediately after learning a second maze. The second maze was learned immediately after the first or 120 days later, just before the test for retention of the first. In Bunch's experiment, learning an interpolated maze right after a first produced decrement. Learning the second after 120 days resulted in improvement. The results appear to favor some kind of practice interpretation for the long-delayed interpolation. The control groups would, of course, not have the benefit of the possible warm-up effect enjoyed by the experimental group. It would be interesting to investigate how effectively the second maze was retained by the experimental group which was tested after 120 days. If the interpolated maze was not really learned well it might suggest that the original learning had not really been retained effectively for other reasons, and that the results in the delayed test do not bear on the problem of retroaction. Minami and Dallenbach (1946) found in their cockroach experiment that interpolation had the most damaging effects either just after original learning or just before the test.

5. DEGREE OF LEARNING. If material is well learned, we would expect it to be less affected by interpolation. This appears to be the case. McGeoch and Irion (1952) review the studies dealing with this aspect of interference and conclude that less interference occurs when either or both original and interpolated materials are well learned. Osgood (1953) interprets these conclusions along the lines of generalization and discrimination. As learning of any kind, including conditioning, proceeds, originally some generalization appears to occur. As training continues, the generalization drops out and the learning becomes more specifically organized. The association units become "discriminated" (Hovland, 1937). With greater discrimination, there appears to be less opportunity for interpolated material to interfere. A number of studies (Melton and Irion, 1940, and Osgood, 1948) indicate that unless interpolated learning is practiced to an efficiency level of about twice as much as original learning, there is interference up to that point. After such a point, however, interference does not increase, and may even decrease.

The affective character of the materials or the learning situation. It is by now commonly accepted (whether or not there is any justification) that emotional factors are involved in retention. When something unpleasant happens we are even told to "forget it." On the other hand, when something unpleasant to us but interesting to others is forgotten, we are accused of having "convenient memories." Freudian theory has been freely applied by psychologist and layman alike in promoting the view that unpleasant matters are forgotten because, somehow, it is uncomfortable or anxiety-producing to remember such things.

In the twenties and thirties there was a rash of experiments designed to demonstrate that unpleasant experiences were more easily forgotten than were pleasant ones. The typical experiment involved asking subjects to write down a list of pleasant and unpleasant events that had occurred during some recent period. Then, allowing some time, for example, a month, to pass, the subjects were asked to recall their previous reports. If they failed to recall as large a percentage of the unpleasant as of the pleasant, it was concluded that some sort of "repressive" force was at work. Such experiments involve a great many uncontrolled variables (see McGeoch and Irion, 1952, pp. 384–389) and results were so contradictory as to offer little support for one conclusion or another. The obvious difficulty is in determining whether the pleasure or lack of it in some real experience has any present emotional loading. At the time of thinking about some prior experience there is no necessity that the recall experience should be emotionally toned.

An improved form of experiment was that of Sharp (1938) in which she used paired associate lists in a learning and retention procedure. The lists were made up of words presumed to be "acceptable," "unacceptable," or "neutral" on the basis of case studies of abnormal subjects. Although the results of this experiment were not confirmed later (see Sears, 1944) for normal subjects, Sharp found that both abnormal and normal subjects had greater difficulty in learning acceptable and unacceptable material (compared with neutral). Unacceptable material was less well retained after 2, 9, and 16 days. Acceptable material was retained better than neutral.

Sharp's words were selected from case-history material and represent an indirect reflection of affective tone. In a more direct study along these lines Feldman (1956) had normal subjects respond to a free association test and selected critical words (long reaction times, failure to repeat on retest) according to the Keet (1948) technique. The critical words then were paired with nonsense syllables as either stimuli or responses. Learning scores showed a significantly greater number of trials to learn the critical than neutral words. Although no measures of retention were obtained, it can be presumed that there would be greater losses in the critical materials on the basis of poor learning scores.

There appears to be no serious reason for doubting that when the learning material is repugnant or otherwise "unacceptable" or actually disturbing at *the time of learning* that the learner should have some difficulty about learning, and if learning is difficult, retention should be correspondingly difficult. Harlow (1953) has indicated that any kind of excitement, even from being too hungry, may interfere with learning and presumably with retention. There is, on the other hand, no reason to suppose that the materials learned have any intrinsic power or force to affect retention. We are still a long way from demonstrating Freudian mechanisms via nonsense syllable learning.

Traumatic experiences and retention. Some learning psychologists in the thirties and forties felt ready to tackle the complex problems of abnormal behavior and the interesting "defense mechanisms" of clinical literature. We shall discuss some of their efforts in Chapter 16. For the present we can consider a problem more related to retention than to learning, the problem of repression. We will not concern ourselves with Freud's description of this mechanism or later interpretations beyond indicating that whatever the fine points involved in clinical debates, the notion of repression includes the proposition that some things are "forgotten" as far as the subject's recall is concerned although it might be possible to show that the material can be made available to recall without relearning. The essential feature to be included is that the recall is being hampered by some kind of emotional blocking mechanism, and, typically, the blocking is presumed to be some sort of traumatic experience associated with the now forgotten material.

There is no great point to reviewing the extensive series of failures to provide a laboratory demonstration of repression. This has already been done by Sears (1943) and later by Zeller (1950a). According to Zeller, nobody has demonstrated repression in a satisfactory manner. Zeller first outlined the logically necessary steps for a suitable repression experiment and then proceeded to perform one (Zeller, 1950b). It may be worth the space to examine his experiment as it throws light on the difficulties of experimental work in this area. Zeller had subjects learn nonsense syllables under ordinary conditions. Later he tested for retention and demonstrated no unusual losses. After this test, an experimental group was subjected to a highly traumatic experience. The subjects were asked to duplicate block-tapping designs and were told that their level of performance was inadequate. Allegedly simpler designs were tried and again failure reported to the subjects. Zeller then proceeded to upbraid the subjects, informed the subjects (college students) they were functioning below an eight-year level, that they did not have sufficient intelligence to complete college, and so on. The subjects were then retested for the nonsense syllables and found to suffer a loss. They were instructed to return later (surprisingly some did) and were again tested for nonsense syllables. This time the scores were still low. Now Zeller gave "therapy" by telling the subjects that he was only fooling in the block-tapping test, that the subjects were good college material, and so on. A retest of the nonsense syllables now showed improvement and Zeller concluded that he had demonstrated repression.

If we examine Zeller's logical development of his experiment we may be tempted to argue that the logic is considerably at fault if he really believes that he is dealing with anything like repression. As far as the writer has been able to ascertain, it is the block-tapping that should have been repressed and items associated with this rather distressing experience. Zeller did not report any, nor did he inquire about any forgetting of the traumatic experience. About all we are able to conclude is that subjects that have been made to believe they are mental incompetents were unable to operate effectively in recalling nonsense syllables which they must, inevitably, have regarded as another test of intelligence. When they were reassured and the emotional distress was removed they operated at a higher efficiency. If this is repression, then Zeller has demonstrated it, although such procedures are known to every mother who ever dried a child's tears.

Ego-involvement and retention. In the same period in which psychoanalytic phenomena were enjoying the attention of learning psychologists, a great number of studies was reported involving personality factors allegedly affecting retention. Most of the studies took their departure in one direction or another from the Zeigarnik (1927) effect. (See McGeoch and Irion, 1952, pp. 390–394.) The usual form of the Zeigarnik experiment consists of having subjects attempt a large number of tasks or problems, say about twenty. The subjects are allowed to complete about half of these, and are interrupted in the others, either by being told that the time is up or because the experimenter wishes them to try another. At the conclusion of the test period, the subjects are asked to recall the tasks worked on and the typical finding of the Lewin (1946) school was that the uncompleted tasks were recalled more effectively. It is possible to introduce a variety of extra conditions into the procedure. For example, the tasks can be described as trivial and something to be done (a "task" orientation), or the tasks can be presented as an intelligence test with various suggestions about the importance of doing well, and so on. (This is an ego-orientation or "stress" situation.)

As the experiments on "ego" and "task" orientations multiplied, the results came to be more and more contradictory so that no prediction about which tasks would be recalled could be made with any confidence. Thelma Alper (1952), in a systematic evaluation of the studies, came to the conclusion that what would happen in a Zeigarnik situation depended basically upon what kind of subject was involved as well as on the "set" given by the instructions. After extensive clinical study of a limited number of subjects she concluded that the nature of the recall depends upon the "ego-pattern" and the task-setting. Strong egos recall incomplete tasks in a nonstressful setting and completed tasks in a stress situation. For weak ego patterns the nature of recalls is reversed.

Osgood (1953) emphasized the circularity of explanations offered by experimenters in this area. Any kind of result is accounted for by a "catch phrase." If subjects recall more completed tasks, it is because "they derived 'ego-enhancement' from them." If they fail to recall uncompleted tasks, they are defending their egos. "How do we know this?" asks Osgood. Simply because they do or do not recall one kind of task or another. The ego defense or enhancement is never measured directly and in advance.

We have touched on these studies at this point because they appear to bear on the general problem of retention. Actually, no measures of learning are ever taken in these studies. In this respect the studies are comparable to the memory-span experiments. If we have no measure of learning we are hard put to talk about retention. In general we can regard these attempts to include the operation of personality variables in retention as worthwhile efforts in an attack on a complicated business. It is probably still premature to hope for much satisfactory data in this area. We will have to have better measures of ego variables before we can look for reliable studies on the personality factors in retention.

Theoretical formulations of forgetting. The preceding discussions have revealed the complicated nature of the problem of forgetting. How are we to organize all the variables in a comprehensive view? We are hard put to it to even state what calls for explanation. If we take McGeoch's (1942) conception of the problem it appears that if we really learn something and do not learn anything else which might interfere, then we will not forget and there will be nothing to explain. If we do forget it is merely because we learned something else. While this view has a large following, it is by no means simple to point to the interfering learning in every instance, as any feature of a stimulus situation can be seized upon as important for association with the unknown interfering responses.

In an experimental situation it should be possible to point out the new associations which have been formed, but most experimenters have failed to look for such. Melton and von Lackum (1941) made a count of the number of interfering responses which occurred in a retroactive inhibition situation and failed to find enough to account for all the retroactive inhibition present. They then resorted to postulating some factor (x) which they interpreted to function as an "unlearning" operation to account for forgetting. According to this interpretation, some kind of unlearning process goes on when we forget. They failed to give any further explanation of this "unlearning" and it seems clear that the assumption rests on a failure to find interference items. Bugelski (1948) criticized this interpretation on the ground that in the ordinary retroactive inhibition experiment college-student subjects normally refrain from pronouncing wrong answers and consequently the interfering items are not observed. When subjects are encouraged to give answers, even wrong ones, they readily offer a great many more than would ordinarily be observed. In a series of learning tasks (10 sets of paired associates) Bugelski found items from the first list interfering with the recall of items from the tenth list. Throughout the learning the materials just learned kept intruding into successive lists so that by the tenth list, the subjects were hardly able to perform at all.

The alternative to a competition or interference theory appears to be a disuse interpretation. Here we must await the eventual unfolding of the neurological investigations which will tell the story. There appears to be no easy behavioral way of establishing the disuse hypothesis. It can always be argued that so long as the passage of time is involved some kind of new learning can take place. If new learning is denied because of some control over the activity of organism, then it is argued that physiological atrophy might have occurred or that it takes time to get back to a normal condition. Take the familiar example of riding bicycles or swimming. We do not forget how to do either. Yet there is no question that a long period of disuse does make us less efficient in these skills, even though we can perform passably. To argue that some kind of new learning interferes with retention of swimming habits seems specious. Disuse may have its place in an eventual comprehensive view. We will encounter many of these same problems in our next chapters. Perhaps an appreciation of some of the factors in extinction will help us appreciate the intricacies of the problem of forgetting.

Chapter

13   *Extinction*

In our examination of the methods of measurement of learning (Chapter 8) we did not discuss one measure which has been used very extensively in this connection, the resistance to "extinction." Before we can consider extinction as a measure of habit strength we had best find out a bit more about it. The other measures are reasonably self-evident in their nature and do not involve the complications that arise in connection with extinction. We have already referred to this process frequently in the past without stopping to analyze it. Now we can examine it in more detail.

Extinction, as Pavlov (1927), pointed out, is nothing more than a laboratory process. Pavlov usually used the term "experimental extinction" as a more correct and proper description of what was involved. Experimental extinction refers to the laboratory procedure of presenting the conditioned stimulus to the trained subject and not following through with the customary unconditioned stimulus. This is all that it means; what happens after that may be thought of as the results of the process but should not be confused with the process itself. The word "extinction" connotes elimination, deterioration, or death of something. Using the term "experimental extinction," or even "extinction" itself without carefully specifying that only the laboratory procedure is referred to, results in considerable confusion from the connotations. It is easy, for example, to get the notion that a habit that has undergone experimental extinction is dead, defunct, or otherwise out of the picture. The truth of this remains to be determined. That the habit has disappeared is debatable. We have seen in connection with retention that the type of test involved is crucial. A relearning procedure may show considerable savings after an extinction.

If this is the case, we can hardly speak of anything corresponding to complete disappearance. It is highly unlikely that two subjects, one previously trained and extinguished, and one naïve, would present the same picture in a new learning session involving the same stimuli and responses. Our problem is to evaluate the difference between them. In what ways have they become different?

ILLUSTRATIONS OF EXPERIMENTAL EXTINCTION

Before we go much further into the problem a few illustrations of experimental extinction might be in order. We might roughly sample the field by choosing a classical conditioning example, a conditioned motor response, an instrumental reward, and an instrumental avoidance response. We can start with Pavlov. In the typical case, a dog is trained to salivate to some CS, for example, a buzzer. When the conditioned response is appropriately established, experimental extinction is initiated. The unconditioned stimulus is no longer presented while the conditioned stimulus is sounded a number of times. The first few trials are followed by salivation, but as the trials continue the amount of salivation decreases until after some 7–10 trials or so, the animal does not salivate at all. Pavlov describes numerous cases, one of which is summarized in Table 2. The conditioned stimulus would be sounded at regular intervals ranging from minutes to half-hour periods. Systematic attempts were made to explore the pattern of diminution in response with various time intervals between trials (see Pavlov, 1927, p. 53.)

The same experimental procedure can be applied to any form of classical conditioning. Once the CR is established, extinction can be initiated by presenting the CS without the UncS. In the conditioned galvanic skin response, for example, the CS can be presented alone for a number of trials and a gradual diminution in the CR is observed. The CR can be measured, as in acquisition, by any of the usual techniques with typically reversed results. Thus, in extinction procedure, frequency of the CR decreases, latency increases, and amplitude decreases.

An example of an extremely interesting kind of extinction is shown in Figure 13.1. In the experiment from which this figure is taken, Hilgard and Marquis (1935) conditioned a dog to blink to a light signal, the UncS being a puff of air to one eye. We have described such experiments before (p. 106) and only a brief statement is required here. Records were taken of the action of both eyes and it is seen from the data that a curious sequence of events took place. At first, when the puff reinforcement was present, both eyes blinked together; gradually the bilateral lid reflex dropped out and the unilateral reflex began to prevail. When conditioning was considered satisfactory, extinction procedure was instituted. Note that the unilateral reflex be-

TABLE 2

Extinction of a Salivary Response at 3-minute Test Intervals
(Pavlov, 1927, p. 55)

Time, P.M.	Conditioned Stimulus *	Salivary Secretion (drops in 30 seconds)
12.07	Metronome	13
12.10	"	7
12.13	"	5
12.16	"	6
12.19	"	3
12.22	"	2.5
12.25	"	0
12.28	"	0
12.31	Tactile	0
12.34	Metronome	0
12.37	Buzzer	2.5

* The response was conditioned to three different stimuli, but more strongly to the buzzer than to the tactile S. Note that extinction with the metronome affected the response to the tactile S.

gins to fall off in frequency while the bilateral reflex begins to return and that eventually the original state of affairs is restored.

In the instrumental reward situation, for example, the Skinner box, we have a variation in that we do not ordinarily present a specific stimulus (CS) unless we are dealing with "discriminated stimuli." The conditioning stimuli, if they are to be considered at all, are in the situation itself. Earlier (p. 93) we have tried to show that the Skinner situation is not so "unstructured" as Skinner makes out, that there are sequences of stimuli whose effectiveness can be separately appraised. For the present we can accept the view that the experimenter, at least, is not presenting conditioned stimuli. Nor is he presenting any unconditioned stimuli, since these are unknown. The experimental extinction procedure consists of simply cutting off the food supply,

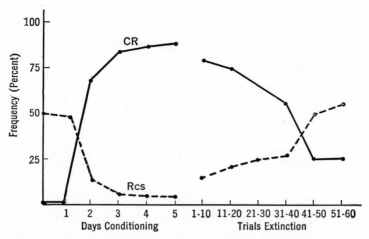

FIG. 13.1. The disappearance and reappearance of a natural response, the bilateral blink (*Rcs*) during the conditioning and extinction
of a new response, the unilateral blink (*CR*). (After Hilgard and
Marquis, 1940, p. 112.)

or "reinforcement," retaining the rest of the situation physically intact. The animal proceeds to press the bar and no reinforcement follows. Ordinarily it continues to press for some time, usually with a decreasing rate until eventually it ceases pressing at all or drops to an
"operant" rate. Since usually the extinction period is relatively prolonged (up to an hour or so) [1] and since the rate declines fairly rapidly within the first few minutes, it becomes a technical question as
to when to terminate the extinction procedure. This question has
been resolved in various ways by different experimenters, some favoring some such measure as the total number of responses in an hour, in
20 minutes, in the first 5, or 2 minutes. Others choose a criterion of
2, 5, or other number of minutes without a response.[2] Figure 13.2
shows a typical extinction curve produced by a pigeon pecking at a
target after reinforcement was discontinued.

Extinction of an instrumental avoidance response will prove to be
somewhat more involved than the types just illustrated. For the moment we will avoid the theoretical difficulties and merely look at an
example of this kind of study. We are already somewhat familiar
with the following study (see p. 65). Woodward (1954) trained rats

[1] Later we will consider the question of prolonged extinction periods and multiple
periods.
[2] Correlations between various criteria are reported by Walker (1948).

FIG. 13.2. Extinction after a periodic reinforcement (arithmetic series, mean: one reinforcement per minute). One pigeon, one continuous period. (After Skinner, 1950.)

to jump over a hurdle in a shuttle box. Various groups of rats were trained with different heights of hurdle (0, 2, 5, and 8 inches) and with various time intervals between the onset of the CS (a light) and the UncS (shock). The intervals were 0, 2, 5, and 10 seconds. Each rat was trained to a criterion of 20 successive avoidance responses. This is a rigid and difficult standard, because a single lapse can prolong the training for some time. It should be observed that as soon as the avoidance response occurs (that is, as soon as it antedates the shock), we have what amounts to an extinction trial since no UncS is present. The last 20 training trials are, therefore, the first 20 extinction trials also. Figure 13.2 shows the latencies of the jumps to the light from the point at which the UncS is omitted until the animals no longer jump to the light. It is obvious that the latencies increase steadily until the time between the onset of the light and the jump exceeds that between light and shock. The animals can then be said to have "extinguished." What has happened apparently is that the time of the response has been delayed more and more until the response fails to occur. (See also Sheffield, 1948.)

Now we have seen four examples of experimental extinction—a Pavlovian CR, a conditioned motor response (eyelid blink), a rewarded operant, and an avoidance response. In each case (save that of the operant) the experimenter fails to supply an UncS at the normal time and we find that the response dwindles off in amount, rate, or frequency.

The instrumental avoidance picture is a bit more complicated than it appears to superficial observation. While it is true that the UncS (that is, shock) is omitted in extinction, it is commonly held (Mowrer, 1950) that the animal also is reinforced through the instrumental response in that this response permits the diminution of the alleged anxiety drive that led to the jump in the first place. During the extinction procedure, the experimenter is doing nothing with respect to this reinforcement. He is not supplying it, nor denying it, nor does he have any independent evidence as to whether it is occurring or not. We can summarize some of the relationships just considered in Table 3.

TABLE 3

Experimental Extinction in Different Types of Learning Situations

	CS	UncS	Reinforcement
Classical (autonomic)	Presented	Omitted	None considered *
Classical (motor, e.g., eyelid)	Presented	Omitted	None considered *
Instrumental reward	Status unknown	Status unknown	Omitted
Instrumental avoidance	Presented	Omitted for "fear"	None considered *
		Unknown for instrumental response	Neither given nor denied

* The Pavlovian CR is usually regarded as a case of substitution learning (see p. 58) but Hull (see p. 61) makes it a special case of the UncS actually operating as a reinforcer. This interpretation could be applied to the eyelid blink and the conditioned avoidance response without positing the fear as an activating agent or drive.

It is evident that as soon as we extend our discussion of extinction beyond Pavlov's laboratory procedure we have a much more complicated problem on our hands. The only common element is that some measures which were taken during acquisition are now observed to diminish.

It might be argued that there is another common element, that in every instance reinforcement has been omitted. While a case can be made out for this position, we must recognize that there is nothing common to the several concepts of reinforcement as they are supposed to operate in the different learning situation.

Before we try to account for the generally increasing deterioration in some features of the response, a number of other aspects of extinction behavior must be described. These other aspects have been related to a number of variables which have been examined over the years by numerous workers. The more important of these variables can be listed as follows:

The variables in experimental extinction
1. Types of stimuli and responses involved
2. Frequency of reinforcement
    a. Amount of reinforcement
    b. Inhibition of reinforcement
    c. Spaced versus massed trials
3. Pattern of reinforcement
    a. Partial—aperiodic, fixed ratio
    b. Periodic
    c. Secondary reinforcement
4. Drive state
    a. During learning
    b. During experimental extinction
5. Frequency of presentation of CS without UncS
    a. Spontaneous recovery
    b. "Below zero" extinction
    c. Results of successive extinction
6. Temporal factors in extinction
    a. Retention of CR's
    b. Effect of intervals between
        (1) Extinction trials
            (a) Classical
            (b) Instrumental
        (2) Extinction sessions
7. Energy expenditure
8. Counterconditioning
9. Punishment
10. Prevention of response

An examination of the above listed variables will reveal some of the facets of the extinction problem. When we find out what we need to explain the task of rendering an account may be clearer.

1. **Stimulus-response relationship.** We cannot catalog all the kinds of responses that have been observed in extinction. It does appear that some kinds of responses are easy and others difficult to extinguish. At this time we will consider only some broad general classes.

Some supporters of dual-factor learning theories intimate that responses involving emotional reactions or autonomic nervous system functions are difficult to extinguish. With a relatively small number of reinforcements, the subjects may continue to respond for many trials in the absence of the original UncS. Thus Miller (1948) reports that his rats would turn a wheel which dropped the door to the black compartment in his white-black box (see p. 14) for as many as 600 trials. This number of "avoidance" reactions would occur after only 4 shock trials. Solomon and Wynne (1953) reported that dogs would jump a hurdle 500 and 600 times after only a few shock trials. In fact, Solomon and Wynne seem to believe that their dogs would never extinguish. It should be noted that they used very intense shock (just below tetanizing strength) and this may have led to something other than ordinary learning. We have already considered the argument (see p. 64) that avoidance is its own reward. We shall have to return to this problem later. In contrast, Brogden (1949) reports a fairly rapid extinction of a leg-withdrawal response in dogs. In 4 days the dogs "extinguished" the response which took an average of 11 days to acquire.

The conditioned eyelid blink appears to be strongly subject to "voluntary" control and extinction can be delayed or facilitated by suitable instructions to human subjects (Miller, 1939). Human hand withdrawal can be extinguished in one trial (Woodworth, 1938). Probably any kind of "voluntary" conditioned responses in human subjects can extinguish in one trial under suitable conditions. Responses of a choice variety in a T-maze or runway extinguish with difficulty; animals continue to run, once they get started, for many trials. Bugelski and Woodward (1951) found that they could control the number of times rats would leave an area where they had been shocked by varying the stimulus situation or environment. Scharlock (1954) found little or no change in activity either at the choice point or any place else after 50 unreinforced trials for albino rats in a T-maze. Extinction of instrumental reward responses depends upon so many factors that no general comment seems warranted here.

GENERALIZATION OF EXTINCTION. Just as the effects of reinforcement generalize to some extent, so do the results of an extinction procedure. The phenomenon has been studied primarily with classical conditioning and not too extensively even in this connection so we have less empirical information than desired. Lack of empirical evidence, however, has not been a hindrance to theoretical speculation and both Hull (1943) and Spence (1937) have made great use of the generalization of extinction. Hull has incorporated it into his analysis of the process of biological adaptation for survival, and Spence has made it fundamental to his analysis of transposition phenomena (see

p. 410). The basic proposition describing the generalization of extinction is that the nonreinforcement of a stimulus to the point where it no longer elicits the conditioned response will also affect the strength of any other stimulus for eliciting that response to the degree that these other stimuli are on some continuum of similarity with the original CS. Thus, after conditioning to a tone of 256 vibrations per second, an organism can be expected, through generalization, to respond to tones of 250, 225, 260, 275, and so forth, on both sides of the original stimulus (see Fig. 7.1, p. 150). The reactions presumably will be weaker as we depart from the original. Now if we "extinguish" the original stimulus, we will also find a decrement in the response to the other stimuli. The loss of effectiveness of the other stimuli will depend upon how close or similar they happen to be to the original. Thus the tone of 250 should show a higher *percentage* of loss than a tone of 240, and so on. Stimuli at the extremes of the generalization range would suffer less proportional drop in response strength. Such stimuli, however, would not have had so much strength to begin with. The nature of the alleged mathematical function describing generalization of extinction has been a matter of concern to Hull. He finally settled on an equation based on the work of Hovland (see p. 149) which describes the generalization of extinction as a negatively accelerated curve, dropping off from the point of origin.

The effects of generalized extinction are particularly important theoretically in the formation of discriminated responses. If the experimenter desires to teach a subject to react to one stimulus but not to another, he will have difficulty to the degree to which the two stimuli are similar or generalizable. Suppose we consider the previous example again. This time we wish a dog to salivate to a tone of 256 but not to one of 260. Every time we reinforce the 256 stimulus, the 260 stimulus enjoys an increase in strength through the generalization of reinforcement. On the other hand, every time we fail to reinforce 260, the 256 stimulus suffers a decrement through generalization of extinction. When the final positive response to 256 is built up, it will have far less strength than if the 260 stimulus had never been presented and can easily be extinguished by a few nonreinforced stimulations. This problem presumably arises at any time we wish to teach someone to do something and not do something else.

We have already raised the question, in connection with generalization of positive effects (see p. 281), as to whether generalization of extinction spreads in both directions from the point of origin as Hull assumes. Wolpe (see p. 155) argues that generalization of extinction is more likely to be a one-sided phenomenon; that, if 256 vibrations per second is a positive signal and we now extinguish responses to 260, there is going to be a deterioration of response to all stimuli beyond 260 to be sure, but little or no deterioration below 256. The argument has been set forth earlier and we need go no further into it at the moment except to note that the experimental evidence is not available from which to form a reasonable judgment.

2. **Number of reinforcements.** Although we might expect that the greater the number of reinforcements, the greater the number of responses to be noted in the extinction period, this is only true to some limiting degree. The evidence is scattered and systematic studies are rare. (Perin, 1943; Williams, 1938.) If we restrict ourselves to mention of the bar press habit, then we find that as far as extinction responses are concerned a point of diminishing returns is reached around 85–100 reinforcements. Reinforcing the bar press beyond 100 times does not assure any greater number of responses in extinction beyond that of 90 reinforcements or so (Hull, 1943). Occasionally an experimenter finds results that appear contradictory to all expectations. Thus, Finger (1942) found that rats that were given 16 reinforced trials on a runway extinguished more rapidly than rats given only 8 reinforcements. Perhaps we would not be disturbed by such data if there had been 160 and 80 trials rather than 16 and 8. Lawrence and Miller (1947) repeated Finger's experiment in an attempt to explain his paradoxical results. They believed that Finger's use of the same box as both starting pen and goal were responsible for his findings and in the Lawrence-Miller apparatus these two boxes were made distinct. With this change in apparatus they found that animals given 16 reinforced runs continued to run for 25 extinction trials. Rats given only 8 reinforced runs extinguished in 13 trials. Lawrence and Miller account for Finger's paradox by suggesting that Finger established two conflicting tendencies in his rats—one to search for food in the goal box and the other to leave the goal box when the door was opened. During learning there would be no conflict because the presence of food assured eating, thus supplying a cue pattern for leaving when the door opened. During extinction these tendencies were in conflict. "The opening of the door coincided with continued searching behavior and so conflict resulted." According to this explanation, Finger's rats had failed to discriminate between start and goal boxes and would hesitate to leave the starting box. Since failure

to leave was the criterion of extinction, the two groups would extinguish quickly. In the Lawrence and Miller experiment, the rats with a greater number of training trials would also benefit from "secondary reinforcement" cues in the goal box. (See Denny, p. 256.)

The Reflex Reserve. In connection with number of reinforcements, Skinner (1938) originally proposed the notion that each reinforcement could be thought of as adding a cumulating habit strength. This habit strength Skinner translates as "resistance to extinction" or a potential for emitting responses, which he called "the Reflex Reserve." The term "reserve" suggests a financial analogy with depositing funds in a bank. Each reinforcement means so much money in the bank to be withdrawn later in the form of extinction responses. The difficulty with the analogy is that there is no one-for-one relationship between deposits and balance. Thus one reinforcement may be worth almost any number of extinction responses. The rate of interest is unknown. Two rats, each given 40 reinforcements, may have widely different extinction reserves. Although Skinner later (1950) admitted that the reserve concept was a poor one in that it implies some sort of hypothetical construct which Skinner has carefully avoided in his empirical nontheorizing, the suggestion that the number of reinforcements is related to habit strength is fairly generally accepted. The reserve, according to Skinner, represents some kind of "resistance to extinction." To speak of "resistance to extinction" is perhaps a poor and even dangerous way of describing habit strength. There is a possibility of dropping into the practice of creating animated entities or forces which operate in some positive fashion to prevent extinction. In the present instance, nothing is served by the construct of "resistance" which cannot just as easily be handled by the more operational practice of developing ratios or formuli to describe the relationship between number of reinforcements and number of responses (or other characteristics) in extinction periods. It is, of course, legitimate to say that, other things being equal, more responses will occur in the experimental extinction of a strong habit than a weaker habit. This is quite different from saying that the stronger habit *resists* extinction. This brief excursion into the logic of the problem is justified because the "reserve" concept has been used by Skinner and his supporters to imply that until the "reserve" is "emptied" or "exhausted" the habit remains some place (within the organism?) and, under proper circumstances, will emerge or be "emitted." This is a purely gratuitous assumption even though, as will be seen shortly, it can be demonstrated that apparently "extinguished" habits will continue to be exercised under some circumstances. To illustrate, if a response has been reinforced to the point where the average subject can be expected to emit, say, 50 responses in extinction and the extinction procedure is terminated at the point where 25 responses have been obtained, the subject still has 25 more "in reserve." These 25 will eventually emerge, given the opportunity. If the extinction has taken place under such circumstances as to eliminate the practical possibility of the responses ever emerging from the reserve (see Counterconditioning, below) Skinner must suppose them to still be "available." Since such reserve responses can make no difference in the behavior of the organism if they never occur, we can perhaps ignore them as of no consequence under the dictum that a difference that makes no difference is no difference.

The facts that the reserve concept does not appear to hold beyond a limited number of reinforcements and that its value cannot be predicted suggest that its usefulness as a principle is of but modest value.

INHIBITION OF REINFORCEMENT. The relationship between extinction and reinforcement frequency is confounded to some degree by the fact that in ordinary training circumstances the use of a food reinforcement gradually reduces the animal's "drive," appetite, or "interest" in the reinforcer, and the presence or absence of the food becomes of less significance. If responses are forced at a rapid rate (massed practice) the effectiveness of each reinforcement is further diminished until, as Hovland (1936) has shown, the rate of learning decreases with additional reinforcements. Hovland calls this "inhibition of reinforcement." It is unlikely that any two reinforcements can be of equal value to a learner, especially if they are given at different times, and any attempt to evaluate the quantity of the reserve is doomed to *post facto* accounting procedures.

3. **Pattern of reinforcement.** Although it is customary to reinforce the learner after every response in numerous learning situations, constant and consistent reinforcement is rare in ordinary human affairs. Even the animal trainer occasionally forgets to reward the seal or runs out of fish. Teachers frequently omit the praises their eager pupils cherish. What is the effect of such lapses in failures to reward? Reinforcement theories generally imply that failure of reinforcement should result in a weakening of the learning. Is this actually the case?

Pavlov (1927) first began to investigate the effect of an occasional omission of the UncS. He found, contrary to what might be expected, that extinction was delayed in such cases beyond the ordinary number of trials.

Skinner (1938) began to study the problem of pattern effects systematically and devised a variety of procedures which produced startling, as well as controversial, results. In one procedure, animals are reinforced at irregular intervals during the training period. A reinforcement might be provided for a bar press which occurred 30 seconds after the last reinforcement. The next reinforcement might be delayed 1½ minutes, the third for 1 minute. Such a schedule, which might provide a pellet of food on the average every minute, is called "aperiodic" reinforcement. In a more common procedure, *Periodic Reinforcement* or PR, a reinforcement is provided at some fixed interval, say 2 minutes after the last response. The usual finding in these procedures is that the animals gradually acquire a pattern of response that is suited to the reinforcement schedule. Thus, if a 2-minute schedule is employed, a rat will press, eat, then press sporadically or not at all for a short period, gradually building up the rate as the time of the next reinforcement approaches.

In a variation of periodic reinforcement, the time between reinforcements is determined by the rate of pressing in that the experimenter decides to reinforce every second, third, or fiftieth response. The animal then gains nothing by waiting but must tap out the required number. Some looseness of thinking occasionally creeps into discussion of such reinforcement at *Fixed Ratios*. Some students get the impression that the animal counts the presses or is otherwise "expecting" in a variety of ways; that is, expecting no rewards, expecting rewards at certain times, and so on. Such impressions lead to confusion in the interpretation of extinction data as will soon become apparent.

When extinction is carried out on subjects that have been trained under one or another form of partial reinforcement the usual finding is that a great many more responses are noted than if the same number of reinforcements had been supplied in continuous fashion during training. This is true for pigeons pecking at targets (Skinner, 1950), for rats pressing bars (Mowrer and Jones, 1945), human gambling (Lewis, 1952), T-maze choices (Denny, 1946), human eyelid blinks (Humphreys, 1939; Grant and Schipper, 1952), alley running (Linton and Miller, 1951). There are contradictory findings, for example by Rubin (1953) who found greater resistance to extinction with 100 percent reinforcement for panel-pushing (a rat study), but in general, as Jenkins and Stanley (1950) concluded in their review of many studies, learning proceeds more rapidly with 100 percent reinforcement and extinction is delayed by training under partial reinforcement.

Various explanations have been offered for this common finding of a greater number of extinction responses under partial reinforcement training. Humphreys (1939) believes that subjects that are reinforced 100 percent of the time in training develop an "expectancy" of continuous reinforcement. As soon as extinction procedure is instituted, the expectancy fails of confirmation and a new expectancy begins to be developed. The partial-reinforcement procedure prevents the development of such expectancies, and during the extinction period the subject continues in a state of doubt or uncertainty which slows the development of a new negative expectancy. Such an explanation, however much it might appear applicable to humans, is of dubious value when applied to animal subjects. As Deese (1952) points out, it is an *ad hoc* explanation and of little predictive value.

Mowrer and Jones (1945) offer another explanation that also appears a little forced although it has some appeal. They argue, for example, that the animal that gets reinforced every fourth trial comes to respond to a different set of circumstances than the constantly reinforced subject.

According to Mowrer and Jones, then, the subject learns a habit of pressing 4 times before eating and his extinction trials should be divided by 4 in comparison with a 100-percent reinforcement subject. The implication of this argument is that in extinction the animal that is reinforced for every fourth response produces 4 responses as a unit, that he has a pattern of pressing 4 times and then eating. This pattern should be considered the real habit or "response." Actually there is no evidence that animals learn to work in bursts of 3 or 4 or any other fixed number of responses. They more probably learn to respond until some cue associated with food presentation impinges on them and then investigate the food compartment.

The writer has been unable to train a rat to press 3 or more times and come to a food bin unless the third tap was accompanied by the sound of dropping food. If no food dropped into the food cup, the rat kept on pressing the bar until interrupted. Following each press, however, the food tray was approached. In the usual Skinner box with the bar just over the food cup, the presence or absence of food can be quickly noted and the experimenter is likely to overlook these tray-inspection responses, especially if he is not observing the rat but is content to let the automatic dispensing device provide the food at appropriate intervals.

The possibility exists that in extinction of partially reinforced subjects some different kinds of cues are operating for continuing pressing or pecking or whatever the case may be, which are not the same as those operating in the 100-percent reinforcement situation. If the situation is one of different cues controlling 100-percent reinforced responses and some other cues controlling partially reinforced responses, there is hardly any point to making comparisons of extinction responses in terms of number. Theoretical explanations of the kind that have been advanced may be wide of the mark.

This is essentially the explanation offered by Hull (1943) and it has the merit of simplicity. He suggests that during the reinforcement stage, the animal is learning to react to a situation in which sometimes the reinforcement is present and sometimes absent. The cue pattern during partial reinforcement is different from the cue pattern during 100-percent reinforcement. In the latter case, the consequences of goal responses provide stimuli for the repetition of the response, that is, eating food, for example, sets the stage for the next response. In the partial reinforcement situation the animal learns to respond in the absence of such goal stimuli. This is much more like the extinction situation than a 100-percent reinforcement schedule. Consequently the animals will have learned different habits in the two situations.

4. **Drive states and extinction.** Two conditions must be differentiated: (a) drive state during learning and (b) drive state during extinction. Drive state during learning studies involve allowing the subjects to learn some habit under different deprivations and then observing extinction behavior under some specific deprivation period such as 24 hours. Results from various studies (Reynolds, 1949; Kendler, 1945; Strassburger, 1950; Meyer, 1951) are contradictory and nondefinitive. Finan's (1940) study employing 1-, 12-, 24-, and 48-hour drives showed a greater number of extinction responses for the 12-hour groups than for any of the others. The only significant finding was that the 1-hour group responded less than the others. The later studies show even less relationship between drive at acquisition and extinction, and we might conclude (see Chap. 8) that there is no relationship here of consequence.

Studies of extinction under different drive levels suggest that longer deprivations result in a greater number of extinction responses. Skinner (1938) shows a higher extinction curve for a 48-hour deprivation than for a 24. The curves are of similar shape and might easily be superimposed one on the other if the lower curve were multiplied by a constant. Skinner, in evaluating such data, and holding to the Reserve concept, shows that if the animals are allowed to continue in the situation the total number of responses in all groups will eventually be equal. If this is actually the case, we must conclude that drive at extinction is also of no consequence as a variable.

5. **Frequency of presentation of the CS without UncS.** From the previous discussions we have already learned that extinction is in some fashion a function of the number of times the response occurs without reinforcement. This appears to be the case in both Pavlovian and operant responses even though we do not control the CS in the latter instance. The relationship is not a simple one, however, and more must be considered than normally meets the eye.

SPONTANEOUS RECOVERY. If we set up as a criterion of extinction the failure to respond after some specific interval of no response, say 5 minutes, we should hardly be surprised if a little later, or a day later, the response again is observed. There is no good reason to believe that failure to respond for 5 minutes or any other time means that the organism will never respond again. The child who has been discouraged from asking for some favor rarely desists permanently. On the contrary, all our experience suggests that persistence is a common feature of behavior in the absence of reinforcement. We frequently look into the same places for lost objects, even when we assure ourselves that they cannot be there.

Pavlov characterized the finding that the "extinguished" response returns at a future test as some process of "spontaneous recovery." This description is unfortunate since it implies some kind of dynamism in the response and places the emphasis on the return of the response, rather than on the fact that the extinction is incomplete, or, rather, on the probability that the response has been temporarily suppressed. The Pavlovian interpretation leads to a search for causes of the recovery instead of a search for factors leading to cessation of the response.

The findings of Pavlov have been confirmed for many other kinds of responses. A rat in a Skinner box, for example, will continue to depress the bar for days on end if he is taken out after some modest criterion of extinction is attained per day. The writer observed one rat press a bar 30 times per day for 34 days with little or no sign of deterioration of the habit. Within a few minutes of being placed in the box, the 30 responses were tapped out and the animal was removed. From all appearances the rat would have continued well into old age.

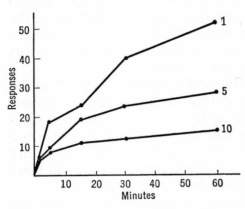

FIG. 13.3. The median cumulative response curves for the 60-minute extinction sessions of Sessions 1, 5, and 10. Rats were reinforced 40 times at each training session and then extinguished for 1 hour. By the tenth session bar-pressing extinguished rapidly. (After Bullock and Smith, 1953.)

When a more rigid criterion is adopted, say 5 minutes without a response, the "recovery" is less complete after 24 hours. Ellson (1938) extinguished rats in a Skinner box for five successive periods. At each succeeding period fewer responses were recorded until, by the fifth period, the animals responded hardly at all. From Skinner's point of view, extinction is not complete until the "reserve" is exhausted. If, for some reason, responses cease temporarily and the reserve is not emptied, the remaining responses will emerge on a later occasion, given the opportunity. The problem, then, is to determine the variables responsible for temporary cessation. In the Ellson study cited above, animals were extinguished without any interpolated retraining. Bullock and Smith (1953) varied this procedure by retraining animals every day in a Skinner box after the previous day's extinction. On every day for 10 days, rats would be given 40 reinforcements and then no further reinforcements for a 1-hour period. With succeeding days the number of extinction responses declined until by the tenth day the rats were responding only infrequently after the forty-first bar press. Presumably with sufficiently prolonged training, animals could learn to stop working as soon as the machine stopped paying. Here we have an indication of a discrimination being acquired in the extinction situation where failure of reinforcement becomes a cue to stay away from the bar (see Fig. 13.3).

BELOW ZERO EXTINCTION. Pavlov (1927) found that spontaneous recovery was diminished if the CS was presented more frequently than necessary to get down to a level of no response in the first extinction period. Thus, if an animal failed to salivate at all after 10 unreinforced presentations of the CS, and Pavlov continued to present the CS for 10 additional trials, the animal would show less recovery on the next day than if stimulation had been halted after the first 10. Pavlov called this procedure "below zero extinction." In an operant situation this would correspond to leaving the animal in a Skinner box, for example, for some time beyond any ordinary criterion. Bullock (1950) kept rats in Skinner boxes for as long as 5 consecutive hours and found responses being made sporadically all through this lengthy period. Spontaneous recovery was minimal in such cases.

If we take the position that there is no spontaneous recovery if extinction is carried out to a sufficient degree (below or to zero) then any recovery observed in other situations suggests that extinction procedure was terminated too quickly even if no responses were observed. When a response does not occur it may be thought of as being "suppressed" or otherwise made unavailable. If the organism is fatigued or emotional, then there may be some temporary incapacity or incompatibility for the response. This is essentially the suggestion of Guthrie (1935) who thinks that the frustration related to nonappearance of reinforcer creates a state or attitude somewhat like that of a "balky mule or obstinate person." This attitude is (like any response) conditioned to the stimuli operating at the time and to that extent represents the development of a new response to a stimulus pattern. This pattern, however, appears fairly late in an extinction session and consequently may not be present at the *beginning* of the next session. In the absence of the stimuli, the balkiness or obstinacy will not be present to interfere with the original reaction which has a chance to occur. Prolonging the extinction provides the opportunity for the negative reaction to be learned to a wider variety of stimulus components. These may bring out the attitude more quickly in a subsequent test.

6. Temporal factors in extinction.

RETENTION OF CR'S IN TIME. If responses are conditioned and no experimental extinction is attempted, what will happen to the CR as time passes, in the absence of any opportunity to practice? It should be observed, before we try to answer the question, that psychologists rarely attempt any long-range investigations in this area for numerous practical reasons. The life span of many animals used in learning experiments is not great and the significance of temporal intervals is somewhat ambiguous. Hilgard and Marquis (1940) observed CR's in dogs after intervals of 4 months. Wendt (1937) reports retention of a CR for 2½ years. We have already mentioned Skinner's (1950) report of substantial retention of a pecking response in pigeons after 4 years. In Skinner's carefully controlled observation there was some decline in the total number of pecks (almost 50 percent) from what could have been expected although there was no control over the sheer age factor (see Fig. 13.4). It may be that older pigeons are less given to tapping at targets which do not "pay off," however well they paid off in their youth. Pavlov also reports prolonged retention of CR's as do Gantt (1936) and Liddell (1944).

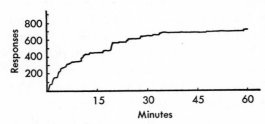

FIG. 13.4. Extinction in a pigeon 4 years after conditioning. Even after 4 years, the pigeon began to peck quickly and within the hour had pecked about 600 times. (After Skinner, 1950.)

THE EFFECT OF TEMPORAL INTERVALS BETWEEN EXTINCTION TRIALS. If extinction procedure is interrupted before a rigid criterion is attained, the CR can be retained over fairly long periods. We noted (above) that if rats are withdrawn from a Skinner box after 30 bar presses, the response may remain available in strength for as long as 30 days or more. In an experiment under the writer's supervision, Kurke (1953) allowed rats to press a bar 10, 20, or 30 times in each extinction period. The situation appears to be superficially analogous to spaced versus massed training. It should not be overlooked, however, that the experimenter is not controlling the rate of response. Most previous studies (Hilgard and Marquis, 1935; Gagne, 1941) suggest that massing extinction trials results in more rapid extinction. Kurke found, on the contrary, that the most rapid extinction (to a 5-minute no-response criterion) was obtained with the 10-press-per-trial group, with the 30-press-per-trial group taking the greatest number of extinction sessions to meet the criterion.

In a similar experiment, Rohrer (1947) spaced the intervals between individual bar presses by withdrawing the bar for different periods for different groups of animals. He found no differences in extinction rates except when the original training had been extensive. When a lot of reinforcements had been given, massed extinction seemed to be more rapid than spaced. Sheffield (1950) found spaced extinction faster than massed in a runway situation. Pavlov's (1927, p. 23) original findings stressed the rapidity of extinction with massed trials. Pavlov reports what appears to be an all-day extinction session with one dog. We report this in some detail to sample the flavor of the early Russian experiments.

The dog was first extinguished with the CS applied every 2 minutes. After a rest and feeding, a 4-minute interval was initiated, then an 8-, 16-, and a final 2-minute interval. Pavlov reports faster extinction with the shorter intervals, but we can see that this finding is at least ambiguous by noting the number of trials until the first zero

TABLE 4

Number of Trials and Total Time to Extinguish a Conditioned Salivary Reaction in One Dog
(Data from Pavlov, 1927, p. 53.)

CS Interval (minutes)	Total Time (minutes)	Responses until First "Zero"
2	15	5
4	20	4
8	54	6
16	Incompletion 2 hrs.	8 (Incomplete)
2	18	6

response (see Table 4). We, of course, also note that with short time intervals more stimuli can be given than with long time intervals. There appears to be no significant trend in the number of trials. Even at the end of what must have been a hard day, the dog responded 6 times.

The results of experiments on spacing extinction trials are contradictory and confused. Various kinds of situations have been employed along with a variety of intervals. What is massing for one experimenter is spacing for another. The problem of spaced versus massed learning will require more extensive treatment (see Chap. 16). For the present we can note that a rapid rate of elicitation of responses may bring about a relatively rapid cessation of response. This cessation, however, is most likely to be of a temporary variety.

7. **Energy expenditure and extinction.** Ordinary experience suggests that we are prone to give up exhausting tasks more readily than lighter work. This conclusion, however, is not easily established by

evidence. Fatigue studies are notoriously indecisive. Boredom in a light task can lead to rapid cessation while extra "motivation" can keep the worker on the job long after he would admit any genuine desire to continue for work's sake alone. When animals are required to exert themselves in physical work, experimental observations suggest that the more exacting tasks are extinguished more rapidly. Thus Solomon (1948b) found that rats would give up jumping a 16-inch gap more rapidly than an 8-inch gap in a Lashley jumping situation when no longer reinforced. In an earlier study, Solomon (1947) demonstrated that the amount of work done could serve as a cue for a turning response. In this experiment rats were trained to enter the fourth of a series of alleys stemming from a long runway. When the rats were later equipped with loaded "saddle bags" and had to do more work in running along, they tended to enter nearer alleys. Mowrer and Jones (1945) found that rats required to depress a Skinner bar with an 80-gram load extinguished sooner than rats pressing 40- or 5-gram loads. It should be noted that only one extinction session was observed. If the reserve concept is to be considered as meaningful in these situations then further sessions might bring out a different picture. Actually the Mowrer-Jones findings have not been confirmed. In fact, in a study by Maatsch, Adelman, and Denny (1954) rats pressing bars with weights of 5, 40, and 80 grams showed no difference in pressing rates and no differences in meeting extinction criteria. Applezweig (1951) had previously shown that when training weights were held constant, rats would extinguish faster on heavier weights. However, if rats were *selected* and specifically trained on heavier weights, there were no differences in extinction trials. Woodward (1954) found that rats jumping 2-, 5-, and 8-inch hurdles to a light-shock setup extinguished in reverse order. That is, an 8-inch fence jump was more readily extinguished than a 2-inch jump. A 2-inch jump would be made significantly more often than a 5-inch jump. When no work of a jump nature was required at all, as in the case of rats that were trained merely to run from one side of a box to the other, the running continued for a significantly greater number of trials. The latter finding may have been due not so much to the lack of work involved as to the lack of discriminability between the two sides of the runway.

Skinner views the labor involved as probably of minor consequences and more a function of the schedule of reinforcement. He himself (Skinner, 1950) found pigeons capable of a tremendous amount of work under suitable schedules. Rates of 4000 pecks per hour could be maintained for as long as 15 hours. In another attack on this question, which Skinner conceives of as "difficulty of response," Skinner arranged a harness on the pigeon in such a way as to serve as a check on the amount of movement. To peck the target the pigeon would have to strain against the harness. Seven units of strain were arranged. When the pigeon strained against 3 units, the rate was fairly rapid. At 7 units the rate dropped markedly. Changing from one unit to another was followed by a sudden drop while the reverse change was followed by a sudden rise. Skinner argues from the rapidity of the adjustment that no cumulative fatigue or difficulty effects were operating. A tired pigeon working against 7 units of strain should not immediately recover to a rate suitable to a lower strain or vice versa. In any event, Skinner claims the only influence of the difficulty variable is to exert a temporary depressing effect on the slope of the curve. It does not alter its curvature.

8. **Counterconditioning.** In ordinary experimental extinction the response that is observed is the CR or the operant in which the experimenter is interested. Little or no attention is paid to what else the subject may be doing. Rarely is any provision made to detect or record any activity that may be associated with the failure of the CR to occur. Occasionally the technique employed by the experimenter happens to provide a record of more than just the CR and some unexpected information may result. The Hilgard and Marquis (1935) experiment described earlier (see p. 340) was of such a nature. Even more to the point is an experiment of Wendt's (1936). Wendt studied the eye movements of men and monkeys subjected to rotation. He found that as the subjects adjusted or "adapted" to rotation, the typical rotational nystagmus disappeared gradually. However, instead of the subsequent eye-movement behavior becoming a minus quantity, Wendt observed the development of a new type of response which could be described as competitive with normal nystagmic responses. Instead of compensatory movements to rotation, the subjects began to make pursuit movements in the direction of rotation. In observing monkeys that were being trained to delay a draweropening response for 8 or 16 seconds, Wendt reports that the delay period, far from being the quiet, somnolent state that Pavlov described, was filled with activity which was specific for the individual monkey. Each monkey developed a pattern of behavior which filled in the delay period and served to prevent premature reactions. What

might ordinarily be termed "inhibition" appears to Wendt to be better described as interference. Miller's (1948) experiment also provides an illustration of the development of a competitive response. In his white-black box problem, when the wheel was made inoperative, subjects quickly learned to depress a bar which was followed by door opening. The above illustrations are more or less unique. Ordinarily advocates of an interference theory leave to the reader's imagination just what the subject might be doing when he fails to give the CR.

In some situations the experimenter deliberately initiates training such as to force a new response to a stimulus which has been associated with the original CR. Thus Kellogg and Walker (1938) conditioned dogs to raise the right paw to a buzzer and then began to shock the left paw. The animals, some with difficulty, learned to make the new response. Attempts at removing conditioned fears by associating fear stimuli with food (Jones, 1924), or the common practice of breaking habits by substitution of other habits, also fit the pattern. In many instances such retraining or counterconditioning is difficult to achieve. The procedure is sometimes called "proactive inhibition" which we have already considered (see p. 165). At the moment we are concerned with pointing out that we can expect a range of difficulty from little to much when counterconditioning is attempted. In those cases where a natural type of response begins to take over, the counterconditioning may be easy. In others, as in the Kellogg-Walker study, the subject may become quite unable to respond effectively for a long time, especially if he actually begins to learn even more and different responses from those recorded by the experimenter.

9. **Punishment.** In some cases of experimental extinction it is possible to administer punishment in some form, say shock, if the CR occurs. This normally leads to relatively rapid cessation of the response. We have already discussed this procedure in connection with negative reinforcement (see p. 274) and will not go into the same detail. The findings of Estes (1944) indicate that the response does not "extinguish," being merely *suppressed.* Such suppression, however, provides a possible situation for the development of counterconditioning or new learning as Dollard and Miller (1950) point out.

10. **Prevention of the CR.** With some situations it is possible to prevent the occurrence of the CR while presenting stimuli which normally bring it out. In an avoidance situation, for example, one might put up a barrier which prevents passage to a "safe" side. When the stimulus is presented the animal might try to scale the barrier, but

if this is impossible he must eventually desist. Bugelski and Coyer (1950) attempted this procedure in a hurdle-jumping avoidance situation. When a buzzer was sounded the animal leaped to the barrier, but after a minute of struggle it withdrew to a corner and remained there for 20 minutes, never jumping or leaving the corner when the previously potent buzzer sounded. A day later, however, "spontaneous recovery" was observed. More study of prevention is needed before we are able to draw serious conclusions about prevention. A similar procedure could be used in an operant situation with a discriminated stimulus which could be presented while the response was prevented. In this connection we recall White's (1953) study in which he showed that presenting 30 click stimuli in a Skinner box when the bar was absent effectively reduced the frequency of pressing the bar on a subsequent occasion when the bar was present. Guthrie (1935) makes a great deal of this type of procedure in his theory of extinction. From his point of view it is necessary to prevent the CR before new habits can be learned to the CS. We will look at his views shortly.

THEORETICAL ANALYSIS OF EXTINCTION

We have examined a number of variables at work in extinction procedure and we have noted a fair number of facts. What do these facts mean? Can we legitimately use the word "extinction" now with its ordinary connotation of death or deterioration?

Pavlov's findings. For Pavlov, the findings of the extinction procedure meant the development of some kind of *internal inhibition*. Since the CR was no longer observable, Pavlov believed it to be held back by a positive inhibitory process which he assumed to operate in the form of a wave, spreading over the cortex and depressing action. A broad spread of inhibition would result in sleep or stupor. A narrow spread would limit inhibition to a restricted range of stimuli. Extinction could be thought of as generalizing in the same way as the corresponding process of excitation. The course of development of inhibition could be disturbed by some novel change in the situation between extinction trials. In such cases, a CR might be observed, due, says Pavlov, to *Disinhibition* (see p. 164). Internal inhibition or extinction is to be discriminated from *external inhibition* which (operating oppositely to disinhibition) is illustrated by some disturbing or novel circumstance affecting the subject during acquisition. Pavlov also introduced the concept of *Conditioned Inhibition* by which he felt he could explain the fact that some stimulus which accompanied the CS during extinction procedure would also take on negative values so that its presence would "inhibit" other CR's if it were introduced along with another CS.

All the above suggestions are Pavlov's conceptualizations and do not refer to any actually observed processes in the nervous system. As such they can neither be proved nor disproved but enjoy status to the extent that they are fruitful in accounting for a variety of phenomena and lead to confirmable predictions. Hilgard and Marquis (1940, pp. 311–312) object to Pavlov's neurological schematizing because his geographical concepts of spatial irradiation do not lend themselves to accounting for generalization of intensity and quality variations in stimuli. Earlier (see p. 150) we have raised the question of the validity of the generalization concept in the form Hilgard and Marquis employ. They further object that evidence for a "sluggish spread of an inhibitory disturbance from one restricted region to surrounding areas" is lacking. It might be noted also that Pavlov's interpretation of hypnosis as a form of partial sleep appears not to square with electroencephalographic evidence (Walter, 1953).

Neurophysiological theorizing about extinction. Neurophysiologists have not been so active in considering extinction as they have in trying to picture acquisition. In Chapter 11 we considered Eccles' (1953) speculation about how conditioning takes place. At this time we can examine his interpretation of extinction.

Eccles recognizes that his picture of conditioning would, on the surface, leave the CS with the power of evoking the CR indefinitely. He knows, of course, that this does not correspond with the facts of extinction and attempts to account for the eventual disappearance of the CR through what he calls a "disuse" hypothesis. The term "disuse" is somewhat paradoxical here as it does not refer to any waiting period or passage of time proposition but deals with what goes on during active stimulation of the organism in a regular extinction procedure. Eccles' discussion is not exactly illuminating in this matter, but we can try to appreciate how he develops a disuse hypothesis out of active stimulation. He starts with the recognition that the CR is not an exact reproduction of the UncR. Harking back to Figure 11.2 (p. 297) we see that the activation of RC by impulses from NN is only part of the impulse pattern that is present when the UncS is also supplied. During experimental extinction, with only the CS presented, the discharge from CC will necessarily be smaller. (There are no impulses from collaterals of the pathway for the UncS.) The result of this smaller discharge is a change in the pattern of impulses in NN. Some synaptic knobs normally activated in NN will not now be activated. "Hence there will not be the same maintenance of synaptic efficacy in the neuronal network." Eccles supposes this general drop in efficacy to spread throughout the network as successive synaptic knobs originally involved now fail to discharge. With less frequent discharge, Eccles presumes these knobs to regress and thus provide for the "gradual extinction of a conditioned reflex when it is not continuously being reinforced by the unconditioned stimulus."

Malmo (1954) criticized Eccles' hypothesis on the ground that if disuse is to be the basic explanation, then leaving the organism alone and free from any stimulation by the CS should be the best way to bring about extinction. But this is patently not so. We have already seen that unused CR's can be retained for long periods. Malmo also brings up the spontaneous recovery argument, which, to the extent that there is such recovery, speaks against a disuse view. Malmo himself espouses a theory of inhibition based on Eccles' own work. It has long been known that when a reflex is elicited in an animal, the reflex activity ordinarily involves cooperation between antagonistic muscle pairs in such a way that, for example, when a flexor contracts, an extensor relaxes and vice versa. Eccles (1949) has demonstrated that when nerve potentials are recorded from the separate innervators, it is found that excitation of the dorsal roots is accompanied by a "depolarization." This is followed by a "hyperpolarization" (a large, positive, postsynaptic potential) in the motor neurones of the antagonistic muscles. The hyperpolarization is hypothesized by Eccles to operate as an inhibitory effect. Malmo uses this hyperpolarization or inhibition as a basis for extinction. He treats the hyperpolarization as analogous to Hull's reactive inhibition (see p. 365) and describes it as having a cumulative inhibitory effect which develops with repeated stimulation.

Reynolds (1955) points out that Malmo misuses the hyperpolarization concept by applying it to the effectors implementing the CR, whereas Eccles's observations apply to antagonistic effectors. In addition, Reynolds notes that any reactive inhibition account could only be of temporary value, and as a result of massed practice. By considering Eccles' hyperpolarization in its proper relations, Reynolds suggests an explanation of extinction that makes use of principles similar to Hull's conditioned inhibition (see p. 365) and the Guthrie-Wendt interference or competition suggestions. The explanation proposed by Reynolds runs along as follows: Whenever a reflex is activated, one set of effectors, for example, flexor muscles, receives excitatory impulses, while the other (antagonistic) set receives inhibitory (hyperpolarizing) impulses. This stimulation of the extensors in turn normally, through the myotactic reflex, results in stimulation of the flexors. This interplay between flexors and extensors results in the normal balanced action involved in ordinary movement, stretching, standing, locomotion, and so on.

When an UncS such as shock is administered in an avoidance experiment, the normal balance is upset and the flexion response dominates the extension reaction which is temporarily suppressed. With repetition of shock and CS, the CS comes to evoke the flexion alone. During extinction, the UncS, not being present, cannot inhibit the extensor response (via cerebral collaterals of the myotactic reflex) so that impulses for an extensor response can now operate as they did before the conditioning ever took place and these impulses can serve as a new UncS, but now for the extension response. We have here a situation where the CS is now being associated with impulses for extension instead of flexion and we have a possible explanation for extinction in terms of competition or "interference." An interesting feature of this interpretation is that the interplay of flexor-extensor antagonism can continue reversing as the CS is presented repeatedly, one reaction inhibiting the other successively until a balance is reached which approximates the prelearning condition with the organism indifferent to the CS. Since the development of the antagonistic reactions is a gradual process it requires repetitions and thereby offers an explanation of the gradual increase in latency and decrease in amplitude of the CR.

While the neurology involved in this account is conceptual rather than specifically factual, the explanation appears to be broad enough to account for the findings of the laboratory insofar as reflex behavior is concerned. The formula is invitingly simple: in the absence of an UncS, the reaction creates a situation which develops new unconditioned stimuli for a competing response. The CS, therefore, accompanies a new UncS and becomes associated with a response which differs from the original. In the Pavlovian salivation experiment, the supply of saliva which cannot be absorbed by now nonavailable food, is presumed to elicit a contrary and opposing nonsalivating reaction. While this antagonistic response cannot be described at present, the formula would require that some such mechanism must operate. "Higher" processes may involve similar competitions between responses at different levels of a habit-family hierarchy. How well the pattern fits more elaborate learning situations may now be observed as we consider more general attempts to account for extinction on somewhat more behavioral levels.

Hull's interpretation of extinction. How does Hull interpret the data obtained from extinction procedures? His basic approach (Hull, 1943) rests on the fact that all responses, reinforced or not, require an expenditure of energy and presumably are accompanied by some type of aftereffect of work. He does not commit himself to any specific type of aftereffect but acknowledges that it might be analogous to fatigue. To adopt the analogy for the moment, any considerable repetition of some response would result in the accumulation of some type of fatigue product or physiological change. Such a change is thought of as a sort of negative drive state which normally is diminished by rest. Presumably the drive state is accompanied by drive stimuli which tend to lead the organism to stop working, or rest. Because the organism tends to stop working, the effect of the drive can be thought of as inhibitory, and since the "inhibition" involved comes from work or reacting, Hull gives it the name of Reactive Inhibition or I_R. As I_R accumulates, then, the organism is less and less inclined to work until it ceases completely even when reinforced. I_R is eliminated by rest.

So far we have only a picture of a gradual disinclination for activity, and this of a temporary nature. Given time, the organism will recuperate and return with normal vigor to the task. Similar observations can be made in numerous other activities where the process of "adaptation" takes place. Thus the eyes stop blinking after a while even though the neighbor continues to shingle his roof. In sensory areas, adaptation is commonplace. We cease smelling the cheese, hearing the ticking clock, and so on. After a rest the sensory reactions or reflexes are freed from this "habituation" and are again functional.

Reactive inhibition, then, is of no significance by itself in the explanation of "extinction" because extinction is not a temporary affair. In order to handle the permanence feature Hull postulates that reactive inhibition corresponds to "drive." Assuming the "drive" nature of I_R, Hull points out that when the organism rests, this drive is reduced. This is the same as saying "when the organism does not respond, the I_R is reduced." Resting or *not making the response* that produces the I_R amounts to the reduction of a drive. When some behavior (resting) is followed by drive reduction, it is strengthened (learned) according to Hull. The organism then can be said to be learning *not to perform* the response in the very process of performing it. Likewise, since the response is not performed in a vacuum the situation in which the work is being done becomes associated with stopping or resting, or not performing. When the organism is exposed to the stimuli or the situation again, there will be a tendency (because of antedating of learned responses) to stop even before the first response is made. If reinforcement follows the response, the tendency to stop is lessened or delayed. Reinforcement, however, cannot prevent the cumulative effect of I_R, and sooner or later the response will not occur. It is also possible that continued reinforcement will lead to satiation and eliminate any "drive" to respond. With no response occurring, there can be no I_R. If no reinforcement follows, as is the case in extinction procedure, there is a strong deterrent to responding with the CR and so the CR drops out in favor of the response of "not working" in accordance with the number of reinforcements for not working just as any learned response. The organism, then, learns to *not respond*, or perhaps, more positively, to "rest" in the presence of a CS. Since the resting is a competitive response, we can classify Hull's solution of the extinction problem as an "interference" theory. We can diagram the Hull view as in Figure 13.5.

Hull calls the results of extinction procedure cI_R which corresponds to Pavlov's "conditioned inhibition." The notion of reactive inhibition as a factor in extinction was first proposed by Mowrer and Jones (1945) and by Miller and Dollard (1941). Hull (1943) incorporated their views into what he called "the Miller-Mowrer hypothesis." According to this hypothesis, extinction develops as a "conditioned inhibition" in that a stimulus becomes associated with a response (of resting) on the basis of drive reduction, the drive in question being generated from the work done by the organism in responding to the original S.

Wolpe (1952b) suggests an interesting possibility of accounting for conditioned inhibition in neurophysiological terms which helps to clarify the possible mechanism involved in showing how *cessation of responding* can bring about a more permanent cessation. Wolpe first presumes that when any response occurs there will be innervation of

First stage, training

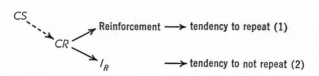

Second stage, extinction

a. Early trials

b. Late trials

FIG. 13.5. The development of conditioned inhibition $(_cI_R)$. (1) The reinforcement, for a while, will counteract the cumulative I_R. (2) The I_R operating as a drive will lead the organism to stop responding with CR and start responding in some other way, resting. (3) Resting is thought of as a response which reduces the I_R drive and, because of this drive reduction, the resting response is learned. (4) Because the resting response follows closely upon the CS and is reinforced, it will begin to come forward in time until it antedates the original CR. The organism has now extinguished the original CR through learning a new CR.

afferent fibers from the muscle system involved by a fatigue associated substance. Such innervation can be considered as in part inhibitory. Sherrington (1925) had shown that if such afferents were cut and their central ends stimulated, reflex action would disappear. After a response has been made, the stimulation of this inhibitory system will diminish. Wolpe now assumes that the cessation of this inhibitory stimulation alters the synapse involved in such a way as to make it more difficult to traverse by impulses from the CS (see Fig. 13.6).

How "real" the Wolpe account may be depends on future investigations of the neural consequences of motor reactions. For the present we must depend on behavioral evidence. In support of his views, Hull draws on evidence like that of Mowrer and Jones, and Solomon (see above).

We have already pointed out the limitations of this evidence and contradictory experiments have been cited. Skinner's (1950) objections (see p. 351) seem particularly apropos. The animals in the experiments of Mowrer and Jones and Solomon had not been tested extensively to determine whether they had in fact "exhausted their reserves" or what they could have done with other work loads. If Skinner is correct, the amount of work done has no effect on the extinction pattern other than changing its slope, not its curvature, and the work output can be varied extensively by arranging the reinforcement schedule. Since it can be shown that some kinds of "extinction" can be brought about more rapidly with fewer responses than with more (Kurke's experiment, see p. 356) there seems to be more reason

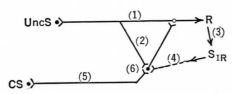

FIG. 13.6. Wolpe's neurophysiological explanation of conditioned inhibition. Impulses at (5) initiate R after conditioning. R leads to fatigue-like substance impulses which now inhibit synapse (6). Cessation of those impulses is assumed to change (6) so as to diminish its conductivity. (After Wolpe, 1952b.)

for doubting the basic role of I_R as operating in the way in which Hull requires. The I_R explanation is, of course, seriously questioned by Tolman followers who try to demonstrate nonresponse extinction (see p. 269). If extinction could occur without the response being made at all, then the I_R theory would have to be sacrificed. Later we may find a modified role for it.

Guthrie's views on extinction. It will be recalled that Guthrie (1935) views the acquisition of any response as a one-trial affair. Making a response to a given situation is tantamount to having learned it. If that response does not alter the situation so that the organism must now do something else, then something else will be learned as soon as it is done. The previous response which had just been learned must now be eliminated, that is, it is extinguished once and for all as soon as the new response is learned. Guthrie's theory, then, explains extinction as ocurring on the basis of elimination of one response by another. This view is usually described as an interference theory or a competition theory. To eliminate one response, another must be made to occur. The man who decides to munch on apples or chewing gum in order to quit smoking illustrates the general implications of the theory.

Critics of Guthrie usually raise the question of how one gets the organism to stop making the original response so that the new one has a chance to occur. Guthrie handles this question easily by pointing out that a number of possible bases for weakening the original tendency can be readily pictured: it is possible to tire the organism out to the point that it fails, from sheer exhaustion, to repeat the original response. Thus wild horses can be taught not to throw the rider by letting them wear themselves out trying to throw securely tied blankets, saddles, and other loads. The rider mounts the fatigued animal which then does not attempt to throw him. Or, the stimuli can be applied so rapidly that they occur within the refractory phase of the response and so it cannot occur (this is unlikely in terms of ordinary responses and techniques for stimulation). Or, the stimuli for the response can be applied in a subthreshold strength, carefully gauged so that the response never does quite come off while other responses are helped to occur in the presence of the old stimuli. This involves considerable manipulative skill and Guthrie is a little weak in illustrative material here. Simply preventing the response by physical blocking or failure to supply the necessary means can also work. A prisoner in solitary confinement without cigarettes *must* learn not to smoke. But this "not something" will be learned only to the prison situation and the nonprison cues will retain full strength. We can expect the prisoner to ask for a cigarette as almost the first response upon release. Solitary confinement does not permit the extinction of any aspects of a smoking habit that are associated with other stimuli. One cannot learn to refuse an offered cigarette if no one makes offers.

The Guthrie view is supported by several of the lines of evidence discussed earlier, such as prevention, counterconditioning, and the energy expenditure studies which are readily adapted to Guthrie's view. Sheffield's (1948) study of avoidance behavior (see p. 63) provides additional evidence as does that of Woodward (1954) on how new habits develop to replace the old. Wendt's studies strongly support Guthrie's analysis. In this connection, the point cannot be made too strongly that most studies of extinction have ignored other behavior in which the animal indulges when undergoing extinction. We have already made the point that if we only observe the original CR by means of some recording device, evidence of other behavior replacing the old will not be forthcoming. It has been only by fortunate selection of responses that Hilgard and Marquis (1935) and Wendt (1936) were able to find the evidence concerning the substitute response in the extinction of the eyelid response and eye movements. Guthrie himself offers numerous anecdotal observations of considerable interest and perhaps of value for personal adjustments and habit-breaking, but actual experimental evidence of counterconditioning is limited. There is much to recommend the Guthrie view and we shall return to it in the summing up.

Tolman on extinction. Tolman has not written specifically on the problem we are now considering. The implications of his views on extinction have been spelled out by at least two interpreters, one of the Tolman school, and one who favored the general Hull orientation. We can start with the latter. Osgood (1950) attempted to give an account of how Tolman would explain avoidance behavior and its extinction. His interpretation is somewhat as follows: If we take as an illustration of avoidance behavior some typical experiment, say that of a dog raising a paw to a buzzer which has previously been paired with shock, the application of Tolman's views would, on the surface, imply that the behavior should continue indefinitely. This is the interpretation that was proposed by Hilgard and Marquis (see p. 62). The reasoning is that the dog raises his leg because he has come to expect a shock following the buzzer. Expecting the shock dictates the next step, that of raising the paw with the additional expectation that if the paw is raised, no shock will be experienced. Since this latter expectancy is constantly confirmed, the behavior should theoretically strengthen and never weaken. Hilgard and Marquis recognized that this is unlikely *in fact* and introduced the possibility that the dog will sometime forget or fail to raise his leg in time and thus accidentally "discover" that no shock is present. This now leads to a contradiction of the expectancy, and the new expectancy of no shock will gradually become stronger.

Osgood chooses another escape clause for Tolman. He suggests that the original expectancy of shock following buzzer is based on the several trials on which they did occur together. The shock probably is accompanied by some fear response which mediates the leg withdrawal. As the buzzer stimulation continues without the shock (because the leg is withdrawn) the original expectancy extinguishes because it is no longer being confirmed. At the same time, the second expectancy is being strengthened because it is being confirmed. Since the second expectancy depends on the first, and since the first is being extinguished, a point is reached when the first expectancy is no longer present in any strength and therefore, the second, although fully established, is no longer functionally appropriate. In Tolman's language, the buzzer is no longer a sign for shock and no motivation exists for doing anything about it. The animal therefore fails to react since, according to Tolman, the behavior is a function of "demand" among other variables and the demand is no longer present. Tolman has not indicated whether he is pleased with Osgood's unsolicited assistance and so we will let it rest for the moment.

Seward and Levy (1949), and Deese (1951) offer an alternative kind of explanation for Tolman to consider. Both these investigators set up a situation wherein animals were trained to arrive at a goal box containing food. Seward and Levy used a runway and Deese used a T-maze. After the animals were suitably trained, they were given an opportunity to examine the goal which now contained no food. Presumably, in the course of this examination they were supposed to acquire an expectancy that the goal box was empty and that there would be no point to running down to it since that would be obviously useless exercise. Both experimenters report positive results. Bugelski, Coyer, and Rogers (1952) repeated the Seward and Levy experiment and found no basis for assuming that the pre-extinction behavior had any influence on the subsequent extinction runs. They criticized the design of both Seward and Levy and Deese and point out that Tolman's position does not require the development of the type of pre-extinction expectancy that was specified. The subjects might very well develop the expectancy that there is no food at the goal end *when they are placed there by hand* and may have no expectancies whatever about what will happen if they run to the goal.

It appears reasonable to presume that for Tolman, the nature of extinction must be explained in terms of the development of new, different, or contrary expectancies if the old ones are not confirmed. This statement, although bare of evidence, is not out of line with the general reorientation the writer has tried to give the Hull and Guthrie views. If the new expectancy is a new habit or a new response, neural or otherwise, there appears to be basis for a general agreement.

Before we try to see to what extent the different views can be consolidated we should examine the points made by Skinner in his evaluation of what takes place during extinction.

The Skinner approach to extinction. The views of Skinner have been made fairly clear in the preceding context but a brief restatement of them is perhaps in order. It will be recalled that Skinner originally (1938) postulated some kind of "reserve" so that each reinforcement could be thought of as adding so many potential responses to the repertoire of the organism. These potential responses, then, would be emitted on suitable occasions in the absence of additional reinforcement. When they were all emitted, the reserve would be exhausted and the habit could be said to be extinguished. Skinner does not consider any other kind of failure to respond as due to anything but temporary suppressive agents or conditions. The facts of temporary cessations and of spontaneous recovery give Skinner little concern. He believes that if conditions are handled properly, the organism will continue emitting at a rate which will decline steadily until the animal is through responding. This is actually more of a belief than a fact because it is probable that regardless of reinforcement schedules and other controls that might be initiated, the organism is going to falter, hesitate, and go through several periods of starting and stopping, particularly if reinserted into the situation. The hesitations and stoppages are put down by Skinner to what he calls emotion and frustration. These are not exactly behavioral terms as Skinner would like to believe but, rather, interpretations. In any case, the animal that fails to get the reinforcement is alleged to be disturbed, distressed, or "emotional" and this kind of reaction is presumed to be incompatible with further reaction of the type that is being extinguished. Because of this competition, the original response is not made again until the emotion is eliminated, presumably through rest or change of stimulus conditions. When the animal is again undisturbed, and conditions are right, the remainder or part of the remainder of the reserve will emerge.

Skinner supports his views with the evidence of Estes (1944) on punishment, and the great variety of extinction curves he has accumulated under different conditions of drive, different schedules of reinforcement, and differing amounts of work done (see above). Before leaving Skinner on this theme, we should recall that he no longer is too pleased with the reserve concept. The data cited earlier (see p. 285) to the effect that there is a point of diminishing returns from reinforcement also makes the concept a bit shaky from an empirical point of view, although, within limits, it does appear that the greater the number of reinforcements, the greater the number of extinction responses. This last point is subject to considerable modification by the action of other variables, like counterconditioning, spacing of trials, possibly the work level involved, and the possible action of emotional factors which may operate in such a way as to make a rapid extinction relatively permanent. On the surface, it appears that

Skinner cannot be included in an interference interpretation. The responses must emerge before extinction is complete. Skinner's data are certainly convincing on this point, yet we cannot easily accept his conclusion if there is no way of knowing when the last response has been given. If the competitive learning that might take place is sufficiently strong, then the responses still in the reserve will never emerge. Skinner's position is virtually unassailable. He can say, "I told you so," whenever an old, long-forgotten response occurs. It is a handy explanation whenever a competitive training program breaks down. When the reformed alcoholic returns to the bottle or the reform-school graduate to his crime we can talk about the unexhausted reserve. It might be equally plausible to talk about the *relearning* of a formerly satisfying habit. After all, there would not be so much to relearn as only certain responses could have been extinguished. The practical habit breaker would do well to follow Skinner by using a prolonged extinction procedure before initiating training in some counterresponse. Unfortunately, it is difficult to arrange for many operants to occur without some kind of reinforcement (secondary or otherwise).

AN INTEGRATIVE ATTEMPT

The various views on extinction which have just been examined appear, at least superficially, to be quite unique. Is there any prospect of reconciling them into one comprehensive view? A closer look at each of the views suggests that there are a great many common concepts which may offer the foundation for a more general and comprehensive interpretation. For example, there appears to be no special disagreement with one another's facts, itself a unique situation in psychology. Even some of the phraseology is common. Hull uses Pavlov's terms with only slight modification of the language. Skinner and Guthrie are not too far apart in their interpretations of the role of emotion in spontaneous recovery. For that matter, Hull goes along with the Guthrie and Skinner notion that the behavior undergoing extinction must first suffer some kind of weakening (reactive inhibition) before some new response is going to replace the original. Skinner, perhaps, wants to be sure about the weakening of the original behavior. None object to the concept of replacement of original behavior by some other although the several kinds of experimental situations do not equally well lend themselves to demonstrations of the nature of the competitive response. The findings of partial reinforcement (longer extinction) seem to be generally interpreted as due to the learning of different kinds of habits and developing in the organism a suitable response in the absence of reinforcement. As we learned earlier, Hull expresses this last point as amounting to teaching the organism a habit which contains the features of the situation that will be encountered during extinction. It is easily enough translated as teaching the organism to expect different results on different occasions. What is the special contribution of each of the theories of extinction we have examined?

For Pavlov and Eccles we have the emphasis on neural processes. For Hull and Guthrie we have the learning of a new habit. For Tolman we have the acquisition of a new expectancy, which we can, for the moment, describe as amounting to a new habit. For Skinner we have the emphasis on suppression through emotion or frustration of the response. Putting these all together, what do they spell?

Going back to our picture of the development of a habit, or the acquisition of some new behavior to some stimulus or situation, we recall that a primary limitation on learning is the capacity of the organism to make the required response. We do not learn what we cannot do. The behavior must be not only potentially present, but it must occur before it is going to be learned, at least when we deal with basic, early, primitive learning. The behavior may be low in the hierarchy (that is, have a low operant rate) but by one means or another the trainer must get this behavior out of the organism whether he waits for it, as Skinner does, or whether he encourages it by limiting the situation more and more narrowly until the organism can do nothing else. We ordinarily do not speak of learning if the organism is fully prepared and performs the required behavior on the first request or stimulation. There must be some sort of change. But change from what? From the more normal or biologically appropriate reaction to the situation. In other words, even before we can begin to talk about learning, we must start talking about extinction. For one thing to be learned another must be extinguished. Learning and extinction seem to be two aspects of the same process. If conditions are adequate, as in the Hilgard and Marquis experiment (see p. 340), we can study both together or pay attention to either side of the picture. Because of our strong interests in positive acquisition, we frequently overlook the other side and make no special efforts to hasten the departure of the competitive behavior. If this were done, perhaps learn-ing would occur much more rapidly. We shall see later how Dollard and Miller (1950) in speaking of therapy suggest just this proposi-tion. Before trying to strengthen some positive approach tendency, they recommend that the negative, avoidance tendency be weakened. The schoolteacher who finds difficulty with teaching some particular material might not do better than to first find out what is holding the acquisition back. Before a student can begin to make decent prog-ress at the piano he must extinguish a host of habits and tendencies acquired from casual observation of pianos, other players, his own un-trained attempts at teasing melodies out of the box, and so on. The child is surprised at being shown how to sit, hold his arms and fingers, how to extend his legs, and so on. After all, he knows how to sit, doesn't he?

If this interpretation is correct, we may be quite a bit ahead. If extinction and learning are two sides of a coin, to the extent that some new habit is going to be difficult to acquire, we can think of the coin as having one biased face. Nowhere is this clearer than in the difficult process of teaching children the refinements of behavior that society imposes on its members. At first infants are allowed, even en-couraged, to behave in biologically normal ways. Later, after perhaps thousands of "reinforcements," a "training" procedure is instituted which makes much that was done before "bad" and calls for a new kind of adjustment. Is this training or retraining? The baby whose burps brought smiles to mother's face now finds frowns for the same performance. Some parents find it amusing to see their children sip the dregs of cocktails or beer glasses. What is funny in a two-year-old may prove embarrassing with a ten-year-old. The artificial standards of a culture sometimes prove distressing to both student and teacher. For our present purpose, however, they point up the fact that much of learning amounts to getting rid of old ways of doing things and adding new ones. Extinction must occur either before or during the new acquisition.

If extinction represents a form of new learning, then we can ap-proach the entire problem from the same point of view as previously presented for acquisition. We can conceive of the response to be ex-tinguished as representing a cell-assembly, or a phase sequence in Hebb's terms. This may be a "natural," built-into-the-organism re-sponse, or a "learned" reaction. The stimuli presented to the organ-ism arouse the sequence of neural activities corresponding to the sensory and motor features of the situation. The sequence normally runs off according to schedule if the reinforcement (subsequent stimulation) is present. The organism can be said to be "expecting" the reinforcement since, in every situation that one observes, it is evident that the organism is making preparatory movements for the execution of the next phase of the response. Thus the animal in the Skinner box, well trained, barely nudges the bar before its head is turned toward the food box. Frequently the bar is missed entirely but the head turning goes on anyway. Such preparatory responses we have previously identified with r_g's or expectancies. It will be recalled that Hebb talks about this as "central facilitation" by which he means that the neural circuit starts running off by itself as soon as any feature of it is excited and that neural stimulation is present in advance of sensory stimulation for making certain movements. Making these movements is facilitated by such prior neural action.

The organism, then, can be said to be expecting to make certain new movements as the behavioral sequence unfolds. In the Skinner box, as the animal turns its head to the food cup it is already prepared to grasp the food that will normally be there by the time its head reaches the cup. Suppose now that no food is present. The expectancy is violated. The animal is prepared for one and only one response, that of eating. It is not prepared for not eating. In Hebb's language, this situation represents the basis for emotion or frustration. It is an interference with the timing of neural impulses and results in a disorganization of the phase sequence. So far, except for the neural reference, we are in line with the common thinking of all the theorists whose views were cited.

The neural disorganization which occurs following the first extinction episode is likely to be of little effect on the organization of the brain's activities as a whole, and the equilibrium will be quickly restored. But the basic pattern for the acquisition of a new reaction to a given situation has already been set down. The next reaction followed by a failure of the expectancy will again create the neural disturbance, the phase sequence cannot run off, and the disorganization may become a little more extensive. We can now expect the situation to begin to deteriorate and to find the organism nonplussed because the original phase sequences cannot be run off. However, the neural action is not a static affair; the impulses will run off into new circuits (or into the older, prelearning circuits if these are still available). Note the rapid extinction of infrequently reinforced habits as well as the rapid extinction of frequently extinguished habits (Bullock and Smith 1953). The new phase sequence will begin to be established. The new phase sequence can represent a variety of possibilities depending on the circumstances introduced by the experimenter. It may, for example, take on the characteristics of periodically reinforced behavior if the experimenter chooses to introduce a reinforcement after a number of unreinforced trials. Counterconditioning will set up different phase sequences. Fatigue and frustration may introduce additional phase sequences of which they are already component parts. The situation will now take on new characteristics as far as the organism is concerned and the behavior in which we happened to be interested is no longer available for inspection. The behavior is extinguished. The experimenter is satisfied and closes his notebook.

EXTINCTION AND FORGETTING

At the end of the last chapter we promised to reconsider the question of forgetting and extinction. We are now ready to return to this problem. It will be remembered that the two processes are alleged to be different (Woodworth, 1938) because in the one case conditioned stimuli are presented (without reinforcement) while in the other case such stimuli are not presented and the response is not elicited. While this may be correct enough as far as laboratory procedure is concerned, the student is now unlikely to agree that it is true outside the laboratory where "forgetting" is more likely to be observed.

If we appreciate the possibilities for counterconditioning outside the laboratory in terms of McGeoch's interference interpretation of forgetting (including the range of stimuli and responses that get into the act through generalization), the differences between extinction and forgetting seem to disappear. The extinction procedure employed in the laboratory appears to be a "speed-up" of the kinds of things that happen more haphazardly outside the laboratory. Certainly there are differences in the behavior of the salivating dog and the poetry-spouting student, and we have taken pains to point out the many variables involved in connection with the kinds of stimuli, kinds of responses, temporal factors, emotional factors, criteria of learning, and on and on that are involved in comparisons between one learning situation and another. The very range of variables certainly should give us pause in any attempt to draw universally valid conclusions. But to draw the conclusion that forgetting and extinction are different processes is just as dangerous as to say that they are the same.

An empirical aside might help us straighten out our reasoning here. If we were interested in getting someone to "forget"something, what would be the best procedure? Would we take a chance on waiting a long time? Or would we be afraid that no matter how long we waited the memory would stubbornly persist? There appears to be no question but that our best insurance against our subject's remembering would be to harrass him, frustrate him, force him to do something different, teach him something else. How we would go about it would depend on the subject, how well he had learned, what else he could do, and the whole gamut of variables we have looked into so far in this text. We could, in short, try to "extinguish" the "memory." It appears that our most-likely-to-succeed procedure would be to counter-train him. In the conditioning laboratory, countertraining, however, is rarely attempted, and the animal is left to countertrain itself (recall here Wendt's monkeys, p. 359). No new sources of reinforcement are provided, no new response is singled out; the animal may learn a succession of reactions, none of which is repeated frequently enough to become established. In an extinction session an animal goes through a multiple-learning experience, as Guthrie might remark, but none of the unreinforced new learning "sticks" very well. Is it any surprise that the old habit may "spontaneously" recover in a later test? Even though seriously weakened, it may be stronger than any of the poorly learned competitive habits. Even if equally learned, the old habit will still edge out the new in a test (Jost's law—see Woodworth, 1938).

Hilgard and Marquis (1940) raised several arguments against the interpretation of extinction as an interference or new learning phenomenon. They state (1940, p. 118) "If the extinction process were essentially similar to the conditioning process, one would expect a positive correlation between the rates of acquisition and extinction, that is, rapid conditioning corresponding to rapid extinction, slow conditioning corresponding to slow extinction. The numerous correlations reported are, however, predominantly negative." But such negative correlations are exactly what an interference hypothesis would predict in the ordinary extinction situation. The interference hypothesis would presume that the rapid learner would be (as is apparently the case) the slow forgetter, that a poor learner would show a rapid disintegration and forget or extinguish quickly, not slowly. Even more to the point, however, a correlation between learning and extinction scores for the same response has only an indirect relationship to extinction. What is demanded is a correlation between the acquisition trials of the first response and the second, the substitute or interference response. Such correlations are not readily available.

The correlations reported by Hilgard and Marquis (1940, p. 119) deal in three cases with eyelid and knee-jerk conditioning. Correlations of −.88, −.66, and −.60 are given between the frequency of CR's during a training series and the frequency of such CR's during experimental extinction. Surely such findings represent just what Hilgard and Marquis say they do not. To rephrase their statement, a *negative* correlation is to be expected if learning and extinction are similar processes. A negative correlation can only be obtained if either good learners have a high number of responses in training and a low number in extinction, or if poor learners have a low score in training and a high score in extinction. Hilgard and Marquis are apparently asking for high frequencies in learning to accompany high frequencies in extinction. This is the only way to get a positive correlation and this is, by their own data, clearly contradicted. Hilgard and Marquis admit that the results of Kellogg and Wolf (1939), where counter-conditioning was employed, show no spontaneous recovery and no loss of the interfering response. The subject still bears study.

Another argument advanced by Hilgard and Marquis deals with the differential effect of drugs on acquisition and extinction. Depressants are found to retard acquisition and hasten extinction while excitants "increase the strength of conditioned responses" but decrease extinction rates. What else could be reasonably expected? Obviously the measures of acquisition and extinction involve activity. Depressants depress all activity and would automatically reflect a slower learning and faster extinction. An adequate dose of a depressant can extinguish the animal along with the habit. Similarly excitants would show an increased activity, and if activity is being measured as symbolic of extinction, then obviously high scores would be recorded.

The arguments of Hilgard and Marquis do not appear to be substantial rebuttals of an interference interpretation of both extinction and forgetting. If we accept the description of interference on the simple anatomical level discussed above (see p. 363) in connection with Eccles' views, then we have a modest foundation on which to base an interference theory of extinction for simple glandular or motor reactions. The inductive leap to forgetting is perhaps a giant step.

But McGeoch (1942) took such a giant step and, while there are difficulties, there appears to be sufficient evidence that the forgetter is having trouble from an embarrassing riches of remembering the wrong things than because of a poverty of responses. Taking into consideration the complexities of both learning and forgetting and the corresponding laboratory operations of conditioning and extinction, there appears to be no real justification for regarding forgetting and extinction as separate biological processes, however much they differ as laboratory procedures. At the same time we suggest the paradoxical proposition that learning and forgetting involve the same processes, if not quite the same operations.

EXTINCTION AND LEARNING: A SUMMARY STATEMENT

Our reasons for excluding extinction scores as a measurement of learning should now be clear. "Resistance to extinction" is hardly a worthy measure of learning strength. Even if we define it "operationally," we have seen in the present chapter sufficient reason for wondering about just what frequency of response during "experimental extinction" means. Our examination of the variables involved in "extinction" suggests that it is a complex affair and hardly something to use as a measure. It is a problem in itself. In our treatment of extinction we found it necessary to consider pretty much the same variables as we did in the consideration of learning in earlier chapters. We found extinction to be a far from simple, negative affair, and that it is instead an intimate component of the learning process, so intimate that it is exceedingly difficult to tease out any but procedural differences. Even the procedural differences are difficult to identify as we examine various levels of complexity of learning.

If the above account bears any semblance of an approximation to reality, then we find the acquisition-extinction problem to be one of levels of complexity. Each new level calls for a consideration of special factors and no particular level represents the whole picture. There is no simple truth of the matter. We find at one place or another that there is meaning and a use for such varied constructs as disuse, adaptation, reactive inhibition, competition, and reserve. No single theorist appears to have the whole answer, nor is anyone of them particularly guilty of error. We need only to recognize that there is no requirement that any particular construct must be applied to any specific set of data and found to fit. To deny that one or another of the suggested constructs *can* apply is equally foolish. Although it is hardly necessary to end with a moral, there appears to be a value to pointing to the moral involved in the understanding of extinction: there are no simple answers to complex questions.

Chapter

14 The Transfer of Training

To some extent, all preceding chapters have been a preparation for this one. We come at last to a problem area
that appears to be more peculiarly human than anything we have
touched on before. It is the area which concerns itself principally
with the problem of the influence of past experience on present behavior. Academically speaking, this area is generally known as that
of the "transfer of training." From the popular point of view, however, the problems we are about to touch are the heart of psychology.
If there is any universal belief (or delusion), it is that the behavior
of adults depends upon how they were treated as children, what their
childhood experiences were, how they were brought up. While most
popular dogma relates to "personality" and emotional behavior patterns (see the next chapter), it is also widely believed that childhood
learning experiences in the more formal sense also determine adult
learning behavior. It is obvious, of course, that there will be but little
experimental data available about human learning experiences in
childhood as they affect the adult learner. Investigation here suffers
for the same reasons as were considered in connection with retention
studies. In view of the broad importance of the subject, we shall try
to widen the scope of the discussion somewhat beyond the usual
academic limitations and venture a bit more boldly into speculations
concerning a wider range of phenomena than are ordinarily discussed
under this heading.

THE INFLUENCE OF PAST EXPERIENCE

What is the influence of past experience? What is the nature of this influence, how does it operate? We can expect offhand that a variety of effects are likely—past experience might help in some cases, hinder in others. "The child is father to the man." Previous experience enables some men to become bankers and presidents, others become bums, criminals, or stamp collectors. Some men solve problems easily, others only with difficulty. The range of problems that can be solved by any one person is normally assumed in some way to reflect his intelligence, but most psychologists are quite prone to attribute a heavy loading to experience in interpreting intelligence-test scores. Even poets recognize that "full many a rose is born to blush unseen." A stimulating environment is normally assumed to be a necessary accompaniment to a healthy brain if an active intelligence is to result. The usual formula for development now commonly accepted is: Behavior $= f$ (heredity $\times$ environment). Unfortunately we have no good mathematical units to insert into the formula on either side of the equation. Verplanck (1955) suggests that we have no real hope of developing an adequate technique for separating "nurture" from "nature." He points out, as Beach (1950) did before, that what is "learned" in one "species" may be "natural" to another. Even with so simple a situation as the Skinner box, Verplanck notes that all our knowledge of rat behavior in bar-pressing does not help a great deal in appreciating what a guinea pig will do in such a situation. Our problem then is the difficult, and perhaps insoluble one, of appraising the role of the environmental factors in the individual case history which affect the present behavioral repertoire of the subject. We leave to the geneticist the problem of evaluating the contribution of the genes. Regardless of how much we are inclined to favor a biological orientation, we are all prone to claim that at least within limits a behavioral pattern depends on "how one was brought up." How can we analyze the role of the previous experiences of a person in relation to his present behavior?

In the last chapter we examined how experience that comes *after* some other experience may come to interfere with the former learned responses to the point where they are unavailable for use. We explained forgetting as due, to some extent, to the interference between new learning and old. We referred to this as a matter of "reproductive interference" or retroactive inhibition. It was noticed, however, that in some cases new learning facilitated the retention of the old, particularly where the interpolated responses were the same and the stimuli similar.

Proactive inhibition and proactive facilitation. In the present problem area, we can set up a formula for laying bare the framework of the problem so that we can proceed to discover the variables which operate to obscure any easy appreciation of what goes on when we learn new materials *after* having learned something else. The basic proposition amounts to an experimental paradigm that has long been known as that of "proactive inhibition." In the typical proactive inhibition experiment we have two groups, one of which learns something, say B, and subsequently learns the material we are really concerned with, material A. Another group, the control, does not learn B at any time, but learns A along with the experimental group. In diagram form:

Group	Original Experience	Test Situation
Experimental	Learn B	Learn A
Control	Do nothing	Learn A

The relative ease or difficulty with which the two groups learn A can then be attributed to the influence of material or experience B, assuming all other variables are under control, particularly that the two groups are equally matched for capacity to learn A in the first place. It is at once apparent that we can expect a range of effects from a negative or debilitating nature, through zero, to a positive facilitative effect. If the effect is negative, we refer to "proactive inhibition," if positive, we speak of "positive transfer"; if zero, we sometimes argue that both effects might have been present but canceled each other, or that material B bears no significant relationship to material A.

Variables operating in proaction. In the proactive inhibition paradigm we have the basic formula by which to appraise the influence of past experience on the present. The formula as such, however, offers no help other than that of a starting point for determining the nature of the variables that can operate in the situation. Before we undertake such a search, we can indulge in a few more generalities which might help set the stage. Suppose that material B happens to be the study of Latin, Greek, and mathematics, and material A happens to be the handling of legal cases, running a hospital, or administering the

United States Treasury. What effects could we anticipate? Suppose that B is a course in French and A is a course in Coptic or Japanese? Would there be any effect? Or suppose that B is participation in high-school football and A is college basketball or debating; what can we expect to find regarding A for an experimental subject? The problem long engaged the attention of educators in this country under the label of "formal discipline." The entire question of a compulsory curriculum versus "free electives" or variously interpreted schemes of "progressive education" was answered by authorities depending on their answers to the question of the influence of "formal discipline" on future activities. Early in the century, Thorndike and Woodworth (1901) attempted the gigantic task of appraising the doctrine of formal discipline by comparing performances on various tests in terms of the backgrounds of the subjects. Their analysis left many questions unanswered or equivocal, although the general finding was that positive transfer occurs only when "identical elements" are involved in B and A. Since the nature of the elements is difficult to appraise, there being such a variety of possibilities, the question of the merit of formal discipline is still unanswered. One might find that study habits, for example, are identical elements in A and B and so positive transfer results, or a variety of capacities might be employed in both A and B, such as computational aptitude or verbal capacity, or simply motivational or practice elements might be present in "identical" form. Osgood (1953) concludes that psychologists are in no position, at the present time, to decide in favor of one view or the other in the question of formal discipline. The doctrine of formal discipline is only one of the many broad questions which psychologists have tried to answer by appealing to past experience. In fact, the problem is not one of showing how past experience accounts for so much as, perhaps, to find behavior samples which are not affected by past experience. Because of our basic interest in those fields of behavior study in which learning psychologists have accumulated some data, however, we cannot branch out here into what would amount to a discourse on general psychology. We will have to confine ourselves to a limited number of general problems. The problems we can hope to throw some light on are the following: (a) The characteristic rapidity of learning in adult life as compared with childhood (we could restate this perhaps as the problem of one-trial learning), (b) The ease of learning meaningful material, (c) The operation of "insight" and responses to relationships, (d) The benefits of practice.

We do not expect to provide definitive answers to these long-puzzling questions. Nor will we attack them directly. Whatever hints we can obtain toward helping toward an understanding of these problems will have to emerge from a more formal investigation of the influence of past experience. We cannot simply inquire into past experience. That is far too formidable an undertaking. Instead we shall look at the experimental paradigm of *proaction* and, by considering the variables involved in investigating proaction, we can remain closer to the laboratory in which occasional glimpses might be had of the answers to the general questions we have listed.

We can leave the broad general questions now and turn to the series of specific questions that arise more or less spontaneously from simply looking at the experimental paradigm of proaction. Leaving aside, for the moment, the question of equal capacity of the two groups, an obvious experimental variable, we can look at the variables that specifically pertain to the problem at hand.

1. **Temporal factors in proaction.** The time at which B is learned relative to A might be of some significance. If B is learned immediately before A the effects may be quite different from those found when B is learned in childhood and A as an adult. Obviously the time factor can range tremendously from immediacy to almost infinity. The learning behavior of aged people, for example, might be a function of how they spent or misspent their youths.

2. **Practice, warm-up, set.** The same factors which were found effective in retroactive facilitation might operate proactively in the learning of A, and must be examined.

3. **The nature of the materials involved.** Materials A and B can be from the same general frame of reference or from widely different selections. Thus A and B can both be sets of nonsense syllables, mazes, code substitution tasks, foreign language vocabularies, and so on. Or A might be one of the kinds of items mentioned while B of another kind. We might arrange for one group, for example, to learn a French-English vocabulary as material B and then test both groups on code substitution. Or using rats in Skinner boxes, we might shock one group of rats prior to inserting the bar and not shock the other group. The rats could then be observed to see if the presumed "anxiety" developed by shocking the rats has any effect on the rate at which they press the bar, on their eating behavior, on extinction patterns. Actually, most experiments in psychology follow the proactive inhibition paradigm with no reference to the fact that it is being em-

ployed. This paradigm exemplifies, in its most general features, the typical experimental procedure followed in behavior studies. One group is held under control, another is given some experience or treatment, and both groups are then compared on some kind of performance, either of a learning nature or of some other kind. We obviously have nothing new here, but may have a wealth of material to draw upon in our attempts to evaluate effects of past experience on present performance.

The proactive inhibition formula fits such a wide variety of experiments that our only problem is the difficulty of selection. Thus, the early experiments of Gesell and Thompson (1941) and McGraw (1935) in training one of a pair of twins while the other was allowed to just grow is a typical example of the kind of investigation that comes under consideration here, when we try to evaluate the influence of past experience. In the maturational studies some kinds of behavior were found to benefit from practice, others not. Our problem is to find out what kind of past experience means something and what kind does not.

4. **The similarity or identity of materials.** We have just considered the question of kinds of materials that are involved in the investigation. The fact that materials can be loosely divided into classes does not indicate in any strict fashion the degree to which these materials are similar or different. Here we encounter the same dilemmas met in the previous chapter. How different are ping-pong and chess, French and algebra, swimming and stair climbing? It is obviously a question of first importance and one that we are as yet in but a poor position to answer. The similarity may reside, not in the content of the materials per se, but in the methods or procedures involved—they may be learned by rote, in various settings, with various instructional sets, or under a variety of motivational circumstances, and in any of these we might be able to argue for similarity or lack of such.

5. **The degree of learning.** The degree to which material B is practiced may have differential effects. If it is learned to a high criterion it may interfere with or facilitate the learning of A in different degrees. Before we can decide the issue, some account must be taken of the strength of the learning. The possibility that A itself may be learned to different strengths in terms of later measures must also be investigated even though the original learning of A is to the same criterion. In other words, the effects of B may not appear at the first learning of A but only afterward, in terms of some retention measure.

Before we investigate the role of the various factors just outlined we must take account of several additional and complicating principles which have been discussed slightly in earlier chapters, but in other connections. Some of these principles can be reduced to the transfer paradigm, perhaps with a little forcing, but in any case their roles, while difficult to pinpoint, must be appreciated in connection with the more general problem to which we are now addressing ourselves.

PRELIMINARY CONSIDERATIONS

Early and late learning. The influence of early learning on later learning experience in terms of early and late, primitive and complex, or child-adult relationships is a relevant problem here. Hebb (1949) has distinguished two kinds of learning which we have already considered in earlier chapters. The basic primitive learning, it will be remembered, is that of the slow development of cell assemblies and the gradual development of more complicated and involved phase sequences which depend upon the development of suitable cell assemblies in the first place. According to Hebb, early infant and child learning is of a more primitive nature than is that of the adult. The infant is chiefly engaged in more or less specific activities and perceptions which correspond to relatively primitive cell asssemblies and simple phase sequences. As the child grows, the cell assemblies and simple phase sequences multiply by a steady process of reacting to the new elements in its environment, and it slowly accumulates a supply of what might be called "behavioral elements" or "reaction systems" which operate in the more or less variegated environment of the child. Thus, the child slowly learns to distinguish, perceive, name, and otherwise react to components of its environment.

We might illustrate with some homely example such as a tomato. The child's first experience may be with the juice of this fruit. Component elements of taste, odor, color, temperature may be reacted to sufficiently frequently for the child to develop a reaction system to the presentation of a glass of the liquid. He may develop responses of acceptance or rejection depending upon a variety of concomitant circumstances, but by his reactions we come to accept the notion that the child "knows" what tomato juice is. This he may indicate long before he can talk and long before he has any "concept" of a tomato or juice. He has a concept, in Hebb's language, of tomato juice.

Sooner or later, he may see pictures of tomatoes and hear the sound of the word "tomato" in the presence of the picture, just as he hears about lions, tigers, owls, and mice, that he never sees in reality but comes to "know" about. He may growl, for example, like his father growls, when asked what does the lion say. His concept of lion, or tomato, to get back to the original illustration, may be fantastically unrealistic and when shown the actual fruit he may be unable to react appropriately but do so to the picture. With more experience, he may get to see, feel, and eat the fruit itself, sliced or whole, salted or with some variety of dressing; he will encounter tomato paste, catsup, cocktail sauce, and pizza pies. His phase sequences of "tomato" will grow enormously as the years go on. Simultaneously, of course, he is developing phase sequences concerning every other kind of element in his environment, his relatives, friends, ways of life, money, and so on. Suppose that one of his relatives is a farmer and wealthy. As the proper phase sequences develop and the child acquires a variety of reactions to money, its shape, feel, exchange value, source, and so on, he may on some occasion, while reflecting upon his wealthy farmer relative, initiate one of the great number of phase sequences dealing with tomatoes. This may set him off onto a whole new train of associations or it may, momentarily, combine with the phase sequences involved in reflecting about the wealthy farmer. A new combination may be set off which behaviorally amounts to a new concept, "There's money in tomatoes."

Here we have an example, perhaps somewhat forced, of what Hebb is saying in his conclusions that there are differences between the learning of children and adults, or more properly, between early and late learning. The first consists of developing phase sequences, the second consists of combining the phase sequences themselves into new patterns, new concepts, new "ideas." If, as we readily recognize, some kinds of behavior patterns are learned slowly and painfully by the child, and, on the other hand, the adult learns some of his reactions or associations fairly quickly, perhaps in one trial, or in no trials at all, we might see not only the difference between the two kinds of learning but also the relationship between them. Late learning is efficient and rapid because it takes advantage of all the slow, hard, elemental learning that has already taken place in the past of the learner. We should expect to find differences, then, in adult and child learning. They are not learning the same kinds of things. One is learning phase sequences, the other is learning to put them together.

The role of generalization. The second general principle which must be taken into account in evaluating past experience is that of generalization. We have met this principle before (p. 146) but in quite another connection. What is its special significance for the transfer of training question?

So long as we think of conditioning or learning as limited to specific S-R connections, it is unlikely that we can begin to explain even a fraction of man's behavior. Obviously no one has time to learn all the possible reactions to all the possible varieties of stimuli to which we are exposed. We rarely hear the same sound twice—with exactly the same pitch, intensity, and timbre, for example, except in a laboratory perhaps. Yet we are able to react appropriately enough to spoken or other auditory signals which may depart in various degrees from the exact stimulus pattern to which we were conditioned. All this is old stuff, or should be, by now. The point to be made, or remade, is that we have a lot of "past experience" available for reacting in a given way without ever having gone through it. It is as if someone were depositing funds to our account without our knowledge. Thus, I might never have seen a specific spider, insect, or snake, yet I treat the specimen with respect and maintain a safe distance. There is no need to be stung by every type of insect before we learn to stay away from unknown varieties.

Putting the matter in another fashion, we can say that we know a lot that we never learned, but which is still and necessarily a function of past experience. The generalization principle fits the proactive inhibition paradigm in that the learning of A (and this may represent a one-trial affair) is a function of previous experience with B.

Mediation in transfer. A third concept must be included before we are ready to consider the role of past experience in present behavior. This concept, too, we have already met (see p. 98 f). It is the notion of "mediation." For our present purposes, we need only appreciate that the learning of A may be facilitated if A is already related to some other material or concept, C, which is also related to B. In effect, an association between B and C can lead more effectively to some behavior A if A also is associated with C. This is really a special case of Hebb's phase sequences becoming related through common relation to a third sequence. Thus, a person who has opened sardine cans with a little wind-up device that accompanies the can, and who has squeezed a tube of toothpaste that soon adopts a wrinkled and rough pattern, might think of a smoothly rolled tube. This in turn might initiate phase sequences of smooth-rolling, wind-up items. The concept of the sardine can might occur, and an invention is born. Obviously such an invention depends on past experience with two separate affairs even though no specific past experience relative to the solution of the problem could be available until after the invention. Such phase sequences as that of thinking of "something rolling up smoothly" can be considered as mediators. They are intervening activities which, based on past experience, unite other past experiences or some feature of the past with a feature of the present.

Armed with the principles of mediation, generalization, early and late learning differences, and the laboratory schema of proactive inhibition, or perhaps better, simply proaction, we are ready to meet the problem of the *transfer of training*.

THE TRANSFER OF TRAINING

The influence of early experience on later-life performance. Experimental attacks on the influence of early experience on later behavior are comparatively new in psychology. The difficulties involved in such an experiment are numerous and complex, and it is no wonder that psychologists have hesitated to embark on programs which by their nature involve long waiting periods for the subjects to grow and age. Experimental control over human infants is, of course, precluded by social restrictions and recourse has been had to animal subjects. When animal subjects are used we have to interpret age levels in terms of life expectancies of the species without full confidence that life patterns unfold in other organisms in the same way as they do in man. We consider a rat of six months too old for ordinary experiments but we do not really know how "old" a six-month rat is. By the time we come to test an animal whose early history has been tampered with, we may not know how many changes have taken place in its behavioral repertoire as a consequence of the tampering so that a pure case is almost impossible to arrange. Thus, in Riesen's (1947) experiments with chimpanzees reared in darkness (see p. 394) we do not know to what extent other sensory modes have come to operate to compensate for lack of vision. We do not have a simple case of functional blindness alone.

The second difficulty is perhaps of even greater consequence. We do not yet know what to test for. The changes involved may be motivational, intellectual, or temperamental. Adequate tests are not available for all possible changes that might be developed by different practices of rearing infant and young organisms. If no change is found in maze learning and we make no other tests, we may be tempted to conclude that no intellectual differences are present. Discrimination tests, on the other hand, might show up differences not found in a maze or other type of problem. Tests of temperament and motivation are as yet poorly developed. It may be some time before we have even an approximation of the effect of early experience on later life patterns. The experiments we shall review must be considered, then, as voyages of exploration into a relatively new territory which has already been endowed by our imaginations with various components.

Beach and Jaynes (1954) have contributed a valuable review of the studies dealing with the effects of early experience on sensory and perceptual functions, reproduction, social and emotional behavior. Their review of early *learning* experience is rather brief, however, and we will have to amplify it here. At the same time we will not attempt to cover the nonlearning areas that they discuss.

Sensory deprivation, perception, and learning. It is not our purpose to attempt a treatment of the many-sided problem of perception. The subject is being attacked by physiologists, phenomenologists, social and clinical psychologists, and almost everyone but learning psychologists. The principles advanced by learning theorists usually are grand attempts to account for all behavior, including perception. Their choice of explanatory principles, however, avoids the traditional introspective and phenomenological language associated with the area of perception. Except for the case of Tolman, one might find it difficult to appreciate that learning psychologists had any concern with perceptual problems. Yet Hull (1952) and Skinner (1953) have by no means voted perception out of their province.

While nonlearning psychologists are usually willing to admit a large if not an overwhelming importance to learning factors in the development of perception, the learning psychologists themselves have pretty generally assumed that perception is primarily a matter of learning. In point of fact, there has been but little experimental investigation of perceptual problems by learning psychologists. They have set the area aside for future study. In the meantime, perception is generally regarded as a matter of *discriminated* response. This amounts to saying that an organism perceives a stimulus when it is able to or does make a specific response to it that is not made to other Ss. Such a proposition may be found unsatisfactory by those concerned with identifying perception with some kind of awareness or other internal activity as Allport (1955) remarks. On the other hand, any objection to this view involves a conflict about the nature of the most proper approach to the scientific study of psychology.

We do not propose to get involved in a debate on this issue at this time. We can recognize that the learning psychologist is operating at a level of assumption and that his experiments in discrimination situations are still at an elementary level. Our real interest at the moment is to consider the limited investigations designed to evaluate how learning affects perception in early life. Perhaps these investigations will open new pathways to the study of more involved perceptual behavior.

The basic question which we can ask now is: What does a newborn infant perceive? For William James (1890) the "experience" of a baby was a "booming, buzzing confusion." It might well be a confusion, but the booming and buzzing might better be put down to poetic license than to scientific observation. For the learning psychologist, at least for what James would have called a "hardheaded" one, the "experience" of the newborn baby is a large *nothing*. We cannot presume that the baby sees, hears, feels, or enjoys any "sensations" whatever. Hebb (1949) has brought this assumption to our consideration most strikingly with his description of the clinical findings of Von Senden.

Von Senden studied the visual behavior of people born with cataracts who had the cataracts removed in later life. According to his findings, such patients, when they recover from the operation, have reasonably adequate eyes. Yet they cannot react to visual stimuli with any approximation to efficiency. For practical purposes, they are still blind. It should not be forgotten that these patients do have other sensorimotor associations with sounds, odors, and cutaneous stimuli, and have some language that has visual connotations. Thus, a blind man can describe a line, curve, or angle in terms of touch. Apparently, visual stimuli in the form of lines and angles (changes of direction) may affect the patient so that he is able to report that "something," a "figure," is "out there" but it is quite impossible for the patient to describe this something as an object of any kind. On the contrary, it appears that weeks, months, and years must pass before such a patient can learn to see adequately. There is some reason to believe that color is reacted to from the first, but what this reaction amounts to is difficult to understand. Color names are learned fairly quickly, according to Hebb. This may be so with adult patients. Children may also re-act to color (Munn, 1938) fairly early in life but color naming is a longer affair.

Numerous questions can be raised (Wertheimer, 1951) about the Von Senden data and it may be that some of the patients he de-scribes were feeble-minded or had additional visual defects. On the other hand, some of them may have had some minimal visual experi-ence in early life before the cataracts formed. Von Senden does not settle the issue.

The study of Riesen (1947, 1950) with chimpanzees raised in dark-ness seems more in line with experimental requirements. Such chim-panzees, when brought out into the light, give every appearance of complete blindness (even though they later respond visually like other chimpanzees). They do not "see" their feeding bottles, nor large disks which are equipped with a shocking device so that the visual stimulus can serve as a CS for an avoidance response. Normal chimpanzees learn to avoid the disk in one trial. The dark-reared require a great many trials before showing any avoidance.

Other experiments have been reported in which other animals have been brought up in the dark with similar results. (Riesen and Kurke, 1954, brought up cats; Hebb, 1937, rats, and Towe, 1954, pigeons.) In general the results confirm the Von Senden generalization al-though rats appear to gain visual control over the environment very quickly (15 minutes).

Other senses have not been studied so extensively as vision. Nissen, Chow, and Semmes (1951) report rearing chimpanzees with their arms and hands encased in tubes which prevented any cutaneous ex-ploration with the hands. Cutaneous sensitivity seemed to be greatly impaired when the cuffs were removed. Grooming behavior was not observed in such subjects although it is a prominent part of a chim-panzee's repertoire.

Hebb, Heath, and Stuart (1954) attempted some preliminary ob-servations on experimental deafness but used adult humans for his subjects. The subjects became extremely irritable and distressed but suffered no apparent permanent effects from the relatively short pe-riods of deafness. Experiments with rats (Wolf, 1943) whose ears were sealed at birth show a deficiency in auditory learning when the ears are "made whole."

The import of the experiments described above is to suggest that we *learn* to perceive. From this point of view, perceiving behavior is subject to the same kinds of principles as any other kind of behavior. As we go higher in the animal scale, learning to perceive takes up more and more time in the developmental life of an infant. The basic discriminations are built up slowly in the early years. When a subject is old enough to talk about his "perceptions" he has already learned a great deal. Learning at an adult stage makes use of this early learning and depends upon it. The fact that such learning goes on, to a considerable degree, before a language stage is reached makes it difficult to discover just what a subject brings with him to an experimental session. Presumably this perceptual learning continues through life as we learn to make finer and finer discriminations. Experimentally we run into trouble in determining any kind of "zero point" from which to start measuring learning. Our subjects have been learning since they were born and perhaps even before this (Spelt, 1948).

With this somewhat lengthy parenthesis we can turn to experiments involving early learning where sensory deprivation is not involved to the same extremes as in the studies just considered. In the experiments we will now examine, the basic concern was with restricting behavior or performance more than the sensory mechanisms. We may find these more pertinent to our basic interest.

One of the best known studies of the influence of infantile experience is that of Hunt (1941) who studied hoarding behavior in young rats. Young rats were deprived of food for two weeks just after weaning, that is, their diets were restricted. Five months later they were given an opportunity to hoard food pellets and proceeded to hoard more than litter-mate controls. Here we have an example of infantile frustration affecting behavior at an adult level. The behavior is normally interpreted as motivational in nature, but we can assume some learning effects. Anderson and Smith (1926) in a much earlier study had found that if infant rats were deprived of food, they showed greater activity and greater learning ability for mazes as adults. Christie (1952) deprived infant rats not only of food, but also of water and found them superior learners as adults in maze problems with food and water reinforcers. When newborn rats were deprived of oxygen (Meier and Bunch, 1950) in the first three hours of life, they showed some deficiency in learning to make appropriate turns in a T-maze in later life. Another form of what might be called "rough treatment" in infancy, the administration of electroconvulsive shock (Porter, Stone, and Ericksen, 1948) also resulted in learning deficiencies in later life in a group of white rats. The small permanent decrement in learning was attributed by the experimenters to probable brain damage. This conclusion is supported by Hurder and Sanders (1953) who did a similar study.

The experiments mentioned above are samples of a variety of studies designed to determine the effect of one kind of intense stimulation or biological deprivation in infancy on later behavior. We are more concerned, however, with studies relating to more behavioral factors, deprivation of stimulation, poverty or richness of environment, early practice opportunities, and so on. Since the publication of Hebb's *The Organization of Behavior* (1949) a number of interesting studies in this area have appeared. As we have already discovered, Hebb makes much of infantile and childhood experience and is responsible for several experiments in this area himself as well as developing a program of research into this problem at McGill. It is to these experiments that we now turn.

In one of these McGill experiments by Clarke *et al.* (1951), six dogs of a Scottish terrier strain were raised (from the close of the weaning period) under different circumstances. Three of the dogs were brought up in normal surroundings, one as a pet at home, the other two as laboratory pets. The other three dogs were raised in a box so constructed as to prevent any vision of the outside world. These three dogs saw only each other and the sides of the box as their "environment." Except for feeding and cleaning periods, they had no contact with humans. At the age of 7½ months, they were released from the box and given the freedom of the laboratory. Two and one-half months later the dogs were given a variety of temperamental and intellectual tests.

In temperamental tests, the restricted dogs showed more subordination in a fighting-for-a-bone test, more "following" behavior, more indifference to strange dogs, less activity in a "stress" situation (watching another dog eat outside a cage when those inside had been deprived for 24 hours), more exploratory activity in a strange environment, more interest in going along with the experimenter to test situations (the "free environment" dogs would tend to run off about their own investigations).

Intellectually, in an *Umweg* problem, none of the restricted dogs reacted correctly in five trials, free dogs averaged three correct solutions and showed more variability in going around a barrier from either side. In a closed field maze test, the free environment dogs were strikingly superior. Even in a stunt such as rolling over, the restricted dogs required an average of 34 trials to learn what the free environment dogs learned in 16. In a ramp-climbing problem (selecting the correct from two ramps which were placed in such a position that one led to the top of a feeding table and the other fell short), the restricted animals averaged 192 errors to the 144 errors of the free dogs.

In a further study of a similar nature, Thompson and Heron (1954a)[1] raised twenty Scottish terriers with three different degrees of restriction, some in a small wooden box with lights on alternate days only, others in cages which permitted only a view of the laboratory ceiling. A third group, mildly restricted, was kept in cages with fronts and tops uncovered; the dogs could look out at the area in front of the cage and had occasional contact with humans. The dogs were taken out of isolation before 1 year of age. The animals were tested in a free environment atmosphere at different periods in their lives (9–10 months, 1½–2 years, 2–4 years) and observations of their general activity were made in bare simple rooms and in a maze situation employing a double-alternation type of structure (although double alternation was not studied). The animals were merely observed for activity for 10-minute periods. The general conclusions of the observers were that the restricted animals showed a significantly greater amount of activity than did the less restricted. (This is interpreted as reflecting exploratory tendencies or curiosity.) The more severe the restriction, the more exploration. Younger animals explored more than the older animals.

In another series of studies, rats were raised in a variety of environments during infancy and then observed as young adults in a variety of test situations. In one of these experiments, Hymovitch (1952) repeated an early experiment of Hebb's (1949) in which rats were blinded in infancy and compared in maze problems with rats blinded at maturity. Hebb found results favoring the rats blinded later in life. Hymovitch confirmed Hebb's findings although his results were not clear-cut. Hymovitch, however, introduced the variation of raising the animals in either free or restricted environments. Restricted rats were raised in stovepipe cages, mesh cages, and enclosed activity wheels. In one experiment rats that were first raised in stovepipe cages were then given free environment experience while a "free environment" group was transferred to stovepipe quarters. Free environment rats were consistently superior to restricted rats and those with early free-

---

[1] A more detailed report is available in another publication by the same authors. See Thompson and Heron, 1954b.

dom were superior to those with later free environment experience.

Donald and Janet Forgays (1952) repeated Hymovitch's work in an attempt to discover factors that work to improve the performance of a free environment rearing. They compared group of rats which were restricted to various degrees with free environment rats. Some of the free environment rats were provided playthings (simple metal and wooden structures), others simply had the run of a relatively large enclosure (4 by 2 feet). The animals were tested on the Hebb-Williams (1946) maze designed to evaluate animal intelligence. Free environment rats with playthings were most superior in the test. The other free environment rats were superior to all varieties of restricted groups. The Forgays conclude: "There seems to be little doubt that free environment experience in early life is reflected in the adult rat by problem solving ability superior to that of rats reared under restricted conditions."

In another free environment study, Forgus (1954) compared the learning scores of three groups of rats brought up under the following circumstances when they were 24 to 84 days old.

Group I: Full free environment with "playthings" available.

Group II: In center of a free environment box but separated from playthings by glass walls.

Group III: Bare black box with one light bulb for illumination.

When tested in a multiple-choice maze, a visual form discrimination, and a problem-solving situation, the rats of Group III were found inferior to the other two groups. Curiously enough, Group II seemed as good as or better than Group I especially on the visual form discrimination test.

The excellent learning of Group II proved paradoxical to Forgus and he repeated the experiment (Forgus 1955) with a modified test. He reasoned that the opportunity for motor activity should have provided a background for better learning but that his former method of evaluation was inadequate for bringing out the superiority of the first group. In the new experiment one group of rats was allowed to gain experience with playthings in a free environment while the other group could only see the objects, being separated from them by plastic walls. At 85 days of age the animals were tested in an 11-unit T-maze. In the early, preliminary training, visual cues could be used and both groups learned equally well. Then the lights were turned out and learning continued in the dark. The animals that had the complex motor experience in early life now proved to be superior to the group that had no such experience. Forgus concludes that the influence of early experience can only be observed when appropriate tests are used and that misunderstanding and controversy arise from the use of inappropriate measures.

Two experiments done at the University of Mississippi by Griffiths and Stringer (1952) and by Bingham and Griffiths (1952) also bear on the transfer problem although they were done in connection with somewhat different purposes, that is, to see how early strong stimulation might affect later reactions to other situations. In the first experiment rats were subjected to loud sounds, rapid rotation, freezing at 10° C. in a refrigerator, heating, and electric shock. The stimulation took place from birth until 57 days of age. At 60 days of age, the animals were tested for maze learning, discrimination, and emotionality. No significant differences were found from control animals. It should be noted here that although the stimuli were relatively extreme, they were presented for brief daily intervals and were not specifically related to the behavior involved in later tests. The second study by Bingham and Griffiths was designed to extend earlier observations by Hebb (1949) on rats raised at home in the care of Hebb's children. The home-reared rats later proved superior to laboratory-reared rats. In the Bingham-Griffiths study some rats were raised in a free environment (a 6 by 9-foot room), others in "squeeze boxes" (2 by 5 by 4 inches), still others in ordinary animal cages. At 51 days all the animals were transferred to standard cages for 14 days and testing began to determine the effects of the different early environments. The free environment rats were found superior in maze learning but no differences were found in temperament, discriminatory learning (Lashley jumping stand), or susceptibility to sound-induced seizures.

The effects of practice. Although we customarily assume that "practice" explains to a considerable degree the level of skill of various types of performance, and we see the evidence of practice in basketball, golf, and playing the piano, we have actually very little purified evidence about the effects of practice. It is easy enough to talk about practice, but to demonstrate how practice itself works, when and how it works, is another matter. The practice variable should not be confused with "frequency" (see p. 283). Learning curves sometimes are called "practice" curves but about all that we can say for certain about such curves is that they will normally rise above a starting point if learning does take place. The appearance of plateaus in some curves appears to suggest that practice is, for the time being, not showing any effect. Erratic rises and falls in individual curves make interpretation difficult. It is awkward to invoke practice to explain a drop in a learning curve.

In the light of the general acceptance of practice as an important determiner of performance, it is surprising how few studies have been devoted to a study of this variable in itself. This is not to discount the enormous number of studies in which practice effects have been observed and reported. It is normally found, for example, that subjects continue to improve in learning nonsense syllables if they proceed to learn successive lists. We have already cited (see p. 326) the studies by Bugelski (1942), Underwood (1945), and the more extensive study by Ward (1937) who found continued improvement over 16 trials although most of the improvement had occurred by trial 6 or 7 (see Fig. 8.3, p. 189). Reports have also been made of similar effects in maze learning by rats that become "maze-wise" so they learn succeeding mazes with more and more ease. Here we have, presumably, some benefits accruing to the learner from improving his *methods* of learning since there is no benefit from the materials. Techniques of learning seem to be the medium through which the learning improves although none of the reports on practice effects spell out the actual mechanisms involved.

The first real break in an appreciation of practice has been provided by a number of studies by Harlow (1949, 1950). In these studies monkeys are offered a choice of two objects on a tray. Under one of these objects, a food reward will be found. The objects vary in color, texture, size, shape, and so on. Harlow undertook to compare the performances of monkeys on 344 such separate choice situations. Thus, a monkey is offered one pair for as many as 50 trials with the position of the positive object varied and random. The first problem takes a number of trials to solve but is eventually mastered. The animal is then given a new problem, then another, and so on. As the problems continue, the animal gets better and better at solving them until by the two hundredth problem, the task is no longer a problem. The monkey solves the problem in one trial. Should he make a chance error (the chances are even that he will) on the first trial, the second choice will be correct. Harlow found similar performances by brain-damaged monkeys and by children. Later his monkeys were trained with discrimination reversal problems in the same fashion. Now the arrangement was such that whichever object was positive on one trial would be negative on the next. Again the monkeys had trouble with the first problems. As the problems continued the monkeys improved until again they reached the level of one-trial solutions. Harlow professed to have no explanation of these findings and contented himself by labeling the results as a demonstration of "learning how to learn" or the "formation of learning sets." The label, however, does not help much and we should inquire somewhat beyond the label.

The fact of the easy late learning gets in the way of an understanding by misdirecting attention. The place to look for an explanation is at the other end, the time of difficulty for the monkey. The first problems are difficult to solve and it is this difficulty that calls for explanation. Why cannot the monkey solve the first problem easily?

One factor in any kind of choice experiments involving naïve animals is the vexing "position habit." The animal turns left or right and thereafter may continue in one of these directions for a long number of trials. Sometimes some other cue, such as color, is hit upon, and a subject may persistently react to one of a number of colors, regardless of the fact that it is not always followed by reinforcement. Krechevsky (1932) has dignified this type of behavior by calling it the "trying out of *hypotheses*." Sometimes an animal persists so much in a fixed pattern as to discourage the experimenter to the point of discarding the subject. One factor in maintaining a position habit or other fixed reaction is that every so often, if the experimenter is varying the position of a reinforcement, the animal will be reinforced for reacting in a fixed manner. This amounts to a partial reinforcement pattern and is consequently difficult to extinguish. We can imagine that Harlow's monkeys were victims of the position habit in the early phases of training. As Hebb (1949, p. 117) points out, a concept of left and right is hard enough for humans to develop and we can conceive of a naïve monkey having no end of trouble developing even a rudimentary concept of direction and alternation with regard to some other aspect of the stimulus situation. It is possible that the animal could solve the problem more easily if the reward was always on one side for the first few trials. In this way a positional cue might be better discriminated and subsequently extinguished more easily. How the monkey finally comes to extinguish the position habit is still a question for study. But there are other features of the situation to consider. Harlow complicated the problem for the monkey by introducing simultaneously a difference between the objects in color, brightness, shape, and size. The animal might have a better chance if only one variable were present because Harlow was asking the monkey to react to "a thing in itself" rather than to some sensory stimulation. In effect, the monkey is asked to extinguish responses to each of the several possible ways in which the objects differ. Thus, if the negative object is blue and this feature momentarily dominates the stimulus situation, the animal must extinguish blue. On a later trial it may have to extinguish a size-relationship—the negative object may be larger. Subsequently, pattern, texture, or any other feature may be momentarily dominant and will have to be extinguished. If the objects are similar in a feature, there will be generalized reinforcement to the negative from the reinforced object, and learning will be delayed.

We cannot pretend this analysis is adequate or even appropriate in the absence of experimental demonstration. However, experiments in concept formation indicate how the problem of acquiring a concept magnifies with the addition of variables. Assuming the correctness of the argument, however, we can conclude that Harlow's monkeys learned how to learn the particular problem form in which they were being trained. How well they would operate in other kinds of problems remains to be seen. Possibly the techniques acquired here might carry over to some other types of problem, but Harlow's monkeys are more than likely narrow specialists. Their curriculum has been over-concentrated with one type of problem. A little experience in solving mechanical puzzles goes a long way in solving other mechanical puzzles as the author has found with numerous classes. Succeeding puzzles of equal difficulty are mastered more and more easily. Students report that they "get the principle" of the puzzles, but their behavior follows the learning pattern of the monkeys. They too learn how to learn, but the experience seems to be limited to the special problem at hand.

We are still without thorough and systematic understanding of the universally acknowledged "practice effect." In subsequent sections of this chapter we will note the operation of practice in other phases of the transfer question. In this section we have already noted a number of considerations that help make insight, one-trial learning, and problem-solving somewhat easier to comprehend in terms of the influence of prior experience.

The kinds of materials. From what kinds of previous experience can we anticipate some effect on present or future behavior? Are there any experiences at all that do not in one way or another affect later reactions? The psychologists' basic assumption, of course, is that all current or future activity is dependent upon what came before. Our present concern is somewhat limited by our more specific subject of learning and so we will try to stick with experimental demonstrations of the influence of learning experiences on future learning, even though the temptation to broaden the scope of the inquiry is constantly present.

The present topic is complicated by aspects of proaction already discussed, such as practice and the nature of early learning. It is further complicated by the fact of inhibitory or negative effects and we will have to proceed carefully if the analysis is to prove fruitful. One element of confusion, that of procedures or techniques, must be disposed of immediately. It is obvious that any learning situation will involve a stimulus complex which will be more or less novel to the subject, and to the extent that the novelty of the circumstances is effective in delaying the learning of some preliminary material, adjustment to this novelty will represent a gain or savings in a subsequent problem in the future. Before subjects in a psychological experiment can begin to react appropriately they have to be reassured that they are not going to be hurt, forced to reveal inadequacies, or private beliefs and feelings, and so on. Unsophisticated sophomores, like naïve rats, require some taming. Taming time must be subtracted from learning time, and this source of variation must be eliminated from the analysis of the benefits of exposure to prior materials in the later test situation.

Assuming the transfer of method (and this includes negative possibilities such as are encountered when some contradictory habit must be learned later) what do we have to say about the transfer of content? Here we have the heart of the transfer problem as we presented it earlier. Does learning one kind of material affect the learning of another? What kinds of materials have been considered in the laboratory?

The consideration of the transfer possibilities of content might be organized effectively by classifying the kinds of materials dealt with in the laboratory in terms of stimuli and responses, and the more general kinds of learning materials such as motor skills, serial reactions, paired associates, and rote or meaningful material.

a. **The influence of prior experience with the stimuli involved.** The concept of a stimulus is not a simple one as it ordinarily involves some response whether this is noted or unobserved. Thus a nonsense syllable is usually treated as both stimulus and response in a serial list, sometimes as a stimulus in paired-associate learning, sometimes as a response in paired-associated presentations (see Gibson, p. 328). So a bell, a light, a shock are also stimuli but some kind of response is usually assumed to occur. We cannot hope to make a clear and clean dichotomy of stimulus and response here, but some studies indicate that familiarity with the stimuli, in terms of previous experience, may affect future learning. Thus Hovland and Kurtz (1952) showed that preliminary familiarization with specific nonsense syllables was helpful in later learning of the syllables when these were arranged in serial lists. It is a common practice in the laboratory to first shock animal subjects in the absence of any other cues if they are to learn to make specific avoidance responses later in connection with some other cue, such as a light. In training rats to press Skinner bars, preliminary training is frequently given in which the clicking of the automatic feeding mechanism is associated with eating behavior. The effects of sensory preconditioning (see p. 256) seem to be achieving some acceptability in this connection.

On the negative side, any extinction procedure serves to illustrate the role of the stimulus which has been associated with some positive reaction and which is now being presented in a manner calculated to result in elimination of that role and the possible adoption of a new one. In Chapter 11 we noted that if the stimuli are nonsense syllables in paired associates and new responses are to be learned to the old stimuli, considerable difficulty is experienced in learning the new reactions. The difficulty appears to increase as the *number* of new reactions is increased. In one study, Bugelski (1948) asked subjects to learn 10 successive lists in which the stimuli were identical but the responses varied with each new list. The learning became progressively worse until by the tenth list almost nothing was being learned relative to the first. Here we have proactive inhibition at its best, or worst.

b. Familiarity or experience with the responses to be learned. The rat that learns to jump to a shock alone and later finds a light paired with the shock learns more readily, as has just been mentioned. Similarly a rat that has learned to press a horizontal Skinner bar is able to learn to press a vertical bar more readily in the same or another box (Ellson, 1938). In considering the matter of familiarity with the response, we run into a problem of some perplexity because the nature of the actual response is frequently unspecified. Are two rats pressing

Skinner bars making the same kind of response? Sometimes a rat presses with one paw or the other or both or with his head, teeth, and so on. We have already discussed the problem of act versus movement (see p. 84) and the variety of questions this problem raises. Similarly, if a monkey opens a box with one paw and then has that arm paralyzed (Jacobsen, 1933), should we wonder if he opens it with another paw or a foot? Lashley appears to have found much to wonder about in this connection. Hebb (1949, p. 153) sees the problem as one of mediation and of "motor equivalence." According to Hebb, much of our early learning consists of bringing a limb from any position in which it happens to be to some point in the line of sight. As the learner grows older he acquires a repertoire of control over his visual-motor patterns of action such that any part of the body can be brought to bear on the line of sight. The story is told of Paderewski that on one occasion some fellow musicians tried to surprise the master by asking him to play a composition which at one place contained 11 notes to be played simultaneously. Paderewski began to play and, as he reached the critical chords, he bent over and tapped the eleventh key with his nose, proceeding clamly on to the end. In terms of "motor equivalence" the performance is understandable even if startling. We have already encountered the problem of mediation and motor equivalence in a number of experiments (see p. 142) and can rest this part of the case after reviewing some common laboratory experiments which make use of distortions of perception by means of mirrors or prisms which force the student subject to modify his normal reactions to visual cues. Thus, in mirror drawing, the subject finds himself unable to trace the pattern of a familiar geometric form when he sees it reflected in a mirror. As he continues to practice his skill improves until he is almost as good at mirror tracing as with normal vision. At this point he is able to "transfer" the skill to his left or unpracticed hand and presumably could do so to his left foot. There is nothing surprising about such transfer, as obviously what is being transferred is not the skill acquired by the right hand but a more general kind of response system which functions as a "motor equivalence" or mediation system. This system amounts to having a new control pattern involving the line of sight. Any previous habits associated with the line of sight become incorporated into the new systems. It takes a number of trials to overcome the brief mirror-tracing practice. Hull (1934b) has attempted a similar account of motor equivalence in his concept of the habit-family hierarchy wherein the mediating agent is an *rg* which is common to numerous responses capable of achieving a final goal response. The experiments of Stratton (1896) and Ewert (1930) on reversing the visual field should be considered in this connection, along with the more common laboratory experiment of learning to aim at targets under water or when viewed through prisms. Here again we note "transfer" when the subjects allegedly acquire the "principle" involved. In the present framework, these experiments again illustrate a mediating process involving a newly acquired motor equivalence.

What happens when subjects learn exactly the same response to a series of different stimuli? The general findings appear to be that efficiency is increased, the learning getting better and better as the stages of new stimulus-old response continue. Here we are obviously gaining from familiarity with the response pattern. How this familiarity operates to our advantage cannot yet be appreciated but apparently some kind of facilitation over the final common path is acquired by repetitions of the responses which permits the reactions to be more readily associated with new stimuli. Perhaps we have here, in addition, some benefits from systematic discrimination of the irrelevant stimuli which might be perplexing to the learner, just as we imagined this to be the case with Harlow's monkeys.

When new responses are not identical but only similar we may have negative transfer, as we saw earlier in connection with Osgood's laws (see p. 327 f). The nature of negative transfer is difficult to predict because of what Osgood (1949) refers to as the "similarity paradox." Some place along the hypothetical continuum from identity through "neutrality" to opposite there is first positive transfer. As identity changes into similarity we begin to get negative transfer; then, as we approach neutrality, the negative effects get smaller (see Figs. 12.2 and 12.3, pp. 329–330).

c. MOTOR SKILLS AND TRANSFER. How does learning one skill, say typing, transfer to some other, for example, piano playing? In this kind of comparison we have little to offer from the laboratory. Some modest experimentation has been done with visual-motor tasks but nothing of significance has yet emerged to throw light on our problem. In one experiment (Gagne and Foster, 1949) subjects first learned to respond in a variety of ways in a pencil-and-paper situation and later made actual motor adjustments—handling various controls when appropriate signals were given in a simulated machine-control situation. Positive transfer was observed. The whole question of simulated training involves the question of transfer. Training prospective pilots on the ground in the well-known Link trainer has proved to be effective (Williams, 1949), as has training on a number of complicated military weapon simulators (Wolfle, 1945). In some cases the designers of the simulator have found such training inadequate or detrimental with negative effects. The high enthusiasm for simulators must be tempered by appreciation of what can and what cannot transfer.

d. MEANINGFUL MATERIAL AND PROACTION. There is considerable emphasis in some educational circles on the teaching of general principles as opposed to drill and rote learning practices. It is held that general principles can carry over or transfer whereas rote training is unlikely to do so. In spite of the firm conviction of "general educators," there is actually little empirical evidence on this question. The usual text harks back to an experiment by Judd (1908) on dart-throwing at a submerged target. Boys who were told about the principle of refraction did better on a new problem than a control group which merely practiced without being told the principle. To what extent knowledge of a principle can transfer to other situations than the one in which it is learned is a complex question. It is possible that the wrong principles may transfer to some new problem situation and prevent its solution, or a situation may exist in which appropriate cues as to the proper principles to apply are hidden or missing. The subject might find himself faced with a problem he cannot solve because he does not recognize it as one for which he is actually quite prepared. Persons with an elementary knowledge of algebra may not be able to solve a simple problem such as: What is the cost of a baseball if the baseball costs twice as much as a bat and the two together cost $1.11? If the individual does not say to himself something along the lines of "Ah, this is an algebra situation—involving one unknown," he may start toying with various imagined costs and go through an empirical approach which delays solution.

It is likely that general principles or "meanings" can transfer to the extent that the learner can also be taught to recognize situations involving general principles and also to recognize situations in which they do not apply. Thus far experimental attacks have proceeded along the lines of solving puzzles which involve similar relationships, cryptograms, and similar problems. McGeoch and Irion (1952) review a number of these studies. Broader investigations of this problem still remain to be made.

e. SIMILARITY AS A FACTOR IN TRANSFER. It will be recalled from the discussion of similarity factors in retention (see p. 324) that the transfer of content and methods or techniques is not a random affair but depends on the relationships between the materials in question. The chief relationship is that of similarity. We have already discussed the awkward problem of the definition of similarity and can do little more to clarify the matter here. All we can be sure about is the first degree of similarity, that of *identity*. Thorndike and Woodworth (1901), as noted earlier, concluded that whatever transfer takes place is a function of identity—identity of control, method, technique, and so on. Since their investigation we have learned to include in the concept of identity some notions of *functional* identity which we derived from the concept of generalization. Thus, to the degree that one stimulus or response generalizes with others, we can expect transfer effects, positive or negative depending on whether the stimuli or responses are involved. Specifying the degree of similarity (or generalization) in advance is impossible and always must be determined by preliminary investigation. Once a scale is derived, however, experimental findings (Yum, 1931; Gibson, 1941; Bruce, 1933; Hamilton, 1943) indicate that positive transfer is a function of the degree of similarity between stimuli (if responses are the same), and negative transfer is a function of the degree of difference between the responses if the stimuli are the same (see p. 330). If, for example, animals are trained to go left on a T-maze for one stimulus condition and right for another, they learn this habit with relative ease compared to the difficulty they have in later learning to do the opposite. Hunter (1932) found the learning of the second habit to take almost three times as long as the first. Rats learn mazes quite easily in which all correct turns are in the same direction. Each succeeding turn is mastered with greater ease (see Fig. 14.1). The similarity of response features is evident.

An experiment by Bruce (1933) illustrates the general conclusions drawn above. Bruce had subjects learn two sets of paired associate nonsense syllables. The syllables making up the two sets were arranged to include all the following possibilities in all possible combinations: both stimuli identical, stimuli similar (one letter changed), stimuli different (all three letters different), responses identical, responses similar, and responses different. The different combinations of the second pairs were learned after 2, 6, or 12 repetitions of the first material, introducing a variable of amount of learning. Positive transfer increased with degree of learning. When responses were identical and stimuli similar, transfer was highest. When stimuli were different, negative transfer occurred with two trials but changed to a modest degree of positive transfer with continued trials. When responses were different but stimuli similar, negative transfer prevailed even with 12 trials. When all terms were different there was no effect with 2 trials, 6 trials yielded negative transfer, and 12 trials gave positive transfer. The results in general bear out the conclusions already described.

The similarity scale employed by Bruce amounted to changes in one letter of a three-letter nonsense syllable. Whether this meets the requirements of a generally acceptable definition might be debated. Other experiments employed rated degrees of similarity with a test of transfer in what amounts to a generalization test. Yum (1931) used rated synonyms in three degrees of rated similarity as stimuli in paired associates after original learning of paired word associates. Transfer effects were of the order of 50, 32, and 11 percent with the three degrees of stimulus similarity.

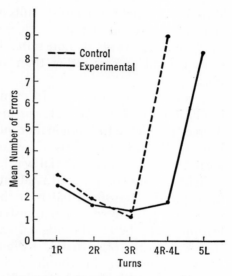

FIG. 14.1. A learning set in maze learning. Rats were trained in a serial fashion to learn first a right turn. When this was learned, the maze was expanded and another right turn was learned. After the rats learned to make three right turns, they were divided into control and experimental groups. The controls went on to learn a fourth right turn while the experimental group learned a left turn. The control learned a left turn at the fifth choice point. Note how learning improves for the second and third turns. Note, further, the difficulty when a left turn must be learned. (From B. Forester, 1955.)

Similarity in behavioral terms may be different from physical similarity. When words are used as stimuli, synonyms might look very different from the original terms, as, for example, "urn" and "vase." Homophones, like "urn" and "earn," might sound much, if not exactly, alike. Which are the more likely to transfer? Razran (1940) used both synonyms and homophones and found synonyms more effective in testing for conditioned salivary responses in humans. An interesting feature of some of Razran's experiments is that, like in some of the early Russian experiments, he found considerable transfer from actual physical stimuli to printed signs carrying word symbols of the original stimuli. The word "light" was effective when substituted for an original conditioned stimulus of a light. Razran's results are more in keeping with a mediation interpretation of transfer than with a generalization hypothesis, as these experiments demonstrate. The similarity here is in terms of some central process rather than along some dimension of a stimulus.

f. AMOUNT OF LEARNING. In examining the business of retroactive inhibition we observed that loss in retention was a function of the degree to which either original or interpolated (or both) material was learned. If the learning was of low or modest amount retroaction was greater than if either material was learned well. In transfer situations a slightly more complicated relationship seems to hold. If conditions favor positive transfer (that is, if the responses to be learned are the same or relatively so) then transfer varies positively with degree of learning. The better the original learning the higher the amount of transfer. On the other hand, if the conditions favor negative transfer (new responses to old stimuli or similar stimuli) then the results of experiments (Siipola and Israel, 1933; Bruce, 1933; Bugelski, 1942) indicate that negative transfer is greatest if the original material is learned rather poorly. If the material is learned well, the initial potential negative transfer is overcome and positive transfer effects are found. McGeoch and Irion (1952) suggest that the degree of learning of the later material is also to be considered. Negative transfer is greatest when both preliminary and secondary materials are learned to about the same degree. We have already noted that generalization experiments seem to follow a somewhat similar pattern in that generalization is greatest early in the learning with a diminution of generalization effects as training proceeds (Hovland, 1937).

Naturally, warm-up effects must be discounted or eliminated by sufficient intervals between the learning periods. It appears that the discriminability of materials (see Gibson, 1941) is a factor in negative transfer just as it is in reproductive interference.

Transposition and transfer. A special type of transfer has been studied in connection with the reactions of subjects to certain *relationships* between stimuli. Bingham (1913) appears to be the first to have called attention to such reactions, although in current literature they are made much of by the Gestalt psychologists. In Bingham's original experiment, chicks were trained to peck corn from a 6-inch circle and to avoid a 4-inch circle where the corn was glued to the pattern. In a later test with a 4-inch and 3-inch circle, the chicks chose the previously avoided 4-inch circle, demonstrating an apparent response to a relationship of "bigger than" although there might have been some other relationship present such as "brighter than" in the larger circle. Later experimenters have demonstrated similar capacities for chicks, rats, monkeys, and children to react to relationship of size and brightness. The usual Gestalt interpretation of such behavior is to assume its innateness as a normal operation, a given in perception. More behavioristically-minded psychologists would like to show the role of learning to be paramount here. Not much progress was made in this direction until Spence (1937, 1942b) analyzed the problem as one of an interaction between the effects of reinforcement and extinction and the generalization features of each. Spence assumed that, to take Bingham's example, reinforcement of the 6-inch circle would spread to all other sizes of circle within the normal perception span of the chick, including the 4-inch circle. The extinction of the 4-inch circle would also generalize and spread to all other sizes of circle also, including the 6-inch positive. The total excitatory strength of the 6-inch circle would then be much less than it would be if no extinction had taken place on the 4 inch. Because the inhibitory effects were generated on a 4-inch circle they could be expected to fall off more rapidly with increasing circle sizes than would the reinforcement effects from the 6-inch circle. But since the reinforcement effects at the extremes would be relatively minimal in strength, a point could be reached, at the extremes, where a smaller circle would have more excitatory strength than the next larger circle. Given a choice at the extreme, then, an animal trained originally to choose a large circle might well react positively to the smaller. Spence tested this hypothesis with chimpanzees. Kuenne (1946) and Alberts and Ehrenfreund (1949) repeated the experiment with young children. Both found some evidence for transposition effects along the lines of Spence's hypothesis, although Kuenne found that the effectiveness of transposition was a function of mental age. Older children showed no tendency to reverse their choices at the extremes of stimuli while younger children did. Here we have evidence, again, of a mediating process at work. The older children could, and did, abstract the principle and say to themselves: "It's the larger," and would then react accordingly. Spence's hypothesis has applicability, then, to lower mental age levels, but cannot operate effectively once language enters the picture.

Actually it is quite impossible to determine what should happen in transposition experiments according to deductions that might be drawn from gradients of excitation and inhibition. The nature of the deduction depends upon the kind of gradient one chooses to assume for the generalization of reinforcement and extinction. Spence chose to make his gradients follow a convex pattern (see Hilgard and Marquis, 1940, p. 191), and so he finds that at one extreme of a continuum there should be a reversal of choice. The learner, having been trained to select the larger of two objects, now chooses the smaller. Hull (1943), on the other hand, following Hovland's data, chose to picture his gradients as concave (negatively accelerated). How Spence's analysis would apply if he adopted Hull's concave gradients of generalization is debatable. It would appear that Spence could not maintain his original interpretation as the values of stimuli would be distributed quite differently so that there would be no possibility of reversals at the extremes. We have already noted that the whole business of generalization is by no means a settled affair, and we are not obliged to presume that the gradients operate in the fashion described by either Hull or Spence.

Hebb (1949) attempted a neurophysiological solution to the problem of transposition in the brightness dimension, which he admits may be of only limited value and probably would only apply at a level where mediated responses were not available. Hebb's solution is more nativistic than that of Spence in that it assumes a special mode of functioning of the neural elements involved in brightness discrimination. According to Hebb, an animal confronted with two brightnesses adapts to one when looking at that and then adapts to the other on changing fixation. The central nervous system is charged with the responsibility of reducing strong intensities and building up weak ones. As the animal changes fixation from one stimulus to the other, then, the central process consists of an adaptation change in one direction or the other. It is this change, argues Hebb, that is the real conditioned stimulus or basis for response. If the animal is rewarded for pecking when it undergoes a lowering of central adaptation, then it can respond appropriately to any pair of stimuli that involves such a lowering process. Hebb admits his views to be tentative and subject to revision as more information is accumulated. In any event, the capacity of an adult human for responding to relationships can readily be interpreted as the result of a mediation process involving language and strongly, if not completely, dependent upon language and learning. It is interesting, in this connection, to note that Woodworth (1938) and Osgood (1953) both explain the Gestalt principle of constancy in a similar fashion. According to their analysis, constancy depends upon a total effect, a comparison between a figure and its ground. If the illumination of both figure and ground is reduced in proportion, they will retain a constant *ratio* of illumination and a subject can confidently report a constant figure. In the choice of a 6-inch over a 4-inch S we might posit a similar ratio factor as the real S. Any change of the actual stimuli would be somewhat irrelevant if the relationship between them remained stable and if it could be assumed that the ratio of stimulation was the effective element in the learning. While Gestaltists might consider this reference to ratios as equivalent to their own views, Hebb would probably make this out to be a specific type of stimulation in a specific brain area and safely within a broadly conceived S-R framework. Until we know more about transposition on both a behavioral and neural level, it is unlikely that we can make any generalizations or predictions that will hold. We must leave this problem to the future.

Insight, one-trial learning, and practice effects. With the problem of transposition "parked" behind us we can return to the general questions raised at the beginning of this chapter. Are we in a better position to understand insight and one-trial learning? How about practice effects? Mediation, generalization, learning-how-to-learn seem adequate principles to handle these questions to some degree. When the proper phase sequences have been separately learned, one-trial association is made possible for some kinds of phase sequences. Without such sequences, learning will be prolonged and amount to learning the phase sequences separately. The ease with which familiar responses are learned to new stimuli argues strongly for the point. The characteristic rapid learning of the adult now seems less mysterious, perhaps, than before. The adult has spent his entire previous life in learning the elements that will take only a short time to combine. An adult can quickly learn that a specific person is named John Smith. He already knows the name. He has merely to associate it with a given stimulus pattern. A child must also learn the name itself. The impatience of the adult at the slow learning of the child seems to be a lack of appreciation of the difficulty of some kinds of tasks for children. Before the child can write he must have language. Before he can eat with a fork, he must learn to eat with his fingers, and only gradually can he learn to use other tools. Even chopsticks can be manipulated by an occidental adult with only a little practice. He has had previous experience with other elements in similar pickup situations.

About "insight" we have already said a good deal (see p. 299). For the moment we can see how one-trial learning and insight can be considered together as manifestations of the same general principle of combining suitable past experiences. Harlow's college-trained monkeys might easily be considered as showing "insight" on problem 344. On problem 3 they were quite uninsightful. The visitor to Harlow's laboratory could hardly recognize the monkeys as being of the same species if he saw one at the beginning of training and another at the end of the course. Insight is usually equated with sudden, one-trial learning, or as behavior that changes after a successful trial. To the extent that it can be shown how previous experiences have entered into the "solution" of a problem, to that extent we can account for some cases of "insight." Along with insight and one-trial learning we can also appreciate why "meaningful" material is acquired more easily than nonsense material. Meaningful material presumably involves mediating responses. The problem is partly if not completely learned before the subject begins to learn. Meaningful material is familiar material, material in which certain stimuli and responses are already available for use and require only a putting together. With the aid of previously acquired mediating responses, learning proceeds apace. Here we find the basis of all mnemonic devices or memory trainers. The subject associates the new material with old or tries to reduce the new to the old. To the extent that he is able to select the appropriate old material, he can successfully remember. If the new girl's name is "Joy" and the first association is "She's a joy to behold," there is no problem in learning the name. Of course, in an instance of this sort there is little likelihood of not learning. Anyone who is a joy to behold is not likely to meet with much "interference." We use mediating devices whether we wish to or not. Associations always occur, the problem is to make them work for instead of against us. Woodworth (1938) gives a number of examples of how student subjects manipulate mediating responses in associating paired associates. Just as we can have insight and one-trial learning in some instances, so can we have complete failure and extensive difficulties from inadequate or inappropriate associations. A student named Woodward always presented a problem to the writer because the first association with him was: name of a psychologist. Unfortunately, the names of Underwood and Woodworth kept recurring inappropriately whenever the occasion arose for calling on the student by name.

The benefits of practice seem also to be more readily appreciated. The question boils down to *practice for what?* We can see how practice can help or hinder depending on how far it goes (see p. 310) and on what is being practiced (Harlow, 1950). At the same time we see how generalization allows us vicariously to practice responses to stimuli that are never presented in the training program but appear only on the test.

Wolfle (1951) suggests how "generalization" can be employed in training programs, and indeed how it probably works in the acquisition of many informally acquired skills, in his review of practical applications of learning theory to training. Wolfle makes use of some earlier proposals by Hull, to show how responses of some types can be associated with a whole range of stimuli even though practice is devoted only to a few points along a stimulus continuum. Thus, if we allow generalization to take care of a range of stimuli on either side of the practiced points, there is no need to practice at the extremes where training will be acquired gratuitously. Assuming a total range of, say, some 50 points from low to high, and an effective generalization spread of 15 points, we would need to practice at only 5 positions on the stimulus continuum to cover the range (see Fig. 7.3, p. 158).

Practice that is to be useful must be related to the use to which it is to be put. If we practice drill, then drill will benefit. Practicing problem solving will benefit problem solving. Practicing taking a general view will aid future general-view-taking. There is no simple statement that covers all considerations.

Other determinants of later learning. At the beginning of the chapter we recognized that it is popularly accepted that child, and perhaps infantile, experience plays a role in later life. The content of this chapter was restricted to the influence of early learning experiences on later learning. The laboratory investigations of learning in infancy are still in *their* infancy. It will be many years before we are able to speak confidently about how a human child should be taught in order to produce an efficient adult learner. Results obtained with rats and dogs are, of course, only suggestive. The important investigations still have to be initiated. There are, of course, other kinds of experiences besides formal learning operations that may affect future learning or behavior in general. In the next chapter we shall consider some of the researches and conclusions relative to the influence of early emotional experience on personality. Again we shall find that while our interest is in humans the research is largely on lower forms. This is the fact of the matter. We must try to get as much out of it as possible.

Chapter

15 Emotion, Learning Theory, and Personality Disorders

LEARNING THEORY AND CLINICAL PSYCHOLOGY

In recent years the profession of psychology has increased at such a rate that one psychologist (Boring, 1954) with a sense of humor estimates that if the present rate of growth of the profession is maintained, and if the world population continues to grow at its present rate, then by 2050, there will be more psychologists in the world than people. What is the reason for this phenomenal increase? There has been an increased demand for psychologists, or at least, an increased number of professional opportunities in the field, particularly in the area of clinical psychology, and the great number of psychologists are now engaged in clinical activities which consist basically of diagnosis of mental illness, and, where permitted, therapy. It should be noted at the outset that the therapy offered by psychologists is ordinarily restricted to working with neurotic as distinguished from psychotic patients although the latter also receive some attention from the psychologist.

Since the concept of mental illness has for ages been a confused one involving various theological interpretations and cultural superstitions and since treatment has been traditionally in the hands of the medical profession, it might be wondered how and why psychologists have gotten involved. The basic reason is the failure of members of the medical profession to develop a rapid and easy cure for mental disorder and their own willingness to introduce into the diagnosis of mental illness a variety of psychological interpretations which take the care of the patient out of the drug and surgery fields and into the atmosphere of "psychotherapy." Some members of the profession have not given up hope of finding a chemical solution of the problems of mental illness or the possibility of a cure by surgery or convulsive therapy in one form or another, but even these medical people are inclined to agree that psychotherapy (however that is defined) is also required, or is, at least, helpful. The medical profession has by no means surrendered its prerogatives in therapy to lay persons and looks with alarm at anyone practicing therapy without a medical degree even if the psychotherapist without an M.D. does nothing different from what a proper psychiatrist might do. Freud (1927), however, felt that nonmedical people could be effective in psychotherapy and decided that, in general, a medical training was not required for psychotherapy.

The separation of mental disorders into structural and functional varieties and the development of psychoanalysis and kindred forms of psychotherapy gradually, but forcefully, led to the now common interpretation that some forms of mental disorder, particularly *neuroses*, are behavioral problems. Such problems are assumed to originate in a faulty environment, particularly in terms of interpersonal relationships, and again, particularly in terms of infantile and early childhood experiences. It is, perhaps, not oversimplification to state that the general assumption of both medical and psychological practitioners is that neurotic disorders are really "personality" problems, that the victim of the disorder is someone who has not *learned* to adjust "normally" to his world, has in fact, *learned* his particular pattern of behavior in order to adjust to a situation which would somehow be unbearable without the protective defenses that have been learned to ward off the difficulties that would otherwise be faced.

Whereas the general public might regard a neurotic as "deranged," "crazy," or "out of his mind," the medical man and the psychologist are prone to accept the formula: diagnosis, faulty bringing up; therapy, retraining. The general medical practitioner frequently is quoted as saying something like "85 percent of my patients are just plain neurotic." Because there is no available pill, and because the general practitioner has neither the time nor the skill to retrain his neurotic patients, the apparently vast number of neurotics have no place to turn except to those who will accept them. Ignoring the large number of swamis, mystics, and palmists, there are only two categories of respectable practitioners who will accept such patients, the psychologist and the psychiatrist. The latter, because of medical licensing, is permitted to introduce drugs, dietary changes, rest cures, and so on. The psychologist is limited to his only tools, his knowledge of the principles of learning. To the extent that the psychologist ventures into the practices of psychoanalysts and adopts their techniques, he is perhaps encroaching upon an area where practice is founded less on scientific knowledge of learning and more on the kinds of interpretations generated by Freud, Jung, and Adler. These interpretations, although presumably arising out of clinical contacts, still amount to an armchair type of psychology which the psychological world itself has long discarded as inadequate methodology.

Regardless of procedures used, all kinds of psychotherapists, including clinical psychologists, claim some degree of success. For one reason or another there is sufficient reinforcement in the situation to keep them at their trades. It is probably safe to say that regardless of theory or technique differences, the "cures" that do occur are accompanied by kinds of changes in personality that can be interpreted as involving learning. That some kind of learning must occur is generally admitted by representatives of all points of view. Shoben (1949) has supported this view by numerous quotations from a variety of therapists. Most of these can be said to subscribe to the generalization that there is a "widespread recognition that psychotherapy is essentially a learning process and should be subject to study as such."

Pavlov and Freud. It is a common practice to refer to Pavlov and Freud as geniuses. Frequently the praise of either is somewhat backhanded in that the inevitable "but" is quickly introduced in any account of their achievements. It is probably too early to appraise the work of either in intellectual history although it is clear enough that Pavlov and Freud really started something. Although they were contemporaries they worked separately, one in the laboratory and the other in his office, and their paths never crossed. In his later years Pavlov became interested in problems of psychiatry and wrote broadly on the implications of his early work with experimental neuroses. It is frequently noted, on the other hand, that Freud was an associationist and that he, from the beginning, emphasized the role of learning in the development of behavior disorders. It is no surprise, then, that in spite of the differences between the methods of the two giants, many efforts have been made to bring the principles of Pavlov and Freud together (Mowrer, 1950; Dollard and Miller, 1950; French, 1933; Sears, 1936). The efforts have not been blessed with much success. Disbelievers in both might remark that "two wrongs do not make a right." Loyal supporters of either will try to show how one anticipated or superseded the other, or how the principles of one can be derived or deduced from the principles of the other.

The current interest of learning theorists in abnormal behavior is not a novel development. Learning psychologists have, ever since Watson (1914), been concerned with emotional disturbances and their cure or elimination. Pavlov's researches on experimental neuroses are ancient history now. In 1936 Hull was looking into Freud's work to see if anything fruitful for learning theory could be found therein. With the end of World War II and some clinical experience behind them, learning psychologists, anxious to help the clinician in his undertaking, have developed a new and stronger interest in clinical problems. Some new approaches developed in learning theory which have been rather broadly applied to clinical problems. Much of the prewar experimentation was expanded in new directions and a substantial volume of experimental data has been accumulated. What it all means for an understanding of abnormal behavior remains to be seen and it is now time to take a look at it.

All lines of investigation into behavior disorders start with Pavlov and we had best begin with him. There are two basic aspects of Pavlov's work that have been exploited by others and each requires separate treatment. These are (a) the fact of conditioning itself, and, (b) the studies of experimental neuroses. We can start with the first and try to follow the complex pattern of developments that Pavlov precipitated.

The early work on conditioning emotions. Pavlov himself did not concern himself directly with conditioning emotion although both he and Bekhterev (1932), his contemporary antagonist, did deal with the defensive reflex (later to be known as "avoidance" behavior). However, Watson and Rayner (1920) in America took over the Pavlovian conditioning paradigm as the basic principle for accounting for the varied emotional life of the adult. Watson assumed an innate equipment of three basic emotions (fear, anger, and love), each of which was a natural, unconditioned response to a limited number of stimuli. Fear was considered a reaction to a sudden loud noise or loss of support, anger to thwarting of bodily movement, and love to strok-ing of erogeneous zones. Other stimuli that happened to occur con-tiguously with any of these natural stimuli became conditioned to the emotional reactions. Thus, a fear of animals would be the normal re-sult of seeing the animal while it was growling or barking loudly. A fear of cats might be presumed to rest on conditioning of the sight of the cat to its loud mewing. Actually, in Watson's views, there need be no specific exposure to the feared object itself if the actual condi-tioning took place with some stimulus which might generalize to such an object. In Watson's famous experiment with little Albert, the young child was presented with a white rat and just as he was about to reach for it Watson made a sudden loud noise behind the child. After seven combined stimulations a fearful withdrawal response re-sulted. This withdrawal or "fear" was then found to generalize to other white fuzzy objects like mittens, fur coats, dogs, rabbits, and the like.

Watson's views might be employed to account for fear of lightning which precedes thunder and any other fears where the history of a possible exposure to a sudden loud noise or loss of support might be traced. It should always be remembered that the possibility of gen-eralization (from barking dog to puppy, cat, horse, and so on) permits broad latitude. Thus a young woman of eighteen might fear cats and have a history of absolutely no contact with cats. An encounter with a noisy dog in childhood might be sufficient explanation. There is also a powerful tool for argument in the principle of secondary or higher order conditioning. Once the dog has had his deadly effect, his owner and any number of other possibilities can begin to be effective fear producers. The theory is, if anything, flexible.

Efforts to repeat Watson's original observations have not been very successful. Bregman (1934) was unable to condition a fear to neutral objects like blocks, curtains, rings, and so on, when the unconditioned stimulus was a bell loud enough to produce a startle or fear reaction in infants. Valentine (1930) found it possible to condition fear to the sight of a caterpillar when combined with a whistle, but a pair of opera glasses proved inadequate as a conditioned stimulus for the same response. The use of a biologically significant conditioned stim-ulus (a living, moving organism) seems to be a possible prerequisite for the Watson type of conditioning. Dennis (1940) criticized Wat-son's views as inadequate to cover the range of emotional response that develops in the normal life of a child and adult. Since Watson's time many attacks have been levied against his tripartite emotional theory (Sherman, 1927a, b; Landis, 1924). Most current views favor a more developmental approach to the broad variety of emotional experience that characterize the older child and adult (Bridges, 1932; Hebb, 1946).

Learning and the development of emotions. One difficulty with Watson's views was the bold specification of the stimuli which originally elicit fear, anger, or love. Most later observers were unable to verify that loud noises or loss of support inevitably produced fear. Any proud father tossing his infant child about in the air is a ready refutation of this claim. To add to the general reluctance to accept Watson's views we have the virtually universal experience of adults or at least older children being frightened by stimuli or situations which never have been accompanied by loud noises or loss of support. Dismissing the rather limp suggestion that generalization might be the explanation, what account could Watson supply for the fear of snakes, spiders, death and corpses, or the fear of the dark? These are all common enough experiences with the rather paradoxical features that young children are not particularly frightened by these stimuli or situations. The baby that will cheerfully try to eat a snake will become the twelve-year-old who will shrink and run from a harmless garter snake. Yet it is most unlikely that anyone has ever gone around beating gongs or "cutting the ground out from under" the child in the presence of reptiles of any kind.

Learning and "natural" fears. Is the answer to this question that such fears are "natural"? Hebb (1946) offers a paradoxical answer of "yes and no." According to Hebb, the fears of death and darkness, snakes and spiders, and so on are natural enough, and yet they depend upon learning. Not, to be sure, the kind of conditioning to which Watson refers. Instead, says Hebb, we have to mature to some degree in terms of experience before some kinds of stimuli can initiate fear reactions. The stimulus for fear, says Hebb, is any *sudden* or *novel* stimulus, or in other words, any *unexpected* stimulus. The unexpected stimulus is one for which we have no ready habit, no dependable reaction. We get used to *living* people, not dead ones. How can anyone react appropriately to a corpse if he has never seen one before? We take pains to shield small children from any contact with corpses. When the time comes for them to participate in wakes and funerals they can hardly be anything but unprepared. Hebb reports his observations on fears displayed by chimpanzees when allowed to view decapitated chimpanzee bodies, chimpanzee skins, and so on.

The usual experience of chimpanzees does not include commerce with such objects. Their terror is explained by Hebb as a natural reaction to the *strange*. What is strange, however, depends on prior experience.

The fear of the dark so characteristic of children above the age of four or five is not due to earlier frightening experiences in the dark. To suspect practically all parents of giving their young children a fright of some sort in the dark seems far too much to expect. Yet children can be counted upon to display such a fear. How does Hebb account for it? He argues that in the early years the child is not asked to fend for himself in the dark. The parents cater to the child's wants. They turn on lights or lead the child when necessary. It is only when a child finds himself responsible for performing his own maneuvers in the dark that he becomes afraid. Now the stimuli about him consist not of chairs, lamps, tables, and so on, but rather vague amorphous shadows, forms to which he never has had to react. He has no suitable habits in what is now a strange situation. It is not the dark that the child fears, it is the lack of ability to make appropriate responses. One of the writer's students reported that as a child he usually went to bed by leaving the family circle in a well-lighted kitchen, dashing as rapidly as possible through dimly illuminated dining and living rooms, and plunging into bed, pulling the covers over his head, and undressing in bed. Only in complete darkness was he comfortable. There was no call to "behave" in the dark under the blankets. The living room and dining room, however, were populated with various spooks and other fearful forms.

While Hebb's suggestions may not prove to be a final or complete answer, we may properly suspect that loud noises and loss of support are not the only, necessary, and inevitable unconditioned stimuli for fear. We can also suspect that any attempt to trace adult fears back to noises or falls in infancy is likely to be fruitless, to say nothing of the naïveté of such an attempt. With these considerations before us we can go back and pick up Watson's ambitious attempt to simplify a complex business.

CONDITIONING AND PSYCHOTHERAPY

It should be noted that Watson's experiment with little Albert showed only some presumed "diagnostic" value of conditioning theory. M. C. Jones (1924) tried to expand the story by showing how *reconditioning* could operate as a therapy. In the Jones therapeutic study, a three-year-old child, Peter, was found to have a broad repertoire of fears of living animals and mechanical toys. A white rat introduced in Peter's crib brought on a paroxysm of fear. Similar reactions were given to fur coats, cotton, and a feathered hat. In reconditioning Peter, the therapists introduced a rabbit in a cage 40 feet away from Peter as the child sat eating. Every day the cage was brought closer to the child until by a slow process of exposure to the rabbit, the child could tolerate the animal without a cage and eventually was able to continue eating with the rabbit in his lap. At this time testing showed that the former fear of feathers, cotton, and fur had also happily disappeared. He was also able to tolerate a rat, mice, frogs, and worms, all of which he formerly feared. It is obvious that therapy of this type must be conducted with great care because of the danger of conditioning the food (or other pleasant stimuli) to the fear reaction. Since the Jones experiment (1924) nothing much has been done in this general framework.

Hilgard and Marquis (1940) mention various sporadic and unsystematic attempts to diagnose hysterical disorders via conditioning techniques and they describe an interesting case of the "cure" of a thirty-two-year-old teacher who came to a psychiatric clinic with a case of "glove" anesthesia involving the left arm. By using shock to the left arm as an alleged CS for the withdrawal to shock of the right arm, the experimenters were able to establish some sensitivity in the left arm. Later, the shock to the right arm was set up as a CS and withdrawal of the left arm was developed as a pseudo-conditioned response. Hilgard and Marquis warn against ill-considered attempts to treat such patients in such fashion because of the danger of treating symptoms instead of the underlying condition. We shall have more to say about this warning later.

Attempts have been made to treat cases of alcoholism by conditioning techniques. Early Russian experiments made use of electric shock accompanying the sights and smells of liquor and the printed words or spoken words signifying drinking and alcohol in attempts to establish avoidance responses to alcohol. More modern treatment involves the use of chemicals which cause unpleasant reactions immediately following the consumption of alcohol. One such drug, Antabuse, is alleged to enjoy some degree of success. There is no theoretical reason why such treatment might not be completely satisfactory from a conditioning viewpoint. The drinker can be made to react to alcohol in an avoidance manner if the stimuli of the drinking situation are made painful enough at the appropriate time.

Guthrie's analysis of conditioning as therapy. Although Guthrie had his differences with Pavlov, his attempts to handle abnormal phenomena can be considered as more or less direct applications of conditioning theory to the special problems involved, with his own modification of Pavlovian doctrine which, as we have seen, amounts to an emphasis on the association of specific movements with particular stimulus situations. In his work on the *Psychology of Human Conflict* (1938), Guthrie treats various types of personality disorder as amounting to learned responses which happen to occur in a given situation but which do not happen to meet the approval of society generally. Thus, a widow who does not get rid of her former husband's possessions and who is moved to tears by these articles will continue to suffer in misery with each exposure to these items, because that is what she did on the last occasion. Therapy consists of either eliminating the stimuli or in changing the reactions to them. This simple formula is carried through for a variety of disorders such as compulsions, fixations, and the rest of the clinical symptomatology. In the matter of getting rid of bad habits (and presumably disorders represent only bad habits for Guthrie) it is necessary to control the S-R relationship so that the *last* response to the stimulus is a desirable one from the therapist's viewpoint. In the case of treating an alcoholic, the problem becomes one of associating stimuli which lead to drinking with a nondrinking reaction. How this is to be accomplished is not specified, but if the therapist attempts to use punishment or some kind of negative stimulation which is calculated to produce an avoidance reaction to alcohol, Guthrie warns the therapist to make sure that the last reaction to the sight of liquor or offers of drink, and so on, is a negative one. It does no good to delay the negative aftereffects beyond the period of most fruitful conditioning because the avoidance will become associated with subsequent stimuli. Hangovers traditionally do not lead to avoidance. The threat of cancer associated with cigarette smoking does not appear to be very effective for those who do not now have the disease. Venereal diseases likewise are but slightly modified in frequency by dire threats about consequences. The consequences must be immediate if they are to work and, in Guthrie's language, the subject must be induced to make some avoidance reaction as the last move to the significant stimuli. In all these circumstances, again, the orthodox clinical psychologist warns against treating symptoms. Although Guthrie's treatment of the problem is intriguing and may be of some practical importance, there is little experimental evidence for his suggestions and we will leave his views for the moment.

Skinner on psychotherapy. Skinner (1953) is very close to Guthrie in his views on abnormal manifestations in behavior. He has not devoted much time to the problem, but in his *Science and Human Behavior* he discusses the logical implications of his systematic thinking about learning for abnormal behavior. In an early article on superstition (1948b), Skinner was able to apply his reinforcement views to accounting for the development of more or less compulsive behavior in rats and pigeons. Skinner contrived situations which produced behavior patterns that, on the surface, seem fantastic, irrational, and absurd. If a pigeon is reinforced at random intervals by having food dropped into the box in which it is confined, and no other stimulation is applied, the pigeon will come to repeat certain specific movements in which it happened to be engaged at the time of reinforcement. Thus, if the pigeon happens to be tucking its head under a wing, while standing on one foot, it will tend to repeat this pattern if grain is dropped into the food bin at that moment. It is possible, of course, to condition the animal to indulge in whatever pattern one cares to reinforce and, after the conditioning takes place, the pattern can be made to appear irrelevant or bizarre by changing some aspects of the situation. Since the pigeon or rat can hardly anticipate the experimenter's purposes, the animal can be made to appear ridiculous. From such modest experiments, Skinner suggests that various maladjustive symptoms might well have an accidental reinforcement history which adequately accounts for them. For Skinner, therapy consists of extinguishing undesirable behavior patterns through the process of nonreinforcement.

It is evident that both Skinner and Guthrie have little use for traditional concepts of clinicians. Skinner describes the clinical concept of "neurosis" as a "linguistic fiction" and takes issue with any suggestion that a neurosis is a clinical entity. He prefers to approach a problem of behavior disorder as just that, a *behavioral* disorder. From his point of view, a clinical patient has learned to behave in a particular way or ways and if one is to "cure" the patient, these ways of behaving must be eliminated.

The Hullian school. Acquired drives. In the line of succession we now arrive at followers of Hull's systematic thinking. Hull himself did not pay much attention to abnormal phenomena in his writings although he did concern himself with some patterns of behavior that might represent some fringe phenomena. For example, Hull (1938) attempted to analyze certain "field" problems that were first described by Lewin (1931). Hull's interest in psychoanalysis has already been mentioned and his work in hypnosis (1933a) is well known. Hull, however, never got around to a serious consideration of the abnormal field. As it is, the application of Hullian theory to problems of personality disorder has been carried on by Hull's students, notably Dollard *et al.* (1939), Mowrer (1950), and Dollard and Miller (1950). For the present, since we are concerned at the moment with the Pavlovian line of development, we will confine ourselves to the conditioning features of Hullian theory as it has been developed in the abnormal area.

Emotion as motivation. Most of the work dealing with maladjustment and behavioral disorder that developed from the Hull approach rests on the assumption that "anxiety" as an acquired *drive* has typical drive characteristics. These drive characteristics are presumed to include the generation of drive stimuli (S_D) which instigate behavior of a trial-and-error nature. One of the responses initiated by the fear-produced stimuli takes the animal out of the fear situation, the anxiety is reduced, and the response is learned.

Ascribing motivational or causal functions to emotion is an ancient human practice. Any layman can explain his or his neighbor's actions in terms of love, hate, jealousy, and so on. The idea is so universally accepted that students in psychology courses are somewhat astounded when first exposed to the James-Lange theory of emotion. In his famous illustration of what happens when one meets a bear, James (1890) gives us the paradoxical formula that "we are afraid because we run" and not vice versa. The implication of James's view in the present connection is that fear or anxiety will not generate any activity, but rather such states will follow the activity and, presumably, enhance it. Of course, it can be argued that James was talking about the "awareness" of the subject, and that the stimuli generated by the physiological changes become important generators of action. James, of course, would not have agreed, since if no action were taken there would be no important physiological changes. In the long history of debate on this subject, Cannon (1929) developed what he claimed to be a counterview in his "emergency" theory of emotion. Cannon, however, found that he could initiate states which resembled fear and anxiety in human subjects by injections of adrenalin without developing any action in them. In his comprehensive review, Lindsey (1951) nowhere brings in evidence about emotional states producing any action. Laboratory studies deal almost exclusively with the *appearance* of the subjects or the operations of their viscera.

Leeper (1948a) tried to make out a case for emotion as a motivating agent but his argument only emphasizes that emotion can represent an *organization* of behavior rather than the commonly assumed *disorganization*. Young (1949) disagrees with Leeper and holds to a disorganization view, but the essential question is not answered by either. Whether emotion operates as an organizing affair or a disorganizing one does not have any bearing on whether or not "emotion" originates behavior. In line with Cannon's homeostatic views and the suggestion of Brown (see p. 218) we might conceive of emotion as *energizing* behavior. Thus, whatever the organism does may be done with more power, energy, and so forth, without there being any directiveness about the behavior except that determined by external stimuli. Considering Leeper's example of the prize fighter we might admit that some modest degree of emotional excitement might facilitate his movements and add some authority to his punches. The motivation for the pugilistic exercise is unlikely, however, to be *initiated* by anger or fear. Experimental evidence that emotions originate behavior is still to be discovered.

ANXIETY AS A DRIVE. In the typical avoidance situation, the shocked animal may well be excited, afraid, or mildly upset depending on strength of shock and so on. In fact, it would be surprising if it were not. But the suggestion that the "anxiety" is activating or "driving" the animal into an avoidance reaction must be regarded as a pure assumption. Theorists continually remind us that they are privileged to assume anything they please, and so they are. It still remains for them to demonstrate that the assumption is not only fruitful but also necessary. If it can be shown that "avoidance" behavior can be obtained in a situation where "anxiety" can be assumed to be absent, the theorist is obliged to re-examine his thinking.

A direct experimental test of the role of fear as a drive could be made if it could be established that an organism could learn an avoidance reaction without first being afraid. Solomon, Kamin, and Wynne (1953) attempted to implement such a test by surgical elimination of the nervous supply for the autonomic reactions presumably mediating fear. Their dog subjects did learn (though more slowly) to make avoidance responses in a hurdle-jumping situation. No report of operative controls is given and the poorer learning of the operated dogs may have been a surgical artifact. It can be argued, of course, that the *entire* physiological mechanism through which fear functions was not eliminated. It should also be noted that Solomon, Kamin, and Wynne used extremely high-level shocks as unconditioned stimuli and the resultant behavior of the dogs appears to have been strongly determined by this shock level. The "avoidance" was extremely prolonged and resisted all ordinary devices to produce extinction. It is highly questionable that after 600 "unreinforced" responses the dogs were avoiding anything. Whatever the explanation of their behavior, it does not appear necessary to assume an intervening anxiety without supporting evidence beyond the jumps themselves.

The writer has recently developed a procedure of training rats to avoid a shock by making either of two responses, depending upon the stimulus presented. Thus, if a light is turned on, the animal is required to pull a chain; if a buzzer is sounded, the rat presses a pedal. The training proceeds by stages with one avoidance response learned well first and the other added later. The problem is a rather difficult one for the rat, but it can be learned (three rats were successfully trained in a week's time). One difficulty involved in the training is to develop both *avoidance* responses. The rats learn quickly what to do to *escape* but some show only slow learning to avoid. The point, however, is that they can learn to avoid with appropriate training. This "discriminated avoidance" appears to pose a problem for the supporters of "anxiety" as a source for the instrumental response. How does the animal discriminate one anxiety learned to a buzzer from another anxiety learned to a light when both anxieties are developed on the same basis, namely, shock? Anxiety theorists can argue that the *pattern* of light-shock is different from that of buzzer-shock and therefore there are subtle differences in the anxiety that develops. How realistic this argument is remains to be seen. For the present we can, at least, appreciate that if the anxiety is mild enough, the average subject will do something appropriate to the *other* stimuli in the picture. The student is urged to reread the sections on avoidance learning in Chapter 4 where it was argued that avoidance learning is not necessarily a separate kind of learning. The present criticisms may help make the earlier argument more comprehensible.

Supporters of the Skinner view who are "anxious" about avoiding references to the physiology of their subjects try to account for avoidance behavior in terms of extraorganismic concepts. Thus, Dinsmoor (1954, 1955) offers an interpretation of avoidance behavior based on the notion that shock is one of a class of "aversive" stimuli. Such "negative reinforcers" operate to strengthen responses through their elimination. An avoidance response is reinforced by the termination of shock. Accompanying stimuli become secondarily negative reinforcers and also serve to maintain the aversive response. Dinsmoor (1955, p. 103) states: "Whether we ever prove or disprove the necessity for supplementing this explanation with an appeal to some form of emotional state remains to be seen; but for the present, the burden of proof seems to rest on those who do maintain the necessity of such an appeal."

We have spent enough time on this question and we can turn now to the work of those who are quite content to accept a hypothetical construct of anxiety as a basic assumption.

ANXIETY AND AVOIDANCE BEHAVIOR. The concept of avoidance learning has been exploited primarily by Hull's students. It will be recalled that Mowrer (p. 66) modified Hull's views on reinforcement to include the notion that emotional reactions, and, generally, any autonomic reactions, are learned by simple association rather than as functions of drive reduction. From Mowrer's point of view, the basic problem in neurotic behavior is the operation of anxiety. Anxiety is conceived of as a natural accompaniment of pain stimulation and is presumed to be learned under circumstances involving painful stimulation or punishment. Thus, whenever an organism is injured or punished in the presence of other, irrelevant, stimuli, such stimuli can take on the role of conditioned stimuli for a fear or anxiety response. Such anxiety is then presumed to function as a drive, an acquired motivation, for the performance of any of a variety of responses that are possible for the organism in the particular situation. If one of these responses happens to reduce the anxiety, it will then be learned because the reduction of anxiety is conceived to be reinforcing, just as the reduction of any other drive would be in Hull's system. If the external and real circumstances no longer call for anxiety, performance of the formerly adjustive response will appear to be irrational, unrealistic, unsatisfying, and so on. The appearance of "symptoms" therefore dictates the analysis that at some time in the past the symptomatic behavior was effective in reducing an anxiety that was based on a reasonably genuine painful or fearful situation. The reinforcement of this behavior, through anxiety reduction, gave it its present strength and accounts for its present performance in the now "safe" situation. We can recall an experimental illustration which may serve to clarify the matter (p. 14). If an animal is shocked in one side of a two-compartment box and escapes to the other side where no shock is present, it will later run to the "safe" side even though no shock is given on the formerly shocked side. The animal, finding himself in the originally shocked side, is presumed to become anxious. The anxiety will provoke restlessness and activity, and, the situation being somewhat limited, it will soon find itself on the other side where the anxiety will be "reduced." The fact that no shock is present anymore is irrelevant to the animal until the fear reaction itself is extinguished through lack of reinforcement (failure of the shock to be administered. See Osgood, 1950). Since Mowrer conceived of the reinforcement of the running behavior to take place after every run, the behavior would acquire tremendous strength and continue long after shock was discontinued. In a sense, the behavior would acquire some autonomy and be self-maintained. We have already discussed this proposition (p. 64).

The experiments of Miller with his white-black box have already been described (see p. 14) and fit the description given above for Mowrer's expansion of Hull's theory. Miller himself (1951) is undecided about whether the fear is learned by Pavlovian principles as Mowrer insists, but the learning of a fear reaction is assumed by Miller, regardless of how it is learned.

Miller's work with the white-black box has received considerable attention as a clear-cut demonstration of derived drives and much theoretical speculation rests on such experiments involving shocked rats in boxes. It should be noted that no other kinds of derived drives have ever been demonstrated, and there may even be some question as to what goes on in the white-black box situation. Earlier (p. 232) we saw that Myers and Miller (1954) tried to demonstrate that hunger, instead of pain, might serve as a basis for acquired drives. In this experiment they found that rats that had been placed in the white compartment once a day for 70 days while hungry, then learned to move a bar which opened the door to the black box while satiated. Unfortunately for the derived drive concept, so did animals that were never in the box before. Rats with no opportunity to develop a drive learned to press the lever as well as rats with 10, 30, or 70 trials of hunger training. The writer has frequently observed rats learn to turn a wheel in a Miller box without ever having been shocked and with no experimenter-induced drive. As a matter of fact, the writer constructed a Miller box with the wheel operative from either white or black compartments. Rats that were shocked on the white side frequently turned the wheel from the black side and ran into the white side where they had been shocked. Clinicians might well be reserved in accepting evidence from rat experiments using shock boxes. The behavior of the rat in such a box can hardly be said to be clearly understood.

If we ignore the critical comments just mentioned we might find that abnormal behavior patterns can (at least in some instances) be diagnosed as involving a prior painful experience of some kind which occurred in the presence of stimuli to which the anxiety component of the pain was associated. Behavior is then engaged in which was found to be successful in reducing the anxiety. Because a drive was reduced, the behavior was reinforced and now is strong.

ANXIETY AND DEFENSE MECHANISMS. With anxiety allegedly established as a learned drive leading to responses which reduce it, Mowrer and Miller are in position to account for any bizarre responses which the clinician will identify as neurotic. The diagnosis is automatically at hand, in that the patient must have learned to fear some situation, and, to defend himself against this fear, he resorted to whatever would reduce it. If the situation was such that the behavior was reasonably appropriate at the time, usually presumed to be in childhood, it is now "neurotic" only because society expects some other more "normal" behavior from the individual at his present age and status. The variety of defense mechanisms as ordinarily described by psychoanalysts is accounted for by the character of the originally learned reaction which reduced the anxiety and which might easily be the resultant of numerous chance variables; thus, if the original reaction was to blame someone else (and successfully get away with it) pathological lying might be accounted for. If the original reaction was running to mama, dependency will have been reinforced.

One of the early experimental programs of learning psychologists interested in abnormal phenomena was to account for the various defense mechanisms on a learning basis. A demonstration that such defenses were learned on the basis of a learned anxiety would strongly support the derived drive hypothesis. Studies of repression, regression, reaction formation, and so on, were attempted. Mowrer (1940a), for example, reported an "experimental analogue of regression." In the experiment designed to demonstrate regression, Mowrer first trained rats to stand on their hind feet whenever a slowly increasing shock developed to threshold strength. As soon as the animals stood on their hind feet the shock was terminated. Later a pedal was placed at the end of the confinement box and standing was no longer adequate to terminate the shock. The pedal had to be depressed. The rats now learned a second (a more advanced?) technique. Now the pedal itself was so wired that touching it would deliver a momentary shock. The experimental question became: what will the rats do now? It turned out that some rats overcame the tendency to avoid the pedal and continued to depress it, taking the brief shock; the rest of the rats "regressed" to the former habit of standing up. As an interesting side feature, Mowrer reported that the rats that remained pedal pressers now retreated as far as possible from the pedal and only ran up to it when it became necessary. Previously they had hovered about in the pedal area. This behavior or markedly avoiding what "you really want to do" was characterized by Mowrer as "Reaction Formation." Whether or not Mowrer's rats were regressing becomes a question of what Freud really meant and the Mowrer demonstration may mean no more than a demonstration of the use of alternate habits. There is no particular objections to analogues if the old logical rule that analogies do not prove anything is remembered.

We have already mentioned (p. 334) a review of such studies by Sears (1943) who arrived at disappointing conclusions regarding the possibility of establishing experimental proof of the operation of learning principles in connection with psychoanalytic phenomena. Since that time little positive work has been done. We have already encountered (p. 335) Zeller's (1950a) review of the literature on repression which concluded with the observation that no one had yet shown repression by laboratory procedures. His own efforts in that direction we have already criticized.

With the derived-drive hypothesis assumed as adequate for explaining abnormal behavior, the treatment or therapy is obviously that of getting rid of the anxiety. Once the stimuli which lead to anxiety have been identified, by whatever means, steps must be taken to extinguish the anxiety to these stimuli and to establish new responses to them. The problem involved is, of course, not simple, and we shall examine the details of this program from a learning point of view later, after additional features of the theoretical structure are presented. For the moment we are dealing with anxiety.

We can conclude this section by contrasting the views of Guthrie and Skinner with those of Mowrer or Miller. How would each go about the process of treating a neurotic?

Both Skinner and Guthrie will have to go after the *behavior* of the patient, extinguishing the "bad habits" and establishing more appropriate ones. Since the habits may represent rather broad categories of behavior such as aggressiveness, depression, shyness, instability, and so on, we can imagine that the difficulty will be great not only in finding the stimuli which lead to such behavior but also the specific responses that must be extinguished. It is obviously easy to talk about extinguishing habits of aggression and equally obvious that the psychologist is going to have a difficult time merely getting started. Guthrie, at least, has the virtue of suggesting that specific behavior units be selected for elimination or counterconditioning. He, at least, knows what he is going to extinguish. Neither Guthrie nor Skinner are going to be concerned over an explanatory fiction like a neurosis or a hidden cause and can proceed immediately to whatever they are able to identify as the undesirable behavior that needs extinction, Guthrie by counterconditioning, Skinner by somehow getting the behavior to occur without reinforcement. Skinner has a twofold problem on his hands. Getting the behavior out is going to prove difficult if the responses are undiscriminated operants. Second, the nature of the reinforcement is certain to be obscure and difficult to eliminate. In his *Walden II*, Skinner (1948a) gives an illustration that may have some relevance. Suppose you wish to extinguish the behavior of telling off-color stories by some vulgar person. You merely form a social group (stimulus situation for telling such stories) and have the group refrain from laughing at the conclusion of each tale. The storyteller presumably exhausts his reserve for *telling* stories (he still may remember them) in that group. If that group can be representative of all groups, the storyteller will soon have to terminate the behavior.

In contrast, Mowrer and Miller will spend a lot of time worrying over the intervening variable of anxiety. The actual overt behavior is irrelevant. It is basic and necessary that the anxiety be extinguished first. Once this is done there will be no motivation (and, therefore, no reinforcement) for the behavior which should drop out of the picture almost immediately. How to extinguish the anxiety is a problem in itself. The Pavlovian analogue applies, of course. Present the CS without the US and extinction is inevitable. While this is hypothetically simple, it may be impossible to identify the CS. At the same time, allowing the anxiety response to occur may have its own dangers.

EXPERIMENTAL NEUROSES AND EXPERIMENTAL CONFLICT

The usual textbook in abnormal psychology devotes some space to the description of Pavlov's early work on "experimental neuroses" and leaves the implication, if it does not say so directly, that this work has a good deal to do with accounting for abnormal behavior. Actually the implications from the laboratory studies are never carried through, even by analogy, to human neurotic or abnormal behavior, although the author of the text has achieved the meritorious status of including some experimental material, giving the text a scientific foundation. What was it that Pavlov had actually done in his laboratory?

In the original findings that have come to be labeled "experimental neuroses" Pavlov was concerned with establishing the limits of the principle of generalization. By employing the "method of contrast" he would systematically reinforce a response to one stimulus and not reinforce a response to some variation of the same stimulus. In the classical experiment, a dog was trained to salivate to a circle and not to an ellipse. The diameters of the ellipse were gradually altered to approach circularity and the procedure was continued until the dog was unable to discriminate between the stimuli. At this point, the animal would necessarily salivate to both or to neither or be sufficiently confused to react in some irregular chance fashion. When the crucial point of inability to discriminate was reached, Pavlov found that some dogs would "break down," that is, behave in a negative manner toward the experimenter, the situation, and everything concerning it. The animals might become aggressive and violent or meek and withdrawn and, in general, reacted in ways that reminded Pavlov of the behavior of dogs caught in cages in a cellar when a flood occurred in Leningrad and Pavlov tried to extricate the animals from the perilous situation. The behavior during the flood might well be considered "abnormal" and so might the behavior of some of the animals in the difficult discrimination situation. In any event, Pavlov saw fit to attach the label "experimental neurosis" to the behavior in the latter situation. The label stuck and psychologists looking for scientific support for their activity in areas of abnormal behavior took over the findings and developed them into support for a theory of conflict. It is this theory that we are going to examine in the present section.

The theory of conflict is the foundation of most psychogenic interpretations of abnormal behavior. It is the basic principle of Freudian psychoanalysis where a conflict is pictured as a battle between evil impulses from the id and noble principles of the superego. According to the conflict theory, neurotics are neurotics because they cannot make up their minds to do one thing or the other, or at least they are unable to react in a socially approved fashion to some stimulus situation(s), presumably because of some tendency to react in a contradictory fashion. They are caught in a perpetual struggle between eating the cake and having it too. They appear to be on the horns of a dilemma and are unable to make progress in any direction. This accounts for their characteristic inefficiency and continual unhappiness, feelings of insecurity and inadequacy, as well as their inappropriate behavior which consists of compromises, evasions, or impulsive reactions which are followed by regret and remorse. Because some neurotics are unable to give a coherent picture of any such battle going on in themselves, because they, in fact, frequently deny having any conflicts beyond the ordinary and normal supply, the psychoanalyst and clinicians generally are disposed to assume that the conflicts are there, but on an unconscious level. The neurotic is then the weary victim of a battle going on in which he, as an individual reporting to the clinician, is only the battleground but not even a spectator. If he does detect and report a conflict of some nature, it is likely to be explained by the clinician as only symbolic of the true and real conflict involving much more significant issues than the superficial problem reported by the patient. Thus the woman who cannot make up her mind between a career and marriage is really, though unconsciously, having a battle between homosexual or father-fixation impulses and various social pressures toward conformity or whatever the clinician decides to call the combatant forces.

Individual and species differences in experimental neuroses. The picture of combat or conflict given above may be extreme but it illustrates the general principle that neurotic behavior results from the antagonism of two forces, impulses, ideas, wishes, and so on. Actually clinicians are not all in agreement about the role of conflict in the development of neurosis. Some emphasize anxiety and its repression instead of conflict per se. Freud (1949) in his later years came to regard most difficulties of personal adjustment as due to the repression of anxiety although he also thought of anxiety as the major cause of repression, and clinicians are not in any formal agreement on the sequence of events involved. Besides conflict and anxiety some theories emphasize frustration as a basic factor in neurotic behavior. It is not our problem to analyze the clinicians' principles so much as to see what the learning psychologists are doing in their relationship to the clinical area and we had best return to it.

In connection with Pavlov's observations of experimental neuroses besides the considerations just referred to, two points stand out strongly but are frequently minimized or ignored:

1. Only certain animals gave way to the disorderly reaction patterns Pavlov called neurotic. Pavlov gave this feature of his findings considerable attention and developed a theory of types, based on the ancient *humour* theory of Hippocrates. Pavlov considered some dogs and breeds to represent personality structures in which different features were more or less dominant. Thus some dogs were sanguine, others choleric, phlegmatic, and melancholic. Pavlov classified the behavior of the dogs as due to different degrees of excitability and inhibition. Choleric dogs were excitable, melancholic dogs were inhibitable. Later, the classification was modified (Frolov, 1937) to include three dimensions: (a) strength-weakness (ability to tolerate strong stimulation), (b) lability-inertia (degree to which behavior would alter), (c) balance-imbalance (degree of excitability or inhibition). An expert observer could classify a dog on the basis of these three characteristic dimensions and predict the probability of the animal developing an experimental neurosis. Anrep, Pavlov's translator, gave convincing demonstrations of his skill in this connection when he visited England to help establish Pavlovian laboratory work there (Walter, 1953). Hilgard and Marquis cite numerous other type classification attempts (1940, p. 308) and give a more detailed picture of Pavlovian typology than here attempted.

H. Mahut (1954) in a study of temperamental differences in dog breeds, observed the reactions of over a hundred dogs in tests of timidity or fearfulness. Her subjects consisted of ten different breeds comprising "working" and "hunting" dogs. Her findings revealed rather striking differences in aggressiveness and fearfulness in the several breeds. Working dogs (shepherd, collie) were significantly more timid than the hunting varieties (scotty, boxer). These differences prevailed even though the environments of the animals were reasonably alike. The fact that dog trainers, on the basis of their own experience, agree almost in detail with Mahut's findings suggest that psychologists might do well to pay some attention to genetic factors before arriving at broad generalizations from observations of a limited species. While we have made the point before and Beach and Jaynes (1954) have repeatedly emphasized it, there appears to be a chronic reluctance among psychologists to recognize the influence of genetic contributions to behavior.

2. The second point to recall from Pavlov's work is that it was a rather peculiar laboratory situation. It involved a discrimination between stimuli, and, therefore, on the surface at least, a kind of clash or conflict between impulses to act and not to act. The point, however, is that the response involved was one of salivation, a response that is under the control of the autonomic nervous system. The response would be given, willy-nilly, many times before it would be successfully extinguished to the inappropriate stimulus. The *history* of the case is usually forgotten by the clinician when dealing with Pavlov's dogs although it is a paramount factor in the clinician's treatment of his patients. This is not a case of being confronted with a difficult decision for the first time without ever having reacted in some fashion to both of the components in the discrimination. It is instead a case of an animal that for many weeks has gone through a particular training procedure involving numerous features of physical restraint, frustration, limited mobility, and, as we shall see, no control over the variable of conflict. In other words, the fact that some of Pavlov's dogs broke down is no evidence for the conclusion that the difficult discrimination was the determining factor in the behavior. White (1949) appreciates the very limited applicability of the Pavlovian experiments to clinical theory. He believes that Pavlov's dogs were not only in a conflict situation, if we can assume this, but also were systematically frustrated and presumably were also disturbed emotionally to a degree which might merit the description of anxiety. If in one experiment we have confounded three different variables (anxiety, frustration, and conflict) it is obvious that we can draw no rigid conclusions from this experiment relative to isolated causal agents in abnormal behavior.

The complications of the apparently simple Pavlovian experiment were gradually impressed on Liddell (1944) who once called Pavlov "the psychiatrist of the future." Liddell began work along Pavlovian lines at Cornell in connection with the effect of thyroxin on intelligence. His experiments were performed with sheep, pigs, and goats and at first made use of the Pavlov frame and conditioning procedure. After many years of observing the behavior of his experimental animals, Liddell came to some interesting conclusions about neurotic breakdowns in experimental situations.

Liddell adopted the defensive leg-withdrawal reflex as his major dependent variable and introduced a simple modification of technique that led to some interesting findings. Instead of permitting an animal to *avoid* a shock by raising its leg, Liddell administered the shock anyhow, regardless of whether or not the animal had raised its leg. He called this procedure "inevitable reinforcement" and found it to be effective in itself in producing an experimental breakdown. According to Liddell, if the animal is shocked, even mildly, every time the CS is presented, it gradually develops a characteristic neurotic pattern. There is no need to present contrasting stimuli for the animal to discriminate. There can be no conflict in terms of what the animal must or must not do. It merely stands and takes the shock on every trial. Perhaps some type of conflict can be read into the situation, but it is not the conflict of discrimination between stimuli that Pavlov introduced.

Liddell found another interesting feature in his "inevitable reinforcement" technique. The experimental neurosis did not develop if the conditioned stimulus (ordinarily a metronome in Liddell's experiments) was presented very frequently or at irregular intervals.

Neurotic behavior did not develop if the experimental animals were allowed to wander freely about the experimental enclosure and received stimuli by remote control. Liddell concluded that strapping the animal into the Pavlov frame in the laboratory represented a restriction of the environment, a form of "encapsulation" and limitation of freedom that strongly contributed to the resulting breakdown.

In another attempt to study the operation of conflict, Maier (1949) employed the Lashley jumping stand with rat subjects. Following a Pavlovian discrimination procedure Maier would bring the animals to a point of difficult discrimination and found that at such times the animal would refuse to jump. Blowing an air blast in the region of the animal's tail would force the animal off the stand. The departure was frequently followed by a convulsive attack and then a comalike state. Maier at first considered the convulsions to be the result of the conflict but later regarded the air blast as the immediate cause of the convulsion with the conflict a predisposing cause. Other experimenters with the situation were able to show that the air blast itself was sufficient as was any high-pitched noise such as key-jingling. Finger (1947), after an exhaustive review of such "audiogenic seizure" experiments, concluded that no one had demonstrated that conflict alone could be considered a cause of the convulsive behavior. In later experiments dealing with "frustration," Maier and Longhurst (1947) would train an animal to jump toward a target card and later lock the doors, holding the positive as well as the negative cards or randomly reinforce either card, preventing learning. In such a situation, Maier noted the development of "fixation." When forced by shock or air blast, animals would begin to jump at one side or the other in complete disregard of the card and continue such behavior indefinitely. Frequently the animals would jump in such a manner as to hit the target sidewise. The resultant drop into the basket was, perhaps, less distressing. As the fixation developed, the animal would fail to jump to a target now made positive again or even to an open door behind which food was in view. Maier interpreted the fixation behavior as corresponding to inadequate, neurotic, reactions which he believes are developed as a result of a history of frustration involving a situation of inevitable failure. Maier finds frustration to be the basic cause of fixations, aggression, and repression in contrast with earlier studies (Dollard *et al.*, 1939) which emphasized only aggression as a consequence of frustration. According to Maier, frustration is a unique state leading to peculiarities of behavior which cannot otherwise be accounted for. He holds that no learning is taking place once the response is fixated. It can be argued, of course, that the fixation persists because it is reinforcing to the animal in that it eliminates the anxious state aroused by finding itself on the stand.

In another line of research, Masserman (1943) used a simple eating-punishment situation with cat subjects. As a cat approached a food dish a blast of air would be blown at its face, or an electric shock given, resulting in a rapid fearful retreat. Here we have a situation in which a pair of drives are arranged to be in conflict. Masserman was more interested in therapeutic techniques than in the principles involved and found a variety of procedures which could bring the cats back to eating. These included gradually forcing cats back to the food (this worked for some), and intoxicating the animals to the point where fear was overcome. Prolonged rest would reduce the fear on a first trial but the fear returned even without additional shocks or air blasts. When the animals were permitted to press pedals which produced feeding signals they also overcame the fear of eating, apparently because they were, to some extent, in control of the situation.

Wolpe (1952b) found that Masserman's technique (which allegedly pitted two conflicting drives against each other) was quite unnecessary to produce the neurotic behavior in cats. All that Wolpe did was to shock cats in a box just after sounding a buzzer. The animals then acquired an anxiety reaction, according to Wolpe, and refused to eat when offered food even after 72 hours of food deprivation. The animals not only failed to eat in the experimental box but would not eat in any room in the laboratory which was similar to the experimental room. The therapy followed by Wolpe consisted of feeding the cat in a very different environment and gradually changing the rooms along some kind of similarity scale until eventually the animal would eat in the laboratory. From there on, the animal would be placed in the box when hungry and small amounts of food would be offered. When eating began, a brief and quiet buzzer was sounded, immediately followed by more food. With continued training, the animal was brought to the point of eating when the full-strength buzzer was sounding continuously.

Wolpe's observations give us a different picture of disturbed behavior. It is by no means necessary to shock the animal in the presence of food. The distressing incident can take place in the absence of otherwise positive stimuli. Later, the distressed animal does not react positively because of an interfering (anxiety?) reaction. Here we have a conflict occurring as a *result*, not a cause of disturbance. It will not do to leap too far into personality problems from the Wolpe demonstration, but the suggestion might be ventured that disorderly behavior does not necessarily call for a search for a hidden conflict or even a history of conscious indecision. Any kind of experience which disturbs the normal course of reaction to stimuli might result in what might be labeled "neurotic" behavior. While a stressful experience involving fear might develop this result, so might a great variety of other circumstances such as illness, faulty diets, exhaustion, endocrine inbalances, accidental injury, or even hereditary factors which eventuate in malfunctioning of the nervous system. We shall return to this suggestion later in the chapter. We have yet to examine Miller's theory of conflict which has been widely endorsed.

MILLER'S ANALYSIS OF CONFLICT. By far the most detailed attempt to work out the principles involved in conflict situations is that of Miller (1944, 1951). Miller considers not only the simple matter of opposed

drives or impulses as Masserman did but goes into the separate characteristics of each opposed tendency. Miller starts out with the notion
of approach and avoidance gradients first described by Hull (1932)
and Bugelski and Miller (1938, see p. 177). The notion of a gradient,
it will be recalled, involves the concept of degrees of strength of conditioning at different distances in space or time from the original
conditioning stimulus. Thus if running behavior is conditioned to a
particular place, say the end of a 6 foot alley, the tendency to run is
assumed to be associated most strongly with the end of the alley
where food or shock have been encountered and lesser tendencies to
run will be associated with places more and more distant from that
end.

By introducing the notion of relative strengths of separate tendencies to react in different ways, Miller is in position to account for a
variety of possible reactions when such tendencies are present but
opposed. The typical situation employed by Miller as a paradigm of
conflict is that of an enclosed alley at one end of which an animal
learns to find food or water. Later the animal is shocked at this end.
The strength of approach can be regulated by the number of learning trials and by the deprivation period, the avoidance by the number
and strength of shocks. An animal can now be placed in the alley at
any desired point and its behavior should consequently be predictable
in terms of the strength of approach and avoidance tendencies at that
point.

To account for the behavior of an animal in the alley, Miller makes
four assumptions, two of which have already been stated as principles,
namely that there are tendencies to approach positive or avoid negative goals and that these tendencies increase with proximity to the
goal objects or locations. The third assumption is that the tendency
to avoid increases more rapidly with proximity to the negative "goal"
or unpleasant stimulus than does the approach tendency. In other
words, the gradient of avoidance is steeper than that of approach. The
fourth assumption is that both tendencies vary with the strengths of
the drives on which they are based. An increased drive may be said
to raise the *height* of the entire gradient. Support for these assumptions comes from Hull's original work on positive gradients and
Brown's (1942) work on drive differences in approach and avoidance
situations. It should be recalled that these gradients are based on
studies involving actual physical space although they are presumed
to function likewise in psychological space or time. Thus the subject

need not actually move physically so long as an impending event draws closer. The approach of Christmas might be presumed to have an effect on the behavior of a child just as examinations or the date and hour of a dental appointment might be assumed to affect behavior. No one has yet developed an experimental methodology for dealing with *psychological* space, and here we must be content (or discontent) with analogy. A study by Rigby (1954), however, did deal with a temporal situation in which rats were confined in cramping quarters with yokes fitted about their heads. A light and buzzer served as positive and negative stimuli. Ten seconds after the light came on, food would be presented to the animal. Similarly, 10 seconds after a buzzer, the animal would be shocked. The activity of the animal in terms of movement of the yoke could be measured during the interval. Rigby found evidence for both positive and negative gradients in this situation. Both gradients appear to be of the same shape after differential training. No greater steepness for the negative gradient (Miller's third assumption) was obtained in this experiment. When both stimuli were presented together (conflict) the animals tended to vacillate at all points during the 10-second interval or sit motionless. For the moment, we can conclude that the evidence in general, especially in spatial situations (Brown, 1942) tends to support Miller's assumptions.

With these assumptions put to work Miller is able to predict and explain what might happen when various combinations of behavioral tendencies are pitted against each other. The several possibilities are described as:

1. Approach-approach conflicts
2. Avoidance-avoidance conflicts
3. Approach-avoidance conflicts
4. Double approach-avoidance conflicts

The first type involves a choice between two positive goal objects and usually offers no real problem, particularly if either goal can be obtained later. Thus, only minor problems can be expected when guests are offered a choice of dessert, unless the guests are problem children to begin with. The second type is translated as "between the devil and the deep blue sea," or a "shotgun wedding," and no resolution is possible if the forces are at all powerful except to "get out of the field." The third and fourth types are presumed to be the situations where real difficulties are encountered. The third type characterizes the problem of wanting something which involves some unpleasantness, for example, asking the unsympathetic boss for a raise, or any circumstance that promises trouble along with the prospect of reward. The cashier with the bag full of bills might conceivably entertain ideas of absconding on occasion but the inevitable pursuit might deter him. In the fourth type the subject desires each of two alternatives which are of such a nature that taking one involves giving up the other (a negative feature). If John wants to marry Susie *and* Mary he may have a difficult time.

Miller assumes that these types of conflict when present in powerful degrees, that is, when the drive states are strong, are representative of the circumstances that result in neurotic behavior. Because the experimental support for his various deductions comes from laboratory situations involving rats (there are some limited observations on children who are faced with choices of candy and toys or pleasant and unpleasant drinks, two unpleasant drinks, and so on), the applications made by Miller remain on an analogy basis, however attractive they may appear.

How frequently such conflicts are faced with any degree of intensity is debatable. The forces involved must be nicely balanced or one will override the other. Of course, Miller's analysis applies only to situations where such forces are balanced. Whether "real life" provides many such occasions is the argument. Perhaps only special kinds of people can get themselves into such spots. Unless John is "neurotic" to begin with, he might not get involved with Mary and Susie at the same time. The employee frequently considers other aspects of the situation besides the presumed surliness of the boss. Of course this is meant by Miller as only an illustration but if this illustration is weak, how can one presume that real situations are any stronger? An employee who seriously believes that a raise depends on the *personality* of an employer and not on his own is in a bad way or is working in the wrong place to begin with, either of which circumstance is suspicious.

The gradients employed by Miller must be thought of as relatively pure, spatial (and temporal) aspects of a limited situation in which *generalization* is the key principle. Bugelski and Woodward (1951) showed that a rat will not run in terms of a gradient from a place in which it was shocked if the shock area is made distinctive enough, any more than spectators at the zoo run from caged lions. To apply gradient principles to behavior in complex human relationships may be on the right path, but to make predictions about the outcomes appears prohibitively complicated. If John leaves town and jilts Jane, we can come through with an *ad hoc* explanation—he left the field.

In their book, *Personality and Psychotherapy*, Dollard and Miller (1950) show how the analysis of conflict can be applied to psychotherapy. One interesting example involves the question of how to bring the subject to handle previously threatening situations. Assuming a high steep negative gradient, one can deduce that forcing a patient too soon to face the formerly unpleasant stimulus or idea will result only in precipitous retreat after some apparent progress has been made. The solution for therapy then is to extinguish the negative features first before trying to achieve positive control. If there is a strong fear of sexual relations the therapist would not urge the patient to try for success in this area until he was confident that the fear was overcome at least to the point where approach tendencies would be strong enough to carry the patient along. Since the possibilities of measurement of such tendencies are lacking, it makes deduction a matter of advice for the art of therapy rather than a working principle.

In the typical experimental pattern followed by Miller and his coworkers we have to recognize again the possible interplay of the three variables of conflict, anxiety, and frustration. It seems logical enough to assume that the hungry rat facing a place where shock has been experienced will become somewhat anxious. Failure to get food is as much a frustration as any other kind of failure. If the three variables cannot be separated it may prove awkward to deduce behavior from conflict principles when one or two or many other variables might, in fact, be determining the reactions.

For the present we must admit that learning psychologists have not produced a handbook or set of formulas for the clinician to use. In the face of the enormous problem of handling the disturbances of personality observed by the clinicians, the harvest from learning theory may seem paltry and useless. We should take account of the conclusions of some clinicians (see Rosenzweig, 1949) who feels that clinicians owe but little to the laboratory and can find little therein to apply. What they need in their work they will largely have to develop for themselves, at least for some time to come. Learning psychologists are just scratching the surface and are greatly handicapped by not being familiar with clinical material and by looking for short cuts to the truth of the matter which, like many other truths, may be vastly complicated. For the learning psychologist to pretend to understand or to be able to alleviate clinical symptoms is dishonest. For the clinician to pretend that his work is based on learning experiments or "learning principles" is equally dishonest. At best they can only offer each other a hand and continue their labors without blinding themselves to the complexity of the problem and to other factors besides learning.

NONLEARNING FACTORS IN PERSONALITY DISTURBANCES

Hebb (1949, p. 261) has courageously suggested that there are other factors. In what amounts to heresy for the ordinary psychologist who has enjoyed his Freud along with a smattering of learning theory and propaganda, Hebb points to the cases of two more or less psychotic chimpanzees (1947) who became so for no apparent good reasons. These are but illustrations, of course, of his general point of view which amounts to considering hereditary and constitutional factors along with experience as determining factors of neurotic or psychotic behavior. Hebb has gone ahead to investigate some of the conditions which produce disturbance, disorientation, and other aspects of "neurotic" behavior. In one study mentioned earlier (p. 209), Bexton, Heron, and Scott (1954) observed the effects of isolation, boredom, and sensory deprivation on subjects who were paid $20 per day to lie on a cot with their eyes goggled, their arms cuffed in large tubes, and obliged to listen to a monotonous tone coming from a pillow speaker. The subjects developed hallucinations and other disturbances and suffered a loss in capacity to handle problems. In another study previously cited (Hebb, *et al.*, 1954) subjects were temporarily deafened and, again, disturbances in reactions were observed. While these studies are modest and certainly only exploratory, they represent a new approach or angle of attack which may add something to our understanding of the "abnormal."

Hebb lists four propositions for serious consideration in his *The Organization of Behavior*, even though they may sound absurd. These four propositions are ridiculous only to the orthodox and to those whose faith has been stronger than their artillery:

1. That there is no separate class of mental illness caused by psychological factors alone—by what was seen and heard in childhood.

2. That we know little about "mental hygiene" or how to achieve it.

3. That it has not been shown that worry and the like can by itself cause any bodily condition such as asthma or stomach ulcers, though it aggravates such conditions.

4. That it has not been shown that any specialized psychotherapy, such as psychoanalysis, has any special value in mental illness.

Of course, Hebb is talking about proof, scientific proof, and he goes on to show that the statements are not ridiculous; in fact, to assert their contraries is more so, according to ordinary concepts of proof.

In connection with the first statement Hebb cites numerous studies which indicate the role of metabolic and structural factors in conditions frequently diagnosed by psychologists and even medical men as "functional" or psychogenic and suggests that it is "possible that a contributing organic cause will be found for all those cases that are now called purely functional." Hebb is strongly impressed with the high incidence (85.18 percent) of schizophrenia for identical twins of schizophrenics compared with the low incidence for fraternal twins (14.7 percent) and the extremely low incidence for stepbrothers and stepsisters (1.8 percent). Hebb regards reports of "experimental neurosis" as apparently "specific to the situation in which it was established," and notes also the fact of differential susceptibility in various breeds and species, pointing to a constitutional factor. The remaining statements are also critically examined and no evidence is found which requires modifying them. In connection with the fourth statement the reader should consult writers like Eysenck (1952a, 1952b) as well as reviewers of clinical success in the *Annual Review of Psychology* (Meehl, 1955). Eysenck (1954), after reviewing the literature on the success of psychotherapy, writes: "If we accept the very doubtful evidence contained in this literature, then our only conclusion can be that there is no evidence whatever to suggest that psychotherapy, Freudian or otherwise, has any ameliorating influence on neurotic disorders." Meehl (1955) in commenting on this conclusion says, "The history of the healing arts furnishes ample grounds for skepticism as to our non-systematic 'clinical' observations."

Hebb stresses the operation of somatophysic factors as of considerable significance in contrast to the popular but experimentally unsupported "psychosomatics."

While psychosomatic viewpoints are extremely popular with clinical psychologists, the writers in this field fail to present an account of how conflict, worry, and other "psychological" operations result in structural or physical symptoms. When Franz Alexander (1950, p. 90) considers that "the stubborn refusal of the nipple by some infants immediately after birth may perhaps be considered as the earliest prototype of anorexia," the critical experimentalist may perhaps be forgiven for raising an eyebrow. Alexander (1950, p. 45) notes the fact that Von Bergmann, who in 1913 claimed that peptic ulcers probably resulted from a chronic gastric neurosis caused by emotional factors, changed his mind in 1927 and "felt it necessary to revise his views . . . he expressed his belief that in most such cases further research would disclose organic causes." It is unfortunate that in spite of giving lip service to the possibility that structural factors might be the important determiners, the psychosomaticists go right on finding psychological origins for tuberculosis, diabetes, and coronary disease. Dunbar (1943) even finds that coronary patients are often "distinguished looking."

It should not be concluded from the above comments that Hebb is in the least antipsychological. He is merely trying to prevent psychologists from rushing into action on the basis of unsupported theories. His major thesis, as he has frequently stated (1949, 1951), is to recognize the role of hereditary and constitutional factors before psychologists get too far out of bounds in staking out their claims. It is not enough to pay lip service to physiology and then proceed as if the organism was merely a bundle of bad habits. Bad habits there might be, but some of them might have to be treated by the surgeon's knife, by changes in diet, by drugs, by electric shock, and by still-to-be-discovered techniques. Hebb's plea is only that the shoemaker stick to his last and learn his trade well.

Dallenbach (1955) has drawn some interesting analogies between the history of phrenology and the history of psychoanalysis. At the conclusion of his paper he quotes from Ernest Jones, Freud's biographer. Freud is reported to have said: "that in time to come it should be possible to cure hysteria and nervous diseases by adminstering a chemical drug without any psychological treatment." Currently the psychiatric world is greatly interested and concerned with the outcomes of therapy involving drugs. Enthusiastic claims for the success of tranquilizing drugs may have to be tempered in the future, but the search for chemical cures for neuroses and psychoses is definitely a major area of research. Dallenbach raises the question of what will be Freud's niche in history if the chemical attack is eventually successful. The question is equally applicable to clinical psychology. If learning theory is to be successfully incorporated into the study of personality and its aberrations, it appears that the path of wisdom is to move slowly, taking account of the simultaneous research in the chemical and physiological areas.

Chapter

16   *Learning and*
       Education

Up to now we have considered a large number of theoretical arguments about the nature and principles of learning. In all that has gone before we have been able to look at experiments which, whether they bore on the issues or not, had the virtue of simplicity and some modest degree of control. To the extent that the experiments were adequately controlled, there are available certain empirical findings which could be used for prediction and control of behavior. We know, for example, under what conditions a rat can be gotten to learn a maze most rapidly or how to make a pigeon peck at a desired rate. We can even make a rat run back and forth in an alley. We can teach dogs to roll over and chickens to walk tightropes.

Unfortunately no one but a psychologist is interested in such activities. The general public is rather more interested in how to bring up and educate their children to be "successful" or to be "good citizens."

Psychologists have not been averse toward studying the problems of education but their efforts in this direction have not been too richly rewarded. Once we leave the narrow and restricted quarters of the rat, the problems of controlled experimentation multiply so rapidly as to leave the issues quite unresolved, and experiments are subject to more alternative explanations than even those previously considered. It is with some misgivings then that we approach the question of how much meaningful and useful information the learning psychologists have accumulated about human learning beyond the conditioned reflex level.

The common interest of the average layman is in the type of learning that deals with the intelligent handling of situations, in the acquisition of what he calls "facts," in the achievement of understanding, and in the acquisition of skills of a variety of types including verbal, manual, and symbolic skills like those involved in mathematics. Some even expect to learn how to think and some instructors are immodest enough to suggest that they can teach students to think.

What have we learned about learning theory that is applicable to the problems facing the parent, the teacher, the supervisor of training in industry or the military? Is it possible to apply some general principles to the great variety of learning situations that crop up everyday in so many different circumstances? Are there any principles which can be applied to teaching someone how to be happy, to be efficient? Do the same principles that apply to teaching a Boy Scout to tie a square knot also apply to teaching someone how to be polite or how to write a theme or how to study? When a military trainee is set to learning the Morse code, will the principles that apply to learning a list of nonsense syllables apply? After all, the series of dots and dashes are so much nonsense at first. What about the child learning to recite the alphabet or a nursery rhyme? Or the fifth-grader learning to multiply fractions or first encountering the decimal system?

It should be quite clear that to expect any small group of principles to cover the range of learning situations that could be enumerated is quite idle and wishful. The student will have learned by now that the learning process itself is but poorly known as yet. Our understanding is confounded by theoretical controversy. There are certain broad generalizations, however, on which most theorists would probably agree.

In this chapter we shall try to make use of those theoretical propositions on which there is most agreement.

We shall not attempt to bring together or develop principles out of the vast fund of empirical observations of teachers and trainers as this would serve little use in the present text as well as create new controversies, for it is commonly observed that one man's empirical meat is another's empirical poison. The discussion will be limited to the contributions to education that have been proposed by learning psychologists rather than those developed by educators. To attempt any greater scope would call for another text. Restricting ourselves to the work of learning psychologists, on the other hand, hardly calls for a chapter. Learning psychologists have not been very active in applying their theoretical principles to practical problems. Only Guthrie

(1953) has written an *Educational Psychology* and this in collaboration with Powers. Skinner (1948a) has offered an educational philosophy in his *Walden II* but he hardly touched on realistic educational problems. Recently, Skinner has worked out a technique and a device for teaching children arithmetical operations. We have not yet had time to evaluate such a device or to consider the possibilities for other kinds of learning situations.

Even when learning psychologists are invited to contribute directly to a volume dealing with educational problems their papers prove to be highly theoretical summaries of their views and hardly the kind of material which a teacher in any kind of educational situation can use. (See the *Forty-first Yearbook* of the National Society for Education, 1942.)

Thorpe and Schmuller (1954) have made a commendable effort to analyze the contributions of learning theorists to education. They reviewed the theoretical formulations and the experimental support for nine different viewpoints. After each theory was presented, the "implications for education" were drawn. We might pause for a moment and consider one such "implication" and see how useful it is.

In deriving the implications for education in Guthrie's theory, the authors mention that "Guthrie pays particular attention in his system to the role of the teacher." Teachers are to select and present subject matter in such a way as to arouse the "native curiosity" of each learner. We can readily imagine a frantic teacher trying to fill this role any better after reading this than before. On what basis is she to select? How is she to present? What if the learner does not appear to have any "native curiosity"? And each learner can receive this individual attention every 1/30th of time at the teacher's disposal if she has 30 pupils and nothing else to do. This amounts to about 10 minutes per pupil in a 5-hour school day. To pursue the point into a specific learning task, Thorpe and Schmuller find Guthrie suggesting that in teaching a child to read, "it is essential that specific stimuli be presented which, once he is motivated (aroused), will elicit the correct reading responses, by trial and error if need be. Subsequently, displacement of correct reading responses is to be guarded against." Now, this is a fair enough interpretation of Guthrie, but what can anyone do with such advice when introducing a five-year-old to the business of reading? How do we present these specific stimuli? What are the specific stimuli for reading? Are they words, as the Teacher's College group (Gates, 1948) maintains, or are they the "phonics" that Flesch (1954) advocates? How do we motivate the student? How do we elicit the "correct reading responses"? And finally, how do we guard against the displacement?

We can hardly blame educators for being annoyed with learning psychologists. Thorpe and Schmuller are to be praised for having the courage to go on through nine such theoretical approaches. Whether they became imbued with the spirit of vagueness and unreality themselves or whether in the nature of the case they felt compelled to make as much practical sense as they could from the work of learning theorists cannot be discovered from their text. Their own summary, however, based on a review of all of the theories considered, is hardly any more "practical" than the remarks of Guthrie. We list now the five practical learning principles Thorpe and Schmuller managed to salvage or discover in current learning theory:

1. Motivation: "Learning proceeds most effectively and tends to be most permanent when the learner is motivated, that is, when he has a stake, as it were, in the activity being undertaken."

2. Adjustment to maturation level: "Learning proceeds most rapidly and tends to be most permanent when the activity involved is geared to the learner's physical and intellectual ability to perform that activity."

3. Pattern learning: "Learning proceeds most effectively and tends to be most permanent when the learner is provided with the opportunity of perceiving meaningful relationships among the elements of the goal toward which he is working."

4. Evaluation of progress: "Learning goes forward with relatively greater effectiveness when the learner is provided with some criterion for indicating specifically what progress he is making."

5. Broad integrated development: "Learning is facilitated when it goes forward under conditions in which the learner also experiences satisfactory personality adjustment and social growth."

These five principles are the harvest of the thousands of experiments performed in the field of learning as they look to educators. Whether these are really principles of learning or just prejudices and platitudes might very well be questioned. As practical propositions, only the fourth (knowledge of results) has any real basis for implementation. We should be able to arrange for a student to know how well he is doing, even though we frequently neglect to do so. The other principles are hardly stated in such a way as to be implemented by the teacher in any practical form.

There is a great gap between the laboratory and the classroom.

Nothing is gained by ignoring this gap. Nor is anything gained by learning theorists mocking educational psychologists or vice versa. Educators frequently enough sneer at learning psychologists as dreamers, ivory-tower inhabitants, and so on. Spence (1954) cautions against any great hopes for practical application of learning theory for a long time to come. Are we to conclude that the laboratory study of learning is, at least for the present, without practical value?

It should be recognized, of course, that what is considered of practical value depends on the frame of reference in which the question is asked. Is it not of value to have recognized the enormous complexity of the learning process? Is it not of value to appreciate that there are no easy answers to difficult questions? Is it not of value to recognize that we still have a great deal to learn about learning? That there are limits to what can be taught, that there are limits to techniques, that there are tremendous individual and species differences, that all our problems are not going to be solved by "better teachers" and "better schools" even if we knew what made a "better" or even a good teacher? There might even be some comfort in the knowledge that psychologists are not quite able to "control" behavior by controlling past or present experience. If the educational system of any country was as successful as some might wish, we could hardly hope for changes, improvements, or progress. Some might be grateful that Watson's early claim to make any normal baby into whatever he desired is in no danger of being realized.

The discussion thus far has been largely negative. Lest the student be too thoroughly dismayed, we should recognize that there are positive findings of considerable importance to education which the psychologists have developed and which can be used effectively if the situation in which these findings are to be applied can be specified. What this amounts to is that if the learning psychologist is permitted to state his conditions, he will be able to secure better results in teaching than one not so trained. The conditions that the psychologist might demand, however, might be impractical in a realistic appraisal of the situation. For example, the psychologist might wish to teach one student at a time instead of having forty or more. The psychologist might hesitate at being asked to teach "good citizenship" or "satisfactory social adjustment" by limiting himself to a classroom. He might feel that it is useless to teach geography at all in a classroom, that the way to teach it is to take around-the-world cruises, or at least some rather expensive facsimiles. The tax-paying and tuition-paying parents might revolt at some of the psychologist's suggestions even though they complain now about how little their children learn. The psychologist might find it undesirable for a child to know the capitals of the 48 states until he knew what a capital was. This would hardly please parents who measure their children's progress by the ability to rattle-off 48 paired-associate nonsense words.

In the remainder of this chapter we shall try to suggest how the discoveries of learning psychologists might or could be applied, given the necessary conditions. Before we do so, however, something should be said about the approach of the psychologist to a learning problem.

THE LEARNING PSYCHOLOGIST'S APPROACH
TO EDUCATION

Education and human engineering. During World War II, psychologists in great numbers were called into service and assigned practical problems, in many cases involving teaching and training both elementary and complex skills. The preparation of an army is a huge educational project and the contribution of psychologists has been acknowledged to be an important one.

As an outcome of their experience during the war, many psychologists have continued in one or another applied fields and their work as practical operators is commonly identified as "human engineering." The basic approach of the human engineer is to improve a product or production process by attempting to adjust the men and machines involved to each other. The first step is to analyze the product, note the deficiencies or lacks, determine the desired goal, and then alter the men, machine, or system as permitted or required to achieve an improved product or process. It is obvious that before the human engineer can go to work effectively, he must know what is desired. If the goal is to produce a better marksman or faster typist it is possible to measure the present level and to determine a desired level or at least to know what would be better in terms of a statistical difference. If the human engineer is asked to produce a better soldier, then we have complications. The latter request would be parallel to asking public-school teachers to produce better citizens. It is obvious that *measurable* criteria of what the goal is to be must be stated. Without such measurable criteria, the psychologist hardly knows which way to turn.

Once the goal is stated, an analysis can be instituted into determining the contribution of the recognizable variables to the present product. The presumption of the human engineer (see Fitts, 1951) is that the present product is a function of the total variance of the several variables that enter into a given product. Thus, poorness of quality or performance is due to errors or variability from some standard. Errors may be constant (more or less built into the man or machine) or variable. Sources of error must be controlled if there is to be a resultant improvement.

When the sources of error are detected and controlled, efforts can be instituted to improve the situation by applying whatever principles are available which bear on the matter. The applications are then subjected to experimental test and, if the results are favorable, the change is instituted. The whole process can then be started again as new principles are suggested until further improvements involve a diminishing return and a prohibitive expense.

How can this approach be applied to education? The essence of the matter is to state clearly what the objective is. So long as the objective is specific and measurable, it is possible to begin work. To take a practical example, psychologists were asked to improve the training of radio operators during the war. Such training has been a common military need since the invention of the telegraph. It might be imagined that training techniques had been established beyond any hope of major improvement. Yet Keller (1943) was able to cut the failure rate among trainees from 15 to 3.4 percent and, more important, he cut the time from former army standards of 41 and 35 hours to 27 hours. Later (p. 478) we shall describe how Keller went about improving code instruction. For the moment we recognize that the task involved was describable and the goal obvious.

Once the preliminary analysis of the problem is completed, the business of developing new procedures must be faced. What principles can be applied? How does the psychologist go about improving Morse code training? He comes prepared, of course, with a background of general principles on which there is considerable agreement even if the principles are vague and far too general to apply directly. He does not, however, deliberately engage in application of procedures that would *violate* the generalizations. This appreciation of the negative, of what not to do, can be of great help and save considerable time and effort. Nor does he engage in application of controversial principles. It is unlikely, for example, that even Tolman would plan to have army trainees learn Morse code by a "latent learning" procedure.

What general principles would the average learning psychologist endorse? We have listed earlier those suggested by Thorpe and Schmuller and found them somewhat vague. Can we do any better?

General principle of learning. While there is no likelihood that any congress of learning psychologists would produce the same list of learning principles on which there would be general agreement, the following list might not prove too different from what might be proposed at such a congress. Perhaps the suggested principles are not entitled to that label. They might even be thought of as biases or prejudices if not as only working assumptions. While universal acceptance is by no means anticipated, and, in fact, misgivings might be more prominent than approval, it might serve a useful purpose to offer a tentative list of such principles. The suggested principles follow:

1. SPECIES AND INDIVIDUAL DIFFERENCES. There are species and individual differences in capacity which must be taken into account before we initiate a learning program. These differences set limits upon what kinds of processes can be acquired. We have previously discussed this under the heading of the A-S ratio (see p. 33).

2. MOTIVATION. The concept of motivation is unquestionably a confused one. If, however, we restate it as essentially a matter of *readiness* for learning, we can include it here as a broad general assumption of major importance. In this restatement, it carries the weight of a concept of attention and includes such equivocal terms as "curiosity," "set," and "expectancy."

3. REINFORCEMENT. Again, whatever the theoretical arguments, a concept of reinforcement as described earlier (see pp. 260–268) in terms of the running-off or completion of an activity which eliminates the stimulation that originated it is a required assumption. In effect, and empirically, a reinforcer in a learning situation can be the occurrence of any event which terminates the stimulus situation. In practice, telling someone that he is correct in some response is such a situation. Telling him that he is incorrect is not such an event since the situation is presumed to contain some stimulus features relating to the subject's self-stimulation which require the "correct" event for their elimination.

4. THE ROLE OF PAST EXPERIENCE. This text has stressed the fact that there is a difference between early or original learning and later learning. We might call it a difference between the learning of a child

and of an adult who is in position to have his childhood experiences, and, in fact, all previous experience work for him. The distinction could be made, as well, in terms of meaningful versus nonmeaningful material where meaningful material is defined as material that is already familiar in some respects in the sense that some kinds of reaction to it will occur on the first occasion of encountering it in a new situation. Thus, it is possible for a person with familiarity with the language to learn the expression "Caesar crossed the Rubicon" in one hearing. A collection of nonsense syllables of equal length would require more trials. We can expect past experience to help or hinder, depending on the special circumstances as described in the chapter on transfer (see p. 391).

5. INTERNALIZATION, OR MEDIATION. (See p. 160.) It must be assumed that the role of past experience is carried on through a process of self-stimulation.

6. LEARNING IS DONE BY THE LEARNER AND NOT BY SOME KIND OF TRANSMISSION PROCESS FROM THE TEACHER. This has been implicit throughout the book. The function of the teacher is to prepare the situation and the chains of events in such a fashion that the learner has the maximum possibilities of acquiring the proper "connections."

It will be observed that only two of the above principles correspond with those of Thorpe and Schmuller (motivation and knowledge of results). The others call attention to aspects of learning not considered in the earlier list. Beyond these limited and general assumptions we cannot go without controversy. With them as "built-in" equipment, the learning psychologist turned human engineer is ready to take the first step in attacking a learning situation. It will be recalled that the human engineer's procedure involves a statement of the problem and the goal in measurable terms, an analysis of the variables determining present performance, and an experimental attack evaluating proposals for eliminating and controlling variables and for testing the value of proposals for improvement. We cannot take the time or space to describe such a program for every conceivable learning situation and will have to content ourselves with a more general coverage, hoping to avoid the frustrating vagueness more or less inherent in a general approach. It appears that the broadest purposes will be served if we attempt a classification of the more common variables and indicate what the learning laboratory has contributed to the control of each.

Our first order of business is then to outline the task that might face the teacher. The variables we will consider deal only with human (mostly children) learning situations in connection with "real life" learning. References to nonsense syllables and animal learning will have to be made on some occasions for lack of any other sources. These references, of course, will have to be taken as of suggestive value only.

Variables in educational situations

1. Kind of learning material and the nature of the learner
2. The learning situation
   a. The learning environment
   b. The role of the teacher
      (1) Motivating function—attention
      (2) Instructing function—reinforcement
         (a) Information
         (b) Guidance
         (c) Imitation
   c. Other instructional devices
      (1) Visual aids
      (2) Mechanical devices
3. Practice operations
   a. Distribution of practice—spacing
   b. Patterning—whole versus part
   c. Active versus passive
   d. Form versus content
   e. Speed versus accuracy
   f. Knowledge of results

The list of variables presented above can serve to orient the discussion in the present chapter. The list is by no means complete and purports to cover only a sample of the learning psychologist's activities. Some variables have been omitted from the present list because they have received consideration in earlier chapters. The present list includes only a few of the more "popular" operations about which controversy is still quite active.

1. KIND OF LEARNING MATERIAL AND THE NATURE OF THE LEARNER

We have already devoted separate chapters to these variables (Chapters 3 and 4). The variables are mentioned here at this time to remind the student that the learning of visual-motor skills is not necessarily going to follow the rules of rote-memory findings, that the learning of facts and the learning of principles may call for different manipulations. Learning emotional control and social graces are problems in their own right. The characteristics of the learner (health, personality, maturation level, special "gifts" or talents or lack of these) must also be taken into account. One learner may grasp at once what another can never learn adequately. The teacher who proceeds to treat everyone alike may be displaying a fine democratic spirit but he may be violating other laws than those guaranteed by the Constitution.

In considering the subject matter and the learner as the first steps, the teacher is covering the initial tasks of the human engineer, the analysis of what the present situation amounts to and what is to be done. The next step is to scrutinize the role the teacher himself is to play.

2. THE LEARNING SITUATION

The learning situation includes at least three variables, the learning environment, the teacher and his relationship with the learner, and the material equipment designed to facilitate the learning.

a. The learning environment. About the learning environment per se the laboratory findings are simply nonexistent. Whereas we all approve of large, airy, well-lighted, nicely decorated schools we have no laboratory evidence that the learning process itself is a function of temperature, humidity, or esthetic surroundings. In the laboratory, the effort has been to simplify the environment so that learning would go on free from distractions. Pavlov (1927) tells about his efforts to reduce the range and nature of irrelevant cues. Leuba's (1941) experiments with hypnosis suggest again that learning is most rapid when the environment is restricted (in his case by sensory deprivation). The Western Electric studies of Roethlesberger and Dickson (1939) again show how productive efficiency is not affected seriously, if at all, by environmental variables. The experiment of Bilodeau and Schlosberg (1951) will be recalled in this connection. Subjects learned equally well in a dingy apparatus room and in a well-lighted room.

Apparently, from the laboratory findings, the environment serves to distract, to provide stimuli which are undesirable and, from Guthrie's point of view, may become parts of a stimulus pattern so that a child may know answers in his classroom seat that he does not know at home. The practice of theater directors of conducting all rehearsals on the stage instead of in living rooms may have strong laboratory support.

None of the above comments is to be interpreted as a plea for a bare and unadorned or dingy classroom, of course. There are other values that must be considered. We must be careful about applying short-term laboratory data to situations where a time span of 16 or more educational years is to be considered.

b. The role of the teacher. It should be apparent that while students do learn, teachers do not teach, at least, not in the sense that the teacher does anything to the student. So far as is known, no teacher has been able to "knock sense into" anyone. When a child does not perform up to parental standards, it is customary to denounce the teacher, and it may even be proper, but not for the usual reasons. The teacher's role must be appreciated before we criticize his methods. What makes a good teacher or a bad one? Are popular teachers good teachers? Should teachers be directive, nondirective, authoritative, democratic? We cannot presume to decide on these questions, but a consideration of the functions of a teacher might make us less dogmatic about our answers.

From the laboratory point of view, the teacher has only two functions. One of these is to motivate learning, the other is to reinforce it. A third function might be presumed to operate between these two, that of arranging the necessary situation, apparatus, stimuli, or provide an opportunity for responses that are to be learned. Let us consider these in order.

(1) THE MOTIVATING FUNCTION. When the psychologist starves a rat, he motivates him. We have already examined what this means (see Chap. 9) and have decided that the starving procedure results in a rat that is inclined or "set" to respond to stimuli related to food. We have also noted that certain so-called secondary reinforcers are more appropriately considered secondary or additional motivators or additional stimuli for responding in specific ways (see p. 93). While some students may be "starved for knowledge" it is not ordinarily the result of having been put on a deprivation schedule. It is not an easy matter to create a "motivating" situation in a classroom. But motivation, in the sense we are using it here, has nothing to do with "wanting" to learn or eagerness to learn or any other state of desiring. De-

siring or wishing has little to do with the case. What is important is that the learner be "set" to react to stimuli and if this is done without his wish it makes little if any difference. The rat certainly does not wish to starve, nor does it wish to learn. It happens to work out that one procedure for creating an appropriate set in human learners might be described as getting them "interested" or "wanting to learn." In either case or in any case, it amounts to creating a situation where a suitable reaction is given to specific stimuli. We have already referred to this as the problem of *attention* or central facilitation (see p. 134). We can afford to talk about attention now without the quotation marks.

The primary function of the teacher, then, is to get the students to "pay" attention. Whether this is done by use of birch rods, electric shock, Chinese water torture, or by promises of ice cream, movies, or money is irrelevant. One procedure or another may involve disastrous side effects or lead to other difficulties, but if attention is secured that problem is solved. Sometimes even screaming at the children to *Pay attention!* may work.

As far as learning psychologists have been able to proceed in this difficult area (Dollard and Miller, 1950) it is pretty generally presumed that attention results when students are made or *become anxious*. How this comes about is not explained by currently prominent learning theorists. No other proposition has been advanced as the "drive" behind ordinary human learning. "Curiosity" itself is based on anxiety, according to Dollard and Miller (1950). The task of the teacher is to create the necessary degree of anxiety. The proposition that anxiety is the basic drive for human learning may appear paradoxical when teachers note that failures in arithmetic are so frequently associated with anxiety. The paradox is easily resolved in theory if we go on and demand that the anxiety must also be relieved at the conclusion of the correct response.

Whether or not anxiety actually plays any separate role (along with its own reduction) it is unlikely that we can find any direct proof for this proposition. That "anxiety" plays some sort of role seems to be borne out by the work of Spence and Taylor (1951), Hilgard, Jones, and Kaplan (1951), and many others who find that "anxious" subjects condition more readily in defensive situations (eyelid blink, galvanic responses). On the other hand, anxious subjects learn verbal and other complicated tasks less well than less anxious subjects. It has been shown that there is a negative correlation between anxiety and IQ (Matarazzo *et al.* 1954) There may be other correlates of anxiety that operate in the learning situation. It is possible, of course, that anxiety operates only in developing a set to learn. When the set developed through anxiety is suitable for certain kinds of responses, a high degree of anxiety may facilitate learning (especially if the measure of learning is itself a measure of the anxiety, as in the case of the PGR). Too much anxiety, on the other hand, may create a set for avoidance or escape behavior and if this is not in the immediate learning program, then the learning will be hampered.

While we are not obliged to accept the notion that anxiety is *the* drive in human learning and the corresponding notion that the reduction of anxiety will reinforce human learning, it seems reasonable to assume that anxiety in some manner helps to create the conditions that generate learning. We have already suggested that anxiety is possibly related to the development of a suitable set. In the following discussion, then, we will consider the function of anxiety *to be restricted to attention-getting* and avoid the theoretical difficulties brought up in the previous chapter. With the above restrictions clearly before us we can define the first obligation of the teacher to be that of creating an appropriate level of anxiety or "curiosity" in the student. The student must be made uneasy or distressed in a situation which he has come to label as one of "not knowing." When the uneasiness or distress is relieved by making certain responses stipulated by the teacher (or text) the student has gone through the basic requirement for learning.

A number of interesting consequences follow from this approach. A student who does not feel uncomfortable in a "not knowing" situation will not, cannot learn. If he can recognize and label the situation and not feel uneasy, he will not proceed to any action. This is, of course, a common, if not universal characteristic of students for most "not knowing" situations. They are not expected to know everything. They are "reinforced" for learning only some kinds of things. Curiosity about others is negatively reinforced and discouraged. Very few aspirants for universal knowledge are discovered. Specialization is a keynote of our civilization. It starts at home with commonly enforced restrictions on activities of the sexes. Girls are not encouraged to use nails and hammers. Even learning psychologists are not inclined to pursue topics outside their area. The teacher has a difficult task in developing a nicely calculated degree of anxiety about the Rosetta Stone or the reign of Charlemagne.

Because most human learning in school situations is bound to be far removed from any direct, physiological needs, the anxiety must be developed by artificial means. The usual means are threats of disapproval, various stimuli that have acquired anxiety value, deprivation of affection and privilege, and so on. A student indifferent to such threats is at best a reluctant learner.

It does not matter what techniques are used or what the threat involves. Hebb (1955), for example, once reversed the usual tactic with a classroom of children and sent all those students who did not care to attend to the lesson out to play. The "freed" students were not allowed to do homework or engage in any educational activity. According to Hebb the students revolted against the technique, demanded homework, and insisted on studying, refusing the opportunities to play.

While we are unable to recommend techniques for controlling the development of controlled degrees of anxiety or curiosity, it perhaps is of value to the teacher to recognize that the "art of teaching" consists of just such manipulation.

(2) THE REINFORCEMENT FUNCTION OF TEACHERS. If the motivating function of teachers is to develop appropriate degrees of "anxiety," the reinforcement function is to allay that anxiety.[1] This operation becomes as complex and devious as the former one in that the reinforcement must be related to the degree of anxiety established and must be given at the appropriate time to have any effect on the learning. The timing might be considered of greatest importance in view of the experimental literature which rather uniformly suggests time intervals on the order of seconds. The reinforcing value of a high grade given at the end of a semester can have little or no direct effect on the learning of skills or content during the semester. If it has any value at all it is in connection with the maintenance of some minimum level of anxiety throughout the learning season on which additional anxiety can be built.

Dollard and Miller (1950) find that the reinforcement effects from successful learning (reduction of anxiety) can come to play a role

---

[1] It should be appreciated that the term "reinforcement" is being employed here in accordance with the meaning attached to it earlier (see p. 260) and not in the sense of some "effect" of drive reduction. How the subject feels about the fact of having given a correct answer or having made a correct response is unimportant in itself. The important feature is that the stimulus pattern involved in the learning situation has been accommodated by the brain activity and is no longer enforcing a change in the pattern of that activity.

such that, after a sufficient number of successes, the learner can come to enjoy a modest anxiety which is encountered in a "not-know" situation. The learner may come to enjoy problems and even seek them out. This behavior we label "curiosity." Curiosity has a high social valuation and the learner learns that it pays to be curious or at least to have that label attached to himself. The label itself comes to carry reinforcement properties.

It is obvious that the handling of the reinforcement function will be a delicate business and calls for the closest supervision of individual performances. To reinforce each child in a class of 30 or so is impossible as far as teachers' operations are concerned. To the extent that learning goes on, it must be assumed that a process of self-reinforcement goes on. There must be some means by which the learner reinforces himself or there could be no learning in a classroom. The learning psychologist finds such a mechanism in the alleged reinforcement value of "knowledge of results." We will consider this mechanism a little later (see p. 477).

As far as the learning psychologist is concerned, then, it is the obligation of the teacher to manipulate the factors of anxiety and reinforcement in such a fashion that positive results are obtained. Any objection to such a proposal on the grounds that it is difficult or impossible with a large class must be met with a shrug. Learning psychologists were not consulted about the size of classes. Ideally, a class should consist of one student and a tutor. Any attempt to go above this limit must be tempered with the realization that provision must be made for self-reinforcement by the rest of the class.

While the reinforcement function calls for the manipulation of rewards and other devices calculated to reduce anxiety, teachers frequently resort to punishment, criticism, and other forms of abuse when appropriate behavior does not emerge. Such activity is not ordinarily condoned by learning psychologists. On the other hand, if it generates useful anxiety which is then reduced after appropriate responses on the part of the learner, then no exception can be taken from it. Punishment for punishment's sake, of course, is not expected to result in learning anything except escape and negative emotional reactions.

(3) THE INSTRUCTING FUNCTION OF THE TEACHER. By the instructing function we mean the process of arranging the necessary conditions, circumstances, and materials by which stimuli are presented and responses generated. This is what is usually meant by "teaching."

How does a teacher go about this? Basically there appear to be at least two techniques of age-old standing: telling the student about something or telling him how to do something and leading him through the procedure by some showing or guiding process, and depending upon some capacity of "imitation" to work. Let us consider each of these in turn.

(a). *The "telling" or talking method.* At the present time there is a rather strong current of feeling opposed to "talking at" the learner. Lectures are considered as basically ineffective and more "active" methods are commonly espoused. We shall have more to say about active and passive methods a bit later (p. 474) but our present concern is with the procedures involved in teaching by talking. While "progressive" educators condemn lecturers, there is no unequivocal evidence that this process is a bad one or even a poor one. In fact, it may be the most effective available for some kinds of learning situations. The trouble is not with the lecturer, however poor he may be, but with the lectures. If the student is not prepared to attend to the material being given out, it is obviously a waste of his time as well as that of the lecturer. When children listen to fairy tales or ghost stories or adults listen to off-color stories the lecture procedure is the only one available and highly effective as far as visible results are concerned. Even one reading of a child's nursery tale is so effectively absorbed that future readings call for precise repetitions in some cases. There is no essential difference between reading nursery tales and reading papers on atomic research except in the audience. Good students emerging from the lecture hall may say, "That was a good lecture." Poor or unprepared students may have a contrary opinion.

The lecture is sometimes criticized as being "directive," and supporters of "nondirective" techniques hold for some sort of inner process of growth that comes from personal activity which they find missing in the lecture method. In one study (Faw, 1949) a lecture method of teaching elementary psychology was compared with a nondirective method. Results measured by an objective test at the end of the semester showed some superiority for the nondirective technique. There is nothing in the study, however, to show that the students in the nondirective class did not spend more time outside trying to learn material that they could not learn inside. It may be that a discussion technique will arouse interest among those who find lectures dull. This, however, is not the fault of the lecture, but of the learners. It is probably true that, as Lewin (1948) found, discussions can lead to more active participation than lectures when there is a question of motivation involved. The motivation, however, is a separate problem and should be kept separate.

There is one major objection to the lecture method, and this objection applies to any one-way teaching process (radio, television, movies, and so on). The student may find himself unable to follow some point, he may have questions to ask which are not answered (unreduced anxiety), or he may have missed parts of the material either for some physical reason such as too rapid a presentation, some interference, or because he is still concerned with a previous point. Unless the lecture can be played back, like a phonograph record, there may be some loss of material. Unless there is some provision for questions or otherwise making the learning session a two-way communication process, the lecture technique may suffer.

At one time student pilots were taught by the process of being told what to do by the pilot who was in the rear seat of a two-cockpit plane while the student sat up front. The pilot spoke through a rubber tube which brought the garbled sound of his voice to the ears of the student. The student had no way of communicating with the instructor. No questions could be asked in the air. While students did learn to fly with this training, it is only a testimonial to their capacity and no credit to the technique. One wonders about how many questions were left in the air.

Before the lecture technique is thrown out of the classroom and a discussion process substituted, it must be recognized that an uninformed discussion is likely to generate more heat than knowledge. Before students are prepared to discuss, there must be some information available. This information can be obtained only by reading or listening, barring the possibility that personal experience might be of some help. The prospect of personal experience in the French and Indian wars is exceedingly remote and one would hardly start a discussion of such a phase of history without the precaution of providing at least a little information. We can conclude the present discussion with the observation that learners are individuals and that education must be an individual matter. If a group of individuals can be brought to some condition of readiness so that the group can operate like or be treated like an individual, then the technique involved can be decided upon the basis of efficiency. It is not a question of lecture or discussion, direction or nondirection, but of what is effective with this learner or group of learners.

(b). *The guidance or "showing how" technique.* When words fail us, we resort to pointing or some sort of push-pull procedure that gets the learner through the motions. If we do not actually manipulate the subject's arms or legs we manipulate our own, hoping that some sort of *imitation* process will operate to bring about the proper sequence of actions. There are two separate problems here, one of guidance, the other of imitation. We can start with the first and see what has been learned about it.

In the laboratory the problem has been examined in terms of evaluating the effect of controlling the action of the learner so that he goes through a correct sequence without error. Thus in a maze the subject can be led through the correct path a number of times and then allowed to try it for himself. The usual finding in some rather old experiments (Koch, 1923; Ludgate, 1923; Carr, 1930) is that learning cannot occur by guidance alone. The subject must be allowed to make his own errors and eliminate these through some extinction process. Guidance does help when given in small doses and fairly early in the learning but not usually on the first trial. Guidance given after learning is well underway appears to be harmful. Here again we recognize the operation of the principle that it is the learner who must learn, he cannot be taught. Guthrie (1935) emphasizes the necessity for permitting the subject to make errors. Only by making errors can the stimuli which lead to erroneous responses be identified, and differentiated. In teaching a child to roller skate or to ride a bicycle, for example, it is important that the child be allowed to fall. (Precautions can be taken to avoid injury, but the falling process must be allowed to occur, at least to some degree.) Only by starting to fall can the child learn what stimuli lead to falling and develop counter-responses. It would probably be wise in many learning situations to make sure that all possible mistakes have been committed in order that each is eliminated. This advice is actually part of the training of aviators who are given specific training in what happens when you do the wrong thing. A beginning student is taken up (to a sufficient altitude to allow for recovery) and put through the paces of stalling, slipping, engine failure, and so on. Such deliberate training for errors is rarely instituted but should be instituted in many if not most kinds of manipulative learning. Instead of telling the beginning pen-and-ink writer to be careful not to smudge and smear there might be some gain from forcing him to get messed up to the point where rather vigorous scrubbing is necessary.

(c). *Learning by imitation.* Although imitation is a universally recognized phenomenon in learning, psychologists have been extremely lax in developing systematic studies of this process. That monkeys and children imitate, or even that children "ape" adults, is so commonly observed as to hardly need mention. Yet we know so little about imitation that we barely have the right to mention it in connection with learning experiments. While imitation is generally admitted for primates it is sometimes denied that animals below the primate imitate. Thorndike (1898) found no reason to assume imitation in chickens, cats, and dogs, and his negative conclusions helped to set a pattern of psychological thinking in which imitation is restricted to higher organisms. Perhaps Thorndike's animals were asked to work out problems where imitation was of little value, or perhaps no opportunity to *learn* to imitate had been provided. Since the experiments of Miller and Dollard (1941) it is commonly accepted that the tendency to imitate is itself learned, at least with animals as low as the rat. Before we consider this problem in greater detail, we should point out that Herbert and Harsh (1944) found that cats could benefit from the process of observing other cats in learning situations. The "learner" cat would be given a series of 30 learning trials. The "observer" cat would then be put to work on the same problem. It appears that the observers benefited if they saw all 30 trials (as against the last 15) and that the benefits were somewhat restricted to simpler problems (as measured by learning scores of the original cats). How the observational process facilitates the learning is a matter for speculation. Somehow the animals learn to discriminate the relevant aspects of the situation and also to persist in working in the relevant areas, according to Herbert and Harsh.

Miller and Dollard find that imitation is a learned process. In their experiments with rats they developed a training technique in which one (a trained rat) would serve as a *leader* while an untrained rat was reinforced for *following.* The learning situation consisted of a T-maze with two feeding stations, one behind the other. When the leader rat made a correct turn it was fed at the far end. If the follower rat happened to go in the same direction, it was fed at the nearer food station. If the follower rat did not follow, it was not reinforced. Miller and Dollard found that learning to imitate appeared to follow the usual course of learning. Learning not to imitate, that is, learning to take the opposite turn from that taken by the leader, was much more difficult. Positive imitation was never perfect (reaching only around 90 percent). The experimenters found that imitators could transfer the learned imitation from one drive to another; thus, when trained on the basis of hunger, they would also follow when thirsty.

Solomon and Coles (1954) challenged the conclusion of Miller and Dollard that any real generalization of imitation took place from drive to drive. They suggest that the thirsty animals might still be hungry in the thirst situation. In their own experiment, they also taught animals to imitate in the T-maze situation and then tried to test for generalization in an avoidance situation. In the latter situation, rats were placed in an avoidance box which contained two sections separated by glass. An imitator rat could presumably observe what the trained rat was doing. The trained rat would then be given a signal for an avoidance response based on shock. The imitator rats were found to show no benefit from the behavior of the trained rats. Solomon and Wynne conclude that there is no generalization across drives and that presumably imitation must be specifically learned in each new need or drive situation. Whether their test is a fair one is difficult to decide. Placing a rat behind a glass plate and expecting it to imitate another may be quite a complex proposition. Further experiments are urgently needed in this much neglected area of study.

For the benefit of the teacher we are in no position to quote experimental literature with worthy applications. The teacher can do as well as the psychologist by observing common-sense rules such as to reduce the necessary maneuvers to the minimum, not to expect a complex performance to be imitated (that is, one beyond the memory span), and orient the imitator to the specific operations involved. The problem is more likely to keep the imitator from imitating too much, from including the irrelevancies that the teacher has not eliminated. The additional danger inherent in learning by imitation is that the learning will not necessarily be accompanied by appreciation or understanding on a verbal level unless that is also included. Children can learn to solve ratio problems by imitating the process displayed by the teacher. This is, of course, no guarantee that they know what it is all about.

We have seen that in implementing his role, the teacher, besides motivating and reinforcing, goes about the process of instructing. This latter process we have seen amounts to providing stimuli (words, actions) to which the student responds. Whether this process is one of lecture, discussion, guidance, or imitation there is one common factor that is an apparent necessity: The student or learner must go through the motions himself if he is to learn. There is apparently no substitute for action. The significance of action is not only related to the fact that reinforcement only follows action. Action itself has a motivational value. Once the action is undertaken, additional stimulation for further activity is available. The role of action is appreciated in the expression: "Interest comes from doing." Some educational programs prosper in that learners are gotten into action (by almost any legitimate or illegitimate means) and find themselves forced to learn if the chain of stimulating sequences is ever to be broken.

The teacher's aids. Modern teachers make use of a variety of devices designed to improve learning efficiency. Such devices include the so-called visual aids, movies, television, radio, wire recorders, and so on. Psychologists have attempted evaluations of some of these devices, frequently with contradictory observations. Some of these devices are essentially one-way communication affairs. It is extremely doubtful that television instruction without additional supervision can be effective. It is possible, of course, for a good television or motion-picture presentation to result in more learning than occurs from the efforts of a poor teacher, but all we have considered so far suggests that unless a teacher of some kind is present to motivate and reinforce for action, little learning will result. There are unquestioned values in mechanical supplements; certainly it is important to provide pictures, diagrams, animation, and sound as illustrative material. Such materials, however, unless they lead to doing serve no purpose. A note of warning should be sounded in connection with professionally produced materials. Their interest may be more in the production of a smooth and finished article than in a realistic and honest presentation. A 20-minute movie about an event that took a month or 10 years to happen can certainly distort the appreciation of the event even without intent to misrepresent. A psychologist's clinical case study with professional actors is a questionable visual aid. There may result a confusion between what is real and what is the psychologist's theory or interpretation.

3. PRACTICE OPERATIONS

In any ordinary learning situation there is some content or lesson to be mastered. The lesson can vary in length from something like learning a nursery rhyme to memorizing the Bible. The time available may vary from a few minutes to a school year and longer. The objective involved and the criteria to be met will also vary. All of these factors present problems to the teacher. How much should the learner attempt to learn at one time? How long a time should he devote to the learning? What should he try to learn? How should he go about it? Apply these questions to something like the learning of a new piano composition a little more difficult than a student has been playing. How should the piano teacher proceed in developing a "lesson plan" or a practice schedule? We can make a beginning toward answering some of these extremely "practical" questions by returning to laboratory findings on special phases or features of practice. These phases have been studied for so long that they have acquired special designations that will serve as topic headings for this section.

a. Spacing versus massing of practice sessions. The problem of spaced versus massed learning has received so much attention that it is a familiar one for practically all students in education and psychology. There is a general appreciation that "spacing" is good and "massing" is bad. In fact, the word "massing" even has a negative connotation. Before we hasten to adopt the general interpretation, let us examine the logical structure of the problem. Just what is meant by "spacing" or "massing"?

For illustrative purposes let us consider a serial order nonsense syllable list. How would we proceed to "space" or "mass" the learning of such a list? It is immediately apparent that we can space the syllables themselves; for example, we can present one syllable every second, every minute, or every day, or any variation in between if we choose. Syllables presented 2 seconds apart are "massed" relative to syllables presented 3 or 4 seconds apart. The latter, in turn, are "massed" relative to 5 seconds or 10 seconds presentation.

Suppose we adopt any particular time between syllables, we can repeat trials immediately or with some rest interval between trials. A 1-minute rest is "spaced" learning compared to no rest at all, whereas it is massed compared with a 2-minute or 2-hour interval. Again we can consider the number of trials within any particular training session in this framework. Five trials per day is spaced compared to ten trials. But 10 trials are spaced compared with 50, and so on. It should be apparent that there is no absolute value which can be labeled as spaced or massed and that we have a problem of relativity on our hands with a relative type of answer inevitable.

In view of the considerations just raised, we can see that no specific answer as to how to arrange practice sessions is going to be available from some handbook. The only answer that can be given will be in terms of comparisons, that is, one arrangement might be shown to be better than another. Our problem is to consider the factors that might make one such arrangement more acceptable than another.

The usual finding in the laboratory is as already implied, that spacing leads to greater efficiency than massing if we indulge ourselves in a broad generalization. Actually there are some tasks (Pyle, 1928) such as code substitution in which massing seems to be better than spacing (within the limits studied). This question of limits must always be considered. Travis (1939), for instance, found that 2-minute practice sessions on a pursuit rotor were better than 1-minute sessions, a finding in favor of massing. On the other hand, a 4-minute session was not so good as the 2-minute, a finding in favor of spacing. If we can discover why spacing is usually favored, then we can attend directly to the causal factors involved and ignore the question of spacing or massing in its usual form.

In his review of human learning, Hovland (1951) finds that massing may occasionally appear favored when the task involved calls for a "warming-up" period. Any interval which fails to account for the warm-up requirement will obviously be too short, and experimental findings would favor massing. It is possible that if the periods between practice sessions are too long some forgetting might occur and again massing would be favored. Hovland also suggests that spacing procedures tend to produce a "fixation of response." Should such fixations interfere with a more variable or versatile performance, massing would be favored.

In contrast, massing may operate against the learner by resulting in an accumulation of reactive inhibition (see p. 365 f) which would tend to reduce the motivation for the responses to be learned and build up a countermotivation (fatigue, boredom). The fatigue effects themselves might result in a work decrement and, if the work output was being measured as the index of learning, results would favor spacing. Another factor suggested by Hovland is that of interference. It is assumed that when a great many associations are being formed at once there will be multiple associations among the individual components. Such associations (most of which will be incorrect) will interfere with the formation of correct associations. Hovland assumes further that with the passage of time the incorrect associations will dissipate, leaving the correct ones. If sufficient time is allowed between trials, then interfering associations will dissipate and findings will favor spacing. We have already discussed (see p. 360) the evidence about interference in serial learning and need not reconsider it here. It should be sufficient to point out that the three factors of motivation, work decrement, and interferences all work to the disadvantage of massing. Their separate roles may be difficult to disentangle, as Hovland points out, but as far as the teacher is concerned he will have them all working together and have no particular need to disentangle the net effects.

When we summarize the situation on the distribution of practice we find that the advice we can give is rather pale and weak to those who are seeking a firm and vigorous answer. We find that spacing is favored if the task involved no great amount of warm-up, if the intervals are not too long to allow forgetting but long enough to permit the forgetting of interfering responses, and if fixation of particular responses is desired. The faults of massing can be countered by rests, by increasing motivation, and by elimination of interfering responses. In the most practical sense the above comments add up to the suggestion that we should not push the learner when he is tired or losing interest. In the most theoretical sense we would stop the learner as soon as his acquisition curve begins to drop from a hypothetical ideal derived from a preliminary study in which the factors of motivation, forgetting, work decrement, and interference (error score) had all been systematically determined.

b. Learning by parts or by wholes. Since 1900 teachers have been told that learning by the "whole" method is better than learning by parts. Students have been resisting this technique for at least as long. Not that there is not some advantage to the whole method sometimes, but the conditions under which the whole method can be effectively used are so circumscribed that the student can hardly be blamed for revolting. We can do no better than quote Hovland (1951) in this connection. In summarizing his interpretation of the relative merits, Hovland states: ". . . The best advice seems to be to learn by using the largest units that are meaningful and within the individual's capacity. The older the individual, the higher his intelligence, the more practice he has had, the greater is the size of the unit he is able to handle." Imagine a teacher with a class of average intelligence and an average age of 10 with individually unknown amounts of practice (but probably none). What procedure should he follow on the basis of this advice?

The whole method, when it applies at all, is restricted to the learning of rote memory material, the learning of poetry, and similar activities. It has little relevance outside of this province and burdening teachers with advice about it seems largely wasteful. There may be some propaganda value to seeing things "as a whole" but it appears that any effective learning will require a mastery of parts and an understanding of the individual components. One does not seek the services of automobile mechanics who know the nature of the internal combustion engine in general.

Students characteristically try to break up the learning process into units; the reinforcements come faster that way. The part method maintains motivation. One appears to be making progress. It takes a supremely confident learner to rely on everything "falling into place" or "clicking" while he struggles along with a "whole" method.

Actually no one ever uses either an absolute whole or absolute part method. A simple sentence consists of parts, but no one would think of memorizing "a man went fishing" by the part method. The situation here, as with spaced and massed learning, is a relative one.

One warning seems in order when parts are learned separately but where a number of parts must be strung together in the final test. If a number of verses of poetry are being memorized or a lengthy piano composition is being learned in sections, there is some danger that associations will not be set up between the end of one section and the beginning of the next. The student would be well advised to practice the connections or transitions even though he believes he knows them, and in a sense finds that there is nothing to practice. It is not unusual, however, to find the classroom orator or even the amateur actor caught in a rut of repetition or waiting for a cue. Once the cue is given, a lengthy speech may follow. The student must learn to make his own cues come from the conclusions of the sections.

c. **Active versus passive learning.** Another old bromide of the elementary psychology texts is that active learning is better than passive. The usual discussion of this proposition is illustrated with reference to some experiments (Bills and Stauffacher, 1937) in which students memorized nonsense syllables better when exerting pressure against dynamometers. It is unlikely that teachers are ever going to get excited about equipping the classroom seats with dynamometers to improve the performances of their charges. As far as experimental evidence is concerned we have little to say on this topic. It is common observation that the good learner is apt to be the one who "sits up and takes notice" and that slouching is a normal correlate of inattention. It is quite likely that all that we mean by "active" learning is that the learner is motivated.

To the extent that active learning involves the process of doing something, we may have additional support for the proposition. While people can learn under hypnosis and, perhaps, while sleeping (see p. 133), the still controversial literature on latent and incidental learning (see p. 225) suggests that more can be expected of the learner who gets into action. Ebbinghaus (1885) was the first to find that attempting to recite material was more effective than merely reading it over. In general, reciting aloud is more effective than silent observation in nonsense syllable learning.

Any kind of effort at rehearsal or self-testing is better than a more passive "reading it over and over" technique. The advantage from activity seems to lie in the fact that such testing reveals the weak spots which need additional time and allows the learner to skip over the already known.

The advantage of active over passive learning does not appear to involve any new principles beyond those of motivation and reinforcement. The teacher who has taken care of these functions probably finds himself with an active learner on his hands. The operations of the teacher will automatically require appropriate action on the part of the learner if the goal of the learner or the criteria of learning are clearly spelled out. To put the matter quite simply, if the learner is expected to recite aloud he should practice reciting aloud; if he is expected to write integrative essays he should practice such performances.

d. Form versus content. Athletic coaches and professional teachers of golf, tennis, swimming, and the like are generally convinced that the first essential of success in a sport of physical prowess is the proper form. What that form should be may be a matter of argument, and one golf professional may disagree with another on just how to hold a club, address the ball, swing, and so on. Frequently it is assumed that the way in which some leading performer operates is the way in which all should practice. Since it is customary for athletic records to be broken by succeeding generations, it may turn out that a new technique may prove to be better than some old one. Here we have to settle for the empirical standards that are available at the time. Most athletes do follow some prescribed form and the unorthodox success is relatively rare.

From the point of view of experimental studies, a number of observations have been made on the development of skills which suggest that attention to form does indeed improve performance beyond what could normally be expected. Thus, in the art of marksmanship, psychologists (English, 1942) were able to improve scores by teaching army recruits to press against the trigger with a uniform pressure instead of squeezing the trigger with a jerk which normally throws the rifle off the target at the crucial moment. It is presumed that the rifleman who squeezes the trigger with a jerky movement is anticipating the explosion and blinks his eyes, due to anticipatory conditioning, just when his eyes should be focused on the target. By exerting slow, even, pressure against the stock of the gun and the trigger, the marksman does not know exactly when the rifle will fire and so he does not blink or throw off the sight. By teaching a pattern of pressure, even with an empty gun, marksmanship improves. In the experimental program involved here, psychologists hollowed out the stock of a gun and replaced it with an arrangement whereby pressure against a plate could be recorded as a marker tracing on a drum. Experts would record their pressure patterns and novices would then press against the stock in the same manner by watching the tracing they developed as compared with that of the expert. When they had learned how to press, they were ready to shoot. In the same fashion, the golf "pro" may not allow the student to swing at a ball for a number of lessons while he concentrates on such things as stance, grip, head position, balances, backswing, and so on.

In a factory production experiment, Lindahl (1945) studied a process in which a workman was required to use his foot in operating a pedal in a series of pressure patterns which in their mechanical translation operated a cut-off wheel. The pattern describing the efforts of a good worker was selected as a correct "form" and novice workers were trained to duplicate this pattern with a large saving in training time, breakage, and general productivity.

Beyond these relatively restricted observations we have little experimental evidence to go on for the present and must be content with the weight of authority of professional athletes and coaches. We can but assume that where form can be demonstrated to be important, attention must be directed to such matters, always reserving the opinion that the form currently in vogue may turn out to be less effective than some other still-to-be-discovered pattern.

e. Speed and accuracy. As in the argument over form and content, the question frequently arises as to whether a learner should begin to operate at the criterion speed or whether he should strive for an accurate performance first. Should telegraphers, for example, start out listening to messages sent at a professional rate or should they start slowly and build up their speed? Common sense and ordinary experience suggest that accuracy should be developed first and that speed will improve more or less spontaneously. In mirror-tracing or maze-running types of tasks, where, in a sense, the errors do not matter except in delaying the arrival at a goal, there might be some merit to working rapidly in the hope that the speed will compensate for the errors and that the errors themselves will drop out. Hovland (1951) cites the conclusion of the Gilbreths that in teaching brick-laying, it is more advisable to start out with the top speed expected because the task in its final form is so different from the task in slow-motion execution that progress is faster with the more rapid work. Hovland concludes from this observation that speed should be emphasized if the final pattern of behavior desired is quite different from the slower performance of the sequences involved. Should a boy learn to hit a baseball thrown slowly or at the speed he can expect in a game? Hovland suggests that the two tasks are sufficiently different to justify the training with faster pitches.

It is obvious that the problem is more complex than it appears to be at firsthand. Before any speed can be considered, there must be some background of experience from which to start. We certainly do not hope that a small child will master the art of catching a rubber ball if it is fired at top speed. It is only after certain basic skills are established that we can afford to introduce speed. The only justifiable conclusion is that the final nature of the task should be taken into account and some attempt at planning the practice program toward this end be made. The policeman who practices firing a revolver by taking careful aim at a target may not be able to do well firing from a moving car at a running fugitive.

f. Knowledge of results. In the ordinary learning situation with human learners it is quite impossible as well as unnecessary that any substantial or objective rewards or reinforcers be employed. The learner appears to derive reinforcement from success. In listening to a long lecture or reading a chapter in a text the learner is continuously reinforced as each item is concluded. Were it not for this possibility, learning itself would be impossible.

This self-reinforcement from success is usually ascribed to "knowledge of results." In line with the Dollard-Miller (1950) approach this would, in turn, be accompanied by some sort of anxiety reduction. We can take it as an empirical fact that learning does not proceed without such knowledge as Thorndike *et al.* (1928) have shown and does occur when knowledge is supplied. Like any other reinforcer, the knowledge of results must be supplied quickly if it is to be effective. The subject or learner must be able to know if he is "right" or "wrong" as soon as he has performed some response. Delaying this knowledge is about as bad as not supplying it at all. In most adult learning situations, the learner will have had sufficient experience to recognize the correctness or wrongness of his responses as soon as they occur, and no outside agency is required.

AN ILLUSTRATIVE SUMMARY

The variables discussed above can now be considered in the framework of a sample learning situation. We take our illustration from the work of Keller (1943) who undertook to improve the army method of training Morse code operators. The original army method consisted of teaching the 10 numerals and 26 letters in several groups; that is, the part method was employed. Soldiers would learn one group, then another, and so on. Keller decided that the whole method could be applied and proceeded on that basis. It should be noted that he worked with a college population. The learners could be presumed to be competent. Motivation could be assumed (certain credit points were assigned for completion of the course). Training sessions were arranged and controlled at the desire of the teacher (five daily 50-minute periods per week). All physical factors were arranged adequately. When training began, Keller relied upon the efficacy of immediate knowledge of results as the reinforcement. Students were required to listen to a code signal and immediately write it down. After 3 seconds, the instructor announced the correct response. If an error was made the student now wrote down the correct reaction and the code signal was given again. By this procedure the learning of code proceeded more effectively than it had by earlier methods. We cannot be sure as to the component contributions of whole method or immediacy of knowledge of results because the two factors were introduced together. We note also the inclusion of the "active" method insofar as the students were required to write not only the original response but also to make corrections when necessary. The record of the students progress was constantly before him in the work sheet.

The procedure so far described was only one aspect of the training story. Keller and Taubman (1943) were able to analyze the work sheets of the students and found it possible to tabulate errors and omissions. By counting up error scores for each letter in the alphabet it was possible to determine which letters were more difficult than others and also which letters were more readily confused with specific other letters. The letters P, W, J, and F, for example, proved to be the most difficult. As an incidental finding of some interest, it was discovered that omissions contributed more heavily to failure on the more difficult letters and erroneous responses (interference) contributed most of the difficulty in the learning of the easier letters. With such information at hand, it became possible to call the attention of students to peculiarities in the dot-dash arrangements that tended to prevent learning (hindered discrimination) and also to provide more practice on difficult letters to allow for more even learning of the entire alphabet without unnecessary overlearning of the easier items.

While our illustration deals with the acquisition of a perceptual-verbal skill, the same procedure could be applied to any selected area of education. The procedure would follow similar lines of attack: a statement of the problem, an analysis of present methods and accomplishments, an appreciation of the variables, innovations of procedure in line with generally accepted learning principles, experimental study and evaluation. To ask for more from the learning psychologist is to ask for something which cannot be delivered. To complain about nondelivery is to show a lack of appreciation of the complexity of the learning process. In spite of the complexity it is probably safe to state that some improvement could be effected in almost any learning situation that is now functioning in the educational systems of the world if learning psychologists were asked to work on specific problems. Their record of achievement during the war suggests that there is great promise for future accomplishments if considerations of expense are not basic obstacles.

Chapter

17 An Invitation to Learning

We have now completed the general task of learning a little about learning. How successful we have been depends upon how much motivation and reinforcement the reader has experienced (ignoring such things as limitations of the text).

There remains a great deal more to be learned about learning. No one text can even begin to summarize all the pertinent literature and every text will reveal a bias of selection. The interested student will go on with other texts and make appropriate comparisons.

The aim of the present text was to spell out the problems and questions with which learning psychologists occupy themselves. The student who finds that he now has a great many questions to ask has arrived at the right point. To those who are unsatisfied because there were not enough answers in the text, we can only suggest that they consider that any science consists of the development of questions. Conant (1953) describes the work of science in his valuable little book *Modern Science and Modern Man* as amounting to finding new questions to answer. The original answers we set out to find become trivial in the face of the new questions that the answers develop.

While answers are important, and in the course of the text we answered all the questions raised in Chapter 2 to one degree of satisfaction or another, the questions are much more interesting. The entire orientation of the present text was to ask the questions and to develop the logic which might help lead to answers and new questions.

In the present text no attempt was made to spell out the complete theory of any one learning psychologist. To do an adequate job would require a great deal of space, almost as much as the original theorists themselves have used. Instead of this approach we tried to concentrate on issues and indicated what at least some of the theorists had to say about each.

Students interested in looking at the various important theorists more intimately might start with Hilgard's (1956) *Theories of Learning*. From this excellent beginning they can turn to the original works themselves.

A word of warning is in order about reading the classics. It should be clear to students that our appreciation of scientific questions develops with time and effort and much that the classical writers have said is no longer considered significant, important, or true. In *Modern Learning Theory* (see Estes *et al.*, 1954) a group of young learning psychologists find serious faults and defects in five major learning theories they examine. There is no doubt but that if they examine any more they will find just as much to criticize as before.

Another warning. Most learning psychologists are fully aware of the weaknesses of some of their principles. They publicly assert the *tentative* nature of these propositions and insist on the need for experimental verification. The reader who uncritically adopts a particular principle as gospel is going beyond the express limitations imposed by the theorist.

The student who has become intrigued by learning problems will welcome the opportunity to acquaint himself with new developments on a theoretical level that have been appearing in recent years. Most of the new developments, however, involve an appreciation of physiology, electronics, mathematics, and some sophistication in symbolic logic.

Spence (1953) for example, has re-examined his own views relative to those of Hull and has come out for specifying all constructs in mathematical terms. Estes (1950) has developed an approach through sampling theory and hopes to be able to predict on a probability basis without recourse to such propositions as reinforcement. Hull's *A Behavior System* (1952) represents his last word on the subject and is heavily mathematical in form. Krech (1950) has turned to a neurophysiological orientation, and we have already noted Hebb's (1955) activities in this area.

Bush and Mosteller (1951a, 1951b) have developed mathematical models dealing with instrumental learning and stimulus generalization. The worth of these models has not yet been fully evaluated, but like Wolpe's (1950, 1952a) neurological models and Walter's (1953) robots, they may lead to new methods of attack on the many-sided problem that learning theory has become.

Olds and Milner (1954) have introduced a new technique of electrical stimulation of the septal region of rats' brains by using implanted electrodes. In this type of research, rats receive brief electrical stimulations in the brain when they press a Skinner bar. According to Olds and Milner the rats work at the bar with great speed and for extensive periods as long as the stimulation is maintained. Olds and Milner consider the electrical stimulation as a kind of reinforcement and suggest that the septal region may contain a "reinforcement center." The technique is too new for evaluation, but already is being extended to other animals. As a technique it is certainly promising and may well affect the future course of research.

The high level of thinking represented in these new theoretical and technical attempts has made new demands on students in their preparation. Underwood (1953) points out "One matter is clear; if the trend toward mathematical models continues to expand, as seems inevitable, the graduate curricula of many schools will have to be revised to allow for considerably more training in higher mathematics. Otherwise these theoretical programs will not provide the stimulation needed for survival simply because they will lack readers." And Mac-Corquodale (1955) states, "Psychologists will have to look to their Mathematics."

These comments have been quoted to help the student who wishes to go forward in his examination of the area of learning. Besides mathematics, the learning student had better be prepared in physics and physiology or he will be unable even to read about the research, much less participate in it. Keeping up with the psychology of learning will not be easy. The picture in learning theory has changed greatly since Thorndike announced the Law of Effect. In the next few years we can expect even greater changes than in the last fifty. The student might note with some satisfaction that the situation in learning theory is at least in some respects keeping pace with the trends in the rest of science.

Bibliography and
Author Index

Bibliography
and
Author Index

1. **Abernethy, E. M.** 1940. The effect of changed environmental conditions upon the results of college examinations. *J. exp. Psychol.*, 10, 293–301. [126]
2. **Adams, D. K.** 1954. In Adams, D. K. *et al.*, *Learning theory, personality theory and clinical research: The Kentucky symposium*. New York: Wiley. Pp. 66–80. [83, 246]
3. **Adelman, H.** *see* Maatsch, J. 1954.
   Adler, A. [419]
4. **Adrian, E. D.** 1947. *Physical background of perception*. New York: Oxford University Press. [235]
5. **Airapetyantz, E. and Bykov, K.** 1945. Physiological experiments and the psychology of the subconscious. *Phil. phenomenol. Res.*, 5, 577–593. [136]

6. **Alberts, E. and Ehrenfreund, D.** 1951. Transposition in children as a function of age. *J. exp. Psychol.*, 41, 30–38. [411]
7. **Alexander, F.** 1950. *Psychosomatic medicine*. New York: Norton. [447–8]
8. **Allport, F. H.** 1955. *Theories of perception and the concept of structure*. New York: Wiley. [393]
9. **Alper, T. G.** 1952. The interrupted task method in studies of selective recall: A reevaluation of some recent experiments. *Psychol. Rev.*, 59, 71–88. [336]
   Alper, T. G. *see* Postman, L. 1946.
   Amatruda, C. S. *see* Gesell, A. 1947.
10. **Ammons, R. B.** 1947. Acquisition of motor skill: I. Quantitative analysis and theoret-

ical formulation. *Psychol. Rev.*, 54, 263–281. [166]

11. **Anderson, J. E. and Smith, A. H.** 1926. The effect of quantitative and qualitative stunting upon maze learning in the white rat. *J. comp. Psychol.*, 6, 337–359. [395]

Anrep, G. V. [437]

Antonitis, J. J. *see* Schoenfeld, W. N. 1950.

12. **Applezweig, M. H.** 1951. Response potential as a function of effort. *J. comp. physiol. Psychol.*, 44, 225–235. [358]

13. **Babkin, B. P.** 1949. *Pavlov, a biography.* Chicago: University of Chicago Press. [279]

Backer, R. *see* Sheffield, F. D. 1951.

14. **Bain, A.** 1870. *Mental science, a compendium of psychology, and the history of philosophy.* New York: Appleton-Century-Crofts. [199]

15. **Baker, L. E.** 1938. The pupillary response conditioned to subliminal auditory stimuli. *Psychol. Monogr.*, 50, No. 223; 32pp. [127]

16. **Ballard, P. B.** 1913. Oblivescence and reminiscence. *Brit. J. Psychol., Monogr. Suppl.*, 1, No. 2. [310]

Barker, A. N. *see* Hull, C. L. 1951

17. **Bartlett, F. C.** 1932. *Remembering: A study in experimental and social psychology.* Cambridge: Cambridge University Press. [316]

18. **Bass, M. J. and Hull, C. L.** 1934. The irradiation of a tactile conditioned reflex in man. *J. comp. Psychol.*, 17, 47–65. [149]

Bateman, D. *see* Leuba, C. 1952.

19. **Beach, F. A.** 1947. A review of physiological and psychological studies of sexual behavior in mammals. *Physiol. Rev.*, 27, 240–307. [210]

20. —— 1950. The snark was a boojum. *Amer. Psychologist*, 5, 115–124. [40, 383]

21. —— 1951. Instructive behavior: Reproductive activities, Chapter 12 in Stevens, S. S. (ed.), *Handbook of experimental psychology.* New York: Wiley. Pp. 387–434. [39, 264]

22. —— **and Jaynes, J.** 1954. Effects of early experience upon the behavior of animals. *Psychol. Bull.*, 51, 239–263. [41, 309, 392, 438]

23. **Bekhterev, V. M.** 1932. *General principles of human reflexology.* New York: International Universities Press. [420]

24. **Bello, F.** 1955. New light on the brain. *Fortune*, 50, 104–108. [38]

25. **Berger, H.** 1929. Über das Electrenkephalogram des Menchen. *Arch. Psychiat. Nervenkr.*, 87, 527–570. [134, 235]

26. **Bergman, G.** 1953. Theoretical psychology. *Annu. Rev. Psychol.*, 4, 435–458. [83]

27. **Berkeley, G.** 1709. *An essay toward a new theory of vision.* Dublin: Jeremy Pepyat (Reprinted 1922. New York: Dutton). [279]

Bergmann, G. von. *see* Alexander, 1950. [448]

28. **Berkun, M. M., Kessen, M. L. and Miller, N. E.** 1952. Hun-

ger-reducing effects of food by stomach fistula versus food by mouth measured by a consummatory response. *J. comp. physiol. Psychol.*, 45, 550–564. [252]

29. **Bernhardt, K. S. and Herbert, R.** 1937. A further study of vitamin B deficiency and learning with rats. *J. comp. Psychol.*, 24, 263–267. [47]

Bersh, P. J. *see* Schoenfeld, W. N. 1950.

30. **Bexton, W. H., Heron, W. and Scott, T. H.** 1954. Effects of decreased variation in the sensory environment. *Canad. J. Psychol.*, 8, 70–76. [209, 223, 446]

31. **Bills, A. G. and Stauffacher, J. C.** 1937. The influence of voluntarily induced tension on rational problem solving. *J. Psychol.*, 4, 261–271. [474]

32. **Bilodeau, I. M. and Schlosberg, H.** 1951. Similarity in stimulating conditions as a variable in retroactive inhibition. *J. exp. Psychol.*, 41, 199–204. [312–3, 459]

33. **Bingham, H. C.** 1913. Size and form perception in *Gallus domesticus*. *J. Anim. Behav.*, 3, 65–113. [410]

34. **Bingham, W. E. and Griffiths, W. J., Jr.** 1952. The effect of different environments during infancy on adult behavior in the rat. *J. comp. physiol. Psychol.*, 45, 307–312. [399]

35. **Birch, H. G. and Bitterman, M. E.** 1949. Reinforcement and learning: The process of sensory integration. *Psychol. Rev.*, 56, 292–308. [256]

Bitterman, M. E. *see* Birch, H. G. 1949.

36. **Blodgett, H. C.** 1929. The effect of the introduction of reward upon the maze performance of rats. *Univ. Calif. publ. Psychol.*, 4, 113–134. [80, 87, 249]

37. **Bonin, G. von, Garol, H. W. and McCulloch, W. S.** 1942. The functional organization of the occipital lobe. In Klüver, H., *Visual mechanisms*. Lancaster, Pennsylvania: Jacques Cattell. [154]

38. **Boring, E. G.** 1954. Material quoted by Sanford, F. H. in *Across the Secretary's Desk* column. *Amer. Psychologist*, 9, 125. [417]

Boycott, B. B. *see* Young, 1951. [238]

39. **Bregman, E. O.** 1934. An attempt to modify the emotional attitudes of infants by the conditioned response technique. *J. genet. Psychol.*, 45, 169–198. [421]

Bregman, E. O. *see* Thorndike, E. L. *et al.* 1928.

Brenall, E. P. *see* Tolman, E. C. 1932.

40. **Bridges, K. M. B.** 1932. Emotional development in early infancy. *Child Develpm.*, 3, 324–341. [422]

Briggs, G. E. *see* Wickens, D. D. 1951.

41. **Brogden, W. J.** 1939. Sensory pre-conditioning. *J. exp. Psychol.*, 25, 323–332. [152, 257]

42. ———— 1947. Sensory pre-conditioning of human subjects. *J. exp. Psychol.*, 37, 527–540. [152]

43. —— 1949. Acquisition and extinction of a conditioned avoidance response in dogs. *J. comp. physiol. Psychol.*, 42, 296–302. [64, 345]

44. —— 1951. Animal studies of learning. Chapter 16 in Stevens, S. S. (ed.), *Handbook of experimental psychology*. New York: Wiley. Pp. 568–612. [6, 73]

45. ——, **Lipman, E. A. and Culler, E.** 1938. The role of incentive in conditioning and extinction. *Amer. J. Psychol.*, 51, 109–117. [62–4]

Brogden, W. J. *see* Chernikoff, R. 1949; Roessler, R. L. 1943.

46. **Brown, J. S.** 1942. The generalization of approach responses as a function of stimulus intensity and strength of motivation. *J. comp. Psychol.*, 33, 209–226. [442–3]

47. —— 1953. Problems presented by the concept of acquired drives. In Brown, J. S. *et al.*, *Current Theory and Research in Motivation*. Lincoln, Nebraska: University of Nebraska Press. Pp. 1–21. [218, 221–2, 232]

48. **Brown, T.** 1820. *Lectures on the philosophy of the human mind*. 4 Vols. Edinburgh: Tait. [278]

49. **Bruce, R. W.** 1933. Conditions of transfer of training. *J. exp. Psychol.*, 16, 343–361. [408, 410]

50. **Bugelski, B. R.** 1938. Extinction with and without subgoal reinforcement. *J. comp. Psychol.*, 26, 121–134. [18, 270]

51. —— 1942. Interference with recall of original responses after learning new responses to old stimuli. *J. exp. Psychol.*, 30, 368–379. [324, 326, 400, 410]

52. —— 1948. An attempt to reconcile unlearning and reproductive inhibition explanations of proactive inhibition. *J. exp. Psychol.*, 38, 670–682. [324, 337, 404]

53. —— 1950. A remote association explanation of the relative difficulty of learning nonsense syllables in a serial list. *J. exp. Psychol.*, 40, 336–348. [189]

54. —— 1951. *A first course in experimental psychology*. New York: Holt. [33, 210]

55. —— and **Cadwallader, T.** 1956. An experimental test of the "Transfer and retroaction surface." *J. exp. Psychol.* (In press.) [328–9]

56. —— and **Coyer, R. A.** 1950. Temporal conditioning vs. anxiety reduction in avoidance learning. *Amer. Psychologist*, 5, 257. [13, 68, 131, 361]

57. ——, **Coyer, R. A. and Rogers, W. A.** 1952. A criticism of pre-acquisition and pre-extinction of expectancies. *J. exp. Psychol.*, 44, 27–30. [97, 249, 371]

58. —— and **Miller, N. E.** 1938. A spatial gradient in the strength of avoidance responses. *J. exp. Psychol.*, 23, 494–505. [177, 282, 442]

59. —— and **Scharlock, D. P.** 1952. An experimental demonstration of unconscious mediated association. *J. exp.*

Psychol., *44*, 334–338. [107, 110, 153]

60. —— and **Woodward, D. P.** 1951. The effect of distinctive cues on the spatial gradient of avoidance. *J. comp. physiol. Psychol.*, *44*, 450–456. [282, 345, 444]

61. —— and **Smith, W. C.** 1953. An effect of repeated conditioning extinction upon operant strength. *J. exp. Psychol.*, *46*, 349–352. [144, 354–5, 377]

62. **Bunch, M. E.** 1946. Retroactive inhibition or facilitation from interpolated learning as a function of time. *J. comp. Psychol.*, *39*, 287–291. [315, 331]

Bunch, M. E. *see* Meier, G. W. 1950.

63. **Burtt, E. A.** 1939. *The English philosophers from Bacon to Mill.* New York: Random House. [278]

64. **Bush, R. R.** and **Mosteller, F.** 1951a. A mathematical model for simple learning. *Psychol. Rev.*, *58*, 313–323. [481]

65. —— and —— 1951b. A model for stimulus generalization and discrimination. *Psychol. Rev.*, *58*, 413–423. [481]

Bykov, K. *see* Airapetyantz, E. 1945.

Cadwallader, T. *see* Bugelski, B. R. 1956.

66. **Campbell, A. A.** 1938. The interrelations of two measures of conditioning in man. *J. exp. Psychol.*, *22*, 225–243. [170]

Campbell, B. A. *see* Sheffield, F. D. 1954.

67. **Cannon, W. B.** 1929. *Bodily changes in pain, hunger, fear and rage.* New York: Appleton-Century-Crofts. [258, 427]

Carpenter, J. A. *see* Deese, J. 1951.

68. **Carr, H. A.** 1925. *Psychology, a study of mental activity.* New York: Longmans, Green. [259]

69. —— 1930. Teaching and learning. *J. genet. Psychol.*, *37*, 189–218. [467]

Chambers, R. M. *see* Coppock, H. W. 1954.

70. **Chernikoff, R.** and **Brogden, W. J.** 1949. The effect of instructions upon sensory preconditioning of human subjects. *J. exp. Psychol.*, *39*, 200–207. [152]

71. **Child, I. L.** 1954. Personality. *Annu. Rev. Psychol.*, *5*, 149–170. [48]

Chow, K. L. *see* Nissen, H. W. 1951.

72. **Christie, R.** 1952. The effect of some early experiences in the latent learning of adult rats. *J. exp. Psychol.*, *43*, 281–288. [395]

73. **Clarke, R. S., Heron, W., Fetherstonhaugh, M. L., Forgays, D. G.** and **Hebb, D. O.** 1951. Individual differences in dogs: Preliminary report on the effects of early experience. *Canad. J. Psychol.*, *5*, 150–156. [396]

Clay, J. *see* Harris, L. J. *et al.* 1933.

74. **Cohen, L. H., Hilgard, E. R.** and **Wendt, G. R.** 1933. Sensitivity to light in a case of hysterical blindness studied by reinforcement-inhibition

and conditioning methods. *Yale J. biol. Med.*, 6, 61–67. [127]

Coles, M. R. *see* Solomon, R. L. 1954.

75. Conant, J. B. 1953. *Modern science and modern man.* Garden City, New York: Doubleday Anchor Books. [280]

76. Coppock, H. W. and Chambers, R. M. 1954. Reinforcement of position preference by automatic intravenous injections of glucose. *J. comp. physiol. Psychol.*, 47, 355–357. [252–3]

77. Cowles, J. T. 1937. Food tokens as incentives for learning by chimpanzees. *Comp. Psychol. Monogr.*, 14, No. 7. [71, 270]

78. Coyer, R. A. 1953. The effect of magnitude of reward and degree of deprivation on the acquisition of a complex maze habit. Unpublished Ph.D. dissertation. The University of Buffalo. [187, 191, 230, 254]

Coyer, R. A. *see* Bugelski, B. R. 1950 and 1952.

79. Crafts, L. W., Schneirla, T. C., Robinson, E. E. and Gilbert, R. W. 1950. *Recent experiments in psychology* (2d. ed.) New York: McGraw-Hill. [12]

80. Crespi, L. P. 1942. Amount of reinforcement and level of performance. *Psychol. Rev.*, 51, 341–357. [177, 190]

Culler, E. *see* Brogden, W. J. 1938; Finch, G. 1934.

81. Dallenbach, K. M. 1955. Phrenology versus psycho-analysis. *Amer. J. Psychol.*, 68, 511–525. [448]

Dallenbach, K. M. *see* Jenkins, J. G. 1924; Minami, G. 1946.

Darwin, C. [157]

82. Dashiell, J. F. 1927. *Fundamentals of objective psychology.* Boston: Houghton Mifflin. [201]

Dealey, W. L. *see* Dvorak, A. 1936.

83. Deese, J. 1951. The extinction of a discrimination without performance of the choice response. *J. comp. physiol. Psychol.*, 44, 362–366. [371]

84. ——— 1952. *The psychology of learning.* New York: McGraw-Hill. [206, 351]

85. ——— and Carpenter, J. A. 1951. Drive-level and reinforcement. *J. exp. Psychol.*, 42, 236–238. [177, 190, 230]

86. ———, Lazarus, R. S. and Keenan, J. 1953. Anxiety, anxiety-reduction and stress in learning. *J. exp. Psychol.*, 46, 55–60. [49]

87. Delafresnaye, J. F. (ed.) 1954. *Brain mechanisms and consciousness.* Springfield, Illinois: Thomas. [38]

88. Dennis, W. 1940. Infant reaction to restraint: An evaluation of Watson's theory. *Trans. N. Y. Acad. Sci.*, Ser. 2, 2, No. 8, 202–218. [421]

89. Denny, M. R. 1946. The role of secondary reinforcement in a partial reinforcement learning situation. *J. exp. Psychol.*, 36, 373–389. [256, 350]

90. ———, Frisbey, N. and Weaver, J., Jr. 1955. Rotary pursuit performance under alternate conditions of dis-

tributed and massed practice. *J. exp. Psychol., 49*, 48–54. [287]

Denny, M. R. *see* Maatsch, J. 1954.

Dickson, W. J. *see* Roethlisberger, F. J. 1939.

91. Dinsmoor, J. A. 1954. Punishment: I. The avoidance hypothesis. *Psychol. Rev., 61*, 34–46. [430]

92. Dinsmoor, J. A. 1955. Punishment: II. Interpretation of empirical findings. *Psychol. Rev., 62*, 96–105. [430]

93. Dollard, J., Doob, L. W., Miller, N. E., Mowrer, O. H. and Sears, R. R. 1939. *Frustration and aggression.* New Haven: Yale University Press. [35, 427, 440]

94. —— and Miller, N. E. 1950. *Personality and psychotherapy: An analysis in terms of learning, thinking and culture.* New York: McGraw-Hill. [72, 275–6, 360, 375, 420, 427, 445, 461, 463, 477]

Dollard, J. *see* Miller, N. E. 1941.

Doob, L. W. *see* Dollard, J. *et al.* 1939.

95. Doré, L. R. and Hilgard, E. R. 1937. Spaced practice and the maturation hypothesis. *J. Psychol., 4*, 245–259. [45]

96. Dunbar, H. F. 1943. *Emotions and bodily changes: A survey of literature on psychosomatic interrelationships, 1910–1933* (2d. ed.). New York: Columbia University Press. [448]

97. Dunlap, K., Gentry, E. and Zeigler, W. 1931. The behavior of white rats under food and electric shock stimulation. *J. comp. Psychol., 12*, 371–378. [127]

98. Dvorak, A., Merrick, N. I., Dealey, W. L. and Ford, G. C. 1936. *Typewriting behavior.* New York: American Book. [46]

99. Ebbinghaus, H. 1885. *Memory: A contribution to experimental psychology.* (*Trans. by Ruger, H. A. and Bussenius, C. E. 1913.* New York: Teachers College, Columbia University). [22, 168, 183, 303, 311, 316, 475]

100. Eccles, J. C. 1949. A review and restatement of the electrical hypotheses of synoptic excitatory and inhibitory action. *Arch. Sci. Physiol., 3*, 567–584. [298, 363]

101. —— 1951. Interpretation of action potentials evoked in the cerebral cortex. *EEG clin. Neurophysiol., 3*, 449–464. [298]

102. —— 1953. *The neurophysiological basis of mind.* New York: Oxford University Press. [295–7, 308, 362]

103. Ehrenfreund, D. 1948. An experimental test of the continuity theory of discrimination with pattern vision. *J. comp. Psychol., 41*, 408–422. [135, 288]

Ehrenfreund, D. *see* Alberts, E. 1951.

104. Eisen, N. H. 1954. The influence of set on semantic generalization. *J. abnorm. soc. Psychol., 49*, 491–496. [153]

105. Elliot, F. R. 1936. Memory for visual, auditory and visual-auditory material.

Arch. Psychol., N. Y., No. 199. 58pp. [125]

106. **Ellson, D. G.** 1938. Quantitative studies of the interaction of simple habits. I. Recovery from specific and generalized effects of extinction. *J. exp. Psychol.*, 23, 339–358. [153, 173, 354, 404]

107. —— 1942. Critical conditions influencing sensory conditioning. *J. exp. Psychol.*, 31, 333–338. [153]

Emmons, W. H. *see* Simon, C. H. 1955.

108. **English, H. B.** 1942. Reminiscence—reply to Dr. Burton's critique. *Psychol. Rev.*, 49, 505–512. [476]

Eriksen, C. W. *see* Porter, P. B. 1948.

109. **Estes, W. K.** 1944. Experimental studies of punishment. *Psychol. Monogr.*, 57, No. 3 (Whole No. 263). [19, 274, 277, 360, 372]

110. —— 1949a. Generalization of secondary reinforcement from the primary drive. *J. comp. physiol. Psychol.*, 42, 286–295. [271]

111. —— 1949b. A study of motivating conditions necessary for secondary reinforcement. *J. exp. Psychol.*, 39, 306–310. [91]

112. —— 1950. Toward a statistical theory of learning. *Psychol. Rev.*, 57, 94–107. [481]

113. ——, Koch, S., MacCorquodale, V. K., Meehl, P. E., Mueller, C. G., Jr., Schoenfield, W. N. and Verplanck, W. S. 1954. *Modern learning theory*. New York: Appleton-Century-Crofts. [78, 83, 143, 149, 481]

114. **Ewert, P. H.** 1930. A study of the effects of inverted retinal stimulation upon spatially coordinated behavior. *Genet. Psychol. Monogr.*, 7, 177–363. [406]

115. **Eysenck, H. J.** 1952a. The effects of psychotherapy: An evaluation. *J. consult. Psychol.*, 16, 319–324. [447]

116. —— 1952b. *The scientific study of personality.* London: Routledge and Kegan Paul. [447]

117. —— 1954. Further comment on "Relations with Psychiatry." *Amer. Psychologist*, 9, 157–158. [447]

118. **Farber, I. E.** 1954. Anxiety as a drive state. In Jones, M. R. (ed.), *Nebraska symposium on motivation, 1954.* Lincoln, Nebraska: University of Nebraska Press. [218]

119. —— and Spence, K. W. 1953. Complex learning and conditioning as a function of anxiety. *J. exp. Psychol.*, 45, 120–125. [49]

120. **Faw, V.** 1949. A psychotherapeutic method of teaching psychology. *Amer. Psychologist*, 4, 104–109. [465]

121. **Feldman, M.** 1956. The effect of emotionally toned words on nonserial order learning. *J. abnorm. soc. Psychol.* (In press.) [333]

Fetherstonhaugh, M. L. *see* Clarke, R. S. *et al.* 1951.

122. **Finan, J. L.** 1940. Quantitative studies in motivation: I. Strength of conditioning in rats under varying degrees of hunger. *J. comp. Psychol.*, 29, 119–134. [230, 352]

123. **Finch, G. and Culler, E.** 1934. Higher order conditioning with constant motivation. *Amer. J. Psychol.*, *46*, 596–602. [124]

124. **Finger, F. W.** 1942. Retention and subsequent extinction of a simple running response. *J. exp. Psychol.*, *31*, 120–133. [347]

125. —— 1947. Convulsive behavior in the rat. *Psychol. Bull.*, *44*, 201–248. [440]

126. **Fitts, P. M.** 1951. Engineering psychology and equipment design. Chapter 35 in Stevens, S. S. (ed.), *Handbook of experimental psychology*. New York: Wiley. Pp. 1287–1340. [455]

127. **Flesch, R.** 1955. *Why Johnny can't read*. New York: Harper. [452]

Foord, E. N. *see* Hebb, D. O. 1945.

Ford, G. C. *see* Dvorak, A. 1936.

128. **Forgays, D. G. and Forgays, J. W.** 1952. The nature of the effect of free-environmental experience in the rat. *J. comp. physiol. Psychol.*, *45*, 322–328. [398]

Forgays, D. G. *see* Clarke, R. S. *et al.* 1951.

Forgays, J. W. *see* Forgays, D. G. 1952.

129. **Forgus, R. H.** 1954. The effect of early perceptual learning on the behavioral organization of adult rats. *J. comp. physiol. Psychol.*, *47*, 331–336. [398]

130. —— 1955. Early visual and motor experience as determiners of complex maze-learning ability under rich and reduced stimulation. *J. comp. physiol. Psychol.*, *48*, 215–220. [398]

131. **Forrester, B.** 1955. A learning set in maze learning. Unpublished M.A. thesis. The University of Buffalo. [409]

Foshee, G. *see* Siegel, P. S. 1953.

Foster, H. *see* Gagne, R. M. 1949.

132. **Fox, B. H. and Robbins, J. S.** 1952. The retention of material presented during sleep. *J. exp. Psychol.*, *43*, 75–79. [227, 231]

133. **French, T. M.** 1933. Interrelation between psychoanalysis and the experimental work of Pavlov. *Amer. J. Psychiat.*, *89*, 1165–1203. [420]

134. **Freud, S.** 1927. *The problem of lay-analysis*. New York: Brentano. [418]

135. —— 1949. *An outline of psychoanalysis*. New York: Norton. [437]

Frisbey, N. *see* Denny, M. R. 1955.

136. **Frolov, J. P.** 1937. *Pavlov and his school: The theory of conditioned reflexes*. New York: Oxford University Press. [437]

137. **Fuller, P. R.** 1949. Operant conditioning of a vegetative human organism. *Amer. J. Psychol.*, *62*, 587–589. [41]

138. **Furchgott, E. and Rubin, R. D.** 1953. The effect of magnitude of reward on maze learning in the white rat. *J. comp. physiol. Psychol.*, *46*, 9–12. [254]

139. **Gagne, R. M.** 1941. The effect of spacing of trials on the acquisition and extinc-

tion of a conditioned operant response. *J. exp. Psychol.*, 29, 201–216. [356]

140. —— and Foster, H. 1949.
Transfer to a motor skill
from practice on a pictured
representation. *J. exp. Psychol.*, 39, 342–355. [406]

141. Gantt, W. H. 1936. An experimental approach to psychiatry. *Amer. J. Psychiat.*, 92,
1007–1021. [170, 356]

Garol, H. W. *see* Bonin, G.
von. 1942.

142. Gates, A. I. 1948. *Educational
psychology.* (3d. ed.) New
York: Macmillan. [451]

Gebhard, P. H. *see* Kinsey,
A. C. *et al.* 1953.

Gentry, E. *see* Dunlap, K.
1931.

143. Gesell, A. and Amatruda, C. S.
1947. *Developmental diagnosis.* New York: Hoeber.
[309]

144. —— and Ilg, F. L. 1943. *Infant and child in the culture
of today.* New York: Har-
per. [309]

145. —— and Thompson, H.
1941. Twins I and C from
infancy to adolescence: A
biogenetic study of individual differences by the method of co-twin control. *Genet.
Psychol. Monogr.*, 24, 2–121.
[387]

146. Gibson, E. J. 1941. Retroactive
inhibition as a function of
degree of generalization between tasks. *J. exp. Psychol.*,
28, 93–115. [173, 324, 408,
410]

147. —— 1942. Intra-list generalization as a factor in verbal learning. *J. exp. Psychol.*,
30, 184–200. [328]

Gilbert, R. W. *see* Crafts,
L. W. *et al.* 1950.

Gilbreth, F. B. *see* Hovland,
1951. [477]

Gilbreth, F. B. *see* Hovland,
1951. [477]

Gleitman, H. *see* Tolman,
E. C. 1949.

148. Grant, D. A. 1939. The influence of attitude on the
conditioned eyelid response.
J. exp. Psychol., 25, 333–346.
[212]

149. —— and Schipper, L. M.
1952. The acquisition and
extinction of conditioned
eyelid responses as a function of the percentage of
fixed-ratio random reinforcement. *J. exp. Psychol.*, 43,
313–320. [350]

Grant, D. A. *see* Warren, A. B.
1955.

150. Grether, W. F. 1938. Pseudo-
conditioning without paired
stimulation encountered in
attempted backward condi-
tioning. *J. comp. Psychol.*,
25, 91–96. [128, 300]

151. Grice, G. R. 1949. Visual discrimination learning with
simultaneous and succes-
sive presentation of stimuli.
J. comp. physiol. Psychol.,
42, 365–373. [288]

152. Griffiths, W. J., Jr. and Stringer, W. F. 1952. The effect of
intense stimulation experienced during infancy on
adult behavior in the rat. *J.
comp. physiol. Psychol.*, 45,
301–306. [399]

Griffiths, W. J., Jr. *see* Bingham, W. E. 1952.

153. Grindley, G. C. 1929–30. Experiments on the influence
of the amount of reward on

learning in young chickens. *Brit. J. Psychol.*, 20, 173–180. [176]

154. **Guthrie, E. R.** 1935. *The psychology of learning.* New York: Harper. [5, 55–6, 84, 126, 129, 150, 165, 246–7, 275, 291, 355, 361, 368, 467]

155. ——— 1938. *Psychology of human conflict.* New York: Harper. [425]

156. ——— 1946a. Psychological facts and psychological theory. *Psychol. Bull.*, 43, 1–20. [3, 219]

157. ——— 1946b. Recency or effect? Reply to V. J. O'Connor. *Harv. educ. Rev.*, 16, 286–289. [293]

158. ——— 1952. *The psychology of learning* (rev. ed.). New York: Harper. [291]

159. ——— and **Horton, G. P.** 1946. *Cats in a puzzle box.* New York: Rinehart. [20, 85, 247]

160. ——— and **Powers, F. F.** 1950. *Educational psychology.* New York: Ronald. [151, 450]

161. **Hall, C. S.** 1951. The genetics of behavior. Chapter 9 in Stevens, S. S. (ed.), *Handbook of experimental psychology.* New York: Wiley. Pp. 304–329. [43]

Hall, C. S. *see* Tolman, E. C. 1932.

Hall, J. F. *see* Page, H. A. 1953.

162. **Hamilton, R. J.** 1943. Retroactive facilitation as a function of degree of generalization between tasks. *J. exp. Psychol.*, 32, 363–376. [324, 327, 408]

Hargreaves, F. J. *see* Harris, L. J. *et al.* 1933.

163. **Harlow, H. F.** 1949. The formation of learning sets. *Psychol. Rev.*, 56, 51–65. [196, 400]

164. ——— 1950. Performance of catarrhine monkeys on a series of discrimination reversal problems. *J. comp. physiol. Psychol.*, 43, 231–239. [400, 415]

165. ——— 1953. Motivation as a factor in the acquisition of new responses. In Brown, J. S. *et al.*, *Current theory and research in motivation.* Lincoln, Nebraska: University of Nebraska Press. Pp. 24–58. [219–21, 232, 245, 254, 267, 333]

166. **Harrell, R. F.** 1947. Further effects of added thiamin on learning and other processes. *Teach. Coll. Contr. Educ.*, 928, 1–102. [48]

167. **Harris, L. J., Clay, J., Hargreaves, F. J.** and **Ward, A.** 1933. Appetite and choice of diet: The ability of the vitamin B deficient rat to discriminate between diets containing and lacking the vitamin. *Proc. Roy. Soc., B, 113*, 161–190. [229]

Harsh, C. M. *see* Herbert, M. J. 1944.

168. **Hayek, F. A.** 1952. *The sensory order.* Chicago: University of Chicago Press. [279]

169. **Hayes, K. J.** 1953. The backward curve: A method for the study of learning. *Psychol. Rev.*, 60, 269–275. [194–5, 197]

Heath, E. S. *see* Hebb, D. O. 1954.

170. **Hebb, D. O.** 1937. The innate organization of visual ac-

tivity: II. Transfer of response in the discrimination of brightness and size by rats reared in total darkness. *J. comp. Psychol.*, 24, 277–299. [394, 397]

171. ——— 1938. Studies of the organization of behavior: I. Behavior of the rat in a field orientation. *J. comp. Psychol.*, 25, 333–352. [132]

172. ——— 1942. The effect of early and late brain injury upon test scores and the nature of normal adult intelligence. *Proc. Amer. Phil. Soc.*, 85, 275–292. [76]

173. ——— 1946. On the nature of fear. *Psychol. Rev.*, 53, 259–276. [422]

174. ——— 1947. Spontaneous neurosis in chimpanzees: Theoretical relations with clinical and experimental phenomena. *Psychosom. Med.*, 9, 3–16. [446]

175. ——— 1949. *Organization of behavior.* New York: Wiley. [2, 8, 33, 46, 74–6, 104, 111–2, 133–4, 161, 182, 204, 211, 215, 224, 234, 258, 264, 268, 295, 308, 388, 393, 396, 399, 401, 405, 412, 446]

176. ——— 1951. The role of neurological ideas in psychology. *J. Personal.*, 20, 39–55. [36]

177. ——— 1955. Drives and the C. N. S. (Conceptual Nervous System). *Psychol. Rev.*, 62, 243–254. [38, 134, 208, 211, 221, 234, 241, 276, 463, 481]

178. ——— and Foord, E. N. 1945. Errors of visual recognition and the nature of the trace. *J. exp. Psychol.*, 35, 335–348. [319]

179. ——— Heath, E. S. and Stuart, E. A. 1954. Experimental deafness. *Canad. J. Psychol.*, 8, 152–156. [223, 394, 446]

180. ——— and Williams, K. 1946 A method of rating animal intelligence. *J. gen. Psychol.*, 34, 59–65. [398]

Hebb, D. O. *see* Clarke, R. S. *et al.* 1951.

181. Herbert, M. J. and Harsh, C. M. 1944. Observational learning by cats. *J. comp. Psychol.*, 37, 81–95. [468]

Heron, W. *see* Bexton, W. H. 1954; Clarke, R. S. *et al.* 1951; Thompson, W. R. 1954a and 1954b.

182. Herrick, C. J. 1926. *Brains of rats and men. A survey of the origin and biological significance of the cerebral cortex.* Chicago: University of Chicago Press. [33]

183. Hilgard, E. R. 1936a. The nature of conditioned response. I. The use for and against stimulus substitution. *Psychol. Rev.*, 43, 366–385. [138]

184. ——— 1936b. The nature of conditioned response. II. Alternatives to stimulus substitution. *Psychol. Rev.*, 43, 547–564. [138]

185. ——— 1951. Methods and procedures in the study of learning. Chapter 15, in Stevens, S. S. (ed.), *Handbook of experimental psychology.* New York: Wiley. Pp. 517–567. [6, 172]

186. ——— 1953. *Introduction to psychology.* New York: Harcourt, Brace. [27, 201, 220]

187. ——— 1956. *Theories of learning* (2nd. ed.). New York:

Appleton-Century-Crofts. [481]

188. —— Jones, L. V. and Kaplan, S. J. 1951. Conditioned discrimination as related to anxiety. *J. exp. Psychol.*, 42, 94–99. [48, 461]

189. —— and Marquis, D. G. 1935. Acquisition, extinction, and retention of conditioned led responses to light in dogs. *J. comp. Psychol.*, 19, 29–58. [339, 356, 359, 369, 374]

190. —— and Marquis, D. G. 1940. *Conditioning and learning.* New York: Appleton-Century-Crofts. [47, 58–9, 62–4, 68, 71–3, 129, 138, 272, 295, 300, 304, 314, 324, 341, 356, 362, 378–9, 412, 424, 437]

191. —— and Smith, M. B. 1942. Distributed practice in motor learning: Score changes within and between daily sessions. *J. exp. Psychol.*, 30, 136–146. [45]

Hilgard, E. R. *see* Cohen, L. H. 1933; Doré, L. R. 1937.

192. Hill, D. and Parr, G. (eds.) 1950. *Electroencephlography: A symposium on its various aspects.* London: Macdonald. [235]

193. Hollingworth, H. L. 1928. *Psychology: Its facts and principles.* New York: Appleton-Century-Crofts. [298]

Horton, G. P. *see* Guthrie, E. R. 1946.

194. Hovland, C. I. 1936. "Inhibition of reinforcement" and phenomena of experimental extinction. *Proc. nat. Acad. Sci., Wash.,* 22, 430–433. [166, 287, 349]

195. —— 1937. The generalization of conditioned responses. I. The sensory generalization of conditioned responses with varying frequencies of tone. *J. gen. Psychol.,* 17, 125–148. [24, 150, 156, 327, 332, 410]

196. —— 1938a. Experimental studies in rote-learning theory: I. Reminiscence following learning by massed and by distributed practice. *J. exp. Psychol.,* 22, 201–224. [310]

197. —— 1938b. Experimental studies of rote-learning: III. Distribution of practice with varying speeds of syllable presentation. *J. exp. Psychol.,* 23, 172–190. [189, 267]

198. —— 1939. Experimental studies in rote-learning theory: IV. Comparison of reminiscence in serial and paired-associate learning. *J. exp. Psychol.,* 24, 466–484. [310]

199. —— 1951. Human learning and retention. Chapter 17 in Stevens, S. S. (ed.), *Handbook of experimental psychology.* New York: Wiley. Pp. 613–689. [7, 310, 472–3, 477]

200. —— and Kurtz, K. H. 1952. Experimental studies in rote-learning theory: X. Pre-learning syllable familiarization and the length-difficulty relationship. *J. exp. Psychol.,* 44, 31–39. [184, 404]

201. Hull, C. L. 1920. Quantitative aspects of the evolution of concepts. *Psychol. Monogr.,* No. 123. [226]

202. —— 1930a. Knowledge and purpose as habit mecha-

nisms. *Psychol. Rev.*, 37, 511–525. [100, 111]

203. ——— 1930b. Simple trial and error learning: A study in psychological theory. *Psychol. Rev.*, 37, 241–256. [104]

204. ——— 1932. The goal gradient hypothesis and maze learning. *Psychol. Rev.*, 39, 25–43. [177, 186, 281, 442]

205. ——— 1933a. *Hypnosis and suggestibility.* New York: Appleton-Century-Crofts. [427]

206. ——— 1933b. Differential habituation to internal stimuli in the albino rat. *J. comp. Psychol.*, 16, 255–273. [205]

207. ——— 1934a. Learning: II. The factor of the conditioned reflex. In Murchison, C. (ed.), *A handbook of general experimental psychology.* Worcester, Massachusetts: Clark University Press. Pp. 382–455. [10, 123, 128, 136, 279]

208 ——— 1934b. The concept of the habit-family hierarchy and maze learning. Part I. *Psychol. Rev.*, 41, 33–54. [139–40, 186, 405]

209. ——— 1935. The conflicting psychologies of learning—a way out. *Psychol. Rev.*, 42, 491–516. [53, 80, 189, 192]

210. ——— 1938. The goal-gradient hypothesis applied to some 'field force' problems in the behavior of young children. *Psychol. Rev.*, 45, 271–300. [427]

211. ——— 1943. *Principles of behavior: An introduction to behavior theory.* New York: Appleton-Century-Crofts. [6, 13, 61, 74, 79, 86–7, 129–30, 139, 148, 156, 166, 169–70, 172–3, 179, 195, 220, 231, 233, 245, 253, 273, 285–6, 345, 347, 352, 365–6, 412]

212. ——— 1945. The place of innate individual and species differences in a natural-science theory of behavior. *Psychol. Rev.*, 52, 55–60. [44]

213. ——— 1947. Reactively heterogeneous compound trial-and-error learning with distributed trials and terminal reinforcement. *J. exp. Psychol.*, 37, 118–135. [186, 273]

214. ——— 1951. *Essentials of behavior.* New Haven: Yale University Press. [66, 220]

215. ——— 1952. A *behavior system.* New Haven: Yale University Press. [83, 86, 170, 253, 287, 392, 481]

216. ——— Livingston, L. R., Rouse, R. O. and Parker, A. N. 1951. True, sham and esophageal feeding as reinforcements. *J. comp. physiol. Psychol.*, 44, 236–245. [251, 267]

Hull, C. L. *see* Bass, M. J. 1934.

217. Humphreys, L. G. 1939. Generalization as a function of the method of reinforcement. *J. exp. Psychol.*, 25, 361–372. [155, 350–1]

218. ——— 1943. Measures of strength of conditioned eyelid responses. *J. gen. Psychol.*, 29, 101–111. [170]

219. Hunt, J. McV. 1941. The effect of infant feeding-frustration upon adult hoarding in the albino rat. *J. abnorm. soc. Psychol.*, 36, 338–360. [395]

220. **Hunter, W. S.** 1932. The effect of inactivity produced by cold upon learning and retention in the cockroach, *Blatella germanica. J. genet. Psychol.*, 41, 253–266. [323, 408]

221. —— 1934. Learning: IV. Experimental studies of learning. In Murchison, C. (ed.), *A handbook of general experimental psychology.* Worcester, Massachusetts: Clark University Press. Pp. 497–570. [7]

222. **Hurder, W. P. and Sanders, A. F.** 1953. The effects of neonatal anoxia on the maze performance of adult rats. *J. comp. physiol. Psychol.*, 46, 61–63. [396]

223. **Hymovitch, B.** 1952. The effects of experimental variations on problem solving in the rat. *J. comp. physiol. Psychol.*, 45, 313–321. [397]

Ilg, F. L. *see* Gesell, A. 1943.

224. **Irion, A. L.** 1948. The relation of 'set' to retention. *Psychol. Rev.*, 55, 336–341. [212]

Irion, A. L. *see* McGeoch, J. A. 1952.

225. **Irwin, F. W., Kauffman, K., Prior, G. and Weaver, H. B.** 1934. On 'learning without awareness of what is learned.' *J. exp. Psychol.*, 17, 823–827. [226]

Irwin, J. M. *see* Melton, A. W. 1940.

Israel, H. C. *see* Rees, H. J. 1935.

Israel, H. E. *see* Siipola, E. M. 1933.

226. **Jacobsen, C. F.** 1933. The influence of extirpation of the motor and premotor areas of the cortex upon the retention and execution of acquired skilled movements in primates. *Amer. J. Physiol.*, 105, 58. [405]

227. **Jacobsen, E.** 1932. Electrophysiology of mental activities. *Amer. J. Psychol.*, 44, 677–694. [234]

228. **James, W.** 1890. *The principles of psychology.* 2 Vol. New York: Holt. [46, 295, 393, 427]

Jarrett, R. F. *see* Postman, L. 1952.

Jaynes, J. *see* Beach, F. A. 1954.

229. **Jenkins, J. G.** 1933. Instruction as a factor in 'incidental' learning. *Amer. J. Psychol.*, 45, 471–477. [225]

230. **Jenkins, J. G. and Dallenbach, K. M.** 1924. Oblivescence during sleep and waking. *Amer. J. Psychol.*, 35, 605–612. [322]

231. —— **and Sheffield, F. D.** 1946. Rehearsal and guessing habits as sources of the 'spread of effect.' *J. exp. Psychol.*, 36, 316–330. [282]

232. —— **and Stanley, J. C.** 1950. Partial reinforcement: A review and critique. *Psychol. Bull.*, 47, 193–234. [351]

Jones, E. [448]

Jones, H. M. *see* Mowrer, O. H. 1945.

Jones, L. V. *see* Hilgard, E. R. 1951.

233. **Jones, M. C.** 1924. The elimination of children's fears. *J. exp. Psychol.*, 7, 382–390. [360, 423–4]

Jost, A. [378]

234. **Judd, C. H.** 1908. The relation of special training to gen-

eral intelligence. *Educ. Rev.*, 36, 28–42. [407]

Jung, C. G. [419]

Kalish, D. *see* Tolman, E. C. 1947.

Kamin, L. J. *see* Solomon, R. L. 1953.

235. **Kantor, J. R.** 1947. *Problems of physiological psychology.* Bloomington, Indiana: Principia Press. [39]

Kaplan, S. J. *see* Hilgard, E. R. 1951.

236. **Kappers, C. U. A.** 1932. Principles of development of the nervous system (neurobiotoxis). In Penfield, W. (ed.), *Cytology and cellular pathology of the nervous system.* New York: Hoeber. [113]

Kauffman, K. *see* Irwin, F. W. 1934.

Keenan, J. *see* Deese, J. 1953.

237. **Keet, C. D.** 1948. Two verbal techniques in a miniature counseling situation. *Psychol. Monogr.*, 62, No. 294. [333]

238. **Keller, F. S.** 1943. Studies in international Morse code. I. A new method of teaching code reception. *J. appl. Psychol.*, 27, 407–415. [455, 478]

239. ——— and Schoenfield, W. N. 1950. *Principles of psychology.* New York: Appleton-Century-Crofts. [144]

240. ——— and Taubman, R. E. 1943. Studies in international Morse code. II. Errors made in code reception. *J. appl. Psychol.*, 27, 504–509. [479]

241. **Kellogg, W. N.** and **Walker, E. L.** 1938. An analysis of the bilateral transfer of con-

ditioning in dogs, in terms of the frequency, amplitude and latency of the responses. *J. gen. Psychol.*, 18, 253–265. [360]

242. ——— and Wolf, I. S. 1939. The nature of the response retained after several varieties of conditioning in the same subjects. *J. exp. Psychol.*, 24, 366–383. [379]

Kellogg, W. N. *see* Spooner, A. 1947.

243. **Kendler, H. H.** 1945. Drive interaction: II. Experimental analysis of the role of drive in learning theory. *J. exp. Psychol.*, 35, 188–198. [352]

244. ——— 1947. A comparison of learning under motivated and satiated conditions in the white rat. *J. exp. Psychol.*, 37, 545–549. [226]

245. ——— 1952. "What is learned?"—a theoretical blind alley. *Psychol. Rev.*, 59, 269–277. [80, 82]

246. **Kennelly, T. W.** 1941. The role of similarity in retroactive inhibition. *Arch. Psychol.*, N.Y., 37, No. 260. [325]

Kessen, M. L. *see* Berkun, M. M. 1952.

247. **Kinsey, A. C., Pomeroy, W. B.** and **Martin, C. E.** 1948. *Sexual behavior in the human male.* Philadelphia: Saunders. [214]

248. ———, ———, ———, and **Gebhard, P. H.** 1953. *Sexual behavior in the human female.* Philadelphia: Saunders. [39, 232]

249. **Koch, H. L.** 1923. The influence of mechanical guidance upon maze learning. *Psy-*

chol. Monogr., 32, No. 5. [467]

250. **Koch, S.** 1954. Clark L. Hull. Chapter 1 in Estes, W. K. *et al, Modern learning theory.* New York: Appleton-Century-Crofts. Pp. 1–176. [233, 254]

251. **Köhler, W.** 1929. *Gestalt psychology.* New York: Liveright. [299]

252. **Konorski, J.** 1948. *Conditioned reflexes and neuron organization.* Cambridge: University Press. [295]

253. **Krawiec, T. S.** 1946. A comparison of learning and retention of materials presented visually and auditorially. *J. gen. Psychol.*, 34, 179–197. [125]

254. **Krech, D.** 1950. Dynamic systems as open neurophysiology systems. *Psychol. Rev.*, 57, 345–361. [481]

255. **Krechevsky, I.** 1932. 'Hypotheses' in rats. *Psychol. Rev.*, 39, 516–532. [401]

256. **Krieg, W. J. S.** 1953. *Functional neuroanatomy* (2d. ed.). New York: Blakiston. [33]

257. **Kuenne, M. R.** 1946. Experimental investigation of the relation of language to transposition behavior in young children. *J. exp. Psychol.*, 36, 471–490. [411]

258. **Kurke, M. I.** 1953. Relative effectiveness of massed versus spaced extinction trials in conditioning inhibition of a bar-pressing habit in the white rat. Unpublished M.A. thesis, The University of Buffalo. [356]

Kurke, M. E. *see* Riesen, A. H. 1953.

Kurtz, K. H. *see* Hovland, C. I. 1952.

259. **Landis, C.** 1924. Studies in emotional reactions. II. General behavior and facial expression. *J. comp. Psychol.*, 4, 447–509. [422]

Lange, C. G. [427]

260. **Lashley, K. S.** 1917. The accuracy of movement in the absence of excitation from the moving organ. *Amer. J. Psychol.*, 43, 169–194. [106]

261. —— 1942. An examination of the 'continuity theory' as applied to discrimination learning. *J. gen. Psychol.*, 26, 241–265. [287]

262. **Lawrence, D. H. and Miller, W. E.** 1947. A positive relationship between reinforcement and resistance to extinction produced by removing a source of confusion from a technique that had produced opposite results. *J. exp. Psychol.*, 37, 494–509. [347–8]

Lazarus, R. S. *see* Deese, J. 1953.

263. **Leavitt, H. F. and Schlosberg, H.** 1944. The retention of verbal and of motor skills. *J. exp. Psychol.*, 34, 404–417. [315–6]

264. **Leeper, R.** 1935. The role of motivation in learning: A study of the phenomenon of differential motivational control of the utilization of habits. *J. genet. Psychol.*, 46, 3–40. [205]

265. —— 1948a. A motivational theory of emotion to replace "Emotion as disorganized

response." *Psychol., Rev.,* 55, 5–21. [217, 428]

266. ——— 1948b. The experiments of Spence and Lippett and by Kendler on the sign-Gestalt theory of learning. *J. exp. Psychol.,* 38, 102–106. [211, 227]

267. **Lepley, W. M.** 1932. A theory of serial learning and forgetting based upon conditioned reflex principles. *Psychol. Rev.,* 39, 279–288. [166]

268. **Lester, O. P.** 1932. Mental set in relation to retroactive inhibition. *J. exp. Psychol.,* 15, 681–699. [22, 313]

269. **Leuba, C. J.** 1940. Images as conditioned sensations. *J. exp. Psychol.,* 26, 345–351. [153]

270. ——— 1941. The use of hypnosis for controlling variables in psychological experiments. *J. abnorm. soc. Psychol.,* 36, 271–274. [133, 258, 267, 459]

271. ——— 1955. Toward some integration of learning theories: The concept of optimal stimulation. *Psychol. Rep.,* 1, 27–33. [209, 221]

272. ——— and Bateman, D. 1952. Learning during sleep. *Amer. J. Psychol.,* 65, 301–302. [227]

Levy, N. *see* Seward, J. P. 1949.

273. **Lewin, K.** 1931. Environmental forces in child behavior and development. In Murchison, C. (ed.), *A handbook of child psychology.* Worcester, Massachusetts: Clark University Press. Pp. 590–625. [427]

274. ——— 1946. Behavior and development as a function of the total situation. In Carmichael, L. (ed.), *Manual of child psychology.* New York: Wiley. Pp. 791–844. [335]

275. ——— 1948. *Resolving social conflicts.* New York: Harper. [465]

276. **Lewis, D. J.** 1952. Partial reinforcement in a gambling situation. *J. exp. Psychol.,* 43, 447–450. [350]

277. **Liddell, H. S.** 1944. Conditioned reflex method and experimental neurosis. In Hunt, J. McV. (ed.), *Personality and the behavior disorders.* Vol. I. New York: Ronald. Pp. 389–412. [314, 356, 438]

278. **Lindahl, L. G.** 1945. Movement analysis as an industrial training method. *J. app. Psychol.,* 29, 420–436. [476]

279. **Lindsley, D. B.** 1951. Emotion. Chapter 14 in Stevens, S. S. (ed.), *Handbook of experimental psychology.* New York: Wiley. Pp. 473–516. [428]

280. **Linton, H. G. and Miller, N. E.** 1951. The effect of partial reinforcement on behavior during satiation. *J. comp. physiol. Psychol.,* 44, 142–148. [350]

Lipman, E. A. *see* Brogden, W. J. 1938.

Lippett, R. O. *see* Spence, K. W. 1946.

Livingston, L. R. *see* Hull, C. L. 1951.

281. **Locke, John.** 1690. *Essay concerning humane understanding* (4th. ed.). In 4 books.

London: Awnsham and John Churchil 1700. [2]

Longhurst, J. V. see Maier, N. R. F. 1947.

Lorenz, K. Z. [264]

282. Lorente de Nó, R. 1938. Synaptic stimulation of motorneurons as a local process. *J. Neurophysiol.*, 1, 195–206. [38, 114, 280, 296]

283. Louchs, R. B. 1935. The experimental delimitation of neural structures essential for learning: The attempt to condition striped muscle responses with faradization of the sigmoid gyri. *J. Psychol.*, 1, 5–44. [284]

284. Luchins, A. S. 1946. Classroom experiments on mental set. *Amer. J. Psychol.*, 59, 295–298. [212]

285. Ludgate, K. E. 1923. The effect of manual guidance upon maze learning. *Psychol. Monogr.*, 33, No. 148. [467]

286. Lumsdaine, A. A. 1939. Conditioned eyelid responses as mediating generalized conditioned finger reactions. *Psychol. Bull.*, 36, 650. [25, 107]

287. Maatsch, J., Adelman, H. and Denny, M. R. 1954. Effort and resistance to extinction of the bar-pressing response. *J. comp. physiol. Psychol.*, 47, 47–50. [358]

288. MacCorquodale, K. 1955. Learning. *Annu. Rev. Psychol.*, 6, 29–62. [482]

289. —— and Meehl, P. E. 1948. On a distinction between hypothetical constructs and intervening variables. *Psychol. Rev.*, 55, 95–107. [82]

290. —— and ——. 1951. On the elimination of cell entries without obvious reinforcement. *J. comp. physiol. Psychol.*, 44, 367–371. [249]

MacCorquodale, K. see Estes, W. K. et al. 1954.

291. McCulloch, W. S. 1944. Cortico-cortical connections. In Bucy, P. C. (ed.), *The precentral motor cortex*. Urbana, Illinois: University of Illinois Press. Pp. 211–242. [154]

McCulloch, W. S. see Bonin, G. von. 1942.

292. McGeoch, G. O. 1935. The conditions of reminiscence. *Amer. J. Psychol.*, 47, 65–87. [310]

293. McGeoch, J. A. 1933. Studies in retroactive inhibitions: II. Relationships between temporal point of interpolation, length of interval, and amount of retroactive inhibition. *J. gen. Psychol.*, 9, 44–57. [331]

294. —— 1936. The direction and extent of intraserial associations at recall. *Amer. J. Psychol.*, 48, 221–245. [189]

295. —— 1942. *The psychology of human learning*. New York: Longmans, Green. [8, 166, 188, 259, 266, 304, 307–8, 312–3, 320, 324, 336, 380]

296. —— and Irion, A. L. 1952. *The psychology of human learning* (2d. ed.). New York: Longmans, Green. [166, 302, 332–3, 335, 407, 410]

297. McGraw, M. B. 1935. *Growth: A study of Johnny and Jimmy*. New York: Apple-

ton-Century-Crofts. [309, 387]

298. **Mahut, H.** 1954. The effect of stimulus position on visual discrimination by the rat. *Canad. J. Psychol.*, 8, 130–138. [437]

299. **Maier, N. R. F.** 1931. Reasoning and learning. *Psychol. Rev.*, 38, 332–346. [138]

300. ———— 1949. *Frustration: The study of behavior without a goal.* New York: McGraw-Hill. [439]

301. ———— and Longhurst, J. V. 1947. Studies of abnormal behavior in the rat. XXI. Conflict and audiogenic seizures. *J. comp. physiol. Psychol.*, 40, 397–412. [440]

302. **Malmo, R. B.** 1954. Eccles' neurophysiological model of the conditioned reflex. *Canad. J. Psychol.*, 8, 125–129. [363]

Marks, M. *see* Worchel, P. 1951.

Marquis, D. G. *see* Hilgard, E. R. 1935 and 1940.

Martin, C. E. *see* Kinsey, A. C. *et al.* 1948 and 1953.

303. **Masserman, J. H.** 1943. *Behavior and neurosis.* Chicago: University of Chicago Press. [440]

304. **Matarazzo, J. D., Ulett, G. A., Guze, S. B. and Saslow, G.** 1954. The relationship between anxiety level and several measures of intelligence. *J. consult. Psychol.*, 18, 201–205. [462]

305. **May, M. A.** 1948. Experimentally acquired drives. *J. exp. Psychol.*, 38, 66–77. [68]

306. **Meehl, P. E.** 1950. On the circularity of the law of effect.

Psychol. Bull., 47, 52–75. [245]

307. ———— 1955. Psychotherapy. *Annu. Rev. Psychol.*, 6, 357–378. [447]

Meehl, P. E. *see* Estes, W. K. *et al.* 1954; MacCorquodale, K. 1948 and 1951.

308. **Meier, G. W. and Bunch, M. E.** 1950. The effects of natal anoxia upon learning and memory at maturity. *J. comp. physiol. Psychol.*, 43, 436–441. [395]

Mellinger, J C. *see* Riesen, A. H. 1953.

309. **Melton, A. W. and Irwin, J. M.** 1940. The influence of degree of interpolated learning on retroactive inhibition and the overt transfer of specific responses. *Amer. J. Psychol.*, 53, 173–203. [332]

310. ———— and Stone, G. R. 1942. The retention of serial lists of adjectives over short time-intervals with varying rates of presentation. *J. exp. Psychol.*, 30, 295–310. [310]

311. ———— and Von Lackum, W. J. 1941. Retroactive and proactive inhibition in retention: Evidence for a two-factor theory of retroactive inhibition. *Amer. J. Psychol.*, 54, 157–173. [337]

Merrick, N. I. *see* Dvorak, A. 1936.

312. **Meyer, D. R.** 1951. Intraproblem-interproblem relationships in learning by monkeys. *J. comp. physiol. Psychol.*, 44, 162–167. [352]

Meyer, D. R. *see* Silver, C. A. 1954.

313. **Miles, W. R.** 1933. Age and human ability. *Psychol. Rev.*, 40, 99–123. [45]

314. **Miller, J.** 1939. The effect of facilitatory and inhibitory ¡attitude on eyelid conditioning. *Psychol. Bull.*, 36, 577–578. [171, 212]

315. **Miller, N. E.** 1935. A reply to "Sign-Gestalt or conditioned reflex?" *Psychol. Rev.*, 42, 280–292. [102, 345]

316. —— 1944. Experimental studies of conflict. In Hunt, J. McV. (ed.), *Personality and the behavior disorders.* Vol. I. New York: Ronald. Pp. 431–465. [441]

317. —— 1946. Comments on multiple-process conceptions of learning. *Psychol. Rev.*, 58, 375–381. [258]

318. —— 1948. Studies of fear as an acquirable drive. I. Fear as motivation and fear-reduction as reinforcement in the learning of new responses. *J. exp. Psychol.*, 38, 89–101. [14, 64, 127, 217, 345, 360]

319. —— 1951. Learnable drives and rewards. Chapter 13 in Stevens, S. S. (ed.), *Handbook of experimental psychology.* New York: Wiley. Pp. 435–472. [15, 65, 232, 431, 441]

320. —— and Dollard, J. 1941. *Social learning and imitation.* New Haven: Yale University Press. [207–8, 210, 241, 248, 366, 468–9]

Miller, N. E. *see* Berkun, M. M. 1952; Bugelski, B. R. 1938; Dollard, J. *et al.* 1939 and 1950; Lawrence, D. H. 1947; Linton, H. B. 1951; Myers, A. K. 1954.

Milner, P. *see* Olds, J. 1954.

321. **Minami, H. and Dallenback, K. M.** 1946. The effect of activity upon learning and retention in the cockroach. *Amer. J. Psychol.*, 59, 1–58. [332]

322. **Mitrano, A. J.** 1939. Principles of conditioning in human goal behavior. *Psychol. Monogr.*, 51, No. 4 (whole No. 230), 70 pp. [41]

323. **Montague, E. K.** 1953. The role of anxiety in serial rote learning. *J. exp. Psychol.*, 45, 91–96. [49]

Mosteller, F. *see* Bush, R. R. 1951a and 1951b.

324. **Mowrer, O. H.** 1938. Preparatory set (expectance)—a determinant on motivation and learning. *Psychol. Rev.*, 45, 62–91. [211]

325. —— 1940a. An experimental analogue of "regression" with incidental observations on "reaction-formation." *J. abnorm. soc. Psychol.*, 35, 56–87. [59, 432]

326. —— 1940b. Anxiety-reduction and learning. *J. exp. Psychol.*, 27, 497–516. [131, 217]

327. —— 1947. On the dual nature of learning—a reinterpretation of "conditioning" and "problem-solving." *Harv. educ. Rev.*, 17, 102–148. [66, 68, 137]

328. —— 1950. *Learning theory and personality dynamics.* New York: Ronald. [65, 138, 342, 420, 427]

329. —— 1953. Motivation and neurosis. Brown, J. S. *et*

al. Current theory and re-search in motivation. Lincoln, Nebraska: University of Nebraska Press. Pp. 162–184. [66]

330. —— and Jones, H. M. 1945. Habit strength as a function of pattern of reinforcement. *J. exp. Psychol.*, 35, 293–311. [350–1, 358, 366–8]

331. —— and Ullman, A. D. 1945. Time as a determinant in integrative learning. *Psychol. Rev.*, 52, 61–90. [130]

Mowrer, O. H. *see* Dollard, J. *et al.* 1939.

Mueller, Jr., C. G. *see* Estes, W. K. *et al.* 1954.

332. Muenzinger, K. F. 1934. Motivation in learning. I. Electric shock for correct responses in the visual discrimination habit. *J. comp. Psychol.*, 17, 267–277. [274]

333. —— 1938. Vicarious trial and error at point of choice. I. A general survey of its relation to learning efficiency. *J. genet. Psychol.*, 53, 75–86. [181]

334. Müller, G. E. and Pilzecker, A. 1900. Experimentelle Beiträge zur Lehre vom Gedächtniss. *Z. Psychol.*, *Ergbd.*, 1, 1–288 (*see* Woodworth, 1938). [266, 320, 331]

335. Munn, N. L. 1938. *Psychological development.* Boston: Houghton Mifflin. [394]

336. Myers, A. K. and Miller, N. E. 1954. Failure to find a learned drive based on hunger; evidence for learning motivated by "exploration."

J. comp. physiol. Psychol., 47, 428–436. [232, 431]

337. Nagge, J. W. 1935. An experimental test of the theory of associative interference. *J. exp. Psychol.*, 18, 663–682. [313]

338. National Society for the Study of Education. *41st. Yearbook.* 1942. Part II. The psychology of learning. [451]

Nelson, A. K. *see* Pratt, K. C. 1930

339. Nissen, H. W. 1954. The nature of the drive as innate determinant of behavioral organization. In Jones, M. R. (ed.), *Nebraska symposium on motivation, 1954.* Lincoln, Nebraska: University of Nebraska Press. [214, 223]

340. ——, Chow, K. L. and Semmes, J. 1951. Effects of restricted opportunity for tactual, kinesthetic, and manipulative experience on the behavior of chimpanzee. *Amer. J. Psychol.*, 64, 485–507. [76, 394]

341. O'Connor, V. J. 1946. Recency or effect? A critical analysis of Guthrie's theory of learning. *Harv. educ. Rev.*, 16, 194–206. [293]

342. Olds, J. and Milner, P. 1954. Positive reinforcement produced by electrical stimulation of septal area and other regions of rat brain. *J. comp. physiol. Psychol.*, 47, 419–427. [482]

343. O'Neill, P. H. 1949. The effect on subsequent maze learning ability of graded amounts of vitamin B₁ in the diet of very young rats.

J. genet. Psychol., 74, 85–95. [48]

344. **Osgood, C. E.** 1946. Meaningful similarity and interference in learning. *J. exp. Psychol.*, 36, 277–301. [326]

345. —— 1948. An investigation into the causes of retroactive interference. *J. exp. Psychol.*, 38, 132–154. [332]

346. —— 1949. The similarity paradox in human learning: A resolution. *Psychol. Rev.*, 56, 132–143. [325, 327, 329, 406]

347. —— 1950. Can Tolman's theory of learning handle avoidance training? *Psychol. Rev.*, 57, 133–137. [370, 431]

348. —— 1953. *Method and theory in experimental psychology.* New York: Oxford University Press. [152, 216, 225, 272–3, 289, 293, 308, 332, 336, 385, 413]

349. **Page, H. A. and Hall, J. F.** 1953. Experimental extinction as a function of the prevention of a response. *J. comp. physiol. Psychol.*, 46, 33–34. [174]

Parr, G. *see* Hill, D. 1950

350. **Pavlov, I. P.** 1927. *Conditioned reflexes.* (Trans. by G. V. Anrep) London: Oxford University Press. [11, 42, 124, 126, 131, 138, 146, 154, 163–4, 166, 274, 283, 295, 338–40, 349, 354, 357, 459]

351. —— 1942. *Lectures on conditioned reflexes. II. Conditioned reflexes and psychiatry.* (Trans. and edited by W. H. Gantt) New York: International Publishers. [54]

352. **Peak, H.** 1933. An evaluation of the concepts of reflex and voluntary action. *Psychol. Rev.*, 40, 71–89. [133]

353. **Penfield, W. and Rasmussen, T.** 1950. *The cerebral cortex of man.* New York: Macmillan. [38, 204]

354. **Perin, C. T.** 1943. A quantitative investigation of the delay-of-reinforcement gradient. *J. exp. Psychol.*, 32, 37–51. [347]

355. **Peters, H. N.** 1935. Mediate association. *J. exp. Psychol.*, 18, 20–48. [109]

Pomeroy, W. B. *see* Kinsey, A. C. *et al.* 1948, 1953.

356. **Porter, P. B., Stone, C. P. and Eriksen, C. W.** 1948. Learning ability in rats given electro-convulsive shocks in late infancy. Part II. *J. comp. physiol. Psychol.*, 41, 423–431. [395]

357. **Postman, L.** 1947. The history and present status of the law of effect. *Psychol. Bull.*, 44, 489–563. [58, 243]

358. —— 1953. The experimental analysis of motivational factors in perception. In Brown, J. S. *et al.*, *Current theory and research in motivation.* Lincoln, Nebraska: University of Nebraska Press. Pp. 59–107. [222–3, 231]

359. —— and **Alper, T. G.** 1946. Retroactive inhibition as a function of the time of interpolation of the inhibitor between learning and recall. *Amer. J. Psychol.*, 59, 439–449. [331]

360. —— and **Jarrett, R. F.** 1952. An experimental analysis of

'learning without awareness.' *Amer. J. Psychol.*, *65*, 244–255. [226]

361. —— and Senders, V. L. 1946. Incidental learning and generality of set. *J. exp. Psychol.*, *36*, 153–165. [225]

Powers, F. F. *see* Guthrie, E. R. 1950.

362. Pratt, K. C., Nelson, A. K. and Sun, K. H. 1930. The behavior of the newborn infant. *Ohio State Univ. Stud. Psychol.*, No. 10, pp. 237.

Prior, G. *see* Irwin, F. W. 1934. [203]

363. Pyle, W. H. 1928. *The psychology of learning*. Baltimore: Warwick and York. [472]

Rasmussen, T. *see* Penfield, W. 1950.

364. Ratliff, M. M. 1938. The varying function of affectively toned olfactory, visual, and auditory cues in recall. *Amer. J. Psychol.*, *51*, 695–701. [301]

Rayner, R. *see* Watson, J. B. 1920.

365. Razran, G. H. S. 1936. Salivating and thinking in different languages. *J. Psychol.*, *1*, 145–151. [153]

366. —— 1939a. A quantitative study of meaning by a conditioned salivary technique (semantic conditioning). *Science*, *90*, 89–90. [153]

367. —— 1939b. Studies in configural conditioning: III. The factors of similarity, proximity, and continuity in configural conditioning. *J. exp. Psychol.*, *24*, 202–210. [151]

368. —— 1939c. Studies in configural conditioning: VI. Comparative extinction and forgetting of pattern and of single-stimulus conditioning. *J. exp. Psychol.*, *24*, 432–438. [314]

369. —— 1939d. A simple technique for controlling subjective attitudes in salivary conditioning of adult human subjects. *Science*, *89*, 160–161. [137]

370. —— 1940. Studies in configurational conditioning: V. Generalization and transposition. *J. genet. Psychol.*, *56*, 3–11. [126, 134, 409]

371. —— 1949. Stimulus generalization of conditioned responses. *Psychol. Bull.*, *46*, 337–365. [152]

372. Rees, H. J. and Israel, H. C. 1935. An investigation of the establishment and operation of mental sets. *Psychol. Monogr.*, *46*, No. 210. [211]

373. Reynolds, B. 1945a. The acquisition of a trace conditioned response as a function of the magnitude of the stimulus trace. *J. exp. Psychol.*, *35*, 15–30. [129]

374. —— 1945b. A repetition of the Blodgett experiment on "latent-learning." *J. exp. Psychol.*, *35*, 504–516. [80, 249]

375. —— 1949. The acquisition of a black-white discrimination habit under two levels of reinforcement. *J. exp. Psychol.*, *39*, 760–769. [352]

376. —— 1950. Acquisition of a simple spatial discrimination as a function of the

amount of reinforcement. *J. exp. Psychol., 40,* 152–160. [254]

377. **Reynolds, R. W.** 1955. Neurophysiological mechanisms for the acquisitions and extinction of conditioned reflexes. *Psychol. Rep., 1,* 279–286. [363]

378. **Riesen, A. H.** 1947. The development of visual perception in man and chimpanzee. *Science, 106,* 107–108. [76, 391, 394]

379. ———— 1950. Arrested vision. *Sci. Amer., 183,* 16–19. [394]

380. ————, **Kurke, M. I. and Mellinger, J. C.** 1953. Interocular transfer of habits learned monocularly in visually naïve and visually experienced cats. *J. comp. physiol. Psychol., 46,* 166–172. [394]

381. **Rigby, W. K.** 1954. Approach and avoidance gradients and conflict behavior in a predominantly temporal situation. *J. comp. physiol. Psychol., 47,* 83–89. [443]

Ritchie, B. F. *see* Tolman, E. C. 1947.

Robbins, J. S. *see* Fox, B. H. 1952.

382. **Roberts, W. H.** 1930. The effect of delayed feeding on white rats in a problem cage. *J. genet. Psychol., 37,* 35–58. [293]

Robinson, E. E. *see* Crafts, L. W. *et al.* 1950.

383. **Robinson, E. S.** 1927. The "similarity" factor in retroaction. *Amer. J. Psychol., 39,* 297–312. [305, 325]

384. ———— 1932. *Association theory today.* New York: Appleton-Century-Crofts. [279, 287, 289, 299–300, 302]

Roby, T. B. *see* Sheffield, F. D. 1950.

Rock, R. T., Jr. *see* Thorndike, E. L. 1934.

385. **Roessler, R. L. and Brogden, W. J.** 1943. Conditioned differentiation of vasoconstriction to subvocal stimuli. *Amer. J. Psychol., 56,* 78–86. [12–3, 15, 22, 29, 229]

386. **Roethlisberger, F. J. and Dickson, W. J.** 1939. *Management and the worker.* Cambridge: Harvard University Press. [459]

Rogers, W. A. *see* Bugelski, B. R. 1952.

387. **Rohrer, J. H.** 1947. Experimental extinction as a function of the distribution of extinction trials and response strength. *J. exp. Psychol. 37,* 473–493. [356]

388. **Rosenzweig, S.** 1949. Clinical practice and personality theory: A symposium. I. The systematic intent of clinical psychology. *J. abnorm. soc. Psychol., 44,* 3–6. [445]

Rouse, R. O. *see* Hull, C. L. 1951.

389. **Rubin, L. S.** 1953. A demonstration of superior resistance to extinction following continuous reinforcement as compared with partial reinforcement. *J. comp. physiol. Psychol., 46,* 28–32. [350]

Rubin, R. D. *see* Furchgott, E. 1953.

390. **Ruch, F. L.** 1937. *Psychology and life.* Chicago: Scott, Foresman. [295]

391. **Russell, W. A. and Storms, L. H.** 1955. Implicit verbal chaining in paired-associate learning. *J. exp. Psychol.*, 49, 287–293. [110]

392. **Saltzman, I. J.** 1949. Maze learning in the absence of primary reinforcement: A study of secondary reinforcement. *J. comp. physiol. Psychol.*, 42, 161–173. [271]

393. ———— 1953. The orienting task in incidental learning. *Amer. J. Psychol.*, 66, 593–597. [225]

Sanders, A. F. *see* Hurder, W. P. 1953.

394. **Scharlock, D. P.** 1954. The effects of a pre-extinction procedure on the extinction of place and response performance in a T-maze. *J. exp. Psychol.*, 48, 31–36. [96–7, 133]

Scharlock, D. P. *see* Bugelski, B. R. 1952.

395. **Scharlock, N. T.** 1952. Mediated association in the learning of paired associate materials: The variable order. Unpublished M.A. thesis, The University of Buffalo. [109]

Schipper, L. M. *see* Grant, D. A. 1952.

396. **Schlosberg, H.** 1937. The relationship between success and the laws of conditioning. *Psychol. Rev.*, 44, 379–394. [138]

Schlosberg, H. *see* Bilodeau, I. M. 1951; Leavitt, H. J. 1944; and Woodworth, R. S. 1954.

Schmuller, A. M. *see* Thorpe, L. P. 1953.

Schneirla, T. C. *see* Crafts, L. W. *et al.* 1950.

397. **Schoenfeld, W. N., Antonitis, J. J. and Bersh, P. J.** 1950. A preliminary study of training conditions necessary for secondary reinforcement. *J. exp. Psychol.*, 40, 40–45. [70, 93]

Schoenfeld, W. N. *see* Estes, W. K. *et al.* 1954; and Keller, F. S. 1950.

Scott, T. H. *see* Bexton, W. H. 1954.

398. **Searle, L. V.** 1949. The organization of hereditary maze-brightness and maze-dullness. *Genet. Psychol. Monogr.*, 39, 279–375. [43]

399. **Sears, R. R.** 1936. Functional abnormalities of memory with special reference to amnesia. *Psychol. Bull.*, 33, 229–274. [420]

400. ———— 1943. Survey of objective studies of psychoanalytic concepts. *Soc. Sci. Res. Coun. Bull.*, No. 51. [334, 433]

401. ———— 1944. Experimental analysis of psychoanalytic phenomena. In Hunt, J. McV. (ed.), *Personality and the behavior disorders.* 2 Vol. New York: Ronald. Pp. 306–332. [333]

Sears, R. R. *see* Dollard, J. *et al.* 1939.

Semmes, Josephine *see* Nissen, H. W. 1951.

402. **Senden, M. von** 1932. *Raum- und Gestaltauffassung bei operierten Blindgeborenen vor und nach der Operation.* Leipzig: Barth. [76, 224]

Senders, V. L. *see* Postman, L. 1946.

403. **Seward, J. P.** 1942. An experimental study of Guthrie's theory of reinforcement. *J. exp. Psychol.*, 30, 247–256. [247]

404. —— **and Levy, N.** 1949. Sign learning as a factor in extinction. *J. exp. Psychol.*, 39, 660–668. [173, 249, 269, 371]

405. **Sharp, A. A.** 1938. An experimental test of Freud's doctrine of the relation of hedonic tone to memory revival. *J. exp. Psychol.*, 22, 395–418. [333]

406. **Sheffield, F. D.** 1948. Avoidance training and the contiguity principle. *J. comp. physiol. Psychol.*, 41, 165–177. [57, 63, 342, 369]

407. —— **and Roby, T. B.** 1950. Reward value of a non-nutritive sweet taste. *J. comp. physiol. Psychol.*, 43, 471–481. [229, 255]

408. ——, **Wulff, J. J. and Backer, R.** 1951. Reward value of copulation without sex drive reduction. *J. comp. physiol. Psychol.*, 44, 3–8. [229, 255]

Sheffield, F. D. *see* Jenkins, W. O. 1946.

409. **Sheffield, V. F.** 1950. Resistance to extinction as a function of the distribution of extinction trials. *J. exp. Psychol.*, 40, 305–313. [357]

410. **Sherman, M.** 1927a. The differentation of emotional responses in infants. I. Judgments of emotional responses from motion picture views and from actual observations. *J. comp. Psychol.*, 1, 265–284. [422]

411. —— 1927b. The differentation of emotional responses in infants. II. The ability of observers to judge emotional characteristics of the crying infants, and of the voice of an adult. *J. comp. Psychol.*, 1, 335–351. [422]

412. **Sherrington, C. S.** 1906. *The integrative action of the nervous system.* London: Constable. [82]

413. —— 1925. Remarks on some aspects of reflex inhibition. *Proc. roy. Soc.*, 97B, 519–545. [164, 367]

414. **Shipley, W. C.** 1935. Indirect conditioning. *J. gen. Psychol.*, 12, 337–357. [124]

Shipley, W. C. *see* Spence, K. W. 1934.

415. **Shoben, E. J.** 1949. Psychotherapy as a problem in learning theory. *Psychol. Bull.*, 46, 366–392. [419]

Shurrager, H. C. *see* Shurrager, P. S. 1946.

416. **Shurrager, P. S. and Shurrager, H. C.** 1946. The rate of learning measured at a single synapse. *J. exp. Psychol.*, 36, 347–354. [183]

417. **Siegel, P. S. and Foshee, G.** 1953. The law of primary reinforcement in children. *J. exp. Psychol.*, 45, 12–14. [41]

418. **Siipola, E. M. and Israel, H. E.** 1933. Habit-interference as dependent upon stage of training. *Amer. J. Psychol.*, 45, 205–227. [410]

419. **Silver, C. A. and Meyer, D. R.** 1954. Temporal factors in sensory preconditioning. *J. comp. physiol. Psychol.*, 47, 57–59. [125, 257]

420. **Simon, C. H. and Emmons, W. W.** 1955. Learning during sleep? *Psychol. Bull.*, 52, 328–342. [228]

421. **Skinner, B. F.** 1938. *The behavior of organisms: An experimental analysis.* New York: Appleton-Century-Crofts. [15, 36, 68, 91, 138–9, 144, 175, 234, 240, 270, 289, 348, 350, 353, 371]

422. ——— 1948a. Walden two. New York: Macmillan. [434, 451]

423. ——— 1948b. "Superstition" in the pigeon. *J. exp. Psychol.*, 38, 168–172. [56, 426]

424. ——— 1950. Are theories of learning necessary? *Psychol. Rev.*, 57, 193–216. [17, 36, 177, 259, 314, 342, 348, 350, 356, 358, 368]

425. ——— 1951. How to teach animals. *Sci. Amer.*, 185 (6), 26–29. [246]

426. ——— 1953. *Science and human behavior.* New York: Macmillan. [139, 392, 426]

427. **Small, W. S.** 1899–1900. An experimental study of the mental processes of the rat. *Amer. J. Psychol.*, 11, 133–164. [185]

Smith, A. H. *see* Anderson, J. E. 1926.

Smith, M. B. *see* Hilgard, E. R. 1942.

428. **Smith, S. A.** 1949. A further reduction of sensory factors in stereoscopic depth perception. *J. exp. Psychol.*, 39, 393–394. [282]

429. **Snoddy, G. S.** 1945. Evidence for a universal shock factor in learning. *J. exp. Psychol.*, 35, 403–417. [45]

430. **Solomon, R. L.** 1947. The role of effect in the performance of a distance discrimination by albino rats. *Amer. Psychologist*, 2, 301. [358]

431. ——— 1948a. Influence of work on behavior. *Psychol. Bull.*, 45, 1–40. [229]

432. ——— 1948b. Effort and extinction rate: A confirmation. *J. comp. physiol. Psychol.*, 41, 93–101. [358]

433. ——— and Coles, M. R. 1954. A case of failure of generalization of imitation across drives and across situations. *J. abnorm. soc. Psychol.*, 49, 7–13. [469]

434. ———, Kamin, L. J. and Wynne, L. C. 1953. Traumatic avoidance learning: The outcomes of several extinction procedures with dogs. *J. abnorm. soc. Psychol.*, 48, 291–302. [428–9]

435. ——— and Wynne, L. C. 1953. Traumatic avoidance learning: Acquisition in normal dogs. *Psychol. Monogr.*, 67, No. 4 (whole No. 354). [64, 301, 345, 469]

436. **Spelt, D. K.** 1948. The conditioning of the human fetus *in utero. J. exp. Psychol.*, 38, 338–346. [395]

437. **Spence, K. W.** 1937. The differential response in animals to stimuli varying within a single dimension. *Psychol. Rev.*, 44, 430–444. [156, 345, 411]

438. ——— 1942a. Theoretical interpretations of learning. Chapter 12 in Moss, F. A. (ed.), *Comparative psychology* (rev. ed.). New

York: Prentice-Hall. Pp. 280–329. [79]

439. ———— 1942b. The basis of solution by chimpanzees of the intermediate size problem. *J. exp. Psychol., 31,* 257–271. [411]

440. ———— 1945. An experimental test of the continuity and non-continuity theories of discrimination learning. *J. exp. Psychol., 35,* 253–266. [288]

441. ———— 1947. The role of secondary reinforcement in delayed reward learning. *Psychol. Rev., 54,* 1–8. [273, 281]

442. ———— 1951. Theoretical interpretations of learning. Chapter 18 in Stevens, S. S. (ed.), *Handbook of experimental psychology.* New York: Wiley. Pp. 690–729. [7, 80, 83, 285]

443. ———— 1953. Mathematical theories of learning. *J. gen. Psychol., 49,* 283–291. [481]

444. ———— 1954. Current interpretations of learning data and some recent developments in stimulus-response theory. In Adams, D. K. *et al., Learning theory, personality theory, and clinical research: The Kentucky symposium.* New York: Wiley. Pp. 1–21. [453]

445. ———— and Lippitt, R. O. 1946. An experimental test of the sign-Gestalt theory of trial-and-error learning. *J. exp. Psychol., 36,* 491–502. [211, 212, 215, 227]

446. ———— and Shipley, W. C. 1934. The factors determining the difficulty of blind alleys in maze learning by the white rat. *J. comp. Psychol., 17,* 423–436. [186]

447. ———— and Taylor, J. A. 1951. Anxiety and strength of the UCS as determiners of the amount of eyelid conditioning. *J. exp. Psychol., 42,* 183–188. [48, 461]

448. ———— and ———— 1953. The relation of conditioned response strength to anxiety in normal, neurotic, and psychotic subjects. *J. exp. Psychol., 45,* 265–272. [48]

Spence, K. W. *see* Farber, I. E. 1953.

449. Spencer, H. 1880. *The principles of psychology.* New York: Appleton-Century-Crofts. [199]

450. Spooner, A. and Kellogg, W. N. 1947. The backward conditioning curve. *Amer. J. Psychol., 60,* 321–334. [129]

Stanley, J. C. *see* Jenkins, W. O. 1950.

Stauffacher, J. C. *see* Bills, A. G. 1937.

451. Stern, W. 1914. The intelligence quotient. In Dennis, W. (ed.), *Readings in general psychology.* New York: Prentice-Hall. 1949. Pp. 338–341. [81]

452. Stevens, H. 1937. Avitaminosis B (B$_1$), maze performance, and certain aspects of brain chemistry. *J. comp. Psychol., 24,* 441–458. [48]

453. Stevens, S. S. 1935. The relation of pitch to intensity. *J. acoust. Soc. Amer., 6,* 150–154. [127]

454. ———— (ed.) 1951. *Handbook of experimental psychology.* New York: Wiley. [6, 167]

455. ——— and Volkmann, J. 1940. The relation of pitch to frequency: A reward scale. *Amer. J. Psychol.*, 53, 329–353. [149]

Stone, C. P. *see* Porter, P. B. 1948.

Stone, G. R. *see* Melton, A. W. 1942.

456. Strassburger, R. C. 1950. Resistance to extinction of a conditioned operant as related to drive level at reinforcement. *J. exp. Psychol.*, 40, 473–487. [352]

457. Stratton, G. M. 1896. Some preliminary experiments on vision without inversion of the retinal image. *Psychol. Rev.*, 3, 611–617. [406]

Stringer, W. F. *see* Griffiths, W. J., Jr. 1952.

Stuart, E. A. *see* Hebb, D. O. 1954.

458. Sullivan, J. J. 1950. Some factors affecting the conditioning of the galvanic skin response. Unpublished Ph.D. dissertation, State University of Iowa. [258]

Sun, K. H. *see* Pratt, K. C. 1930.

459. Switzer, S. A. 1935. The effect of caffeine on experimental extinction of conditioned reactions. *J. gen. Psychol.*, 12, 78–94. [47]

Taubman, R. E. *see* Keller, F. S. 1943.

Taylor, J. A. *see* Spence, K. W. 1951 and 1953.

460. Thistlethwaite, D. L. 1951. A critical review of latent learning and related experiments. *Psychol. Bull.*, 48, 97–129. [80]

Thompson, H. *see* Gesell, A. 1941.

461. Thompson, W. R. and Heron, W. 1954a. The effects of restricting early experience on the problem-solving capacity of dogs. *J. Psychol.*, 8, 17–31. [397]

462. ——— and ——— 1954b. The effects of early restriction on activity in dogs. *J. comp. physiol. Psychol.*, 47, 77–82. [397]

463. Thorndike, E. L. 1898. Animal intelligence. An experimental study of the associative processes in animals. *Psychol. Monogr.*, 2, No. 8, 109pp. [55, 139, 174, 468]

464. ——— 1911. *Animal intelligence: Experimental studies.* New York: Macmillan. [200]

465. ——— 1914. *The psychology of learning.* New York: Teachers College, Columbia University. [299]

466. ——— 1931. *Human learning.* New York: Appleton-Century-Crofts. [58, 137, 243–4]

467. ——— 1932. *The fundamentals of learning.* New York: Teachers College, Columbia University. [19, 58, 244, 285, 301]

468. ——— 1933. A proof of the law of effect. *Science*, 77, 173–175. [282]

469. ——— 1946. Expectation. *Psychol. Rev.*, 53, 277–281. [97]

470. ———, Bregman, E. O., Tilton, J. W. and Woodyard, E. 1928. *Adult learning.* New York: Macmillan. [45, 478]

471. —— and Rock, R. T., Jr. 1934. Learning without awareness of what is being learned or intent to learn it. *J. exp. Psychol.*, 17, 1–19. [226]

472. —— and Woodworth, R. S. 1901. The influence of improvment in one mental function upon the efficiency of other functions. *Psychol. Rev.*, 8, 247–261. [385, 408]

473. Thorpe, L. P. and Schmuller, A. M. 1953. *Contemporary theories of learning*. New York: Ronald. [451–2, 456–7]

Tilton, J. W. *see* Thorndike, E. L. *et al.* 1928.

474. Tinklepaugh, O. L. 1928. An experimental study of representative factors in monkeys. *J. comp. Psychol.*, 8, 187–236. [103]

475. Tolman, E. C. 1930. Maze performance, a function of motivation and of reward as well as of knowledge of the maze paths. *J. genet. Psychol.*, 4, 338–342. [19]

476. —— 1932. *Purposive behavior in animals and men*. New York: Appleton-Century-Crofts. [73, 79–80]

477. —— 1933. Sign-Gestalt or conditioned reflex? *Psychol. Rev.*, 40, 246–255. [102]

478. —— 1936. Operational behaviorism and current trends in psychology. *Proc. 25th. Anniv. Inauguration Graduate Studies*. Los Angeles: University of Southern California. Pp. 89–103. [80]

479. —— 1938a. The determiners of behavior at a choice point. *Psychol. Rev.*, 45, 1–41. [43, 63, 80, 82, 87, 187, 270]

480. —— 1938b. The law of effect: A roundtable discussion. II. *Psychol. Rev.*, 45, 200–203. [248]

481. —— 1948. Cognitive maps in rats and men. *Psychol. Rev.*, 55, 189–208. [88]

482. —— 1949. There is more than one kind of learning. *Psychol. Rev.*, 56, 144–155. [59, 73, 268]

483. —— and Gleitman, H. 1949. Studies in learning and motivation. I. Equal reinforcements in both end-boxes, followed by shock in one end-box. *J. exp. Psychol.*, 39, 810–819. [21–2, 102, 268–9]

484. —— Hall, C. S. and Brenall, E. P. 1932. A disproof of the law of effect and a substitution of the laws of emphasis, motivation, and disruption. *J. exp. Psychol.*, 15, 601–614. [274]

485. —— Ritchie, B. F., and Kalish, D. 1947. Studies in spatial learning. V. Response learning vs. place learning by the non-correction method. *J. exp. Psychol.*, 37, 285–292. [95, 290]

486. Towe, A. L. 1954. A study of figural equivalence in the pigeon. *J. comp. physiol. Psychol.*, 47, 283–287. [394]

487. Travis, R. C. 1939. Length of the practice period and efficiency in motor learning. *J. exp. Psychol.*, 24, 339–345. [472]

488. Tryon, R. C. 1942. Individual differences. In Moss, F. A. (ed.), *Comparative Psychol-*

ogy (2d. ed.). New York: Prentice-Hall.

Ullman, A. D. *see* Mowrer, O. H. 1945. [43]

489. **Underwood, B. J.** 1945. The effect of successive interpolations on retroactive and proactive inhibition. *Psychol. Monogr.*, 59, No. 3. [326, 400]

490. —————— 1953. Learning. *Annu. Rev. Psychol.*, 4, 31–58. [228, 311, 482]

491. **Valentine, C. W.** 1930. The innate bases of fear. *J. genet. Psychol.*, 37, 394–419. [421]

492. **Verplanck, W. S.** 1954. Burrhus F. Skinner. Chapter 3 in Estes, W. K. *et al.*, *Modern learning theory.* New York: Appleton-Century-Crofts. Pp. 267–316. [179, 194]

493. —————— 1955. Since learned behavior is innate, and vice versa, what now? *Psychol. Rev.*, 62, 139–144. [2, 383]

Vincent, S. B. [188]

494. **Voeks, V. W.** 1948. Postremity, recency, and frequency as basis for prediction in the maze situation. *J. exp. Psychol.*, 38, 495–510. [291]

Volkmann, J. *see* Stevens, S. S. 1940.

Von Lackum, W. J. *see* Melton, A. W. 1941.

495. **Walker, E. L.** 1948. Variability in extinction scores in Skinner-box problems. *J. comp. physiol. Psychol.*, 41, 432–437. [341]

Walker, E. L. *see* Kellogg, W. N. 1938.

496. **Walter W. G.** 1953. *The living brain.* New York:

Norton. [235, 237, 262, 294, 362, 437, 482]

Ward, A. *see* Harris, L. J. *et al.* 1933.

497. **Ward, L. B.** 1937. Reminiscence and rote learning. *Psychol. Monogr.*, 49, No. 220. [188, 310, 321, 400]

498. **Warden, C. J.** 1931. *Animal motivation: Experimental studies on the albino rat.* New York: Columbia University Press. [229]

499. **Warren, A. B. and Grant, D. A.** 1955. The relation of conditioned discrimination to the MMPI *Pd* personality variable. *J. exp. Psychol.*, 49, 23–27. [48, 50]

500. **Watson, J. B.** 1914. *Behavior. An introduction to comparative psychology.* New York: Holt. [147, 420]

501. —————— 1919. *Psychology from the standpoint of a behaviorist.* Philadelphia: Lippincott. [283]

502. —————— 1924. *Psychology from the standpoint of a behaviorist.* Philadelphia: Lippincott. [54]

503. —————— 1928. *Behaviorism.* New York: Norton. [216]

504. —————— 1930. *Behaviorism* (rev. ed.). New York: Norton. [3]

505. —————— and Rayner, R. 1920. Conditioned emotional reactions. *J. exp. Psychol.*, 3, 1–14. [420]

Weaver, H. B. *see* Irwin, F. W. 1934.

Weaver, J., Jr. *see* Denny, M. R. 1955.

506. **Weiss, R.** 1955. Effects of a 'set for speed' on 'learning with-

out awareness.' *Amer. J. Psychol.*, 68, 425–431. [226]

507. **Wendt, G. R.** 1930. An analytical study of the conditioned kneejerk. *Arch. Psychol., N. Y.*, 19, No. 123, 97pp. [137]

508. —— 1936. An interpretation of inhibition of conditioned reflexes as competition between reaction systems. *Psychol. Rev.*, 43, 258–281. [359, 369]

509. —— 1937. Two and one-half year retention of a conditioned response. *J. genet. Psychol.*, 17, 178–180. [314, 356]

Wendt, G. R. *see* Cohen, L. H. 1933.

510. **Wertheimer, M.** 1951. Hebb and Senden on the role of learning in perception. *Amer. J. Psychol.*, 64, 133–137. [394]

511. **Wheeler, R. H.** 1940. *The science of psychology* (2d. ed.). New York: Crowell. [45]

512. **White, R. K.** 1936. The completion hypothesis and reinforcement. *Psychol. Rev.*, 43, 396–404. [166]

513. **White, R. T.** 1953. Analysis of the function of a secondary reinforcing stimulus in a serial learning situation. Unpublished Ph.D. dissertation, The University of Buffalo. [91, 361]

514. **White, R. W.** 1949. *The abnormal personality*. New York: Ronald. [438]

515. **Wickens, D. D. and Briggs, G. E.** 1951. Mediated stimulus generalization as a factor in sensory pre-conditioning. *J. exp. Psychol.*, 42, 197–200. [152–3, 257]

516. **Wiener, N.** 1948. *Cybernetics*. Cambridge: Technology Press. [235]

517. **Williams, A. C., Jr.** 1949. Evaluation of the school link as an aid in primary flight instruction. *Univ. Ill. Aeronautics Bull.*, 46, (5), 22pp. [407]

Williams, K. *see* Hebb, D. O. 1946.

518. **Williams, O.** 1926. A study of the phenomenon of reminiscence. *J. exp. Psychol.*, 9, 368–387. [310]

519. **Williams, S. B.** 1938. Resistance to extinction as a function of the number of reinforcements. *J. exp. Psychol.*, 23, 506–522. [347]

520. **Wolf, A.** 1943. The dynamics of the selective inhibition of specific functions in neurosis. *Psychosom. Med.*, 5, 27–38. [394]

Wolf, I. S. *see* Kellogg, W. N. 1939.

521. **Wolfe, J. B.** 1936. Effectiveness of token-rewards for chimpanzees. *Comp. Psychol. Monogr.*, 12, 1–72. [270]

522. **Wolfle, D.** 1945. The use and design of synthetic trainers for military training. *OSRD, Appl. Psychol. Panel, NDRC*, Rep. No. 5426, 36pp. [407]

523. —— 1951. Training. Chapter 34 in Stevens, S. S. (ed.), *Handbook of experimental psychology*. New York: Wiley. Pp. 1267–1286. [158, 415]

524. **Wolfe, H. M.** 1930. Time factors in conditioned finger withdrawal. *J. gen. Psychol.,* 4, 372–378. [129]

525. ——— 1932. Conditioning as a function of the material between the conditioned and the original stimulus. *J. gen. Psychol.,* 7, 80–103. [128]

526. **Wolpe, J.** 1949. An interpretation of the effects of combinations of stimuli (patterns) based on current neurophysiology. *Psychol. Rev.,* 56, 277–283. [155]

527. ——— 1950. Need-reduction, drive-reduction and reinforcement: A neurophysiological view. *Psychol. Rev.,* 57, 19–26. [155, 207, 482]

528. ——— 1952a. Primary stimulus generalization: A neurophysiological view. *Psychol. Rev.,* 59, 8–10. [155, 482]

529. ——— 1952b. The formation of negative habits: A neurophysiological view. *Psychol. Rev.,* 59, 290–299. [155, 366, 368, 441]

530. **Woodward, D. P.** 1954. Temporal and effort factors in the acquisition and extinction of an avoidance response. Unpublished Ph.D. dissertation, The University of Buffalo. [64–5, 67, 341, 358, 369]

Woodward, D. P. *see* Bugelski, B. R. 1951.

531. **Woodworth, R. S.** 1938. *Experimental psychology.* New York: Holt. [266, 304, 320, 345, 377–8, 413–4]

532. ——— and **Schlosberg, H.** 1954. *Experimental psychology* (rev. ed.). New York: Holt. [230, 308]

Woodworth, R. S. *see* Thorndike, E. L. 1901.

Woodyard, E. *see* Thorndike, E. L. *et al.* 1928.

533. **Worchel, P.** and **Marks, M.** 1951. The effect of sleep prior to learning. *J. exp. Psychol.,* 42, 313–316. [323]

Wulff, J. J. *see* Sheffield, F. D. 1951.

Wynne, L. C. *see* Solomon, R. L. 1953a.

534. **Yoshioka, J. G.** 1929. Weber's law in the discrimination of maze distance by the white rat. *Univ. Calif. Publ. Psychol.,* 4, 155–184. [186, 192]

535. **Young, J. Z.** 1951. *Doubt and certainty in science. A biologist's reflections on the brain.* New York: Oxford University Press. [235, 238–9, 246, 260, 264, 289]

536. **Young, P. T.** 1948. Studies of food preference, appetite and dietary habit. VIII. Food-seeking drives, palatability and the law of effect. *J. comp. physiol. Psychol.,* 41, 269–300. [229]

537. ——— 1949. Emotion as disorganized response—a reply to Professor Leeper. *Psychol. Rev.,* 56, 184–191. [428]

538. **Youtz, R. E. P.** 1938a. Reinforcement, extinction and spontaneous recovery in a non-Pavlovian reaction. *J. exp. Psychol.,* 22, 305–318. [57]

539. ——— 1938b. The change with time of a Thorndikian response in the rat. *J. exp. Psychol.,* 23, 128–140. [57]

540. **Yum, K. S.** 1931. An experimental test of the law of

assimilation. *J. exp. Psychol.*, 14, 68–82. [408–9]

541. **Zeaman, D.** 1949. Response latency as a function of the amount of reinforcement. *J. exp. Psychol.*, 39, 466–483. [230]

542. **Zeigarnik, B.** 1927. III. *Das Behalten erledigter und unerledigter Handlungen.* In Lewin, K. (ed.), *Untersuchungen zur Handlungs— und Affektpsychologie. Psychol. Forsch.*, 9, 1–85. [335]

Zeigler, W. *see* Dunlap, K. 1931.

543. **Zeller, A. F.** 1950a. An experimental analogue of repression: I. Historical summary. *Psychol. Bull.*, 47, 39–51. [334, 433]

544. ———— 1950b. An experimental analogue of repression: II. The effect of individual failure and success on memory measured by relearning. *J. exp. Psychol.*, 40, 411–422. [334]

Zeuthen, P. L. A., see Jul, M.,
734, 735, 736.

741. Zeuthen, P. 1945, Rev., also
744. X-rays, A. F. 1956, An exam-
strive, to a function of the
smooth inte flow current.
J. exp. Psychol. 50, 506 473,
630.

742. Zukunick, D. 1972, 111, 124, 544,
Relative relation and
metabolism (Tand mental
Imb syn, As also F. Later
mechanism for handling
and distances (integge L
chol. Exp. 8, 1-5 651.

Ziegler, W., see Dunlap, K.

Zubin, N. F. 1956, An exam-
strive to a function of
feels 6 Statistical summer
Psychosom Bull. 7, 39 57,
1934 454.

—— Psychol. Bib.: exact
normal relation of poster
son, P. The effect of mf
equilibrium and access on
motor threshold by the
footrum. J. exp. Psychol.
40, 121-127, 543.

Index

Subject Index